FOUNDATIONS OF MODERN POLITICAL SCIENCE SERIES

Robert A. Dahl, Editor

FOUNDATIONS OF MODERN POLITICAL SCIENCE SERIES

PRENTICE-HALL, INC., Englewood Cliffs, New Jersey

READINGS IN AMERICAN POLITICAL BEHAVIOR

Second Edition

Edited by

RAYMOND E. WOLFINGER

Stanford University

FOUNDATIONS OF MODERN POLITICAL SCIENCE SERIES

Robert A. Dahl, Editor

READINGS IN AMERICAN POLITICAL BEHAVIOR, Second Edition
edited by Raymond E. Wolfinger

P-13–755512–1   C–13–755520–2

PRENTICE-HALL INTERNATIONAL, INC., London
PRENTICE-HALL OF AUSTRALIA, PTY. LTD., Sydney
PRENTICE-HALL OF CANADA, LTD., Toronto
PRENTICE-HALL OF INDIA PRIVATE LTD., New Delhi
PRENTICE-HALL OF JAPAN, INC., Tokyo

Current printing (last number):

10 9 8 7 6 5 4 3 2 1

PREFACE

This is a book of readings on the processes of American national government. The selections are based on empirical research or practical experience. Most of these articles are systematic and general treatments of recurring features of modern American politics; the others are case studies that illustrate important generalizations and evoke the mood and flavor of political life.

This focus on the systematic, empirical study of political processes excludes not only analyses of current policy issues, but also speculative essays, discussions of research methods, and conceptual schemes dealing with abstract variables. Everything in this book concerns what *is*, not what ought to be. There are no articles urging citizens to vote more intelligently or presidents to dedicate themselves to history rather than to politics. These selections describe; they do not cheer or deplore. This is not to shut moralism out of politics, much less out of political science. Nor does it betray a commitment to a clinical, "value-free" science of politics. What it does betray is a belief in the virtues of understanding the world as it is and a conviction that it is futile to seek the ideal without understanding the feasible. By "political behavior," then, I mean nothing more than the politically relevant perspectives and actions of individual persons, be they voters or presidents.

Thus, while these readings include many "behavioral" selections, they are not presented as examples of a certain species of political science. Rather, they reflect a mood or approach shared by many political scientists who would not consider themselves "behaviorists." (Indeed, among the contributors are a congressman, a law professor, and several journalists.) The chief elements in this approach are a desire to look past the formal structure of government to the reality of how politicians actually think and work; a desire to ignore storybook notions of democracy for study of how the average citizen makes his voting decisions; and a desire to accumulate general knowledge rather than tell anecdotes that quickly become obsolete. The trend in this direction is firmly established in political science. The fruits of such research are already found in many textbooks on American government. But as the pace of research has accelerated, a gap has opened between what scholars have discovered and the material incorporated in even the most modern textbook. The selections in this reader deal with information and ideas that, for the most part, have not been presented in textbooks.

Most of the selections are reprinted intact, although some excerpts from books have been edited to delete repetitious or extraneous material or references to other chapters. Neither the subject matter nor the writing style is esoteric and numbers are used only to summarize facts.

The selections are grouped by conventional headings—Congress, the president, and so on—but most of them are germane to a variety of subjects. For example, the articles by Fenno and Wildavsky can be used together in studying either the appropriations process or presidential-congressional relations; all of Part Five is helpful in understanding the role of the president; most of Part Four concerns Congress; half a dozen selections deal with political parties.

Twelve of the selections in the first edition of this book have been retained unchanged, three more have been shortened or revised, four have been omitted, and twelve new selections have been added. This edition has a stronger emphasis on the executive branch and on interest groups, and includes a new section on political stability and dissent.

There is a great deal about American politics that is not yet known to scholars. These readings reveal not only the advances that have been made in the past generation, but also the vast stretches of ground that must be covered before we will have an adequate understanding of the workings of our political system.

Many people have given me helpful advice on this reader. I am especially indebted to James David Barber, Fred I. Greenstein, Theodore J. Lowi, Nelson W. Polsby, Martin Shapiro, and my students at Stanford University for their comments and suggestions.

Raymond E. Wolfinger

CONTENTS

PART THREE

THE COURTS   163

PART FOUR

POLICY FORMATION AND INTEREST GROUPS   227

PART ONE

CONGRESS

When a man is elected to Congress, at least some of his constituents expect him to represent their district's interests. The country as a whole expects him to help legislate and investigate according to the national interest. To do either of these jobs, the congressman must obtain the help of his colleagues, all of whom are also expected to represent local interests and have their own ideas of what will best serve the national interest. Few local interests are similar, and some are conflicting; and needless to say, there are many conceptions of the national interest.

Neither local nor national interests as such are likely to be at the front of the congressman's mind, however. He is probably most worried about such questions as: How can he maintain and improve his political position back home? How can he get the committee assignments he wants? How can he achieve the personal prestige that he must have if he is to be an effective legislator? Perhaps he wants to go from the House to the Senate, or from Congress to the governor's mansion, or even to the White House. Perhaps he is concerned about how he can influence government policies. Here also the help of his colleagues is essential if he wants to achieve his ambitions.

In "The Job of the Congressman" Lewis A. Dexter discusses some of the things that any member of Congress must take into consideration as he goes about his work. This selection, based on several hundred interviews with senators, representatives, congressional staff members, and lobbyists, is taken from a ten-year study of the politics of foreign trade legislation. Dexter describes the incredible work load the congressman bears. There is so much to be done that, paradoxically, his burden gives him a measure of freedom. Because he cannot attend to everything, he must choose where he will concentrate his limited time and energy. This does not mean, however, that he can act as he pleases; with so many strong-willed men pursuing so many different goals, elaborate rules are necessary if anything is to be accomplished. The formal rules—the committee system, floor procedure, and the like—have been described in most textbooks; but there are also informal rules that are no less important in determining how Congress works and how congressmen behave. Many of these customs are politically loaded: they help some political interests more than they help others. But the fact that the folkways help congressmen grapple with their problems makes them very hard to change. The articles by Richard F. Fenno, Jr. and Ralph K. Huitt are concerned with different aspects of these crucial, unwritten rules.

Fenno's article on the House Appropriations Committee shows that Congress is not an undifferentiated mass, but is made up of many parts which themselves are complex political systems. The Appropriations Committee is a particularly distinctive and cohesive group, with its own rules and customs. Unlike most other committees, which can either produce new legislation or bottle it up, the Appropriations Committee *must* report a series of highly complicated money bills each session, or the government would not function. Not only must the Committee handle a huge work load, but it must also present a united front to the whole House, or see its carefully worked out appropriations upset by every member's attempts to get more money for his district. Therefore Committee disunity cannot easily be tolerated. Fenno describes how the selection process and training undergone by new Committee members instills in them a common "committee" point of view that is distinct from (although not irrelevant to) partisan politics. This unity gives the Committee enormous strength in dealing with other congressmen. Although individual congressmen are often frustrated in their dealings with the Committee, the fact that it continues to be so independent indicates that the arrangement is, on the whole, acceptable to the House.

While Fenno is concerned with the strict folkways of a specialized committee, Huitt looks at the permissive habits of the Senate. His point of departure is the famous characterization of the Senate as dominated by a "club" which admits or rejects other senators on the basis of their conformity to Senate norms. Huitt shows that there are other parts to play in the Senate; that the role of maverick may not be such a dishonored one as many observers have suggested; and that the "outsider's" contribution to the legislative process may be as important as is the "club" member's. These two articles raise an intriguing question: Why is there such harsh intolerance of mavericks in the House Appropriations Committee and such acceptance of them in the Senate?

Traditional theories of representative government assume that a legislator's constituents will vote for or against him on the basis of their opinion of his performance in Congress. In the fourth article Donald

E. Stokes and Warren E. Miller cast doubt on this assumption. They show how little most voters know about the two parties' legislative records, much less the part played by individual congressmen, and suggest some of the reasons for election-day defeats and victories. Their article describes the basic problems and opportunities that comprise the congressman's political environment. Their findings about constituent ignorance reinforce one of Dexter's main points: congressmen are fairly free to make most decisions about not only how they will vote, but also how they will spend their time. The ignorance of most voters is one of the conditions in which interest groups flourish: the scanty knowledge and interest of the majority provide opportunities for alert, intense, well-organized minorities. Examples of how lobbies take advantage of these opportunities are found in Chapters 16 and 17.

CHAPTER ONE

THE JOB OF
THE CONGRESSMAN

LEWIS ANTHONY DEXTER

THE JOB OF THE CONGRESSMAN

Choosing a Job

It is a cliché that the main job of a Congressman is to be reelected. There is much truth to it, but there are various ways of getting reelected. Somehow, the Congressman must do things which will secure for him the esteem and/or support of significant elements of his constituency. This he can achieve in many ways. He can seek for himself a reputation as a national leader, which may sometimes impress his constituents. He can work at press relations, creating and stimulating news stories and an image of activity. He can be a local civic leader, attending and speaking at community functions. He can make a reputation for himself in the field of legislation. In some states, he can be a party wheel horse and rely on the organization to back him. He can get people jobs and do social work and favors. He can become a promoter of certain local industries. He can conduct investigations and set himself up as a defender of public morals. He can take well-publicized trips to international hot spots. He can befriend moneyed interests to assure himself a well-financed campaign. He can befriend labor unions, veterans' organizations, or other groups with a numerous clientele and many votes. The one thing he cannot do is much of all these things. He must choose among them; he has to be a certain kind of Congressman.

The reason he must choose is the scarcity of resources. Resources are

Reprinted by permission of the publisher from Raymond A. Bauer, Ithiel de Sola Pool, and Lewis Anthony Dexter, AMERICAN BUSINESS AND PUBLIC POLICY: THE POLITICS OF FOREIGN TRADE *(New York: Atherton Press, 1963), pp. 406–32. Mr. Dexter has taught at a number of universities.*

various; they include time, money, energy, staff, information, and good will. All these have one common characteristic—there is never enough. They must all be budgeted and used with discretion. Opportunity is striking constantly or at least standing outside the door, but it is only occasionally that one has the wherewithal to capitalize on it. The skill of a Congressman is to make the choices which, with the resources at hand, will get him the greatest results in doing the kind of congressional job he has chosen to do. . . .

For these reasons, a rational Congressman who has decided what kind of Congressman he wants to be would then use his resources according to strategies consisting of whole packages of related acts. His stand on a particular issue would be far less dependent on what was specifically involved in that issue than on its role in a general policy or strategy on which he was working. . . .

A skillful Congressman also takes account of the strategies of the other players in the Capitol arena and the rules of the game there. He is part of a multiperson game in which the goals of the different players vary and in which each defines them for himself; in which the pieces are the scarce resources which can be allocated; and in which the optimal strategies depend on the coalitions which can be formed, the procedural rules of the house in which the game is being played, and the power and the goals of the other players. Voting strategies depend on many things besides the pros and cons of issues. A senior Senator, for example, can seek for himself the mantle of statesman with some chance of success, thanks to unlimited debate and his ability to balance special interests in one part of the state against those in another. A Representative has far less chance of playing that particular kind of game. Again, a Congressman can afford to vote the popular position in his constituency although he believes it wrong when he knows that there will be enough congressional votes to defeat him anyway. He may have to vote his principles with courage when he thinks his vote is going to count. But, even then, he may, if skilled at parliamentary procedure, satisfy his constituents by dramatic votes and gestures at moments when they cannot succeed.

How a Congressman defines his job, the importance of choice in the use of his time and resources, the continuing character of Congress as a social system, and the constraints of procedure and interaction form the substance of this section. The Congressman is typically thrust unprepared into a specialized milieu and confronted with a massive volume of highly technical legislation, with most of which he can deal only superficially. Counting on the assistance of a modest staff, he must work within the framework of a committee structure and is burdened with the additional task of servicing myriad personal requests from his constituents. These pressures combine to make time one of the Congressman's most critical resources and the study of its allocation and husbanding a key to the legislative process.

Allocating Time

The scholar tends to approach his problem as though it had equal salience in the minds of men dealing with it on a practical basis. But we have already observed, in our study of the business community, that foreign-trade policy was only one of many issues crying for the American businessman's attention and not one of the most pressing. What has been said of the businessman must be said double of the Congressman. There are infinite demands on him, which he must meet with finite means. Both the scholar and the newsman often miss this point in their assumption that Congressmen can pay attention to all issues of national policy. We began our study with two major interests: legislation and communication. We wanted to know what Congressmen did about tariff legislation, and we wanted to know what and who influenced them in what they did. We tended to assume that the issues of public policy which were crucial to us were as crucial to the men with whom we were talking. Yet, few Congressmen viewed tariff legislation as their primary concern, and the way in which many of them noticed what they read and heard about reciprocal trade was in large part a consequence of the fact that tariff legislation was simply one of several competing interests for them.

The low priority assigned tariff matters and the effect of that on what Congressmen heard and did may be examined by considering their allocation of time. . . . A Congressman is a member of what sociologists call a free profession, in that he makes his working schedule for himself. His job is undefined and free, not only in schedule, but also in content and in standards of achievement. As a result, he lives under a heavy burden of multiple choices, and, what is more, the choices he has to make are far more fateful than those most citizens make. The citizen may conceive of the Congressman tackling his highly responsible choices with the same care and awe with which the citizen imagines himself tackling the few really responsible choices which he makes. But, by the very nature of their busy lives, Congressmen cannot do this.

Let us consider the ways in which a Congressman may occupy his time. He may concentrate on any of the following aspects of his job:

1. Legislative planning—the working out of legislation in committee
2. Legislative criticism—an unpopular role in the House, but one common in the Senate

3. Parliamentary procedure—specializing in rules and regulations for the conduct of congressional business

4. Legislative tactics—like Lyndon Johnson when he was majority leader, or James Byrnes in an even earlier period

5. Investigation

6. Public education—rallying support for causes through forums, speeches, articles

7. Personal advertisement and campaigning—birthday and condolence letters to constituents, congratulations to graduating high school seniors, newsletters, press releases, trips back home

8. Seeing visitors and shaking hands

9. Personal service—rectification of bureaucratic injustices; facilitating immigration of relatives of constituents; arranging military leaves, transfers, and hardship releases; helping confused constituents to route their inquiries to the right administrative offices; providing information on social security rights, etc.

10. Representation of local or state interests—Senator Wiley (R., Wis.), ranking Republican on the Foreign Relations Committee, reported: "In 1939 on the occasion of the 75th anniversary of the Wisconsin cheese industry, it was my pleasure to preside over an appropriate celebration in Washington. It featured the world's largest cheese. . . . The cheese was eventually cut up and distributed . . . to Senators, Representatives, congressional employees, newspapermen and others. . . . I am satisfied that advancing the interests of one of the foremost food industries of my state . . . is one of the jobs for which I was sent to Washington. . . ."[1]

11. Participating in national political organization or campaigning—for example, Senator A. S. Mike Monroney (D., Okla.) has been chairman of the Speakers Division of the Democratic National Committee

12. Development of local political organization and leadership—many Senators are state political bosses, for example, the late Senator Pat McCarran in Nevada.

A Congressman might decide that his chief responsibility is, after all, legislation. Even so, there is far too much legislation for any particular legislator to attend to all of it. During the Eighty-third Congress, 1953–1955, which we were studying, the following legislative issues were among those considered:

1. Reciprocal Trade Extension acts of 1953 and 1954
2. Customs simplifications bills
3. Cargo Preference Act of 1954
4. Excise tax

[1] A. Wiley, *Laughing with Congress* (New York: Crown Publishers, Inc., 1947), pp. 136–41. This book probably has the best treatment of the congressional work load. It is one of the indispensable books about Congress for anybody trying to find out what Congress does. Especially valuable is Ch. 6, "The Office Inferno," particularly pp. 90–96.

5. Complete overhauling of federal tax system
6. Social security revision
7. Unemployment compensation measures
8. Appropriations measures
9. Amendment to the Constitution[2]
10. Civil service pay raises
11. The lease-purchase bill
12. Revision of health-welfare-grant formulas
13. Flexible price supports
14. Reduction of wheat acreage
15. Reduction of the Air Force
16. Establishment of an Air Academy
17. Building of twenty merchant ships
18. Upper Colorado development
19. Niagara Falls development
20. Highway aid
21. Commercial use of atomic-energy patents
22. Range improvement by private interests on public lands
23. Alaskan statehood
24. Hawaiian statehood
25. End of price controls
26. Revision of the Taft-Hartley Act
27. New health insurance law
28. Windfall profits
29. The Bricker amendment
30. Wiretap bills
31. Suffrage for eighteen-years-olds
32. Raising the federal debt ceiling
33. Tidelands oil
34. Sale of government rubber plants
35. Abolition of the Reconstruction Finance Corporation
36. The St. Lawrence Seaway
37. Special Refugee Immigration Law
38. Interest rate rise for Federal Housing Administration
39. Excess profits tax
40. Bill for twenty-six new judgeships
41. Witness immunity measures
42. Ten plans for government reorganization
43. Rise in postal rates.

In addition, during the Eighty-third Congress members of the Senate were confronted with a number of other time-consuming issues which were not properly legislative but were more important than many laws in terms of policy. Prominent among these were the censuring of

[2]A resolution providing for the replacement of House members killed in a national emergency.

Senator Joseph McCarthy (R., Wis.), the proposal to unseat Senator Dennis Chavez (D., N.M.), and the confirmation of appointments to major commissions, cabinet and diplomatic posts, and judgeships. Some appointments were highly controversial. . . .

In the same session, the Senate and House conducted at least sixty-five investigations, some of which had specific legislative purposes. Finally, it should be considered that interested members of the House and Senate may and do devote long hours of work to legislative proposals that never reach the floor or achieve serious consideration in committee.

Only painstaking and continuous study can give a legislator command of the often complex details of any one of the many proposed pieces of legislation. Few Congressmen can or do master more than a handful of them. A Congressman with years of service may in time develop expertness in a particular field of legislation, but the best-informed of our lawmakers are fully acquainted with only a fraction of the bills that come before each session.

Furthermore, even if some particular legislation is the major focus of interest of a given Congressman, usually, if he is to be reelected, he cannot completely ignore other aspects of his job.[3] Said one administrative assistant:

> You know this business; it is like trying to deal with a great immovable beast or cleanse the Augean stables . . . you just cannot do much. . . . The Senator is now a member of fourteen important subcommittees, and he just cannot split up his time. . . . Now there is the [particular] subcommittee—. . . and all those questions are tremendous and vital questions. . . . Yet, you try to get these Senators [members of the subcommittee] even to agree to meet at any one time and you cannot even do that . . . they are so independent and rushed and all doing things their own way.[4]

Not only is the Congressman himself overcommitted, but he is surrounded by similarly busy men. A salient fact about the Congressman's job is that what he does is invariably accomplished through other people, most of whom are as busy as himself. He becomes involved in a complex web of interdependence with colleagues and constituents as a

---

[3]For a variety of reasons, House members, if they are so minded, are freer to "take it easy" than members of the upper body. They represent a smaller constituency. Crucial decisions in the House are usually made by the leadership. Also, each member of the larger House is on fewer committees.

[4]A senatorial assistant rejected the idea of having an intern from the American Political Science Association in his office because "the intern has lots of ideas—mostly good—but every single one of them means more work." We should note that among the duties of a Congressman is running his own office and staff. By 1959, House members received approximately $40,000 a year for the maintenance of staffs. They were permitted to employ as many as eight persons. In addition, members were allowed $1,200 per session for stationery, 2,700 minutes of telephone service, 12,000 words of

result of the fact that each must work through the other to get what he wants, whether it be reelection, the passage of a piece of legislation, or service from a Congressman. To anticipate a point which we shall develop later, it is highly naïve to think of a Congressman as being under pressure from one direction or even as being under cross-pressure from two opposing directions. More typically, he is under simultaneous influence and demands from many directions, a large number of which are relevant to the issue with which the scholar or interest group is concerned only in that they compete with that issue for the Congressman's time and energies.

However, our purpose is not to argue that Congressmen are busy people but to show specifically that their busyness affected their reaction to the reciprocal-trade extension.

Busyness blocked effective communication of constituents' views to their Congressmen. A Congressman can seldom readily inform himself as to how his constituents feel about any issue. A sense of acting in the dark about public opinion plagued many of the legislators we interviewed. On the simplest level, communications with respect to foreign-trade policy had to compete with, and frequently were lost in, the welter of other communications. This is particularly true of conversations which Congressmen and their assistants had with other people. In 1955, a Senator's assistant commented:

> You know, so many people have come into the office in the last two weeks on all these things—rubber disposal, stock market, reciprocal-trade extensions, and taxes—I just haven't been able to keep in mind which was which; and I think it is pretty difficult for the Senator to keep track, too.

One Representative who was very much concerned with the Reciprocal Trade Act complained about his impossible work load. He had recently been back to his district; he could remember vaguely that a number of people had talked to him about tariff and foreign-trade policy, but he could not recall who had wanted what.

Both these men belonged to the committees which handled reciprocal-trade extension. Yet, even for them, it was but one issue among

---

telegraph service, $600 a year for official office expenses in the district, and $200 a year for airmail and special-delivery stamps. Very few members employ as many as eight persons or spend quite the maximum. Few Congressmen receive office space adequate for that number, and the use of a staff that large is likely to involve the personal financing of some office expenses.

The amount available to Senators for staff purposes varies from state to state. The average expense appeared to be more than $50,000 a year. This usually permits the Senator to employ two or three professional persons as legislative and administrative assistants and two or three clerks. [By 1965, even Senators from the smallest states had staffs twice this size—Ed.]

many. They had no time to give more than a hurried glance to communications about it. As a result, they, too, had only the haziest notion of what public opinion in their constituency really was. The communications they received were poorly remembered and ill-understood. Most messages left only the impression that something had been said, not a clear recollection of what was said. We find that the net effect of communication was to heighten attention to an issue, rather than to convey specific content about it.

SOME AREAS OF INITIATIVE

Congressmen feel much freer than most outsiders think. They need not be unduly constrained by demands from constituents, interest groups, or party. Their freedom is secured by a number of conditions. For one thing, constituents and pressure groups are often satisfied with a fair hearing, not insisting on a specific conclusion. For another thing, American political parties seldom impose discipline in regard to issues.

Among all the conditions that make Congressmen free, there is one that deserves special attention; that is the fact that a Congressman's own decisions largely determine what pressures will be communicated to him. Paradoxical as it may seem, their "freedom" comes from the excessive demands made on them. The complexity of their environment which seems to Congressmen to rob them of initiative thrusts initiative back on them, for, when the demands on a man's resources clearly exceed his capacity to respond, he *must* select the problems and pressures to which to respond.

A Congressman Determines What He Will Hear

There are additional ways in which a Congressman largely determines for himself what he hears from the public. Several mechanisms converge to place a Congressman in a closed communication circuit. For one thing, like anyone else, a Congressman indulges in selective perception and recall of what he hears. Most messages received by a Congressman change saliency more than they change his attitudes on the subject with which they deal. They raise its saliency so that he thinks about it more and becomes more prone to express whatever predispositions he has regarding it. Beset by competing stimuli, he perceives the original message hurriedly, seeing in it what he expects is there. The effect of the stimulus is thus that he reacts more, but reacts in terms of his own accumulated predispositions, not in terms of the content of the communication. Messages serve more as triggers than as persuaders.[5]

[5]See Raymond A. Bauer, "The Communicator and the Audience," *Journal of Conflict Resolution*, Vol. 2 (March, 1958), pp. 67–77.

Second, a Congressman must select those persons within his constituency on whom he is going to build his following; he cannot react to all equally. Third, a Congressman must discount as phony much of the material he receives, and the discounting process can lead to a variation of readings. Last, and perhaps most significant, the attitudes of a Congressman in large measure control what messages will be sent to him, because they determine, often overdetermine, the image people have of him.

Of course, Congressmen do get mail of all kinds, including some with which they are bound to disagree. Although the large bulk of issues mail is supportive, there are exceptions, and sometimes there may be large sacks of mail demanding that a Congressman take a difficult or unpalatable stand. When that happens, the Congressman wants to know how seriously to take those demands on him. Do they represent his constituents' deep feelings or are they the product of a slick promotion? He wants to know something of the degree of spontaneity, sincerity, and urgency of these communications. The Congressman's experience with other communications on the same and other issues is his touchstone for assessing the degree to which his mail is stimulated or spontaneous. Thus, a Senate mail clerk commented on one set of letters: "This mail is surprisingly unstereotyped; . . . although the stationery may have been given out, the message was not. It is quite different from other heavy pressure mail."

. . . In general, experienced Congressmen and their staffs are quite tough-minded and skilled at assessing their mail. They are unlikely to feel pressure from the mere existence of numerous demands on them. That being the case, the demands that seem compelling to Congressmen are apt to be those which fit their own psychic needs and their images of the world.

One way or another, the Congressman must simplify the complex world. We interviewed two Congressmen from the vicinity of New Anglia [New Anglia is a fictious name.]. It will be remembered that there was considerable unemployment in the textile industry around New Anglia. Northern textile unemployment may be interpreted in a variety of ways—as a result of technological obsolescence, foreign competition, Southern competition, and so on. Congressman Second, in virtually these words, said: "Unemployment and the need for protection are the same issue." He saw textile unemployment as the result of foreign competition. But Congressman First, when asked about foreign-trade policy, began immediately to talk about Southern competition and about the failure of the administration to grant defense contracts to the distressed New Anglia area. Rather than seeking relief via tariffs, he was trying to get from the Office of Defense Mobilization a "certificate of necessity" for a steel mill in New Anglia. He commented: "By and large, on . . . the tariff . . . New Anglia businesses feel it is New Anglia against the South, and New Anglia is getting a raw deal every time."

. . . In the Senate Office Building, the mail rooms were in the basement, a long walk from the Senators' offices. That fact, added to the volume of mail a Senator receives, made it far less likely for him to be aware of what was in his mail than was a Representative, whose mail clerk was right in his office. In one senatorial office, the Senator's administrative assistant was under the impression that they had received no mail on foreign-trade policy. One of us took a walk over to the Senator's mail room. The mail clerk said that the mail on foreign-trade policy was first or second in volume of mail on any issue. However, the Senator and his assistants were heavily involved in several other issues, and the mail clerk had not forwarded the reciprocal-trade mail, since, in her judgment, there was nothing that the Senator could do about the issue at the moment. . . .

We add another point that reinforces the notion that Congressmen interpret the pressures on them. Many communications to Congressmen leave the recipient in the dark as to precisely what is wanted of him. Communications to Congress are frequently ambiguous, and it is not surprising if the ambiguities are resolved in consonance with the Congressman's other interests and activities. A letter reporting industrial distress might be seen as a plea for tariff protection by Congressman Second and as a plea for selective allocation of defense contracts by Congressman First. Yet, both would regard themselves as truly and effectively expressing the plea of the constituent.

The work load of the Congressman and his staff reduces the precision with which Congressmen interpret that high proportion of mail which is only partially on target. For example, a large volume of protectionist mail was received from employees of the Westinghouse Corporation in protest against U.S. government purchase of foreign electrical installations. Although the mail was ostensibly directed against the extension of the Reciprocal Trade Act, it is probable that the issue confronting Westinghouse—government purchasing of foreign electrical equipment—should have called for mail asking an administrative tightening-up of the Buy-American Act, not for tariff legislation. But few Congressmen had the time or staff resources to investigate this problem. Our impression was that many Congressmen were not clear as to what was wanted of them by the Westinghouse Corporation. The mail might have had some effect on trade-legislation votes, but the effect, if any, may have been quite unrelated to the specific situation affecting Westinghouse.

The fact that a large part of the mail, and other communications, too, are only partly on target is one which cannot be too strongly emphasized. Sometimes it makes action to meet the request impossible, for many writers ask for something that is procedurally or otherwise impracticable. They may ask a Congressman to support a bill which is still in a committee of which he is not a member and where he has little influence with any member. For him to comply in any way other than by a polite reply to the correspondent would require a major investment of effort and good will. He would have to go out of his way to testify or to approach some of his better-placed colleagues.

On the other hand, the fact that petitioners are vague about what they want also helps make political action possible. Political action requires the formation of coalitions. Coalitions are held together by the glue of ambiguity which enables persons to perceive diverse goals as somehow akin. There are not enough people with an interest in the Buy-American regulations, for example, to produce congressional action. Nor are there enough who care about oil quotas to get such action. Nor are there enough who care about specific tariff rates as such. The only way any of them could achieve legislative effectiveness was to mobilize all of them as a coalition around some issue which might serve at least as a wedge for those whom it did not serve directly. . . .

Indeed, it happens more often than not in public-policy debates that the issues around which mass opinion is mobilized are not the crucial ones in the minds of those who frame legislative policy. This happens often enough so that Congressmen are well attuned to grievances as an index to the sources of public alarm, rather than as specific guidance on legislative drafting. A Congressman is concerned to allay the discontent of those who appeal to him. The complaint is a signal to him to do something, not a command as to what to do. Like a doctor, having made a diagnosis, he often has a range of choices of treatment open to him.

We consider now another range of alternatives among which a Congressman must choose. Almost every district is composed of a complex of interests, and Congressmen are faced with the task of deciding just whom they represent. They cannot give attention and energy equally to all. They must select some for whom they can become valued allies and from whom they can command more than passive support. They must find groups which have money, votes, media of communication, influence, and political desires which a Congressman can further. A Congressman must seek to make himself an important figure to some such groups within his constituency. These may change over time. A Congressman elected by labor votes may throw off this harness by turning to business support. But at any one moment, a Congressman must relate to some key groups within his constituency, for a constituency is a social structure, not an amorphous mass. Thus, Representative Henderson Lanham (D., Ga.) came from a district with both farming and business interests. He had associated himself with the business group. Their protectionist interests, rather than the farmers' stake in international trade, were communicated to him, for people write and talk more to a Congressman whom they know, and he listens more to them.

Although a Congressman's established relationship to a particular group may increase the probability of its members communicating with him, this established relationship does not necessarily make him more compliant to their interests on a specific issue. This is a point so important and so overlooked in the pressure-group model of the democratic process that it deserves emphasis.

In the first place, the direction of influence is as apt to be from the Congressman to his closer constituents as the other way around. Citizens value a relation to a Congressman and are apt to be guided by him.

Second, established favorable relationships between Congressmen and groups in the constituency are invariably based on a range of issues. It is rare that any one of these is of such paramount importance that a group would renounce its allegiance to a Congressman who had pleased them on many other issues. . . . A Congressman wins the allegiance of multipurpose interest groups through both legislation and services. This allegiance, then, can buy him freedom from pressure on almost any individual issue on which he has firm personal convictions.

We may thus enunciate the general principle that whether a group will communicate with a Congressman and whether the Congressman will respond to the interests of that group are functions of the relationship between the group and the Congressman on a *range* of issues. . . .

Belief that a Congressman is busy with other matters will dry up the flow of communication to him on a given subject. The late Senator Joseph McCarthy had twice succeeded in getting the Reciprocal Trade Act amended to place a quota on the importation of foreign furs. But this was before he became involved in the investigation of communism. In 1954, an informed source commented: "None of the Wisconsin dairy or fur people would go see Joe. He's too busy and out of that world. They'd go see Wiley or Thye or Humphrey's assistant, but not Joe—he doesn't follow that sort of thing any more." The image of Senator McCarthy had become that of investigator of communism rather than that of representative of local and state interests.

In making that assertion, we take leave of the traditional theory of pressure politics as expounded both by the politician and the political scientist. The political scientist observing Congress gives too much credence to the way the Congressman himself describes the situation. The Congressman often sees himself as buffeted by a torrent of inexorable demands on his time and effort. Like any busy executive, he sees himself responding to stimuli that come to him from without. What he does not realize is that the nature of these forces on him are largely self-made. . . . One Congressman with an eye on issues will listen with concern to arguments put forward by constituents, whereas another Congressman with an eye on local social groups will feel no pressure from pompous statements about issues as he tries to keep track of births, marriages, and deaths. The Representative who is known to have arranged for the nonquota entrance of relatives of members of a given ethnic group will receive similar requests from other such persons. The Congressman who establishes his home office in a working-class section, where his secretary gives advice on social-security cases, will get such cases, which perhaps take more time than any other service. The Congressman who has interested himself in taxes will hear about taxes, and the one who has cultivated groups interested in foreign trade will hear about tariffs. . . .

A Congressman Is Relatively Free
One implication of the fact that the Congressman makes his own job and hears what he chooses to hear is that he can be a relatively free man, not the unwilling captive of interest groups or parties. There may seem to be a conflict between the two pictures we paint of the Congressman harassed by many demands and of the Congressman relatively free. But, as suggested above, it is precisely because the demands on him are excessive that he must be selective, and therein lies his relative freedom.

Early in our study we talked with a veteran Congressman who said:

> You know, I am sure you will find out a Congressman can do pretty much what he decides to do, and he doesn't have to bother too much about criticism. I've been up here where a guy will hold one economic or political position and get along all right; and then he'll die or resign, and a guy comes in (from the same district) who holds quite a different economic or political position, and he gets along all right, too. That's the fact of the matter.

The reasons for this are many. In American political practice, neither the party nor the executive branch exercises more than slight control over a member of Congress. . . .

The sanction that counts much more than party or executive leadership in the congressional picture is that of reelection by the voters of one's district. But in that regard, too, the Congressman is quite free. There are limits on what is morally or sociologically conceivable. Few, if any, Congressmen could announce adherence to communism and be reelected. But the latitude is wide and of course wider on any one given issue than on all issues put together. A Congressman creates an image on the full range of issues which affects his chances of reelection, although even over the full range his freedom is much more substantial than is often realized.

A Congressman is free, as we have already noted, because each district is ordinarily a complex and he can choose the elements out of which he wishes to build his coalition. As Congressman Stubborn said about his district: "It is a good district, because, if the farmers are mad at you, the cities won't be; and, if the cities are, the farmers won't be; so you can be free."

He is freed from a slavish dependence on the elements in his coalition, not only because he can change it, but, even more, because, once he has built a coalition, he tends to lead it. His closest supporters, who may originally have rallied around him because they wanted him to take certain stands, come to be his men. Within very broad limits, when he shifts, they shift. They gain prestige by being close to a Congressman, and they fear to break a relationship which may some day be useful for important purposes. Once the leader has committed himself, his supporters are inclined to go along.

He is free also because the voters seldom know just what they want. Mostly they want evidence that he is concerned with their problem and is addressing himself effectively to it. Often he is viewed as the doctor who should recommend the appropriate cure. The larger number of constituents, and the ones the Congressman likes, are the ones who come in to say, "Congressman, this is my problem." Those, such as the League of Women Voters, who come in with a list of recommended votes are, fortunately for the comfort of the Congressman, fewer.

Indeed, even where the constituent frames his appeal to his Congressman as a highly specific demand, the Congressman is quite free to disregard it. Few constituents deny their vote to a Congressman who generally listens to them just because he differs on any one issue. Furthermore, for every demand on one side, there is a demand on the other. The Congressman who saw his job in no more imaginative light than doing what his constituents or large groups of them wanted would not only face impossible problems of doing that job, but would also soon find himself offending enough other constituents to undermine his chances of remaining in office.[6] He must view the demands with a more creative eye, seeking to invent formulas that will catch the imagination of constituents rather than taking all requests at face value.

Finally, a Congressman is free also because, as we shall see in the sections to come, the procedure of Congress is so complex that it is easy for him to obfuscate where he stands on any issue and what he has done about it.

CONGRESS AS A SOCIAL SYSTEM

We have confined our attention to the way in which the context of other activities affects incoming information and the way in which the Con-

---

[6]*Cf.* Anthony Downs, *An Economic Theory of Democracy* (New York: Harper & Row, Publishers, 1957), for a demonstration of the proposition that, by following the majority on each issue, a legislator is likely to court defeat by a coalition of passionate minorities.

gressman perceives and interprets it. The action which he takes on the basis of such information must also be placed in the context of his other activities. Though it is easy enough for the scholar to abstract one vote on one issue, Congressmen act on a complex of issues, rather than on a single one. The typical Congressman acts, not as if some bill were the only one to be decided, but as if it must be disposed of in such a way as simultaneously to facilitate desired actions on other issues, too.

In the first place, any one bill compounds many issues. Thus, one Congressman who indicated general support for the Reciprocal Trade Act voted against it in the House. In his district, there was considerable unemployment related to foreign imports. He was disgruntled that the Ways and Means Committee had not given him something he could represent as a token of his concern for the problems of business in his district. Then he added: ". . . and then there is another thing, that damn Eisenhower. I just cannot see why we should give him more power, can you? He . . . is so incapable." Where some people might see one issue, he saw three: national interest in a liberal-trade policy, his district's interest in protection from foreign imports (which he wanted to acknowledge on a token basis), and the delegation of powers to the president.

In the second place, action on any one bill affects action on other bills, too. The single enduring issue that complicates the consideration of all individual issues is the necessity for the Congressman to maintain effective working relationships with other Congressmen. In the words of Speaker Sam Rayburn, you have to "go along" to "get along." . . .

Few issues present themselves as a clear legislative black and white, and there are few uncompromising fighters on any issue. In an interview with Stewart Alsop, then Vice President Nixon stated forcefully the requirements for compromise in politics: "You know, you come to Washington, you have great ideas and there you are in the committees or on the floor of the House, and you have an inability to implement your ideas. . . . You've got to learn how to play the game."[7]

The complication of other issues, role conflict, and the realization that there are infinite demands on Congress' finite time result in Congressmen usually being interested in a viable, rather than in a definitive, solution to the problems with which they are faced. . . .

A legislative enactment is seldom a clean decision of important issues. It is normally a verbal formula which the majority of Congressmen find adequate as a basis for their continuing a policy struggle. It sets up new ground rules within which the issue may be fought out. The ground rules will reflect the balance of forces, but the minority is seldom so weak on a major issue that it has to accept a once-and-for-all decision. The formula must usually offer them the chance of later reversal, keeping the big issue alive. The trade bills were just such formulas. They only

[7]"Nixon on Nixon," *Saturday Evening Post*, July 12, 1958, p. 26.

authorized executive consideration of trade policy, leaving it open to further politics and propaganda to influence what administrative action would actually be and whether it would be liberal or protectionist. They allowed the Congressmen and their followers on both sides to continue their efforts on behalf of the policies about which they cared. The large majority of Congressmen of all tendencies agreed that some bill had to be passed. The old bill was about to expire, and having no bill at all would have created the worst possible situation in the eyes of all but a handful of protectionist extremists. Some bill was required, if only for the sake of having a functioning escape clause. Failure to pass some act would also have harmed the congressional system in ways having nothing to do with foreign trade. It would have damaged the public image of Congress, as similar failures to act have hurt in such countries as France. It would have brought the congressional leadership into bitter conflict with the White House. It would have injured American prestige abroad and thus have had severe consequences for foreign policy and defense spending. It would have tied up other bills in a legislative log jam. There was agreement on the need for action, but none on what action to take. Thus, the framers of the bill had to get some bill out so that the system could continue to function, but a bill that would force Congress as little as possible to make determinations on the issues which divided it the most. Once such a bill had been hammered out, it was helped through by members on both sides of the main issue, for example, Senator Eugene Millikin (R., Colo.) and Representative Robert Kean (R., N.J.). Each had other business to get on with, to which he could proceed on the basis of the text adopted.[8] Not the least of these goals was achievement of an effective, smooth-running congressional system, a goal far more important than almost any one bill and one to which we now turn our attention.

Congress is not a temporary convocation. It is an ongoing social system which must preserve itself intact and which deals with problems on a long-run, rather than a one-shot, basis.

Because Congress is a social system, what comes out in the form of legislation often, and probably usually, differs from what one would predict from an enumeration of the opinions of individual Congressmen.

Suppose that, in the elections of 1954, a voter wished to cast a ballot to facilitate protectionist legislation by Congress. Suppose that, in his district, he faced the choice between a protectionist Democrat and

---

[8]In the interviews, a recurrent theme by partisans of each side was that their struggle, though unsuccessful, was justified by the effect it would have at the next renewal. The protectionist theme in 1955 was: this is the last time "they" will be able to get through a tariff-cutting bill; the corner has been turned. The administration theme was: this is the last gasp of protectionism; "we have laid the basis for a liberal-trade policy." Judging by the ease of the 1958 renewal, the administration may have been right in 1955. Failure to resolve issues in 1954 and 1955 may have bought the time needed for public opinion to mature.

a free-trading Republican, either of whom would be a freshmen.[9] He would probably have been ill-advised to vote for the protectionist Democrat. The Democrat might have added one protectionist vote in the House. We say *might* have because, being a freshman, he might also have given in to the persuasive efforts of Sam Rayburn *et al.* and gone along with a liberal-trade policy in the hope of digging himself in with the Democratic leadership. But, in the House in particular, legislation is written mainly in the committees, and our freshman, a protectionist Democrat, would certainly have not got on the cherished Ways and Means Committee, where tariff legislation is written. The free-trading Republican, however, might have contributed to a Republican majority in the House. Had a Republican majority organized the House, the Ways and Means Committee would have been chaired by a Republican and dominated by a majority of Republicans ranging from mildly to militantly protectionist. Considering the composition of that committee in that period and the protectionist inclinations of Republican Congressmen James Utt (Calif.) and Victor Knox (Mich.), who were in fact displaced from their committee positions by the Democratic victory in 1954, the chances of a protectionist bill being fashioned by the Ways and Means Committee would have been greater with a Republican House. Thus, our hypothetical voter might have been well-advised to vote for a free-trade Republican if he wanted a protectionist law to come out of the House.

Of course, there is no logical reason why tariff legislation should at present be considered by the Ways and Means Committee of the House. Historically it made sense, since the tariff was an important source of revenue. In the present, tariff legislation could just as reasonably, and perhaps more reasonably, be considered by the Foreign Affairs Committee, which, incidentally, is burdened with far less work. However, to make this shift would raise very delicate questions. If some members of the Ways and Means Committee who are more interested in foreign-trade policy than in taxation wanted to shift to the Foreign Affairs Committee, problems of seniority would arise. All in all, such a shift could cause considerable disequilibrium in the social organization of the House of Representatives, and it is not likely.

But it made a good deal of difference that tariff legislation was considered, not by the Foreign Affairs Committee, but by the Ways and Means Committee, if only because of its heavy work load, let alone the difference in committee memberships on the Republican side. The deferment of a decision in 1954 was to a large part due to the fact that the Ways and Means Committee was occupied with tax reform and other legislation dear to the heart of Chairman Daniel Reed (R., N.Y.) and did not have sufficient time for hearings. In 1955, additional legislation was introduced which might have taken much of the steam out of protectionist arguments. But, because of the work load, Ways and Means never got around to considering this legislation.

The fact that Congress is an organized body with its own institutions and procedures was far from a self-evident proposition to the people who were trying to influence Congress on foreign-trade policy in 1953–1955.

We have commented on the importance of committees for the passage of legislation. In the House, this is especially true, since bills are often reported out of committee under the closed rule, which makes it impossible to amend the bill on the floor. A member can vote either for or against the bill as presented. There are two principles which can be deduced from this simple circumstance. First, Committee members on Ways and Means are much more important on foreign-trade measures than are other representatives. However, so far as we could ascertain, Ways and Means members received but little extra mail on the issue by virtue of their Committee membership. The picture is slightly complicated,[10] but there was by no means the concentration of mail one would expect, were this simple principle grasped. Second, there was little or no point in writing the average Congressman advocating amendments to the Reciprocal Trade Act for specific products. (In 1955, there was a brief possibility that the bill would be opened to amendments from the floor, but this was an unusual circumstance.) Nevertheless, Congressmen from Michigan, for example, were confronted with mail which asked them to vote for the Reciprocal Trade Act, but to except cherries by giving them a protective tariff. Many other Congressmen were petitioned for protection for specific products and industries. Given the way in which legislation is passed in the House, these instructions constituted something less than a clear-cut mandate to the Congressmen. They could not vote for reciprocal trade and for protection for the cherry industry or any other interest. They had to vote for or against HR 1 as reported out of committee.

Congressmen specialize according to their committee assignments far more than most laymen realize. Most legislative work is done in committee. A Congressman can therefore ordinarily be effective in drafting and pushing legislation only in a field covered by his committee. Over

---

[10]It looks as though Committee members received a disproportionate number of press releases and other canned communications. This suggests that some interest groups were thinking at least in part of the importance of the Committee. However, such canned communications are precisely the type of communication that is least effective with most Congressmen.

the years, members of committees become experts in their subjects. Other Congressmen follow the lead of committee members in whose general point of view they have confidence. Thus, a generally protectionist Representative who was not on Ways and Means might not do anything about tariff legislation, except that when it got on the floor he would vote for those amendments supported by Dan Reed. Most creative work in framing amendments and strategy and congressional in-fighting would have been done by committee members.

That the pressure groups were not fully alert to exactly how Congress functions may also be demonstrated by their inattention to the conference committee. The Senate and House versions of HR 1 were referred to a joint conference committee, as happens when the bills passed by the two Houses do not agree. That committee had a good deal of leeway. For example, it could have settled on substantially the original House bill and dropped most or all of the senatorial amendments. Would this, then, not have resulted in a bill which the Senate would reject? Not necessarily. In the interests of keeping the system moving, there is a strong congressional bias against rejecting a conference committee report. Amendments which a large majority of either House has inserted as an absolute condition for passing a bill may be quietly dropped if the conference committee has not accepted them. Congressmen, knowing that, will often propose and/or vote for some measure with the intent of demonstrating that they are alert to their constituents' needs, tacitly understanding that it will be amended in conference. Oregon's Senator Wayne Morse (D.) inserted into the Senate bill such an amendment to protect the cherry-and nut-growers.

The opportunity for modifying the bill in conference existed not only in the abstract. It was known that Jere Cooper (D., Tenn.) and Wilbur Mills (D., Ark.), the major House conferees, were dissatisfied with the Senate version and were apparently ready to fight for a substantial revision. This was an attractive opportunity for pressure groups to converge on a small group of men, the Senate-House conferees. But nothing of the sort happened. Perhaps the pro-reciprocal-trade groups were simply tired and had in effect disbanded their effort when the amended bill passed the Senate. Perhaps they were guilty of neglect or a political blunder, although they certainly knew the basic facts. In any event, they seem to have been inadequately sensitive to established institutions and procedures of Congress.

There are many other examples of how communications with Congress fail because the public has too simple a notion of what goes on there. Congressman Amiable, commenting on his wide experience in a state legislature and in Congress, complained, "You always hear from business too late." Businessmen and their representatives respond to the news. They write to protest a bill when their newspaper or magazine reports it, and that is when it is reported out of committee for general debate. But, by that time, especially in the House, it is difficult to amend. If a communication arrives while the committee is still meeting, a member may feel free to work for the adoption of an amendment. But once he has voted, he is under obligation to go along with other members of the committee. He can scarcely afford to sacrifice his long-term working arrangements with the other Congressmen for this one issue. The very petitioners from his district have many interests. If he wants to serve his district, not only at the moment, but over the years, he must preserve his colleagues' respect.

Sometimes an alert trade-association secretary warns his members to write soon enough. In practice, we found relatively few who did so. However, what such a trade association gains in superior tactics it may lose in the appearance of being organized in its efforts.

When mail does come in time to influence the decision on a bill, subsequent amendments to the original bill may make it irrelevant. A communication which was initially clear in its intentions may become unclear in its implications as the congressional process wends its way. A note which said simply, "Vote for free trade," was presumably in favor of HR 1 as originally reported out, a reasonably liberal trade measure. But what about HR 1 as amended by the Senate? At least one Representative voted against it as a protectionist measure. Would our hypothetical Congressman make his free-trade correspondent happy by voting for or against the amended version?

There is one more relevant point which bears directly on the workings of Congress. Its established procedures are sufficiently complicated to make it often hard to tell exactly what stand a Congressman did take on a particular issue. In many instances, a Congressman will cast a record vote for a proposal only when he is sure it will be defeated, or against it when he is sure it will pass. The reason for this may be twofold. The leadership may release him if his vote does not matter, recognizing his need to impress his constituents. He may in fact be opposed to the measure, but want to get a vote in favor of it on his record. If he has guessed wrongly on how the votes divide, he can usually change his vote when the count is totted up. On the crucial votes in the House in 1955, the leadership in fact won by one vote, according to *The Congressional Record*. But at one time, members report, it had lost by seven votes. The leadership usually has enough of a reservoir of political credit to have a few votes switched if it would otherwise lose by a narrow margin.

A particular measure may involve a complex of issues. For example, the open-rule proposal was defended on grounds that the House should not be gagged. Certainly, whether in good conscience or not, a Congressman could have voted for debate under an open rule and claimed that he was nonetheless for HR 1. Such things happen and they happen regularly. We cannot help but remember the bemused comment of a trade-association representative who said, "I don't know what the hell happend with 'em," referring to several Senators who promised to vote "his way" but apparently did not. Aware of the complexities of the congressional process, he knew that he could not take their apparent reneging on a promise as deception on their part, for they may have been hoping to serve him later.

If pressure is to be effective, there must be some clear criterion of yielding to the pressure. In view of the complexity of the congressional process, we suspect that an adroit Congressman could confuse the issue in a majority of instances. A look at the voting pattern of HR 1 suggests that a considerable number of Congressmen were doing just that. That is one reason why, after the open rule and the protectionist Reed amendment were beaten by the narrowest of squeaks, HR 1 went through with a considerable margin. How can one account for the Representatives who first voted to kill the bill and then to pass it? Among other things, they were putting themselves on record on both sides of the issue. To protectionists, they could say that they voted to have the bill changed, but when they were beaten they had no choice but to vote for it, rather than have no bill at all. To freer traders they could say that they voted for the bill. If challenged on their earlier votes, they could defend these in terms of desiring freer debate and improvements in the law.

The complexity of the organization and procedures of Congress reduces the effect of external voices on it. Its social organization exerts constraints on what any single Congressman can do. It also enables him to confuse the issue as to what he has in fact done and why he did it. Clearly, influencing Congress is more than a matter of pressuring individual Congressmen. The job is to approach the right Congressman at the right time and in the right way.

THE HOUSE APPROPRIATIONS COMMITTEE AS A POLITICAL SYSTEM: THE PROBLEM OF INTEGRATION

RICHARD F. FENNO, JR.

Studies of Congress by political scientists have produced a time-tested consensus on the very considerable power and autonomy of congressional committees. Because of these two related characteristics, it makes empirical and analytical sense to treat the congressional committee as a discrete unit for analysis. This paper conceives of the committee as a political system (or, more accurately as a political sub-system) faced with a number of basic problems which it must solve in order to achieve its goals and maintain itself. Generally speaking these functional problems pertain to the environmental and the internal relations of the committee. This study is concerned almost exclusively with the internal problems of the committee and particularly with the problem of self-integration.[1] It describes how one congressional committee—the Committee on Appropriations of the House of Representatives—has dealt with this

The author wishes to acknowledge his indebtedness to the Committee on Political Behavior of the Social Science Research Council for the research grant which made possible this study, and the larger study of legislative behavior in the area of appropriations of which it is a part. This is a revised version of a paper read at the Annual Meeting of the American Political Science Association at St. Louis, September, 1961.

[1]On social systems, see George Homans, *The Human Group* (New York: Harcourt, Brace & World, Inc., 1950); Robert K. Merton, *Social Theory and Social Structure* (New York: Free Press of Glencoe, 1957); Talcott Parsons and Edward Shils, *Toward a General Theory of Action* (Cambridge, Mass.: Harvard University Press, 1951), pp. 190–234. Most helpful with reference to the political system has been David Easton, "An Approach to the Analysis of Political Systems," *World Politics* (April, 1957), pp. 383–400.

Reprinted by permission from the AMERICAN POLITICAL SCIENCE REVIEW, 56 *(June 1962), 310–24. Mr. Fenno is Professor of Political Science at the University of Rochester.*

problem in the period 1947–1961. Its purpose is to add to our understanding of appropriations politics in Congress and to suggest the usefulness of this type of analysis for studying the activities of any congressional committee.

The necessity for integration in any social system arises from the differentiation among its various elements. Most importantly there is a differentiation among subgroups and among individual positions, together with the roles that flow therefrom.[2] A committee faces the problem, how shall these diverse elements be made to mesh together or function in support of one another? No political system (or sub-system) is perfectly integrated; yet no political system can survive without some minimum degree of integration among its differentiated parts. Committee integration is defined as the degree to which there is a working together or a meshing together or mutual support among its roles and subgroups. Conversely, it is also defined as the degree to which a committee is able to minimize conflict among its roles and its subgroups, by heading off or resolving the conflicts that arise.[3] A concomitant of integration is the existence of a fairly consistent set of norms, widely agreed upon and widely followed by the members. Another concomitant of integration is the existence of control mechanisms (*i.e.*, socialization and sanctioning mechanisms) capable of maintaining reasonable conformity to norms. In other words, the more highly integrated a committee, the smaller will be the gap between expected and actual behavior.

This study is concerned with integration both as a structural characteristic of, and as a functional problem for, the Appropriations Committee. First certain basic characteristics of the Committee need description, to help explain the integration of its parts. Second comes a partial description of the degree to which and the ways in which the Committee achieves integration. No attempt is made to state this in quantitative terms, but the object is to examine the meshing together or the minimization of conflict among certain subgroups and among certain key roles. Also, important control mechanisms are described. The study concludes with some comments on the consequences of Committee integration for appropriations politics and on the usefulness of further congressional committee analysis in terms of functional problems such as this one.

[2] On the idea of sub-groups as used here, see Harry M. Johnson, *Sociology* (New York: Harcourt, Brace & World, Inc., 1960), Ch. 3. On role, see specifically Theodore M. Newcomb, *et al.*, *Social Psychology* (New York: Holt, Rinehart & Winston, Inc., 1951), p. 280; see generally N. Gross, W. Mason, and A. McEachern, *Explorations in Role Analysis: Studies of the School Superintendency Role* (New York: John Wiley & Sons, Inc., 1958). On differentiation and its relation to integration, see Scott Greer, *Social Organization* (New York: Random House, Inc., 1955).

[3] The usage here follows most closely that of Merton, *op. cit.*, pp. 26–29.

I

Five important characteristics of the Appropriations Committee which help explain Committee integration are (1) the existence of a well-articulated and deeply rooted consensus on Committee goals or tasks; (2) the nature of the Committee's subject matter; (3) the legislative orientation of its members; (4) the attractiveness of the Committee for its members; and (5) the stability of Committee membership.

Consensus

The Appropriations Committee sees its tasks as taking form within the broad guidelines set by its parent body, the House of Representatives. For it is the primary condition of the Committee's existence that it was created by the House for the purpose of assisting the House in the performance of House legislative tasks dealing with appropriations. Committee members agree that their fundamental duty is to serve the House in the manner and with the substantive results that the House prescribes. Given, however, the imprecision of House expectations and the permissiveness of House surveillance, the Committee must elaborate for itself a definition of tasks plus a supporting set of perceptions (of itself and of others) explicit enough to furnish day-to-day guidance.

The Committee's view begins with the preeminence of the House —often mistakenly attributed to the Constitution ("all bills for raising revenue," Art. I, sec. 7) but nevertheless firmly sanctioned by custom—in appropriations affairs.

It moves easily to the conviction that, as the efficient part of the House in this matter, the Constitution has endowed it with special obligations and special prerogatives. It ends in the view that the Committee on Appropriations, far from being merely one among many units in a complicated legislative-executive system, is *the* most important, most responsible unit in the whole appropriations process.[4] Hand in hand with the consensus on their primacy goes a consensus that all of their House-prescribed tasks can be fulfilled by superimposing upon them one, single, paramount task—to *guard the Federal Treasury*. Committee members

---

[4]This and all other generalizations about member attitudes and perceptions depend heavily on extensive interviews with Committee members. Semi-structured interviews, averaging 45 minutes in length, were held with 45 of the 50 Committee members during the 86th Congress. Certain key questions, all open-ended, were asked of all respondents. The schedule was kept very flexible, however, in order to permit particular topics to be explored with those individuals best equipped to discuss them. In a few cases, where respondents encouraged it, notes were taken during the interviews. In most cases notes were not taken, but were transcribed immediately after the interview. Where unattributed quotations occur in the text, therefore, they are as nearly verbatim as the author's power of immediate recall could make them. These techniques were all used so as to improve *rapport* between interviewer and respondent.

state their goals in the essentially negative terms of guardianship—screening requests for money, checking against ill-advised expenditures, and protecting the taxpayer's dollar. In the language of the Committee's official history, the job of each member is, "constantly and courageously to protect the Federal Treasury against thousands of appeals and imperative demands for unnecessary, unwise, and excessive expenditures."[5]

To buttress its self-image as guardian of public funds the Committee elaborates a set of perceptions about other participants in the appropriations process to which most members hold most of the time. Each executive official, for example, is seen to be interested in the expansion of his own particular program. Each one asks, therefore, for more money than he really needs, in view of the total picture, to run an adequate program. This and other Committee perceptions—of the Budget Bureau, of the Senate, and of their fellow Representatives—help to shape and support the Committee members in their belief that most budget estimates can, should, and must be reduced and that, since no one else can be relied upon, the House Committee must do the job. To the consensus on the main task of protecting the Treasury is added, therefore, a consensus on the instrumental task of *cutting whatever budget estimates are submitted.*

As an immediate goal, Committee members agree that they must strike a highly critical, aggressive posture toward budget requests, and that they should, on principle, reduce them. In the words of the Committee's veterans: "There has never been a budget submitted to the Congress that couldn't be cut." "There isn't a budget that can't be cut 10 per cent immediately." "I've been on the Committee for 17 years. No subcommittee of which I have been a member has ever reported out a bill without a cut in the budget. I'm proud of that record." The aim of budget-cutting is strongly internalized for the Committee member. "It's a tradition in the Appropriations Committee to cut." "You're grounded in it. . . . It's ingrained in you from the time you get on the Committee." For the purposes of a larger study, the appropriations case histories of 37 executive bureaus have been examined for a 12-year period, 1947–1959.[6] Of 443 separate bureau estimates, the Committee reduced 77.2 per cent (342) of them.

It is a mark of the intensity and self-consciousness of the Committee consensus on budget-cutting that it is couched in a distinctive vocabulary. The workaday lingo of the Committee member is replete with

---

[5]"History of the Committee on Appropriations," House Doc. 299, 77th Cong., 1st sess., 1941–1942, p. 11.

[6]The bureaus being studied are all concerned with domestic policy and are situated in the Agriculture, Interior, Labor, Commerce, Treasury, Justice, and Health, Education and Welfare Departments. For a similar pattern of Committee decisions in foreign affairs, see Holbert Carroll, *The House of Representatives and Foreign Affairs* (Pittsburgh, Pa.: University of Pittsburgh Press, 1958), Ch. 9.

negative verbs, undesirable objects of attention, and effective instruments of action. Agency budgets are said to be filled with "fat," "padding," "grease," "pork," "oleaginous substance," "water," "oil," "cushions," "avoirdupois," "waste tissue," and "soft spots." The action verbs most commonly used are "cut," "carve," "slice," "prune," "whittle," "squeeze," "wring," "trim," "lop off," "chop," "slash," "pare," "shave," "fry," and "whack." The tools of the trade are appropriately referred to as "knife," "blade," "meat axe," "scalpel," "meat cleaver," "hatchet," "shears," "wringer," and "fine-tooth comb." Members are hailed by their fellows as being "pretty sharp with the knife." Agencies may "have the meat axe thrown at them." Executives are urged to put their agencies "on a fat boy's diet." Budgets are praised when they are "cut to the bone." And members agree that, "You can always get a little more fat out of a piece of pork if you fry it a little longer and a little harder."

To the major task of protecting the Treasury and the instrumental task of cutting budget estimates, each Committee member adds, usually by way of exception, a third task—*serving the constituency to which he owes his election*. This creates no problem for him when, as is sometimes the case, he can serve his district best by cutting the budget requests of a federal agency whose program is in conflict with the demands of his constituency.[7] Normally, however, members find that their most common role-conflict is between a Committee-oriented budget-reducing role and a constituency-oriented budget-increasing role. Committee ideology resolves the conflict by assigning top, long-run priority to the budget-cutting task, and making of the constituency service a permissible, short-run exception. No member is expected to commit electoral suicide; but no member is expected to allow his district's desire for federal funds to dominate his Committee behavior.

Subject Matter

Appropriations Committee integration is facilitated by the subject matter with which the group deals. The Committee makes decisions on the same controversial issues as do the committees handling substantive legislation. But a money decision—however vitally it affects national policy—is, or at least seems to be, less directly a policy decision. Since they deal immediately with dollars and cents, it is easy for the members to hold to the idea that they are not dealing with programmatic questions, that theirs is a "business" rather than a "policy" committee. The subject matter, furthermore, keeps Committee members relatively free agents, which promotes intra-Committee maneuvering and, hence, conflict avoidance. Members do not commit themselves to their constituents in terms

[7]See, for example, Philip A. Foss, "The Grazing Fee Dilemma," Inter-University Case Program, No. 57 (University of Alabama, 1960).

of precise money amounts, and no dollar sum is sacred—it can always be adjusted without conceding that a principle has been breached. By contrast, members of committees dealing directly with controversial issues are often pressured into taking concrete stands on these issues; consequently, they may come to their committee work with fixed and hardened attitudes. This leads to unavoidable, head-on intra-committee conflict and renders integrative mechanisms relatively ineffective.

The fact of an annual appropriations process means the Committee members repeat the same operations with respect to the same subject matters year after year—and frequently more than once in a given year. Substantive and procedural repetition promotes familiarity with key problems and provides ample opportunity to test and confirm the most satisfactory methods of dealing with them. And the absolute necessity that appropriations bills do ultimately pass gives urgency to the search for such methods. Furthermore, the House rule that no member of the Committee can serve on another standing committee is a deterrent against a fragmentation of Committee member activity which could be a source of difficulty in holding the group together. If a committee has developed (as this one has) a number of norms designed to foster integration, repeated and concentrated exposure to them increases the likelihood that they will be understood, accepted, and followed.

Legislative Orientation

The recruitment of members for the Appropriations Committee produces a group of individuals with an orientation especially conducive to Committee integration. Those who make the selection pay special attention to the characteristics which Masters has described as those of the "responsible legislator"—approval of and conformity to the norms of the legislative process and of the House of Representatives.[8]

Key selectors speak of wanting, for the Appropriations Committee, "the kind of man you can deal with" or "a fellow who is well-balanced and won't go off half-cocked on things." A Northern liberal Democrat felt that he had been chosen over eight competitors because, "I had made a lot of friends and was known as a nice guy"—especially, he noted, among Southern Congressmen. Another Democrat explained, "I got the blessing of the Speaker and the leadership. It's personal friendships. I had done a lot of things for them in the past, and when I went to them and asked them, they gave it to me." A Republican chosen for the Committee in his first term recalled,

> The Chairman [Rep. Taber] I guess did some checking around in my area. After all, I was new and he didn't know me. People told me that they were

[8]Nicholas A. Masters, "House Committee Assignments," *American Political Science Review*, Vol. 55 (June 1961), pp. 345–57.

called to see if I was—well, unstable or apt to go off on tangents . . . to see whether or not I had any preconceived notions about things and would not be flexible—whether I would oppose things even though it was obvious.

A key criterion in each of the cases mentioned was a demonstrable record of, or an assumed predisposition toward, legislative give-and-take.

The 106 Appropriations Committee members serving between 1947 and 1961 spent an average of 3.6 years on other House committees before coming to the Committee. Only 17 of the 106 were selected as first term Congressmen. A House apprenticeship (which Appropriations maintains more successfully than all committees save Ways and Means and Rules[9]) provides the time in which legislative reputations can be established by the member and an assessment of that reputation in terms of Appropriations Committee requirements can be made. Moreover, the mere fact that a member survives for a couple of terms is some indication of an electoral situation conducive to his "responsible" legislative behavior. The optimum bet for the Committee is a member from a sufficiently safe district to permit him freedom of maneuver inside the House without fear of reprisal at the polls.[10] The degree of responsiveness to House norms which the Committee selectors value may be the product of a safe district as well as an individual temperament.

Attractiveness

A fourth factor is the extraordinarily high degree of attractiveness which the Committee holds for its members—as measured by the low rate of departure from it. Committee members do not leave it for service on other committees. To the contrary, they are attracted to it from nearly every other committee.[11] Of the 106 members in the 1947–1961 period, only two men left the Committee voluntarily; and neither of them initiated the move.[12] Committee attractiveness is a measure of its capacity

[9]In the period from 1947 through 1959 (80th to 86th Congresses), 79 separate appointments were made to the Appropriations Committee, with 14 going to freshmen, The Committee filled, in other words, 17.7 per cent of its vacancies with freshmen. The Rules Committee had 26 vacancies and selected no freshmen at all. The Ways and Means Committee had 36 vacancies and selected 2 freshmen (5.6 per cent). All other committees had a higher percentage of freshmen appointments. Armed Services ranked fourth, with 45 vacancies and 12 freshmen appointed, for a percentage of 26.7. Foreign Affairs figures were 46 and 14, or 30.4 per cent; Un-American Activities figures were 22 and 7, or 31.8 per cent. *Cf.* Masters, *op. cit.*

[10]In the 1960 elections, 41 out of the current 50 members received more than 55.1 per cent of the vote in their districts. By a common definition, that is, only 9 of the 50 came from marginal districts.

[11]The 106 members came to Appropriations from every committee except Ways and Means.

[12]One was personally requested by the Speaker to move to Ways and Means. The other was chosen by a caucus of regional Congressmen to be his party's representative on the Rules Committee. Of the 21 members who were forced off the Committee for lack of seniority during a change in party control, or who were defeated for reelection and later returned, 20 sought to regain Committee membership at the earliest opportunity.

to satisfy individual member needs—for power, prestige, recognition, respect, self-esteem, friendship, etc. Such satisfaction in turn increases the likelihood that members will behave in such a way as to hold the group together.

The most frequently mentioned source of Committee attractiveness is its power—based on its control of financial resources. "Where the money is, that's where the power is," sums up the feeling of the members. They prize their ability to reward or punish so many other participants in the political process—executive officials, fellow Congressmen, constituents, and other clientele groups. In the eyes of its own members, the Committee is either the most powerful in the House or it is on a par with Ways and Means or, less frequently, on a par with Ways and Means and Rules. The second important ingredient in member satisfaction is the government-wide scope of Committee activity. The ordinary Congressman may feel that he has too little knowledge of and too little control over his environment. Membership on this Committee compensates for this feeling of helplessness by the wider contacts, the greater amount of information, and the sense of being "in the middle of things" which are consequent, if not to subcommittee activity, at least to the full Committee's overview of the federal government.

Thirdly, Committee attractiveness is heightened by the group's recognizable and distinctive political style—one that is, moreover, highly valued in American political culture. The style is that of *hard work*; and the Committee's self-image is that of "the hardest working Committee in Congress." His willingness to work is the Committee member's badge of identification, and it is proudly worn. It colors his perceptions of others and their perceptions of him.[13] It is a cherished axiom of all members that, "This Committee is no place for a man who doesn't work. They have to be hard working. It's a way of life. It isn't just a job; it's a way of life."

The mere existence of some identifiable and valued style or "way of life" is a cohesive force for a group. But the particular style of hard work is one which increases group morale and group identification twice over. Hard work means a long, dull, and tedious application to detail, via the technique of "dig, dig, dig, day after day behind closed doors"—in an estimated 460 subcommittee and full Committee meetings

---

[13] A sidelight on this attitude is displayed in a current feud between the House and Senate Appropriations Committees over the meeting place for their conference committees. The House Committee is trying to break the century-old custom that conferences to resolve differences on money bills are always held on the Senate side of the Capitol. House Committee members "complain that they often have to trudge back to the House two or three times to answer roll calls during a conference. They say they go over in a body to work, while senators flit in and out. . . . The House Appropriations Committee feels that it does all the hard work listening to witnesses for months on each bill, only to have the Senate Committee sit as a court of appeals and, with little more than a cursory glance, restore most of the funds cut." *Washington Post*, April 24, 1962, p. 1.

a year. And virtually all of these meetings are in executive session. By adopting the style of hard work, the Committee discourages highly individualized forms of legislative behavior, which could be disruptive within the Committee. It rewards its members with power, but it is power based rather on work inside the Committee than on the political glamour of activities carried on in the limelight of the mass media. Prolonged daily work together encourages sentiments of mutual regard, sympathy, and solidarity. This *esprit* is, in turn, functional for integration on the Committee. A Republican leader summed up,

> I think it's more closely knit than any other committee. Yet it's the biggest committee, and you'd think it would be the reverse. I know on my subcommittee, you sit together day after day. You get better acquainted. You have sympathy when other fellows go off to play golf. There's a lot of *esprit de corps* in the Committee.

The strong attraction which members have for the Committee increases the influence which the Committee and its norms exercise on all of them. It increases the susceptibility of the newcomer to Committee socialization and of the veteran to Committee sanctions applicable against deviant behavior.[14]

Membership Stability

Members of the Appropriations Committee are strongly attracted to it; they also have, which bears out their selection as "responsible legislators," a strong attraction for a career in the House of Representatives. The 50 members on the Committee in 1961 had served an average of 13.1 years in the House. These twin attractions produce a noteworthy stability of Committee membership. In the period from the 80th to the 87th Congress, 35.7 per cent of the Committee's membership remained constant. That is to say, 15 of the 42 members on the Committee in March, 1947, were still on the Committee in March, 1961.[15] The 50 members of the Committee in 1961 averaged 9.3 years of prior service on that Committee. In no single year during the last fourteen has the Committee had to absorb an influx of new members totalling more than one-quarter of its membership. At all times, in other words, at least three-fourths of the members have had previous Committee experience. This extraordinary stability of personnel extends into the staff as well. As of June, 1961,

[14]This proposition is spelled out at some length in J. Thibaut and H. Kelley, *The Social Psychology of Groups* (New York: John Wiley & Sons, Inc., 1959), p. 247; and in D. Cartwright and A. Zander, *Group Dynamics: Research and Theory* (2nd ed) (New York: Harper & Row, Publishers, 1953), p. 420.

[15]This figure is 9 per cent greater than the next most stable House Committee during this particular period. The top four, in order, were Appropriations (35.7%), Agriculture (26.7%), Armed Services (25%), Foreign Affairs (20.8%).

its 15 professionals had served an average of 10.7 years with the Committee.[16]

The opportunity exists, therefore, for the development of a stable leadership group, a set of traditional norms for the regulation of internal Committee behavior, and informal techniques of personal accommodation. Time is provided in which new members can learn and internalize Committee norms before they attain high seniority rankings. The Committee does not suffer from the potentially disruptive consequences of rapid changeovers in its leadership group, nor of sudden impositions of new sets of norms governing internal Committee behavior.

II

If one considers the main activity of a political system to be decision making, the acid test of its internal integration is its capacity to make collective decisions without flying apart in the process. Analysis of Committee integration should focus directly, therefore, upon its subgroups and the roles of its members. Two kinds of subgroups are of central importance—subcommittees and majority or minority party groups. The roles which are most relevant derive from: (1) positions which each member holds by virtue of his subgroup attachments, e.g., as subcommittee member, majority (or minority) party member; (2) positions which relate to full Committee membership, e.g., Committee member, and the seniority rankings of veteran, man of moderate experience, and newcomer[17]; (3) positions which relate to both subgroup and full Committee membership, e.g., Chairman of the Committee, ranking minority member of the Committee, subcommittee chairman, ranking subcommittee member. Clusters of norms state the expectations about subgroup and role behavior. The description which follows treats the ways in which these norms and their associated behaviors mesh and clash. It treats, also, the internal control mechanisms by which behavior is brought into reasonable conformity with expectations.

Subgroup Integration

The day-to-day work of the Committee is carried on in its subcommittees each of which is given jurisdiction over a number of related governmental units. The number of subcommittees is determined by the Committee Chairman and has varied recently from a low of 9 in 1949

[16]The Committee's permanent and well integrated professional staff (as distinguished from its temporary investigating staff) might be considered as part of the sub-system though it will not be treated in this paper.

[17]"Newcomers" are defined as men who have served no more than two terms on the Committee. "Men of moderate experience" are those with 3–5 terms of service. "Veterans" are those who have 6 or more terms of Committee service.

to a high of 15 in 1959. The present total of 14 reflects, as always, a set of strategic and personal judgments by the Chairman balanced against the limitations placed on him by Committee tradition and members' wishes. The Chairman also determines subcommittee jurisdiction, appoints subcommittee chairmen, and selects the majority party members of each group. The ranking minority member of the Committee exercises similar control over subcommittee assignments on his side of the aisle.

Each subcommittee holds hearings on the budget estimates of the agencies assigned to it, meets in executive session to decide what figures and what language to recommend to the full Committee (to "mark up" the bill), defends its recommendations before the full Committee, writes the Committee's report to the House, dominates the debate on the floor, and bargains for the House in conference committee. Within its jurisdiction, each subcommittee functions independently of the others and guards its autonomy jealously. The Chairman and ranking minority member of the full Committee have, as we shall see, certain opportunities to oversee and dip into the operations of all subcommittees. But their intervention is expected to be minimal. Moreover, they themselves operate importantly within the subcommittee framework by sitting as chairman or ranking minority member of the subcommittee in which they are most interested. Each subcommittee, under the guidance of its chairman, transacts its business in considerable isolation from every other one. One subcommittee chairman exclaimed,

> Why, you'd be branded an impostor if you went into one of those other subcommittee meetings. The only time I go is by appointment, by arrangement with the chairman at a special time. I'm as much a stranger in another subcommittee as I would be in the legislative Committee on Post Office and Civil Service. Each one does its work apart from all others.

All members of all subcommittees are expected to behave in similar fashion in the role of subcommittee member. Three main norms define this role; to the extent that they are observed, they promote harmony and reduce conflict among subcommittees.[18] Subcommittee autonomy gives to the House norm of *specialization* an intensified application on the Appropriations Committee. Each member is expected to play the role of specialist in the activities of one subcommittee. He will sit on from one to four subcommittees, but normally will specialize in the work, or

---

[18]A statement of expected behavior was taken to be a Committee norm when it was expressed by a substantial number of respondents (a dozen or so) who represented both parties, and varying degrees of experience. In nearly every case, moreover, no refutation of them was encountered, and ample confirmation of their existence can be found in the public record. Their articulation came most frequently from the veterans of the group.

a portion of the work, of only one. Except for the Chairman, ranking minority member and their confidants, a Committee member's time, energy, contacts and experience are devoted to his subcommittees. Specialization is, therefore, among the earliest and most compelling of the Committee norms to which a newcomer is exposed. Within the Committee, respect, deference, and power are earned through subcommittee activity and, hence to a degree, through specialization. Specialization is valued further because it is well suited to the task of guarding the Treasury. Only by specializing, Committee members believe, can they unearth the volume of factual information necessary for the intelligent screening of budget requests. Since "the facts" are acquired only through industry, an effective specialist will, perforce, adopt and promote the Committee's style of hard work.

Committee-wide acceptance of specialization is an integrative force in decision making because it helps support a second norm—*reciprocity*. The state at which a subcommittee makes its recommendations is a potential point of internal friction. Conflict among subcommittees (or between one subcommittee and the rest of the Committee) is minimized by the deference traditionally accorded to the recommendation of the subcommittee which has specialized in the area, has worked hard, and has "the facts." "It's a matter of 'You respect my work and I'll respect yours.' " "It's frowned upon if you offer an amendment in the full Committee if you aren't on the subcommittee. It's considered presumptuous to pose as an expert if you aren't on the subcommittee." Though records of full Committee decisions are not available, members agree that subcommittee recommendations are "very rarely changed," "almost always approved," "changed one time in fifty," "very seldom changed," etc.

No subcommittee is likely to keep the deference of the full Committee for long unless its recommendations have widespread support among its own members. To this end, a third norm—*subcommittee unity* —is expected to be observed by subcommittee members. Unity means a willingness to support (or not to oppose) the recommendations of one's own subcommittee. Reciprocity and unity are closely dependent upon one another. Reciprocity is difficult to maintain when subcommittees themselves are badly divided; and unity has little appeal unless reciprocity will subsequently be observed. The norm of reciprocity functions to minimize inter-subcommittee conflict. The norm of unity functions to minimize intra-subcommittee conflict. Both are deemed essential to subcommittee influence.

One payoff for the original selection of "responsible legislators" is their special willingness to compromise in pursuit of subcommittee unity. The impulse to this is registered most strongly at the time when the subcommittee meets in executive session to mark up the bill. Two ranking minority members explained this aspect of markup procedure in their subcommittees:

> If there's agreement, we go right along. If there's a lot of controversy we put the item aside and go on. Then, after a day or two, we may have a list of ten controversial items. We give and take and pound them down till we get agreement.

> We have a unanimous agreement on everything. If a fellow enters an objection and we can't talk him out of it—and sometimes we can get him to go along—that's it. We put it in there.

Once the bargain is struck, the subcommittee is expected to "stick together."

It is, of course, easier to achieve unity among the five, seven, or nine members of a subcommittee than among the fifty members of the full Committee. But members are expected wherever possible to observe the norm of unity in the full Committee as well. That is, they should not only defer to the recommendations of the subcommittee involved, but they should support (or not oppose) that recommendation when it reaches the floor in the form of a Committee decision. On the floor, Committee members believe, their power and prestige depend largely on the degree to which the norms of reciprocity and unity continue to be observed. Members warn each other that if they go to the floor in disarray they will be "rolled," "jumped," or "run over" by the membership. It is a cardinal maxim among Committee members that, "You can't turn an appropriations bill loose on the floor." Two senior subcommittee chairmen explain,

> We iron out our differences in Committee. We argue it out and usually have a meeting of the minds, a composite view of the Committee. . . . If we went on the floor in wide disagreement, they would say, "If you can't agree after listening to the testimony and discussing it, how can we understand it? We'll just vote on the basis of who we like the best."

> I tell them (the full Committee) we should have a united front. If there are any objections or changes, we ought to hear it now, and not wash our dirty linen out on the floor. If we don't have a bill that we can all agree on and support, we ought not to report it out. To do this is like throwing a piece of meat to a bunch of hungry animals.

One of the most functional Committee practices supporting the norm of unity is the tradition against minority reports in the subcommittee and in the full Committee. It is symptomatic of Committee integration that custom should proscribe the use of the most formal and irrevocable symbol of congressional committee disunity—the minority report. A few have been written—but only 9 out of a possible 141 during the 11 years, 1947–1957. That is to say, 95 per cent of all original appropriations bills in this period were reported out without dissent. The technique of "reserving" is the Committee member's equivalent for the registering of dissent. In subcommittee or Committee, when a member reserves, he goes on record informally by informing his colleagues that he reserves the right to disagree on a specified item later on in the proceedings. He may seek a change or support a change in that particular item in full Committee or on the floor. But he does not publicize his dissent. The subcommittee or the full Committee can then make an unopposed recommendation. The individual retains some freedom of maneuver without firm commitment. Often a member reserves on an appropriations item but takes no further action. A member explained how the procedure operates in subcommittee,

> If there's something I feel too strongly about, and just can't go along, I'll say, "Mr. Chairman, we can have a unanimous report, but I reserve the right to bring this up in full Committee. I feel duty bound to make a play for it and see if I can't sell it to the other members." But if I don't say anything, or don't reserve this right, and then I bring it up in full Committee, they'll say, "Who are you trying to embarrass? You're a member of the team, aren't you? That's not the way to get along."

Disagreement cannot, of course, be eliminated from the Committee. But the Committee has accepted a method for ventilating it which produces a minimum of internal disruption. And members believe that the greater their internal unity, the greater the likelihood that their recommendations will pass the House.

The degree to which the role of the subcommittee member can be so played and subcommittee conflict thereby minimized depends upon the minimization of conflict between the majority and minority party sub-groups. Nothing would be more disruptive to the Committee's work than bitter and extended partisan controversy. It is, therefore, important to Appropriations Committee integration that a fourth norm— *minimal partisanship*—should be observed by members of both party contingents. Nearly every respondent emphasized, with approval, that "very little" or "not much" partisanship prevailed on the Committee. One subcommittee chairman stated flatly, "My job is to keep down partisanship." A ranking minority member said, "You might think that we Republicans would defend the Administration and the budget, but we don't." Majority and minority party ratios are constant and do not change (*i.e.*, in 1958) to reflect changes in the strength of the controlling party. The Committee operates with a completely non-partisan professional staff, which does not change in tune with shifts in party control. Requests for studies by the Committee's investigating staff must be made by the Chairman and ranking minority member of the full Committee and by the chairman and ranking minority member of the subcommittee involved. Subcommittees can produce recommendations without dissent and the full Committee can adopt reports without dissent precisely because party conflict is (during the period 1947–1961) the exception rather than the rule.

The Committee is in no sense immune from the temperature of party conflict, but it does have a relatively high specific heat. Intense party strife or a strongly taken presidential position will get reflected in subcommittee and in Committee recommendations. Sharp divisions in party policy were carried, with disruptive impact, into some areas of Committee activity during the 80th Congress and subsequently, by way of reaction, into the 81st Congress.[19] During the Eisenhower years, extraordinary presidential pleas, especially concerning foreign aid, were given special heed by the Republican members of the Committee.[20] Partisanship is normally generated from the environment and not from within the Committee's party groups. Partisanship is, therefore, likely to be least evident in subcommittee activity, stronger in the full Committee, and most potent at the floor stage. Studies which have focused on roll-call analysis have stressed the influence of party in legislative decision making.[21] In the appropriations process, at any rate, the floor stage probably represents party influence at its maximum. Our examination, by interview, of decision making at the subcommittee and full Committee level would stress the influence of Committee-oriented norms—the strength of which tends to vary inversely with that of party bonds. In the secrecy and intimacy of the subcommittee and full Committee hearing rooms, the member finds it easy to compromise on questions of more or less, to take money from one program and give it to another and, in general, to avoid yes-or-no type party stands. These decisions, taken in response to the integrative norms of the Committee, are the most important ones in the entire appropriations process.

Role Integration

The roles of subcommittee member and party member are common to all.

Other more specific decision-making positions are allocated among the members. Different positions produce different roles, and in an inte-

[19]See, for example, the internal conflict on the subcommittee dealing with the Labor Department. 93 *Cong. Rec.*, pp. 2465–562 passim; 94 *Cong. Rec.*, pp. 7605–7.

[20]See, for example, the unusual minority report of Committee Republicans on the foreign aid appropriations bill in 1960. Their protest against Committee cuts in the budget estimates was the result of strenuous urging by the Eisenhower Administration. House Report No. 1798, *Mutual Security and Related Agency Appropriation Bill*, 86th Cong., 2d sess., 1960.

[21]David Truman, *The Congressional Party* (New York: John Wiley & Sons, Inc., 1959); Julius Turner, *Party and Constituency: Pressures on Congress* (Baltimore, Md.: Johns Hopkins Press, 1951).

grated system these too must fit together. Integration, in other words, must be achieved through the complementarity or reciprocity of roles as well as through a similarity of roles. This may mean a pattern in which expectations are so different that there is very little contact between individuals; or it may mean a pattern in which contacts require the working out of an involved system of exchange of obligations and rewards.[22] In either case, the desired result is the minimization of conflict among prominent Committee roles. Two crucial instances of role reciprocity on the Committee involve the seniority positions of old-timer and newcomer and the leadership positions of Chairman and ranking minority member, on both the full Committee and on each subcommittee.

The differentiation between senior and junior members is the broadest definition of who shall and who shall not actively participate in Committee decisions. Of a junior member, it will be said, "Oh, he doesn't count—what I mean is, he hasn't been on the Committee long enough." He is not expected to and ordinarily does not have much influence. His role is that of apprentice. He is expected to learn the business and the norms of the Committee by applying himself to its work. He is expected to acquiesce in an arrangement which gives most influence (except in affairs involving him locally) to the veterans of the group. Newcomers will be advised to "follow the chairman until you get your bearings. For the first two years follow the chairman. He knows." "Work hard, keep quiet, and attend the Committee sessions. We don't want to listen to some new person coming in here." And newcomers perceive their role in identical terms: "You have to sit in the back seat and edge up little by little." "You just go to subcommittee meetings and assimilate the routine. The new members are made to feel welcome, but you have a lot of rope-learning to do before you carry much weight."

At every stage of Committee work, this differentiation prevails. There is remarkable agreement on the radically different sets of expectations involved. During the hearings, the view of the elders is that "Newcomers . . . don't know what the score is and they don't have enough information to ask intelligent questions." A newcomer described his behavior in typically similar terms: "I attended all the hearings and studied and collected information that I can use next year. I'm just marking time now." During the crucial subcommittee markup, the newcomer will have little opportunity to speak—save in locally important matters. A subcommittee chairman stated the norm from his viewpoint this way: "When we get a compromise, nobody's going to break that up. If someone tries, we sit on him fast. We don't want young people who throw

---

22The ideas of "reciprocity" and "complementarity," which are used interchangeably here, are discussed in Alvin Gouldner, "The Norm of Reciprocity," *American Sociological Review* (April 1960). Most helpful in explaining the idea of a role system has been the work of J. Wahlke, H. Eulau, W. Buchanan, L. Ferguson. See their study, *The Legislative System* (New York: John Wiley & Sons, Inc., 1962), esp. Intro.

bricks or slow things down." And a newcomer reciprocated, describing
his markup conduct: "I'm not provocative. I'm in there for information.
They're the experts in the field. I go along." In full Committee, on the
floor, and in conference committee, the Committee's senior members
take the lead and the junior members are expected to follow. The apprentice role is common to all new members of the House. But it is
wrong to assume that each Committee will give it the same emphasis.
Some pay it scant heed.[23] The Appropriations Committee makes it a
cornerstone of its internal structure.

Among the Committee's veterans, the key roles are those of Committee Chairman and ranking minority member, and their counterparts
in every subcommittee. It is a measure of Committee integration and the
low degree of partisanship that considerable reciprocity obtains between
these roles. Their partisan status nevertheless sets limits to the degree of
possible integration. The Chairman is given certain authority which he
and only he can exercise. But save in times of extreme party controversy,
the expectation is that consultation and cooperation between the Chairman and ranking minority member shall lubricate the Committee's entire work. For example, by Committee tradition, its Chairman and
ranking minority member are both *ex officio* voting members of each subcommittee and of every conference committee. The two of them thus
have joint access at every stage of the internal process. A subcommittee chairman, too, is expected to discuss matters of scheduling and agenda
with his opposite minority number. He is expected to work with him during the markup session and to give him (and, normally, only him) an
opportunity to read and comment on the subcommittee report.[24] A
ranking minority member described his subcommittee markup procedure approvingly:

> Frequently the chairman has a figure which he states. Sometimes he will
> have no figure, and he'll turn to me, and say, "———, what do you think?"
> Maybe I'll have a figure. It's very flexible. Everyone has a chance to say
> what he thinks, and we'll move it around. Sometimes it takes a long
> time. . . . He's a rabid partisan on the floor, but he is a very fair man in
> the subcommittee.

Where influence is shared, an important exchange of rewards occurs. The chairman gains support for his leadership and the ranking
minority member gains intra-Committee power. The Committee as a
whole insures against the possibility of drastic change in its internal
structure by giving to its key minority members a stake in its operation.
Chairmen and ranking minority members will, in the course of time, exchange positions; and it is expected that such a switch will produce no

[23]For example, the Committee on Education and Labor; see footnote 28.
[24]See the exchange in 101 *Cong. Rec.*, pp. 3832, 3844, 3874.

form of retribution nor any drastic change in the functioning of the Committee. Reciprocity of roles, in this case, promotes continued integration. A ranking minority member testified to one successful arrangement when he took the floor in the 83d Congress to say:

> The gentleman and I have been seesawing back and forth on this Committee for some time. He was Chairman in the 80th Congress. I had the privilege of serving as Chairman in the 81st and 82nd Congresses. Now he is back in the saddle. I can say that he has never failed to give me his utmost cooperation, and I have tried to give him the same cooperation during his service as Chairman of this Committee. We seldom disagree, but we have found out that we can disagree without being disagreeable. Consequently, we have unusual harmony on this Committee.[25]

Reciprocity between Chairmen and ranking minority members on the Appropriations Committee is to some incalculable degree a function of the stability of membership which allows a pair of particular individuals to work out the kind of personal accommodation described above. The close working relationship of Clarence Cannon and John Taber, whose service on the Committee totals 68 years and who have been changing places as Chairman and ranking minority member for 19 years, highlights and sustains a pattern of majority-minority reciprocity throughout the group.

Internal Control Mechanisms

The expectations which apply to subcommittee, to party, to veterans and to newcomers, to chairmen and to ranking minority members prescribe highly integrative behaviors. We have concentrated on these expectations, and have both illustrated and assumed the close correlation between expected and actual behavior. This does not mean that all the norms of the Committee have been canvassed. Nor does it mean that deviation from the integrative norms does not occur. It does. From what can be gathered, however, from piecing together a study of the public record on appropriations from 1947 to 1961 with interview materials, the Committee has been markedly successful in maintaining a stable internal structure over time. As might be expected, therefore, changes and threats of change have been generated more from the environment—when outsiders consider the Committee as unresponsive—than from inside the sub-system itself. One source of internal stability, and an added reason for assuming a correlation between expected and actual behavior, is the existence of what appear to be reasonably effective internal control mechanisms. Two of these are the socialization processes applied to newcomers and the sanctioning mechanisms applicable to all Committee members.

[25] *Cong. Rec.*, p. 4933.

Socialization is in part a training in perception. Before members of a group can be expected to behave in accordance with its norms, they must learn to see and interpret the world around them with reasonable similarity. The socialization of the Committee newcomer during his term or two of apprenticeship serves to bring his perceptions and his attitudes sufficiently into line with those of the other members to serve as a basis for Committee integration. The Committee, as we have seen, is chosen from Congressmen whose political flexibility connotes an aptitude for learning new lessons of power. Furthermore, the high degree of satisfaction of its members with the group increases their susceptibility to its processes of learning and training.

For example, one half of the Committee's Democrats are Northerners and Westerners from urban constituencies, whose voting records are just as "liberal" on behalf of domestic social welfare programs as non-Committee Democrats from like constituencies. They come to the Committee favorably disposed toward the high level of federal spending necessary to support such programs, and with no sense of urgency about the Committee's tasks of guarding the Treasury or reducing budget estimates. Given the criteria governing their selection, however, they come without rigid preconceptions and with a built-in responsiveness to the socialization processes of any legislative group of which they are members. It is crucial to Committee integration that they learn to temper their potentially disruptive welfare-state ideology with a conservative's concern for saving money. They must change their perceptions and attitudes sufficiently to view the Committee's tasks in nearly the same terms as their more conservative Southern Democratic and Republican colleagues. What their elders perceive as reality (*i.e.,* the disposition of executives to ask for more money than is necessary) they, too, must see as reality. A subcommittee chairman explained:

> When you have sat on the Committee, you see that these bureaus are always asking for more money—always up, never down. They want to build up their organization. You reach the point—I have—where it sickens you, where you rebel against it. Year after year, they want more money. They say, "Only $50,000 this year"; but you know the pattern. Next year they'll be back for $100,000, then $200,000. The younger members haven't been on the Committee long enough, haven't had the experience to know this.

The younger men, in this case the younger liberals, do learn from their Committee experience. Within one or two terms, they are differentiating between themselves and the "wild-eyed spenders" or the "free spenders" in the House. "Some of these guys would spend you through the roof," exclaimed one liberal of moderate seniority. Repeated exposure to Committee work and to fellow members has altered their perceptions and their attitudes in money matters. Half a dozen Northern Democrats of low or moderate seniority agreed with one of their number who said: "Yes, it's true. I can see it myself. I suppose I came here a flaming liberal; but as the years go by I get more conservative. You just hate like hell to spend all this money. . . . You come to the point where you say, 'By God, this is enough jobs.' " These men will remain more inclined toward spending than their Committee colleagues, but their perceptions, and hence their attitudes, have been brought close enough to the others to support a consensus on tasks. They are responsive to appeals on budget-cutting grounds that would not have registered earlier and which remain meaningless to liberals outside the Committee. In cases, therefore, where Committee selection does not and cannot initially produce individuals with a predisposition toward protecting the Treasury, the same result is achieved by socialization.

Socialization is a training in behavior as well as in perception. For the newcomer, conformity to norms in specific situations is insured through the appropriate application, by the Committee veterans, of rewards and punishments. For the Committee member who serves his apprenticeship creditably, the passage of time holds the promise that he will inherit a position of influence. He may, as an incentive, be given some small reward early in his Committee career. One man, in his second year, had been assigned the task of specializing in one particular program. However narrow the scope of his specialization, it had placed him on the road to influence within the Committee. He explained with evident pleasure:

> The first year, you let things go by. You can't participate. But you learn by watching the others operate. The next year, you know what you're interested in and when to step in. . . . For instance, I've become an expert on the ———— program. The chairman said to me, "This is something you ought to get interested in." I did; and now I'm the expert on the Committee. Whatever I say on that, the other members listen to me and do what I want.

At some later date, provided he continues to observe Committee norms, he will be granted additional influence, perhaps through a prominent floor role. A model Committee man of moderate seniority who had just attained to this stage of accomplishment, and who had suffered through several political campaigns back home fending off charges that he was a do-nothing Congressman, spoke about the rewards he was beginning to reap.

> When you perform well on the floor when you bring out a bill, and members know that you know the bill, you develop prestige with other members of Congress. They come over and ask you what you think, be-

cause they know you've studied it. You begin to get a reputation beyond your subcommittee. And you get inner satisfaction, too. You don't feel that you're down here doing nothing.

The first taste of influence which comes to men on this Committee is compensation for the frustrations of apprenticeship. Committee integration in general, and the meshing of roles between elders and newcomers in particular, rest on the fact that conformity to role expectations over time does guarantee to the young positive rewards—the very kind of rewards of power, prestige, and personal satisfaction which led most of them to seek Committee membership in the first place.

The important function of apprenticeship is that it provides the necessary time during which socialization can go forward. And teaching proceeds with the aid of punishments as well as rewards. Should a new member inadvertently or deliberately run afoul of Committee norms during his apprenticeship, he will find himself confronted with negative sanctions ranging in subtlety from "jaundiced eyes" to a changed subcommittee assignment. Several members, for example, recalled their earliest encounter with the norm of unity and the tradition against minority reports. One remembered his attempt to file a minority report. "The Chairman was pretty upset about it. It's just a tradition, I guess, not to have minority reports. I didn't know it was a tradition. When I said I was going to write a minority report, some eyebrows were raised. The Chairman said it just wasn't the thing to do. Nothing more was said about it. But it wasn't a very popular thing to do, I guess." He added that he had not filed one since.

Some younger members have congenital difficulty in observing the norms of the apprentice's role. In the 86th Congress, these types tended to come from the Republican minority. The minority newcomers (described by one of the men who selected them as "eight young, energetic, fighting conservatives") were a group of economy-minded individuals some of whom chafed against any barrier which kept them from immediate influence on Committee policy. Their reaction was quite different from that of the young Democrats, whose difficulty was in learning to become economy-minded, but who did not actively resent their lack of influence. One freshman, who felt that, "The appropriations system is lousy, inadequate, and old fashioned," recalled that he had spoken out in full Committee against the recommendations of a subcommittee of which he was not a member. Having failed, he continued to oppose the recommendation during floor debate. By speaking up, speaking in relation to the work of another subcommittee and by opposing a Committee recommendation, he had violated the particular norms of his apprentice role as well of the generally applicable norms of reciprocity and unity. He explained what he had learned, but remained only partially socialized:

They want to wash their dirty linen in the Committee and they want no opposition afterward. They let me say my piece in Committee. . . . But I just couldn't keep quiet. I said some things on the floor, and I found out that's about all they would take. . . . If you don't get along with your Committee and have their support, you don't get anything accomplished around here. . . . I'm trying to be a loyal, cooperative member of the Committee. You hate to be a stinker; but I'm still picking at the little things because I can't work on the big things. There's nothing for the new men to do, so they have to find places to needle in order to take some part in it.

Another freshman, who had deliberately violated apprenticeship norms by trying to ask "as many questions as the chairman" during subcommittee hearings, reported a story of unremitting counteraction against his deviation:

In the hearings, I have to wait sometimes nine or ten hours for a chance; and he hopes I'll get tired and stay home. I've had to wait till some pretty unreasonable hours. Once I've gotten the floor, though, I've been able to make a good case. Sometimes I've been the only person there. . . . He's all powerful. He's got all the power. He wouldn't think of taking me on a trip with him when he goes to hold hearings. Last year, he went to ———. He wouldn't give me a nudge there. And in the hearings, when I'm questioning a witness, he'll keep butting in so that my case won't appear to be too rosy.

Carried on over a period of two years, this behavior resulted in considerable personal friction between a Committee elder and the newcomer. Other members of his subcommittee pointedly gave him a great lack of support for his non-conformity. "They tried to slow him down and tone him down a little," not because he and his subcommittee chairman disagreed, but on the grounds that the Committee has developed accepted ways of disagreeing which minimize, rather than exacerbate, interpersonal friction.

One internal threat to Committee integration comes from new members who from untutored perceptions, from ignorance of norms, or from dissatisfaction with the apprentice role may not act in accordance with Committee expectations. The seriousness of this threat is minimized, however, by the fact that the deviant newcomer does not possess sufficient resources to affect adversely the operation of the system. Even if he does not respond immediately to the application of sanctions, he can be held in check and subjected to an extended and (given the frequency of interaction among members) intensive period of socialization. The success of Committee socialization is indicated by the fact that whereas wholesale criticism of Committee operations was frequently voiced among junior members, it had disappeared among the men of moderate experience. And what these middle seniority members now accept as the facts of Committee life, the veterans vigorously assert and defend as the essentials of a smoothly functioning system. Satisfaction with the Committee's internal structure increases with length of Committee service.

An important reason for changing member attitudes is that those who have attained leadership positions have learned, as newcomers characteristically have not, that their conformity to Committee norms is the ultimate source of their influence inside the group. Freshman members do not as readily perceive the degree to which interpersonal influence is rooted in obedience to group norms. They seem to convert their own sense of powerlessness into the view that the Committee's leaders possess, by virtue of their positions, arbitrary, absolute, and awesome power. Typically, they say: "If you're a subcommittee chairman, it's your Committee." "The Chairman runs the show. He gets what he wants. He decides what he wants and gets it through." Older members of the Committee, however, view the power of the leaders as a highly contingent and revocable grant, tendered by the Committee for so long and only so long as their leaders abide by Committee expectations. In commenting on internal influence, their typical reaction is: "Of course, the Committee wouldn't follow him if it didn't want to. He has a great deal of respect. He's an able man, a hard-working man." "He knows the bill backwards and forwards. He works hard, awfully hard, and the members know it." Committee leaders have an imposing set of formal prerogatives. But they can capitalize on them only if they command the respect, confidence and deference of their colleagues.

It is basic to Committee integration that members who have the greatest power to change the system evidence the least disposition to do so. Despite their institutional conservatism, however, Committee elders do occasionally violate the norms applicable to them and hence represent a potential threat to successful integration. Excessive deviation from Committee expectations by some leaders will bring counter-measures by other leaders. Thus, for example, the Chairman and his subcommittee chairmen exercise reciprocal controls over one another's behavior. The Chairman has the authority to appoint the chairman and members of each subcommittee and fix its jurisdiction. "He runs the Committee. He has a lot of power," agrees one subcommittee chairman. "But it's all done on the basis of personal friendship. If he tries to get too big, the members can whack him down by majority vote."

In the 84th Congress, Chairman Cannon attempted an unusually broad reorganization of subcommittee jurisdictions. The subcommittee chairman most adversely affected rallied his senior colleagues against the Chairman's action—on the ground that it was an excessive violation of role expectations and threatening to subcommittee autonomy. Faced with the prospect of a negative Committee vote, the Chairman was forced to act in closer conformity to the expectations of the other leaders. As one participant described the episode,

> Mr. Cannon, for reasons of his own, tried to bust up one of the subcommittees. We didn't like that. . . . He was breaking up the whole Committee. A couple of weeks later, a few of the senior members got together and worked out a compromise. By that time, he had seen a few things, so we went to him and talked to him and worked it out.

On the subcommittees, too, it is the veterans of both parties who will levy sanctions against an offending chairman. It is they who speak of "cutting down to size" and "trimming the whiskers" of leaders who become "too cocky," "too stubborn," or who "do things wrong too often." Committee integration is underwritten by the fact that no member high or low is permanently immune from the operation of its sanctioning mechanisms.

III

Data concerning internal committee activity can be organized and presented in various ways. One way is to use key functional problems like integration as the focal points for descriptive analysis. On the basis of our analysis (and without, for the time being, having devised any precise measure of integration), we are led to the summary observation that the House Appropriations Committee appears to be a well-integrated, if not an extremely well-integrated, committee. The question arises as to whether anything can be gained from this study other than a description of one property of one political sub-system. If it is reasonable to assume that the internal life of a congressional committee affects all legislative activity involving that committee, and if it is reasonable to assume that the analysis of a committee's internal relationships will produce useful knowledge about legislative behavior, some broader implications for this study are indicated.

In the first place, the success of the House Appropriations Committee in solving the problem of integration probably does have important consequences for the appropriations process. Some of the possible relationships can be stated as hypotheses and tested; others can be suggested as possible guides to understanding. All of them require further research. Of primary interest is the relationship between integration and the power of the Committee. There is little doubt about the fact of Committee power. Of the 443 separate case histories of bureau appropriations examined, the House accepted Committee recommendations in 387, or 87.4 per cent of them; and in 159, or 33.6 per cent of the cases, the House Committee's original recommendations on money amounts were the exact ones enacted into law. The hypothesis that the greater the degree of Committee unity the greater the probability that its recommendations will be accepted is being tested as part of a larger study.[26] House Committee integration may be a key factor in producing House victories in conference committee. This relationship, too, might be tested. Integration appears to help provide the House conferees with a feeling of confidence and superiority which is one of their important advantages in the mix of psychological factors affecting conference deliberations.

Another suggested consequence of high integration is that party groups have a relatively small influence upon appropriations decisions. It suggests, too, that Committee-oriented behavior should be duly emphasized in any analysis of congressional oversight of administrative activity by this Committee. Successful integration promotes the achievement of the Committee's goals and doubtless helps account for the fairly consistent production of budget-cutting decisions. Another consequence will be found in the strategies adopted by people seeking favorable Committee decisions. For example, the characteristic lines of contact from executive officials to the Committee will run to the chairman and the ranking minority member (and to the professional staff man) of the single subcommittee handling their agency's appropriations. The ways in which the Committee achieves integration may even affect the success or failure of a bureau in getting its appropriations. Committee members, for instance, will react more favorably toward an administrator who conforms to their self-image of the hard-working master-of-detail than to one who does not—and Committee response to individual administrators bulks large in their determinations.

Finally, the internal integration of this Committee helps to explain the extraordinary stability, since 1920, of appropriations procedures—in the fact of repeated proposals to change them through omnibus appropriations, legislative budgets, new budgetary forms, item veto, Treasury borrowing, etc. Integration is a stabilizing force, and the stability of the House Appropriations Committee has been a force for stabilization throughout the entire process. It was, for example, the disagreement between Cannon and Taber which led to the indecisiveness reflected in the short-lived experiment with a single appropriations bill.[27] One need only examine the conditions most likely to decrease Committee integration to ascertain some of the critical factors for producing changes in the appropriations process. A description of integration is also an excellent base-line from which to analyze changes in internal structure.

All of these are speculative propositions which call for further re-

[26]*Cf.* Dwaine Marvick, "Congressional Appropriations Politics," unpublished manuscript (Columbia University, 1952).

[27]See Dalmas Nelson, "The Omnibus Appropriations Act of 1950," *Journal of Politics* (May, 1953).

search. But they suggest, as a second implication, that committee integration does have important consequences for legislative activity and, hence, that it is a key variable in the study of legislative politics. It would seem, therefore, to be a fruitful focal point for the study of other congressional committees.[28] Comparative committee analysis could usefully be devoted to (1) the factors which tend to increase or decrease integration; (2) the degree to which integration is achieved; and (3) the consequences of varying degrees of integration for committee behavior and influence. If analyses of committee integration are of any value, they should encourage the analysis and the classification of congressional committees along functional lines. And they should lead to the discussion of interrelated problems of committee survival. Functional classifications of committees (*i.e.*, well or poorly integrated) derived from a large number of descriptive analyses of several functional problems may prove helpful in constructing more general propositions about the legislative process.

[28]This view has been confirmed by the results of interviews conducted by the author with members of the House Committee on Education and Labor, together with an examination of that Committee's activity in one policy area. They indicate very significant contrasts between the internal structure of that Committee and the Appropriations Committee—contrasts which center around their comparative success in meeting the problem of integration. The House Committee on Education and Labor appears to be a poorly integrated committee. Its internal structure is characterized by a great deal of subgroup conflict, relatively little role reciprocity, and minimally effective internal control mechanisms. External concerns, like those of party, constituency, and clientele groups, are probably more effective in determining its decisions than is likely to be the case in a well-integrated committee. An analysis of the internal life of the Committee on Education and Labor, drawn partly from interviews with 19 members of that group, appears in *National Politics and Federal Aid to Education* (Syracuse, N.Y.: Syracuse University Press, 1962), by Professor Frank Munger and the author. See also Nicholas R. Masters, *op. cit.*, note 8 above, pp. 354–55; and Seymour Scher, "Congressional Committee Members as Independent Agency Overseers: A Case Study," *American Political Science Review*, Vol. 54 (December 1960), pp. 911–20.

CHAPTER THREE

THE OUTSIDER
IN THE SENATE:
AN ALTERNATIVE ROLE

RALPH K. HUITT

The growing concern of students of politics with the social structure of official bodies and the behavior expected of their members promises to make the Senate of the United States a prime target of research. Two recent books make notable contributions and suggest the trend. One is William S. White's *Citadel: The Story of the U.S. Senate*,[1] an "insider's" impressions based on years of close observation; and the other is Donald R. Matthews' *U.S. Senators and Their World*,[2] the work of a political scientist. One (though not the only) concern of both books is the system of norms for behavior of members of the Senate.[3] Although reached through different routes (White's largely inferred from observed behavior, Matthews' principally from interviews), their statements of Senate norms and the way they work have much in common. The norms (or "folkways," as Matthews calls them) are viewed as cultural "oughts" upon which there is a high degree of consensus. The members who conform most closely to the norms are, generally speaking, the most influential and effective members. This general view is almost certainly correct, as

The author gratefully acknowledges his indebtedness to Senator William Proxmire of Wisconsin for invaluable assistance in the preparation of this paper, and to the Rockefeller Foundation for a grant which made possible the theoretical work on it. The author is, of course, solely responsible for all statements of fact and judgment.

[1](New York: Harper & Row, Publishers, 1957).
[2](Chapel Hill, N.C.: University of North Carolina Press, 1960).
[3]See especially White, *op. cit.*, Chs. 5–10, and Matthews, *op. cit.*, Ch. 5.

Reprinted by permission from the AMERICAN POLITICAL SCIENCE REVIEW, *55 (September 1961), 566–75. Mr. Huitt is Professor of Political Science at the University of Wisconsin.*

it would be for any stable human group; in this the Senate is not unique (as White sometimes seems to suggest it is) but typical.[4]

But what about the Senator who does not conform? What is his place in the Senate and what happens to him there? This study will explore these questions through a case study of such a Senator. But first it may be useful to try to restate the relevant parts of the analysis of White and Matthews (without holding them in any way responsible for the restatement) in terms of role theory, which will provide the conceptual framework for the analysis of the Senator's experience.[5] In this the Senators will be seen as actors in a political sub-system called the Senate, vested with an official position (or status) called "Senator." The analyst's problem then is to describe the "Senator" role—the dynamic, behavioral aspect of the official position. The new Senator, with different motivations, faces much the same problem: he must learn or be taught the norms which define the rights and obligations of his position in order to take the actions which will validate, poorly or well, his occupancy of the position. White and Matthews, in effect, describe the Senator role by stating the norms which prescribe how persons who occupy the Senator position are expected to behave. Needless to say, it is essential to identify *whose* expectations are meant—who, that is, prescribes the appropriate behavior. For White the expectations apparently emanate from a powerful elite he calls the "Inner Club" whose members, appropriately referred to as the "Senate type," most nearly fulfill the requirements of the role, and who wield the internal sanctions. Matthews suggests that the expectations are widely shared by the membership as a whole.

What is the "Senator" role (White's "Senate type" or "Senate man," Matthews' effective Senator) which emerges from these two books? It is one of a prudent man, who serves a long apprenticeship before trying to assert himself, and talks infrequently even then. He is courteous to a fault in his relations with his colleagues, not allowing political disagreements to affect his personal feelings. He is always ready to help another Senator when he can, and he expects to be repaid in kind. More than anything else, he is a Senate man, proud of the institution and ready to de-

---

[4]George Homans, *The Human Group* (New York: Harcourt, Brace & World, Inc., 1950), pp. 147, 169–70, 426–28.

[5]"Role" and related concepts are defined in a great variety of ways by social scientists, depending upon the discipline of the definer and the special problems which engage his interest. For an excellent clarification of the definitional problem see Neal Gross, Ward S. Mason, and Alexander W. McEachern, *Explorations in Role Analysis: Studies of the School Superintendency Role* (New York: John Wiley & Sons, Inc., 1958), Ch. 2. Because the purpose of the present study is not to refine role theory but to employ it rather crudely to gain some insights into the behavior of Senators, concepts are stated with as little elaboration as possible. For the theoretical formulation principally relied on see Theodore Sarbin, "Role Theory," in Gardner Lindzey (ed.), *Handbook of Social Psychology*, (Cambridge, Mass.: Addison-Wesley, 1954), Vol. I, pp. 223–58.

fend its traditions and perquisites against all outsiders. He is a legislative workhorse who specializes in one or two policy areas, says Matthews. He has a deep respect for the rights of others, says White, making his institution the last citadel of individualism. In this composite, the Senator as an ideal type is a man of accommodation who knows that "you have to go along to get along"; he is a conservative, institutional man, slow to change what he has mastered at the expense of so much time and patience.

But what of the man who does not play by the rules? What sanctions, if any, does the system impose? White suggests small inconveniences: the formal rules, for instance, may be closely applied to him.[6] But the Senate is disinclined to proceed against *any* Senator; the "great ones" do about as they please and the others, except for a few who are not acceptable at all, can get away with almost anything so long as it is not directed against a member of the Inner Club.[7] The whole thrust of this book nevertheless suggests that the non-Senate type who does not make the Inner Club never amounts to much in the Senate. This is essentially Matthews' point, too, which he arrives at through some ingenious measurements showing on their face, that the Senator who violates the folkways is less effective in getting his bills passed.[8] Neither is bothered much by cases of spectacularly successful Senators who do not altogether fit the type —the talkative Humphrey, whom White firmly locates in the Inner Club; the domineering Taft and Johnson, who leapt immediately to leadership. White explains them simply as "authentic geniuses among Senate types,"[9] which indeed is consistent with his emphasis on sentiment and feeling rather than overt behavior. In Matthews' collective profile they cause hardly a wrinkle.

This study is a participant-observer analysis of a single case of presumptively deviant senatorial behavior, that of William Proxmire, Democrat of Wisconsin, in his first year in the Senate. The observer was legislative assistant to Senator Proxmire that year. The observer's assumption was that one way to gain insights into the structure and working rules of a social system is to learn what the neophyte has to learn during his "initiation" period. Senator Proxmire was an ideal subject. He went to the Senate keenly aware of the importance of learning its norms and constructing with care the role he should play there. His interest was theoretical as well as practical; as a person trained in the social sciences he was self-conscious about his learning experiences and determined to rationalize them in order to develop a consistent view of the Senate and

---

[6]*Op. cit.*, p. 82.
[7]*Ibid.*, pp. 122, 126.
[8]*Op. cit.*, pp. 114–17. More will be said about this later.
[9]*Op. cit.*, p. 82.

his place in it.[10] More than that, he was willing to share his experiences and discuss them regularly with the observer.

Because this is a study of an individual in his relations with an institution, an attempt will be made first to suggest some of the relevant personality factors. Then Proxmire's choice of role will be recounted. After that some inferences will be drawn and hypotheses suggested about the role systems of the Senate.

I

A complex human being like William Proxmire cannot be psychologically categorized by a layman. Nevertheless, analysis begins with simplification; from the whole man must be abstracted some elements which shape him as a political personality, which identify him as a political type. In Proxmire's case, the first would seem to be a driving ambition to succeed, to which almost everything else in his life is subordinated, coupled with a puritan's belief in the sanctity of unremittent work.

Only a man with Proxmire's bottomless ambition and faith in the efficacy of effort would have believed he had any prospects at all in Wisconsin politics. His disabilities were perhaps best summed up in an apocryphal story given wide currency in the state in 1952, when he first ran for governor. It relates a conversation between his opponent, Governor Walter Kohler, and, say, Driscoll of New Jersey, at the governors' conference that year.

"Have you an opponent, Walter?" asks Driscoll.

"Yes," replies Kohler. "He's the son of an Illinois Republican. He graduated from Yale and Harvard, worked for J. P. Morgan and married a Rockefeller, and just moved into Wisconsin three years ago."

"My God, Walter," explodes Driscoll. "Did you pick him yourself?"

The presumed liabilities bear closer inspection.[11] The Illinois Republican father was a physician who worked long hours seven days a week until his death at 79, who taught his son that it is morally wrong as well as inefficient to be awake and not at work. At Yale Proxmire learned the rewards of perseverance: too light for football, he nevertheless made every practice, spring and fall, for four years and finally got his letter by participating in one play in a "letter" game. His experience at the Harvard graduate school confirmed what Proxmire had

---

[10]Proxmire has a B.A. degree from Yale, an M.B.A. from the Harvard Graduate School of Business Administration, and he carried his doctoral program in government at Harvard to the dissertation-writing stage.

[11]See the sketch of Proxmire's life and personality by Godfrey Sperling, Jr., in *The Christian Science Monitor*, August 31, 1957; or the Chicago *Sun-Times*, August 25, 1957.

suspected while working for Morgan, that the financiers no longer made the decisions that mattered; the politicians did. The public life therefore offered the largest opportunities for a man who would make his mark. There also his political values crystallized. ("I didn't raise my son to be a Democrat," said Dr. Proxmire. "Harvard did it to Bill."[12]) To decide to be governor of his newly adopted state did not seem preposterous to Proxmire; experience had taught him that he could reach his goals because he wanted to more than most people and would pay a higher price.

Another lesson of experience, reenforced by temperament, was that he did better alone. The second personality trait—and I think the decisive one—which affected Proxmire's choice of role in the Senate is his compulsive independence. No group can contain him long; he does not trust it to take care of him nor make his decisions, and he cannot abide the restrictions on his actions which would go with truly belonging. Claims upon him which would limit his freedom of action, even those of friends and supporters, are onerous. His position in the Democratic Party of Wisconsin is a case in point.

The value of Proxmire's winning a Senate seat in 1957 to a party which had won only one other statewide race in 25 years can hardly be overstated.[13] Nevertheless, before the election an astute political reporter said in his syndicated column that it was no secret that there were "some pretty substantial Democrats who would not mind Proxmire's defeat in the senatorial election, considering their personal feelings alone and not the welfare of the party to which they owe their allegiance."[14] Some understanding of this estrangement is crucial to an explanation of Proxmire's political personality.

After World War II a group of Wisconsin Democrats, many of them Madison [University of Wisconsin] intellectuals, undertook the seemingly impossible task of rejuvenating their moribund and reactionary party. Their success, after a decade of effort, was spectacular; in 1958 the Democrats captured the state Assembly, all statewide offices but one, and half the congressional seats. These organization people naturally would like a dominant voice in party affairs, and at the minimum they expect to be consulted. Proxmire has not done much consulting, the plain fact being that if he had, he almost surely would never have gone to the Senate. He had barely qualified to vote in the state when he won his first office—from a Democratic assemblyman who had lived all his 65 years in one Wisconsin county. After that Proxmire ran as he pleased (three

---

[12]Chicago *Daily News*, August 8, 1957, p. 22.

[13]Proxmire was elected in August, 1957, to the unexpired term of Senator McCarthy, and to his first full term in 1958.

[14]John Wyngaard, August 17, 1957.

times for governor before going to the Senate) without heeding pointed suggestions that he had "had his chance."

His indefatigable campaigning undoubtedly did much to rebuild the party, but as usual he made his own calculations along the way. He discovered very early that time spent hunting up a county chairman is, on the average, enough to shake two hundred hands downtown. Whether the chairman would get him any votes was problematical; not so with the handshaking. With Democratic politicians at that time virtually ignored by communication media in large areas of this Republican state, direct personal contact through continuous campaigning seemed the one sure way to make himself known. This piece of practical wisdom, acted upon, did not endear him to the organization but it made him unbeatable in a primary.

More important, a strong hold on the electorate, which can control him only in the most general sense, enables him to resist any group (including his staunch supporters) which might seek to exercise specific influence. Two incidents will illustrate. The morning after his first election to the Senate Proxmire stood with his wife before daybreak in the rain at a plant gate in Milwaukee, thanking the workers for their help. A couple of weeks later, when a labor leader dared to suggest that he was the union's man, Proxmire chose a state CIO convention as the place to declare his independence of labor. One act was as significant as the other and they were not unrelated.

II

Throughout the spring of 1958, for roughly half his first session in the Senate, Proxmire strove earnestly to be a model freshman Senator. He worked hard on his committees and took care of his constituents. He accepted cheerfully a mammoth portion of the burden of freshmen of the majority party, presiding over the Senate. He did much more than his share; an unofficial tabulation midway in the session showed that he had sat in the chair longer than anyone else and about sixteen times as long as Vice President Nixon. The club apparently approved of him. No Senator can ask his colleagues how he is doing, but his staff members can and do check with *their* peers. The reports at first were always the same: He's doing fine; he hasn't made a single mistake.

But Proxmire had not satisfactorily answered the question that mattered most to him: How much could he talk on the floor? Ordinary prudence, as well as Senate practice, counsel a neophyte to bide his time before exercising very freely his undoubted right to speak at any time. But to a man like Proxmire the life of the Senate is the debate on the floor. Not to be there and participate is to deny himself equal membership in the Senate. Proxmire said of a freshman colleague who seldom spoke: "He might as well not be a Senator!"

Nevertheless he forbore, trying to find socially acceptable ways to take some part. The "morning hour," that period at the beginning of each day when Senators introduce bills and insert material in the *Congressional Record*, seemed safe enough so he quickly became a regular contributor to the *Record*. He entered colloquies on the floor only when specifically invited to do so by senior members. He cautiously scheduled his first major speech for the day before the Easter recess when most members would be gone, having been assured that this was an appropriate time for a freshman to talk. Only two members heard him through, the presiding officer and Senator Douglas (who canceled an appointment in order to give Proxmire an audience) .[15]

But almost as if he could not help himself, Proxmire became steadily more active in debate until he was one of the busiest men on the floor. Then came the first warnings that he was "talking too much." The warnings were characteristic of the operations of the Senate. None of them was direct. They came in friendly tips: someone heard an unnamed person say it; the report was passed on to a Proxmire staff man for what it was worth. Or a very senior Senator in the chair would pointedly overlook Proxmire standing at his desk, to recognize other members ahead of him out of turn.

Proxmire retired, brooding, to his office. He was puzzled and frustrated. He believed that he *had* exercised great restraint. He had kept his speeches short, except when asked by a party floor man to help kill time. So he sat mute. Not even a debate on unemployment compensation, in which he was deeply interested, could make him speak.

Then the dam broke. In the first week of June Proxmire offered six amendments to the Mutual Security Act and pressed them to a vote.[16] Inasmuch as Proxmire was not a member of the Foreign Relations Committee, and four of his amendments were first introduced on the floor so the Committee had no chance to consider them, the performance was hardly a demonstration of modesty and withdrawal. Criticism was sharp and immediate (though indirect, as always), and it spurred Proxmire to a decision: he would "be a Senator like Wayne [Morse] and Paul [Douglas]"; he would talk when he pleased on whatever he chose and would not worry about his influence in the Senate. He had found his role.

The Senate soon learned what that meant. In mid-July, for instance, Proxmire served notice that "I intend to rise every day, from now on un-

[15]104 *Cong. Rec.* (April 3, 1958), pp. 6200–14.
[16]*Ibid.* (May 26, 1958), pp. 9424–25; (May 28), p. 9655; (June 4–5), pp. 9868–69, 10157–63, 10260–62, 10266–70.

til social security improvement is adopted, to plead for it,"[17] which he did, on 27 consecutive occasions. But if the club was unused to being lectured by a freshman member, it must have been wholly unprepared for his threat to hold them beyond adjournment by the very antithesis of freshmanlike behavior, a filibuster.

The provocation was a bill to allow the Metropolitan Sanitary District of Chicago to increase the amount of water it may withdraw from Lake Michigan by a thousand cubic feet per second for a three-year test period.[18] Similar bills had been passed by both houses twice before (by the Senate in the closing hours of a session with scant debate) only to be vetoed by the President because of objections raised by Canada. Once more it appeared that the bill would come up in the flood of last-minute legislation, and with committee and leadership support it seemed sure to slide through the tired Senate. Moreover, because the Canadian position was now ambiguous the President might sign the bill.

But the pressure for adjournment which was the greatest factor in favor of the bill's passage could also be its doom—if its opponents had sufficient nerve. Their hope was to stall consideration as long as possible, then make it clear that the cost of passage was extended debate. It was a simple, time-proven strategy, but not one designed to make friends.

Proxmire was by no means the only man fighting the bill—there was a militant bipartisan coalition on each side—but he was probably the most determined and certainly the most conspicuous. It was he who blocked unanimous consent to allow any deviation from the rules in handling the bill. Thus he objected to a meeting of the Public Works Committee while the Senate sat, and to the bill's being reported to the Senate after the expiration of the morning hour—tactics which brought sharp rebukes from two senior members but delayed the bill a day.[19] And it was he who held the floor from nine till midnight the last night of the session, until the water-diversion bill was put aside for other business;[20] and he who sat through the early morning hours, armed with a score of amendments and great piles of materials, ready to resume the debate. When the session ended at 4:11 A.M. the unfinished business of the Senate was a Proxmire amendment to the bill. It is not likely that anyone on the floor that night doubted that Proxmire was ready to talk on through Sunday if need be, but probably few present realized how eager he was to do just that.

---

[17]*Ibid.* (July 18, 1958), p. 14187.
[18]H.R. 2, 85th Cong. See S. Rept. 2482, 104 *Cong. Rec.* (August 20, 1958), p. 18606.
[19]*Ibid.* (August 19, 1958), p. 18457.
[20]*Ibid.* (August 23, 1958), pp. 19464–66, 19469–78, 19522–39, 19554–55.

III

What may be suggested about the "Senator" role from this summary statement of the first stage of Proxmire's socialization in the Senate?

First, at a certain point in his first session, Proxmire selected the role he would play. He did not play badly the role associated with the member of the Inner Club; he rejected it. He did not fail in an effort to make himself acceptable to the Inner Club; he decided he did not want to try to be one of them. The role he chose was one suited to his personality and temperament, one he had played before.[21] In his opinion it offered him the best opportunities to attain his goals in the Senate. Conformity with the folkways would not have allowed him, for instance, to associate himself so persistently with expansion of social security nor to make his Horatio-like stand against the water-diversion bill. Moreover, the independent role clearly was congenial to his constituency—Proxmire's seat had been held successively by "Old Bob" La Follette and his son and by Joe McCarthy—and Proxmire was up for reelection. But it is important that his performance was not simply a bid for votes; it was rather a deliberately adopted legislative style which he has followed consistently since reelection.[22]

Second, he had a model to go by. He mentioned two Senators and could have named others. The norms for his behavior were furnished by a small group within the Senate, just as the norms of the "Senate type" are likewise furnished by another, perhaps much larger, group within the Senate. The model, moreover, is rooted in Senate history. There have always been members of the Senate labelled variously as "independents," "mavericks," and the like. They have come from all sections of the country, although the Midwest seems to have produced more than its share. It is not necessary to try to establish a roster of such Senators; a voluminous popular literature and common knowledge

[21]In his first press conference after winning the special election in 1957, Proxmire shunned labels such as "liberal" and "Douglas Democrat," but mentioned approvingly that some labor leaders had described him as a "maverick." Chicago *Daily News*, August 29, 1957.

[22]Representative actions are not hard to find. In 1959 Proxmire made three speeches criticizing the Democratic party leadership in the Senate, with support from four other Senators. 105 *Cong. Rec.* (February 23), pp. 2814–2820; (March 9), pp. 3559–3578; (April 15), pp. 5956–5959. In 1960 he opposed the judicial nomination of a Wisconsin man who had massive support from within and outside the state, with no one else from Wisconsin in opposition. (Proxmire said: "I have had more visits and phone calls in connection with this nomination than with any other matter I have dealt with since I came to the Senate.") Hearings, Senate Judiciary Subcommittee, 86th Cong., 2d Sess., *Nomination of James R. Durfee*; 106 *Cong. Rec.* (January 25, 1960); pp. 1027–33; (April 19), pp. 7577–78; (April 20), p. 7750. In 1961 he was the first to make a fight against a Kennedy nominee. *Ibid.* (daily edition, January 23, 1961), pp. 1086–1100.

support the contention that the "loner," the man who conspicuously walks his own way, is a familiar figure in the Senate.[23] What is more important is to try to sharpen the description of the role and to distinguish it from its opposite, the "Senate type" which makes up the membership of the Inner Club.

Because the most significant characteristic of the role is its conscious rejection of the behavior associated with belonging to the Inner Club, we might tentatively label it the "Outsider." The term is not meant, however, to apply indiscriminately to all members of what White calls the Outer Club (*i.e.*, all Senators not in the Inner Club), who may simply have failed somehow to be taken into the inner communion, but to the man who does not *want* to be in.

If the "Senate type" who belongs to the Inner Club is distinguished by his sensitiveness to Senate moods, his regard for Senate traditions and norms, and his spirit of accommodation, the Outsider is notable for his determination to speak out wherever he pleases on whatever subject he chooses without regard to whether he can get any vote but his own. And if the "Senate type" cares more for the esteem of like-minded colleagues than any other kind of approval, the Outsider typically looks elsewhere— to his constituents and to his ideological allies across the nation, perhaps more than to those other members of the Senate whose norms he shares.

The difference between the Outsider and the Senate type is not so much in ideology or issue orientation (although the Outsider is more likely to be liberal, as his opposite number is apt to be conservative) as in legislative style. The popular literature of forty years has drawn a sharp picture of that style. The Outsider feels impelled to stand for principle absolutely, preferring defeat on those terms to half-a-loaf. He

---

[23]"Borah and Johnson, Disturbers of the Senatorial Peace," *The Literary Digest*, August 23, 1919, pp. 52, 55; Austin Haines, "Smith W. Brookhart, Dissenter," *Nation*, November 1, 1922, pp. 465–67; Richard Barry, "A Radical in Power: A Study of La Follette," *Outlook*, November 29, 1922, pp. 564–67; Chester H. Rowell, "La Follette, Shipstead, and the Embattled Farmers," *World's Work*, August, 1923, pp. 408–20; F. E. Haynes, "La Follette and La Follettism," *Atlantic Monthly*, October 1924, pp. 536–44; Bruce Bliven, "Robert M. La Follette's Place in Our History," *Current History*, August, 1925, pp. 716–22; Charles Merz, "Androcles and the Lion: The Silent President and the Roaring Borah," *Century*, April, 1926, pp. 698–703; Richard Washburn Child, "He Rides Alone," *Saturday Evening Post*, May 21, 1927, pp. 6–7, 187, 189; Dixon Merritt, "Four Senators," *Outlook*, December, 28, 1927, pp. 531, 534; Ray T. Tucker, "Those Sons of Wild Jackasses," *North American Review*, February, 1930, pp. 225–33; Frederick R. Barkley, "The Voice of the Corn Belt: Senator Norris—Square Peg in the G.O.P.," *Outlook*, January 14, 1931, pp. 52–54, 74–75; Louis H. Cook, "Brookhart, Insurgent," *North American Review*, February, 1931, pp. 178–84; Oswald Garrison Villard, "Borah Goes on the War Path," *Nation*, July 25, 1934, p. 91; "Borah: Political History-Maker," *Literary Digest*, February 1, 1936, p. 9; Richard L. Neuberger, "Wayne Morse: Republican Gadfly," *American Mercury*, July, 1947, pp. 16–24; Robert L. Riggs, "Wayne Morse: The Peril of Independence," *The New Republic*, March 2, 1953, pp. 10–12; Robert L. Riggs, "That Maverick Morse," *Nation*, May 5, 1956, pp. 380–82.

likes to tell people what they should and frequently do not want to hear. He is never so confident of the soundness of his opinions as when he holds them alone. He is as comfortable alone against the crowd as the Senate type is in the bosom of the club; indeed he is probably happiest when he stands by himself against powerful and wrong-headed foes. As a consequence few people, in the body or outside, are lukewarm toward him; they tend to like or dislike him strongly. He is like the "sons of the wild jackasses" who came out of the Midwest thirty years ago, of whom it was said that "theirs is not a compromising spirit, and this lack of the give-and-take philosophy may, with their want of a sense of humor, be their greatest weakness but it has often proved to be their strength."[24]

The characterization is not really adequate. For one thing, it is undoubtedly too harsh. Many who helped shape it were deeply unsympathetic with the goals and tactics of the men they described, among whom there were, then and now, attractive as well as powerful personalities. Nevertheless there is more than a suggestion that unpopularity was not unknown to them and they were not dismayed by it. Even if it were wholly fair, the description obviously would not apply in all its details to any individual. What we have sketched here is an "ideal type"; real people are only more or less like it.[25] Its relevance is that it suggests what I shall argue here, that the Outsider is not a deviant at all but a person playing a recognizable and recognized role, a legitimate alternative to some others which he might select.

Deviant behavior has been defined as "behavior which violates institutionalized expectations—that is, expectations which are shared and recognized as legitimate in a social system."[26] My argument is that the Outsider role has been accepted and esteemed by a considerable part, at least, of the general public and by the specialized publics of close students of the Senate, and that within the Senate itself it is recognized as legitimate whether it is popular with a majority or not. Most theories of deviant behavior postulate an effort (even if ineffective) by the social system to eliminate or at least control the offending behavior. The Senate has proved that it can and will take telling measures against what it considers deviant behavior, but the kind of behavior associated with the Outsider role is remarkably free of institutional inhibitions.

[24]Tucker, *op. cit.*, pp. 226–27.

[25]This should be emphasized. No classification of individuals is intended. Where individuals are mentioned it is only to illustrate a characteristic in the construction of a type.

[26]Albert K. Cohen, "The Study of Social Disorganization and Deviant Behavior," in Robert K. Merton, *et al.* (eds.), *Sociology Today* (New York: Basic Books, 1959), pp. 461–84. Robert A. Dentler and Kai T. Erickson argue that deviants are functional to the group, testing and tracing its boundaries, as opposed to the notion of deviance as a dysfunctional aspect of group or society; but they accept Cohen's definition and it is clear that they are talking about behavior which is regarded as illegitimate by the group. "The Function of Deviance in Groups," *Social Problems*, Vol. 7 (Fall 1960), pp. 98–107.

One piece of evidence supporting the assertion of widespread public acceptance of the role is the long tenure in office usually enjoyed by the established maverick. Approval by the special publics is suggested by the frequency with which close observers rank men noted for their independence at or close to the top of lists of outstanding Senators. Thus a group of political scientists who specialized in legislation (presumed to be able to make informed judgments largely free from provincial, partisan, or emotional bias) were asked in 1950 to "grade" all members of the Senate; they consistently put Douglas first, and the next three in order were Kefauver, Morse, and Lehman.[27] The same year *Time* included Douglas among the "Senate's most valuable ten," calling him, among other things, "maverick liberal."[28] *Collier's* congressional award for 1946 went to Robert La Follette, Jr., "as notable an independent as the Senate has known since his fiery father, Wisconsin's famous Old Bob . . ." who always "has been free to do his stuff as he thought it should be done."[29] One of two awards made by the American Political Science Association in 1959 to outstanding members of the Senate went to John J. Williams of Delaware, who is noted for his lone-wolf assaults on wasteful spending, subsidies, and tax privileges.[30]

More than that, the Senate itself has in a sense put its *imprimatur* on the role. In 1955 the Senate set about selecting "five outstanding persons, but not a living person, who have served as members of the Senate" whose portraits would be painted in oval spaces left blank for that purpose when the Reception Room was decorated a century earlier.[31] A committee of five Senators chaired by John F. Kennedy considered nominations for two years with advice from many people.[32] The Senators finally selected were Webster, Calhoun, Clay, Taft, and the senior La Follette. The names fall almost automatically into slots—the nationalist,

[27]Byron L. Johnson and W. E. Butt, "Rating the Senators," *New Republic*, March 3, 1952, pp. 10–11.

[28]"Senate's Most Valuable Ten," *Time*, April 3, 1950, p. 20.

[29]James C. Derieux, "For Distinguished Congressional Service," *Collier's*, April 26, 1947, pp. 78–79. The awards, made each year for four years to one member of each house consisted of a $10,000 cash prize and a gold medal presented by the President of the United States. Other Senators chosen were Arthur H. Vandenberg (1945), Alben W. Barkley (1947), and Vandenberg again (1948). Young Bob's style in the Senate was not his father's; indeed, by the time the *Collier's* award was made he probably was a valued member of the Inner Club. But the point is that his independence was stressed in the article announcing the award.

[30]105 *Cong. Rec.* (September 11, 1959), pp. 19085–86. See also William Benton, "For Distinguished Service in Congress," *New York Times Magazine*, July 24, 1955, pp. 14 ff.

[31]*New York Times*, May 5, 1957, IV, p. 2.

[32]The original committee was made up of Lyndon B. Johnson, chairman; Richard B. Russell, Styles Bridges, Mike Mansfield, and Eugene D. Millikin. 101 *Cong. Rec.* (August 2, 1955), p. 12967. Johnson later was replaced by Kennedy and Millikin by John W. Bricker. For a description of the selection process, see John F. Kennedy, "Search for the Five Greatest Senators," *New York Times Magazine*, April 14, 1957, pp. 14–18.

the sectionalist, the compromiser, the arch Republican, the maverick liberal.[33] Was the committee—perhaps consciously—filling historic roles? The choice of La Follette is striking. It is doubtful that any man ever aroused more bitter antagonisms in the Senate or was ever more reviled by his colleagues than he.[34] That La Follette was selected as a protype seems more likely from the fact that his closest competitor was George W. Norris, a man not like any of the other "outstanding persons" but the most like La Follette.[35]

What happens inside the Senate to the Outsider? Not much; as White observed, the Senate is not a body disposed to impose sanctions on any behavior but the most outrageous. The point is important. A group may be expected to punish deviant behavior, and the Senate has proved that it can and will do so with dreadful finality.[36] Calculated and continued flouting of the dignity and good order of the Senate, easier to recognize than define, is deviance which compels sanctions. It will be punished finally, as Huey Long and Joe McCarthy learned, by a spiritual banishment more conclusive than formal censure and more galling, in its daily erosion of ego, than physical expulsion. But the Senate is of all official bodies (again, as White remarked) perhaps the most tolerant of individualistic, even eccentric, behavior.

Institutional arrangements, both formal and informal, encourage tolerance. An external system determines who shall be members and confers upon them an equal official status, and the seniority system softens the contest for status and preference internally. The Senate is a relatively large group (though its smallness has always been emphasized); it *does* have a hundred members and the staff people who share intimately in the work of the body multiply that number several times. Differences in style, temperament, and goals therefore may be softened by simple avoidance if not by the sharing of committee tasks, or by the temporary alliances of mutual interest which account for much legislation. And because the Senate agenda is managed largely by unanimous consent a majority judiciously refrains from employing against irksome behavior the small sanctions which serve merely to irritate the offending member.

---

[33]See S. Rept. No. 279, 85th Cong., 1st Sess., 103 *Cong. Rec.* (May 1, 1957), pp. 6206–8.

[34]This was frankly acknowledged in the committee report, *ibid.,* p. 6205, which says of La Follette, in part: "Ceaseless battler for the underprivileged in an age of special privilege, courageous independent in an age of partisan conformity; he fought memorably against tremendous odds and stifling inertia for social and economic reforms which ultimately proved essential to American progress in the twentieth century. . . . The bitter antagonisms stirred by his unyielding opposition to international commitments and conflict were ultimately submerged by widespread admiration for his dedicated life-long fight against political corruption and corporate greed." An editorial criticism of the selections characterizes La Follette as "the champion of lost causes." "What Makes These Senators Great?" *Christian Century,* May 15, 1957, p. 612.

[35]103 *Cong. Rec.,* pp. 6212–13.

[36]White, *op. cit.,* pp. 121–35.

The imposition of censure or ostracism is a rare and traumatic action reserved for really deviant behavior usually borne a long time.

The evidence is strong that the Senate accepts as legitimate a wide range of behavior. Its members advance without hindrance to the perquisites of seniority, and some of the most powerful committees have had rather odd chairmen. Relations among subgroups appear to be easy; an Outsider who fights with only a handful of friends on one issue may, because of personal expertness on the subject, be chosen by the leadership to lead the party on a crucial measure the next week. Proxmire has said that no sanctions have been imposed on him; on the contrary, the leadership gave him substantial help in 1960 in the passage of a dairy price support bill which was helpful to his constituents.[37] Proxmire, like other Outsiders, readily joins subgroups in support of common interests and frequently votes with the majority. The behavior associated with the Outsider role seems to fall well within the bounds of what most members of the Senate regard as tolerable.

If this analysis is correct, an assumption of role consensus in the Senate is incorrect; there is variability not only in the behavior of occupants of the Senator position but in the expectations—the "ideal patterns"—of behavior to which members may conform.[38] The Outsider therefore is not a deviant but an alternative role. It would be a mistake also to assume, without empirical justification, a bimodal distribution of acceptable behaviors—the Inner Club member and the Outsider. What is more probable is the existence of several legitimate "Senator" roles. One thinks, for instance, of the persistence of the pure service type, the "Errand Boy," who eschews controversy and distinguishes himself neither in committee nor on the floor, but renders himself unbeatable by causing his beneficence to fall like gentle rain on all his constituents, Democrats and Republicans alike. The identification and conceptualization of alternative roles will in turn provide important clues to strains and conflicts or to the existence of sub-systems within the body.[39]

It should be emphasized, however, that the successful performance of this task would by no means exhaust the sets of role orientations in the Senate which are worth analysis.[40] What we are dealing with here—the

[37]S. 2917, S. Rept. 1592, 86th Cong., 2d sess.; P.L. 86–799. See *Cong. Rec.* (daily edition, August 19, 1960), pp. 15594–600.

[38]See the discussion of "the postulate of role consensus" in Gross, *et al., op. cit.,* Ch. 2.

[39]*Ibid.*, pp. 25–26.

[40]The most perceptive and elaborate statement of the interrelated sets of roles within a legislative sub-system is found in the comparative study of four state legislatures by Heinz Eulau, John C. Wahlke, LeRoy C. Ferguson, and William Buchanan, "The Role of the Representative: Some Empirical Observations on the Theory of Edmund Burke," *American Political Science Review,* Vol. 53 (September 1959), pp. 742–56; "The Legislator as Specialist," *Western Political Quarterly,* Vol. 13 (September 1960), pp. 636–51; and especially their mimeographed working paper, "The Role Concept in the Comparative Study of State Legislatures," pp. 3–17. See also my "The Congressional Committee: A Case Study," *American Political Science Review,* Vol. 48 (June 1954), pp. 340–65.

way the Senator relates himself generally to his colleagues and the obligations of his office, or better the *style* of his performance in chamber, committee room, and office—is concerned with only one set, albeit an important one. Externally it is the image of himself as Senator which he projects to his publics. Within the Senate it is the cluster of attitudes and
modes of behavior toward other members which identify him to them
and stimulate and shape their attitudes and behavior toward him. The
choice of this role among available alternatives is therefore crucial to the
successful performance of his other roles and to his self-esteem, and its
importance is heightened by the fact that, once adopted, it is not easy
to change.

IV

The disability usually supposed to be associated with the Outsider role
is that the Senator who chooses it is thereby doomed to be less effective in
the Senate. White puts it indirectly: the Inner Club runs the Senate;[41]
the Outsider would be then, by definition, not of much consequence.
Matthews goes further, attempting to test the proposition that the more
effective member abides by the folkways. He constructs an index of "Legislative Effectiveness" by calculating the proportion of all public bills
and resolutions introduced by each Senator in two successive Congresses
that were passed by the Senate, arguing that "to the extent that the concept as used on Capitol Hill has any distinct meaning, 'effectiveness' seems
to mean the ability to get one's bills passed." He then plots the effectiveness index against indexes measuring conformity with two Senate folkways and concludes: "The less a Senator talks on the Senate floor, and
the narrower a Senator's area of legislative interest and activity, the
greater is his effectiveness.' "[42]

It should be said at once that Matthews is as modest in his claims for
his statistical test as he is resourceful in constructing it. Nevertheless the
effectiveness index raises questions too important to ignore. To the individual Senator, to whom being a Senator is part of a professional career,
the ability to get reelected might be considered a fair test of effectiveness
and any behavior judicious which helps him pass the test. From the
point of view of society, the conception of the Senate as a bill-and-resolu-
tion factory where the individual members are paid on a piece-work basis
seems both too narrow and contrary to fact. To take the last point first,
the passage of a bill is a collective process in which the introducer may
have played a very small part, if indeed his bill was not changed beyond
recognition.[43] Conversely, bill introduction may be no more than a form

[41]*Op. cit.*, pp. 86–87.
[42]*Op. cit.*, pp. 114–17.
[43]In determining standards for the selection of the five outstanding Senators,
Kennedy rejected the notion of choosing those whose names are prominently associated

of advocacy, or a way to state a personal platform, or simply a bid for publicity. Or again, a Senator may persistently sponsor legislation he knows can pass only well in the future, if at all, as George Norris did the TVA.[44] But more important, the enactment of legislation is but one and perhaps not the most important function of either house of Congress, let alone of all members individually. An adequate assessment of the effectiveness of alternative Senate roles or individual role-takers must await an analysis of the political functions performed by the Senate.[45]

Suppose, for instance, that one function of the legislature should prove to be "the institutionalization, crystallization, and resolution of conflicts."[46] Might not then the Outsider's outspoken championship of minority, perhaps unpopular, views contribute to the process? The analysis would have to take account of the latent functions—the unintended and unrecognized consequences—as well as the manifest functions.[47] A latent function of the legislature might be to provide catharsis for fringe views which never will prevail.[48] If so, what better agent than the lone fighter against hopeless odds (regardless of his motivations or what he fights for) who, as he afflicts the mighty, may serve as the psychological representative of all the Outsiders in the great society?[49] To turn the question around, is it likely that certain modes of legislative behavior should persist over long periods of time *without* having relevance for the political functions the legislature is called upon to perform?

It may be that Senate role and Senate function are directly linked and either may be approached through the other. The "ideal pattern" of behavior which we have called "role" may embrace one or more basic functions of the Senate, performed in greater or less degree by all the members, writ large and personified in the "ideal" role-taker. Thus the Errand Boy, if we may assume there is such a role, simply is performing

---

with legislation. He pointed out that the Senator whose name a bill bears may not be for the bill and may not even have read it, while a Senator whose legislative efforts fail may find that later on someone else will take up his bill and succeed. John F. Kennedy, *op. cit.*

44Stephen K. Bailey and Howard D. Samuel, *Congress at Work* (New York: Holt, Rinehart & Winston, 1952), Ch. 8; Henry C. Hart, "Legislative Abdication in Regional Development," *The Journal of Politics*, Vol. 13 (1951), pp. 393–417.

45Robert K. Merton, *Social Theory and Social Structure* (New York: Free Press of Glencoe, Inc., 1957), pp. 19–84.

46In their forthcoming comparative study of four state legislatures, Eulau, Wahlke, Ferguson, and Buchanan use this phrase to define the legislative process.

47Merton, *op. cit.*, pp. 60–84. Merton makes "the distinction between manifest functions and latent functions; the first referring to those objective consequences for a specified unit (person, sub-group, social or cultural system) which contribute to its adjustment or adaptation and were so intended; the second referring to unintended and unrecognized consequences of the same order."

48David B. Truman suggests this as one of the functions of the public hearing of the congressional committee. *The Governmental Process* (New York: Knopf, 1951), pp. 372–77.

49This is suggested by Proxmire's mail from all over the country when, for instance, he criticized his party's leadership in the Senate.

to the virtual exclusion of everything else a function which by all accounts has always consumed a great deal of energy and time of Senators and (especially since the Legislative Reorganization Act) their staff. In any event, what is important is that a functional analysis be made, and that it take into account what the legislators actually do and not just putative functions ascribed to them. Not until such an analysis has been satisfactorily performed can anyone say what senatorial role is "effective" and what is not.

Any sophisticated assessment of Senate roles, moreover, must recognize that any role, or even a single item of behavior, may have "diverse consequences, functional and dysfunctional, for individuals, for subgroups, and for the more inclusive social structure and culture."[50] Thus the behavior of the Senate type who is in the Inner Club may be functional for groups which benefit from preserving the status quo, dysfunctional for those seeking change; functional for the preservation of harmony within the body, dysfunctional for conflict resolution in the larger society. The behavior associated with the Outsider may be functional for protest groups seeking a spokesman, dysfunctional for groups needing leverage inside the legislative body. It may even be functional for the leadership to the degree that it makes more persuasive the middle position usually taken by the leaders. A given role may be functional in some respects for the role-taker, dysfunctional in others. Proxmire, for example, unquestionably has paid a price for choosing the Outsider role (as he would if he had chosen another) which he believes to be justified by the increased freedom of action it gives him. The important thing would seem to be not what role is chosen but what the role-taker uses it for, what goals are served by it. The Inner Club member may get little more than the personal satisfaction of belonging, the Outsider no more than personal publicity. Either may, on the other hand, choose his role self-consciously with the probable consequences clearly in mind, in order to maximize the advantages to be gained toward legislative goals he has set himself.

[50]Merton, *op. cit.*, p. 30.

CHAPTER FOUR

PARTY GOVERNMENT AND THE SALIENCY OF CONGRESS

DONALD E. STOKES AND WARREN E. MILLER

Any mid-term congressional election raises pointed questions about party government in America. With the personality of the President removed from the ballot by at least a coattail, the public is free to pass judgment on the legislative record of the parties. So the civics texts would have us believe. In fact, however, an off-year election can be regarded as an assessment of the parties' record in Congress only if the electorate possesses certain minimal information about what that record is. The fact of possession needs to be demonstrated, not assumed, and the low visibility of congressional affairs to many citizens suggests that the electorate's actual information should be examined with care.

How much the people know is an important, if somewhat hidden, problem of the normative theory of representation. Implicitly at least, the information the public is thought to have is one of the points on which various classical conceptions of representation divide. Edmund Burke and the liberal philosophers, for example—to say nothing of Hamilton and Jefferson—had very different views about the information the public could get or use in assessing its government. And the periods of flood tide in American democracy, especially the Jacksonian and Progressive eras, have been marked by the most optimistic assumptions as to what the people could or did know about their government. To put the mat-

The research from which this report is drawn was supported by grants of the Rockefeller Foundation and the Social Science Research Council. The authors also gratefully acknowledge the skilled assistance of Ralph Bisco, John Faily, Julie Crowder, and Arthur Wolfe.

Reprinted by permission from the PUBLIC OPINION QUARTERLY, *26 (Winter 1962), 531–46. Messrs. Stokes, and Miller are Professors of Political Science at the University of Michigan.*

ter another way: any set of representative institutions will work very differently according to the amount and quality of information the electorate has. This is certainly true of the institutional forms we associate with government by responsible parties. A necessary condition of party responsibility to the people is that the public have basic information about the parties and their legislative record. Without it, no institutional devices can make responsibility a fact.

To explore the information possessed by those who play the legislative and constituent roles in American government, the Survey Research Center of the University of Michigan undertook an interview study of Congressmen and their districts during the mid-term election of Eisenhower's second term. Immediately after the 1958 campaign the Center interviewed a nationwide sample of the electorate, clustered in 116 congressional districts, as well as the incumbent Congressmen and other major-party candidates for the House from the same collection of districts.[1] Through these direct interviews with the persons playing the reciprocal roles of representative government, this research has sought careful evidence about the perceptual ties that bind, or fail to bind, the Congressman to his party and district. We will review some of this evidence here for the light that it throws on the problem of party cohesion and responsibility in Congress.

THE RESPONSIBLE-PARTY MODEL AND THE AMERICAN CASE

What the conception of government by responsible parties requires of the general public has received much less attention than what it requires of the legislative and electoral parties.[2] The notion of responsi-

---

[1] The 116 districts are a probability sample of all constituencies, although the fact that the study was piggy-backed onto a four-year panel study of the electorate extending over the elections of 1956, 1958, and 1960 made the design of the 1958 representation sample unusually complex. In particular, since metropolitan areas and non-metropolitan counties or groups of counties, rather than congressional districts, were used as primary sampling units when the panel sample was originated in 1956, the districts represented in our 1958 sample did not have equal probability of selection and the efficiency of the sample of districts was somewhat less than that of a simple random sample of equal size. Descriptions of the sample design may be obtained from the Survey Research Center.

[2] For example, the 1950 report of the American Political Science Association's Committee on Political Parties, the closest approach to an official statement of the responsible-party view as applied to American politics, concentrates on the organization of Congress and the national parties and deals only very obliquely with the role of the public. See American Political Science Association, *Toward a More Responsible Two-party System* (New York: Holt, Rinehart & Winston, 1950). In general, theoretical and empirical treatments of party government have focused more on the nature of party *appeals*—especially the question of whether the parties present a real "choice"—than on the cognitive and motivational elements that should be found in the *response* of an electorate that is playing its correct role in a system of

bility generally is understood to mean that the parties play a mediating role between the public and its government, making popular control effective by developing rival programs of government action that are presented to the electorate for its choice. The party whose program gains the greater support takes possession of the government and is held accountable to the public in later elections for its success in giving its program effect.

Two assumptions about the role of the public can be extracted from these ideas. *First*, in a system of party government the electorate's attitude toward the parties is based on what the party programs are and how well the parties have delivered on them. The public, in a word, gives the parties *programmatic* support. And, in view of the importance that legislative action is likely to have in any party program, such support is formed largely out of public reaction to the legislative performance of the parties, especially the party in power.

Second, under a system of party government the voters' response to the local legislative candidates is based on the candidates' identification with party programs. These programs are the substance of their appeals to the constituency, which will act on the basis of its information about the proposals and legislative record of the parties. Since the party programs are of dominant importance, the candidates are deprived of any independent basis of support. They will not be able to build in their home districts an electoral redoubt from which to challenge the leadership of their parties.[3]

How well do these assumptions fit the behavior of the American public as it reaches a choice in the off-year congressional elections? A first glance at the relation of partisan identifications to the vote might give the impression that the mid-term election is a triumph of party government. Popular allegiance to the parties is of immense importance in all our national elections, including those in which a President is chosen, but its potency in the mid-term congressional election is espe-

---

responsible-party government. For example, see the excellent discussion in Austin Ranney and Willmoore Kendall, *Democracy and the American Party System* (New York: Harcourt, Brace & World, 1956), pp. 151–52, 384–85, 525–27.

It should be clear that the data of this report are taken from a particular election of a particular electoral era. We would expect our principal findings to apply to most recent off-year elections, but they are of course subject to modification for earlier or later periods.

[3]This assumption does not imply that pressures toward party cohesion come *only* from the mass public. Other sanctions against party irregularity are of equal or greater importance, especially those available in the nominating process and within the legislative parties themselves. To cite the most celebrated empirical case, the cohesiveness of the British parliamentary parties is not enforced primarily, if at all, by the British electorate. Nevertheless, the public ought not to give aid and comfort to the legislative party irregular; the idea of the candidate building a local bastion of strength from which he can challenge the party leadership is clearly contradictory to the party-government model.

Table 1   1958 Vote for House Candidates, by Party Identification

	Party Identification[a]			
	Democratic	Independent	Republican	Total
Voted Democratic	53%[b]	2%	6%	61%
Voted Republican	5	3	31	39
TOTAL	58%	5%	37%	100%

[a]The Democratic and Republican party identification groups include all persons who classify themselves as having some degree of party loyalty.
[b]Each entry of the table gives the per cent of the total sample of voters having the specified combination of party identification and vote for the House in 1958.

cially pronounced. This fact is plain—even stark—in the entries of Table 1, which break down the vote for Congress in 1958 into its component party elements. The table makes clear, first of all, how astonishingly small a proportion of the mid-term vote is cast by political independents. Repeated electoral studies in the United Sates have indicated that somewhat fewer than 1 American in 10 thinks of himself as altogether independent of the two parties.[4] But in the off-year race for Congress only about a twentieth part of the vote is cast by independents, owing to their greater drop-out rate when the drama and stakes of the presidential contest are missing.

Table 1 also makes clear how little deviation from party there is among Republicans and Democrats voting in a mid-term year. The role of party identification in the congressional election might still be slight, whatever the size of the party followings, if partisan allegiance sat more lightly on the voting act. But almost 9 out of every 10 partisans voting in the off-year race support their parties. Indeed, something like 84 per cent of *all* the votes for the House in 1958 were cast by party identifiers supporting their parties. The remaining 16 per cent is not a trivial fraction of the whole—standing, as it did in this case, for 8 million people, quite enough to make and unmake a good many legislative careers. Nevertheless, the low frequency of deviation from party, together with the low frequency of independent voting, indicates that the meaning of the mid-term vote depends in large part on the nature of party voting.

THE SALIENCY OF THE PARTIES' LEGISLATIVE RECORDS

If American party voting were to fit the responsible-party model it would be *programmatic* voting, that is, the giving of electoral support according to the parties' past or prospective action on programs that con-

[4]See Angus Campbell, Philip E. Converse, Warren E. Miller, and Donald E. Stokes, *The American Voter* (New York: Wiley, 1960), p. 124.

sist (mainly) of legislative measures. There is little question that partisan voting is one of the very few things at the bottom of our two-party system; every serious third-party movement in a hundred years has foundered on the reef of traditional Republican and Democratic loyalties. But there is also little question that this voting is largely nonprogrammatic in nature. A growing body of evidence indicates that party loyalties are typically learned early in life, free of ideological or issue content, with the family as the main socializing agency. Certainly the findings of adult interview studies show that such loyalties are extremely long-lived and, summed across the population, give rise to extraordinarily stable distributions.[5] The very persistence of party identification raises suspicion as to whether the country is responding to the parties' current legislative actions when it votes its party loyalties.

That this suspicion is fully warranted in the mid-term election is indicated by several kinds of evidence from this research. To begin with, the electorate's perceptions of the parties betray very little information about current policy issues. For the past ten years the Survey Research Center has opened its electoral interviews with a series of free-answer questions designed to gather in the positive and negative ideas that the public has about the parties. The answers, requiring on the average nearly ten minutes of conversation, are only very secondarily couched in terms of policy issues. In 1958, for example, more than six thousand distinct positive or negative comments about the parties were made by a sample of 1,700 persons. Of these, less than 12 per cent by the most generous count had to do with contemporary legislative issues. As this sample of Americans pictured the reasons it liked and disliked the parties, the modern battlefields of the legislative wars—aid-to-education, farm policy, foreign aid, housing, aid to the unemployed, tariff and trade policy, social security, medical care, labor laws, civil rights, and other issues—rarely came to mind. The main themes in the public's image of the parties are not totally cut off from current legislative events; the political activist could take the group-benefit and prosperity-depression ideas that saturate the party images and connect them fairly easily with issues before Congress. The point is that the public itself rarely does so.

How little awareness of current issues is embodied in the congressional vote also is attested by the reasons people give for voting Republican or Democratic for the House. In view of the capacity of survey respondents to rationalize their acts, direct explanations of behavior should be treated with some reserve. However, rationalization is likely to increase, rather than decrease, the policy content of reasons for voting. It is therefore especially noteworthy how few of the reasons our respond-

[5]For evidence on this point, see *ibid.*, pp. 120–67.

ents gave for their House votes in 1958 had any discernible issue content. The proportion that had—about 7 per cent—was less even than the proportion of party-image references touching current issues.

Perhaps the most compelling demonstration of how hazardous it is to interpret party voting as a judgment of the parties' legislative records is furnished by the evidence about the public's knowledge of party control of Congress. When our 1958 sample was asked whether the Democrats or the Republicans had had more Congressmen in Washington during the two preceding years, a third confessed they had no idea, and an additional fifth gave control of the Eighty-fifth Congress to the Republicans. Only 47 per cent correctly attributed control to the Democrats. These figures improve somewhat when nonvoters are excluded. Of those who voted in 1958, a fifth did not know which party had controlled Congress, another fifth thought the Republicans had, and the remainder (61 per cent) correctly gave control to the Democrats. However, when a discount is made for guessing, the proportion of voters who really *knew* which party had control of the Eighty-fifth Congress probably is still not more than half.[6]

It would be difficult to overstate the significance of these figures for the problem of party government. The information at issue here is not a sophisticated judgment as to what sort of coalition had *effective* control of Congress. It is simply the question of whether the country had a Democratic or a Republican Congress from 1956 to 1958. This elementary fact of political life, which any pundit would take completely for granted as he interpreted the popular vote in terms of party accountability, was unknown to something like half the people who went to the polls in 1958.

It is of equal significance to note that the parties' legislative record was no more salient to those who *deviated* from party than it was to those who voted their traditional party loyalty. It might be plausible to suppose that a floating portion of the electorate gives the parties programmatic support, even though most voters follow their traditional allegiances. If true, this difference would give the responsible-party model

---

[6]Plainly, some deduction has to be made for guessing. One model of the situation would be to think of the sample as composed of three types of people: those who knew, those who didn't know and said so, and those who didn't know but guessed. Assuming that for those who guessed $p = q = \frac{1}{2}$, where p is the probability of guessing Republican, we would deduct from the Democratic answers a percentage equal to the 18 per cent who guessed Republican incorrectly, hence reducing the proportion of voters who really knew which party controlled Congress to 43 per cent. This model may be too severe, however, in view of the presence of the Republican President. It may be more reasonable to admit a fourth type of person, those who did not guess but were misled by Republican control of the White House. Or we might think of the guessers as following a probability law in which $p > \frac{1}{2} > q$. In either of these cases something less than 18 per cent would be deducted from the Democratic answers; hence, the proportion of voters who *knew* which party controlled Congress would lie somewhere between 43 and 61 per cent.

Table 2   Issue Responses and Awareness of Which Party Controlled 85th Congress Among Party Supporters and Voters who Deviated from Party

| | Of Party Identifiers Who | |
	Voted for Own Party	Voted for Other Party
Aware of party control:		
Uncorrected	61%	60%
Corrected for guessing[a]	44	35
Giving issue reasons for House vote	6	7

[a]This correction deducts from the proportion attributing control to the Democrats a percentage equal to the proportion attributing control to the Republicans. See footnote 6.

some factual basis, whether or not the greater part of the electorate lived in darkness. But such a theory finds very little support in these data. In 1958 neither the issue reasons given for the Congressional vote nor the awareness of party control of the Eighty-fifth Congress was any higher among those who voted *against* their party identification than it was among those who voted *for* their party, as the entries of Table 2 demonstrate. If anything, correcting perceived party control for guessing suggests that voters who deviated from their party in 1958 had poorer information about the course of political events over the preceding two years.

Nor do the perceptions of party control of Congress that *are* found supply a key to understanding the congressional vote. Whatever awareness of control the electorate had in 1958 was remarkably unrelated to its support of candidates for the House. To make this point, Table 3 analyzes deviations from party according to three perceptions held by party identifiers voting in 1958: *first*, whether they thought the country's recent domestic affairs had gone well or badly; *second* (to allow for the complication of divided government), whether they thought Congress or President had the greater influence over what the government did;

Table 3   Percentage of Party Identifiers Voting Against Party in 1958, by Perception of Party Control of Government and Course of Domestic Affairs

| Thought That Domestic Affairs | Thought That More Effective Branch of Government Was Controlled by | |
	Own Party	Other Party
Had gone well	I 16 (N = 43)	II 22 (N = 46)
Had gone badly	III 14 (N = 152)	IV 13 (N = 122)

and, *third*, whether they thought the Democrats or Republicans had controlled Congress. To recreate the basis on which the voter might assign credit or blame to the parties, the second and third of these perceptions may be combined; that is, partisans may be classified according to whether they thought their own party or the opposite party had controlled the more effective branch of government. Crossing this classification with perceptions of whether domestic affairs had gone well yields four groups for analysis, two of which (I and IV) might be expected to show little deviation from party, the other two (II and III) substantially more. In fact, however, the differences between these groups are almost trifling. According to the familiar lore, the groups that thought affairs had gone badly (III and IV) are the ones that should provide the clearest test of whether perceptions of party control are relevant to voting for the House. Moreover, with a recession in the immediate background, most people who could be classified into this table in 1958 fell into one of these two groups, as the frequencies indicate. But when the two groups that felt there had been domestic difficulties are compared, it seems not to make a particle of difference whether the Democrats or Republicans were thought to have controlled the actions of government. And when the two groups (I and II) that felt things had gone well are compared, only a slight (and statistically insignificant) difference appears. Interestingly, even this small rise in the rate of deviation from party (in cell II) is contributed mainly by Democratic identifiers who wrongly supposed that the Congress had been in Republican hands.

The conclusion to be drawn from all this certainly is not that national political forces are without *any* influence on deviations from party in the mid-term year. Clearly these forces do have an influence. Although the fluctuations of the mid-term party vote, charted over half a century or more, are very much smaller than fluctuations in the presidential vote or of the congressional vote in presidential years, there is *some* variation, and these moderate swings must be attributed to forces that have their focus at the national level.[7] Even in 1958 one party received a larger share of deviating votes than the other. Our main point is rather that the deviations that do result from national forces are not

[7]A simple but persuasive comparison is this: from 1892 to 1960 the standard deviation of the two-party division of the mid-term congressional vote was 3.9 per cent; of the presidential-year congressional vote, 5.5 per cent; of the presidential vote, 8.2 per cent. Moreover, if the realignment of party loyalties that occurred in the early 1930's is taken into account by computing deviations from pre- and post-1932 means, rather than from a grand mean for the whole period, the standard deviation of the mid-term congressional vote is found to have been 2.4 per cent, compared with a standard deviation of 7.5 per cent for the presidential vote. Some of the remaining variability of the mid-term vote may be due to fluctuations of turnout that do not involve deviation from party. Yet, even ignoring this possibility, the bounds within which national political forces can have influenced the off-year vote by inducing deviations from party appear narrow indeed.

in the main produced by the parties' legislative records and that, in any case, the proportion of deviating votes that can be attributed to national politics is likely to be a small part of the total votes cast by persons deviating from party in a mid-term year. This was specifically true in 1958.

If the motives for deviations from party are not to be found primarily at the national level, the search moves naturally to the local congressional campaign. A third possibility—that deviations are by-products of state-wide races—can be discounted with some confidence. Despite the popular lore on the subject, evidence both from interview studies and from aggregate election statistics can be used to show that the influence of contests for Governor and Senator on the outcome of House races is slight in mid-term elections, although these contests can have an immense influence on turnout for the House.[8] In our 1958 sample, a majority of those who deviated from party in voting for the House *failed* to deviate also at the state level; more often than not, what had moved them into the other party's column at the House level was dissociated from the contests for Governor or Senator in which they voted. Moreover, the fact that an elector deviates from his party in voting both for the House and some office contested on a state-wide basis is not conclusive evidence that the state race has influenced his choice for the House, rather than the other way round. When the possibility of *reverse* coattail effects is allowed for, the reasons for believing that the state-wide race is a potent force on the House vote seem faint indeed.[9] As we search for the motives for deviation from party, analysis of the local congressional race pays greater dividends.

THE SALIENCY OF CONGRESSIONAL CANDIDATES

By the standards of the civics text, what the public knows about the candidates for Congress is as meager as what it knows about the parties'

---

[8]A remarkable fact is that while the total vote for the House increased by 3 million between 1954 and 1958, more than 2 million of this increase was contributed by New York, where Rockefeller sought the governorship; by Ohio, where a fierce referendum battle was fought over the issue of "right-to-work"; and by California, where the fantastic Knight-Knowland-Brown free-for-all was held.

[9]This conclusion is fully supported by an analysis of the variance of turnout and party vote in the mid-term congressional elections of the 1950's. If state-wide races have a major influence on local House races, the election results for the several congressional districts of a state should vary together; similar changes of turnout and party division should be seen in the districts that are influenced by the same state-wide contests. An analysis of the variance of the differences between the 1954 and 1958 turnout level and partisan division for all congressional districts in states having at least two districts indicates the state races have a large effect on turnout; the intraclass correlation expressing the ratio of the between-state variance to the total variance of turnout was more than .45. But this analysis shows, too, that statewide races have almost no effect whatever on the party division of the House vote; the intraclass correlation expressing the ratio of the between-state variance to the total variance of the party division was not more than .02.

legislative records. Of the people who lived in districts where the House seat was contested in 1958, 59 per cent—well over half—said that they had neither read nor heard anything about either candidate for Congress, and less than 1 in 5 felt that they knew something about both candidates. What is more, these remarkable proportions are only marginally improved by excluding nonvoters from the calculations. Of people who went to the polls and cast a vote between rival House candidates in 1958, fully 46 per cent conceded that they did so without having read or heard any- thing about either man. What the other half *had* read or heard is illu- minating; we will deal with its policy content presently. Many of our re- spondents said they knew something about the people contesting the House seat on the basis of very slender information indeed.

The incumbent candidate is by far the better known. In districts where an incumbent was opposed for reelection in 1958, 39 per cent of our respondents knew something about the Congressman whereas only 20 per cent said they knew anything at all about his nonincumbent op- ponent. The incumbent's advantage of repeated exposure to the electo- rate is plain enough. In fact, owing to the greater seniority and longer exposure of Congressmen from safe districts, the public's awareness of incumbents who were unopposed for reelection in 1958 was as great as its awareness of incumbents who had had to conduct an election cam- paign that year.

The saliency of a candidate is of critical importance if he is to at- tract support from the opposite party. However little the public may know of those seeking office, any information at all about the rival party's candidate creates the possibility of a choice deviating from party. That such a choice occurs with some frequency is shown by the entries of Table 4, whose columns separate party identifiers in contested districts in 1958 according to whether they were aware of both candidates, the candidate of their own party or the other party only, or neither candi- date. The condition of no information leads to fairly unrelieved party- line voting, and so to an even greater degree does the condition of in-

Table 4   Percentage Voting for Own Party Candidate and Other Party Candidate for House in 1958, by Saliency of Candidates in Contested Districts

		Voter Was Aware of		
Voted for Candidate	*Both Candidates* (N = 196)	*Own Party Candidate Only* (N = 166)	*Other Party Candidate Only* (N = 68)	*Neither Candidate* (N = 368)
Of own party	83%	98%	60%	92%
Of other party	17	2	40	8
TOTAL	100%	100%	100%	100%

formation only about the candidate of the voter's own party. But if partisan voters know something about the opposition's man, substantial deviations from party appear. In fact, if such voters know *only* the opposition candidate, almost half can be induced to cast a vote contrary to their party identification. In the main, recognition carries a positive valence; to be perceived at all is to be perceived favorably. However, some *negative* perceptions are found in our interviews, and when these are taken into account the explanation of deviation from party becomes surer still. For example, if we return to Table 4 and select from the third column only the voters who perceived the candidate of the other party *favorably*, a clear majority is found to have deviated from party allegiance in casting their votes. And if we select from the first column only the handful of voters who perceived the candidate of their own party *negatively* and of the opposite party *positively*, almost three-quarters are found to have deviated from their party loyalty in voting for the House.

What our constituent interviews show about the increment of support that accrues to the salient candidate is closely aligned to what the candidates themselves see as the roots of their electoral strength. Our interviews with incumbent and nonincumbent candidates seeking election to the House explored at length their understanding of factors aiding—or damaging—their electoral appeal. In particular, these interviews probed the candidates' assessment of four possible influences on the result: traditional party loyalties, national issues, state and local contests, and the candidate's own record and personal standing in the district. Caution is in order in dealing with answers to questions that touch the respondent's self-image as closely as these. Specifically, we may expect some overstatement of the candidate's own importance, particularly from the victors, and we may expect, too, that too large a discount will be applied to party allegiance, since this "inert" factor, having little to do with increments of strength, is so easily taken for granted.

After these allowances are made, it is still impressive how heavy a weight the incumbent assigns his personal record and standing. The Congressman's ranking of this and the other factors in the election is shown in Table 5. As the entries of the table indicate, more than four-fifths of the incumbents reelected in 1958 felt that the niche they had carved out in the awareness of their constituents had substantial impact on the race, a proportion that exceeds by half the percentage who gave as much weight to any of the three other factors. This difference is more than sheer puffing in the interview situation, and the perceptual facts it reveals deserve close attention. Among the forces the Representative feels may enhance his strength at the polls, he gives his personal standing with the district front rank.

Table 5   Relative Importance of Factors in Reelection
As Seen by Incumbent Candidates in 1958

Perceived As	Personal Record and Standing	National Issues	Traditional Party Loyalties	State and Local Races
Very important	57%	26%	25%	14%
Quite important	28	20	21	19
Somewhat important	9	20	24	27
Not very important	3	27	18	19
Not important at all	3	7	12	21
TOTAL	100%	100%	100%	100%

In view of the way the saliency of candidates can move the electorate across party lines, great stress should be laid on the fact that the public sees individual candidates for Congress in terms of party programs scarcely at all. Our constituent interviews indicate that the popular image of the Congressman is almost barren of policy content. A long series of open-ended questions asked of those who said they had any information about the Representative produced mainly a collection of diffuse evaluative judgments: he is a good man, he is experienced, he knows the problems, he has done a good job, and the like. Beyond this, the Congressman's image consisted of a mixed bag of impressions, some of them wildly improbable, about ethnicity, the attractiveness of family, specific services to the district, and other facts in the candidate's background. By the most reasonable count, references to current legislative issues comprised not more than a thirtieth part of what the constituents had to say about their Congressmen.

The irrelevance of legislative issues to the public's knowledge of Representatives is underscored by the nature of some primary *determinants* of saliency. A full analysis of the causes of constituent awareness of candidates goes beyond the scope of this paper. Although our investigation has given a good deal of attention to communication factors and to characteristics of Congressmen and constituents themselves that determine the probability a given Congressman will be known to a given constituent, this interplay of causes cannot be explored very deeply here. However, it *is* noteworthy in the present discussion that many factors increasing the saliency of candidates are unlikely to enhance what the public knows about their stands on issues. An excellent example is sex. Both for incumbents and nonincumbents, a candidate property that is related to saliency is gender; one of the best ways for a Representative to be known is to be a Congress*woman*. How irrelevant to policy issues this property is depends on what we make of the causal relation between sex and salience. The fact of being a woman may make a candidate more visible, but a woman may have to be unusually visible (like a Congressman's widow, say) before she can be elected to the House, or even become a serious candidate. If the first of these inferences is even partially right, the salience of the candidate is not likely to be in terms of positions taken on legislative issues.

Given the number of women who run for Congress, the role of sex may seem a trivial example to demonstrate the irrelevance of issue stands to saliency. However, the same point can be made for a much wider set of districts by the greater saliency of candidates who live in the constituent's home community. Just as there is enormous variety in the communities that make up the American nation, so there is the widest possible variation in how well a congressional district coincides with a natural community, and the goodness of this fit is a fundamental way of typing districts. At one extreme is the constituency whose area is lost within one of the country's great metropolitan centers comprising at best a small fraction of the whole community. At the middle of the range is the district that is itself a natural community, consisting of a single medium-sized city and its environs. At the other extreme is the district whose territory includes a great number of small communities, as well as surrounding open country that goes on, in some cases, for hundreds of miles. In all but the metropolitan districts the salience of the candidate for the voter differs markedly according to whether candidate and voter live in the same community. The fact of common residence—of being "friends and neighbors"—stands for important facts of communication and community identification. Candidates will be joined by formal and informal communication networks to many of the voters living in the same community, and they may also be objects of considerable community pride.

The reality of this local effect is demonstrated by Table 6. As the entries of the table show, dividing a nationwide sample of constituents according to whether they live in the same community as their Congressman or his opponent produces marked differences of saliency. The

Table 6   Influence of "Friends and Neighbors" Factor on Saliency of Candidates for Voters[a]

	Incumbent Candidate Lives in		Non-incumbent Candidate Lives in	
Voter Is	Same Community as Voter (N = 269)	Other Community than Voter (N = 414)	Same Community as Voter (N = 304)	Other Community than Voter (N = 447)
Aware of candidate	67%	45%	47%	22%
Not aware of candidate	33	55	53	78
TOTAL	100%	100%	100%	100%

[a]Metropolitan and large urban districts, for which the notion of the candidate living outside the voter's community has no clear meaning, are excluded from the analysis.

"friends and neighbors" effect made familiar by studies of primary voting in one-party areas has a counterpart in voting for Representatives throughout the country, apart from the large metropolitan areas.[10] And despite the fact that localism is found here in the context of as tightly party-determined an election as any in American politics, the irrelevance of local appeal to legislative issues is probably as great as it is in the wide-open, one-party primary.

CONCLUSION

What the public knows about the legislative records of the parties and of individual congressional candidates is a principal reason for the departure of American practice from an idealized conception of party government. On the surface the legislative elections occurring in the middle of the President's term appear to be dominated by two national parties asking public support for their alternative programs. Certainly the electorate whose votes they seek responds to individual legislative candidates overwhelmingly on the basis of their party labels. Despite our kaleidoscopic electoral laws, the candidate's party is the one piece of information every voter is guaranteed. For many, it is the only information they ever get.

However, the legislative events that follow these elections diverge widely from the responsible-party model. The candidates who have presented themselves to the country under two party symbols immediately break ranks. The legislative parties speak not as two voices but as a cacophony of blocs and individuals fulfilling their own definitions of the public good. Party cohesion by no means vanishes, but it is deeply eroded by the pressures external to party to which the Congressman is subject.

The public's information about the legislative record of the parties and of members of Congress goes far toward reconciling these seemingly contradictory facts. In the congressional election, to be sure, the country votes overwhelmingly for party symbols, but the symbols have limited meaning in terms of legislative policy. The eddies and cross-currents in Congress do not interrupt a flow of legislation that the public expects but fails to see. The electorate sees very little altogether of what goes on in the national legislature. Few judgments of legislative performance are associated with the parties, and much of the public is unaware even of which party has control of Congress. As a result, the absence of party discipline or legislative results is unlikely to bring down

[10]See V. O. Key, Jr., *Southern Politics* (New York: Knopf, 1949), pp. 37ff. We have demonstrated the "friends and neighbors" effect in terms of candidate salience because of our interest in the policy content of candidate perceptions. However, owing to the impact of salience on the vote, living in the same community with the candidate has a clear effect on voting as well.

electoral sanctions on the ineffective party or the errant Congressman.

What the public's response to the parties lacks in programmatic support is not made up by its response to local congressional candidates. Although perceptions of individual candidates account for most of the votes cast by partisans against their parties, these perceptions are almost untouched by information about the policy stands of the men contesting the House seat. The increment of strength that some candidates, especially incumbents, acquire by being known to their constituents is almost entirely free of policy content. Were such content present, the Congressman's solidarity with his legislative party would by no means be assured. If the local constituency possessed far greater resources of information than it has, it might use the ballot to pry the Congressman away from his party quite as well as to unite him with it. Yet the fact is that, by plying his campaigning and servicing arts over the years, the Congressman is able to develop electoral strength that is almost totally dissociated from what his party wants in Congress and what he himself has done about it. The relevance of all this to the problem of cohesion and responsibility in the legislative party can scarcely be doubted.

The description of party irresponsibility in America should not be overdrawn. The American system *has* elements of party accountability to the public, although the issues on which an accounting is given are relatively few and the accounting is more often rendered by those who hold or seek the Presidency than by the parties' congressional delegations. Especially on the broad problem of government action to secure social and economic welfare it can be argued that the parties have real differences and that these have penetrated the party images to which the electorate responds at the polls.

Nevertheless, American practice does diverge widely from the model of party government, and the factors underlying the departure deserve close analysis. An implication of the analysis reported here is that the public's contribution to party irregularity in Congress is not so much a matter of encouraging or requiring its Representatives to deviate from their parties as it is of the public having so little information that the irregularity of Congressmen and the ineffectiveness of the congressional parties have scant impact at the polls. Many of those who have commented on the lack of party discipline in Congress have assumed that the Congressman votes against his party because he is forced to by the demands of one of several hundred constituencies of a superlatively heterogeneous nation. In some cases, the Representative may subvert the proposals of his party because his constituency demands it. But a more reasonable interpretation over a broader range of issues is that the Congressman fails to see these proposals as part of a program on which the party—and he himself—will be judged at the polls, because he knows the constituency isn't looking.

PART TWO

THE PRESIDENT

As his administration was drawing to an end, Harry Truman predicted what would happen when Dwight Eisenhower became President: "He'll sit here and he'll say, 'Do this! Do that!' *And nothing will happen.*" This is the key problem for any American president. Both political ambition and the public interest require him to undertake many more responsibilities than he can discharge simply by commanding that his will be done. This is not a problem faced only by vigorous, innovating presidents; even the feeblest do-nothing president has innumerable tasks thrust upon him.

One of the president's difficulties lies in the very governmental apparatus at whose head he stands; it is so vast and complicated that coordination and harmony are difficult to achieve. Roger Hilsman explores this situation in the realm of foreign policy, where the variety of agencies and points of view inevitably poses problems of control for the chief executive. Hilsman discusses the sources of conflict, techniques of bureaucratic skirmishing, and some of the resources contending officials use in advising the president, i.e., in trying to have their proposals adopted as American foreign policy. As Hilsman's account suggests, the principal agencies concerned with foreign policy—the CIA, the Defense Department, and the State Department—play somewhat the same role that private interest groups do in domestic policy.

Every president faces the same challenge: How can he overcome the cruel imbalance between his goals and the means available to accomplish them? Richard Neustadt, a former member of President Truman's White House staff, explores this question in his book, *Presidential Power*, from which the second selection in this section is taken. In the chapter before the one reprinted here, Neustadt described three "cases of command" by the president. The first was Truman's dismissal of General MacArthur because the General persisted in making public statements that undercut American foreign policy. The second was President Eisenhower's order sending troops to enforce school desegregation in Little Rock. And the third was Truman's seizure of the steel mills to avert a strike. Neustadt presents all three cases as examples of presidential weakness and political ineptness in that Truman and Eisenhower had to take such drastic steps because they were incapable of getting their way by more limited action.

In "The Power to Persuade" Neustadt argues that a successful president accumulates adequate power by convincing other people that it is in their interest to go along with him. ("Persuade" may be too narrow a word, since it includes everything from the president's symbolic position as steward of the nation's destiny to, say, his opportunity to inspect anyone's income tax returns.) Neustadt's capsule account of the creation of the Marshall Plan shows how a president, if he is to achieve some of his goals, must work with men whose overall political aims are different from his, but who share with him some particular common interest on which a mutually beneficial alliance can be based.

Richard Fenno's description of the relationship between Franklin D. Roosevelt and Jesse Jones illustrates this point in greater detail. Jones was a successful businessman with important connections in the southern conservative wing of the Democratic party. Although unsympathetic to most of the New Deal, he was appointed to a series of major posts. Jones pursued his conservative inclinations while in these positions, yet Roosevelt kept him in office for more than ten years. He did so because Jones's conservatism was overbalanced by his willingness to endorse some of Roosevelt's policies and by his service as a kind of character witness for the President to the business community. When Jones's support was no longer as important as his divergent political beliefs, Roosevelt fired him.

It is not surprising that the Democratic party's ideological limits were wide enough to include Roosevelt and Jones; both our parties are collectivities of clashing interests, often sharing little beyond the common label "Democrat" or "Republican." In the process of winning nomination an elected president builds a coalition of his party's factions strong enough to wage a successful election campaign and then provide the political foundation for his administration. When Lyndon B. Johnson became President after John F. Kennedy's assassination, he faced a similar problem of coalition building, but one that had to be solved in days rather than months. Rowland Evans and Robert Novak's account of Johnson's response to this challenge provides a remarkably clear illustration of the two parties' fragmented character, as well as of the techniques by which the president, as his party's leader, must keep its various factions' support if he is to govern effectively. The sum total of this support makes up most of the "public confidence" that any president needs. Johnson skillfully won this confidence in his first days in office; its gradual dissipation in later years gravely undermined his influence during the last years of his presidency.

In the 1962 steel price crisis, described in the last selection, the circle of people whom the president must persuade grows from a few political leaders to the steel industry and, finally, the general public. This case also demonstrates how far-flung the president's responsibilities have become. Nothing in the Constitution or the law authorizes a president to set the price of steel. But since President Kennedy had just induced the steel unions to accept a modest increase in wages—evidently without complaints from the companies that such a step was an unjustifiable intrusion of governmental power—he could certainly expect repercussions from the unions if he did not oppose the price increase. Once he decided to do so, Kennedy fought this battle on two very different fronts. He tried to convince the public that his position was proper, and he exerted pressure on the steel industry by rewarding firms that held prices steady while threatening the companies that had raised prices. These two efforts were not independent of each other. If public response had been unfavorable, Republican politicians would not have hesitated to denounce Kennedy as a dictator, and this in turn would have strengthened the position of the companies that had raised prices. Apparently favorable public opinion led the Republicans to lie low until they could attack the President on the peripheral issue of awakening reporters in the middle of the night. After the steel episode, Kennedy's popularity among businessmen appeared to decline considerably. A subsequent temporary drop in the stock market was blamed on his steel policy.

This case illustrates the formidable array of resources that the president can employ to get his way. The wholehearted employment of these powers may involve political cost to the president. In fact, any exercise of his powers may damage the president's position: He faces endless demands on his time and energy; a decision to pay attention to one subject means that a dozen others are neglected. The president, therefore, must weigh priorities carefully, facing the fact that many desirable things cannot be accomplished because he must spend his political resources on those policies that he considers most important for the country and for his own political position. This is not "just playing politics," for a president who is politically weak will be unable to carry out even the noblest conceptions of the public interest.

PROBLEMS OF COMMAND IN MAKING FOREIGN POLICY

ROGER HILSMAN

In the years following World War II, Princeton University established what was probably the most unlikely university post in the Western world—a professorship combining sculpture and boxing. The job was set up for a man named Joseph Brown, who was equally competent in both fields and who was drawn to things that called for both talents. As a boxer, he was interested in strong bodies, and as a sculptor he was interested in strong lines. Designing playground equipment combined the two nicely, and Professor Brown conceived and built some unusual pieces in free-form concrete. But his greatest achievement came when he discovered nylon rope woven around a core of steel wire. He built a spider web of this special rope in the shape of a pyramid, and then tightened the strands until each was in vibrating tension with every other. The results were dramatic: if an impish child in a crowd of climbers plucked a strand on one side of the pyramid, some startled innocent on the other would find himself flung violently in several directions at once. The taut nylon web was so intricately interwoven that there was no sure way of telling who had been the original culprit, so the game of retaliation and counterretaliation usually led to what can be described as complex pandemonium. But since most of the chil-

Reprinted by permission from Roger Hilsman, TO MOVE A NATION: THE POLITICS OF FOREIGN POLICY IN THE ADMINISTRATION OF JOHN F. KENNEDY *(New York: Doubleday & Company, Inc., 1967), pp. 3–8, 10–13, 63–68. A Professor of Political Science at Columbia University, Mr. Hilsman was Director of the Bureau of Intelligence and Research at the State Department and Assistant Secretary of State for Far Eastern Affairs during the Kennedy administration.*

dren succeeded in hanging on and the one or two who didn't were never more than shaken up, the apparatus was a huge success.

But Professor Brown's greatest pride was neither in the fun nor the body-building, but in what he liked to call the educational contribution. "The children," he said, "learn two profound truths about life. The first is that there are so-and-so's in the world. The second, and more important, is that it's not easy to be sure just who they are."

In these two respects, if in no other, Washington resembles life. Anyone who has lived and worked there knows beyond doubt that the town is full of so-and-so's. But it would be impossible to get agreement on a definitive list.

"Washington," I remember Secretary of State Dean Rusk saying when one of our colleagues was cruelly and unfairly attacked in the press, "is an *evil* town." It is, but not because the people who inhabit it are evil by nature, but because of the struggle that is inherent in the fact that the capital of a nation is the nerve center of the nation's power. Where power is, there also are conflict and turmoil. Thus the reasons that Washington is the way it is lie deep in the heart of both the nature of the business of Washington and of the political and governmental process by which that business is carried out. . . .

THE PROCESS OF POLICY-MAKING

The nature and importance of the business done in Washington are obvious. The process by which that business is done and the nation is moved is more obscure.

As Americans, with our flair for the mechanical and love of efficiency combined with a moralistic Puritan heritage, we would like to think not only that policy-making is a conscious and deliberate act, one of analyzing problems and systematically examining grand alternatives in all their implications, but also that the alternative chosen is aimed at achieving overarching ends that serve a high moral purpose. Evidence that there is confusion about goals or evidence that the goals themselves may be competing or mutually incompatible is disquieting, and we hear repeated calls for a renewed national purpose, for a unifying ideology with an appeal abroad that will rival Communism, or for a national strategy that will fill both functions and set the guidelines for all of policy. As Americans, we think it only reasonable that the procedures for making national decisions should be orderly, with clear lines of responsibility and authority. We assume that what we call the "decisions" of government are in fact decisions—discrete acts, with recognizable beginnings and sharp, decisive endings. We like to think of policy as rationalized, in the economist's sense of the word, with each step leading logically and economically to the next. We want to be able to find out who makes decisions, to feel that they are the proper, official, and authorized persons, and to know that the really big decisions will be made at the top, by the President and his principal advisers in the formal assemblage of the Cabinet or the National Security Council and with the Congress exercising its full and formal powers. And we feel that the entire decision-making process ought to be a dignified, even majestic progression, with each of the participants having roles and powers so well and precisely defined that they can be held accountable for their actions by their superiors and eventually by the electorate.

The reality, of course, is quite different. Put dramatically, it could be argued that few, if any, of the decisions of government are either decisive or final. Very often policy is the sum of a congeries of separate or only vaguely related actions. On other occasions, it is an uneasy, even internally inconsistent compromise among competing goals or an incompatible mixture of alternative means for achieving a single goal. There is no systematic and comprehensive study of all the implications of the grand alternatives—nor can there be. A government does not decide to inaugurate the nuclear age, but only to try to build an atomic bomb before its enemy does. It does not make a formal decision to become a welfare state, but only to take each of a series of steps—to experiment with an income tax at some safely innocuous level like 3 per cent, to alleviate the hardship of men who have lost their jobs in a depression with a few weeks of unemployment compensation, or to lighten the old age of industrial workers with a tentative program of social security benefits. Rather than through grand decisions on grand alternatives, policy changes seem to come through a series of slight modifications of existing policy, with the new policy emerging slowly and haltingly by small and usually tentative steps, a process of trial and error in which policy zigs and zags, reverses itself, and then moves forward in a series of incremental steps.[1] Sometimes policies are formulated and duly ratified only to be skewed to an entirely different direction and purpose by those carrying them out—or they are never carried out at all. And sometimes issues are endlessly debated with nothing at all being resolved until both the problem and the debaters disappear under the relentless pyramiding of events. . . .

THE POWER OF THE PRESIDENT

. . . On some occasions presidents do not succeed in getting [other officials] to come around, and they must then either pay the political costs of public disunity or make some concession to achieve the unity of

[1]See Charles E. Lindblom, "The Science of 'Muddling Through,'" *Public Administration Review*, Vol. 19 (Spring 1959); and his book, *The Intelligence of Democracy* (New York: The Free Press, 1965).

compromise. In the Kennedy administration, for example, the State Department was convinced that high-level visits to Vietnam were politically bad. They felt, in particular, that visits by so high-ranking an official as Secretary of Defense McNamara would get United States prestige hooked too tightly to the roller coaster of events in Vietnam in spite of the fact that we had only limited influence on those events. Visits by so high-ranking an official would also tend to make a bad situation look even worse by showing our concern too openly. And, finally, such visits would tend to make a Vietnamese struggle conducted with only our aid and advice look in the world's eyes like a purely American war.

The President was only too well aware of these probable consequences, but in the circumstances, he indicated that he was prepared to pay the price. For the only way of keeping the higher-ranking military officers in the Pentagon from an increasingly public display of discontent with the President's decision not to enlarge the war was to keep the Secretary of Defense fully content with the policy. And the only way to do that, apparently, was to let him see for himself.

On some occasions, the President clearly makes the decision, even if he cannot make it exactly as he might wish. On other occasions, the decision is just as clearly made by Congress. But in action after action, responsibility for decision is as fluid and restless as quicksilver, and there seems to be neither a person nor an organization on whom it can be fixed. At times the point of decision seems to have escaped into the labyrinth of governmental machinery, beyond layers and layers of bureaucracy. Other times it seems never to have reached the government, but remained in either the wider domain of a public opinion created by the press or in the narrower domain dominated by the maneuverings of special interests.

TURMOIL

Just as our desire to know who makes a decision is frustrated, so is our hope that the process of policy-making will be dignified. A decision, in fact, may be little more than a signal that starts a public brawl by people who want to reverse it. President Eisenhower's "New Look" decision to concentrate on air power at the expense of ground forces, for example, had no visible result for the first year except semipublic fights with the Joint Chiefs of Staff, an eruption of the so-called "Colonels' revolt," and frequent leaks of top secret information. The whole strategy was completely reversed when the Kennedy administration came into responsibility in 1961, and the reversal was fought by the same technique of leaks, but this time it was Air Force rather than Army partisans doing the leaking. At the very beginning of the Kennedy administration, for example, Rusk wrote McNamara a memorandum seeking an interdepartmental discussion of the basic problem, and a distorted version of the memo was promptly given to Air Force sympathizers in the press in an obvious attempt at sabotage.

Leaks, of course, are the first and most blatant signs of battle, and they are endemic in the policy process. When it became clear, for example, that the report of the Gaither Committee, set up by Eisenhower in 1957 to study civil defense in terms of the whole of nuclear strategy, would be critical of the "New Look" and the entire Eisenhower defense policy, the crucial battle between the different factions within the administration took place, not on the substance of the report, but on the issue of whether there would be two hundred top secret copies of the report or only two. For everyone knew without saying so that if the President did not accept the Gaither Committee's recommendations, it might be possible to keep the report from leaking to the press if there were only two copies, but never if there were two hundred. The committee won the battle, and two hundred top secret copies were distributed within the Executive Branch. The President did not accept the recommendations; and, sure enough, within a few days Chalmers Roberts of the Washington *Post* was able to write a story, covering almost two newspaper pages, that contained an accurate and comprehensive version of both the top secret report and its recommendations.

Not surprisingly, it was these continual leaks that especially puzzled and angered Eisenhower. In 1955, he said, "For some two years and three months I have been plagued by inexplicable undiscovered leaks in this Government." But so are all presidents, before and after Eisenhower. Not only are there leaks of secret information, but leaks that distort secret information so as to present a special view that is often totally false. There flows out of Washington a continuous stream of rumor, tales of bickering, speculation, stories of selfish interest, charges and counter-charges. Abusive rivalries arise between the government agencies engaged in making policy, and even within a single agency different factions battle, each seeking allies in other agencies, among the members of Congress, from interest associations, and among the press. Officialdom, whether civil or military, is hardly neutral. It speaks, and inevitably it speaks as an advocate. The Army battles for ground forces, the Air Force for bombers; the "Europe faction" in the State Department for policy benefiting NATO, and the "Africa faction" for anti-colonialist policies unsettling to our relations with Europe. All of these many interests, organizations, and institutions—inside and outside the government—are joined in a struggle over the goals of governmental policy and over the means by which these goals shall be achieved. Instead of unity, there is conflict. Instead of a majestic progression, there are erratic zigs and zags. Instead of clarity and decisiveness, there are tangle and turmoil, instead of order, confusion. . . .

POLICY CONVICTIONS

. . . Among the principal findings of a British government committee appointed to study the powers of ministers was that most men find it easier to go against their own pecuniary interests than they do to go against a deep conviction on policy. As we have said, in the business of Washington, the stakes are high and the issues fundamental, both to our society and to the question of war and peace for the entire world. In such circumstances it is not surprising that passions run strong and full. It is not even surprising that men occasionally feel so deeply that they take matters into their own hands, leaking secret materials to the Congress or the press in an attempt to force the President to adopt what they are convinced is the only right path, the salvation of the nation. When in the late 1950s, for example, intelligence officials leaked secret information foreshadowing an upcoming "missile gap" to Democratic senators and sympathetic members of the press, it was not because they were disloyal, but because they were deeply convinced that the nation was in peril. They had tried and failed to convince the top levels of the Eisenhower administration of the validity of their projections, and they felt completely justified in taking matters into their own hands by going over the President's head to Congress, the press, and the public. Colonel Billy Mitchell was doing the same in the 1920s when he provoked a court-martial so he could present the case for air power to the nation at large. But none of this is new. Throughout history, the motive for such deeds—for mankind's greatest achievements, but also, unhappily, for mankind's greatest crimes—has rarely been to benefit the individual, but for the glory of something the individual thinks of as bigger than himself, for his God, his nation, or his ideology.

There is nothing in this to nullify the point that selfish interests are also involved in these decisions, and that the decisions affect such powerful interests as labor, the farmers, the medical profession, and the "military-industrial complex." But society is made up of its different parts, and it is not merely a rationalization when farmers, for example, argue that a healthy nation depends on a healthy agriculture. There is nothing wrong in the people of a democracy expressing their interests, their values, hopes, and fears through "interest" organizations. How else, save through some such hierarchy of representative organizations, can the needs and desires of so many millions of people be aggregated?

Nor is there anything wrong in the fact that the bureaucracy itself is divided, that it represents special interests, and that its parts speak as advocates, fighting hard for their constituencies. The Department of Labor is inevitably and rightly more oriented toward workingmen than management; the Bureau of Mines more toward extractive industry than the industrial users of minerals; the Children's Bureau more toward restrictions on employers than permissiveness. Indeed some segments of society that are poorly organized for exercising leverage on either public opinion or the Congress would have a much smaller voice if the bureaucracy of the federal government did not represent their interests, and many of the long-range, more general interests of society as a whole have no other spokesman at all. But all this also contributes to the turbulence of the Washington scene.

INADEQUACY OF KNOWLEDGE

Still another dimension of the confusion and turbulence of the policy-making process is the complexity of the problems and the inadequacy of our knowledge of how and why things work in the social affairs of men, our limited capacity to foresee developments that bring problems or to predict the consequences of whatever action we do take. Partly this is because in the field of foreign affairs, especially, there are so many other people and nations involved, friends and enemies, with goals of their own and tactics of their own. But it is more than this. More and better understanding will not always or necessarily lead to sure solutions to knotty problems, but it sometimes does. If our understanding of the workings of a modern industrial economy had been better in the 1920s, the Great Depression could very probably have been avoided; and if our knowledge had been only slightly greater in the 1930s than it was, the measures to meet the Depression would probably have been more effective and quicker-acting. Winston Churchill called World War II the "unnecessary war," by which he meant that if we had better understood what Hitler and Nazism were really about and particularly their compelling dynamism leading toward war, it would have been politically possible to take the necessary preventive measures—which however hard and costly, would have been better than the horror of what actually occurred.

When knowledge is inadequate, when problems are complex, and especially when they are also new—presenting a challenge with which there has been no experience—there is in such circumstances room to spare for disagreement, conflict, and turmoil. It is not the only cause of disagreement, much less the central cause, but it is one of them. McGeorge Bundy once said that policy in Vietnam was "the most divisive issue in the Kennedy administration." He meant *inside* the administration, and he was right. And the cause of the dissension was precisely inadequate understanding and a failure of analysis. Modern guerrilla warfare, as the Communists practice it, is *internal* war, an ambiguous aggression that avoids direct and open attack violating international frontiers but combines terror, subversion, and political action with hit-and-run guerrilla raids and ambush. It is new to the Western world, and not yet fully understood. In the Kennedy administration there were those who saw it as a modified form of traditional war, but war nevertheless to be fought primarily with traditional military measures. Others saw guerrilla warfare as essentially political in nature, aimed at winning the people while terrorizing the government, and they believed that in fighting against a guerrilla insurgency military measures should be subordinated to political action. But there was simply not enough knowledge and experience with such matters to prove who was right, and the struggle within the administration became increasingly bitter.

POLICY-MAKING IS POLITICS

These are some of the facets of policy-making and the decisions that move nations—separate institutions sharing powers, the press, experts, and others who influence policy without holding formal power, selfish and unselfish interest groups that exert a different kind of power, the difficulties and complexities of analysis, prediction, and judgment. These many facets help to explain the turmoil, and they flag a warning to those who would be cynical about Washington and the hurly-burly that is disquieting or even repugnant to so many. But they do not completely explain even the surface phenomena of Washington, nor is what explanation they do give completely satisfying. As Americans, we aspire to a rationalized system of government and policy-making. This implies that a nation can pursue a single set of clearly perceived and generally agreed-to goals, as a business organization is supposed to pursue profits. Yet is this realistic? Is the problem of making policy in a highly diversified mass society really one of relating the different steps in making a decision to a single set of goals or is it precisely one of choosing goals—of choosing goals not in the abstract but in the convoluted context of ongoing events, with inadequate information, incomplete knowledge and understanding, and insufficient power—and doing so, in all probability, while we are pitted against opposition both at home and abroad? If so, the making of national decisions is not a problem for the efficiency expert, or of assembling different pieces of policy logically as if the product were an automobile. Policy faces inward as much as outward, seeking to reconcile conflicting goals, to adjust aspirations to available means, and to accommodate the different advocates of these competing goals and aspirations to one another. It is here that the essence of policy-making seems to lie, in a process that is in its deepest sense political.

Recognizing the political nature of policy-making might help us to a better understanding of the diversity and seeming inconsistency of the goals that national policy must serve. It might also help us to understand

the powerful but sometimes hidden forces through which these competing goals are reconciled, why the pushes and pulls of these crosscurrents
are sometimes dampened or obscured, and why they are sometimes so
fiercely public. Even the roles of such "unrational" procedures as bargaining and power might also become more clear.

President Kennedy once said, "There will always be the dark and
tangled stretches in the decision-making process—mysterious even to
those who may be most intimately involved. . . ."[2] Yet it is equally true
that we can understand better than we now do how a nation is moved
and that better understanding can lead to more effective policy and
perhaps even to improvements in the policy-making process itself. Understanding comes in looking at the vital stuff of events themselves,
in the interaction of the President, the Congress, the press, and special
interests and in the rivalries of the great Executive departments, State,
Defense, and the Central Intelligence Agency, as they clash in the actual
making of policy, in the crucible of events—in the struggle over organizational mandates, in the crisis of Soviet nuclear missiles in Cuba, of the
Congo, Laos, and the guerrilla struggle in Vietnam. . . .

THE PROBLEM OF CIA

"It's a hell of a way to learn things," President Kennedy said immediately after the Bay of Pigs, "but I have learned one thing from this business—that is, that we will have to deal with the CIA."

That something was wrong about the CIA had become increasingly
clear for several years. When President Kennedy was still a senator, he
and everyone else on Capitol Hill, where it was all common gossip, had
known the general outlines of a number of fiascoes—aid to the 1958 re-
bellion in Indonesia, where an American pilot, Allen L. Pope, was still
held prisoner; the allegation that CIA was deeply involved in maintaining Chinese Nationalist, Kuomintang troops on the territory of Burma;
and a variety of situations, such as Laos, where the CIA was reported to
be pursuing policies undercutting the ambassador.

Kennedy had also been aware that the trouble was more fundamental than particular mistakes. President Truman, who had been responsible for setting up the CIA, some years later expressed the nature of
this concern in a public statement. "For some time I have been dis-
turbed," he wrote, "by the way CIA has been diverted from its original
assignment. It has become an operational and at times a policy-making
arm of the government." Truman went on to say that he never had any
thought when he set up the CIA that it would be injected into peace-

<hr/>

[2]In his foreword to Theodore C. Sorensen's *Decision-Making in the White House*
(New York: Columbia University Press, 1963).

time cloak-and-dagger operations, but that he intended for it to be confined to intelligence work. "Some of the complications and embarrassment that I think we have experienced are in part attributable to the fact that this quiet intelligence arm of the President has been so removed from its intended role that it is being interpreted as a symbol of sinister and mysterious foreign intrigue—and a subject for Cold War enemy propaganda." President Truman's conclusion was that he would like to see the CIA restored to its original assignment as the intelligence arm of the President. "We have grown up as a nation," he wrote, "respected for our free institutions and for our ability to maintain a free and open society. There is something about the way the CIA has been functioning that is casting a shadow over our historic position and I feel that we need to correct it."[3]

President Truman's role in creating the CIA makes his criticism all the more sobering. But, stiff though his criticism was, others were even harsher. Article after article in magazines and newspapers catalogued a long list of charges: that the CIA was a mass of bumbling inefficiency; that it was a citadel of extreme conservatism; that it had vast sums of money at its disposal for which it made no accounting; that it had such an extensive empire and so many employees that in some of our embassies overseas the CIA agents outnumbered regular foreign service officers; that the pervasive secrecy of intelligence activities permitted CIA to pursue its own policies without regard for the rest of the government; that when an intelligence agency combined policy and operations with intelligence-gathering, as the CIA did, there was an inevitable tendency to warp the intelligence it gathered to suit its particular policies; and that the atmosphere of plot and intrigue inevitably spilled over into the domestic arena, threatening the very system the intelligence agency was supposed to protect. Some of these charges were undoubtedly motivated by nothing more than sensationalism. But some of the concern was very real. Two responsible journalists, one the head of the *Herald Tribune*'s Washington bureau, later went so far as to write a book which charged that there were "two governments in the United States today," one visible and the other invisible. They were convinced that "the Invisible Government has achieved a quasi-independent status and a power of its own," with the result that one cannot help suspecting "that the foreign policy of the United States often works publicly in one direction and secretly through the Invisible Government in just the opposite direction"—sometimes, they seem to suggest, against the wishes of the President himself.[4]

[3]Harry S Truman in an article syndicated by the North American Newspaper Alliance, as it appears in the Washington *Post*, December 22, 1963.

[4]David Wise and Thomas B. Ross, *The Invisible Government* (New York: Random House, Inc., 1964).

The root fear was that the CIA represented a *Staat-im-Staat*, a state within a state, and certainly the basis for fear was there. In its network of agents overseas, the CIA had the means for gathering the necessary information on which policy must be based. In its staff of researchers and in the Board of National Estimates in Washington, which are all under the Deputy Director for Intelligence, it had a "little State Department" of people qualified to analyze that information and reach policy conclusions. Because of its method of operating out of embassies— which all intelligence services do, incidentally—it had representation abroad and contact with high officials of foreign governments through which policy could be implemented. Indeed, because the CIA could keep its men in a particular country longer than most ambassadors stay, CIA station chiefs frequently had been able to make closer friendships with prime ministers and kings and presidents than ambassadors did, and thus to be more influential. In many countries, especially the more backward countries on the firing line of Communist expansionism, where money is used freely in ways that the State Department budget does not provide for and where intrigue is a way of life, most nationals of the country sincerely believed that it was the CIA station chief who really represented the United States. The CIA also had all the facilities of an information and propaganda agency—including powerful radio transmitters. It also had independent communications facilities, as mentioned earlier, by which either information or instructions could be sent without any other part of the American government being aware of it. For the implementation of policy, indeed, the CIA had military training centers that had frequently been used to train guerrillas and on at least one occasion—for the Bay of Pigs operation—a brigade of regular troops equipped with artillery. It had airplanes and the pilots to fly them. It had naval vessels and the crews to man them. With all of this it is not surprising that there should be fear that the CIA might develop into a state within a state.

From my own personal experience, I know that it had not and that most of the more extreme charges about CIA were not valid. Although the people in CIA, in common with all other human beings, have made mistakes, the organization possesses a more able staff than most. Far from being a haven of extreme conservatism, the CIA during the Eisenhower administration was the one place that Senator McCarthy was unable to touch in his witch hunt and was in fact the only place in the Eisenhower administration that had room for the young activists who wanted to work with youth and labor movements abroad. Through its intelligence-gathering effort, which has relied on scholarly research as much as on cloak-and-dagger operations, the CIA has played a large part, though not the only part, in making the United States Government the best informed in the world. In a patient though sometimes painful educational campaign waged through the tedious procedures by which National Intelligence Estimates are developed, it has succeeded in bringing an objectivity—and an over-all point of view rising above the parochial interests of the individual military services—that was previously unknown in the American government's analyses of events abroad. The United States, in fact, owes the men and women of the CIA an extraordinary debt.

But the CIA still represented a most serious problem, as President Truman said. And the problem was one of power.

"The National Security Act of 1947 . . . has given Intelligence," Allen Dulles once said, "a more influential position in our government than Intelligence enjoys in any other government of the world."[5] By the time the Kennedy administration came into office, Allen Dulles had been Director of the CIA for almost eight years, and the CIA's power was at an all-time high.

The CIA, first of all, had people. Where the State Department, for example, at one time had three people on its Laos desk, the CIA had six. This meant that the CIA could always afford to be represented at an interdepartmental meeting, that it could spare the manpower to prepare the papers that would dominate the meeting, and that it could explore the byways and muster the information and arguments that gave its men authority at those meetings.

What is more, the people in CIA were outstandingly able, which was itself a source of power. As mentioned above, the agency had stoutly protected its people from McCarthy and was one of the few parts of government in the Eisenhower era where new ideas were encouraged and activists permitted to do things, and these facts also helped in attracting still more active and able people. Promotion was fast.

CIA also had money. The exact amount of its budget is still secret. But various newsmen have estimated the total for all United States intelligence activities at about two billion dollars per year, and it is obvious that CIA's share of the total would be large, certainly amounting to more than the State Department had to spend per year. CIA's freedom from normal accounting and auditing procedures gave it a flexibility in the use of its money that also gave it power. Paradoxically, CIA became involved in many activities that its critics considered to be outside its legitimate purview at the urging of other agencies, such as the State Department, who would normally be responsible for the activity but whose budget did not provide for it. Buying books abroad was one example and helping the impoverished leader of a government-in-exile come to New York to present his case to the UN General Assembly was another. Unhappily, however, where both activities would be ac-

---

[5] In a speech at Yale University, February 3, 1958.

cepted as a matter of course if the State Department money had been available, they became sinister when CIA money was used.

CIA'S command of information was also a source of power. Quite apart from the issue of whether or not information is bent to support a particular point of view, in Washington the first to have a tidbit of information is the first to interpret its significance, and is the first to be on the scene when discussion starts on what the policy implications of the information might be. Where information is an asset, command over information is the power to grant or withhold that asset—to a congressman or the press, for example.

Even the need for secrecy can be power. Quite apart from the phenomenon mentioned earlier that in countries where intrigue is a way of life the mere fact of being the secret intelligence service gives prestige that translates into power, the need to keep certain operations or sources of information secret gives those who "need to know" a further dimension for making judgments or understanding the why of what is happening. Those who knew of the peripheral reconnaissance flights that probed Soviet air defenses during the Eisenhower administration and the U-2 flights over the Soviet Union itself, for example, were better able to understand some of the things the Soviets were saying and doing than people who did not know of these activities.

The CIA also derived power from the fact that the function they performed, like that of the FBI, is by its nature politically appealing. The CIA was in the forefront of the Cold War. Its job was to smite our enemies, not to negotiate with them, or compromise with them, or make agreements with them. It had the appeal of patriotism. In Congress, the CIA's natural allies were also the "inner club," the power center of Congress—the men at the heart of the long-standing coalition of Southern Democrats and right-wing Republicans, the men of long tenure and conservative outlook. A natural alliance with the congressional power center, a mandate so broad that it is called upon to testify as often before the Committees on Armed Services and Science and Technology as before the Committee on Foreign Relations, and a command of secret information that can itself enhance the position of the members of the congressional committee that receives it—all of these are levers which a politically astute Director of the CIA can use to great effect on Capitol Hill. And most have done so. It is no accident that the two men John F. Kennedy immediately named as carry-overs into his new administration were J. Edgar Hoover and Allen W. Dulles.

Political leverage is power. Information is power. Secrecy is power. Speed in communications is power. Ability is power. And the sheer number of people is power. CIA had all these, and during the years of the Eisenhower administration it had still another source of power—the fact that the Secretary of State, John Foster Dulles, and the Director of the

CIA, Allen W. Dulles, were brothers. Allen Dulles probably never presumed on this relationship, but it inevitably had its effects, if only because people believed it did, and behaved accordingly. When the Kennedy administration took office, resentment of the CIA in the Foreign Service and the State Department was high. They resented what they thought was high living abroad, the better communication, the more ample travel funds, and the encroachment on what was regarded as traditional State Department functions. But it was the relationship of the two brothers that had become the focus of the resentment. John Foster Dulles said that he carried the State Department in his hat, by which he meant that he did not rely very heavily on the department and its bureaucracy. Allen Dulles, on the other hand, did rely heavily on his bureaucracy. He liked to have his own man in every capital of the world, if possible, and in allied and friendly capitals, he liked to have his man on close personal terms with the chief of state who was also in some cases under some obligation to the CIA of one form or another. As mentioned above, in many cases the CIA's station chief had been in the country much longer than the ambassador, knew more of the nationals more intimately, knew conditions in the country better, had more money to spend, more favors to do, and may well have been a more able person than the ambassador. In differences of judgment, in other words, it might well have been that the CIA man was more often right. But quite apart from the facts of the matter, many people in the department and the foreign service were convinced that CIA would win disputes no matter what the merits were and there were persistent rumors that this or that ambassador had been relieved not for the reasons given but because he had taken issue with the judgment of the CIA station chief in his country.

What people in the State Department did not so often realize was that there was a basis for resentment in the CIA as well. CIA, as we have said, had a large number of exceptionally able people. It was undoubtedly frustrating to some of these men to have to take a back seat to some less able foreign service officer who occupied the front position solely because he was the State Department representative. The State Department was jealous of its policy-making role, and instead of leading in foreign policy it sometimes merely excluded others from participating. And as the CIA people got older, they saw a ceiling on their own advancement. Unlike a foreign service officer, a CIA career man could have little hope of ever becoming an ambassador—his long service in intelligence alone precluded it.

All these questions of morale were a matter of concern to the Kennedy administration when it came into office, but it was the greater issue of the power of CIA and its role—the problem that Truman later described—that was paramount. . . .

CHAPTER SIX

THE POWER
TO PERSUADE

RICHARD E. NEUSTADT

I

The limits on command suggest the structure of our government. The constitutional convention of 1787 is supposed to have created a government of "separated powers." It did nothing of the sort. Rather, it created a government of separated institutions *sharing* powers.[1] "I am part of the legislative process," Eisenhower often said in 1959 as a reminder of his veto.[2] Congress, the dispenser of authority and funds, is no less part of the administrative process. Federalism adds another set of separated in-situations. The Bill of Rights adds others. Many public purposes can only be achieved by voluntary acts of private institutions; the press, for one, in Douglass Cater's phrase is a "fourth branch of government."[3] And with the coming of alliances abroad, the separate institutions of a London, or a Bonn, share in the making of American public policy.

[1]The reader will want to keep in mind the distinction between two senses in which the word *power* is employed. When I have used the word (or its plural) to refer to formal constitutional, statutory, or customary authority, it is either qualified by the adjective "formal" or placed in quotation marks as "power(s)." Where I have used it in the sense of effective influence upon the conduct of others, it appears without quotation marks (and always in the singular). Where clarity and convenience permit, *authority* is substituted for "power" in the first sense and *influence* for power in the second sense.

[2]See, for example, his press conference of July 22, 1959, as reported in the *New York Times* for July 23, 1959.

[3]See Douglass Cater, *The Fourth Branch of Government* (Boston: Houghton Mifflin Company, 1959).

Reprinted by permission from PRESIDENTIAL POWER *(New York: John Wiley & Sons, Inc., 1960), pp. 33–57, 198–200. Mr. Neustadt was a member of the White House staff during the Truman administration and is now Director of the John F. Kennedy Institute of Politics and Professor of Government at Harvard University.*

What the Constitution separates our political parties do not combine. The parties are themselves composed of separated organizations sharing public authority. The authority consists of nominating powers. Our national parties are confederations of state and local party institutions, with a headquarters that represents the White House, more or less, if the party has a President in office. These confederacies manage presidential nominations. All other public offices depend upon electorates confined within the states.[4] All other nominations are controlled within the states. The President and Congressmen who bear one party's label are divided by dependence upon different sets of voters. The differences are sharpest at the stage of nomination. The White House has too small a share in nominating Congressmen, and Congress has too little weight in nominating Presidents for party to erase their constitutional separation. Party links are stronger than is frequently supposed, but nominating processes assure the separation.[5]

The separateness of institutions and the sharing of authority prescribe the terms on which a President persuades. When one man shares authority with another, but does not gain or lose his job upon the other's whim, his willingness to act upon the urging of the other turns on whether he conceives the action right for him. The essence of a President's persuasive task is to convince such men that what the White House wants of them is what they ought to do for their sake and on their authority.

Persuasive power, thus defined, amounts to more than charm or reasoned argument. These have their uses for a President, but these are not the whole of his resources. For the men he would induce to do what he wants done on their own responsibility will need or fear some acts by him on his responsibility. If they share his authority, he has some share in theirs. Presidential "powers" may be inconclusive when a President commands, but always remain relevant as he persuades. The status and authority inherent in his office reinforce his logic and his charm.

Status adds something to persuasiveness; authority adds still more. When Truman urged wage changes on his Secretary of Commerce while the latter was administering the steel mills, he and Secretary Sawyer were not just two men reasoning with one another. Had they been so, Sawyer probably would never have agreed to act. Truman's status gave him special claims to Sawyer's loyalty, or at least attention. In Walter Bagehot's charming phrase "no man can *argue* on his knees." Although there is no kneeling in this country, few men—and exceedingly few Cabinet officers—are immune to the impulse to say "yes" to the President of the

---

[4]With the exception of the Vice-Presidency, of course.

[5]See David B. Truman's illuminating study of party relationships in the 81st Congress, *The Congressional Party* (New York: John Wiley & Sons, Inc., 1959), especially Chs. 4, 6, and 8.

United States. It grows harder to say "no" when they are seated in his oval office at the White House, or in his study on the second floor, where almost tangibly he partakes of the aura of his physical surroundings. In Sawyer's case, moreover, the President possessed formal authority to intervene in many matters of concern to the Secretary of Commerce. These matters ranged from jurisdictional disputes among the defense agencies to legislation pending before Congress and, ultimately, to the tenure of the Secretary, himself. There is nothing in the record to suggest that Truman voiced specific threats when they negotiated over wage increases. But given his *formal* powers and their relevance to Sawyer's other interests it is safe to assume that Truman's very advocacy of wage action conveyed an implicit threat.

A President's authority and status give him great advantage in dealing with the men he would persuade. Each "power" is a vantage point for him in the degree that other men have use for his authority. From the veto to appointments, from publicity to budgeting, and so down a long list, the White House now controls the most encompassing array of vantage points in the American political system. With hardly an exception, the men who share in governing this country are aware that at some time, in some degree, the doing of *their* jobs, the furthering of *their* ambitions may depend upon the President of the United States. Their need for presidential action, or their fear of it, is bound to be recurrent if not actually continuous. Their need or fear is his advantage.

A President's advantages are greater than mere listing of his "powers" might suggest. The men with whom he deals must deal with him until the last day of his term. Because they have continuing relationships with him, his future, while it lasts, supports his present influence. Even though there is no need or fear of him today, what he could do tomorrow may supply today's advantage. Continuing relationships may convert any "power," any aspect of his status, into vantage points in almost any case. When he induces other men to do what he wants done, a President can trade on their dependence now *and* later.

The President's advantages are checked by the advantages of others. Continuing relationships will pull in both directions. These are relationships of mutual dependence. A President depends upon the men he would persuade; he has to reckon with his need or fear of them. They too will possess status, or authority, or both, else they would be of little use to him. Their vantage points confront his own; their power tempers his.

Persuasion is a two-way street. Sawyer, it will be recalled, did not respond at once to Truman's plan for wage increases at the steel mills. On the contrary, the Secretary hesitated and delayed and only acquiesced when he was satisfied that publicly he would not bear the onus of decision. Sawyer had some points of vantage all his own from which to resist presidential pressure. If he had to reckon with coercive implications in the President's "situations of strength," so had Truman to be mindful of the implications underlying Sawyer's place as a department head, as steel administrator, and as a Cabinet spokesman for business. Loyalty is reciprocal. Having taken on a dirty job in the steel crisis Sawyer had strong claims to loyal support. Besides, he had authority to do some things that the White House could ill afford. . . . He might have resigned in a huff (the removal power also works two ways). Or . . . he might have declined to sign necessary orders. Or, he might have let it be known publicly that he deplored what he was told to do and protested its doing. By following any of these courses Sawyer almost surely would have strengthened the position of management, weakened the position of the White House, and embittered the union. But the whole purpose of a wage increase was to enhance White House persuasiveness in urging settlement upon union and companies alike. Although Sawyer's status and authority did not give him the power to prevent an increase outright, they gave him capability to undermine its purpose. If his authority over wage rates had been vested by a statute, not by revocable presidential order, his power of prevention might have been complete. So Harold Ickes demonstrated in the famous case of helium sales to Germany before the Second World War.[6]

The power to persuade is the power to bargain. Status and authority yield bargaining advantages. But in a government of "separated institutions sharing powers," they yield them to all sides. With the array of vantage points at his disposal, a President may be far more persuasive than his logic or his charm could make him. But outcomes are not guaranteed by his advantages. There remain the counter pressures those whom he would influence can bring to bear on him from vantage points at their disposal. Command has limited utility; persuasion becomes give-and-take. It is well that the White House holds the vantage points it does. In such a business any President may need them all—and more.

[6]As Secretary of the Interior in 1939, Harold Ickes refused to approve the sale of helium to Germany despite the insistence of the State Department and the urging of President Roosevelt. Without the Secretary's approval, such sales were forbidden by statute. See *The Secret Diaries of Harold L. Ickes* (New York: Simon and Schuster, Inc., 1954), Vol. 2, especially pp. 391–93, 396–99. See also Michael D. Reagan, "The Helium Controversy," in Harold Stein (ed.), *American Civil-Military Decisions* (University, Ala.: University of Alabama Press, 1963), pp. 43–59.

In this instance the statutory authority ran to the Secretary as a matter of *his* discretion. A President is unlikely to fire Cabinet officers for the conscientious exercise of such authority. If the President did so, their successors might well be embarrassed both publicly and at the Capitol were they to reverse decisions previously taken. As for a President's authority to set aside discretionary determinations of this sort, it rests, if it exists at all, on shaky legal ground not likely to be trod save in the gravest of situations.

II

This view of power as akin to bargaining is one we commonly accept in the sphere of congressional relations. Every textbook states and every legislative session demonstrates that save in times like the extraordinary Hundred Days of 1933—times virtually ruled out by definition at mid-century—a President will often be unable to obtain congressional action on his terms or even to halt action he opposes. The reverse is equally accepted: Congress often is frustrated by the President. Their formal powers are so intertwined that neither will accomplish very much, for very long, without the acquiescence of the other. By the same token, though, what one demands the other can resist. The stage is set for that great game, much like collective bargaining, in which each seeks to profit from the other's needs and fears. It is a game played catch-as-catch-can, case by case. And everybody knows the game, observers and participants alike.

The concept of real power as a give-and-take is equally familiar when applied to presidential influence outside the formal structure of the federal government. . . . When he deals with such people a President draws bargaining advantage from his status or authority. By virtue of their public places or their private rights they have some capability to reply in kind.

In spheres of party politics the same thing follows, necessarily, from the confederal nature of our party organizations. Even in the case of national nominations a President's advantages are checked by those of others. In 1944 it is by no means clear that Roosevelt got his first choice as his running mate. In 1948 Truman, then the President, faced serious revolts against his nomination. In 1952 his intervention from the White House helped assure the choice of Adlai Stevenson, but it is far from clear that Truman could have done as much for any other candidate acceptable to him.[7] In 1956 when Eisenhower was President, the record

[7]Truman's *Memoirs* indicate that having tried and failed to make Stevenson an avowed candidate in the spring of 1952, the President decided to support the candidacy of Vice President Barkley. But Barkley withdrew early in the convention for lack of key Northern support. Though Truman is silent on the matter, Barkley's active candidacy nearly was revived during the balloting, but the forces then aligning to revive it were led by opponents of Truman's Fair Deal, principally Southerners. As a practical matter, the President could not have lent his weight to *their* endeavors and could back no one but Stevenson to counter them. The latter's strength could not be shifted, then, to Harriman or Kefauver. Instead the other Northerners had to be withdrawn. Truman helped withdraw them. But he had no other option. See *Memoirs* by Harry S. Truman, *Years of Trial and Hope*, Vol. 2 (Garden City, N.Y.: Doubleday, 1956, copr. 1956 Time Inc.), pp. 495–96.

leaves obscure just who backed Harold Stassen's effort to block Richard Nixon's renomination as Vice President. But evidently everything did not go quite as Eisenhower wanted, whatever his intentions may have been.[8] The outcomes in these instances bear all the marks of limits on command and of power checked by power that characterize congressional relations. Both in and out of politics these checks and limits seem to be quite widely understood.

Influence becomes still more a matter of give-and-take when Presidents attempt to deal with allied governments. A classic illustration is the long unhappy wrangle over Suez policy in 1956. In dealing with the British and the French before their military intervention, Eisenhower had his share of bargaining advantages but no effective power of command. His allies had their share of counter pressures, and they finally tried the most extreme of all: action despite him. His pressure then was instrumental in reversing them. But had the British government been on safe ground *at home*, Eisenhower's wishes might have made as little difference after intervention as before. Behind the decorum of diplomacy—which was not very decorous in the Suez affair—relationships among allies are not unlike relationships among state delegations at a national convention. Power is persuasion and persuasion becomes bargaining. The concept is familiar to everyone who watches foreign policy.

In only one sphere is the concept unfamiliar: the sphere of executive relations. Perhaps because of civics textbooks and teaching in our schools, Americans instinctively resist the view that power in this sphere resembles power in all others. Even Washington reporters, White House aides, and Congressmen are not immune to the illusion that administrative agencies comprise a single structure, "the" Executive Branch, where presidential word is law, or ought to be. Yet . . . when a President seeks something from executive officials his persuasiveness is subject to the same sorts of limitations as in the case of Congressmen,

[8]The reference is to Stassen's public statement of July 23, 1956, calling for Nixon's replacement on the Republican ticket by Governor Herter of Massachusetts, the later Secretary of State. Stassen's statement was issued after a conference with the President. Eisenhower's public statements on the vice-presidential nomination, both before and after Stassen's call, permit of alternative inferences: either that the President would have preferred another candidate, provided this could be arranged without a showing of White House dictation, or that he wanted Nixon on condition that the latter could show popular appeal. In the event, neither result was achieved. Eisenhower's own remarks lent strength to rapid party moves which smothered Stassen's effort. Nixon's nomination thus was guaranteed too quickly to appear the consequence of popular demand. For the public record on this matter see reported statements by Eisenhower, Nixon, Stassen, Herter, and Leonard Hall (the Republican National Chairman) in the *New York Times* for March 1, 8, 15, 16; April 27; July 15, 16, 25–31; August 3, 4, 17, 23, 1956. See also the account from private sources by Earl Mazo in *Richard Nixon: A Personal and Political Portrait* (New York: Harper & Row, Publishers, 1959), pp. 158–87.

or governors, or national committeemen, or private citizens, or foreign governments. There are no generic differences, no differences in kind and only sometimes in degree. The incidents preceding the dismissal of Mac- Arthur and the incidents surrounding seizure of the steel mills make it plain that here as elsewhere influence derives from bargaining advantages; power is a give-and-take.

Like our governmental structure as a whole, the executive establishment consists of separated institutions sharing power. The President heads one of these; Cabinet officers, agency administrators, and military commanders head others. Below the departmental level, virtually independent bureau chiefs head many more. Under mid-century conditions, federal operations spill across dividing lines on organization charts; almost every policy entangles many agencies; almost every program calls for interagency collaboration. Everything somehow involves the President. But operating agencies owe their existence least of all to one another—and only in some part to him. Each has a separate statutory base; each has its statutes to administer; each deals with a different set of subcommittees at the Capitol. Each has its own peculiar set of clients, friends, and enemies outside the formal government. Each has a different set of specialized careerists inside its own bailiwick. Our Constitution gives the President the "take-care" clause and the appointive power. Our statutes give him central budgeting and a degree of personnel control. All agency administrators are responsible to him. But they *also* are responsible to Congress, to their clients, to their staffs and to themselves. In short, they have five masters. Only after all of those do they owe any loyalty to each other.

"The members of the Cabinet," Charles G. Dawes used to remark, "are a President's natural enemies." Dawes had been Harding's Budget Director, Coolidge's Vice President, and Hoover's Ambassador to London; he also had been General Pershing's chief assistant for supply in the First World War. The words are highly colored, but Dawes knew whereof he spoke. The men who have to serve so many masters cannot help but be somewhat the "enemy" of any one of them. By the same token, any master wanting service is in some degree the "enemy" of such a servant. A President is likely to want loyal support but not to relish trouble on his doorstep. Yet the more his Cabinet members cleave to him, the more they may need help from him in fending off the wrath of rival masters. Help, though, is synonymous with trouble. Many a Cabinet officer, with loyalty ill-rewarded by his lights and help withheld, has come to view the White House as innately hostile to department heads. Dawes's dictum can be turned around.

A senior presidential aide remarked to me in Eisenhower's time: "If some of these Cabinet members would just take time out to stop and ask themselves 'What would I want if I were President?', they wouldn't give him all the trouble he's been having." But even if they asked themselves the question, such officials often could not act upon the answer. Their personalf attachment to the President is all too often overwhelmed by duty to their other masters.

Executive officials are not equally advantaged in their dealings with a President. Nor are the same officials equally advantaged all the time. . . . The vantage points conferred upon officials by their own authority and status vary enormously. The variance is heightened by particulars of time and circumstance. In mid-October 1950, Truman, at a press conference, remarked of the man he had considered firing in August and would fire the next April for intolerable insubordination:

> Let me tell you something that will be good for your souls. It's a pity that you . . . can't understand the ideas of two intellectually honest men when they meet. General MacArthur . . . is a member of the Government of the United States. He is loyal to that Government. He is loyal to the President. He is loyal to the President in his foreign policy. . . . There is no disagreement between General MacArthur and myself. . . .[9]

MacArthur's status in and out of government was never higher than when Truman spoke those words. The words, once spoken, added to the General's credibility thereafter when he sought to use the press in his campaign against the President. And what had happened between August and October? Near-victory had happened, together with that premature conference on *post*war plans, the meeting at Wake Island.

If the bargaining advantages of a MacArthur fluctuate with changing circumstances, this is bound to be so with subordinates who have at their disposal fewer "powers," lesser status, to fall back on. And when officials have no "powers" in their own right, or depend upon the President for status, their counter pressure may be limited indeed. White House aides, who fit both categories, are among the most responsive men of all, and for good reason. As a Director of the Budget once remarked to me, "Thank God I'm here and not across the street. If the President doesn't call me, I've got plenty I can do right here and plenty coming up to me, by rights, to justify my calling him. But those poor fellows over there, if the boss doesn't call them, doesn't ask them to do something, what *can* they do but sit?" Authority and status so conditional are frail reliances in resisting a President's own wants. Within the White House precincts, lifted eyebrows may suffice to set an aide in motion; command, coercion, even charm aside. But even in the White House a President does not monopolize effective power. Even there persuasion is akin to bargaining. A former Roosevelt aide once wrote of Cabinet officers:

[9]Stenographic transcript of presidential press conference, October 19, 1950, on file in the Truman Library at Independence, Missouri.

Half of a President's suggestions, which theoretically carry the weight of orders, can be safely forgotten by a Cabinet member. And if the President asks about a suggestion a second time, he can be told that it is being investigated. If he asks a third time, a wise Cabinet officer will give him at least part of what he suggests. But only occasionally, except about the most important matters, do Presidents ever get around to asking three times.[10]

The rule applies to staff as well as to the Cabinet, and certainly has been applied *by* staff in Truman's time and Eisenhower's.

Some aides will have more vantage points than a selective memory. Sherman Adams, for example, as The Assistant to the President under Eisenhower, scarcely deserved the appelation "White House aide" in the meaning of the term before his time, or as applied to other members of the Eisenhower entourage. Although Adams was by no means "chief of staff" in any sense so sweeping—or so simple—as press commentaries often took for granted, he apparently became no more dependent on the President than Eisenhower on him. "I need him," said the President when Adams turned out to have been remarkably imprudent in the Goldfine case, and delegated to him even the decision on his own departure.[11] This instance is extreme, but the tendency it illustrates is common enough. Any aide who demonstrates to others that he has the President's consistent confidence and a consistent part in presidential business will acquire so much business on his own account that he becomes in some sense independent of his chief. Nothing in the Constitution keeps a well-placed aide from converting status into power of his own, usable in some degree even against the President—an outcome not unknown in Truman's regime or, by all accounts, in Eisenhower's.

The more an officeholder's status and his "powers" stem from sources independent of the President, the stronger will be his potential pressure *on* the President. Department heads in general have more bargaining power than do most members of the White House staff; but bureau chiefs may have still more, and specialists at upper levels of established career services may have almost unlimited reserves of the enormous power which consists of sitting still. As Franklin Roosevelt once remarked:

[10]Jonathan Daniels, *Frontier on the Potomac* (New York: The Macmillan Company, 1946), pp. 31–32.

[11]Transcript of presidential press conference, June 18, 1958, in *Public Papers of the Presidents: Dwight D. Eisenhower, 1958* (Washington, D.C.: The National Archives, 1959), p. 479. In the summer of 1958, a congressional investigation into the affairs of a New England textile manufacturer, Bernard Goldfine, revealed that Sherman Adams had accepted various gifts and favors from him (the most notoriety attached to a vicuña coat). Adams also had made inquiries about the status of a Federal Communications Commission proceeding in which Goldfine was involved. In September 1958, Adams was allowed to resign. The episode was highly publicized and much discussed in that year's congressional campaigns.

> The Treasury is so large and far-flung and ingrained in its practices that I find it is almost impossible to get the action and results I want—even with Henry [Morgenthau] there. But the Treasury is not to be compared with the State Department. You should go through the experience of trying to get any changes in the thinking, policy, and action of the career diplomats and then you'd know what a real problem was. But the Treasury and the State Department put together are nothing compared with the Na-a-vy. The admirals are really something to cope with—and I should know. To change anything in the Na-a-vy is like punching a feather bed. You punch it with your right and you punch it with your left until you are finally exhausted, and then you find the damn bed just as it was before you started punching.[12]

In the right circumstances, of course, a President can have his way with any of these people. . . . Between a President and his "subordinates," no less than others on whom he depends, real power is reciprocal and varies markedly with organization, subject matter, personality, and situation. The mere fact that persuasion is directed at executive officials signifies no necessary easing of his way. Any new Congressmen of the Administration's party, especially if narrowly elected, may turn out more amenable (though less useful) to the President than any seasoned bureau chief "downtown." *The probabilities of power do not derive from the literary theory of the Constitution.*

III

There is a widely held belief in the United States that, were it not for folly or for knavery, a reasonable President would need no power other than the logic of his argument. No less a personage than Eisenhower has subscribed to that belief in many a campaign speech and press-conference remark. But faulty reasoning and bad intentions do not cause all quarrels with Presidents. The best of reasoning and of intent cannot compose them all. For in the first place, what the President wants will rarely seem a trifle to the men he wants it from. And in the second place, they will be bound to judge it by the standard of their own responsibilities, not his. However logical his argument according to his lights, their judgment may not bring them to his view.

The men who share in governing this country frequently appear to act as though they were in business for themselves. So, in a real though not entire sense, they are and have to be. When Truman and MacArthur fell to quarreling, for example, the stakes were no less than the substance of American foreign policy, the risks of greater war or military stale-

---

[12]As reported in Marriner S. Eccles, *Beckoning Frontiers* (New York: Alfred A. Knopf, Inc., 1951), p. 336.

mate, the prerogatives of Presidents and field commanders, the pride of a proconsul and his place in history. Intertwined, inevitably, were other stakes, as well: political stakes for men and factions of both parties; power stakes for interest groups with which they were or wished to be affiliated. And every stake was raised by the apparent discontent in the American public mood. There is no reason to suppose that in such circumstances men of large but differing responsibilities will see all things through the same glasses. On the contrary, it is to be expected that their views of what ought to be done and what they then should do will vary with the differing perspectives their particular responsibilities evoke. Since their duties are not vested in a "team" or a "collegium" but in themselves, as individuals, one must expect that they will see things *for* themselves. Moreover, when they are responsible to many masters and when an event or policy turns loyalty against loyalty—a day-by-day occurrence in the nature of the case—one must assume that those who have the duties to perform will choose the terms of reconciliation. This is the essence of their personal responsibility. When their own duties pull in opposite directions, who else but they can choose what they will do?

When Truman dismissed MacArthur, the latter lost three posts: the American command in the Far East, the Allied command for the occupation of Japan, and the United Nations command in Korea. He also lost his status as the senior officer on active duty in the United States armed forces. So long as he held those positions and that status, though, he had a duty to his troops, to his profession, to himself (the last is hard for any man to disentangle from the rest). As a public figure and a focus for men's hopes, he had a duty to constituents at home, and in Korea and Japan. He owed a duty also to those other constituents, the UN governments contributing to his field forces. As a patriot he had a duty to his country. As an accountable official and an expert guide he stood at the call of Congress. As a military officer he had, besides, a duty to the President, his constitutional commander. Some of these duties may have manifested themselves in terms more tangible or more direct than others. But it would be nonsense to argue that the last *negated* all the rest, however much it might be claimed to override them. And it makes no more sense to think that anybody but MacArthur was effectively empowered to decide how he, himself, would reconcile the competing demands his duties made upon him.

Similar observations could be made about the rest of the executive officials encountered in Chapter 2. Price Director Arnall, it will be recalled, refused in advance to sign a major price increase for steel if Mobilization Director Wilson or the White House should concede one before management had settled with the union. When Arnall did this, he took his stand, in substance, on his oath of office. He would do what he had sworn to do in *his* best judgment, so long as he was there to do it.

This posture may have been assumed for purposes of bargaining and might have been abandoned had his challenge been accepted by the President. But no one could be sure and no one, certainly, could question Arnall's right to make the judgment for himself. As head of an agency and as a politician, with a program to defend and a future to advance, *he* had to decide what he had to do on matters that, from his perspective, were exceedingly important. Neither in policy nor in personal terms, nor in terms of agency survival, were the issues of a sort to be considered secondary by an Arnall, however much they might have seemed so to a Wilson (or a Truman). Nor were the merits likely to appear the same to a price stabilizer and to men with broader duties. Reasonable men, it is so often said, *ought* to be able to agree on the requirements of given situations. But when the outlook varies with the placement of each man, and the response required in his place is for each to decide, their reasoning may lead to disagreement quite as well—and quite as reasonably. Vanity, or vice, may weaken reason, to be sure, but it is idle to assign these as the cause of Arnall's threat or MacArthur's defiance. Secretary Sawyer's hesitations, cited earlier, are in the same category. One need not denigrate such men to explain their conduct. For the responsibilities they felt, the "facts" they saw, simply were not the same as those of their superiors; yet they, not the superiors, had to decide what they would do.

Outside the Executive Branch the situation is the same, except that loyalty to the President may often matter *less*. There is no need to spell out the comparison with Governors of Arkansas, steel company executives, trade union leaders, and the like. And when one comes to Congressmen who can do nothing for themselves (or their constituents) save as they are elected, term by term, in districts and through party structures *differing* from those on which a President depends, the case is very clear. An able Eisenhower aide with long congressional experience remarked to me in 1958: "The people on the Hill don't do what they might *like* to do, they do what they think they *have* to do in their own interest as *they* see it. . . ." This states the case precisely.

The essence of a President's persuasive task with Congressmen and everybody else, *is to induce them to believe that what he wants of them is what their own appraisal of their own responsibilities requires them to do in their interest, not his.* Because men may differ in their views on public policy, because differences in outlook stem from differences in duty—duty to one's office, one's constituents, oneself—that task is bound to be more like collective bargaining than like a reasoned argument among philosopher-kings. Overtly or implicitly, hard bargaining has characterized all illustrations offered up to now. This is the reason why: persuasion deals in the coin of self-interest with men who have some freedom to reject what they find counterfeit.

IV

A President draws influence from bargaining advantages. But does he always need them? The MacArthur, steel strike, and Little Rock episodes were instances where views on public policy diverged with special sharpness. Suppose such sharp divergences are lacking, suppose most players of the governmental game see policy objectives much alike, then can he not rely on logic (or on charm) to get him what he wants? The answer is that even then most outcomes turn on bargaining. The reason for this answer is a simple one: most men who share in governing have interests of their own beyond the realm of policy *objectives*. The sponsorship of policy, the form it takes, the conduct of it, and the credit for it separate their interest from the President's despite agreement on the end in view. In political government, the means can matter quite as much as ends; they often matter more. And there are always differences of interest in the means.

Let me introduce a case externally the opposite of my previous examples: the European Recovery Program of 1948, the so-called Marshall Plan. This is perhaps the greatest exercise in policy *agreement* since the Cold War began. When the then Secretary of State, George Catlett Marshall, spoke at the Harvard commencement in June of 1947, he launched one of the most creative, most imaginative ventures in the history of American foreign relations. What makes this policy most notable for present purposes, however, is that it became effective upon action by the 80th Congress, at the behest of Harry Truman, in the election year of 1948.[13]

Eight months before Marshall spoke at Harvard, the Democrats had lost control of both Houses of Congress for the first time in fourteen years. Truman, whom the Secretary represented, had just finished his second troubled year as President-by-succession. Truman was regarded with so little warmth in his own party that in 1946 he had been urged *not* to participate in the congressional campaign. At the opening of Congress in January 1947, Senator Robert A. Taft, "Mr. Republican," had somewhat the attitude of a President-elect. This was a vision widely shared in Washington, with Truman relegated, thereby, to the role of

[13]In drawing together these observations on the Marshall Plan, I have relied on the record of personal participation by Joseph M. Jones, *The Fifteen Weeks* (New York: The Viking Press, Inc., 1955), especially pp. 89–256; on the recent study by Harry Bayard Price, *The Marshall Plan and Its Meaning* (Ithaca: Cornell University Press, 1955), especially pp. 1–86; on the Truman *Memoirs*, Vol. 2, Chs. 7–9; on Arthur H. Vandenberg, Jr. (ed.), *The Private Papers of Senator Vandenberg* (Boston: Houghton Mifflin Company, 1952), especially pp. 383 ff.; and on notes of my own made at the time. This is an instance of policy development not covered, to my knowledge, by any of the university programs engaged in the production of case studies.

caretaker-on-term. Moreover, within just two weeks of Marshall's commencement address, Truman was to veto two prized accomplishments of Taft's congressional majority: the Taft-Hartley Act and tax reduction.[14] Yet scarcely ten months later the Marshall Plan was under way on terms to satisfy its sponsors, its authorization completed, its first-year funds in sight, its administering agency in being: all managed by as thorough a display of executive-congressional cooperation as any we have seen since the Second World War. For any President at any time this would have been a great accomplishment. In years before mid-century it would have been enough to make the future reputation of his term. And for a Truman, at this time, enactment of the Marshall Plan appears almost miraculous.

How was the miracle accomplished? How did a President so situated bring it off? In answer, the first thing to note is that he did not do it by himself. Truman had help of a sort no less extraordinary than the outcome. Although each stands for something more complex, the names of Marshall, Vandenberg, Patterson, Bevin, Stalin, tell the story of that help.

In 1947, two years after V-J Day, General Marshall was something more than Secretary of State. He was a man venerated by the President as "the greatest living American," literally an embodiment of Truman's ideals. He was honored at the Pentagon as an architect of victory. He was thoroughly respected by the Secretary of the Navy, James V. Forrestal, who that year became the first Secretary of Defense. On Capitol Hill Marshall had an enormous fund of respect stemming from his war record as Army Chief of Staff, and in the country generally no officer had come out of the war with a higher reputation for judgment, intellect, and probity. Besides, as Secretary of State, he had behind him the first generation of matured foreign service officers produced by the reforms of the 1920's, and mingled with them, in the departmental service, were some of the ablest of the men drawn by the war from private life to Washington. In terms both of staff talent and staff's use, Marshall's year began a State Department "golden age" which lasted until the era of McCarthy. Moreover, as his Under Secretary, Marshall had, successively, Dean Acheson and Robert Lovett, men who commanded the respect of the professionals and the regard of Congressmen. (Acheson had been brilliantly successful at congressional relations as Assistant Secretary in the war and postwar years.) Finally, as a special undersecretary Marshall had Will Clayton,

14Secretary Marshall's speech, formally suggesting what became known as the Marshall Plan, was made at Harvard on June 5, 1947. On June 20 the President vetoed the Taft-Hartley Act; his veto was overridden three days later. On June 16 he vetoed the first of two tax reduction bills (HR 1) passed at the first session of the 80th Congress; the second of these (HR 3950), a replacement for the other, he also disapproved on July 18. In both instances his veto was narrowly sustained.

a man highly regarded, for good reason, at both ends of Pennsylvania Avenue.

Taken together, these are exceptional resources for a Secretary of State. In the circumstances, they were quite as necessary as they obviously are relevant. The Marshall Plan was launched by a "lame duck" Administration "scheduled" to leave office in eighteen months. [Most people thought that the Democrats would be defeated in the 1948 election, particularly if President Truman ran for reelection.] Marshall's program faced a congressional leadership traditionally isolationist and currently intent upon economy. European aid was viewed with envy by a Pentagon distressed and virtually disarmed through budget cuts, and by domestic agencies intent on enlarged welfare programs. It was not viewed with liking by a Treasury intent on budget surpluses. The plan had need of every asset that could be extracted from the personal position of its nominal author and from the skills of his assistants.

Without the equally remarkable position of the senior Senator from Michigan, Arthur H. Vandenberg, it is hard to see how Marshall's assets could have been enough. Vandenberg was Chairman of the Senate Foreign Relations Committee. Actually, he was much more than that. Twenty years a Senator, he was the senior member of his party in the Chamber. Assiduously cultivated by F.D.R. and Truman, he was a chief Republican proponent of "bipartisanship" in foreign policy, and consciously conceived himself its living symbol to his party, to the country, and abroad. Moreover, by informal but entirely operative agreement with his colleague Taft, Vandenberg held the acknowledged lead among Senate Republicans in the whole field of international affairs. This acknowledgment meant more in 1947 than it might have meant at any other time. With confidence in the advent of a Republican administration two years hence, most of the gentlemen were in a mood to be responsive and responsible. The war was over, Roosevelt dead, Truman a caretaker, theirs the trust. That the Senator from Michigan saw matters in this light, his diaries make clear.[15] And this was not the outlook from the Senate side alone; the attitudes of House Republicans associated with the Herter Committee and its tours abroad suggest the same mood of responsibility. Vandenberg was not the only source of help on Capitol Hill. But relatively speaking, his position there was as exceptional as Marshall's was downtown.

Help of another sort was furnished by a group of dedicated private citizens who organized one of the most effective instruments for public information seen since the Second World War: the Committee for the Marshall Plan, headed by the eminent Republicans whom F.D.R., in 1940, had brought to the Department of War—Henry L. Stimson as

[15]Vandenberg, *op. cit.*, pp. 378–79 and 446.

honorary chairman and Robert P. Patterson as active spokesman. The remarkable array of bankers, lawyers, trade unionists, and editors, who had
drawn together in defense of "internationalism" before Pearl Harbor and
had joined their talents in the war itself, combined again to spark the
work of this committee. Their efforts generated a great deal of vocal
public support to buttress Marshall's arguments, and Vandenberg's, in
Congress.

But before public support could be rallied, there had to be a purpose tangible enough, concrete enough, to provide a rallying ground.
At Harvard, Marshall had voiced an idea in general terms. That this
was turned into a hard program susceptible of presentation and support
is due, in major part, to Ernest Bevin, the British Foreign Secretary.
He well deserves the credit he has sometimes been assigned as, in effect,
co-author of the Marshall Plan. For Bevin seized on Marshall's Harvard
speech and organized a European response with promptness and concreteness beyond the State Department's expectations. What had been
virtually a trial balloon to test reactions on both sides of the Atlantic
was hailed in London as an invitation to the Europeans to send Washington a bill of particulars. This they promptly organized to do, and the
American Administration then organized in turn for its reception without further argument internally about the pros and cons of issuing the
"invitation" in the first place. But for Bevin there might have been trouble
from the Secretary of the Treasury and others besides.[16]

If Bevin's help was useful at that early stage, Stalin's was vital from
first to last. In a mood of self-deprecation Truman once remarked that
without Moscow's "crazy" moves "we never would have had our foreign
policy . . . we never could have got a thing from Congress."[17] George
Kennan, among others, has deplored the anti-Soviet overtone of the case
made for the Marshall Plan in Congress and the country, but there is
no doubt that this clinched the argument for many segments of Ameri-

[16]The initial reluctance of Secretary of the Treasury, John Snyder, to support
large-scale spending overseas became a matter of public knowledge on June 25, 1947.
At a press conference on that day he interpreted Marshall's Harvard speech as a call
on Europeans to help themselves, by themselves. At another press conference the same
day, Marshall for his own part had indicated that the U.S. would consider helping
programs on which Europeans agreed. The next day Truman held a press conference
and was asked the inevitable question. He replied, "General Marshall and I are in
complete agreement." When pressed further, Truman remarked sharply, "The Secretary
of the Treasury and the Secretary of State and the President are in complete agreement." Thus the President cut Snyder off, but had programming gathered less
momentum overseas, no doubt he would have been heard from again as time passed
and opportunity offered.

The foregoing quotations are from the stenographic transcript of the presidential
press conference June 26, 1947, on file in the Truman Library at Independence,
Missouri.

[17]A remark made in December, 1955, three years after he left office, but not
unrepresentative of views he expressed, on occasion, while he was President.

can opinion. There also is no doubt that Moscow made the crucial contributions to the case.

By 1947 events, far more than governmental prescience or open action, had given a variety of publics an impression of inimical Soviet intentions (and of Europe's weakness), and a growing urge to "do something about it." Three months before Marshall spoke at Harvard, Greek-Turkish aid and promulgation of the Truman Doctrine had seemed rather to crystallize than to create a public mood and a congressional response. The Marshall planners, be it said, were poorly placed to capitalize on that mood, nor had the Secretary wished to do so. Their object, indeed, was to cut across it, striking at the cause of European weakness rather than at Soviet aggressiveness, per se. A strong economy in Western Europe called, ideally, for restorative measures of continental scope. American assistance proffered in an anti-Soviet context would have been contradictory in theory and unacceptable in fact to several of the governments that Washington was anxious to assist. As Marshall, himself, saw it, the logic of his purpose forbade him to play his strongest congressional card. The Russians then proceeded to play it for him. When the Europeans met in Paris, Molotov walked out. After the Czechs had shown continued interest in American aid, a communist coup overthrew their government while Soviet forces stood along their borders within easy reach of Prague. Molotov transformed the Marshall Plan's initial presentation; Czechoslovakia assured its final passage, which followed by a month the take-over in Prague.

Such was the help accorded Truman in obtaining action on the Marshall Plan. Considering his politically straitened circumstances he scarcely could have done with less. Conceivably, some part of Moscow's contribution might have been dispensable, but not Marshall's, or Vandenberg's, or Bevin's, or Patterson's, or that of the great many other men whose work is represented by their names in my account. Their aid was not extended to the President for his own sake. He was not favored in this fashion just because they liked him personally, or were spellbound by his intellect or charm. They might have been as helpful had all held him in disdain, which some of them certainly did. The Londoners who seized the ball, Vandenberg and Taft and the congressional majority, Marshall and his planners, the officials of other agencies who actively supported them or "went along," the host of influential private citizens who rallied to the cause—all these played the parts they did because they thought they had to, in their interest, given their responsibilities, not Truman's. Yet they hardly would have found it in their interest to collaborate with one another, or with him, had he not furnished them precisely what *they* needed from the White House. Truman could not do without their help, but he could not have had it without unremitting effort on his part.

The crucial thing to note about this case is that despite compatibility of views on public policy, Truman got no help he did not pay for (except Stalin's). Bevin scarcely could have seized on Marshall's words had Marshall not been plainly backed by Truman. Marshall's interest would not have comported with the exploitation of his prestige by a President who undercut him openly, or subtly, or even inadvertently, at any point. Vandenberg, presumably, could not have backed proposals by a White House which begrudged him deference and access gratifying to his fellow-partisans (and satisfying to himself). Prominent Republicans in private life would not have found it easy to promote a cause identified with Truman's claims in 1948—and neither would the prominent New Dealers then engaged in searching for a substitute [for Truman].

Truman paid the price required for their services. So far as the record shows, the White House did not falter once in firm support for Marshall and the Marshall Plan. Truman backed his Secretary's gamble on an invitation to all Europe. He made the plan his own in a well-timed address to the Canadians. He lost no opportunity to widen the involvements of his own official family in the cause. Averell Harriman, the Secretary of Commerce; Julius Krug, the Secretary of the Interior; Edwin Nourse, the Economic Council Chairman; James Webb, the Director of the Budget—all were made responsible for studies and reports contributing directly to the legislative presentation. Thus these men were committed in advance. Besides, the President continually emphasized to everyone in reach that he did not have doubts, did not desire complications and would foreclose all he could. Reportedly, his emphasis was felt at the Treasury, with good effect. And Truman was at special pains to smooth the way for Vandenberg. The Senator insisted on "no politics" from the Administration side; there was none. He thought a survey of American resources and capacity essential; he got it in the Krug and Harriman reports. Vandenberg expected advance consultation; he received it, step by step, in frequent meetings with the President and weekly conferences with Marshall. He asked for an effective liaison between Congress and agencies concerned; Lovett and others gave him what he wanted. When the Senator decided on the need to change financing and administrative features of the legislation, Truman disregarded Budget Bureau grumbling and acquiesced with grace. When, finally, Vandenberg desired a Republican to head the new administering agency, his candidate, Paul Hoffman, was appointed despite the President's own preference for another. In all of these ways Truman employed the sparse advantages his "powers" and his status then accorded him to gain the sort of help he had to have.

Truman helped himself in still another way. Traditionally and practically, no one was placed as well as he to call public attention to the task of *Congress* (and its Republican leadership). Throughout the fall and winter of 1947 and on into the spring of 1948, he made repeated use of presidential "powers" to remind the country that congressional action was required. Messages, speeches, and an extra session were employed to make the point. Here, too, he drew advantage from his place. However, in his circumstances, Truman's public advocacy might have hurt, not helped, had his words seemed directed toward the forthcoming election. Truman gained advantage for his program only as his own endorsement of it stayed on the right side of that fine line between the "caretaker" in office and the would-be candidate. In public statements dealing with the Marshall Plan he seems to have risked blurring this distinction only once, when he called Congress into session in November 1947 asking both for interim aid to Europe *and* for peacetime price controls. The second request linked the then inflation with the current Congress (and with Taft), becoming a first step toward one of Truman's major themes in 1948. By calling for both measures at the extra session he could have been accused—and was—of mixing home-front politics with foreign aid. In any event no harm was done the European program (or his politics). But in advance a number of his own advisers feared that such a double call would jeopardize the Marshall Plan. Their fears are testimony to the narrowness of his advantage in employing his own "powers" for its benefit.[18]

It is symptomatic of Truman's situation that "bipartisan" accommodation by the White House then was thought to mean congressional consultation and conciliation on a scale unmatched in Eisenhower's time. Yet Eisenhower did about as well with opposition Congresses as Truman did, in terms of requests granted for defense and foreign aid. It may be said that Truman asked for more extraordinary measures. But it also may be said that Eisenhower never lacked for the prestige his predecessor had to borrow. It often was remarked, in Truman's time, that he seemed a "split-personality," so sharply did his conduct differentiate domestic politics from national security. But personality aside, how else could *he*, in his first term, gain ground for an evolving foreign policy? The plain fact is that Truman had to play bipartisanship as he did or lose the game.

V

Had Truman lacked the personal advantages his "powers" and his status gave him, or if he had been maladroit in using them, there probably would not have been a massive European aid program in 1948. Some-

---

[18]This might also be taken as testimony to the political timidity of officials in the State Department and the Budget Bureau where that fear seems to have been strongest. However, conversations at the time with White House aides incline me to believe that there, too, interjection of the price issue was thought a gamble and a risk. For further comment see my "Congress and the Fair Deal: A Legislative Balance Sheet," *Public Policy* (Cambridge, Mass.: Harvard University Press, 1954), Vol. 5, 362–64.

thing of the sort, perhaps quite different in its emphasis, would almost certainly have come to pass before the end of 1949. *Some* American response to European weakness and to Soviet expansion was as certain as such things can be. But in 1948 temptations to await a Taft Plan or a Dewey Plan might well have caused at least a year's postponement of response had the "outgoing" Administration bungled its congressional, or public, or allied, or executive relations. Quite aside from the specific virtues of their plan, Truman and his helpers gained that year, at least, in timing the American response. As European time was measured then, this was a precious gain. The President's own share in this accomplishment was vital. He made his contribution by exploiting his advantages. Truman, in effect, lent Marshall and the rest the perquisites and status of his office. In return they lent him their prestige and their own influence. The transfer multiplied *his* influence despite his limited authority in form and lack of strength politically. Without the wherewithal to make his bargain, Truman could not have contributed to European aid.

Bargaining advantages convey no guarantees. Influence remains a two-way street. In the fortunate instance of the Marshall Plan, what Truman needed was actually in the hands of men who were prepared to "trade" with him. He personally could deliver what they wanted in return. Marshall, Vandenberg, Harriman, *et al.* possessed the prestige, energy, associations, staffs, essential to the legislative effort. Truman himself had a sufficient hold on presidential messages and speeches, on budget policy, on high-level appointments, and on his own time and temper to carry through all aspects of his necessary part. But it takes two to make a bargain. It takes those who have prestige to lend it on whatever terms. Suppose that Marshall had declined the Secretaryship of State in January 1947; Truman might not have found a substitute so well-equipped to furnish what he needed in the months ahead. Or suppose that Vandenberg had fallen victim to a cancer two years before he actually did; Senator Wiley of Wisconsin would not have seemed to Taft a man with whom the world need be divided. Or suppose that the Secretary of the Treasury had been possessed of stature, force, and charm commensurate with that of his successor in Eisenhower's time, the redoubtable George M. Humphrey. And what if Truman then had seemed to the Republicans what he turned out to be in 1948, a formidable candidate for President? It is unlikely that a single one of these "supposes" would have changed the final outcome; two or three, however, might have altered it entirely. Truman was not guaranteed more power than his "powers" just because he had continuing relationships with Cabinet secretaries and with senior Senators. Here, as everywhere, the outcome was conditional on who they were and what he was and how each viewed events, and on their actual performance in response.

Granting that persuasion has no guarantee attached, how can a President reduce the risks of failing to persuade? How can he maximize his prospects for effectiveness by minimizing chances that his power will elude him? The Marshall Plan suggests an answer: he guards his power prospects in the course of making choices. Marshall himself, and Forrestal, and Harriman, and others of the sort held office on the President's appointment. Vanderberg had vast symbolic value partly because F.D.R. and Truman had done everything they could, since 1944, to build him up. The Treasury Department and the Budget Bureau—which together might have jeopardized the plans these others made—were headed by officials whose prestige depended wholly on their jobs. What Truman needed from those "givers" he received, in part, because of his past choice of men and measures. What they received in turn were actions taken or withheld by him, himself. The things they needed from him mostly involved his own conduct where his current choices ruled. The president's own actions in the past had cleared the way for current bargaining. His actions in the present were his trading stock. Behind each action lay a personal choice, and these together comprised *his* control over the give-and-take that gained him what he wanted. In the degree that Truman, personally, affected the advantages he drew from his relationships with other men in government, *his power was protected by his choices.*

By "choice" I mean no more than what is commonly referred to as "decision": a President's own act of doing or not doing. Decision is so often indecisive and indecision is so frequently conclusive, that choice becomes the preferable term. "Choice" has its share of undesired connotations. In common usage it implies a black-and-white alternative. Presidential choices are rarely of that character. It also may imply that the alternatives are set before the choice-maker by someone else. A President is often left to figure out his options for himself. Neither implication holds in any of the references to "choice" throughout this book.

If Presidents could count upon past choices to enhance their current influence, as Truman's choice of men had done for him, persuasion would pose fewer difficulties than it does. But Presidents can count on no such thing. Depending on the circumstances, prior choices can be as embarrassing as they were helpful in the instance of the Marshall Plan. . . .

Assuming that past choices have protected influence, not harmed it, present choices still may be inadequate. If Presidents could count on their own conduct to provide them *enough* bargaining advantages, as Truman's conduct did where Vandenberg and Marshall were concerned, effective bargaining might be much easier to manage than it often is. In the steel crisis, for instance, Truman's own persuasiveness with companies and union, both, was burdened by the conduct of an independent Wage Board and of government attorneys in the courts, to say nothing of Wilson, Arnall, Sawyer, and the like. Yet in practice, if not theory, many of *their* crucial choices never were the President's to make. Decisions that are legally in others' hands, or delegated past recall, have an unhappy way of proving just the trading stock most needed when the White House wants to trade. One reason why Truman was consistently more influential in the instance of the Marshall Plan than in the steel case, or the MacArthur case, is that the Marshall Plan directly involved Congress. In congressional relations there are some things that no one but the President can do. His chance to choose is higher when a message must be sent, or a nomination submitted, or a bill signed into law, than when the sphere of action is confined to the Executive, where all decisive tasks may have been delegated past recall.

But adequate or not, a President's own choices are the only means *in his own hands* of guarding his own prospects for effective influence. He can draw power from continuing relationships in the degree that he can capitalize upon the needs of others for the Presidency's status and authority. He helps himself to do so, though, by nothing save ability to recognize the pre-conditions and the chance advantages and to proceed accordingly in the course of the choice-making that comes his way.

CHAPTER SEVEN

THE PRESIDENTIAL COALITION: THE CASE OF JESSE JONES

RICHARD F. FENNO, JR.

Conflict between President-oriented actions and department-oriented actions inheres in the American political system. It is as evident in the administrative realm as in the legislative. The Cabinet member is subject to strong non-presidential or extra-presidential influences, creating a gap between fact and theory in the formal power-responsibility relationship. The case study of Jesse Jones illustrates the general problem as it has been stressed in this chapter.

Jesse Jones's behavior as a Cabinet officer must be set in the context of his previous experience in government. A Texas Democrat, he was appointed by President Hoover in 1932 as a Director of the Reconstruction Finance Corporation. One year later he became its Chairman, a position he held until 1939 when President Roosevelt designated him to be Federal Loan Administrator. In this post he was given general supervision over several loan agencies in addition to the RFC. In 1940, Jones was made Secretary of Commerce, and by a special, unanimous resolution of Congress he was allowed to remain as Federal Loan Administrator.[1] That agency was formally incorporated into the Department of Commerce in 1942. Three features of his RFC experience shed light on Jones's perception of his job and his pattern of behavior as Secretary of Commerce.

In the *first* place, the RFC was a creature of the Congress, a government corporation whose authority and functions were determined by

[1] House Joint Resolution 602, approved September 13, 1940.

Reprinted with permission of Harvard University Press from THE PRESIDENT'S CABINET, *Caravelle edition (New York: Vintage Books, 1959), pp. 234–48, 307–9. Copyright 1959 by the President and Fellows of Harvard College.*

the legislature. With the exception of the appointment of its Directors, it was relatively independent of the President. A statutory relationship thus bound Jones closely to the Congress during his entire thirteen years of government service. He assiduously cultivated and strengthened these ties at every opportunity in order "to make the RFC a dependable favorite of Congress."[2] At the forefront of his accomplishments Jones always spoke, not a bit modestly, of his smooth relationships with that body:

> Throughout the entire period, we received in a manner probably unique in the history of federal agencies, the complete cooperation and confidence of each successive Congress. Not a single request that I made of Congress during those thirteen years was refused. On the other hand, Congress increased and broadened our power from year to year.[3]

Under congressional authorization, and subject only to the routine approval of the President, Jones lent between 1940 and 1945 "anything that we think we should . . . any amount, any length of time, any rate of interest."[4] The following remark by Senator Adams bespeaks the unusual willingness of Congress to grant discretionary authority to him: "Of course, the credit you are using comes from the Congress, and we have heard it said across this table and in the Senate and House that these vast credits were being extended largely because of the confidence the Congress has in Jesse Jones. Now that has been said time after time."[5] Senator Taft described the incorporation of the RFC into the Commerce Department as "an extraordinary precedent, justified only by the character of the man."[6]

For Jones, congressional hearings were not inquisitions or ordeals about which to become apprehensive; they were informal, friendly, laudatory—almost clubby—interchanges.[7] Frequently he would sit on the witness table and chat in an off-the-cuff manner. Or, if there happened to be a vacant seat between committee members, he would take it and the "hearing" would begin. Indeed, so comfortable did this executive official feel among congressional committees that he designed, bought, and presented to the Senate Committee on Banking and Currency a new

---

[2]Bascom Timmons, *Jesse H. Jones* (New York: Holt, Rinehart & Winston, Inc., 1956), p. 259.

[3]Jesse Jones and Edward Angly, *Fifty Billion Dollars* (New York: The Macmillan Company, 1951), p. vii.

[4]*New York Times*, January 25, 1945, p. 14.

[5]Senate Banking and Currency Committee, *Hearings on H.R. 5667*, 77th Cong., 1st sess. (Washington, D.C., 1941), p. 14.

[6]86 *Cong. Rec.* (1940), p. 11862.

[7]When they did subject him to a normally (for others) warm interrogation, Jones was quick to show a hair shirt and to take personal offense. For example, see House Subcommittee of the Committee on Foreign and Domestic Commerce, *Hearings on Petroleum Investigation*, 77th Cong., 2d sess. (Washington, D.C., 1942), pp. 105–7.

table for their hearing room—one is tempted to say their clubroom—in order that he might see them all better while testifying.[8] Jones pursued this cordial alliance in casual, day-to-day contacts. Once a week he would lunch on Capitol Hill with members of the legislature, in the office of Vice-President Garner, Speaker Rayburn, or Senate Secretary Biffle. On other occasions he would come to Garner's office for morning or afternoon coffee. "I guess it's *our* office," commented Garner, "Jones uses it as much as I do."[9]

A *second* crucial element in Jones's RFC experience was its nonpartisan character. Like most independent agencies, its plural executive was composed of members of both political parties. Jones himself had been a very active Democrat as Director of Finance for the Democratic National Committee in 1924, as a favorite son candidate for President in 1928, and as a faithfully heavy contributor to party causes. He had influential Democratic friends like fellow-Texan John Nance Garner and Senator Carter Glass. And though he retained these ties the RFC acquired a reputation for nonpartisanship. Jones, moreover, was a conservative in politics, and as the Republican-Southern Democratic coalition took shape within Congress, his Democratic politics became less of a liability. He continually stressed the nonpartisan nature of his organization and won the support of Republicans as well as Democrats. The ranking Republican member of the House Banking and Currency Committee spoke of Jones as "a man whom I so much respect for his wisdom, his intelligence, and his patriotism that without giving it much consideration, I would accept almost any proposal he might make."[10] Or, consider this colloquy between the ranking Republican and the ranking Democrat on the Senate Appropriations Committee:

> SEN. WHITE: . . . I have to confess that there is a disposition for me to favor anything that Mr. Jones recommends.
> SEN. MCKELLAR: That is for me, too. I do not think that there is a finer man anywhere in the world.[11]

Jones's extraordinary standing with Congress was built partly on his success in keeping his organization in close touch with that body and yet outside party conflict.

A *third* factor, intertwined with the other two, was the close *entente* between Jones's organization and a powerful social constituency—the business community. During Jones's government service, agencies under his supervision authorized expenditures of fifty billion dollars to assist

[8]Timmons, *op. cit.*, pp. 263–65.
[9]*Ibid.*, p. 264.
[10]83 *Cong. Rec.* (1938), p. 1988.
[11]Senate Subcommittee of Committee on Appropriations, *Hearings on Department of Commerce Appropriation Bill for 1943*, 77th Cong., 2d sess. (Washington, D.C., 1942), p. 64. See also Jones and Angly, *op. cit.*, p. 545.

various enterprises in business, industry, and banking. He was in constant contact with representatives of this group, as consciously and as inevitably reaching out for their support as they did for his. His public speeches were aimed at this particular clientele, and the groups which gave him a forum were business groups—the Chamber of Commerce, the American Bankers Association, the National Wholesale Association Council, the Economic Development Committee, the Department of Commerce's Business Advisory Council. Jones himself was a businessman who had become by 1929 "the best known private citizen in Texas," due to his ownership of a newspaper, several hotels, a bank, several skyscrapers, and other assorted real estate.[12] He identified himself completely with business, and he considered the RFC to be "America's largest corporation and the world's biggest and most varied banking agency."[13]

Jones never passed up the opportunity, before Congress, to attribute the success of the RFC wholly to the fact that it was a "businesslike, nonpolitical organization." Again and again he reiterated that "Our agency is a business agency composed entirely of business people."[14] He was tireless in his praise of his agencies as paragons of businesslike efficiency and economy, and he loved to make invidious comparisons between himself and the "do-gooders," "idealists," and "screwballs" in the government who did not possess the same virtues. His organizations were run as businesses, by businessmen, and for businessmen. Jones fastened himself to a powerful constituency which cut across party lines and which gave him leverage both in and out of Congress. Moreover, his appeals to Congress and to his business constituency were mutually reinforcing. Throughout the Roosevelt Administration the executive branch had not been especially hospitable to business, and its channels of access to government coursed mostly through the legislature. Members of Congress tended to be very sympathetic to Jones's emphasis on business and identified themselves with his efforts to help it, especially small business.[15]

As head of the RFC, Jones developed lines of responsibility and areas of support which had few presidential dimensions. On the basis of his personal and institutional resources, he had fashioned a substantial enclave of power and, hence, a considerable degree of political independence. As Secretary of Commerce, however, he was brought into a different, and theoretically more dependent, relationship to the President. He joined the "official family" at Cabinet meetings; his for-

[12]Timmons, *op. cit.*, p. 153.

[13]Jones and Angly, *op. cit.*, p. 3.

[14]Senate Committee on Expenditures in the Executive Branch, *Hearings on Amendment of Budget and Accounting Act of 1921*, 78th Cong., 1st sess. (Washington, D.C., 1943), p. 104.

[15]House Subcommittee of Committee on Appropriations, *Hearings on Department of Commerce Appropriation Bill for 1944*, 78th Cong., 1st sess. (Washington, D.C., 1943), p. 11.

mal responsibility now ran directly up the hierarchy to the Chief Executive; and with a closer relationship came greater opportunities for him to help the President. Jones himself had no intention of allowing either of the two patterns of relationships—least of all the President-oriented one—to absorb the other. And as if to underscore the point, he refused to accept the Commerce post until Roosevelt agreed to let him retain all his RFC functions.[16]

However this may be, the key idea is that Jones's network of relations with Congress, with a social constituency, and with political partisans is the kind of network within which nearly every department Secretary must operate. It is the essence of his extra-Cabinet activity. The vividness, perhaps, but not the validity of this proposition depends upon Jones's particular RFC background and his perception of his new role. His situation, faced with alternative lines of responsibility to the President and to the Congress, is a normal one in the American political system. In his first appearance before the House Appropriations Committee, he spoke as any Secretary of Commerce would when he said, "If the Department of Commerce means anything, it means as I understand it, the representation of business in the councils of the administration, at the Cabinet table, and so forth."[17] The duality of roles, as presidential lieutenant and departmental executive, promotes ambiguity, conflict, and, as the Jones case illustrates, a pattern of behavior quite unknown to any hierarchial image of President-Cabinet relations.

In 1943, Congress was considering legislation to set up a single agency to coordinate the disposal of surplus government property. It provided for coordination by the President and, as a practical matter, by the Bureau of the Budget. With an eye to uniformity and control, the Budget Bureau desired that all agencies in the executive branch be tied into the program. This, of course, included the RFC and its various subsidiary corporations, which comprised one of the largest government purchasers and holders of property. In the Senate hearings, the Bureau expressed its wish that ". . . the disposal policies of these corporations should be subject to review under this bill, for assurance that they are tied in, that there is cohesion and coordination, and that they are not out in a competitive status."[18] Jones was willing to listen to the advice of a unifying agency but fought for the complete autonomy of the RFC in disposing of its property. In effect, he argued against the wishes

[16]Jones and Angly, *op. cit.*, pp. 257, 536; Timmons, *op. cit.*, p. 250; *New York Times*, January 25, 1945, p. 14.

[17]House Subcommittee of Committee on Appropriations, *Hearings on Department of Commerce Appropriation Bill for 1942*, 77th Cong., 1st sess. (Washington, D.C., 1941), p. 9.

[18]Senate Committee on Expenditures in the Executive Branch, *Hearings on Amendment of Budget and Accounting Act of 1921*, 78th Cong., 1st sess. (Washington, D.C., 1943), pp. 29–31.

of the Chief Executive, and did so without even consulting Roosevelt. Before the committee, Jones stated his own position and appealed for support to his favorite constituencies, Congress and business.

Arguing from the standpoint of business, he said,

> I don't see any excuse for a new agency to handle and dispose of these properties. You have a perfectly good one. . . . I should think that you would use the RFC and give it such additional manpower as it needs, because it is a business agency and this is a business proposition. There would be no purpose in setting up a new one, but Congress can do it if it wants.

At the suggestion of the Committee, he was "willing" even to enlarge his own domain and leave out the Budget Bureau altogether in the area of real property.

> SEN. FERGUSON: Could the RFC become the agency and dispose of all properties? Is that the logical place to place it, because it is a business organization?
>
> SECRETARY JONES: I think that is where it belongs; that is all plants, equipment, machinery, machine tools, and so forth. *I have not discussed the matter with anyone in authority in the government.* Those are my views and they are very strong. . . . I do not understand why they (Budget Bureau) would be a natural agency to do this job.
>
> FERGUSON: Who would be the natural agency in the government?
>
> JONES: The RFC. . . . When I say the RFC, I mean also the Department of Commerce, because they are the business end of the government.[19]
>
> [19]*Ibid.*, pp. 113–14.

The hearings closed on a familiar note: Jones's appeal to the Congress and reciprocated congressional sentiments of affection for him.

> CHAIRMAN (Senator Hill): You feel that your agency, having built these plants and secured this property, is the agency to make this disposition?
>
> JONES: The RFC is your agency, an agency of the Congress.
>
> CHAIRMAN: Mr. Jones, when you first appeared here this morning, I spoke about your many different titles. I am going to confer another title on you, and that is that you are a great diplomat, too. That was a fine way to put it. But as you say, it is Congress' agency that has secured this property. It is your feeling that it is the agency that Congress should use for the disposition of this property better than anybody else?
>
> JONES: Yes, sir. . . . I do not intend to be immodest.
>
> CHAIRMAN: We would not have you immodest. We do not want you to be.
>
> SEN. FERGUSON: The entire country is going to be very fortunate if all the other agencies feel about Congress as you do I am sure.

CHAIRMAN: I want to say this, too, since the Senator has said what he has, that Mr. Jones's actions always square with his words. He is always most considerate of the Congress.[20]

One point at which Jones's double-barreled efforts to mitigate presidential control were effective was in the appropriations process. The major purpose of the executive budget is to provide for coordination of the expenditures of the executive branch in the name of economy and efficiency. The reverse side of the coin is the President's central control over programming through his control over expenditures. The Budget Bureau, as a staff arm of the President, prepares a document which expresses unity in policy as well as in finance. Reductions that it makes in agency requests represent the complex judgment of the President and his staff on matters of priority, cohesion, and purpose. Insofar as Cabinet members can make successful appeals to the Congress against this judgment, they can operate their departments with little dependence on the President and, virtually, if not literally, in defiance of him.

In drawing up the Department of Commerce budget for fiscal 1944, the decision was made to eliminate the field service of the Bureau of Foreign and Domestic Commerce. This was done because wartime restrictions on trade had reduced the usefulness of this service, and because that part of the job which needed to be done could, in the eyes of those dealing with the budget, be performed better by a wartime agency. To Jones, the reduction represented an attack upon his domain by people who were ignorant of his problems, and he lobbied strenuously before the appropriations committees in the House and Senate to restore the cut of $430,000 in the interests of his clientele.

In the House Subcommittee hearings, Jones began by stressing the efficiency and economy of his own agency while taking pot shots at others, both tactics designed to identify his aims with those of Congress.

> We have a seasoned organization, which would work in cooperation with the RFC and its agencies. We have been in the government a long time. You don't hear much fuss about us. We get along pretty well and we think we know how to do the job better than some big shot that you would get in as temporary head, building up an organization which would be partly made up of volunteers and inexperienced people who do not know how to work together. . . . Of course, we do not spend any money which does not seem to be necessary. I believe in economy, but there are apparently not a great many people who do. There seem to be a good many in Congress who do, but not the boys on the spending line.[21]

[20]*Ibid.*, pp. 118–19.
[21]House Subcommittee of Committee on Appropriations, *Hearings on Department of Commerce Appropriation Bill for 1944*, 78th Cong., 1st sess. (Washington, D.C., 1943), p. 8.

With a little legislative arm-twisting, Jones freely stated his position on the budget cut.

> MR. HARE: Mr. Secretary. . . . we all know of your wide business experience, and I wonder if you would give us the advantage of your judgment as to what extent and in what way these district offices would be able to contribute in giving assistance to small business activity?
> JONES: If we had that money, we would expand the present organization instead of closing it. *But we have had advice from the Budget Bureau that this does not fit into the President's program. Of course, we are not trying to oppose the President, but we think the Budget is wrong.*22

Before the Senate Committee, Jones concluded his appeal for the restoration of the cut in terms of his particularistic clientele and without reference to any overall presidential program.

> I think that the Department of Commerce has got to carry the ball for business. That is what it is set up to do. If we haven't got the right people to do the job, then others should be gotten to do it. But the Department is the representative of business at the Cabinet table and in the administration whatever the administration is. So I say that I think it is of importance that we not destroy or diminish this service by one iota, that it really ought to be expanded and encouraged.23

Of the $430,000, Congress restored $295,000, and only four of the thirty field offices were closed.24

Jones's consciousness of his high standing contributed to a psychological hypersensitivity to any attempt "to horn in on our RFC operations." He communicated this sensitivity to the Congress and they responded in kind. They were irritated when a wartime agency like the Office of Production Management or the Board of Economic Warfare infringed in any way on the discretionary authority of Jones over the money which they had appropriated.25 Their solicitude, while a blessing to Jones, was a distinct burden to the President, for it allowed the Secretary of Commerce to prosecute, before friendly committees, an internecine warfare with other agencies of the executive branch, casting

22*Ibid.*, p. 10.

23Senate Subcommittee of Committee on Appropriations, *Hearings on Department of Commerce Appropriations Bill for 1944*, 78th Cong., 1st sess. (Washington, D.C., 1943), p. 63.

24House Subcommittee of Committee on Appropriations, *Hearings on Department of Commerce Appropriations Bill for 1945*, 78th Cong., 2d sess. (Washington, D.C., 1944), p. 107. Jones argued again in 1944 for the restoration of the original amount, using the same rationale. *Ibid.*, pp. 2, 6, 9, 13–14.

25Senate Committee on Banking and Currency, *Hearings on Increasing the Borrowing Authority of the RFC*, 77th Cong., 1st sess. (Washington, D.C., 1941), pp. 12–14, 20.

about for non-presidential support as he went. The most obvious of these adventures was that which resulted in the "acrimonious public debate" between Jones and Henry Wallace, who was head of the BEW, in June of 1943. This quarrel between subordinates obviously hurt and annoyed the President and hampered his direction of the war effort.

At least as early as December of 1942 Jones had been engaged in sidewise combat with the BEW before Congress. In an appearance before the Senate Banking and Currency Committee, Jones allowed himself, with little encouragement, to complain that he was really "working under" the BEW and was very dissatisfied with the arrangement. One of those informal gestures which seldom break into print provided Senator Tobey with an opening.

> SEN. TOBEY: This matter of working with the BEW was enough to cause you to *raise your eyebrows,* as you did the first time it was mentioned here, is that right?
> JONES: That is right, I suppose, but I don't quite know what you mean.[26]

Of course, Jones knew very well, and only had to be coaxed a little more to reveal that "we negotiate contracts and arrange financing and none of them (other agencies) except the BEW ever interferes with our negotiations. They leave it to us, feeling that we are the business organization with experience, preferring to have us negotiate the contracts; and because of our responsibility to Congress, we quite naturally prefer to do it."

> TOBEY: But the BEW does interfere.
> JONES: They do a great deal of the negotiating, yes. . . .
> TOBEY: Would you want to answer this question, having in mind the talk here this morning about the BEW and its extraordinary powers? Would you feel that if the BEW were curbed . . . it would be a wise procedure?
> JONES: The Executive Order is made by the President.
> TOBEY: Yes, I know.
> JONES: I think I would not care to discuss that.
> TOBEY: But here is a nation and we are all striving to serve it. . . . *Such a thing as I suggest might contravene the President . . .* but whether the nation would be better served by having a better setup . . . would you feel that some other arrangement would be wiser than the present arrangement?
> JONES: *Inasmuch as you press the question, I will say I think it could be improved.*[27]

[26]Senate Committee on Banking and Currency, *Hearings on Increasing the Borrowing Authority of the RFC,* 77th Cong., 2d sess. (Washington, D.C., 1942), p. 6.
[27]*Ibid.,* p. 8. See also *ibid.,* pp. 10, 41.

Jones did not consider his relationship with Roosevelt in terms of subordination or hierarchy. He saw it, instead, as a marriage of convenience between co-equal potentates. "I never considered that I was working *for* him, but *with* him for the country."[28]

> In the twelve years I worked with him, we never had an argument. We did not always see alike. If he asked me to do something which in my opinion we could not or should not—and that happened only a few times—we just did not do it. For me that was the only way to operate without having a break with the President.[29]

His biographer describes how Jones "layered" Roosevelt's proposals.

> He granted such demands as he deemed wise or safe, but when Roosevelt wanted something that Jones considered wrong or clearly unwise, he listened, withheld argument, and then contrived an escape by inconspicuous inaction.[30]

Neither was there any feeling of intimacy between the two men.

> In no sense did I feel his superiority over other men except that he was President and the greatest politician our country has ever known, and ruthless when it suited his purpose.[31]

Roosevelt, for his part, was willing to work on a relatively thin margin of loyalty, both personal and programmatic—which is undoubtedly one reason that their association lasted as long as it did. Ultimately, however, the personalities of the two men cannot explain the difficulties or the endurance of the relationship.

Roosevelt retained Jones in the Cabinet because his presence was helpful—not in spite of his independent strength, but because of it. The most persistent political problem facing any President is that of consolidating enough support for his policies. From this standpoint, Jones's influence with groups in and out of the government was an asset on which Roosevelt could trade. He saw Jones's conservatism as "a good thing for this administration," "a good antidote for the extreme liberals, a sort of balance as it were."[32] In 1940, Jones spoke over a nation-wide radio hookup to his business constituency, urging that the reelection of the President was in their best interests. Roosevelt realized, too, that Jones's strength in Congress, with its hard core in the influential Texas

[28]Timmons, *op. cit.*, p. 249.
[29]Jones and Angly, *op. cit.*, p. 262.
[30]Timmons, *op. cit.*, p. 394. See also Jones and Angly, *op. cit.*, p. 257.
[31]Jones and Angly, *op. cit.*, p. 290. See also p. 283.
[32]*Ibid.*, pp. 262–63; Timmons, *op. cit.*, p. 252.

delegation,[33] was useful to him. It was a strength calculated by some as "ten votes in the Senate and forty in the House" on matters within Jones's area of competence.[34] He was able on one occasion, for instance, to persuade reluctant legislators to vote a huge export-import loan to South America.[35] Thus the total picture of the Jones-Roosevelt relationship was an admixture of help and hindrance. Neither assets nor liabilities were constants, and the ultimate judgment, of participant and observer alike, is one of subtle calculation.

As the 1944 Democratic Convention approached, Roosevelt's calculations "convinced" him that Jones's influence was being used to support a conservative revolt, and to persuade the Texas delegation to vote against a fourth-term nomination. Jones denies it, but whatever the case, the decisive thing is that Roosevelt believed it was true. Moreover, it was the kind of behavior which touched his most sensitive political nerve. Jonathan Daniels writes that in 1944 the President was speaking contemptuously of "Jesus H. Jones," and that he was planning then to remove him from the Cabinet.[36] Judge Rosenman feels that the move was a mistake and that "Roosevelt would never have made it under ordinary circumstances, but the vindictiveness aroused by the reports of Jones's activity impaired his usually clear political insight."[37] The puzzle of the curt Roosevelt-to-Jones note after the election can best be explained in this way. It stressed Henry Wallace's "utmost devotion to the cause, travelling almost incessantly and working for the success of the ticket in a great many parts of the country."[38] As Joseph Harris says, "Roosevelt chose this means of letting it be known that Jones was dismissed because of his failure to support Roosevelt politically. On any other grounds, the dismissal of Jones would have caused a great furor."[39]

Jones did not go down without a fight in which he uncontestably demonstrated his independent power. Divorced of the prestige of office, he nonetheless could summon enough political support to keep his base of operations, the RFC, out of the hands of his successor. His letter blasting Henry Wallace and his testimony on the George Bill were in the nature of a valedictorian appeal to business and to the Congress. Con-

[33]It is not without importance to note that between January 2, 1932, and the date of the United States's entrance into the war, the RFC authorized loans of almost $180,000,000 in Texas. *Report of the RFC*, Third Quarter, 1941 (Washington, D.C., 1942).

[34]John Gunther, *Roosevelt in Retrospect* (New York: Harper & Row, Publishers, 1950), p. 128.

[35]Timmons, *op. cit.*, pp. 266–67.

[36]Jonathan Daniels, *Man of Independence* (Philadelphia: Lippincott, 1950), p. 243.

[37]Samuel Rosenman, *Working with Roosevelt* (New York: Harper & Row, Publishers, 1952), pp. 84–85.

[38]Jones and Angly, *op. cit.*, p. 218.

[39]Joseph Harris, *The Advice and Consent of the Senate* (Berkeley, Calif.: University of California Press, 1953), p. 147.

gress responded with majorities of 400–2 and 74–12 in favor of removing the RFC from the Department of Commerce. Wallace, with that lack of perspective so common to a man who has been run over by a steamroller, but with the sure knowledge that he had been thoroughly flattened, said later that "Jesse Jones wielded greater power for a longer period than any human being in the history of the United States."[40]

A more sober and pertinent comment, perhaps, would be that the denouement, like the rest of the story, illustrates something of the fragmented, decentralized nature of power in the American political system. Norton Long has written that "to deny that political power is derived exclusively from superiors in the hierarchy is to assert that subordinates stand in a feudal relation in which to a degree they fend for themselves and acquire support peculiarly their own."[41] Jesse Jones built, inhabited, and manipulated a political fiefdom with a degree of independence which brought a heavy burden to his lord-President. But the feudal analogy is only partially correct, for within the democratic political process there are no laws of primogeniture and entail. Jones's fiefdom was, in the final accounting, a web of relationships peculiarly his own, held only for so long as he could hold it. It was not a transferable property. At the very end, he boasted facetiously about his two-headed job that "I do not believe there is another man in the world that will do it except me."[42] It was an accurate assessment not alone of the man, but of the system. Power in the American political system is both fragmented and, in David Riesman's description, "mercurial." It can quite easily and logically be won by the Cabinet member, but as the Jones case demonstrates, no particular constellation can be held, or held together, permanently. The Jones case also demonstrates that the winning, the holding, and the losing are not likely to make the tasks of the Chief Legislator-Chief Administrator any easier.

The investigations which we have made into Cabinet-member activity in the areas of public prestige, party, Congress, and departmental administration lead to a few conclusions about the Cabinet and the political system in which it operates. One striking circumstance is the extent to which the Cabinet concept breaks down in the course of the members' activities outside the Cabinet meeting. In matters of prestige, partisan politics, and legislative relations alike, the Cabinet as a collectivity has only a symbolic value, a value which readily disappears when the need for action supersedes the need for a show window. In the day-to-day work of the Cabinet member, each man fends for himself without much consideration for Cabinet unity. His survival, his support, and his

[40]Timmons, *op. cit.*, p. 330.
[41]Norton Long, "Power and Administration," *Public Administration Review*, Vol. 9 (Autumn 1949), p. 258.
[42]*New York Times*, January 25, 1945, p. 15.

success do not depend on his fellow members. His performance is judged separately from theirs. This condition is but another result of the combination of the centrifugal tendencies in our political system with the low degree of institutionalization which characterizes the Cabinet.

The political help which the President receives comes not from the group but from individual Cabinet members, who can and do augment the President's effectiveness in his leadership roles. It would be a serious mistake not to emphasize the possibilities for crucial assistance by individuals. But probably most striking is the fact that the possibilities for such assistance are very frequently negated by the number of limitations which surround them. There are pervasive limitations of a personal or a situational nature, and there are limitations inherent in the political system—all of which make it neither easy for a Cabinet member to help the President nor axiomatic that he should do so. In the final reckoning, the President receives much less assistance of a positive, non-preventive type from his individual Cabinet members than one might expect. This fact serves to accent the high degree of success which is represented by preventive assistance. It also helps to underline the tremendous gap which separates the presidential level of responsibility from that of his subordinates. It demonstrates, too, the extent to which the two levels are subject to the pulls of different political forces.

CHAPTER EIGHT

LBJ BUILDS
HIS COALITION

ROWLAND EVANS AND ROBERT NOVAK

Lyndon Johnson, trained to the use of power, his whole life geared to his driving ambition, had come now to the presidency itself, but under circumstances that could not conceivably have been more ominous. Driving through the sunny streets of Dallas in a motorcade on November 22, 1963, President John F. Kennedy was murdered by a mail-order rifle fired by Lee Harvey Oswald. Tragedy struck in Johnson's own Texas, in the very city where, almost exactly three years earlier, he himself had been mobbed by screaming Republicans.

Now, when the nation mourned its dead President, the burden of binding the wound, of creating a sympathetic response between the new President and the millions of American citizens who loved the old, of reassuring Kennedy's Administration that he was worthy of its support, of showing a resolute face to the world, of moving a nation wrapped in sorrow out of its tears—the whole burden fell on this one man.

Here was Lyndon Johnson, the first Southern President since the Civil War, not elected but come to the office by an assassin's bullet; Lyndon Johnson, born in Texas and now the sudden repository of all the hopes of twenty million Negroes battling for equality; Lyndon Johnson, hotly opposed for the *second* office at the last convention by the liberal core of his own party; Lyndon Johnson, the legislative genius now challenged with the highest responsibility of *executive* power. Paradox crowded on paradox. The forbidding quality of these paradoxes was forgotten after the event, but they bore heavily on Johnson that November day.

Of all the imperatives for Johnson in that worst of times, there was one that towered highest; that was the imperative of confidence. Here was his preeminent concern, first as he waited in a cubicle with the blinds drawn near the emergency room at Parkland Hospital, minutes later as he sat stone-faced in the car of Dallas Police Chief Jesse Curry who drove him, incognito, to the President's Air Force One—now *his* Air Force One—at Love Field; still later, now sworn in as President, as the great plane took off and returned to the Capital. Johnson knew that above all else, he needed the confidence of the American people. He knew how that other Johnson, Andrew Johnson, who succeeded Abraham Lincoln in another time of racial crisis, was vilely accused of having himself plotted against Lincoln. He knew, too, that that other Johnson had lost the confidence of the people before he had fairly had a chance to gain it. And so this Johnson, Lyndon Baines Johnson, the Thirty-sixth President, began at once, as by instinct, to restore the confidence of the people in their country and to gain their confidence for himself.

Yet, in those days and early weeks of transition between the Kennedy and Johnson Administrations, the new President's quest for confidence was always accompanied by the reality of his power. Although he knew he had yet to gain the confidence of the nation and the world, he did not hesitate to use his new power. He was the lawful President, and he made the decisions and gave the orders from the very outset of those fearful early moments.

Air Force One waited at the end of the runway at Love Field in Dallas. Brigadier General Chester V. Clifton, President Kennedy's Army aide, ordered the pilot to take off immediately. Malcolm Kilduff, Kennedy's assistant press secretary, canceled the order and told the pilot to delay. Johnson had ordered Kilduff to keep the plane on the field until Federal Judge Sarah Hughes arrived to swear him in as President.

Back in the main compartment of the plane where Kennedy's body lay in its casket and where Jacqueline Kennedy and her husband's former aides—Dave Powers, Kenny O'Donnell, and Larry O'Brien—huddled together in their grief, there was first surprise, then consternation at the long delay. Brigadier General Godfrey T. McHugh, President Kennedy's Air Force aide, rushed up to the pilot's cabin to repeat Clifton's order. "Mrs. Kennedy and Kenny O'Donnell want it," he said, his voice edged with impatience and emotion.

But again, Mac Kilduff countermanded the order. "But, Mac," McHugh said, "Mrs. Kennedy and Kenny want it." Kilduff, acting under higher authority, said what had to be said: "General, they're not in charge anymore."

Johnson *was* in charge. For he had become President, not when sworn in aboard Air Force One by Sarah Hughes, but the moment Kennedy died. . . .

There were the Kennedy men in and out of the government proper: the Irish Mafia, Harvard professors, labor leaders, the Kennedy Cabinet, the White House technicians, big-city politicians. All these, with no time to lose, had to be brought within the compass of the new President. Those in the government had to be persuaded to stay on the job. For if, as Johnson moved into his new job, some or most of these moved out of their old jobs, the country would draw an obvious conclusion: these Kennedy men did not choose to work for Johnson. That could destroy confidence. Thus, Johnson's first important move as President was to prevent even the appearance of an exodus, and to reinforce his still-tentative ties with the Northern power blocs that made up the power of the Democratic party: Negro organizations, labor unions, big-city machines—plus the liberal intellectuals.

From the beginning as President, Johnson never entertained the remote possibility of following Harry Truman's example when he succeeded to the presidency in 1945 at the death of Franklin Roosevelt. Truman cleaned out his predecessor's Cabinet and White House staff and moved in his own. For two reasons, Johnson simply did not enjoy the option that had been open to Truman. First, it was too late in Kennedy's term and the mood of the hour was too black. And second, he would have been hard put to find replacements. He *had* to keep the Kennedy team intact.

The extraordinary intensity and persistence of the new President in carrying out this job was symbolic of the extraordinary success of the transition period. There was no hesitation, no ceremony, no delay. As President, Johnson could now persuade with an authority never before possessed, and persuasion had always been a sharp instrument in his exercise of power.

But persuasion, in the first few days at least, could not be too exuberant. Johnson subdued his energy, lowered his voice, and assumed a posture of humility. The merest semblance of exuberance in a period of a national grief and mourning could trigger the mass exodus of New Frontiersmen that he must avoid at all costs. It could mean an abrupt resignation as Attorney General by Robert F. Kennedy that would split the Democratic party in two. For immediately upon the death of his brother, Bobby Kennedy assumed leadership not only of the family but of a substantial portion of the Democratic party.

Thus, in those early days of Johnson's presidency, the old acrimony between him and Bobby Kennedy was absent. Talking to Kennedy on the telephone from Dallas and then in Washington on Saturday, November 23, at his first Cabinet meeting, the new President was thoughtful and understanding of the young Attorney General's personal loss. As Johnson told another New Frontiersman that evening, he had kept the Saturday Cabinet meeting short mainly out of respect for Bobby Kennedy. Eventually deep discord between these two figures who had been on the ragged edge of civility for some three years was inevitable, rather sooner than later. But the fact that Johnson was able to maintain that civility on November 23, 1963, saved the transition from disaster at the outset. Bobby stayed.

Bobby Kennedy was not the only potentially troubling member of the administration inherited by Johnson. He distrusted the brisk Ivy League manner of two Eastern Establishment Republicans who played vital policy-making roles for President Kennedy: Douglas Dillon, Secretary of the Treasury, and McGeorge Bundy, White House aide for National Security. He resented the fact that he was greeted in his first hours in the White House by memoranda pleading with him not to reduce expenditures from two Cabinet members: Secretary of Agriculture Orville Freeman and Secretary of Labor Willard Wirtz. The speculation throughout Washington was that Dillon, Bundy, Freeman, Wirtz, Secretary of the Interior Stewart Udall and quite likely many, many more would be gone by year's end. The fact that they stayed is testimony to the magnificent restraint of Johnson in those transition days. Old friends and aides remarked they had never seen him so self-possessed, so humble. Talking to a quick-witted New Frontiersman on Saturday night, Johnson asked for patience. He could not, he said, absorb things as swiftly as Jack Kennedy.

With each key Kennedy man, Johnson used a different technique to try to make him a Johnson man. Walter Heller, the chairman of the President's Council of Economic Advisers, had sat next to Vice-President Johnson regularly at President Kennedy's weekly "briefing sessions" preceding his press conferences. For three years, Heller invariably made a point of giving Johnson a copy of his economic briefing paper for Kennedy when the President called in his experts to bone up for the press conference. As a result, Johnson developed a special relationship with the lean professor from the University of Minnesota whose New Economics set the tone of domestic policy in the Kennedy Administration.

Late in the evening on Saturday, November 23, Heller was called to the temporary office of the new President in the Executive Office Building just across West Executive Avenue from the White House. What ensued there was an essence of the new President's first few weeks in office as, one by one, he exerted the highly individualistic Johnsonian charm and persuasion to prevent the exceptional men brought to Washington by Kennedy from leaving.

As his chat with Heller progressed, Johnson was particularly anxious about the stock market decline following the assassination. Was there anything he could do or say to instill confidence? Heller told him the number of points the market had dropped in the few moments between the assassination and the close of the market and was mentally computing the percentage of decline when Johnson himself figured it out. The drop had been about 3 percent, Johnson said, and now the important thing was to create a general sense of confidence and assurance that the Johnson Administration was going to "move forward," not slide backward.

After touching on economic subjects, President Johnson came to the important point. Heller had left his chair and was walking to the door to leave, when Johnson came over, pulled him away from the door and shut it. He wanted to tell Heller what he had told a dozen others already: that he was not a conservative, a budget-slasher, who would take the government back to the laissez-faire of the Eisenhower Administration. No, far from it. The new President was, he said, a Roosevelt New Dealer, and anyone who studied his record would find that out. It was, he continued, vital that the economic and political liberals understand that fact. He asked Heller to make that clear to his liberal friends, to such Kennedy intellectuals from Harvard as historian Arthur Schlesinger, Jr., a White House assistant, and economist J. Kenneth Galbraith, Ambassador to India, who was in Washington for Kennedy's funeral.

As for Heller, said the President, there must be no question about his leaving the administration. Johnson needed him—needed him more than Kennedy had because Johnson had far more to learn than Kennedy. Heller's response echoed the words that the new President was hearing that day, and for many days thereafter, from every Kennedy man he appealed to: Heller would stay, he was eager to do everything he could to smooth the transition period for the new President, and he would stay not just out of a sense of duty but with a sense of warmth and friendship. That, Johnson knew, was establishing confidence.

Heller was essential to the new President not only because he had friends throughout the academic community and was a symbol of the New Economics, but because an indispensable part of government was in his charge and Johnson could not do without him all at once. In establishing confidence he must, then, establish a confidential relationship with Heller, with the Cabinet, and with the other main blocks in the arch of which Johnson himself had now become the keystone.

With Schlesinger, the emphasis was different. Schlesinger was important not because of what he was doing in the White House but because of his symbolic quality as a liberal's liberal. If Johnson could not let a Heller leave because the departure would make a gaping hole in the government itself, he could not let a Schlesinger leave because the departure would make a gaping hole in the new administration's ideological image.

On Tuesday, November 26, he asked Schlesinger, who had sent in his resignation the day after the assassination, to join him in the East Room of the White House, where the President made a speech to the Latin American ambassadors, pledging his support of the Alliance for Progress in graceful, sensitive words that evoked the memory both of John F. Kennedy and Franklin D. Roosevelt. Now, as he walked out of the East Room, he took Schlesinger back with him to the Oval Office in the White House, where by now Johnson was installed. Sitting on opposite sofas by the fireplace, the President made what must have been a difficult appeal to Schlesinger. He and Schlesinger had never been close, and the man from the Texas frontier on occasion resented the blunt rhetoric and intellectualism of the Harvard professor on the New Frontier. He needed Schlesinger, said Johnson, because Schlesinger had a profound knowledge of the programs, the purposes, and the history of this country and of the progressive policies that distinguished Democratic administrations. Schlesinger knew the writers and the liberals, and Johnson needed that. He had Schlesinger's letter of resignation, he said, but he regarded it as nothing but a gesture, a formal offer. He rejected it. "If you act on it," Johnson told Schlesinger, "I will have you arrested."

Schlesinger, who really *wanted* to resign when he submitted his letter to Johnson, pointed out that every President had a right to have his own people, particularly in the White House. Johnson replied that he now regarded Schlesinger as one of his own men, that he had complete confidence in him, and that although it undoubtedly would be a sacrifice for Schlesinger, he must stay for the President's sake and for the country's. Johnson said all this with simplicity, dignity, and conviction.

Schlesinger stayed on for four months. He was given no jobs to do and saw the President only infrequently before he left. He was, then, a symbol, but an important one for Johnson.

Johnson's wooing of administration officials went to extremes at times, as it did with Adlai Stevenson, Ambassador to the United Nations and still an idol to the Democratic party's liberal wing. Johnson's private opinion of Stevenson had never been high, but their relations had generally been cordial and now he needed him. So ardent was his wooing that Stevenson, who had far less policy-making influence under Kennedy than he had hoped for, felt a new and major role was destined for him in this new administration.

Stevenson went to President Johnson's office in the Executive Office Building on Monday, November 25, the day of Kennedy's funeral. "I know and you know that you should be sitting behind this desk rather than me," Johnson told Stevenson. "You could have had the vice-presidential nomination in Los Angeles, but you kept your word to me that you wouldn't back any of the candidates and as a result I am here instead of you." What Johnson was saying—correctly or not—was that if

Stevenson had endorsed Kennedy, the second place on the ticket would have been his for the asking.

Then Johnson went on: the late President had not been consulting Stevenson, but "all that is going to be changed from now on." Stevenson must not hesitate to telephone Johnson any time he had a recommendation. "I want you to play a large role in the formation of policy," Johnson said. Recalling that conversation to a friend a few weeks later, Stevenson said he genuinely believed that if he had given the word, Johnson would have replaced both Secretary of State Dean Rusk and McGeorge Bundy. But Stevenson told the President he should retain both Rusk and Bundy. Notwithstanding the President's glowing invitation for Stevenson to play that "large role" in policy-making, he found his influence progressively reduced, even below its level with Kennedy.[1]

The effort to encompass the entire New Frontier was so successful that no Kennedy man left until Ted Sorensen, Kennedy's Special Counsel at the White House, resigned effective February 29 to write a history of the Kennedy Administration. Nor was Sorensen's departure followed by a mass exodus. The key faces of the New Frontier remained in Washington into 1965 and even beyond.

Yet, Johnson's valiant achievement in retaining the entire Kennedy team had its unpleasant side. Edward R. Murrow, the brilliant radio-television commentator, had come to government from broadcasting in 1961 to take over the United States Information Agency. Some time in early 1963, he became ill. The illness was diagnosed as cancer, and from that moment, it was simply a question of picking an appropriate time to resign. Shortly before President Johnson went to Texas for the Christmas holiday, Murrow was advised by his doctors he must soon leave Washington for good and enter a clinic. Murrow had not wanted to resign during the transition, but now he had no choice. He informed Johnson that he would remain for one more month and that, three or four days before leaving, he would alert the President so that the usual statement could be issued at the White House.

But Murrow's health deteriorated faster than expected. Soon after New Year's Day his doctors ordered him into a clinic. On each of seven successive days, Murrow attempted to arrange an appointment with the President. He could not contact the President on the telephone. He booked a seat on a plane to California for January 17. Still the White House was silent. Finally, less than six hours before he left for the airport, Johnson telephoned him to say good-by and read the statement that the White House would issue.

Why did Johnson handle Murrow's departure in that way? Not because he wasn't sensitive to Murrow's health (although obviously he had

[1] By 1965, Stevenson was reduced to asking Vice-President Hubert Humphrey for advice on how to get in touch with the President. Humphrey suggested that Stevenson try to work through Bill Moyers, the leading presidential aide.

not been fully briefed on its seriousness). Not because he didn't appreciate Murrow's work in the government. What concerned Johnson was the prestige of the presidency after the shock of Dallas. Johnson wanted to delay Murrow's departure until he could find an appropriate replacement. He felt the presidency could not risk top-level vacancies. *Any* vacancy could impair confidence, and confidence after Dallas was the first imperative. . . .

But the high point of Johnson's bid for confidence came two days later, when he rode to the Capitol to address a joint session of Congress. That, the first full-dress presidential message to the nation, was of supreme importance to Johnson. How it was to be made—as a "fireside chat" from the White House or from the rostrum of the House to a joint session of Congress—was the subject of a most serious discussion. Ted Sorensen preferred the congressional approach, and Johnson, his roots deep on Capitol Hill, agreed.

On Saturday, November 23, Johnson asked Sorensen to write this first major speech—the same task he had performed so well for Kennedy. Later that day, Johnson by accident ran into Galbraith in an elevator in the Executive Office Building. Worried about the speech to Congress four days later, Johnson asked Galbraith whether he worked well with Sorensen. When the answer was yes, Johnson asked him to collaborate on the address. That night, Sorensen and Galbraith got together in the handsome Georgetown house of Katherine Graham, widow of Philip Graham and now publisher of the *Washington Post*. Galbraith hatched ideas and Sorensen put them in writing.

When Sorensen prepared his speeches for Kennedy, the draft was circulated, amendments were made, and it was then returned to Sorensen for final polishing. With Johnson, it was different. After the Sorensen-Galbraith draft was submitted to Johnson, they never saw it again. Johnson gave it to Abe Fortas, who did a top-to-bottom rewrite. "I corned it up a little," Fortas said later. The result was an amalgam that was neither pure Kennedy nor pure Johnson. It was a transition address.

But in those days when appearances meant so much, the speech itself was only part of a larger ceremony. There was the ritualistic question of who would accompany the new President during the slow ride up Pennsylvania Avenue to Capitol Hill. The fact that Johnson's old friend, Representative Joe Kilgore, was *not* in the presidential limousine on November 27 was a sign of the mood in Washington during the transition.

On November 22, Kilgore put away his tan Stetson hat. For Joe Kilgore sensed what Johnson was seeking after the assassination. The image of Texas had always irritated and sometimes infuriated the Eastern Seaboard, and the Eastern Seaboard dominated Washington and the New Frontier. Thus, Kilgore knew how important it was to dilute the old image of Texas now that a Texan was President. The worst service his friends could perform for Johnson would be to strut around the streets of Washington and in and out of the White House wearing Stetson hats.

When the President announced he would address Congress November 27, Kilgore telephoned Elizabeth Carpenter, Mrs. Johnson's press secretary and one of the most prominent Texans in Washington. He told Mrs. Carpenter that the speech Johnson would make to Congress was the most important speech he would ever give. This speech, said Kilgore, would fix the President forever in the minds of millions of Americans who, until November 22, had been all but unaware of his existence. Not only that, said Kilgore, but it also would set the tone of his administration and establish its credentials. Every American who could find a television set would be watching and every American would form his first impression of the new President on the basis of this first speech. Kilgore asked Mrs. Carpenter to tell the President all that, and to tell him further that he must not wave his arm from the rostrum of the House, he must not shout or speak too fast, and he must say the right things.

Informed of Kilgore's call, the President invited him to the White House to hear the draft of the all-important speech. Then, he invited the conservative Texas Congressman to ride to Capitol Hill with him when he went to give his speech. No, said Kilgore, that wouldn't do. The best help he could give his old friend, he told the President, was to stay away from him in public. Everything was changed now, and the President must do nothing to convey the impression that his closest friends were conservative Texas politicians. The next day, when Johnson went to the Capitol to deliver his speech, Ted Sorensen was in the presidential limousine. Joe Kilgore took a taxicab.

Speaking from the rostrum of the House, President Johnson achieved a tour de force in the most important address of his life. The words that counted were these: "Today, in this moment of new resolve, I would say to all my fellow Americans, *let us continue.*" Who could not recapture, on hearing those words, the phrase that gave them birth, uttered by John Kennedy on the steps of the Capitol January 20, 1961: "*Let us begin.*" The new President, with that link between the dead and the quick, rang with conviction and captured precisely the mood of the country. The speech had been written by Sorensen, Galbraith, and Fortas, but the heart of it—"let us continue"—was President Johnson's own. And then the President examined the unfinished business: "Our most immediate tasks," he said, "are here on this Hill." He moved quickly to show that Kennedy's projects were his projects. He told Congress:

First, no memorial oration or eulogy could more eloquently honor President Kennedy's memory than the earliest possible passage of the civil rights bill for which he fought so long. We have talked long enough about equal rights in this country. We have talked for one hundred years or more. It is time now to write the next chapter and to write it in the books of law. I urge you again, as I did in 1957 and again in 1960, to enact a civil rights law so that we can move forward to eliminate from this nation every trace of discrimination and oppression that is based upon race or color.

And then to the next unfinished task that Kennedy had placed high on his congressional program:

> And second, no act of ours could more fittingly continue the work of President Kennedy than the early passage of the tax bill for which he fought all this long year. . . . This is no time for delay. It is a time for action.

Finally, a strong appeal to the nation's hope and faith:

> Let us put an end to the teaching and the preaching of hate and evil and violence. Let us turn away from the fanatics of the far left and the far right, from the apostles of bitterness and bigotry, from those defiant of law and those who pour venom into our nation's bloodstream. . . . So let us here highly resolve that John Fitzgerald Kennedy did not live—or die—in vain.

Sitting with Mrs. Johnson, in the place of honor in the overflowing galleries of the House chambers, were three men: Governor Carl Sanders of Georgia, a voice of the New South; Mayor Robert Wagner of New York, a Catholic and a voice of the big-city Democrats; and Arthur Schlesinger, Jr., a voice of the third great component of the Democratic party: the liberal-intellectuals.

Who had the time and forethought to make those selections? Probably Johnson himself. It was a last minute decision. Schlesinger was telephoned from the White House with his invitation late Tuesday evening, the night before the speech. He was out but returned the call at 1:00 A.M. Clifton Carter, Johnson's long-time political agent in Texas, gave him the invitation. Schlesinger had not intended to go to the speech. As it was, he returned from Capitol Hill convinced the President had "achieved a genuine success." Johnson, thought Schlesinger, had never spoken so well before.

By the time Lyndon Johnson finished his address to Congress on November 27, he had indisputably gained the confidence not only of the nation but of the liberals who had always distrusted him. Johnson went out of his way to be pleasant to Joseph Rauh of the Americans for Democratic Action, inviting his arch-critic aboard Air Force One to attend Senator Lehman's funeral in New York.

CHAPTER NINE

THE STEEL PRICE CRISIS OF 1962

WALLACE CARROLL

TUESDAY

It was peaceful at the White House on the afternoon of Tuesday, April 10—so peaceful, that the President of the United States thought he might have time for a nap or a little relaxed reading.

Just to be sure, he called his personal secretary, Mrs. Evelyn Lincoln, and asked what the rest of the day would bring.

"You have Mr. Blough at a quarter of six," said Mrs. Lincoln.

"Mr. Blough?" exclaimed the President.

"Yes," said Mrs. Lincoln.

There must be a mistake thought the President. The steel negotiations had been wound up the previous week.

"Get me Kenny O'Donnell," he said.

But there had been no mistake, at least not on the part of Kenneth O'Donnell, the President's appointments secretary.

Whether Mr. Blough—Roger I. Blough, chairman of the board of United States Steel Corporation—had made a mistake was a different question.

For when he walked into the President's office two hours later with the news that his company had raised the price of steel, he set off seventy-two hours of activity such as he and his colleagues could not have expected.

During those seventy-two hours, four antitrust investigations of the steel industry were conceived, a bill to roll back the price increases was seriously considered, legislation to impose price and wage controls on the steel industry was discussed, agents of the Federal Bureau of Investigation questioned newspapermen by the dawn's early light, and the Defense Department—biggest buyer in the nation—began to divert purchases away from United States Steel.

Also in those seventy-two hours—and this was far more significant—the Administration maintained its right to look over the shoulders of capital and labor when they came to the bargaining table and its insistence that any agreement they reached would have to respect the national interest.

And in those seventy-two hours, new content and meaning were poured into the magnificent abstraction, "the Presidency," for the historically minded to argue about as long as men remained interested in the affairs of this republic.

A full and entirely accurate account of those seventy-two hours may never be written. The characters were many. They moved so fast that no one will be able to retrace all of what they did.

Understandably, industry participants—facing official investigation now—would not talk much. Nor were Government participants willing to tell all.

Nevertheless, a team of *New York Times* reporters undertook to piece the tale together while memories were fresh.

Here is what they learned.

Early on that afternoon of April 10, Roger Blough had met with his colleagues of United States Steel's executive committee in the board room on the twentieth floor at 71 Broadway, New York. Three of the twelve members were absent, but Leslie B. Worthington, president of the company, and Robert C. Tyson, chairman of the finance committee, were there.

For several months these men had been giving out hints, largely overlooked in Washington, that the company would have to raise prices to meet increasing costs.

The Kennedy Administration had pressed for no increase in prices last fall, and there had been no increase. It had pressed again for a modest wage contract this year, and a modest contract had been signed a few days earlier. The Administration expected no price increase now.

The company's executive committee reviewed the situation. The sales department had concurred in a recommendation to increase prices by 3½ percent—about $6 on top of the going average of $170 a ton.

Mr. Blough had taken soundings within the company on the public relations aspects. Everyone realized that the move would not win any popularity prize, but the committee voted unanimously to go ahead.

With the decision made, Mr. Blough took a plane to Washington. Word was telephoned to the White House that he wanted to see the President and had something "important" to say about steel.

A few minutes after 5:45 the President received him in his oval office, motioned him to a seat on a sofa to his right, and made himself comfortable in his rocking chair.

With little preliminary, Mr. Blough handed the President a four-page mimeographed press release that was about to be sent to newspaper offices in Pittsburgh and New York.

The President read:

"Pittsburgh, Pa., April 10—For the first time in nearly four years United States Steel today announced an increase in the general level of its steel prices."

Mr. Kennedy raced through the announcement. Then he summoned Arthur J. Goldberg, the Secretary of Labor. Minutes later Mr. Goldberg reached the President's office from the Labor Department four blocks away.

Grimly, the President gave the paper to Mr. Goldberg and said it had been distributed to the press. Mr. Goldberg skimmed over it and asked Mr. Blough what was the point of the meeting, since the price decision had been made.

Mr. Blough replied that he thought he should personally inform the President as a matter of courtesy. Mr. Goldberg retorted it was hardly a courtesy to announce a decision and confront the President with an accomplished fact.

In the half-hour discussion that followed, President Kennedy seems to have kept his temper. But Mr. Goldberg lectured Mr. Blough with some heat. The price increase, the Secretary said, would jeopardize the Government's entire economic policy. It would damage the interests of United States Steel itself. It would undercut responsible collective bargaining. Finally he said, the decision could be viewed only as a double-cross of the President because the company had given no hint of its intentions while the Administration was urging the United Steelworkers of American to moderate its wage demands.

Mr. Blough, a former high school teacher turned lawyer and company executive, defended himself and the company in a quiet voice.

When he had gone President Kennedy called for the three members of his Council of Economic Advisers. Dr. Walter W. Heller, the chairman, a lean and scholarly looking man, came running from his office across the street. Dr. Kermit Gordon followed in three minutes. James Tobin, the third member, hurried back to his office later in the evening.

Into the President's office came Theodore C. Sorenson, the White House special counsel, Mr. O'Donnell, and Andrew T. Hatcher, acting press secretary in the absence of Pierre Salinger, who was on vacation.

Now the President, who usually keeps his temper under rein, let go.

He felt he had been double-crossed—deliberately. The office of the President had been affronted. The national interest had been flouted.

Bitterly, he recalled that:

"My father always told me that all businessmen were sons-of-bitches but I never believed it till now!"

It was clear that the Administration would fight. No one knew exactly what could be done, but from that moment the awesome power of the Federal Government began to move.

To understand the massive reaction of the Kennedy Administration a word of background is necessary.

Nothing in the range of domestic economic policy had brought forth a greater effort by the Administration than the restraint it sought to impose on steel prices and wages.

Starting last May the Administration worked on the industry, publicly and privately, not to raise its prices when wages went up in the fall. And when the price line held, the Administration turned its efforts to getting an early and "noninflationary" wage contract this year.

Above all, the Administration constantly tried to impress on both sides that the national interest was riding on their decisions. A price increase or an inflationary wage settlement, it argued, would set off a new wage-price spiral that would stunt economic growth, keep unemployment high, cut into export sales, weaken the dollar and further aggravate the outflow of gold.

On Friday and Saturday, April 6 and 7, the major steel companies had signed the new contract. President Kennedy had hailed it as "noninflationary." Privately, some steel leaders agreed with him.

Thus, the President confidently expected that the companies would not increase prices. And the standard had been set, he hoped, for other industries and unions.

This was the background against which the group in the President's office went to work.

By about 8 P.M. some decisions had been reached.

President Kennedy would deliver the first counterattack at his news conference scheduled for 3:30 the following afternoon.

Messrs. Goldberg, Heller, and Sorensen would gather material for the President's statement. Other material of a statistical nature would be prepared in a longer-range effort to prove the price increase was unjustified.

While the discussion was going on, the President called his brother, Robert F. Kennedy, the Attorney General; Secretary of Defense Robert S. McNamara, and the Secretary of the Treasury, Douglas Dillon, who had just arrived in Hobe Sound, Fla., for a short vacation.

At his home on Hillbrook Lane, Senator Estes Kefauver of Tennessee, chairman of the Senate Antitrust Subcommittee, was getting ready to go out for the evening. The phone rang. It was the President. Would Senator Kefauver publicly register "dismay" at the price increase and consider an investigation?

The Senator certainly would. He promised an investigation. So did the Justice Department.

In the President's office, meanwhile, there had been some talk of what could be done to keep other steel companies from raising prices. Most of the discussion centered on the economic rebuttal of the case made by United States Steel.

Mr. Goldberg and Dr. Heller decided to pool resources. Mr. Goldberg called Hyman L. Lewis, chief of the Office of Labor Economics of the Bureau of Labor Statistics, and asked him to assemble a crew.

Mr. Lewis reached three members of the bureau—Peter Henle, special assistant to the Commissioner of Labor Statistics; Arnold E. Chase, chief of the Division of Prices and Cost of Living; and Leon Greenberg, chief of the Productivity Division.

He told them what was wanted and asked them to go to Dr. Heller's office in the old State Department Building.

Dr. Heller, who had been working on the problem in his office, hurried off after a few minutes to the German Ambassador's residence on Foxhall Road.

The Ambassador was giving a dinner, a black tie affair, in honor of Prof. Walter Hallstein, president of the European Common Market. The guests were well into the meal when Dr. Heller arrived, looking, as one of the guests remarked, like Banquo's ghost in a tuxedo.

Back at the White House the President had also changed to black tie. The members of Congress and their wives were coming to his annual reception at 9:45. Ruefully, the President recalled that the news of the Cuban disaster had arrived during his reception in 1961.

"I'll never hold another Congressional reception," he remarked.

But as he and Mrs. Kennedy received the leaders of Congress and their wives, he easily relaxed into small talk.

What did the men think, he asked, of the break with tradition by making this a black tie, instead of a white tie, affair? Republicans and Democrats unanimously favored the change. Many of the younger members of Congress, they pointed out, did not have a white tie and all that went with it.

With the party spread through three rooms, no one could tell how many times Mr. Kennedy slipped out to talk about steel. The President stayed until 12:08 A.M. Then he retired.

By that time, the White House staff, the Council of Economic Advisers, and the Departments of Labor, Justice, Defense, Commerce, and the Treasury were all at work on the counterattack.

WEDNESDAY

Midnight had struck when Walter Heller, still in black tie, returned to his office from the German Embassy. With him, also in black tie, came another dinner guest, George W. Ball, Under Secretary of State.

Dr. Heller's two colleagues in the Council of Economic Advisers, Dr. Gordon and Dr. Tobin, were already there. So were the four men from the Bureau of Labor Statistics.

At about 2:45 A.M. the four men from the Bureau of Labor Statistics left the session. Their assignment from then on was to bring up to date a fact book on steel put out by the Eisenhower Administration two years ago.

The idea was to turn it into a kind of "white paper" that would show that the price increase was unjustified.

Toward 4 o'clock Dr. Heller and Dr. Tobin went home for two or three hours' sleep. Dr. Gordon lay down on the couch in his office for a couple of hours.

As the normal working day began, President Kennedy held a breakfast meeting at the White House with Vice President Johnson; Secretary of State Dean Rusk (who played no part in the steel crisis); Secretary Goldberg; Mr. Sorensen; Myer Feldman, Mr. Sorensen's deputy; Dr. Heller and Andrew Hatcher.

The meeting lasted an hour and forty-five minutes. Mr. Goldberg and Dr. Heller reported on the night's work. Mr. Sorensen was assigned to draft the President's statement on steel for the news conference. Mr. Goldberg gave him a two-page report from the Bureau of Labor Statistics headed: "Change in Unit Employment Costs in the Steel Industry 1958 to 1961."

It said in part:

> While employment costs per hour of all wage and salaried employes in the basic iron and steel industry rose from 1958 to 1961, there was an equivalent increase in output per man-hour.
>
> As a result, employment cost per unit of steel output in 1961 was essentially the same as in 1958.

The latter sentence was quoted that afternoon in the President's statement.

During the morning the President had called Secretary Dillon in Florida and discussed with him the Treasury's work on tax write-offs that would encourage investment in more modern plant and machinery. The two decided that the course would not be altered.

The President also telephoned Secretary of Commerce Luther H.

Hodges, who was about to testify before a House Maritime subcommittee. After giving his testimony Secretary Hodges spent most of the day on the phone to businessmen around the country.

In Wall Street that morning United States Steel shares opened at 70¾, up 2¾ from the day before. But on Capitol Hill the company's stock was down.

Senator Mike Mansfield, the majority leader, called the price increase "unjustified." Speaker John W. McCormack said the company's action was "shocking," "arrogant," "irresponsible." Senator Hubert H. Humphrey, the Democratic whip, spoke of "an affront to the President."

Senator Albert Gore of Tennessee suggested a law that would empower the courts to prohibit price increases in basic industries such as steel until there had been a "cooling-off period."

Representative Emanuel Celler of Brooklyn, chairman of the House Antitrust Subcommittee, scheduled a broad investigation of the steel industry. So did Senator Kefauver.

The pressures on United States Steel were beginning to mount. But now some of the other titans of the industry began to fall in line behind Big Steel.

As the President came out of the White House shortly before noon to go to the airport where he was to welcome the Shah of Iran, he was shown a news bulletin. Bethlethem Steel, second in size only to United States Steel, had announced a price increase.

Others followed in short order—Republic, Jones and Laughlin, Youngstown, and Wheeling. And Inland, Kaiser, and Colorado Fuel & Iron said they were "studying" the situation.

When he faced the newsmen and television cameras at 3:30, President Kennedy spoke with cold fury. The price increase, he said, was a "wholly unjustifiable and irresponsible defiance of the public interest." The steel men had shown "utter contempt" for their fellow citizens.

He spoke approvingly of the proposed investigations. But what did he hope to accomplish that might still save the Administration's broad economic program?

In his conference statement the President had seemed to hold out no hope that the price increases could be rolled back. If the increases held, what imminent comfort could there be in possible antitrust decrees that would take three years to come from the courts?

Actually, the possibility of making United States Steel retract the increase had been considered early in the consultation.

Drs. Heller and Gordon, and possibly some of the other economists, had argued that the principal thrust of the Administration's effort should be to convince one or two significant producers to hold out. In a market such as steel, they said, the high-priced sellers would have to come down if the others did not go up.

This suggested a line of strategy that probably proved decisive.

As one member of the Big Twelve after another raised prices, only Armco, Inland, Kaiser, C F & I, and McLouth remained holding the line. These five hold-outs represented 14 per cent of total industry capacity, or 17 per cent of the capacity of the Big Twelve.

Everything pointed to Inland as the key to the situation.

Inland Steel Corporation, with headquarters in Chicago, is a highly efficient producer. It could make a profit at lower prices than those of some of the bigger companies. And any company that sold in the Midwest, such as United States Steel, would feel Inland's price competition.

Moreover, there was a tradition of public service at Inland. Clarence B. Randall, a former chairman of the board, had served both the Eisenhower and Kennedy Administrations. (But he played no part in this crisis.)

Joseph Leopold Block, Inland's present chairman, who was in Japan at the moment, had been a member of President Kennedy's Labor-Management Advisory Committee.

At 7:45 that Wednesday morning, Philip D. Block, Jr., vice chairman of Inland, was called to the telephone in his apartment at 1540 North Lake Shore Drive in Chicago.

"Hello, P. D.," said Edward Gudeman, Under Secretary of Commerce, a former schoolmate and friend of Mr. Block's, calling from Washington.

"What do you think of this price increase of United States Steel's?"

Mr. Block said he had been surprised.

"I didn't ask P. D. what Inland might do," said Mr. Gudeman several days later. "I didn't want them to feel that the Administration was putting them on the spot. I just wanted him to know how we felt and to ask his consideration."

Inland officials agreed to consider. They said they had not been coaxed or threatened by any of the officials who called them.

The approach, which seems to have developed rather spontaneously in many of the calls that were made to businessmen, was to ask their opinion, state the Government's viewpoint, and leave it at that.

But there also were calls with a more pointed aim—to steel users, asking them to call their steel friends and perhaps even issue public statements.

Another call to Inland was made by Henry H. Fowler, Under Secretary of the Treasury and Acting Secretary in Mr. Dillon's absence.

After Mr. Kennedy's afternoon news conference Mr. Fowler called John F. Smith, Jr., Inland's president. Like other Treasury officials who telephoned other businessmen, Mr. Fowler talked about the effect of a steel price increase on imports and exports and the further pressure it would place on the balance of payments.

A third call went to Inland that day. It was from Secretary Goldberg to Leigh B. Block, vice president for purchasing.

Both Inland and Government officials insist that there was no call from the White House or from any Government office to Joseph Block in Japan.

Though no concrete assurance was asked or volunteered in these conversations, the Administration gathered assurance that Inland would hold the line for at least another day or two.

Next came Armco, sixth largest in the nation. Walter Heller had a line into that company. So did others. Calls were made. And through these channels the Administration learned that Armco was holding off for the time being, but there would be no public announcement one way or the other.

Meanwhile, Mr. Gudeman had called a friend in the upper reaches of the Kaiser Company. Secretary McNamara had called a number of friends, one of them at Allegheny-Ludlum, a large manufacturer of stainless.

How many calls were made by President Kennedy himself cannot be told. But some time during all the activity he talked to Edgar Kaiser, chairman of Kaiser Steel, in California.

According to one official who was deeply involved in all this effort, the overall objective was to line up companies representing 18 per cent of the nation's capacity. If this could be done, according to friendly sources in the steel industry, these companies with their lower prices soon would be doing 25 per cent of the business. Then Big Steel would have to yield.

Parallel with this "divide-and-conquer" maneuver, the effort moved forward on the antitrust line.

During the morning someone had spotted in the newspapers a statement attributed to Edmund F. Martin, president of Bethlehem Steel. Speaking to reporters on Tuesday after a stockholder's meeting in Wilmington, Del., Mr. Martin was quoted as having said: "There shouldn't be any price rise. We shouldn't do anything to increase our costs if we are to survive. We have more competition both domestically and from foreign firms."

If Mr. Martin had opposed a price rise on Tuesday, before United States Steel announced its increase, and if Bethlehem raised its prices on Wednesday after that announcement, his statement might prove useful in antitrust proceedings. It could be used to support a Government argument that United States Steel, because of its bigness, exercised an undue influence over other steel producers.

At about 6 o'clock Wednesday evening, according to officials of the Justice Department, Attorney General Kennedy ordered the Federal Bureau of Investigation to find out exactly what Martin had said.

At about this same time, Paul Rand Dixon, chairman of the Federal Trade Commission, told reporters that his agency had begun an informal investigation to determine whether the steel companies had violated a consent decree of June 15, 1951.

That decree bound the industry to refrain from collusive price fixing or maintaining identical delivered prices. It provided penalties running up to $5,000 a day.

Meanwhile, more calls were going out from Washington.

The Democratic National Committee called many of the Democratic Governors and asked them to do two things:

First, to make statements supporting the President and, second, to ask steel producers in their states to hold the price line.

Among those called were David L. Lawrence of Pennsylvania, Richard J. Hughes of New Jersey, and Edmund G. Brown of California. But the National Committee said nothing in its own name. The smell of "politics" was not to be allowed to contaminate the Administration's efforts.

Another call was made by Robert V. Roosa, an Under Secretary of the Treasury, to Henry Alexander, chairman of Morgan Guaranty Trust Company in New York. Morgan is represented on United States Steel's board of directors and is widely considered one of the most powerful influences within the company.

Thus by nightfall on Wednesday—twenty-four hours after Mr. Blough's call on the President—the Administration was pressing forward on four lines of action:

First, the rallying of public opinion behind the President and against the companies.

Second, a divide-and-conquer operation within the steel industry.

Third, antitrust pressure from the Justice Department, the Federal Trade Commission, the Senate, and the House.

Fourth, the mobilization of friendly forces within the business world to put additional pressure on the companies.

That night at the White House the Kennedys gave a state dinner for the visiting Shah and his Empress.

In a toast to his guests, President Kennedy, a man seemingly without a care in the world, observed that he and the Shah shared a common "burden." Each of them had made a visit to Paris and each of them might as well have stayed at home, for the Parisians had eyes only for their wives.

When the guests had gone, the President put in a call to Tucson, Ariz. It came through at 12:15 A.M.

THURSDAY

Archibald Cox, the Solicitor General, had left by plane on Wednesday afternoon for Tucson, where he was to make two speeches to the Arizona Bar.

On arriving at his hotel that night, he received a message to call the President. When he called he was asked what suggestions did he have for rolling back steel prices?

Mr. Cox had been chairman of the Wage Stabilization Board during the Korean War and had worked with young Senator Kennedy on statements about steel prices and strikes of the past.

After the call, Mr. Cox stayed up all night, thinking and making notes, mostly about legislation. From past experience Mr. Cox had concluded that the antitrust laws could not cope with the steel problem and that special legislation would be necessary.

Mr. Cox made his two speeches, flew back to Washington, and stayed up most of that night working on the legislative draft.

But Mr. Cox was not the only one at work on the steel problem in the early hours of Thursday.

At 3 A.M. Lee Linder, a reporter in the Philadelphia bureau of the Associated Press, was awakened by a phone call. It was the F.B.I. At first Mr. Linder thought he was being fooled. Then he determined that the call was genuine. The agents asked him a question or two and then told him: "We are coming right out to see you."

Mr. Linder had been at the stockholders' meeting of Bethlehem Steel in Wilmington on Tuesday and had quoted Mr. Martin about the undesirability of a price increase. Bethlehem Steel later called the quotation incorrect.

The agents were checking on that quotation. Mr. Linder said later that he had given them the same report he had written for the Associated Press.

At 6:30 A.M. James L. Parks, Jr., of the *Wilmington Evening Journal* arrived at his office. Two F.B.I. agents were waiting for him. He had talked to Mr. Martin after the meeting, together with Mr. Linder and John Lawrence of the *Wall Street Journal*. Later in the day the Federal agents interviewed Mr. Lawrence.

This descent of the F.B.I. on the newsmen was the most criticized incident in the seventy-two frenzied hours.

Republicans, who had kept an embarrassed silence up to this point, pounced on this F.B.I. episode. Representative William E. Miller of upstate New York, chairman of the Republican National Committee, compared it to the "knock on the door" techniques of Hitler's Gestapo.

In Chicago, as the day progressed, Philip Block and two other high officials of Inland reached a decision: prices would not be raised. They called Joseph Block in Kyoto. He concurred and they agreed to call a directors' meeting to ratify their decision the next morning.

No announcement was to be made until the morning and no one in Washington was told.

Back in Washington, the President was holding an early meeting in the Cabinet Room at the White House. Present were Attorney General

Kennedy; Secretaries McNamara, Goldberg, Hodges; Under Secretary of the Treasury Fowler; Mr. Dixon, chairman of the Federal Trade Commission; Dr. Heller, and Mr. Sorensen.

Roger Blough was scheduled to hold a televised news conference in New York at 3:30 that afternoon. The White House meeting decided that the Administration should put in a speedy rebuttal to his case for United States Steel.

Secretary Hodges had long-scheduled engagements that day in Philadelphia and New York. It was decided that he would hold a news conference in New York at 5 P.M. and try to rebut Mr. Blough point by point.

Meanwhile two of the most secret initiatives of the entire seventy-two hours had been set in motion.

The first involved a newspaperman—Charles L. Bartlett, the Washington correspondent of the *Chattanooga Times*. All Mr. Bartlett would say later was: "I helped two friends get in touch with each other again."

One friend was President Kennedy—Mr. Bartlett and his wife are members of the Kennedy social set. The other friend was an officer of United States Steel. His identity has not been definitely established, but Mr. Bartlett knows Mr. Blough.

What came of this effort to reopen "diplomatic relations" is not known, although at least one Cabinet member thought it was useful. What came of the second secret initiative, however, can be reported.

At noon or earlier on Thursday President Kennedy phoned Clark Clifford, a Washington lawyer who had first come to national prominence as counsel for President Truman.

Secretary Goldberg, said the President, knew the officers of United States Steel very well and could, of course, talk to them on behalf of the Administration. But Mr. Goldberg, he went on, was known to the steel men mainly as an adversary.

For years he had been the counsel for the steel workers' union and one of their chief strategists in negotiations with the company. In view of this would Mr. Clifford, familiar as he was with the outlook of corporation executives through his law work, join Mr. Goldberg in speaking to United States Steel?

Mr. Clifford agreed, flew to New York, and met Mr. Blough. He presented himself as a friend of the disputants, but he made clear that he was in 100 per cent agreement with the President. His purpose, he said, was to see if a tragic mistake could be rectified. The mistake, he left no doubt, was on the company's side.

For fourteen months, he continued, President Kennedy and Mr. Goldberg had worked for healthy conditions in the steel industry. They had tried to create an atmosphere of cooperation in the hope of protecting the national interest. Now all this was gone.

The President, he went on, believed there had been a dozen or more occasions when the company's leaders could easily have told him that despite all he had done they might have to raise prices. But they never had told him. The President, to put it bluntly, felt doubled-crossed.

What Mr. Blough said in reply could not be learned. But he indicated at the end that he would welcome further talks and he hoped Mr. Clifford would participate in them. Mr. Clifford returned to Washington the same day.

Secretary Hodges, meanwhile, arrived at the University Club in New York at about 3:40, ten minutes after Mr. Blough had begun his news conference.

While Mr. Hodges shaved and changed his shirt, his assistant, William M. Ruder, tried to take notes on Mr. Blough's broadcast, but the static he heard sounded like the Grand Central shuttle.

The Blough news conference was held in the ground floor auditorium at 71 Broadway.

"Let me say respectfully," Mr. Blough began, "that we have no wish to add acrimony or misunderstanding."

On several occasions, he said, he had made it clear that United States Steel was in a cost-price torque that could not be tolerated forever, that a company without profits is a company that cannot modernize, and that the price increase would add "almost negligibly" to the cost of other products—$10.64 for the steel in a standard automobile, 3 cents for a toaster.

One question and answer in the fifty-eight-minute session caught the ears of people in Washington: Could United States Steel hold its new price if Armco and Inland stood pat?

"It would definitely affect us," conceded Mr. Blough. "I don't know how long we could maintain our position."

A half-hour after Mr. Blough finished, Secretary Hodges held his news conference in the Empire State Building.

But the words that probably hit Big Steel the hardest came that day from two Pennsylvania Republicans—Representatives William W. Scranton, the party's candidate for Governor, and James E. Van Zandt, the candidate for Senator.

"The increase at this time," they wired Mr. Blough, "is wrong—wrong for Pennsylvania, wrong for America, wrong for the free world. The increase surely will set off another round of inflation. It will hurt people most who can least afford to be hurt."

Meanwhile, Justice Department agents appeared at the headquarters of United States Steel, Bethlehem, Jones & Laughlin, and other companies and served subpoenas for documents bearing on the price increase and other matters.

And at 7 P.M. Attorney General Kennedy announced that the Justice Department had ordered a grand jury investigation of the increase.

By that time, President and Mrs. Kennedy were getting ready for another state dinner with the Shah and Empress—this time at the Iranian Embassy.

FRIDAY

The first big news of the day came from Kyoto, Japan. Joseph Block, Inland's chairman, had told a reporter for the *Chicago Daily News*: "We do not feel that an advance in steel prices at this time would be in the national interest."

That news heartened the Administration but it did not stop planning or operations. Nor did Inland's official announcement from Chicago at 10:08 A.M., Washington time, that it would hold the price line.

At 10:15 Solicitor General Cox met in Mr. Sorensen's office with representatives of the Treasury, Commerce, and Labor Departments, Budget Bureau, and Council of Economic Advisers.

The discussion was on emergency wage-price legislation of three broad kinds:

First, ad hoc legislation limited to the current steel situation; second, permanent legislation imposing some mechanism on wages and prices in the steel industry alone; and third, permanent legislation for steel and other basic industries, setting up "fact-finding" procedures.

At 11:45 Secretary McNamara said at his news conference that the Defense Department had ordered defense contractors to shift steel purchases to companies that had not raised prices. Later in the day the department awarded to the Lukens Steel Company, which had not raised prices, a contract for more than $5,000,000 worth of a special armor plate for Polaris-missile submarines.

At 12:15 President Kennedy and most of the Thursday group met again in the Cabinet Room. It was estimated at that time that the price line was being held on 16 per cent of the nation's steel capacity.

Inland had announced. Armco had decided to hold but not announce. Kaiser's announcement came in while the meeting was on. This might be enough to force the bigger companies down again, but the sentiment of the meeting was that the retreat would not come soon.

Accordingly, preparations continued for a long struggle. Lists of directors of the companies that were holding the line were distributed, and each man present was asked to call men he knew.

Notably absent from this meeting was Secretary Goldberg. He was on his way to New York with Mr. Clifford in a Military Air Transport plane.

A secret rendezvous had been arranged with Mr. Blough and some of the other leaders of United States Steel at the Carlyle Hotel.

At this meeting, as in Mr. Clifford's talk with Mr. Blough on the previous day, no demands or threats or promises came from the Government side.

The discussion seems to have been a general one about what lay ahead. The outlook, said Mr. Clifford, was "abysmal."

United States Steel, he contended, had failed to weigh the consequences of its action. If it held this position, its interest and those of the industry would inevitably be damaged, and the nation as a whole would suffer.

While the talk was going on, Mr. Blough was called to the phone. Then Mr. Goldberg was called. Each received the same message. Bethlehem Steel had rescinded the price increase—the news had come through at 3:20 P.M.

President Kennedy heard the news while flying to Norfolk for a weekend with the fleet. It was unexpected.

The Administration had made no special effort with Bethlehem. To this day, officials here are uncertain what did it.

Among other things, Bethlehem's officials were struck by the Inland and Kaiser announcement that morning. Inland posed direct competition to Bethlehem's sales in the Midwest—the largest steel market—and Kaiser posed it on the West Coast.

Further, special questions were raised by the Pentagon's order to defense industries to shift their steel buying to mills that did not raise prices. What did this mean for Bethlehem's vast operations as a shipbuilder?

Whatever the compelling factors were, Bethlehem's decision brought the end of the battle clearly in sight. The competitive situation was such that United States Steel's executive committee was not called into session to reverse its action of the previous Tuesday. The company's officers acted on their own.

The big capitulation came at 5:28. Mrs. Barbara Gamarekian, a secretary in the White House press office, was checking the Associated Press news ticker. And there was the announcement—United States Steel had pulled back the price increase.

Mrs. Gamarekian tore it off and ran into the office of Mr. Sorensen, who was on the phone to the acting press secretary, Mr. Hatcher, in Norfolk.

"Well" Mr. Sorensen was saying, "I guess there isn't anything new."

Mrs. Gamarekian put the next bulletin under his eye.

"Wait a minute!" shouted Mr. Sorensen.

Mr. Hatcher gave the news to the President as he came off the nuclear submarine, *Thomas A. Edison,* in Norfolk.

It was just seventy-two hours since Roger Blough had dropped in on Mr. Kennedy.

PART THREE

THE COURTS

The federal judiciary is popularly thought to be "above politics."
Congress and the president are the political branches of government;
the courts are different. Although most political scientists knew better,
they acted, until recently, as if they shared the belief that the judiciary
is immune to the pulling and hauling of private interests and ambitious
politicians. The study of the Supreme Court was limited to the study of
constitutional law. Specialists in the field analyzed the way the Court
applied general principles to the solution of individual cases; no attention was paid to how these issues were raised or how the Court reached
its decisions or, for that matter, how the justices were appointed to the
Court in the first place. Since they were the law of the land, the decisions
were obeyed by all good citizens and were permanent unless the Court
itself overturned them. There was a good deal of debate over how democratic it was to have nine (or five) justices, *appointed* for life, overruling
the will of the people as expressed by the *elected* branches of government. But, although this subject was debated endlessly, no one seemed
to know how often or for how long the will of the people had been frustrated.

Political scientists have begun to act on the realization that the
courts are part of the political process. The first article, by Sheldon Goldman, makes this point abundantly clear in describing the considerations
involved in appointing judges to the Circuit Courts of Appeals, the level
of the federal judiciary just below the Supreme Court. Goldman's research is based on an extraordinary opportunity: he was able to examine
the Justice Department's files on the appointment of all judges sitting
on the appeals courts in the early 1960s. He shows that while legal qualifications (as measured by the American Bar Association) are important,

so are the candidates' previous partisan activity, their support from key party leaders and senators, and the Justice Department's assessment of their ideological orientation. In discussing the kind of high-level patronage represented by judicial appointments, Goldman also casts some light on one type of incentive to political party activity.

The second selection is concerned with the internal politics of the Supreme Court. David J. Danelski has examined several Justices' private papers in order to analyze the inner workings of the Court. By thinking of the Court as a small group, Danelski makes profitable use of the theoretical formulations of past research on small group behavior. He describes the Chief Justice's influence and shows how the personalities and abilities of different men in this position have had an impact on the Court's work.

The final two selections deal with the relation of the Supreme Court's decisions to the other branches of government and to the people whose behavior they are supposed to control. Implicit in both of these articles is the thought that interest groups pursue their goals through litigation, just as they lobby Congress or exert pressure on the president. Indeed, this view has even been explicitly stated by the Supreme Court in a decision holding that attempts to interfere with this process are in conflict with the First Amendment:

> Groups which find themselves unable to achieve their objectives through the ballot frequently turn to the courts. Just as it was true of the opponents of New Deal legislation during the 1930's, for example, no less is it true of the Negro minority today. And under the conditions of modern government, litigation may well be the sole practicable avenue open to a minority to petition for redress of grievances.[1]

In this context Robert A. Dahl writes about judicial review of national legislation. He considers the Court one element in the political process, sometimes allied with the dominant forces in Congress and the White House, and sometimes opposed to them. He puts the old moralistic arguments about majority rule and minority rights in a new and more sensible light by spelling out what "majority rule" means and by actually looking at the cases where the Court has overruled Congress. He finds that the Court has seldom been able to balk a determined majority in the other branches of government, and rarely is at odds with them for very long.

Scholars used to assume that the story of a Supreme Court case ended with the decision. Frank J. Sorauf begins his article at this point and reports some of the events that followed a decision on religious in-

[1] NAACP v. Button, *Supreme Court Reporter*, 83, 336.

struction in public schools. His study is a specific illustration of Dahl's point that Court decisions are not final rulings, but episodes in continuing political controversies. He also shows that, far from obeying a Court decision, the interested parties often cannot even agree on what the decision means.

CHAPTER TEN

JUDICIAL APPOINTMENTS TO THE UNITED STATES COURTS OF APPEALS

SHELDON GOLDMAN

. . . This article seeks to explore the complex judicial selection process for appointments to the United States Courts of Appeals. The data utilized have been largely gathered from a systematic study of certain Justice Department files[1] for each of the eighty-four judges in active service on the appeals courts during part or all of the period between 1961 and 1964.[2] The object of this paper is to analyze the various components

This paper draws not only on the Justice Department files but also on interview data. Attorney General Nicholas deB. Katzenbach and his former assistant Joseph Dolan, former Deputy Attorney General Lawrence Walsh, and ABA Committee on Federal Judiciary chairmen Bernard G. Segal and Robert W. Meserve graciously allowed me to interview them. So did twenty-seven appeals court judges (some of whom were associated with the Justice Department) whose names must remain unlisted. In addition, various newspapers and published materials were consulted. Among the latter were WHO'S WHO IN AMERICA (1956, 1958, 1960, 1962, 1964) and SENATE COMMITTEE ON THE JUDICIARY, LEGISLATIVE HISTORY OF THE UNITED STATES CIRCUIT COURTS OF APPEALS AND THE JUDGES WHO SERVED DURING THE PERIOD 1801 THROUGH MARCH 1958 (1958).

[1]The files examined . . . [included] biographical data sheets; the report of the ABA [American Bar Association] Standing Committee on Federal Judiciary; memoranda written by the ABA committee chairman, Justice Department officials, the White House staff, or, on rare occasions, even the President; letters from important people that contain pertinent information or an assessment of the candidate; and newspaper clippings relevant to the appointment or impending appointment . . . [and] letters from senators and congressmen as well as memoranda concerning either the positions taken by the senators regarding the appointment or developments in negotiations with the senators. Also contained in this file are letters to the President from congressmen concerning the appointment.

[2]The eighty-four judges included thirty-eight Eisenhower appointees . . . ; 21 Kennedy appointees . . . ; 14 Truman appointees; 10 Roosevelt appointees; and 1 Hoover appointee.

Reprinted by permission from the WISCONSIN LAW REVIEW *(Winter 1967), pp. 186–214. Some text and footnotes have been omitted. Mr. Goldman is Associate Professor of Government at the University of Massachusetts.*

of the selection process and, in particular, to examine the role of politics and ideology in the process and thus the kind of people appointed.[3] Our attention is focused on the Eisenhower and Kennedy Administrations. The first section contains an overview of the process, the second section focuses on particular aspects of judicial selection, and the third section attempts to assess the relative importance of these selection components.

I

The judges on the United States Courts of Appeals were nominated for their positions by the President and were appointed by him after the United States Senate had given its advice and consent. Behind this simple statement lies a complex reality of customs, pressures, expectations, and constraints that operate on the participants in the appointment process. The first reality—and an obvious one to casual observers of the process—is that the President's men in the Justice Department, *i.e.* the Attorney General and especially the Deputy Attorney General and his assistants, are primarily responsible for judicial selection. Thus, our attention must focus on the Justice Department rather than the White House.

The appointment process "begins" (at least analytically) by the President's men considering various lawyers or judges for a particular vacancy. The sources of names of prospective candidates for appeals court judgeships are varied. The President occasionally will have his personal choice whom the Justice Department will then promote. But, in more cases, the Deputy, or, indeed, the Attorney General, will take the initiative and activate candidacies of those thought to be well suited for the particular vacancy. This appears to have been the case during the Eisenhower Administration when assistants to the Attorney General Stanley Barnes and Warren Burger, Solicitor General Simon Soboloff, and Chief Counsel of the Treasury Department Elbert Tuttle were appointed to appeals court positions. During the Kennedy Administration, for example, the influence of the Deputy and the Attorney General was apparent in the selection of Carl McGowan for a post on the District of Columbia Circuit.[4]

[3]For data on the socio-economic and political backgrounds of the Eisenhower and Kennedy appointees, see Goldman, *Characteristics of Eisenhower and Kennedy Appointees to the Lower Federal Courts*, 18 WESTERN POLITICAL Q. 755 (1965). Analysis of the relationship of background characteristics to judicial decisional behavior is reported in Goldman, *Voting Behavior on the United States Courts of Appeals, 1961–1964*, 60 AM. POL. SCI. REV. 374 (1966). See also Grossman, *Social Backgrounds and Judicial Decision-Making*, 79 HARV. L. REV. 1551 (1966).

[4]"McGowan probably was the personal choice of Attorney General Kennedy, perhaps on the recommendation of Deputy Attorney General Nicholas deB. Katzenbach, a former University of Chicago law professor." *Chicago Sun Times*, Aug. 17, 1962, p. 42, col. 3 (four star ed.). McGowan, also a noted law school professor in the same city, had known the deputy for many years.

Justice officials use their vast network of friends, acquaintances, and friends of friends as a source for possible appointees. This is not done out of personal favoritism but out of a desire to insure the selection of highly competent people who will reflect credit on the administration. Illustrative of the personal involvement of a high Justice official is a letter to the Attorney General from a candidate who was later appointed to the bench. The candidate had been extremely active in the preceding presidential campaign and had made the acquaintance of the Attorney General, who had also been active in the campaign. The letter began with a first name salutation and continued:

> Further in connection with our conversation of last week regarding the vacancy on the United States Court of Appeals for the —— Circuit, this is to advise that both Senators —— and —— will support me. You will be receiving letters from them within a few days, and I told them, as you suggested, to send copies to [the deputy].
>
> Enjoyed visiting with you and hope to see you again before too long.

It is hard to determine the number of appeals court judges who were initially selected and promoted by the Justice Department officials on their own or at the instigation of the President. The difficulty is that for political reasons the department prefers its suggestions to become the recommendations of the senators of the President's party from the appointee's state. However, it is probably no exaggeration to suggest that close to one out of five Eisenhower or Kennedy appeals court appointees had his nomination initiated by the Justice Department.

The next obvious source of names of potential judicial candidates is the senator or senators from the President's party representing the state for which the appointment is slated. Typically, the senator will suggest several or possibly only one candidate in a formal letter written to the Attorney General or the Deputy. Justice officials, however, know that such letters are often written only to satisfy certain constituents or to pay political debts. Only by personal conversation with the senator can the Justice officials know which candidate, if any, the senator really favors.[5]

Another source of suggestions for candidates is the political leaders in the President's party, such as veteran congressmen, state party chairmen, governors, national committeemen, and mayors of large cities. Prospective candidates are also often suggested by high-level administration men, by law school deans responding to queries from Justice officials or writing on their own initiative, by friends of Justice officials, and by

[5]Interview with Joseph Dolan, Assistant Deputy Attorney General (1961–1964), February 18, 1964.

friends of friends. Indeed, those desiring their own appointment have been known to directly inform the Justice Department of their availability. Still another source of suggestions is the judiciary; about forty percent of the Justice Department files of the Eisenhower and Kennedy appointees contained letters of recommendation from state or federal judges.

When a vacancy occurs on an appeals court due to death or retirement, the sources mentioned will readily suggest candidates to fill the vacancy. The Justice Department maintains files on some of the likely candidates. Usually the Department will consider those candidates proposed by the senators and the party organization before promoting its own candidate. Often it turns out that the varied sources will independently recommend the same individual for a particular vacancy. This is ordinarily taken as evidence of a strong candidacy.[6]

The problem for the President's men is to investigate informally and evaluate the proposed candidates in the light of certain expectations and constraints. Frequently, the Deputy and his assistants will canvass the lawyers in the Justice Department. Often Justice lawyers will independently volunteer information. These lawyers come from all sections of the country and usually have extensive professional and political contacts in their home states. It is not at all uncommon for several Justice lawyers to survey different lawyers from their home states concerning the candidates. . . .

The American Bar Association's Standing Committee on Federal Judiciary also conducts informal investigations of the major candidates being considered for both district and appeals court posts, a practice begun during the Eisenhower Administration. The committee reports the results of its investigations and its tentative ratings to the Justice Department.

When the senator(s) and party leaders from the state scheduled to receive the appointment agree on one candidate who subsequently appears qualified by the Justice Department's and the ABA's standards, that candidate's nomination is virtually certain, and confirmation by the Senate is only a matter of time. However, when Justice officials select a man from many submitted names, or have their own candidate to promote and are willing to challenge the senator(s) and state party's nominee, extensive negotiations have to be undertaken with these political leaders. Once the Justice officials have secured the necessary political clearance for the selected candidate, the FBI report is in and nothing adverse has unexpectedly been uncovered, the Attorney General makes his recommendation to the President. Shortly thereafter, the nomination is announced from the White House and sent to the Senate.

6Interview with Lawrence Walsh, Deputy Attorney General (1957–1960), May 27, 1964.

The Senate Judiciary Committee is usually briefed on impending nominations, and committee members, particularly the chairman, may indicate what trouble, if any, there will be in having the committee render its approval. The committee meets in closed sessions to discuss the nominations and to decide when to hold hearings. The committee chairman, presently Senator Eastland, has been known deliberately to delay confirmation proceedings for numerous reasons, such as the nomination of a Negro.

In all, it is not unusual for the time span between the opening of a vacancy and the administration of the judicial oath to the appointee to be approximately one year or longer. The average time it took to appoint the eighty-four appeals judges actively serving during part or all of the 1961-1964 period was seven months. The process is long and involved, yet, for appointments to the appeals courts, the Justice Department ordinarily has much leeway in determining who will finally be appointed. Therefore, it is useful to focus our attention on the expectations and constraints, some of which have been mentioned in passing, within which the President's men in the Justice Department operate.

II

A. "Qualified" Appointees

The President's men in the Justice Department strive to appoint competent people to appeals court posts. They strive because they wish to do a "good" job, *i.e.* to support these important courts, and, in general, avoid the damaging image of "playing politics" with the judiciary. The criteria for being "qualified" or "well qualified" are ambiguous and difficult to define but include being a "respected" lawyer or judge and having the professional competence and judicial temperament thought to befit an appointee to the appeals courts. Trial court experience is usually a plus mark in the evaluation of candidates. Public legal experience seems to be prominent in the backgrounds of the appointees.[7]

There are also external pressures to appoint unquestionably qualified people to appeals court posts. Newspaper editorial writers are fond of delivering sermons on the necessity of "high quality" judicial apointments. By lauding good appointments, newspapers help cultivate an image that most administrations presumably seek.

While Justice officials would like to appoint the "magnas" [exceptionally well qualified candidates] and "summas" of the legal-judicial profession, they often find that only "cums" [qualified candidates]

---

[7]About half of the Eisenhower and Kennedy appointees were either federal district judges or state judges at the time of their appointment. See Goldman, *Characteristics of Eisenhower and Kennedy Appointees to the Lower Federal Courts,* 18 WESTERN POLITICAL Q. 755, 758 (1965).

have survived the hurdles of the appointment process. The American Bar Association, through its Standing Committee on Federal Judiciary, believes it can discern the "magnas" and "summas" of the profession and has taken upon itself the task of promoting such candidates for federal court appointments. The committee has played an active role in the appointment process since the Eisenhower Administration. Lawyers and judges from the states of the leading contenders (whose names are supplied by Justice officials) are canvassed, and the candidates are given ratings. . . . From 1957 through 1960 Judge Walsh was Deputy Attorney General and was on exceptionally cordial terms with committee chairman Bernard Segal.[8] The committee and the Kennedy Administration were also on friendly terms, but members of the Justice Department, in several instances, would find that only the "Wall Street type" lawyers in the large cities were being initially contacted by the committee. "Wall Street types" are presumably different in attitudes or values from labor union or individually practicing lawyers.

. . . On those occasions when both the committee and the President's men agree that among the contenders there are many "cums" but only one "summa," other constraints on Justice officials might encourage them to bypass the "summa" and support a "cum." In such cases, the committee can help Justice officials withstand the political pressures to bypass the "summa" by exerting and rallying outside pressure in favor of the "summa." The committee, it would then seem, could define its role as that of providing countervailing power to the political pressures inherent in the appointment process that might be impelling the Justice Department towards the nomination of a "cum" instead of an acknowledged "summa."

In practice, the ABA committee works with Justice officials and often strengthens the hand of the Department in dealings with senators and other political actors. The following example, perhaps unusual in the amount and direction of the committee's activity, is illustrative. Justice officials wished to nominate a lawyer they believed highly capable ("summa" quality) but who did not have political backing from the state party leaders (the senators were of the opposition party). The committee forwarded to the Justice officials an informal report that was highly laudatory of the candidate and contained a tentative rating of "well qualified." The party officials in the candidate's home state, however, favored other candidates who were apparently less qualified. The Deputy informed the committee chairman of the developments, and the chairman indicated in a handwritten memo, "I am hopeful I can raise him [Justice's preferred candidate] to an 'exceptionally well qualified'

---

[8]Judge Walsh in a 1959 address before the House of Delegates of the ABA notes: "Your chairman [Segal] has become, next to the Attorney General himself, I think, my most intimate associate in Washington. I work with him and spend more time with him and talk longer with him than anybody else in the Department. . . .

status." The reasons for this were presented in the letter the chairman sent to a member of the committee:

> We should now encourage this type of nomination by giving him [the candidate] our highest classification. I am impressed, too, by the fact that he is under serious consideration although he has never held political office or been active in the party. Since there is going to be such a scramble for this position, I have the feeling we ought to accord the top man our top classification if he deserves it.

The chairman, after consulting with the Deputy, secured editorial support for the Justice candidate from the editor of one of the major newspapers in the candidate's home state. The editor, according to the chairman, was "most cooperative, showed a keen appreciation of the problem, demonstrated a willingness to be guided as to what should appear in the editorial. . . ." These efforts were successful, and the candidate was nominated and appointed.

It is of interest to look at the ABA ratings of the Eisenhower and Kennedy appeals court appointees (the ABA committee did not rate candidates prior to the Eisenhower Administration). . . . While the Eisenhower Administration appointed more "summas" and "magnas" than the Kennedy Administration, still approximately sixty percent of the Kennedy appointees received the high ratings. Only one appointee from each administration failed to receive committee approval—and the qualifications of these appointees had caused considerable division among lawyers and judges.[9]

Although the data are limited, the preceding analysis of the committee's role in the appointment process involving appeals judges appears to be supported by Table 1. We can assume that the Eisenhower and Kennedy appointees categorized as non-activists were likely not to have received strong political backing at the time they were candidates for appeals posts. Table 1 indicates that the non-activist group had relatively higher ABA ratings than the partisan activist group.[10] Of course, this does not suggest that an appointee's prior partisan activism in some way soiled his professional quality, but rather that the committee may

[9]Public controversies can be expected if a president nominates for a judgeship someone who has received a "Not Qualified" rating by the ABA committee. Two prominent examples of such controversies concerned the nominations of Irving Ben Cooper and Francis X. Morrissey for federal district judgeships. The Cooper controversy (Cooper was subsequently appointed) is recounted in GROSSMAN, *op. cit. supra* note 3, at 181–95 (1965). The Morrissey controversy (Morrissey withdrew his nomination) is related in ROCHE, COURTS AND RIGHTS 32 (1966).

[10]Partisan activists were those engaged in one or more of the following activities at any time prior to judicial appointment: party or campaign office; candidate for, or elected to, political office; closely associated with a political figure; active party worker. . . .

have undertaken to accord its highest ratings to the non-activists in situations where they were the "best" available for the vacancy. Whatever interpretation one may draw from the data, Table 1 suggests that non-activists are more likely than activists to receive highest ratings by the committee. This seems reasonable (assuming that the committee can pinpoint those who are actually the "summas" and "magnas"), for there would be little reason for the Justice Department to want to consider a man without political backing in preference to one *with* backing and of roughly the same "quality."

In sum, there is often great difficulty in defining not only who is qualified, but who is *best* qualified for a particular post. In the final analysis, the ABA committee provides the major external pressure on the Justice Department to appoint obviously qualified people to the federal courts. The expectations of the committee, as spokesman for the legal fraternity, as well as the desire of the President's men in the Justice Department to make "good" appointments, provide a major constraint underlying the appointment process: only those with solid professional credentials can be appointed to the United States Courts of Appeals.

B. Political Considerations: Party as a Factor

Of the 84 judges in active service during part or all of the 1961-1964 period, 79 (ninety-four percent) were affiliated with the same political party as the President who appointed them.[11] Furthermore, about 4 out of 5 appointees, during some portion of their pre-judicial careers,

Table 1   ABA Committee Ratings of Eisenhower and Kennedy Appointees to Appeals Courts Compared to Prior Partisan Activism of Appointees

	Eisenhower Appointees				Kennedy Appointees			
	Partisan Activist		Nonactivist		Partisan Activist		Nonactivist	
ABA Rating	No.	%	No.	%	No.	%	No.	%
Exceptionally Well Qualified[a]	7	21.2	6	50.0	3	17.6	1	25.0
Well Qualified	14	42.4	2	16.7	7	41.2	2	50.0
Qualified	3	9.1	—	—	6	35.3	1	25.0
Neutral or Not Qualified	1	3.1	—	—	1	5.9	—	—
Unavailable or Not Indicated	8	24.2	4	33.3	—	—	—	—
Total	33	100.0%	12	100.0%	17	100.0%	4	100.0%

[a]Included in this category is the one Eisenhower appointee rated by the ABA as "very well qualified."

[11]During the past forty years, 9 out of 10 federal court appointees were members of the appointing President's political party. See 20 CONGRESSIONAL Q. 1175 (1962).

were political activists. It is evident that party organizations expect that qualified lawyers or judges with some record of partisan activism and party affiliation be given preferential consideration for appointment. The Justice Department files, in fact, contain letters from party officials exhorting Justice officials to remember their partisans. For example, a Republican state chairman wrote as follows to the Deputy Attorney General about a vacancy on the appeals court scheduled to be filled by an appointment from his state: "We hear rumblings from our congressmen that rumors are rife about the appointment of a Democrat to this position. When we have a man of Judge [X's] competence this strikes terror in our hearts."[12]

On occasion, the President's supporters in the state from which the appointee is to be chosen will remind Justice officials of the stakes involved in ignoring their wishes. The following excerpt is from a letter written by a state leader to the Attorney General:

> If [X] is not named this would damage seriously the Kennedy forces in [the state]. [X] was openly for Kennedy before L.A. and stood strong and voted there. He is known as one of my closest friends. He is an excellent lawyer—and on the merits alone, better qualified than Judge [Y].
> The Senators will give you no trouble, but we have put this on the line in public and if [X] is not appointed it will be a mortal blow.

X was appointed.

Patronage-minded politicians often favor the elevation of a federal district judge to the appeals court because this means that two jobs are filled rather than one. But if a preference must be stated, the local party organizations apparently prefer having their say in the filling of federal district judgeships because "a good deal of patronage, some involving big fees, often develops in bankruptcy proceedings," a large part of the business of the federal district courts.[13]

While there has not been an administration in our history whose judicial appointments were equally divided between both political parties, there is still the tradition that a few appointments to the federal courts are made to persons affiliated with the opposition party. Both the Eisenhower and Kennedy administrations attempted to make such "nonpartisan" appointments to both the federal district courts and the appeals courts. The "nonpartisan" appointments occurred when there were multiple vacancies, almost all of which involved the elevation of a district judge to an appeals court vacancy. In many cases the Justice Department had to negotiate "package" arrangements with the political

---

[12]The appointment went to Judge X.
[13]N.Y. Times, March 10, 1964, p. 44, col. 1. See also JACOB, JUSTICE IN AMERICA 88 (1965).

actors in the process so that "nonpartisan" appointments could be made.[14]

C. Political Considerations: Political Clearance

If the formal system for judicial appointments only required appointment by the President, partisans acceptable to the administration would no doubt still be primarily among those chosen. That the system requires the "advice and consent" of the Senate insures that the party leaders and, particularly, the senator(s) of the President's party from the state from which the prospective appointee is to be chosen, will have a say about which partisans are chosen. The formal procedures for judicial appointments imply a negotiations process involving senators and the administration. In practice, senators have a veto power in the appointment process so that the judicial appointments, at the very least, must be "cleared" with the senator(s) of the President's party from whose state the appointee will be picked. In addition the state party organization and party leaders will, in some situations, also "clear" the prospective nominee.[15]

Political "clearance" implies a passive role that occasionally is actually played by the senators. Frequently a senator will submit a list of acceptable people to fill a vacancy. If many names are submitted by different sources, the senator will then be asked to "clear" the candidate selected by the Justice officials. Occasionally the senator may refuse to "clear" the candidate pending either some form of "package" understanding with the Justice Department involving district court positions or pending an understanding between both senators concerning the candidate to back for any district judgeship vacancies.

In some cases, shortly after a vacancy occurs, the congressional delegation and the state's political leaders will meet for the purpose of choosing one candidate to support. Such a united front is usually very persuasive when the backed candidate is clearly qualified. In such situations, of course, "clearance" is but an euphemism for a more powerful role played in the selection process. But, typically, the state's political leaders and congressional delegation cannot agree on one candidate to sup-

---

[14]This sort of "package" arrangement was typically an understanding that out of the two or more vacancies, all but one would be party appointments. An example of this occurred during the Eisenhower administration when a Republican senator sent a statement to the Justice Department in which he announced his backing of the elevation of District Judge X, a former Democratic congressman, provided that Y, a Republican lawyer, received the district court post vacated by X.

[15]This is especially the case when there are no senators of the President's party in a particular state. For example, the *New York Times* reported that Mayor Robert Wagner of New York City, the recent victor in a mayoralty primary battle, would be consulted by the Kennedy Administration on patronage appointments. The Administration, the article reported; would be "very receptive to suggestions from the Mayor on judgeships or other patronage appointments." *N.Y. Times*, Sept. 10, 1961, p. 76, col. 4.

port, and when the state party is torn by bitter personal rivalries, a situation approaching chaos can develop.[16]

Political clearance is not necessarily synonymous with active support of particular candidacies. Rather, political clearance is considered an exercise of patronage and it is important for the prestige and power of the senator and other party leaders of the President's party to be able to "clear" all appointments made to individuals from their state. That senators, and in many cases, state party leaders of the President's party expect to be able to "clear"—and conversely veto—prospective appointees, provides a major constraint upon the President's men at Justice.[17]

D. State Representation

Party leaders expect that their state will be represented on their federal court of appeals by a citizen of their state. Consider, for example, the following excerpt from a national committeeman's letter to the Deputy Attorney General: "I feel that because of our very rapid growth, industrial development, importance in mining, etc. [name of state] is entitled to, and should have, a representative on the Court who is fully familiar and conversant with the problems, development, and growth of this state."

More typical is the case in which the state's only member on the appeals court dies or retires, and the senator(s) of the President's party respond with a claim for their state phrased similarly to this one: "I assume that the position made vacant by Judge [X]'s retirement will be filled by a [name of state] appointment. . . . I might also say that I have received indications from many of the [state] lawyers who are anxious that [the state] continues to be represented on the second circuit court of appeals."[18]

16This occurred, for example, when Judge J. Earl Major retired from the Seventh Circuit Court of Appeals on March 23, 1956. The vacancy was slated for Indiana, and a bitter and lengthy fight among the Republican factions in that state over the appointment resulted in the vacancy existing for well over a year. For some of the juiciest, although undoubtedly exaggerated details, see *Chicago Tribune*, March 16, 1956, § 1, p. 23, col. 2; *id.*, March 15, 1957, § 1, p. 17, col. 1.

17Failure to clear appointments with state party leaders can result at the very least in ill will. Failure to clear a nomination with the senator(s) is ordinarily fatal to a nomination and can result in (1) indefinite delay of the nomination within the Senate Judiciary Committee; (2) reprisals by the senator against the President's program; or (3) ultimately, perhaps, a public battle in the Senate over the nomination. For this reason, of the eighty-four appeals court appointees studied, every one from a state with one or two senators of the President's party was "cleared" by the senators concerned.

18Judges have also expressed the usefulness of the state representation concept on the appeals courts. For example, a chief judge from one circuit wrote to the Justice Department and urged the appointment of a candidate who was from a state that lacked representation on the circuit. The judge argued: "The court's prestige and effectiveness . . . would be enhanced if a judge of the court came from each of [the] states [encompassed by the Circuit]."

Occasionally, when there is only one vacancy and two states lack "representation" on the appeals court, an understanding is reached concerning which state should be recognized. Note the remarks of Judge Walter Pope recorded at a press conference upon his appointment to the Court of Appeals for the Ninth Circuit. "I seem to be the accidental beneficiary of a circumstance," Judge Pope observed. "Only two states were not represented on the Ninth Circuit's eight man board—Oregon and Montana. It seemed to be Montana's turn so I got it."[19] When the senators involved in such a situation are from the President's party, there is typically an understanding that the state receiving the appointment will support the "deprived" state's claim when the next vacancy occurs. However, with the Judgeships Acts of 1961[20] and 1966[21] there are enough seats on all but the First Circuit for every state to be represented. . . .

When the senators are not of the President's party, their state's claim can be ignored by the Justice Department. However, this can bring unforeseen and unwanted consequences, as was demonstrated by the Eisenhower Administration's appointment of Simon Sobeloff of Maryland to the Fourth Circuit Court of Appeals. South Carolina had been in line for that appointment. The Democratic controlled Senate Judiciary Committee obliged the Democratic senators from South Carolina by delaying confirmation proceedings for close to one year. The nomination was finally forced out of committee and onto the floor, where it was approved, although not without a bitter fight. Apparently the Eisenhower Administration got the point, for the next vacancy on the Fourth Circuit was filled by a South Carolinian.

The custom of state representation on the appeals courts, then, places a constraint upon the President's men in their efforts to find a suitable candidate for nomination. The efficacy of this custom is underscored by the fact that close to seventy percent of the judges in active service during 1961-1964 (filling other than newly created seats) came from the same states as the judges they replaced.

E. Pressures from Contenders

The prospective nominees themselves are a source of pressure on Justice officials. Most typically, they urge their senators, their friends, and their friends' friends to write letters of recommendation to the Justice Department. Frequently, when urged by the candidates, local bar associations will issue endorsements or circulate petitions supporting candidates for judicial office. The candidates expect that such activity will encourage the Justice Department to consider them seriously.

Anthony Lewis, in a front page *New York Times* article of March

[19]*San Francisco Chronicle*, March 14, 1949, p. 2, col. 1 (early ed.).

[20]28 U.S.C. § 44 (1964).

[21]Pub. L. No. 372, 89th Cong., 2d sess. (March 18, 1966).

24, 1958, described the activities of Judge Kaufman when he was actively campaigning for a position on the Court of Appeals for the Second Circuit. The story centered around the "fact" that Judge Kaufman, then a distinguished district court judge, was slated for appointment to a vacancy on the Second Circuit. Lewis observed that Judge Kaufman had many friends in Congress who were backing him for the vacancy, including Senators Styles Bridges (New Hampshire) and Estes Kefauver (Tennessee) and Representative Emanuel Celler (New York), chairman of the House Judiciary Committee. The previous year Judge Kaufman had aspired to the vacancy created by the death of Judge Jerome Frank, but the Eisenhower Administration had appointed Judge Moore. "Judge Kaufman, who had made no secret in legal circles of his desire for promotion, was disappointed. His congressional supporters were sufficiently annoyed to hold up the confirmation of Judge Moore for the rest of the session." Lewis concluded his article by observing: "Among lawyers here Judge Kaufman is regarded as ambitious, hard-working and exceptionally able as a trial judge. The one criticism heard has been that he has taken too active a part in seeking the promotion to the Second Circuit."[22] One year after the above appeared, the Eisenhower Administration nominated a brilliant lawyer and Republican, Henry J. Friendly, to the vacancy. Judge Kaufman, a Democrat, and noted jurist, was elevated two years later by the Kennedy Administration.

In general, when judicial candidates themselves initiate their candidacies by encouraging a barrage of recommendations from lawyers, political activists, and judges to the Justice Department, the resulting pressures provide another constraint on the Justice officials. This constraint may result in prolonging the appointment process. An avalanche of recommendations for one serious contender cannot be tactfully answered by the immediate appointment of another serious contender. The Justice Department officials may feel it important for each serious contender to make his move and articulate his backing so that they can then better grasp the politics involved as well as assess the qualifications of the candidates.

F. Quasi-Ideology[23] and Policy Orientation
In general, Justice officials from both administrations stood ready to reject "extremists," but "extremism" was somewhat differently defined by the two administrations. The Kennedy Administration, a Justice of-

22Lewis, *Kaufman Slated for Higher Bench*, N.Y. Times, March 24, 1958, p. 1, col. 4, and p. 16, cols. 3–5.

23The term "quasi-ideology" refers to American "liberalism" and "conservatism." To consider American "liberalism" and "conservatism" as distinct ideologies is to plunge into controversy. By using the term "quasi-ideology" we acknowledge the probable existence of differently structured "liberal" and "conservative" value hierarchies without assuming an intellectual rigor or doctrinaire pervasiveness to them. . . .

ficial revealed, would not consider a Democrat who was a "Goldwater Conservative" type. Although candidates during the Kennedy Administration, according to one official, were not given "a saliva test for their liberalism," judicial philosophy was an important consideration in the evaluation of candidates, especially for candidates on the "leading" circuits. A close observer of the Kennedy Administration noted that the President's men wanted to appoint Democrats with the "liberal" point of view of the administration but in many cases were not able to do so—or else made some bad guesses.

The Justice Department files yield some evidence that quasi-ideology was an articulated consideration for a few appointments made by the Kennedy Administration. For example, the following was written to Attorney General Robert Kennedy by a federal district judge concerning a particular candidate (subsequently appointed) : "He is our kind of Democrat. . . . I am well acquainted with his views for we have had many occasions upon which to exchange them."

The quasi-ideological assessment of candidates is, of course, a tricky business, and such assessments are usually made under the general standard of "our kind" of Democrat (or Republican). There was one appointment made by the Kennedy Administration for which quasi-ideology was the decisive consideration. The Democratic senators and the Justice officials had narrowed the list of candidates to two, and the senators (friends of both candidates) decided to leave the final selection to the President's men. A Washington, D.C., attorney, himself once a member of the Justice Department, wrote a letter to the Attorney General that undoubtedly crystallized the alternatives faced by the President's men. The letter began by noting that the choice of candidates involved two: "X" and "Y."

Both of these men would make competent judges and are quite superior to the present composition of the—Circuit bench, which is not saying much. . . .

Assuming that I exaggerate and that these men are actually comparable in competence and judicial temperament, there are I think the intangibles which weigh more heavily in favor of [X] than [Y]. I must tread softly here for, by definition, intangibles are hard to weigh. Nonetheless, I submit the trend as toward [X] and against [Y]:

First, not only is the—Circuit a weak bench, it is a conservative bench quite out of step with the premises of the New Frontier as almost all of us understand those premises. In the great run of cases it does not matter whether a judge is liberal or conservative if he is a good judge. There are a handful of cases, however,—and, Heaven knows, they always seem to be the important ones!—where the judicial mind can go either way, with probity, with honor, self-discipline and even with precedent. This is where the "liberal" cast of mind (we all know it, few of us can define it) can move this nation forward, just as the conservative mind can and does hold it back. This is intangible truth, but every lawyer knows it as reality! [X] would go forward, [Y] would hold back.

Second, the political point of view of a candidate deserves weight when other things are equal, or almost equal. . . . I know of [X's] devotion to the Democratic Party . . . I personally know that over the years he has contributed vast amounts of time and money to good Democrats. On this point, both of his Senators will strongly attest. . . .

[Y] is entitled, as aren't we all, to his convictions and if his convictions in the 1950's happened to be Eisenhower that was not only his privilege, it was his duty. But I also think privilege and duty carry with them the consequences of their acts. I do not think it is unduly partisan of me if I feel a good man cannot and should not live in both worlds.

The President's men chose "X."

In general, however, the Kennedy Administration probably did not use a "liberalism" checklist as part of the selection process. Indeed, the President's men would probably have scorned any suggestion that only the most ideological "liberal" should be chosen. However, there is an indication that the President's men were alert to the candidacies of those harboring a "conservative" orientation. In practice, those appointed by the Kennedy Administration were likely to be categorized as "liberal" in newspaper articles, while the Eisenhower appointees were more likely to be labeled "conservative."

It seems evident from an inspection of the files of the Eisenhower appointees that President Eisenhower's men in the Justice Department proceeded cautiously when considering candidates with a "liberal" orientation, although again it should be emphasized that the Justice officials were not interested in using a candidate's "conservatism" as a criterion. However, just as with the Kennedy Administration, friends of the administration would write letters recommending certain candidates and espouse quasi-ideological reasons for so doing. For example, one letter on behalf of a candidate contained the following: "His [the candidate's] great belief in the democratic form of Government and its protection through the courts is something that is greatly needed in our judicial system today after twenty years of neglect." Or note the following from a former senator:

> [X] is conservative in politics and one who would not have radical social theories that would influence his interpretations of the Constitution. . . . I sincerely believe that the administration wants to appoint to all of our courts young men of good quality who will hold the fort against New Dealism as it develops in the future.

In a few cases, apparently, the President's men made special efforts to discover the orientation of particular candidates. In one case, for example, this was done by an appeals judge who, at the request of the Attorney General, made some discreet inquiries and reported that the candidate's views "are not those of [Y, a quasi-ideological liberal] and are quite different." . . .

The Eisenhower Administration was considering elevating a federal district judge, and the Deputy Attorney General instructed one of his assistants to report on the judge's record, presumably because the informal investigation had yielded the allegation that the judge was "anti-government" in litigation handled by the Justice Department. The memo presented an analysis of the judge's decisions and concluded:

> His decisions uniformly manifest respect for legal precedent, appreciation of the problems of law enforcement and awareness of the rights of an accused. There is nothing in his decisions that would indicate an anti-prosecution bias; where concern for the rights of individuals is shown, it is more than justified by the evidence he adduces in support of his decisions. The five opinions which resulted in the dismissal of criminal charges all seem well grounded and do not indicate a predilection against the enforcement of any particular statute or class of statutes. . . . Nor do Judge [X's] dispositions of petitions for habeas corpus from accused or convicted criminals support a conclusion that he is reticent to enforce the criminal law. . . .
>
> Lastly, it should be noted that Judge [X] most decidedly has not shown any anti-government bias in civil cases involving the government.

Another Justice lawyer reported to the Deputy as follows:

> The *New York Times Index* from 1933 to date reveals no statements or actions by Judge [X] which indicate disfavor of the federal government or any enforcement agency thereof. A search of the Index of Legal Periodicals, the Journal of the American Bar Association and Vital Speeches from 1933 to date revealed nothing written or spoken by Judge [X]. . . .

The Justice Department is, in effect, the federal government's law firm and is involved in litigation on behalf of the Government that accounts for a substantial number of all cases on the dockets of the federal courts. A large portion of these cases are criminal cases. As an organization concerned with its prestige and public image, the Justice Department does not like to lose cases. During the Roosevelt Administration, "liberalism" was in large part synonymous with supporting the federal government; thus quasi-ideolgical considerations coincided with the Department's organizational needs. But after the Second World War, and in no small measure due to the shift in focus of the Supreme Court itself, "liberalism" and support of the federal government diverged in the broad area of civil liberties, which subsumes the criminal law area. The above example drawn from the Eisenhower Administration suggests that a "conservative" oriented administration could find its "right of center" quasi-ideology compatible with the organizational needs of the Justice Department. But what happens to a "liberal" oriented administration, such as Kennedy's?

It appears from an investigation of the Justice files that the Kennedy Administration did not specifically examine particular judges' decisions, although undoubtedly the Department generally was familiar with the records of the federal district judges being considered for elevation, if only through the informal investigation. However, there was perhaps some pull between the Department's organizational needs and the preference of the President's men for those with a "liberal" orientation. This was articulated in an interview with a Justice official who expressed dismay with some of the criminal decisions of a particular circuit, although he insisted, "I'm not in favor of 'hanging judges.' " The next appointment to that circuit, he noted, "will be a lawyer or a judge who is a careful liberal, a good technician."

The specific policy area that occupied most, if not all, of the attention of the Kennedy people in the Justice Department was that of segregation. The Kennedy Administration appointed six men to appeals courts who were citizens of southern states. In every case, the administration sought to discover the candidate's views on racial segregation. A Justice official emphasized that it was determined policy of the Department not to appoint a racist to the Fourth or Fifth Circuits. Concern with the candidates' views on this policy area was in evidence in the southern candidates' files. Consider, for example, this memo to the Attorney General in reference to a candidate: "The contact says that he has no doubt whatever that [X] will be all right on civil rights questions." The Justice official noted in his memo that he had met with the candidate who "volunteered that he has no feelings of racial bias or prejudice whatever, and that if appointed he would apply the law in the civil rights field as laid down by the Supreme Court without any hesitation, and would feel quite comfortable about it." . . .

III

Any assessment of the relative importance of the components of the appointment process—particularly the six expectations and constraints discussed in this article—must be tentative and imprecise. . . .

Two types of appointment situations seem to be typical: (1) where one or both senators of the state from which the appointee will be selected belong to the President's party; and (2) where both senators belong to the opposition party. In the first situation, senatorial clearance is of overriding importance, and senators generally narrow the range of candidates to be considered. In the second situation, clearance with important congressmen or party leaders is considered "good politics," but unless there is a united front of the state party leaders and congressmen, Justice officials can select their own candidate and can ordinarily secure "clearance" for that candidate.

In both types of appointment situations (and especially the second type) the Justice officials can choose among several qualified candidates. Other considerations then come into play: Is the candidate "our kind" as evidenced by past partisan activism or quasi-ideological outlook? Who (party organizations, politicians, bar groups, newspapers) will be happy or unhappy with a particular apointment? If the elevation of a district judge is involved, is the elevation part of a "package" that must be worked out with local party leaders or senators? Could a particular circuit bench be strengthened by a certain kind of appointment (such as a legal scholar or a lawyer with extensive trial experience)? Which of these considerations will carry more weight than the others depends entirely upon specific circumstances. In general, though (and with some exceptions), political considerations have taken precedence over quasi-ideological considerations, and "our kind" considerations have been more important than the appointment of brilliant legal scholars or ABA designed "summas." No doubt Justice officials are delighted to appoint brilliant or "summa" type lawyers or judges who have strong political backing and are "our kind." But the process tends to produce the appointment of qualified people who best satisfy the particular political requirements of the specific situation.

Generally, then, the judges on the appeals courts were appointed largely due to fortuitous circumstances; they were in the right place at the right time. Many had the right contacts, or friends with contacts, who could influence Justice officials to consider seriously their candidacies. Some received their appointments though a process of elimination. In general, the appointment process can be characterized as a highly complex negotiations process consisting of several components. Those selected for appointment have tended to be political activists reflecting (to some extent) the values and outlook of the appointing administration. This undoubtedly has far-reaching consequences for judicial decisional behavior and for the development of law in the United States.

CHAPTER ELEVEN

THE INFLUENCE OF THE CHIEF JUSTICE IN THE DECISIONAL PROCESS

DAVID J. DANELSKI

The Chief Justice of the United States has a unique opportunity for leadership in the Supreme Court. He presides in open court and over the secret conferences where he usually presents each case to his associates, giving his opinion first and voting last. He assigns the Court's opinion in virtually all cases when he votes with the majority; and when the Court is divided, he is in a favorable position to seek unity. But his office does not guarantee leadership. His actual influence depends upon his esteem, ability, and personality and how he performs his various roles.

IN CONFERENCE

The conference is the matrix of leadership in the Court.[1] The Court member who is able to present his views with force and clarity and defend them successfully is highly esteemed by his associates. When perplexing questions arise, they turn to him for guidance. He usually makes more suggestions than his colleagues, gives more opinions, and orients the discussion more frequently, emerging as the Court's task leader. In

[1]This study is based largely on private papers of members of the Supreme Court from 1921 to 1946. The theory of conference leadership is derived primarily from the work of Robert F. Bales. See his "Task Roles and Social Roles in Problem-Solving Groups" in Eleanor Maccoby *et al.*, *Readings in Social Psychology* (New York: Holt, Rinehart & Winston, Inc., 1958), pp. 437–47.

Reprinted by permission of the publisher and with revisions by the author from Walter F. Murphy and C. Herman Pritchett, eds., COURTS, JUDGES, AND POLITICS: AN INTRODUCTION TO THE JUDICIAL PROCESS *(New York: Random House, Inc., 1961), 497–508. Copyright © 1961 by Random House, Inc. Mr. Danelski is Associate Professor of Political Science at Yale University.*

terms of personality, he is apt to be somewhat reserved; and, in concentrating on the decision of the Court, his response to the emotional needs of his associates is apt to be secondary.

Court members frequently disagree in conference and argue their positions with enthusiasm, seeking to persuade their opponents and the undecided brethren. And always, when the discussion ends, the vote declares the victor. All of this gives rise to antagonism and tension, which, if allowed to get out of hand, would make intelligent, orderly decision of cases virtually impossible. However, the negative aspects of conference interaction are more or less counterbalanced by activity which relieves tension, shows solidarity, and makes for agreement. One Court member usually performs more such activity than the others. He invites opinions and suggestions. He attends to the emotional needs of his associates by affirming their value as individuals and as Court members, especially when their views are rejected by the majority. Ordinarily he is the best-liked member of the Court and emerges as its social leader. While the task leader concentrates on the Court's decision, the social leader concentrates on keeping the Court socially cohesive. In terms of personality, he is apt to be warm, receptive, and responsive. Being liked by his associates is ordinarily quite important to him; he is also apt to dislike conflict.

As presiding officer of the conference, the Chief Justice is in a favorable position to assert task and social leadership. His presentation of cases is an important task function. His control of the conference's process makes it easy for him to invite suggestions and opinions, seek compromises, and cut off debate which appears to be getting out of hand, all important social functions.

It is thus possible for the Chief Justice to emerge as both task and social leader of the conference. This, however, requires the possession of a rare combination of qualities plus adroit use of them. Normally, one would expect the functions of task and social leadership to be performed by at least two Court members, one of whom might or might not be the Chief Justice. As far as the Chief Justice is concerned, the following leadership situations are possible:

	Task Leadership	*Social Leadership*
I	+	+
II	−	+
III	+	−
IV	−	−

In situation I, the Chief Justice is a "great man" leader, performing both leadership functions. The consequences of such leadership, stated as hypotheses, are: (1) conflict tends to be minimal; (2) social cohesion tends to increase; (3) satisfaction with the conference tends to increase; (4) production, in terms of number of decisions for the time spent, tends to increase; and (5) expression of dissent tends to be minimal. The consequences in situations II and III are the same as in I, particularly if the Chief Justice works in coalition with the associate justice performing complementary leadership functions. However, in situation IV, unless the task and social functions are adequately performed by associate justices, consequences opposite to those in situations I, II, and III tend to occur.

Situation II prevailed in the Taft Court (1921–1930): Chief Justice Taft was social leader, and his good friend and appointee, Justice Van Devanter, was task leader. Evidence of Van Devanter's esteem and task leadership is abundant. Taft, for example, frequently asserted that Van Devanter was the ablest member of the Court. If the Court were to vote, he said, that would be its judgment too. The Chief Justice admitted that he did not know how he could get along without Van Devanter in conference, for Van Devanter kept the Court consistent with itself, and "his power of statement and his immense memory make him an antagonist in conference who generally wins against all opposition." At times, Van Devanter's ability actually embarrassed the Chief Justice, and he wondered if it might not be better to have Van Devanter run the conference himself. "Still," said Taft, "I must worry along until the end of my ten years, content to aid in the deliberation when there is a difference of opinion." In other words, Taft was content to perform the social functions of leadership. And he did this well. His humor soothed over the rough spots in conference. "We are very happy with the present Chief," said Holmes in 1922. "He is good-humored, laughs readily, not quite rapid enough, but keeps things moving pleasantly."

Situation I prevailed in the Hughes Court (1930–1941) : task and social leadership were combined in Chief Justice Hughes. He was the most esteemed member of his Court. This was due primarily to his performance in conference. Blessed with a photographic memory, he would summarize comprehensively and accurately the facts and issues in each case he presented. When he finished, he would look up and say with a smile: "Now I will state where I come out." Then he would outline his views as to how the case should be decided. Sometimes that is all the discussion a case received, and the justices proceeded to vote for the disposition suggested by the Chief. Where there was discussion, the other Court members gave their views in order of seniority without interruption, stating why they concurred or dissented from the views of the Chief Justice. After they had their say, Hughes would review the discussion, pointing out his agreement and disagreement with the views expressed. Then he would call for a vote.

As to the social side of Hughes's leadership, there is the testimony of Justice Roberts: never in the eleven years Roberts sat with Hughes in conference did he see him lose his temper. Never did he hear him pass a personal remark or even raise his voice. Never did he witness him interrupting or engaging in controversy with an associate. Despite Hughes's popular image of austerity, several of his associates have said that he had a keen sense of humor which aided in keeping differences in conference from becoming discord. Moreover, when discussion showed signs of deteriorating into wrangling, Hughes would cut it off. On the whole, he was well-liked. Justice Roberts said: "Men whose views were as sharply opposed as those of Van Devanter and Brandeis, or those of Sutherland and Cardozo, were at one in their admiration and affectionate regard for their presiding officer." Roberts could have well added Justices Holmes, Black, Reed, Frankfurter, Douglas, McReynolds, and perhaps others.

Situation IV prevailed during most of Stone's Chief Justiceship (1941–1946). When Stone was promoted to the center chair, Augustus Hand indicated in a letter to Hughes that Stone did not seem a sure bet as task leader because of "a certain inability to express himself orally and maintain a position in a discussion." Hand proved to be correct. Stone departed from the conference role cut out by Hughes. When he presented cases, he lacked the apparent certitude of his predecessor; and, at times, his statement indicated that he was still groping for a solution. In that posture, cases were passed on to his associates for discussion. Court members spoke out of turn, and Stone did little to control their debate. Instead, according to Justice Reed, he would join in the debate with alacrity, "delighted to take on all comers around the conference table." "Jackson," he would say, "that's damned nonsense." "Douglas, *you* know better than that."

In other words, Stone was still acting like an associate justice. Since he did not assume the Chief Justice's conference role as performed by Hughes, task leadership began to slip from his grasp. Eventually, Justice Black emerged as the leading contender for task leadership. Stone esteemed Black, but distrusted his unorthodox approach; thus no coalition occurred as in the Taft Court. Justices Douglas, Murphy, Rutledge, and, to a lesser degree, Reed acknowledged Black's leadership which he was able to reinforce by generally speaking before them in conference. Justices Roberts, Frankfurter, and Jackson, however, either looked to Stone for leadership or competed for it themselves.

The constant vying for task leadership in the Stone conference led to serious conflict, ruffled tempers, severe tension, and antagonism. A social leader was badly needed. Stone was well-liked by his associates and could have performed this function well, but he did not. He did not use his control over the conference process to cut off debates leading to irreconcilable conflict. He did not remain neutral when controversies arose so that he could later mediate them. As his biographer, Alpheus T. Mason, wrote: "He was totally unprepared to cope with the petty bickering and personal conflict in which his Court became engulfed." At times, when conference discussion became extremely heated, Justice Murphy suggested that further consideration of certain cases be postponed. Undoubtedly others also performed social functions of leadership, but in this regard, Stone was a failure.

A consideration of the personalities of the task and social leaders on the Court from 1921 to 1946 is revealing. Of his friend, task leader Van Devanter, William D. Mitchell said: "Many thought him unusually austere, but he was not so with his friends. He was dignified and reserved." Of task leader Black, his former law clerk, John P. Frank, wrote: "Black has firm personal dignity and reserve. . . . [He] is a very, very tough man. When he is convinced, he is cool hard steel. . . . His temper is usually in close control, but he fights, and his words may occasionally have a terrible edge. He can be a rough man in an argument." On the other hand, social leader Taft was a warm, genial, responsive person who disliked conflict of any kind. Stone had a similar personality. He, too, according to Justice Jackson, "dreaded conflict." Hughes's personality contained elements conducive to both task and social leadership. He was "an intense man," said Justice Roberts; when he was engrossed in the work of the Court, "he had not time for lightness and pleasantry." Nonetheless, added Roberts, Hughes's relations with "his brethren were genial and cordial. He was considerate, sympathetic, and responsive."

The consequences of the various Court leadership configurations from 1921 to 1946 may be summarized as follows:

	Taft (II)	Hughes (I)	Stone (IV)
Conflict	Present but friendly	Present but bridled by CJ	Considerable; unbridled and at times unfriendly
Cohesion	Good; teamwork and compromise	Fair; surface personal cordiality; less teamwork than in Taft Court	Poor; least cohesion in 25-year period; personal feuds in the Court
Satisfaction	Considerable	Mixed; Stone dissatisfied prior to 1938; Frankfurter, Roberts, and others highly satisfied	Least in 25-year period; unrelieved tension and antagonism
Production	Fair; usually one four- to five-hour conference a week with some items carried over	Good; usually one conference a week	Poor; frequently more than one conference a week; sometimes three and even four
Dissent	Low; .27 recorded dissenting votes per decision	Fairly low; .58 recorded dissenting votes per decision	High; 1.23 recorded dissenting votes per decision

Except in production, the Taft Court fared better than the Courts under his two successors. The consequences of leadership in the Stone Court were predictable from the hypotheses, but Hughes's "great man" leadership should have produced consequences more closely approximating those in the Taft Court. The difference in conflict, cohesion, satisfaction, and expression of dissent in the two Courts can be perhaps attributed to the fact that Taft was a more effective social leader than Hughes.

OPINION ASSIGNMENT

The Chief Justice's power to assign opinions is significant because his designation of the Court's spokesman may be instrumental in:

(1) Determining the value of a decision as a precedent, for the grounds of a decision frequently depend upon the justice assigned the opinion.
(2) Making a decision as acceptable as possible to the public.
(3) Holding the Chief Justice's majority together when the conference vote is close.
(4) Persuading dissenting associates to join in the Court's opinion.

The Chief Justice has maximal control over an opinion when he assigns it to himself; undoubtedly Chief Justices have retained many important cases for that reason. The Chief Justice's retention of "big cases" is generally accepted by his associates. In fact, they expect him to speak for the Court in those cases so that he may lend the prestige of his office to the Court's pronouncement.

When the Chief Justice does not speak for the Court, his influence lies primarily in his assignment of important cases to associates who generally agree with him. From 1925 to 1930, Taft designated his fellow conservatives, Sutherland and Butler, to speak for the Court in about half of the important constitutional cases[2] assigned to associate justices. From 1932 to 1937, Hughes, who agreed more with Roberts, Van Devanter, and Sutherland than the rest of his associates during this period, assigned 44 per cent of the important constitutional cases to Roberts and Sutherland. From 1943 to 1945, Stone assigned 55.5 per cent of those cases to Douglas and Frankfurter. During that period, only Reed agreed more with Stone than Frankfurter, but Douglas agreed with Stone less than any other justice except Black. Stone had high regard for Douglas' ability, and this may have been the Chief Justice's overriding consideration in making these assignments.

It is possible that the Chief Justice might seek to influence dis-

---

[2]"Important constitutional cases" were determined by examination of four recent leading works on the Constitution. If a case was discussed in any two of the works, it was considered an "important constitutional case."

senting justices to join in the Court's opinion by adhering to one or both of the following assignment rules:

> *Rule 1*: Assign the case to the justice whose views are the closest to the dissenters on the ground that his opinion would take a middle approach upon which both majority and minority could agree.
>
> *Rule 2*: Where there are blocs on the Court and a bloc splits, assign the opinion to a majority member of the dissenters' bloc on the grounds that (a) he would take a middle approach upon which both majority and minority could agree and (b) the minority justices would be more likely to agree with him because of general mutuality of agreement.

There is some evidence that early in Taft's Chief Justiceship he followed Rule 1 occasionally and assigned himself cases in an effort to win over dissenters. An analysis of his assignments from 1925 to 1930, however, indicates that he apparently did not adhere to either of the rules with any consistency. The same is true for Stone's assignments from 1943 to 1945. In other words, Taft and Stone did not generally use their assignment power to influence their associates to unanimity. However, an analysis of Hughes's assignments from 1932 to 1937 indicates that he probably did. He appears to have followed Rule 1 when either the liberal or conservative blocs dissented intact. When the liberal bloc dissented, Roberts, who was then a center judge, was assigned 46 per cent of the opinions. The remaining 54 per cent were divided among the conservatives, apparently according to their degree of conservatism: Sutherland, 25 per cent; Butler, 18 per cent; McReynolds, 11 per cent. When the conservative bloc dissented, Hughes divided 63 per cent of those cases between himself and Roberts.

Hughes probably also followed Rule 2. When the left bloc split, Brandeis was assigned 22 per cent of the cases he could have received compared with his 10 per cent average for unanimous cases. When the right bloc split, Sutherland was assigned 16 per cent of the decisions he could have received compared with his 11 per cent average for unanimous cases. He received five of the six cases assigned the conservatives when their bloc split.

Of course, there are other considerations underlying opinion assignment by the Chief Justice, such as equality of distribution, ability, and expertise. It should be noted that opinion assignment may also be a function of social leadership.

UNITING THE COURT

One of the Chief Justice's most important roles is that of Court unifier. Seldom has a Chief Justice had a more definite conception of that role than Taft. His aim was unanimity, but he was willing to admit that at times dissents were justifiable and perhaps even a duty. Dissents were proper, he thought, in cases where a Court member strongly believed the majority erred in a matter involving important principle or where a dissent might serve some useful purpose, such as convincing Congress to pass certain legislation. But, in other cases, he believed a justice should be a good member of the team, silently acquiesce in the views of the majority, and not try to make a record for himself by dissenting.

Since Taft's conception of the function of the dissent was shared by most of his associates, his efforts toward unity were well received. Justices joining the Taft Court were indoctrinated in the no-dissent-unless-absolutely-necessary tradition, most of them learning it well. Justice Butler gave it classic expression on the back of one colleague's opinions in 1928:

> I voted to reverse. While this sustains your conclusion to affirm, I still think reversal would be better. But I shall in silence acquiesce. Dissents seldom aid in the right development or statement of the law. They often do harm. For myself I say: "lead us not into temptation."

Hughes easily assumed the role of Court unifier which Taft cut out for him, for his views as to unanimity and dissent were essentially the same as Taft's. Believing that some cases were not worthy of dissent, he would join in the majority's disposition of them, though he initially voted the other way. For example, in a 1939 case involving statutory construction, he wrote to an associate: "I choke a little at swallowing your analysis, still I do not think it would serve any useful purpose to expose my views."

Like Taft, Hughes mediated differences of opinion between contending factions, and in order to get a unanimous decision, he would try to find common ground upon which all could stand. He was willing to modify his own opinions to hold or increase his majority; and if this meant he had to put in some disconnected thoughts or sentences, in they went. In cases assigned to others, he would readily suggest the addition or subtraction of a paragraph in order to save a dissent or a concurring opinion.

When Stone was an associate justice, he prized the right to dissent and occasionally rankled under the no-dissent-unless-absolutely-necessary tradition of the Taft and Hughes Courts. As Chief Justice, he did not believe it appropriate for him to dissuade Court members from dissenting in individual cases by persuasion or otherwise. A Chief Justice, he thought, might admonish his associates generally to exercise restraint in the matter of dissents and seek to find common ground for decision, but beyond that he should not go. And Stone usually went no further. His activity or lack of it in this regard gave rise to new expectations on the part of his associates as to their role and the role of the Chief Justice regarding unanimity and dissent. In the early 1940's, a new tradition of freedom of individual expression displaced the tradition of the Taft and Hughes Courts. This explains in part the unprecedented number of dissents and separate opinions during Stone's Chief Justiceship.

Nonetheless, Stone recognized that unanimity was desirable in certain cases. He patiently negotiated a unanimous decision in the Nazi Saboteurs case.[3] It should be pointed out, however, that this case was decided early in his Chief Justiceship before the new tradition was firmly established. By 1946, when he sought unanimity in the case of General Yamashita,[4] the new tradition of freedom was so well established that Stone not only failed to unite his Court, but the dissenters, Murphy and Rutledge, apparently resented his attempt to do so.

The unprecedented number of dissents and concurrences during Stone's Chief Justiceship can be only partly attributed to the displacing of the old tradition of loyalty to the Court's opinion. A major source of difficulty appears to have been the free-and-easy expression of views in conference. Whether the justices were sure of their grounds or not, they spoke up and many times took positions from which they could not easily retreat; given the heated debate which sometimes occurred in the Stone conference, the committment was not simply intellectual. What began in conference frequently ended with elaborate justification as concurring or dissenting opinions in the United States Reports. This, plus Stone's passiveness in seeking to attain unanimity, is probably the best explanation for what C. Herman Pritchett characterized as "the multiplication of division" in the Stone Court.

CONCLUSION

Interpersonal influence in the Supreme Court is an important aspect of the judicial process which has been given little attention. Of course, the "why" of the Court's decisions cannot be explained solely or even predominantly in those terms. Yet interpersonal influence is a variable worthy of consideration. Take, for example, the Court's about-face in the flag salute cases. With task leader Hughes presiding in 1940, not a single justice indicated in conference that he would dissent in the Gobitis[5] case. Subsequently, Stone registered a solo dissent, but such militant civil libertarians as Black, Douglas, and Murphy remained with Hughes. Only three years later, the Court reversed itself in the Barnette[6] case with Black, Douglas, and Murphy voting with Stone. One might seriously ask whether the presence of Hughes in the first case and not in the second had something to do with the switch. Much more work has to be done in this area, but it appears that in future analyses of the Court's work, task and social leadership will be useful concepts.

[3]Ex parte Quirin, 317 U.S. 1 (1942).
[4]In re Yamashita, 327 U.S. 1 (1946).
[5]Minersville School District v. Gobitis, 310 U.S. 586 (1940).
[6]West Virginia v. Barnette, 319 U.S. 624 (1943).

The importance of the Chief Justice's power to assign opinions is obvious. Equally if not more important is his role in unifying the Court. Taft's success in this regard greatly contributed to the Court's prestige, for unanimity reinforces the myth that the law is certain. In speaking of the Court in 1927, Hughes said that "no institution of our government stands higher in public confidence." As Court unifier, he sought to maintain that confidence after his appointment in 1930. That the Court's prestige is correlated with unanimity was demonstrated in Stone's Chief Justiceship: as dissent rose, the Court's prestige declined.

Thus the activity of the Chief Justice can be very significant in the judicial process. If he is the Court's task leader, he has great influence in the allocation of political values which are inevitably involved in many of the Court's decisions. More than any of his associates, his activity is apt to affect the Court's prestige; this is important, for ultimately the basis of the Court's power is its prestige.

CHAPTER TWELVE

THE SUPREME COURT AND MAJORITY CONTROL

ROBERT A. DAHL

In the course of its one hundred and sixty-seven years, in eighty-five cases, the Court has struck down ninety-four different provisions of federal law as unconstitutional, and by interpretation it has significantly modified a good many more. It might be argued, then, that in all or in a very large number of these cases the Court was, in fact, defending the legitimate constitutional rights of some minority against a 'tyrannical' majority. There are, however, some exceedingly serious difficulties with this interpretation of the Court's activities.

To begin with, it is difficult to determine when any particular Court decision has been at odds with the preferences of a national majority. Adequate evidence is not available, for scientific opinion polls are of relatively recent origin; and, strictly speaking, national elections cannot be interpreted as more than an indication of the first choice of about 40 to 60 per cent of the adult population for certain candidates for public office. The connection between preferences among candidates and preferences among alternative public policies is highly tenuous. On the basis of an election, it is almost never possible to adduce whether a majority does or does not support one of two or more *policy* alternates about which candidates are divided. For the greater part of the Court's history, then, there is simply no way of establishing with any high degree of confidence whether a given alternative was or was not supported by a majority or a minority of adults or even of voters.

Reprinted by permission from PLURALIST DEMOCRACY IN THE UNITED STATES *(Chicago: Rand McNally & Co., 1967), pp. 154–70. An earlier version of this selection, "Decision-Making in a Democracy: The Role of the Supreme Court as a National Policy-Maker," was reprinted in the first edition of this reader. Mr. Dahl is Sterling Professor of Political Science at Yale University.*

In the absence of relatively direct information, we are thrown back on indirect tests. The ninety-four provisions of federal law that have been declared unconstitutional were, of course, initially passed by majorities of those voting in the Senate and in the House. They also had the President's formal approval. One could, therefore, speak of a majority of those voting in the House and Senate, together with the President, as a 'law-making majority.' It is not easy to determine whether a law-making majority actually coincides with the preferences of a majority of American adults, or even with the preferences of a majority of that half of the adult population which, on the average, votes in congressional elections. Such evidence as we have from opinion polls suggests that Congress is not markedly out of line with public opinion, or at any rate with such public opinion as there is after one discards the answers of people who fall into the category, often large, labelled "no response" or "don't know." If we may, on these somewhat uncertain grounds, take a law-making majority as equivalent to a 'national majority,' then it is possible to test the hypothesis that the Supreme Court is shield and buckler for minorities against tyrannical national majorities.

Under any reasonable assumptions about the nature of the political process, it would appear to be somewhat naive to assume that the Supreme Court either would or could play the role of Galahad. Over the whole history of the Court, one new Justice has been appointed on the average of every twenty-three months. Thus a President can expect to appoint two new Justices during one term of office; and if this were not enough to tip the balance on a normally divided Court, he would be almost certain to succeed in two terms. For example, Hoover made three appointments; Roosevelt, nine; Truman, four; Eisenhower, five; Kennedy in his brief tenure, two. Presidents are not famous for appointing Justices hostile to their own views on public policy; nor could they expect to secure confirmation of a man whose stance on key questions was flagrantly at odds with that of the dominant majority in the Senate. Typically, Justices are men who, prior to appointment, have engaged in public life and have committed themselves publicly on the great questions of the day. As the late Mr. Justice Frankfurter pointed out, a surprisingly large proportion of the Justices, particularly of the great Justices who have left their stamp upon the decisions of the Court, have had little or no prior judicial experience. Nor have the Justices—certainly not the great Justices—been timid men with a passion for anonymity. Indeed, it is not too much to say that if Justices were appointed primarily for their 'judicial' qualities without regard to their basic attitudes on fundamental questions of public policy, the Court could not play the influential role in the American political system that it does in reality play.

It is reasonable to conclude, then, that the policy views dominant on the Court will never be out of line for very long with the policy views dominant among the law-making majorities of the United States. And it would be most unrealistic to suppose that the Court would, for more than a few years at most, stand against any major alternatives sought by a law-making majority. The judicial agonies of the New Deal will, of course, come quickly to mind; but President Franklin D. Roosevelt's difficulties with the Court were truly exceptional. Generalizing over the whole history of the Court, one can say that the chances are about two out of five that a President will make one appointment to the Court in less than a year, two out of three that he will make one within two years, and three out of four that he will make one within three years (Table 1). President Roosevelt had unusually bad luck: he had to wait four years for his first appointment; the odds against this long interval are about five to one. With average luck, his battle with the Court would never have occurred; even as it was, although his 'court-packing' proposal did formally fail, by the end of his second term in 1940 Roosevelt had appointed five new Justices and he gained three more the following year [Table 1]. Thus by the end of 1941, Mr. Justice Roberts was the only remaining holdover from the pre-Roosevelt era.

It is to be expected, then, that the Court would be least successful in blocking a determined and persistent lawmaking majority on a major policy. Conversely, the Court is most likely to succeed against 'weak' law-making majorities: transient majorities in Congress, fragile coalitions, coalitions weakly united upon a policy of subordinate importance or congressional coalitions no longer in existence, as might be the case when a law struck down by the Court had been passed several years earlier.

Table 1   The Interval Between Appointments to the Supreme Court, 1789–1965

Interval In Years	Number of Appointments	Percentage of Total	Cumulative Percentage
Less than 1 Year	38	41	41
1	22	24	65
2	10	11	76
3	9	10	86
4	6	6.5	92.5
5	6	6.5	99
12	1	1	100
Total	92	100	100

Note: The table excludes six Justices appointed in 1789. It includes only Justices who were appointed and confirmed and served on the Court. All data through 1964 are from *Congress and the Nation*, 1452–53.

THE RECORD

An examination of the cases in which the Court has held federal legislation unconstitutional confirms these expectations. Over the whole history of the Court, about half the decisions have been rendered more than four years after the legislation was passed (Table 2). Thus the congressional majorities that passed these laws went through at least two elections before the decision was handed down and may well have weakened or disappeared in the interval. In these cases, then, the Court was probably not directly challenging current law-making majorities.

Of the twenty-four laws held unconstitutional within two years, eleven were measures enacted in the early years of the New Deal. Indeed, New Deal measures comprise nearly a third of all the legislation that has ever been declared unconstitutional within four years of enactment.

It is illuminating to examine the cases where the Court has acted on legislation within four years of enactment—where the presumption is, that is to say, that the lawmaking majority is not a dead one. Of the twelve New Deal cases, two were, from a policy point of view, trivial; and two, although perhaps not trivial, were of minor importance to the New Deal program.[1] A fifth involved the NRA, which was to expire within three weeks of the decision.[2] Insofar as the unconstitutional provisions allowed "codes of fair competition" to be established by industrial groups, it is

Table 2   Supreme Court Cases Holding Federal Legislation Unconstitutional: by time between legislation and decision

	Supreme Court Cases Involving:					
Number of Years	New Deal Legislation		Other		All Federal Legislation	
	N	%	N	%	N	%
2 or less	11	92	13	17.5	24	28
3–4	1	8	13	17.5	14	16
5–8	0	0	20	27	20	24
9–12	0	0	10	14	10	12
13–16	0	0	7	10	7	8
17–20	0	0	2	3	2	2
21 or more	0	0	8	11	8	10
Total	12	100%	73	100%	85	100%

[1]*Booth* v *United States*, 291 U.S. 339 (1934), involved a reduction in the pay of retired judges. *Lynch* v *United States*, 292 U.S. 571 (1934), repealed laws granting to veterans rights to yearly renewable term insurance; there were only twenty-nine policies outstanding in 1932. *Hopkins Federal Savings & Loan Assn'* v *Cleary*, 296 U.S. 315 (1935), granted permission to state building and loan associations to convert to federal ones on a vote of 51 per cent or more of votes cast at a legal meeting. *Ashton* v *Cameron County Water Improvement District*, 298 U.S. 513 (1936), permitted municipalities to petition federal courts for bankruptcy proceedings.

[2]*Schechter Poultry Corp.* v *United States*, 295 U.S. 495 (1935).

fair to say that President Roosevelt and his advisers were relieved by the Court's decision of a policy that they had come to find increasingly embarrassing. In view of the tenacity with which FDR held to his major program, there can hardly be any doubt that, had he wanted to pursue the policy objective involved in the NRA codes, as he did for example with the labor provisions, he would not have been stopped by the Court's special theory of the Constitution. As to the seven other cases,[3] it is entirely correct to say, I think, that whatever some of the eminent Justices might have thought during their fleeting moments of glory, they did not succeed in interposing a barrier to the achievement of the objectives of the legislation; and in a few years most of the constitutional dogma on which they rested their opposition to the New Deal had been unceremoniously swept under the rug.

The remainder of the thirty-eight cases where the Court has declared legislation unconstitutional within four years of enactment tend to fall into two rather distinct groups: those involving legislation that could reasonably be regarded as important *from the point of view of the law-making majority* and those involving minor legislation. Although the one category merges into the other, so that some legislation must be classified rather arbitrarily, probably there will be little disagreement with classifying the specific legislative provisions involved in eleven cases as essentially minor from the point of view of the law-making majority (however important they may have been as constitutional interpretations).[4] The specific legislative provisions involved in the remaining fifteen cases are by no means of uniform importance, but with one or two possible exceptions it seems reasonable to classify them as major policy issues from the point of view of the law-making majority.[5] We would expect that cases involving major legislative policy would be pro-

---

[3] *United States* v *Butler*, 297 U.S. 1 (1936); *Perry* v *United States*, 294 U.S. 330 (1935); *Panama Refining Co.* v *Ryan*, 293 U.S. 388 (1935); *Railroad Retirement Board* v *Alton R. Co.*, 295 U.S. 330 (1935); *Louisville Joint Stock Land Bank* v *Radford*, 295 U.S. 555 (1935); *Rickert Rice Mills* v *Fontenot*, 297 U.S. 110 (1936); *Carter* v *Carter Coal Co.*, 298 U.S. 238 (1936).

[4] *United States* v *Dewitt*, 9 Wall. (U.S.) 41 (1870); *Gordon* v *United States*, 2 Wall. (U.S.) 561 (1865); *Monongahela Navigation Co.* v *United States*, 148 U.S. 312 (1893); *Wong Wing* v *United States*, 163 U.S. 228 (1896); *Fairbank* v *United States*, 181 U.S. 283 (1901); *Rassmussen* v *United States*, 197 U.S. 516 (1905); *Muskrat* v *United States*, 219 U.S. 346 (1911).

[5] *Ex parte Garland*, 4 Wall. (U.S.) 333 (1867); *United States* v *Klein*, 13 Wall. (U.S.) 128 (1872); *Pollack* v *Farmers' Loan & Trust Co.*, 157 U.S. 429 (1895), rehearing granted 158 U.S. 601 (1895); *Employers' Liability Cases*, 207 U.S. 463 (1908); *Keller* v *United States*, 213 U.S. 138 (1909); *Hammer* v *Dagenhart*, 247 U.S. 251 (1918); *Eisner* v *Macomber*, 252 U.S. 189 (1920); *Knickerbocker Ice Co.* v *Stewart*, 253 U.S. 149 (1920); *United States* v *Cohen Grocery Co.*, 255 U.S. 81 (1921); *Weeds, Inc.* v *United States*, 255 U.S. 109 (1921); *Bailey* v *Drexel Furniture Co.*, 259 U.S. 20 (1922); *Hill* v *Wallace*, 259 U.S. 44 (1922); *Washington* v *Dawson & Co.*, 264 U.S. 219 (1924); *Trusler* v *Crooks*, 269 U.S. 475 (1926).

Table 3   Number of Cases Involving Legislative Policy Other
Than Those Arising Under New Deal Legislation Holding Legislation
Unconstitutional Within Four Years After Enactment

Interval In Years	Major Policy	Minor Policy	Total
2 or less	11	2	13
3 to 4	4	9	13
Total	15	11	26

pelled to the Court much more rapidly than cases involving minor policy, and, as Table 3 shows, this is in fact what happens.

Thus a law-making majority with major policy objectives in mind usually has an opportunity to seek ways of overcoming the Court's veto. It is an interesting and highly significant fact that Congress and the President do generally succeed in overcoming a hostile Court on major policy issues (Table 4). It is particularly instructive to examine the cases involving major policy. In two cases involving legislation enacted by radical Republican Congresses to punish supporters of the Confederacy during the Civil War, the Court faced a rapidly crumbling majority whose death knell as an effective national force was sounded after

Table 4   Type of Congressional Action Following Supreme Court Decisions
Holding Legislation Unconstitutional Within Four Years After Enactment
(Other Than New Legislation)[6]

Congressional Action	Major Policy	Minor Policy	Total
Reverses Court's Policy	10[a]	2[d]	12
Changes Own Policy	2[b]	0	2
None	0	8[e]	8
Unclear	3[c]	1[f]	4
Total	15	11	26

[6]The cases in each category are: (a) *Pollock* v *Farmers' Loan & Trust Co.*, 157 U.S. 429 (1895); *Employers' Liability Cases*, 207 U.S. 463 (1908); *Keller* v *United States*, 213 U.S. 138 (1909); *Hammer* v *Dagenhart*, 247 U.S. 251 (1918); *Bailey* v *Drexel Furniture Co.*, 259 U.S. 20 (1922); *Trusler* v *Crooks*, 269 U.S. 475 (1926); *Hill* v *Wallace*, 259 U.S. 44 (1922); *Knickerbocker Ice Co.* v *Stewart*, 253 U.S. 149 (1920); *Washington* v *Dawson & Co.*, 264 U.S. 219 (1924); (b) *Ex parte Garland*, 4 Wall. (U.S.) 333 (1867); *United States* v *Klein*, 13 Wall. (U.S.) 128 (1872); (c) *United States* v *Cohen Grocery Co.*, 255 U.S. 81 (1921); *Weeds, Inc.* v *United States*, 255 U.S. 109 (1921); *Eisner* v *Macomber*, 252 U.S. 189 (1920); (d) *Gordon* v *United States*, 2 Wall. (U.S.) 561 (1865); *Evans* v *Gore*, 253 U.S. 245 (1920); (e) *United States* v *Dewitt*, 9 Wall. (U.S.) 41 (1870); *Monongahela Navigation Co.* v *United States*, 148 U.S. 312 (1893); *Wong Wing* v *United States*, 163 U.S. 228 (1896); *Fairbank* v *United States*, 181 U.S. 283 (1901); *Rassmussen* v *United States*, 197 U.S. 516 (1905); *Muskrat* v *United States*, 219 U.S. 346 (1911); *Choate* v *Trapp*, 224 U.S. 665 (1912); *United States* v *Lovett*, 328 U.S. 303 (1946); (f) *Untermyer* v *Anderson*, 276 U.S. 440 (1928).

the election of 1876.[7] Three cases are difficult to classify and I have labelled them "unclear." Of these, two were decisions made in 1921 in volving a 1919 amendment to the Lever Act to control prices.[8] The legislation was important, and the provision in question was clearly struck down, but the Lever Act terminated three days after the decision and Congress did not return to the subject of price control until the Second World War, when it experienced no constitutional difficulties arising from these cases (which were primarily concerned with the lack of an ascertainable standard of guilt). The third case in this category successfully eliminated stock divdends from the scope of the Sixteenth Amendment, although a year later Congress enacted legislation taxing the actual income from such stocks.[9]

The remaining ten cases were ultimately followed by a reversal of the actual policy results of the Court's action, although not necessarily of the specific constitutional interpretation. In four cases,[10] the policy consequences of the Court's decision were overcome in less than a year. The other six required a long struggle. Workmen's compensation for longshoremen and harbor workers was invalidated by the Court in 1920;[11] in 1922 Congress passed a new law which was, in its turn, knocked down by the Court in 1924;[12] in 1927 Congress passed a third law, which was finally upheld in 1932.[13] The notorious income tax cases of 1895[14] were first somewhat narrowed by the Court itself;[15] the Sixteenth Amendment was recommended by President Taft in 1909 and was ratified in 1913, some eighteen years after the Court's decisions. The two child labor cases represent the most effective battle ever waged by the Court against legislative policy-makers. The original legislation outlawing child labor, based on the commerce clause, was passed in 1916 as part of Wilson's New Freedom. Like Franklin Roosevelt later, Wilson was somewhat unlucky in his Supreme Court appointments; he made only three appointments during his eight years, and one of these was wasted, from a policy point of view, on Mr. Justice McReynolds. Had McReynolds voted 'right,' the subsequent struggle over the problem of child labor

---

[7]Ex parte *Garland*, 4 Wall. (U.S.) 333 (1867); *United States* v *Klein*, 13 Wall. (U.S.) 128 (1872).

[8]*United States* v *Cohen Grocery Co.*, 255 U.S. 81 (1921); *Weeds, Inc.* v *United States*, 255 U.S. 109 (1921).

[9]*Eisner* v *Macomber*, 252 U.S. 189 (1920).

[10]*Employers' Liability Cases*, 207 U.S. 463 (1908); *Keller* v *United States*, 213 U.S. 138 (1909); *Trusler* v *Crooks*, 269 U.S. 475 (1926); *Hill* v *Wallace*, 259 U.S. 44 (1922).

[11]*Knickerbocker Ice Co.* v *Stewart*, 253 U.S. 149 (1920).

[12]*Washington* v *Dawson & Co.*, 264 U.S. 219 (1924).

[13]*Crowell* v *Benson*, 285 U.S. 22 (1932).

[14]*Pollock* v *Farmers' Loan & Trust Co.*, 157 U.S. 429 (1895).

[15]*Nicol* v *Ames*, 173 U.S. 509 (1899); *Knowlton* v *Moore*, 178 U.S. 41 (1900); *Patton* v *Brady*, 184 U.S. 608 (1902); *Flint* v *Stone Tracy Co.*, 220 U.S. 107 (1911).

need not have occurred, for the decision in 1918 was by a Court divided five to four, McReynolds voting with the majority.[16] Congress moved at once to circumvent the decision by means of the tax power, but in 1922 the Court blocked that approach.[17] In 1924, Congress returned to the engagement with a constitutional amendment that was rapidly endorsed by a number of state legislatures before it began to meet so much resistance in the states remaining that the enterprise miscarried. In 1938, under a second reformist President, new legislation was passed twenty-two years after the first; this a Court with a New Deal majority finally accepted in 1941,[18] and thereby brought to an end a battle that had lasted a full quarter-century.

The entire record of the duel between the Court and the law-making majority, in cases where the Court has held legislation unconstitutional within four years after enactment, is summarized in Table 5.

A consideration of the role of the Court as defender of minorities, then, suggests the following conclusions:

First, judicial review is surely inconsistent with democracy to the extent that the Court simply protects the policies of minorities from reversal or regulation by national majorities acting through regular law-making procedures.

Second, however, the frequency and nature of appointments to the Court inhibits it from playing this role, or otherwise protecting minorities against national law-making majorities. National law-making majorities—*i.e.*, coalitions of the President and a majority of each house of Congress—generally have their way.

Third, although the court evidently cannot hold out indefinitely against a persistent law-making majority, in a very small number of important cases it has succeeded in delaying the application of a policy for as long as twenty-five years.

Table 5   Type of Congressional Action After Supreme Court Decisions Holding Legislation Unconstitutional Within Four Years After Enactment (Including New Deal Legislation)

Congressional Action	Major Policy	Minor Policy	Total
Reverses Court's Policy	17	2	19
None	0	12	12
Other	6*	1	7
Total	23	15	38

*In addition to the actions in Table 4 under "Changes Own Policy" and "Unclear," this figure includes the NRA legislation affected by the *Schechter Poultry* case.

[16]*Hammer* v *Dagenhart*, 247 U.S. 251 (1918).
[17]*Bailey* v *Drexel Furniture Co.*, 259 U.S. 20 (1922).
[18]*United States* v *Darby*, 312 U.S. 100 (1941).

JUDGES AS POLICY-MAKERS

How can we appraise decisions of the third kind just mentioned? It might be argued that the one function of the Court is to protect rights that are in some sense basic or fundamental. Thus (the argument might run), in a country where basic rights are, on the whole, respected, one would expect only a small number of cases where the Court has had to plant itself firmly against a law-making majority. But majorities may, on rare occasions, become 'tyrannical'; when they do, the Court intervenes; and although the constitutional issue may, strictly speaking, be technically open, the Constitution assumes an underlying fundamental body of rights and liberties which the Court guarantees by its decisions.

Even without examining the actual cases, however, it is somewhat unrealistic to suppose that a Court whose members are recruited in the fashion of Supreme Court Justices would long adhere to norms of abstract Right or Justice substantially at odds with those of a majority of elected leaders. Moreover, in an earlier day it was perhaps easier to believe that certain rights are so natural and self-evident that their fundamental validity is as much a matter of definite knowledge, at least to all reasonable creatures, as the color of a ripe cherry.

But today we know that the line between abstract Right and policy is extremely hard to draw. A policy decision might be defined as an effective choice among alternatives about which there is, at least initially, some uncertainty. This uncertainty may arise because of inadequate information as to (a) the alternatives that are thought to be 'open'; (b) the consequences that will probably ensue from choosing a given alternative; (c) the level of probability that these consequences will actually ensue; and (d) the relative value of the different alternatives.

No one, I imagine, will quarrel with the proposition that the Supreme Court, or indeed any Court, must make and does make policy decisions in this sense. But such a proposition is not really useful to the question before us. What is critical is the extent to which a court can and does make policy decisions by going outside established 'legal' criteria found in precedent, statute, and Constitution. Now in this respect the Supreme Court occupies a most peculiar position, for it is an essential characteristic of the institution that from time to time its members decide cases where legal criteria are not in any realistic sense adequate to the task. The distinguished legal scholar and member of the Court, the late Mr. Justice Frankfurter, once described the business of the Supreme Court in these words:

It is essentially accurate to say that the Court's preoccupation today is with the application of rather fundamental aspirations and what Judge

Learned Hand calls "moods," embodied in provisions like the due process clauses, which were designed not to be precise and positive directions for rules of action. The judicial process in applying them involves a judgment . . . that is, on the views of the direct representatives of the people in meeting the needs of society, on the views of Presidents and Governors, and by their construction of the will of legislatures the Court breathes life, feeble or strong, into the inert pages of the Constitution and the statute books.[19]

Very often, then, the cases before the Court involve alternatives about which there is severe disagreement in the society, as in the case of segregation or economic regulation; the very setting of the case is, then, "political." Moreover, these are usually cases where competent students of constitutional law, including the learned Justices of the Supreme Court themselves, disagree; where the words of the Constitution are general, vague, ambiguous, or not clearly applicable; where precedent may be found on both sides; and where experts differ in predicting the consequences of the various alternatives or the degree of probability that the possible consequences will actually ensue. Typically, in other words, although there may be considerable agreement as to the alternatives thought to be open, there is very serious disagreement—both as to questions of fact bearing on consequences and probabilities and as to questions of value.

If the Court were assumed to be a 'political' institution, no particular problems would arise, for it would be taken for granted that the members of the Court would resolve questions of fact and value by introducing assumptions derived from their own predispositions or those of influential clienteles and constituents. However, since much of the legitimacy of the Court's decisions rests upon the belief that it is not a political institution but exclusively a legal one, to accept the Court as a political institution would solve one set of problems at the price of creating another. Nonetheless, if it is true that the nature of the cases arriving before the Court is sometimes of the kind I have described, then the Court cannot act strictly as a legal institution. It must, that is to say, choose among controversial alternatives of public policy by appealing to at least some criteria of acceptability on questions of fact and value that cannot be found in or deduced from precedent, statute and Constitution.

In making these choices does the Court rise to a level of abstract Right or Justice above the level of mere policy? The best rebuttal to this view of the Court will be found in the record of the Court's decisions. Surely the six cases referred to a moment ago, where the policy consequences of the Court's decisions were overcome only after long battles, will scarcely appeal to many contemporary minds as evidence for the

[19]Frankfurter, "The Supreme Court in the Mirror of Justices," 105 *U. of Pa. Law Review* 781, 793 (1957).

proposition under examination. A natural right to employ child labor in mills and mines? To be free of income taxes by the federal government? To employ longshoremen and harbor workers without the protection of workmen's compensation? The Court itself did not rely upon such arguments in these cases, and it would do no credit to their opinions to reconstruct them along such lines.

So far, however, our evidence has been drawn from cases in which the Court has held legislation unconstitutional within four years after enactment. What of the other forty cases? Do we have evidence in these that the Court has protected fundamental or natural rights and liberties against the dead hand of some past tyranny by the lawmakers? The evidence is not impressive. In the history of the Court there has never been a single case arising under the First Amendment in which the Court has held federal legislation unconstitutional.[20] If we turn from these fundamental liberties of religion, speech, press, and assembly, we do find a handful of cases—something less than ten—arising under Amendments Four to Seven in which the Court has declared acts unconstitutional that might properly be regarded as involving rather basic liberties.[21] An inspection of these cases leaves the impression that, in all of them, the lawmakers and the Court were not very far apart; moreover, it is doubtful that the fundamental conditions of liberty in this country have been altered by more than a hair's breadth as a result of these decisions.

Over against these decisions we must put the fifteen or so cases in which the Court used the protections of the Fifth, Thirteenth, Fourteenth, and Fifteenth Amendments to preserve the rights and liberties of a relatively privileged group at the expense of the rights and liberties of a submerged group: chiefly slaveholders at the expense of slaves,[22] white people at the expense of colored people,[23] and property holders at the expense

[20]It is at least debatable whether *Aptheker* v *Secretary of State* 378 U.S. 500 (1964) might be considered an exception. A divided court held that the passport provisions of the Subversive Activities Control Act of 1950 were invalid because they were too broad. If Congress wanted to forbid or regulate travel it would have to be more specific.

[21]The candidates for this category would appear to be *Boyd* v *United States*, 116 U.S. 616 (1886); *Rassmussen* v *United States*, 197 U.S. 516 (1905); *Wong Wing* v *United States*, 163 U.S. 228 (1896); *United States* v *Moreland*, 258 U.S. 433 (1922); *Kirby* v *United States*, 174 U.S. 47 (1899); *United States* v *Cohen Grocery Co.*, 255 U.S. 81 (1921); *Weeds, Inc.* v *United States*, 255 U.S. 109 (1921); *Justices of the Supreme Court* v *United States* ex rel. *Murray*, 9 Wall. (U.S.) 274 (1870); *United States* ex rel. *Toth* v *Quarles*, 350 U.S. 11 (1955). It would be only fair to add one case not involving the first ten amendments: *U.S.* v *Brown*, 381 U.S. 437 (1965). Section 504 of the Labor-Management Reporting and Disclosure Act of 1959 made it a crime for a Communist Party member to serve as an officer or an employee (other than in a clerical or custodial position) of a labor organization. By a vote of 5-4 the Court held this section unconstitutional on the rather narrow ground that it constituted a bill of attainder, a holding that rested on the Court's conclusion that the intent of the statute was punitive. The prohibition against bills of attainder is not contained in the Bill of Rights but in Article I, Section 9.

[22]*Dred Scott* v *Sanford*, 19 How. (U.S.) 393 (1857).

[23]*United States* v *Reese*, 92 U.S. 214 (1876); *United States* v *Harris*, 106 U.S.

of wage earners and other groups.[24] These cases, unlike the relatively innocuous ones of the preceding set, all involved liberties of genuinely fundamental importance, where an opposite policy would have meant thoroughly basic shifts in the distribution of rights, liberties, and opportunities in the United States—where, moreover, the policies sustained by the Court's action have since been repudiated in every civilized nation of the Western world, including our own. Yet, if our earlier argument is correct, it is futile—precisely because the basic distribution of privilege was at issue—to suppose that the Court could have acted much differently in these areas of policy from the way in which it did in fact act.

SOME CONCLUSIONS

Thus the role of the Court is not simple and it is an error to suppose that its functions can be either described or appraised by means of simple concepts drawn from democratic or moral theory. It is possible, nonetheless, to derive a few general conclusions about the Court's role as a policy-making institution.

National politics in the United States, as in other stable democracies, is dominated by relatively cohesive alliances that endure for long periods of time. One recalls the Jeffersonian alliance, the Jacksonian, the extraordinarily long-lived Republican dominance of the post-Civil-War years, and the New Deal alliance shaped by Franklin Roosevelt. Each is marked by a break with past policies, a period of intense struggle, followed by consolidation, and finally decay and disintegration of the alliance.

Except for short-lived transitional periods when the old alliance is disintegrating and the new one is struggling to take control of political institutions, the Supreme Court is inevitably a part of the dominant national alliance. As an element in the political leadership of the dominant alliance, the Court of course supports the major policies of the alliance. Acting solely by itself with no support from the President and Congress, the Court is almost powerless to affect the course of national policy.

The Supreme Court is not, however, simply an *agent* of the alliance. It is an essential part of the political leadership and possesses some bases

---

629 (1883); *United States* v *Stanley (Civil Rights Cases)*, 109 U.S. 3 (1883); *Baldwin* v *Franks*, 120 U.S. 678 (1887); *James* v *Bowman*, 190 U.S. 127 (1903); *Hodges* v *United States*, 203 U.S. 1 (1906); *Butts* v *Merchants & Miners Transportation Co.*, 230 U.S. 126 (1913).

24*Monongahela Navigation Co.* v *United States*, 148 U.S. 312 (1893); *Adair* v *United States*, 208 U.S. 261 (1908); *Adkins* v *Children's Hospital*, 261 U.S. 525 (1923); *Nichols* v *Coolidge*, 274 U.S. 531 (1927); *Untermyer* v *Anderson*, 276 U.S. 440 (1928); *Heiner* v *Donnan*, 285 U.S. 312 (1932); *Louisville Joint Stock Land Bank* v *Radford*, 295 U.S. 555 (1935).

of power of its own, the most important of which is the unique legitimacy attributed to its interpretations of the Constitution. This legitimacy the Court jeopardizes if it flagrantly opposes the major policies of the dominant alliance; such a course of action, as we have seen, is one in which the Court will not normally be tempted to engage.

It follows that within the somewhat narrow limits set by the basic policy goals of the dominant alliance, the Court *can* make national policy. Its discretion, then, is not unlike that of a powerful committee chairman in Congress who cannot, generally speaking, nullify the basic policies substantially agreed on by the rest of the dominant leadership, but who can, within these limits, often determine important questions of timing, effectiveness, and subordinate policy. Thus the Court is least effective against a current law-making majority—and evidently least inclined to act. It is most effective when it sets the bounds of policy for officials, agencies, state governments, or even regions, a task that has come to occupy a very large part of the Court's business.[25]

Few of the Court's policy decisions can be interpreted sensibly in terms of a 'majority' versus a 'minority.' In this respect the Court is no different from the rest of the political leadership. Generally speaking, policy at the national level is the outcome of conflict, bargaining, and agreement among minorities; the process is neither minority rule nor majority rule but what might better be called *minorities* rule, where one aggregation of minorities achieves policies opposed by another aggregation.

The main objective of presidential leadership is to build a stable and dominant aggregation of minorities with a high probability of winning the Presidency and one or both houses of Congress. Ordinarily the main contribution of the Court is to confer legitimacy on the fundamental policies of the successful coalition.

But if this were the only function of the Supreme Court, would it have acquired the standing it has among Americans? In fact, at its best —and the Court is not always at its best—the Court does more than merely confer legitimacy on the dominant national coalition. For one thing, by the way it interprets and modifies national laws, perhaps but not necessarily by holding them unconstitutional, the Supreme Court sometimes serves as a guide and even a pioneer in arriving at different standards of fair play and individual right than have resulted, or are likely to result, from the interplay of the other political forces. Thus in recent years the Court has modified by interpretation or declared unconstitutional provisions of federal law restricting the rights of unpopular and

[25]"Constitutional law and cases with constitutional undertones are of course still very important, with almost one-fourth of the cases in which written opinions were filed (in recent years) involving such questions. Review of administrative action . . . constitutes the largest category of the Court's work, comprising one-third of the total cases decided on the merits. The remaining . . . categories of litigation . . . all involve largely public law questions." Frankfurter, *op. cit.*

even widely detested minorities—military deserters, Communists, and alleged bootleggers, for example.[26] The judges, after all, inherit an ancient tradition and an acknowledged role in setting higher standards of justice and right than the majority of citizens or their representatives might otherwise demand. If the standards of justice propounded by the Court are to prevail, for reasons we have already examined they cannot be too remote from general standards of fairness and individual right among Americans; but though some citizens may protest, most Americans are too attached to the Court to want it stripped of its power.

There are times, too, when the other political forces are too divided to arrive at decisions on certain key questions. At very great risk, the Court can intervene in such cases; and sometimes it may even succeed in establishing policy where President and Congress are unable to do so. Probably in such cases it can succeed only if its action conforms to a widespread set of explicit or implicit norms held by the political leadership: norms which are not strong enough or are not distributed in such a way as to insure the existence of an effective law-making majority but are nonetheless sufficiently powerful to prevent any successful attack on the legitimacy and power of the Court. This is probably the explanation for the relatively successful work of the Court in enlarging the freedom of Negroes to vote during the past three decades and in its famous school integration decisions,[27] and the reapportionment cases. . . .[28]

Yet the Court does even more than this. Considered as a political system, democracy is a set of basic procedures for arriving at decisions. The operation of these procedures presupposes the existence of certain rights, obligations, liberties, and restraints; in short, certain patterns of behavior. The existence of these patterns of behavior in turn presupposes widespread agreement (particularly among the politically active and influential segments of the population) on the validity and propriety of the behavior. Although its record is by no means lacking in serious blemishes, at its best the Court operates to confer legitimacy, not simply on the particular and parochial policies of the dominant political alliance, but upon the basic patterns of behavior required for the operation of a democracy.

Yet in order to *confer* legitimacy, the Court must itself *possess* legitimacy. For in a political society thoroughly permeated by the democratic

[26]*Trop* v *Dulles*, 356 U.S. 86 (1958); *Kennedy* v *Mendoza-Martinez*, 372 U.S. 147 (1963); *Schneider* v *Rusk*, 377 U.S. 163 (1964); *Aptheker* v *Secretary of State*, 378 U.S. 500 (1964); *U.S.* v *Brown* 381 U.S. 437; *Alberston* v *Subversive Activities Control Bd.*, Sup. Ct. 194 (1965); *U.S.* v *Romano*, 86 Sup. Ct. 279 (1965).

[27]*Rice* v *Elmore*, 165 F. 2d 387 (C.A. 4th, 1947), cert. denied 333 U.S. 875 (1948); *United States* v *Classic*, 313 U.S. 299 (1941); *Smith* v *Allwright*, 321 U.S. 649 (1944); *Grovey* v *Townsend*, 295 U.S. 45 (1935); *Brown* v *Board of Education*, 347 U.S. 483 (1954); *Bolling* v *Sharpe*, 347 U.S. 497 (1954).

[28]The leading decisions were *Baker* v *Carr*, 369 U.S. 186 (1962); *Wesberry* v *Sanders*, 376 U.S. 1 (1964); and *Reynolds* v *Sims*, 377 U.S. 533 (1964).

ethos, where the legitimacy of every political institution depends finally on its consistency with democracy, the legitimacy of judicial review and the Court's exercise of that power must stem from the presumption that the Court is ultimately subject to popular control. The more the Court exercises self-restraint and the less it challenges the policies of law-making majorities, the less the need or the impulse to subject it to popular controls. The more active the Court is in contesting the policies of law-making majorities, the more visible becomes the slender basis of its legitimacy in a democratic system, and the greater the efforts will be to bring the Court's policies into conformity with those enacted by law-making majorities.

To the extent that the Supreme Court accepts the policies of law-making majorities, then, it retains its own legitimacy and its power to confer legitimacy on policies; yet to that extent it fails to protect minorities from control or regulation by national majorities. To the extent that it opposes the policies of national law-making majorities in order to protect minorities, it threatens its own legitimacy. This is the inescapable paradox of judicial review in a democratic political order.

CHAPTER THIRTEEN

ZORACH v. CLAUSON: THE IMPACT OF A SUPREME COURT DECISION

FRANK J. SORAUF

It has become a commonplace that the Constitution is what the Supreme Court says it is. Scholars of American constitutional law have, therefore, focused their studies largely on the Court's opinions as indices of the Constitution's current meaning. But however well established may be the Court's role as the expounder of the constitutional document, the impact of a decision will depend on many individuals and circumstances far beyond the confines of the Court. This paper will examine the effects of the decision in Zorach v. Clauson[1] on public policy in the seven years since its announcement. It will attempt to follow the repercussions of one Supreme Court decision though the entire political process within one area of political conflict—in this case the conflict over church-state relationships.[2]

The impact of the Zorach decision on state court decisions, on administrative rulings, on legislative action, and on the educational policies of local school districts may also be viewed as a case study in federalism. Within the federal system, what limits affect the power of the Court to dictate adherence to the Constitution throughout the states? How effec-

I am indebted for assistance in this project to both the Council on Research and the Social Science Research Center of the Pennsylvania State University.

[1]343 U.S. 306 (1952).

[2]For somewhat similar studies see Walter Murphy, "Civil Liberties and the Japanese American Cases: A Study in the Uses of *Stare Decisis,*" *Western Political Quarterly,* Vol. 11 (March, 1958), pp. 3–12; Jack W. Peltason, *Federal Courts in the Political Process* (Garden City, N.Y.: Doubleday, 1955), Ch. 6; and Gordon Patric, "The Impact of a Court Decision: Aftermath of the McCollum Case," *Journal of Public Law,* Vol. 6 (Fall, 1957), pp. 455–64.

Reprinted by permission from the AMERICAN POLITICAL SCIENCE REVIEW, *53 (September 1959), 777–91. Mr. Sorauf is Professor of Political Science at the University of Minnesota.*

tively does it function as an instrument of national supremacy? How responsive are state and local authorities to shifting constitutional interpretations?

THE DECISION

Despite considerable diversity in detail, "released time" programs of religious education have one principle in common: release from ordinary classroom attendance for students wishing to attend religious classes. Generally one hour a week is set aside for the purpose, and those students whose parents do not elect the religious classes for them are herded to study halls or given make-work exercises for the hour. The classes provided by the religious bodies of the community are referred to in religious education circles as "weekday church schools."

From a modest beginning shortly before World War I the released time movement expanded irregularly through the '20s and '30s, and then surged ahead dramatically in the wartime and postwar religious renaissance.[3] In the late '40s, however, one Mrs. Vashti McCollum pressed a suit through the Illinois courts and to the Supreme Court of the United States, challenging the constitutionality of the released time program of the Champaign schools, as a breach in the wall of separation between church and state. The Supreme Court, in an 8–1 decision, agreed.[4] Justice Black, speaking for the Court, noted: "Here not only are the State's tax-supported public school buildings used for the dissemination of religious doctrines. The State also affords sectarian groups an invaluable aid in that it helps to provide pupils for their religious classes through use of the State's compulsory public school machinery. This is not separation of Church and State."[5]

Public reaction to the McCollum decision was distinctly hostile. A number of communities across the country defied the Court and continued to hold religious classes in school rooms. A brief examination of the periodical indexes for the next few years indicates the extent of the wrath and condemnation heaped on the Court in leading journals. More particularly, in the constitutional uncertainty about released time that the McCollum case created, school districts and religious bodies began to cast about for acceptable programs and to test in the courts the applicable limits of the McCollum rule. During this period of constitutional sparring another test case, Zorach v. Clauson, emerged from Brooklyn.

This case questioned the released time program of the New York

[3]For the best brief but authoritative survey of released time in America, see Erwin L. Shaver, *The Weekday Church School* (Boston: Pilgrim, 1956). Dr. Shaver served for many years as the Executive Director of Weekday Religious Education of the National Council of Churches.

[4]McCollum v. Board of Education, 333 U.S. 203 (1948).

[5]*Ibid.*, p. 212.

City schools. Unlike the Champaign plan the New York program required that religious classes be held off the school premises, that all costs (even of application blanks) be borne by the organizations, and that there be no announcements or comments on the program during regular school sessions. The churches were, however, to make weekly attendance reports to the schools. Taxpayer-parents challenged the arrangement on the ground that the weight and influence of the public schools were placed squarely in support of released time, since the program depended on the schools' suspending classes and enforcing attendance. The New York courts swept aside these contentions to uphold it. In a 6-3 decision the U.S. Supreme Court sustained the state courts and the New York plan itself.

Writing for the majority, Justice Douglas first dismissed the argument that coercion had been used to get students into religious classes, and then turned to expound a theory of the separation of church and state quite at odds with the Court's earlier statement of an absolute separation in the Everson[6] and McCollum cases:

> The First Amendment, however, does not say that in every and all respects, there shall be a separation of Church and State. Rather, it studiously defines the manner, the specific ways, in which there shall be no concert or union or dependency one on the other. That is the common sense of the matter. Otherwise the state and religion would be aliens to each other—hostile, suspicious, and even unfriendly.[7]

For further support Douglas listed current instances of church-state cooperation, noting that even the Supreme Court's sessions begin with a plea for Divine guidance. Following this enunciation of new doctrine, he uttered his frequently quoted dictum on religion in American life and institutions:

> We are a religious people whose institutions presuppose a Supreme Being. . . . When the state encourages religious instruction or cooperates with religious authorities by adjusting the schedule of public events to sectarian needs, it follows the best of our traditions. For it then respects the religious nature of our people and accommodates the public service to their spiritual needs. To hold that it may not would be to find in the Constitution a requirement that the government show a callous indifference to religious groups. That would be preferring those who believe in no religion over those who do believe. . . . [W]e find no constitutional requirement which makes it necessary for government to be hostile to religion and to throw its weight against efforts to widen the effective scope of religious influence.[8]

Government must, therefore, not coerce religious observance, but it may cooperate with religious bodies, accommodate itself to their con-

[6]Everson v. Board of Education, 330 U.S. 1 (1947).
[7]343 U.S. 306 (1952), p. 312.
[8]*Ibid.*, p. 314.

venience, and even encourage programs of religious instruction. "[I]t can close its doors or suspend its operations," Douglas wrote, "as to those who want to repair to their religious sanctuary for worship or instruction. No more than that is undertaken here."[9] In conclusion Douglas reaffirmed the McCollum precedent and distinguished the facts there at issue from those before the Court.

Each of the three dissenters spoke individually. Justice Black, the Court's spokesman in the Everson and McCollum cases, could find no significant differences between the Brooklyn and Champaign programs—at least not enough to justify upholding the Brooklyn plan. He concluded by reaffirming his doctrine of an absolute separation, pressing its wisdom upon the Court. Justice Frankfurter argued the coercive elements of a system in which the nonreligious student was compelled to remain in school and regretted that the appellants had been denied an opportunity to prove coercion in the lower courts. Justice Jackson's dissent—which can at best be called intemperate—deals as much with the Court itself as with religious education. After reiterating the argument that the program rested on state coercion, Jackson turned to remind his "evangelistic brethren" that "what should be rendered to God does not need to be decided and collected by Caesar."[10] He agreed, too, that the distinction between the Champaign and Brooklyn programs was "trivial, almost to the point of cynicism" and concluded his philippic by supposing that the majority opinion would "be more interesting to students of psychology and of the judicial processes than to students of constitutional law."[11]

So much for the case and decision itself. We turn now to the impact of the Zorach decision on released time programs and on church-state relations in general.

INITIAL REACTION AND RECEPTION

The friends of released time reacted immediately to the Zorach decision with extravagant praise. It was tritely hailed as the "*magna carta* for the weekday religious education movement,"[12] "a landmark in the history of America,"[13] and "a great piece of jurisprudence."[14] Justice Douglas was saluted for averting the dangers of advancing secularism. Even the date of the decision was commemorated: "during the week of April 28 each year . . . some weekday classes hold special observances and con-

[9]*Ibid.*
[10]*Ibid.*, pp. 324–25.
[11]*Ibid.*, p. 325.
[12]Erwin L. Shaver, "Weekday Religious Education Secures Its Charter and Faces a Challenge," *Religious Education*, Vol. 48 (January–February, 1953), p. 43.
[13]Walter Howlett, *A Review and Challenge of Sixteen Years* (published by the Greater New York Coordinating Committee on Released Time, no date), p. 6.
[14]Robert C. Hartnett, "Religious Education and the Constitution," *America*, Vol. 87 (May 24, 1952), 225.

tribute to a fund to help bring weekday church schools to communities which do not have them."[15]

In their attempts to explain the general doctrine of church-state relations in the Zorach decision to their readers and members, the supporters of released time programs were generally agreed in their interpretations. Most noted with triumph that the decision "radically revised the Everson-McCollum doctrine on 'separation' "[16] and that the Court had had to retreat from its unrealistic doctrine of complete separation. One well-known religious educator went so far as to observe that "the principle of friendly cooperation between the state and religious bodies was substituted for that of absolute separation" and that the whole issue of separation "may be said to be wide open."[17]

Enthusiasm and wide-sweeping interpretation also mark these commentators' development of the narrow legal issues in the decision. The "shadow of illegality has been dispelled,"[18] the decision "removes the apparent stigma that weekday religious education has been under in the minds of many,"[19] the decision "established without a doubt the legality of releasing pupils from the public schools"[20]—so went announcements of the good tidings. At least in the initial burst of optimism, the local religious leader or educator might easily have gathered that all released time programs had been sanctioned and that the McCollum precedent was no more. For instance, one commentator noted simply that the Court "reversed" itself in the Zorach case,[21] and another thought it had "cut the heart out of the McCollum decision" and "greatly modified, if not virtually overruled" it.[22] To be sure, Erwin L. Shaver, the generally recognized leader of the released time movement, cautioned that there was "no contradiction" between the two cases, explaining the "seeming reversal" on the basis of two differing sets of facts.[23] His was, however, a lone counsel of caution.

The exuberance of released time advocates was matched by the disappointment of its opponents. Varied in approach, their comments reflected both a generalized dissatisfaction with the decision, and a desire to minimize its effect. The *Christian Century* in its initial editorial reaction went to great pains to point out that the New York program differed

---

[15]Shaver, *op. cit.*, note 3 above, p. 60.

[16]Hartnett, *op. cit.*, p. 225.

[17]F. Ernest Johnson, "Religion and Education," *Progressive Education*, Vol. 33 (September 1956), 146.

[18]Shaver, *op. cit.*, note 3 above, p. 31.

[19]"Following the Best of Our Traditions," *National Council Outlook*, Vol. 2 (June 1952), 20.

[20]*Introducing the Weekday Church School* (published by the Division of Christian Education of the National Council of Churches, no date), p. 15.

[21]Herbert B. Mulford, "A Pattern for Religion in Public Education," *Religious Education*, Vol. 49 (September–October, 1954), 333.

[22]Robert F. Drinan, "The Supreme Court and Religion," *The Commonweal*, Vol. 56 (September 12, 1952), 554.

[23]Shaver, *op. cit.*, note 12 above, p. 40.

fundamentally from the one invalidated in Champaign. Unlike the favorable commentaries, it concluded that the McCollum precedent had certainly not been overruled. It also thought, contrary to the supporters, that Justice Douglas' opinion "will not clarify the church-and-state issue, but will produce much future litigation."[24] *Church and State*, publication of the Protestants and Other Americans United for the Separation of Church and State, ran only a brief news item devoted largely to excerpts from the dissenting opinions.[25]

For his part, Professor R. Freeman Butts attempted to underplay the Court's dictum, quoted above, by distinguishing between "we as a people" and "we as a government" and by insisting that "we as a government" must be neutral on all religious issues.[26] Another authority on school law, while deploring that the Court had "really muddied" the waters of constitutional doctrine in the Zorach case, nonetheless concluded that it was not a reversal of the earlier Champaign precedent.[27] Finally, some among the opponents of released time avoided or ignored the force of the Zorach decision entirely. The chairman of the Anti-Defamation League, for instance, has observed that the Zorach decision reaffirms the doctrine of church-state separation laid down in the earlier Everson and McCollum cases.[28]

This brief excursion into the reactions to the Zorach decision indicates that representatives of interest groups on the two sides of the issue have, by perceiving within the bounds of a distinct frame of reference, really divided the Court's precedent into sharply contrasting images. Readers who overlap these self-selected audiences are confronted by two "precedents" rather than one. Whether McCollum was reversed or followed, whether the separation doctrine is clarified or confused, whether all or only some released time programs have judicial approval seems to depend on the commitments one brings to his appraisal of the decision.

THE IMPACT ON RELEASED TIME PROGRAMS

The impact of a Supreme Court decision should be most obvious in its direct and primary effect on the policies in question. In this instance the Zorach opinion, touted as a "magna charta" for the released time movement, rescued certain programs from the constitutional limbo to which they presumably had been consigned by the McCollum case. The em-

---

[24]"The Court Concurs," *Christian Century*, Vol. 69 (May 14, 1952), 582.

[25]*Church and State Newsletter*, Vol. 5 (May 1952), 2. This account gives 21 lines of type to the majority opinion and 76 to the dissenters.

[26]"The Relation between Religion and Education," *Progressive Education*, Vol. 33 (September 1956), 142.

[27]Lee O. Garber, "Confusing Decisions on Released Time," *Nation's Schools*, Vol. 50 (August 1952), 72.

[28]Henry E. Schultz, *Religious Education and the Public Schools* (New York: Anti-Defamation League, 1955), p. 5.

pirical question, then, is whether it has in fact stimulated and accelerated the growth of these programs. This turns out to be not an easy question to answer.

Aggregate statistical totals of the number of children receiving released time religious training are impossible to come by. Several commentators seem to agree that after the McCollum decision in 1948 the released time programs fell off by some 20 per cent, accounting for a pupil loss of about 10 per cent.[29] By 1953 the total attendance was variously estimated between 2,000,000 and 2,500,000—back just about to the pre-McCollum total. Three to five years later, leaders of the movement were setting enrolments at about 3,000,000 in programs in over 3,000 communities in 45 or 46 states.[30] All of the losses after the McCollum decision were apparently recouped by 1953, and in the last five years enrolments have risen to an all-time high. Dr. Shaver sums up the growth in recent years as "a modest increase since 1952, although not a great one."[31]

Enrolment statistics from scattered states and communities also confirm the general impression of a modest overall growth since Zorach, with more substantial increases in some instances. The United Lutheran Church, for example, reports a 28 per cent growth in weekday church schools and a 13 per cent increase in pupils between the years 1951 and 1953.[32] And if one accepts various data from the state of New York at face value, enrolments there have doubled from 225,000 in 1952 to 450,000 in 1956.

Accounts of the impact of Zorach in specific communities supplement these statistical indications. The school board in Pittsfield, Massachusetts, was reported (in a journal that can hardly be called friendly) to have inaugurated a released time program immediately after the decision of the Brooklyn case. "Protestant and Jewish leaders represented in the local Council of Churches withdrew their formal opposition to the plan after the April 28 Supreme Court decision upholding the New York system of 'released time,' but voted not to participate themselves during the coming school year."[33] Finally, in these community policy debates the impact of the decision is reflected in the determination of some religious groups to press their newly won advantage. The *New York*

---

[29]"State Support of Church Schools" (mimeographed excerpts from the reports of the Board for Parish Education of the Lutheran Church—Missouri Synod), p. 19; and Shaver, *op. cit.*, note 12 above, p. 41.

[30]Shaver, *op. cit.*, note 12 above; Erwin L. Shaver letter to the author, March 14, 1958; various mimeographed press releases of the Confraternity of Christian Doctrine of the National Catholic Welfare Conference; and Charles H. Tuttle, "No Poor Relation in the House of the State," *National Council Outlook*, Vol. 2 (June 1952), 4.

[31]Shaver letter to the author, March 14, 1958.

[32]W. Kent Gilbert, *Suggested Procedures for an Evaluation of the Weekday Church School Series of the United Lutheran Church in America* (Columbia University, D.Ed. thesis, 1955).

[33]*Church and State Newsletter*, Vol. 5 (June 1952), 3.

Times reported in late 1952 the efforts of the United Lutheran Church "at increasing church pressure on public schools to permit children to receive weekday religious education under the released-time system."[34]

The ability of local authorities to begin released time programs may depend to some extent on the willingness of state legislatures to authorize or tolerate them. Yet no new legislation on the subject has been enacted by any state since the Zorach case decision. Bills to authorize released time programs in New Hampshire were beaten down in the 1953, 1955, and 1957 legislative sessions. Similar proposals have also been introduced in the Michigan and Arizona legislatures with similar results. Evidently, the Court's permissive opinion has failed to influence legislative policy making in the states. However, enabling legislation is not usually necessary; only 13 states have laws expressly permitting absence for religious instruction.[35] In most states the localities simply begin their programs under the regular educational authority with some vague assurances that they are not violating any state statutory or constitutional restrictions on religious education. Even in Virginia, where released time flourishes as in no other state, no explicit state authority for it exists.

In these circumstances the states' attorneys general, as the construers and appliers of state limitations, assume an important role in charting the legal progress of released time programs. Here the impact of Zorach is easier to assess. In only four instances, apparently, has a state attorney general found occasion to mention the Zorach precedent in dealing with released time or similar programs of religious education. The attorney general of Iowa upheld a released time plan in Dubuque that was virtually identical to the Brooklyn plan.[36] An opinion in Indiana reaffirmed the constitutionality of a state statute that an earlier attorney general had held to be in grave doubt after McCollum. Here again there were no significant differences between the program authorized and the one the Court upheld in Zorach.[37] Thirdly, the Vermont attorney general in 1954 cited Zorach v. Clauson in holding unconstitutional any religious classes in the schools during school hours. He hastened to add, however, that there would be no federal or state constitutional ob-

---

[34]October 14, 1952, p. 35.

[35]See Research Division of the National Educational Association, "The State and Sectarian Education," *Research Bulletin*, Vol. 34 (December, 1956) for the best summary of state legislation. It cites 14 states with permissive legislation, but the New Mexico listing turns out to involve a favorable ruling by the attorney general on the basis of ordinary school legislation. The 13 are: California, Indiana, Iowa, Kentucky, Maine, Massachusetts, Minnesota, New York, North Dakota, Oregon, Pennsylvania, South Dakota, and West Virginia.

[36]Opinion of August 18, 1953, *Thirtieth Biennial Report of the Iowa Attorney General* (1954), pp. 73–76.

[37]Opinion No. 24 of June 1, 1956, *Opinions of the Attorney General of Indiana* (1956), pp. 105–14.

jection to classes held off school premises and made available to all sects.[38] Finally, the Oregon attorney general referred to Zorach somewhat ambiguously in holding that local school boards are not free under the Oregon released time law to refuse requests for a released time program in a local community.[39] Reports persist that attorneys general in several other states have informally decided such issues since 1952 but these are unconfirmed and too sketchy and fugitive to deal with here.

To round out the picture, mention ought also to be made of the uncertainties the decision has created. In relaxing the stringencies of the McCollum decision, it has still not resolved the status of such a program as Utah has adopted. Released time classes in that state extend to five hours a week, receive high school credit in some parts of the state, and are taught by special, state-accredited teachers. A learned observer therefore suggests:

> Elements showing some degree of control by the state of released time teachers, the degree of identification and coercion inherent in granting credit, some danger of unconstitutional administration, a possibility of attack on the ground of state preference for one religion, plus an unusual amount of time allowed for religious studies tend toward a stronger case for unconstitutionality than Zorach.[40]

This compilation indicates that the impact of Zorach on local policy decisions has been a tonic to the movement, although it has hardly revolutionized the pattern of religious education.

THE ISSUE OF COMPLIANCE

It is no secret that after the McCollum decision, and despite it, many communities continued to hold released time classes in public school buildings. The most conservative estimate places non-compliance at 15 per cent of the programs,[41] and other estimates run up to 40 and 50 per cent in some states. Five years later in the Zorach case the Court reaffirmed the McCollum ruling but offered the localities a clearly constitutional alternative: religious education off school premises. Have local religious and educational groups met the Court half-way and given up released time in the school room?

The answer is "no—not entirely." In 1956 a knowledgeable authority on school law wrote that "school systems in virtually every state violate in some way the legal principles concerning religious instruction in the

38Opinion No. 14 of July, 1954, *Biennial Report of the Attorney General of Vermont* (1954–1956), pp. 95–98.

39Opinion No. 2890 of December 2, 1954, *Biennial Report and Opinions of the Attorney General of Oregon* (1954–1956).

40Ruth W. Wilkins, "Constitutionality of Utah Released Time Program," *Utah Law Review*, Vol. 3 (Spring 1953), 339.

41Shaver, *op. cit.*, note 12 above.

public schools." Some of the violations are unwitting, he wrote, but knowing violators include "some persons holding responsible church or school positions."[42] Apart from such generalizations, precise estimates of noncompliance are not easy to make. Apparently, all or most of the programs run by the Virginia Council of Churches still use school rooms,[43] many communities in Texas also,[44] and there are many reports of school room use in scattered places. Released time programs are conducted in school rooms in five Pennsylvania counties of which I am aware. Finally, *Religious Education* two years ago disclosed that a casual poll of released time programs indicated that 32 percent were still holding classes in school buildings, although some were paying token rentals of from $5 to $100 a year.[45]

Uncertainty about what constitutes noncompliance complicates this assessment. The transparent ruse of "renting" community educational facilities for five dollars a year is an obvious evasion of the Zorach rule. But what of holding religious instruction in schools during the lunch hour?[46] Or after school hours? Or what of giving high school credit for Bible classes? Or of holding released time classes in publicly owned community centers? Or of giving class credit for otherwise acceptable released time programs?[47] Apparently, in this "twilight area," the very groups that are most adept in expanding aid to religion by analogous application of the precedent have been unwilling at the same time to apply the limitations of Zorach.

Dr. Shaver and the Division of Christian Education of the National Council of Churches, to be sure, have clearly and repeatedly urged compliance. The very vigor of their urgings may, in fact, be taken as some indication of the degree of non-compliance. In a 1956 speech Shaver urged the need for dispelling

> . . . the mood of illegality which still pervades the weekday church school movement in some quarters. Much of this is due to the same attitude of defiance or indifference to decisions of the Supreme Court that one finds

[42]E. C. Bolmeier, "Legality and Propriety of Religious Instruction in the Public Schools," *Educational Forum*, Vol. 20 (May 1956), 480.

[43]Luther Flynn, *A Study of Moral, Spiritual, and Religious Values in the Public Schools of Virginia* (University of Virginia: D.Ed. thesis, 1956).

[44]William A. Flachmeier, *Religious Education and the Public Schools of Texas* (University of Texas: Ph.D. thesis, 1955).

[45]Edwin L. Shaver, "A Look at Weekday Church Schools," *Religious Education*, Vol. 51 (January–February, 1956), 18–39.

[46]*New York Times*, February 20, 1955, p. 88. The program then reached 100 of 280 high school pupils in Bangor, Michigan.

[47]*Church and State Newsletter* and the releases and memos of the Confraternity of Christian Doctrine, though obviously parties to the dispute, repeatedly carry stories of such local practices. See also Flachmeier, *op. cit.*; and Jack J. Early, *Religious Practices in the Public Schools in Selected Communities in Kentucky* (University of Kentucky: D.Ed. thesis, 1956).

in the segregation issue. Such an attitude toward the Zorach decision should be opposed just as strongly as the non-conforming attitude toward the segregation decision.[48]

Other writings and speeches of his repeatedly urge local religious groups to refuse the help of school authorities in recruiting and registering students, to avoid the use of public school machinery and buildings for any aspect of the program, and to refrain from trying "to 'get by' with legal infractions because their communities may not object."[49]

Conceivably, what appears to be non-compliance to an outside observer may be only the ignorance of some local officials. To get some limited information on this possibility, I sent questionnaires to the county superintendents of schools in Pennsylvania's 67 counties. One question confronted them with five possible forms of released time program and asked them to mark the alternatives they thought the Supreme Court would presently consider unconstitutional. The results, summarized in Table 1, indicate that nearly all the 50 county superintendents who responded to this question were well aware of the prevailing constitutional law on released time. If anything, they lean to a rigid interpretation of separation, as their overwhelming judgment on the uncertain third alternative indicates.[50] If this degree of constitutional sophistication prevails in the other states, noncompliance with the Zorach decision must be knowing evasion. In fact, in Pennsylvania the five county superintendents indicating classroom use for released time in their counties are even more aware of the constitutional niceties in this area than the average superintendent.

THE PRECEDENT EXPANDS

The impact of the Zorach rule does not stop with its direct consequences. Contrary to the gloomy expectations of Justice Frankfurter and others, there has been no further ardent rash of released time litigation following Zorach, nor has the decision fired up old debates on the issue. All sides in the general controversy over church-state relations have apparently decided that released time is now a settled issue, and have shifted

[48]Frank M. McKibben, *Report and Interpretation of the First National Conference on Weekday Religious Education* (National Council of Churches, no date), p. 12.

[49]Erwin L. Shaver, "A New Day Dawns for Weekday Religious Education," *International Journal of Religious Education*, Vol. 28 (July–August 1952), 8. For his other warnings, see *The Weekday Church School; Introducing the Weekday Church School* (National Council of Churches, no date); and *Remember the Weekday to Teach Thereon* (National Council of Churches, no date).

[50]A total of 59 of 67 answered the questionnaire, although only 50 responded to this question. A total of 33 superintendents reported they have released time programs in their counties, and 26 reported they do not. Of the 33 counties with released time, at least five still use school rooms, and two use community centers. The respondents making "correct" judgments on the issues of constitutionality are evenly divided between counties with released time programs and those without.

Table 1   Judgments of Fifty Pennsylvania School Superintendents on the Unconstitutionality of Released Time Plans

Released Time Plan	Responses of "Unconstitutional"	"Unconstitutional"
Classes in school rooms, taught by regular teacher	49	98%
Classes in school rooms, taught by representatives of religions	47	94
Classes in school rooms, taught after regular school hours	41	82
Classes taught off school premises by representatives of religions	8	16
Classes taught off school premises when all classes dismissed	1	2

their efforts to more advanced proposals. In this shifting of debate the Zorach decision has served both as legal precedent and political symbol and has had, consequently, a far-reaching influence quite beyond the particular facts on which it originally rested. The possibility of exactly this sort of application of the decision prompted the editors of the official organ of the National Council of churches to warn:

> . . . it is perhaps inevitable that some will uncritically assume that now "anything goes." This unwarranted implication will and ought to be stoutly resisted. This decision deals only with a specific case before the court. The decision says nothing explicitly about public aid to parochial schools, about required Bible reading and prayer in the public schools, or about the chaplaincy system of the Armed Services, military hospitals, and government schools.[51]

But their advice went unheeded.

At the very least, the Zorach precedent has been applied by analogy to validate or support varieties of religious education other than released time programs. When, for instance, the New York Board of Regents in March, 1955, recommended the injection of moral and spiritual values into public school curricula of the state, it cited the Zorach dicta to buttress its assumptions about the relevance of religious education to the Republic.[52] One scholar, proposing programs of teaching "about" religion in a "non-denominational" manner in the public schools, surmises that in light of the Zorach decision "there is good reason to believe that non-indoctrinational study of religion as a part of the culture will not fall under the ban."[53] Speaking also of this kind of program, another scholar ap-

---

[51]"Following the Best of Our Traditions," *National Council Outlook*, June 1952, p. 20.

[52]Mentioned in Joseph F. Costanzo, "Religion in Public School Education," *Thought*, Vol. 31 (Summer, 1956), p. 218.

[53]F. Ernest Johnson (ed.), *American Education and Religion: The Problem of Religion in the Schools* (New York: Harper & Row, 1952), p. 190.

praises the Zorach decision and declares that now "we have *carte blanche* to do what we think is morally, educationally, and philosophically sound in this field on the college level."[54] For another commentator permissive cooperation is quickly transformed to compulsory alliance:

> If, as the Court said, the state follows the best of our traditions when it encourages religious instruction or cooperates with religious authorities by adjusting the schedule of public events to sectarian needs (off public property), how much more faithful to American tradition is the state when it requires that its own schools teach America's [religious] heritage to its young citizens and future guardians of our Republic?[55]

Similar expansions of the Zorach rule to cover other issues of religion in education have occurred in the courts. A Massachusetts court in reaffirming the legality of Bible reading in the public schools drew attention to Zorach as sanctioning a similar religious activity in the schools.[56] A year later the Kentucky Court of Appeals held that employment of members of religious orders, wearing religious garb and symbols, to teach in public schools did not violate the church-state separation. In so holding, it cited the Zorach case as an example of the Supreme Court's approval of analogous aid to religion.[57] The Tennessee Supreme Court also recently ruled that reciting the Lord's Prayer, reading a verse of the Bible, or singing an "inspiring song" in the public schools did not breach the constitutional separation. In the course of its opinion the Court cited Zorach, but only to refer to its insistence that in cooperating with religion government be "neutral when it comes to competition between sects."[58]

The outward expansion of the Zorach precedent does not stop here. Courts and interest groups have taken its new doctrine of a "part-way" separation of church and state to expand the permissible area of government aid to and cooperation with organized religion. At the minimum some commentators edge cautiously away from the new doctrine to assert that "the legality of a friendly governmental attitude toward religious sects and institutions is now solidly affirmed."[59] And at the other extreme, one scholar found in the Zorach decision proof that the separa-

[54]David W. Louisell, "Constitutional Limitations and Supports for Dealing with Religion in Public Higher Education," *Religious Education*, Vol. 50 (September–October, 1955), p. 289.

[55]Costanzo, *op. cit.*, pp. 237–38.

[56]Commonwealth v. Renfrew, 126 N.E. 2d 109 (1955).

[57]Rawlings v. Butler, 290 S.W. 2d 801 (1956).

[58]Carden v. Bland, 288 S.W. 2d 718 (1956), p. 722. I should also note that in one state case the Zorach decision was used to deny an expansion of church-state cooperation. The New Jersey Supreme Court held the distribution of Gideon Bibles in the public schools to be preferential aid for some religious sects. See Tudor v. Board of Education, 100 A. 2d 857 (1953). This is, however, the only instance of the restrictive use of the precedent in state or federal courts of which I am aware.

[59]Paul N. Elbin, "Religion in State Schools," *Christian Century*, September 17, 1952, p. 1061.

tion of church and state can in reality amount to a denial of religious liberty: "If and where a community feels so strongly about religion in relation to the education of its children that it insists on some token of religious faith within the school, what we are dealing with is an elemental demand for religious liberty."[60] The California Supreme Court, in ruling that aid to religions in the form of property tax exemptions was not unconstitutional, also took note of the Court's new and relaxed doctrine of separation.[61]

Beyond these influences on other forms of religious education and on the issue of church-state relations, the precedent has spread slowly outward to touch more general questions of religious liberty. And no part of the decision has contributed so much to this inflation of the precedent as Justice Douglas' gratuitous assertion that "we are a religious people whose institutions presuppose a Supreme Being."[62] One could, in fact, discuss the Zorach decision simply as a study in the misadventures of a dictum, for the courts have been as uncritical and unrestrained as laymen in embracing it.

The Pennsylvania Supreme Court, for instance, turned to it to support its contention that "immoral" has a sufficient precise and definite meaning for satutory use.[63] A Federal district court used the dictum to support a denial of a petition for naturalization to an atheist who refused to take the statutory oath of allegiance. In the Zorach case, wrote the judge, the Supreme Court "has not deemed it to be old fashioned to declare, 'We are a religious people whose institutions presuppose a Supreme Being.'"[64] The same phrase has also helped a New York Judge find meaning for "immorality" in a concurring opinion,[65] and in another case supported the upholding of a pledge of allegiance to "one nation, under God."[66] Similarly, a member of the New York Board of Regents notes that in the Zorach ruling the Court proclaimed that "belief and dependence upon Almighty God is still the basic law of this great nation."[67] So the Court's dictum is turned from a statement of social fact to a constitutional imperative.

Finally, one ought to note that the Zorach precedent has in the hands of laymen expanded curiously in another direction. From its pages the friends of released time have fashioned two spurious constitutional doctrines. One of these comes from Erwin Shaver, who in several of his writings has read the Court's decision to demand rather than permit released time in the states. "It is now," he writes, "the 'unalienable right'

[60] Johnson, *op. cit.*, p. 195.
[61] Lundberg v. County of Alameda, 298 P. 2d 1 (1956), p. 7.
[62] 343 U.S. 306, p. 314.
[63] Commonwealth v. Randall, 133 A. 2d 276 (1957).
[64] Petition of Plywacki, 107 F. Supp. 593 (1952), p. 593.
[65] Commercial Pictures v. Board of Regents, 113 N.E. 2d 502 (1953), p. 511.
[66] Lewis v. Allen, 159 N.Y.S. 2d 807 (1957).
[67] *New York Times*, June 16, 1952, p. 13.

of every parent of a public school child, if he so requests it, to have his child excused for 'religious observance and education.' In no state or local community can this right be denied."[68] The other is voiced by a number of partisans who have convinced themselves that the decision "reaffirms the right of parents to determine the content and method of their children's education,"[69] and that "parental rights in education—a longstanding American tradition—received new vindication" in the decision.[70] There has been no judicial support for these two constitutional excursions.

The impact of Zorach beyond the bounds of the facts it decided and the rules it enunciated illustrates how Supreme Court precedents, as soon as they leave judicial hands, enter another realm of policy-making and become symbols in political debate and deliberation. A certain expansion and exaggeration of doctrine in this process is normal and expected. But the expansion is encouraged and accelerated when the decision is as freighted with sweeping dicta and legal homilies as Zorach. It is no overstatement to say that in their rush to embrace Justice Douglas' comforting words the friends of the decision have smothered its legal distinctions.

THE PRECEDENT VANISHES

On the other hand, there have been several instances where the Zorach decision has, surprisingly, been ignored when directly relevant; and ignored not only by interested groups and individuals but also in opinions of state courts and attorneys general. Since 1953 several such courts and officials have omitted mention of the Zorach rule in deciding the very questions of religious education and separation in which technicians of the law might be expected to consult the precedent. The fact that one finds the Zorach precedent serving in unlikely cases and failing to serve in other, more likely ones, lends credence to the old proposition that, contrary to the canons of jurisprudence, judges may deduce precedents from decisions.

The Virginia Supreme Court of Appeals, in holding state payments to sectarian training schools invalid, in 1955 cited the Everson and Mc-Collum cases as the last words on the separation of church and state.[71] And a dissent in a Kentucky case in 1956 cited the Everson case at length on the issue of separation without mentioning the Court's relaxation of the doctrine in Zorach.[72] In response to a 1954 query about the denominational use of public school facilities, with or without rental fee, the

68Shaver, *op. cit.*, note 49 above.
69Shaver, *op. cit.*, note 12 above, p. 39.
70Msgr. John S. Middleton, Secretary of Education for the New York Archdiocese, in *New York Times*, April 29, 1952, p. 23.
71Almond v. Day, 89 S.E. 2d 851 (1955), p. 858.
72Rawlings v. Butler, 290 S.W. 2d 801 (1956), pp. 812–13.

Nevada attorney general held such practices to breach the separation of church and state. After confessing he could find no cases deciding these particular facts, he cited the general dicta of the Everson and McCollum cases without mentioning the Court's less rigorous standards in Zorach.[73] Finally, the Illinois attorney general, approving the holding of sectarian classes on school premises by regular school teachers before or after school hours, did not mention Zorach. The McCollum precedent stands curiously alone in his opinion, even though for this purpose it is probably a less favorable precedent than Zorach.[74]

IN CONCLUSION

Initially, a precedent such as Zorach v. Clauson legalizes certain policies within the states, and interested parties and officials of the state apply the precedent to identical or similar programs. This much is the immediate and intended result of the Court's action, and it can be measured in terms of the growth of the program. More important, however, may well be the secondary impact of the decision on new and unsettled issues. The expansion of the Zorach precedent illustrates the tendency of an opinion to radiate constitutional sanctions far beyond its original boundaries. Its history ought also to suggest that a Supreme Court precedent is in no sense an objective fact, that its interpretations and application depend as much on the goals and involvements of the groups concerned as on the words of the decision itself. To rephrase the old saw, the precedent in reality consists of what influential partisans and decision-makers say the Supreme Court says it is.

In effect, the Zorach precedent represents a continuation and extension, rather than a resolution, of conflict in the arena of church-state relations. By altering the balance among the contending interests the decision has reframed the issue, shifted somewhat the focus of the conflict, triggered new interest group activity, and brought other policy-making organs into action. Released time programs are sanctioned and grow modestly with greatly diminished opposition, and their proponents take a cue from Zorach to press for new policies in the area of greater lenience the Court appeared to open up in the decision. So a decision such as this, especially one so thickly larded with popular dicta, creates a political and constitutional climate which encourages new goals and further innovations in aid to religion, thereby leading to the next test case. Beyond resolving old policy conflicts, then, the precedent has been used to advance and sanction new policy goals.

The evidence of noncompliance with the Zorach ruling indicates

---

[73]Opinion No. 316 of February 19, 1954, *Reports and Official Opinions of Attorney General of Nevada* (1952–1954), pp. 232–35.

[74]Opinion No. 204 of March 12, 1955, *Illinois Attorney General's Opinions for 1955*, pp. 84–86.

the limited effectiveness of the Court in maintaining constitutional uniformity within the federal system. Especially in religiously homogeneous communities where there are no dissident elements strong enough to protest or begin court action, the McCollum and Zorach rules are evaded and ignored. Although centralized judicial review of the litigation of such controversies has brought some uniformity of doctrine, the highly decentralized machinery of compliance thwarts real national uniformity of practice.

Finally, this analysis of the impact of Zorach v. Clauson illustrates once again that the doctrines of sociological jurisprudence cut two ways. Doubtless the Court felt forced by prevailing values to retreat in the Zorach case from its earlier absolutist position on the separation of church and state. But in so accommodating the mores of the time, it has created a symbol and an endorsement—the Zorach precedent—that is at the moment reshaping and molding the very values which the Court will have to attend to in later decisions.

POLICY FORMATION AND INTEREST GROUPS

Policy formation is the heart of government and also the most diffi-cult aspect for political scientists to study empirically in any but an anec-dotal fashion. There are numerous articles and books that set forth ideal systems for making decisions "scientifically" and that exhort pub-lic administrators to follow principles of rationality in formulating policy goals, but systematic descriptions of how officials actually do make policy are scarce.

Charles E. Lindblom's "The Science of 'Muddling Through' " is an attempt to do just this. Lindblom begins by outlining the supposedly ideal decision-making procedure: an official ranks values, collects and organizes all relevant information, compares the alternative policies, and then makes his decision. In fact, this ideal is rarely attained. The actual process is more casual: means and ends are mixed together, neither values nor policies are compared, and the result is likely to represent only an "incremental" departure from the status quo. Lindblom argues that this reality is not so deplorable. The scientific method is impossible except for the simplest of problems because it requires too much time and money and "assumes intellectual capacities and sources of information that men simply do not possess."

In the second selection Theodore J. Lowi analyzes policy forma-tion from a different standpoint: the character of the interest groups affected by a particular decision. His point of departure is the simple ob-servation that the outlines of struggles over what the government should do change fundamentally from one kind of policy area to another. In other words, the *subject matter* has a good deal to do with the *process* by which decisions are made. Lowi sees two important dimensions of domestic policies: (1) whether those who benefit from a policy and those who pay for it are identifiable individuals or groups and "come into direct confrontation" with each other; and (2) whether the benefits and/ or costs of the policy apply evenly to broad categories of people or can be "disaggregated," i.e., divided piecemeal and distributed to specific persons. From this starting point Lowi develops a theory that explains how politics differs so much from an issue area where policy decisions are obscure and almost unopposed to another issue area where publicity and controversy are omnipresent.

The steel price case and the Marshall Plan are examples of the latter type of decision. The third selection gives an illustration of esoteric politics, in this case, interest groups which quietly seek special tax provisions unopposed by any force but the Treasury Department. In this article Stanley S. Surrey shows that the officials resisting these requests are handicapped by the absence of interest group opposition to such provisions. In such cases, where all the intense participants are on one side, decisions are likely to be made without publicity by relatively specialized politicians, in this example, members of the House Ways and Means Committee and the Senate Finance Committee. Surrey's article reveals interrelationships between the congressional committee system, the administration, and lobbyists.

The same themes are followed in the selection by Clem Miller contrasting effective and ineffective lobbying by various groups of distressed farmers. This account of lobbying from the receiving end by a perceptive congressman demonstrates in a highly specific way how lobbying works—or doesn't work.

The last selection is also concerned with lobbying, but by officials in the executive branch rather than by private interests. This passage from Aaron Wildavsky's *The Politics of the Budgetary Process* describes the techniques used by agencies to get more funds from the Appropriations Committees. It can be used as a companion piece to Fenno's, for it shows how bureaucrats respond to the congressional obsession with budget cutting. Wildavsky's research is also valuable as an example of the interaction between private interests, political ambition, and the problems of effective calculation and control in a complex government. The two principal factors in success with the Appropriations Committee are support for the program from specific interests and ability to ease the Committee's problems of making valid decisions. The latter consideration explains the importance of mutual trust between bureaucrats and congressmen, while the former is illustrated by agency officials' attempts to find "clienteles" whom their programs can serve, which then can be counted on to supply political reinforcement when dealing with Congress.

CHAPTER FOURTEEN

THE SCIENCE OF "MUDDLING THROUGH"

CHARLES E. LINDBLOM

Suppose an administrator is given responsibility for formulating policy with respect to inflation. He might start by trying to list all related values in order of importance, e.g., full employment, reasonable business profit, protection of small savings, prevention of a stock market crash. Then all possible policy outcomes could be rated as more or less efficient in attaining a maximum of these values. This would of course require a prodigious inquiry into values held by members of society and an equally prodigious set of calculations on how much of each value is equal to how much of each other value. He could then proceed to outline all possible policy alternatives. In a third step, he would undertake systematic comparison of his multitude of alternatives to determine which attains the greatest amount of values.

In comparing policies, he would take advantage of any theory available that generalized about classes of policies. In considering inflation, for example, he would compare all policies in the light of the theory of prices. Since no alternatives are beyond his investigation, he would consider strict central control and the abolition of all prices and markets on the one hand and elimination of all public controls with reliance completely on the free market on the other, both in the light of whatever theoretical generalizations he could find on such hypothetical economies.

Finally, he would try to make the choice that would in fact maximize his values.

An alternative line of attack would be to set as his principal ob-

Reprinted by permission from the PUBLIC ADMINISTRATION REVIEW, *19 (Spring 1959), 79–88. Mr. Lindblom is Professor of Economics and Political Science at Yale University.*

jective, either explicitly or without conscious thought, the relatively simple goal of keeping prices level. This objective might be compromised or complicated by only a few other goals, such as full employment. He would in fact disregard most other social values as beyond his present interest, and he would for the moment not even attempt to rank the few values that he regarded as immediately relevant. Were he pressed, he would quickly admit that he was ignoring many related values and many possible important consequences of his policies.

As a second step, he would outline those relatively few policy alternatives that occurred to him. He would then compare them. In comparing his limited number of alternatives, most of them familiar from past controversies, he would not ordinarily find a body of theory precise enough to carry him through a comparison of their respective consequences. Instead he would rely heavily on the record of past experience with small policy steps to predict the consequences of similar steps extended into the future.

Moreover, he would find that the policy alternatives combined objectives or values in different ways. For example, one policy might offer price level stability at the cost of some risk of unemployment; another might offer less price stability but also less risk of unemployment. Hence, the next step in his approach—the final selection—would combine into one the choice among values and the choice among instruments for reaching values. It would not, as in the first method of policy-making, approximate a more mechanical process of choosing the means that best satisfied goals that were previously clarified and ranked. Because practitioners of the second approach expect to achieve their goals only partially, they would expect to repeat endlessly the sequence just described, as conditions and aspirations changed and as accuracy of prediction improved.

BY ROOT OR BY BRANCH

For complex problems, the first of these two approaches is of course impossible. Although such an approach can be described, it cannot be practiced except for relatively simple problems and even then only in a somewhat modified form. It assumes intellectual capacities and sources of information that men simply do not possess, and it is even more absurd as an approach to policy when the time and money that can be allocated to a policy problem are limited, as is always the case. Of particular importance to public administrators is the fact that public agencies are in effect usually instructed not to practice the first method. That is to say, their prescribed functions and constraints—the politically or legally possible—restrict their attention to relatively few values and relatively few alternative policies among the countless alternatives that might be imagined. It is the second method that is practiced.

Curiously, however, the literatures of decision making, policy formulation, planning, and public administration formalize the first approach rather than the second, leaving public administrators who handle complex decisions in the position of practicing what few preach. For emphasis I run some risk of overstatement. True enough, the literature is well aware of limits on man's capacities and of the inevitability that policies will be approached in some such style as the second. But attempts to formalize rational policy formulation—to lay out explicitly the necessary steps in the process—usually describe the first approach and not the second.[1]

The common tendency to describe policy formulation even for complex problems as though it followed the first approach has been strengthened by the attention given to, and successes enjoyed by, operations research, statistical decision theory, and systems analysis. The hallmarks of these procedures, typical of the first approach, are clarity of objective, explicitness of evaluation, high degree of comprehensiveness of overview, and, wherever possible, quantification of values for mathematical analysis. But these advanced procedures remain largely the appropriate techniques of relatively small-scale problem solving where the total number of variables to be considered is small and value problems restricted. Charles Hitch, head of the Economics Division of RAND Corporation, one of the leading centers for application of these techniques, has written:

> I would make the empirical generalization from my experience at RAND and elsewhere that operations research is the art of sub-optimizing, i.e., of solving some lower-level problems, and that difficulties increase and our special competence diminishes by an order of magnitude with every level of decision making we attempt to ascend. The sort of simple explicit model which operations researchers are so proficient in using can certainly reflect most of the significant factors influencing traffic control on the George Washington Bridge, but the proportion of the relevant reality which we can represent by any such model or models in studying, say, a major foreign-policy decision, appears to be almost trivial.[2]

Accordingly, I propose in this paper to clarify and formalize the second method, much neglected in the literature. This might be described

[1] James G. March and Herbert A. Simon similarly characterize the literature. They also take some important steps, as have Simon's recent articles, to describe a less heroic model of policy making. See *Organizations* (New York: Wiley, Inc., 1958), p. 137.

[2] "Operations Research and National Planning—A Dissent," *Operations Research*, Vol. 5 (October 1957), 718. Hitch's dissent is from particular points made in the article to which his paper is a reply; his claim that operations research is for low-level problems is widely accepted.

For examples of the kind of problems to which operations research is applied, see C. W. Churchman, R. L. Ackoff, and E. L. Arnoff, *Introduction to Operations Research* (New York: Wiley, 1957); and J. F. McCloskey and J. M. Coppinger, eds., *Operations Research for Management*, Vol. II (Baltimore: Johns Hopkins Press, 1956).

as the method of *successive limited comparisons.* I will contrast it with the first approach, which might be called the rational-comprehensive method.[3] More impressionistically and briefly—and therefore generally used in this article—they could be characterized as the branch method and root method, the former continually building out from the current situation, step-by-step and by small degrees; the latter starting from fundamentals anew each time, building on the past only as experience is embodied in a theory, and always prepared to start completely from the ground up.

Let us put the characteristics of the two methods side by side in simplest terms.

Rational-Comprehensive (Root)	Successive Limited Comparisons (Branch)
1a. Clarification of values or objectives distinct from and usually prerequisite to empirical analysis of alternative policies.	1b. Selection of value goals and empirical analysis of the needed action are not distinct from one another but are closely intertwined.
2a. Policy formulation is therefore approached through means-end analysis: First the ends are isolated, then the means to achieve them are sought.	2b. Since means and ends are not distinct, means-end analysis is often inappropriate or limited.
3a. The test of a "good" policy is that it can be shown to be the most appropriate means to desired ends.	3b. The test of a "good" policy is typically that various analysts find themselves directly agreeing on a policy (without their agreeing that it is the most appropriate means to an agreed objective).
4a. Analysis is comprehensive; every important relevant factor is taken into account.	4b. Analysis is drastically limited: i) Important possible outcomes are neglected. ii) Important alternative potential policies are neglected. iii) Important affected values are neglected.
5a. Theory is often heavily relied upon.	5b. A succession of comparisons greatly reduces or eliminates reliance on theory.

Assuming that the root method is familiar and understandable, we proceed directly to clarification of its alternative by contrast. In explaining the second, we shall be describing how most administrators do in fact approach complex questions, for the root method, the "best" way as a blueprint or model, is in fact not workable for complex policy ques-

---

[3]I am assuming that administrators often make policy and advise in the making of policy and am treating decision making and policy making as synonymous for purposes of this paper.

tions, and administrators are forced to use the method of successive limited comparisons.

INTERTWINING EVALUATION AND EMPIRICAL ANALYSIS (1b)

The quickest way to understand how values are handled in the method of successive limited comparisons is to see how the root method often breaks down in *its* handling of values or objectives. The idea that values should be clarified, and in advance of the examination of alternative policies, is appealing. But what happens when we attempt it for complex social problems? The first difficulty is that on many critical values or objectives, citizens disagree, Congressmen disagree, and public administrators disagree. Even where a fairly specific objective is prescribed for the administrator, there remains considerable room for disagreement on sub-objectives. Consider, for example, the conflict with respect to locating public housing, described in Meyerson and Banfield's study of the Chicago Housing Authority[4]—disagreement which occurred despite the clear objective of providing a certain number of public housing units in the city. Similarly conflicting are objectives in highway location, traffic control, minimum wage administration, development of tourist facilities in national parks, or insect control.

Administrators cannot escape these conflicts by ascertaining the majority's preference, for preferences have not been registered on most issues; indeed, there often *are* no preferences in the absence of public discussion sufficient to bring an issue to the attention of the electorate. Furthermore, there is a question of whether intensity of feeling should be considered as well as the number of persons preferring each alternative. By the impossibility of doing otherwise, administrators often are reduced to deciding policy without clarifying objectives first.

Even when an administrator resolves to follow his own values as a criterion for decisions, he often will not know how to rank them when they conflict with one another, as they usually do. Suppose, for example, that an administrator must relocate tenants living in tenements scheduled for destruction. One objective is to empty the buildings fairly promptly, another is to find suitable accommodation for persons displaced, another is to avoid friction with residents in other areas in which a large influx would be unwelcome, another is to deal with all concerned through persuasion if possible, and so on.

How does one state even to himself the relative importance of these partially conflicting values? A simple ranking of them is not enough; one needs ideally to know how much of one value is worth sacrificing

---

[4] Martin Meyerson and Edward C. Banfield, *Politics, Planning and the Public Interest* (New York: Free Press of Glencoe, 1955).

for some of another value. The answer is that typically the administrator chooses—and must choose—directly among policies in which these values are combined in different ways. He cannot first clarify his values and then choose among policies.

A more subtle third point underlies both the first two. Social objectives do not always have the same relative values. One objective may be highly prized in one circumstance, another in another circumstance. If, for example, an administrator values highly both the dispatch with which his agency can carry through its projects *and* good public relations, it matters little which of the two possibly conflicting values he favors in some abstract or general sense. Policy questions arise in forms which put to administrators such a question as: Given the degree to which we are or are not already achieving the values of dispatch and the values of good public relations, is it worth sacrificing a little speed for a happier clientele, or is it better to risk offending the clientele so that we can get on with our work? The answer to such a question varies with circumstances.

The value problem is, as the example shows, always a problem of adjustments at a margin. But there is no practicable way to state marginal objectives or values except in terms of particular policies. That one value is preferred to another in one decision situation does not mean that it will be preferred in another decision situation in which it can be had only at great sacrifice of another value. Attempts to rank or order values in general and abstract terms so that they do not shift from decision to decision end up by ignoring the relevant marginal preferences. The significance of this third point thus goes very far. Even if all administrators had at hand an agreed set of values, objectives, and constraints, and an agreed ranking of these values, objectives, and constraints, their marginal values in actual choice situations would be impossible to formulate.

Unable consequently to formulate the relevant values first and then choose among policies to achieve them, administrators must choose directly among alternative policies that offer different marginal combinations of values. Somewhat paradoxically, the only practicable way to disclose one's relevant marginal values even to oneself is to describe the policy one chooses to achieve them. Except roughly and vaguely, I know of no way to describe—or even to understand—what my relative evaluations are for, say, freedom and security, speed and accuracy in governmental decisions, or low taxes and better schools than to describe my preferences among specific policy choices that might be made between the alternatives in each of the pairs.

In summary, two aspects of the process by which values are actually handled can be distinguished. The first is clear: evaluation and empirical analysis are intertwined; that is, one chooses among values and among policies at one and the same time. Put a little more elaborately, one simultaneously chooses a policy to attain certain objectives and chooses the objectives themselves. The second aspect is related but distinct: the administrator focuses his attention on marginal or incremental values. Whether he is aware of it or not, he does not find general formulations of objectives very helpful and in fact makes specific marginal or incremental comparisons. Two policies, X and Y, confront him. Both promise the same degree of attainment of objectives a, b, c, d, and e. But X promises him somewhat more of f than does Y, while Y promises him somewhat more of g than does X. In choosing between them, he is in fact offered the alternative of a marginal or incremental amount of f at the expense of a marginal or incremental amount of g. The only values that are relevant to his choice are these increments by which the two policies differ; and, when he finally chooses between the two marginal values, he does so by making a choice between policies.[5]

As to whether the attempt to clarify objectives in advance of policy selection is more or less rational than the close intertwining of marginal evaluation and empirical analysis, the principal difference established is that for complex problems the first is impossible and irrelevant, and the second is both possible and relevant. The second is possible because the administrator need not try to analyze any values except the values by which alternative policies differ and need not be concerned with them except as they differ marginally. His need for information on values or objectives is drastically reduced as compared with the root method; and his capacity for grasping, comprehending, and relating values to one another is not strained beyond the breaking point.

RELATIONS BETWEEN MEANS AND ENDS (2b)

Decision making is ordinarily formalized as a means-ends relationship: means are conceived to be evaluated and chosen in the light of ends finally selected independently of and prior to the choice of means. This is the means-ends relationship of the root method. But it follows from all that has just been said that such a means-ends relationship is possible only to the extent that values are agreed upon, are reconcilable, and are stable at the margin. Typically, therefore, such a means-ends relationship is absent from the branch method, where means and ends are simultaneously chosen.

Yet any departure from the means-ends relationship of the root method will strike some readers as inconceivable. For it will appear to them that only in such a relationship is it possible to determine whether

[5]The line of argument is, of course, an extension of the theory of market choice, especially the theory of consumer choice, to public policy choices.

one policy choice is better or worse than another. How can an administrator know whether he has made a wise or foolish decision if he is without prior values or objectives by which to judge his decisions? The answer to this question calls up the third distinctive difference between root and branch methods: how to decide the best policy.

THE TEST OF "GOOD" POLICY (3b)

In the root method, a decision is "correct," "good," or "rational" if it can be shown to attain some specified objective, where the objective can be specified without simply describing the decision itself. Where objectives are defined only through the marginal or incremental approach to values described above, it is still sometimes possible to test whether a policy does in fact attain the desired objectives; but a precise statement of the objectives takes the form of a description of the policy chosen or some alternative to it. To show that a policy is mistaken one cannot offer an abstract argument that important objectives are not achieved; one must instead argue that another policy is more to be preferred.

So far, the departure from customary ways of looking at problem solving is not troublesome, for many administrators will be quick to agree that the most effective discussion of the correctness of policy does take the form of comparison with other policies that might have been chosen. But what of the situation in which administrators cannot agree on values or objectives, either abstractly or in marginal terms? What then is the test of "good" policy? For the root method, there is no test. Agreement on objectives failing, there is no standard of "correctness." For the methods of successive limited comparisons, the test is agreement on policy itself, which remains possible even when agreement on values is not.

It has been suggested that continuing agreement in Congress on the desirability of extending old age insurance stems from liberal desires to strengthen the welfare programs of the federal government and from conservative desires to reduce union demands for private pension plans. If so, this is an excellent demonstration of the ease with which individuals of different ideologies often can agree on concrete policy. Labor mediators report a similar phenomenon: the contestants cannot agree on criteria for settling their disputes but can agree on specific proposals. Similarly, when one administrator's objective turns out to be another's means, they often can agree on policy.

Agreement on policy thus becomes the only practicable test of the policy's correctness. And for one administrator to seek to win the other over to agreement on ends as well would accomplish nothing and create quite unnecessary controversy.

If agreement directly on policy as a test for "best" policy seems a poor substitute for testing the policy against its objectives, it ought to be remembered that objectives themselves have no ultimate validity other than they are agreed upon. Hence agreement is the test of "best" policy in both methods. But where the root method requires agreement on what elements in the decision constitute objectives and on which of these objectives should be sought, the branch method falls back on agreement wherever it can be found.

In an important sense, therefore, it is not irrational for an administrator to defend a policy as good without being able to specify what it is good for.

NON-COMPREHENSIVE ANALYSIS (4b)

Ideally, rational-comprehensive analysis leaves out nothing important. But it is impossible to take everything important into consideration unless "important" is so narrowly defined that analysis is in fact quite limited. Limits on human intellectual capacities and on available information set definite limits to man's capacity to be comprehensive. In actual fact, therefore, no one can practice the rational-comprehensive method for really complex problems, and every administrator faced with a sufficiently complex problem must find ways drastically to simplify.

An administrator assisting in the formulation of agricultural economic policy cannot in the first place be competent on all possible policies. He cannot even comprehend one policy entirely. In planning a soil bank program, he cannot successfully anticipate the impact of higher or lower farm income on, say, urbanization—the possible consequent loosening of family ties, possible consequent eventual need for revisions in social security and further implications for tax problems arising out of new federal responsibilities for social security and municipal responsibilities for urban services. Nor, to follow another line of repercussions, can he work through the soil bank program's effects on prices for agricultural products in foreign markets and consequent implications for foreign relations including those arising out of economic rivalry between the United States and the U.S.S.R.

In the method of successive limited comparisons, simplification is systematically achieved in two principal ways. First, it is achieved through limitation of policy comparisons to those policies that differ in relatively small degree from policies presently in effect. Such a limitation immediately reduces the number of alternatives to be investigated and also drastically simplifies the character of the investigation of each. For it is not necessary to undertake fundamental inquiry into an alternative and its consequences; it is necessary only to study those respects in which the proposed alternative and its consequences differ from the status quo. The empirical comparison of marginal differences among alternative policies that differ only marginally is, of course, a counterpart of the incremental or marginal comparison of values discussed above.[6]

Relevance As Well As Realism

It is a matter of common observation that in Western democracies public administrators and policy analysts in general do largely limit their analyses to incremental or marginal differences in policies that are chosen to differ only incrementally. They do not do so, however, solely because they desperately need some way to simplify their problems; they also do so in order to be relevant. Democracies change their policies almost entirely through incremental adjustments. Policy does not move in leaps and bounds.

The incremental character of political change in the United States has often been remarked. The two major political parties agree on fundamentals; they offer alternative policies to the voters only on relatively small points of difference. Both parties favor full employment, but they define it somewhat differently; both favor the development of water power resources, but in slightly different ways; and both favor unemployment compensation, but not the same level of benefits. Similarly, shifts of policy within a party take place largely through a series of relatively small changes, as can be seen in their only gradual acceptance of the idea of governmental responsibility for support of the unemployed, a change in party positions beginning in the early 30's and culminating in a sense in the Employment Act of 1946.

Party behavior is in turn rooted in public attitudes, and political theorists cannot conceive of democracy's surviving in the United States in the absence of fundamental agreement on potentially disruptive issues, with consequent limitation of policy debates to relatively small differences in policy.

Since the policies ignored by the administrator are politically impossible and so irrelevant, the simplification of analysis achieved by concentrating on policies that differ only incrementally is not a capricious kind of simplification. In addition, it can be argued that, given the limits on knowledge within which policy-makers are confined, simplifying by limiting the focus to small variations from present policy makes the most of available knowledge. Because policies being considered are like present and past policies, the administrator can obtain information and claim some insight. Non-incremental policy proposals are therefore typically not only politically irrelevant but also unpredictable in their consequences.

[6]A more precise definition of incremental policies and a discussion of whether a change that appears "small" to one observer might be seen differently by another is to be found in my "Policy Analysis," *American Economic Review*, Vol. 48 (June 1958), 298.

The second method of simplification of analysis is the practice of ignoring important possible consequences of possible policies, as well as the values attached to the neglected consequences. If this appears to disclose a shocking shortcoming of successive limited comparisons, it can be replied that, even if the exclusions are random, policies may nevertheless be more intelligently formulated than through futile attempts to achieve a comprehensiveness beyond human capacity. Actually, however, the exclusions, seeming arbitrary or random from one point of view, need be neither.

Achieving a Degree of Comprehensiveness
Suppose that each value neglected by one policy-making agency were a major concern of at least one other agency. In that case, a helpful division of labor would be achieved, and no agency need find its task beyond its capacities. The shortcomings of such a system would be that one agency might destroy a value either before another agency could be activated to safeguard it or in spite of another agency's efforts. But the possibility that important values may be lost is present in any form of organization, even where agencies attempt to comprehend in planning more than is humanly possible.

The virtue of such a hypothetical division of labor is that every important interest or value has its watchdog. And these watchdogs can protect the interests in their jurisdiction in two quite different ways: first, by redressing damages done by other agencies; and, second, by anticipating and heading off injury before it occurs.

In a society like that of the United States in which individuals are free to combine to pursue almost any possible common interest they might have and in which government agencies are sensitive to the pressures of these groups, the system described is approximated. Almost every interest has its watchdog. Without claiming that every interest has a sufficiently powerful watchdog, it can be argued that our system often can assure a more comprehensive regard for the values of the whole society than any attempt at intellectual comprehensiveness.

In the United States, for example, no part of government attempts a comprehensive overview of policy on income distribution. A policy nevertheless evolves, and one responding to a wide variety of interests. A process of mutual adjustment among farm groups, labor unions, municipalities and school boards, tax authorities, and government agencies with responsibilities in the fields of housing, health, highways, national parks, fire, and police accomplishes a distribution of income in which particular income problems neglected at one point in the decision processes become central at another point.

Mutual adjustment is more pervasive than the explicit forms it takes in negotiation between groups; it persists through the mutual impacts of groups upon each other even where they are not in communication. For all the imperfections and latent dangers in this ubiquitous process of mutual adjustment, it will often accomplish an adaptation of policies to a wider range of interests than could be done by one group centrally.

Note, too, how the incremental pattern of policy making fits with the multiple pressure pattern. For when decisions are only incremental —closely related to known policies, it is easier for one group to anticipate the kind of moves another might make and easier too for it to make correction for injury already accomplished.[7]

Even partisanship and narrowness, to use pejorative terms, will sometimes be assets to rational decision making, for they can doubly insure that what one agency neglects, another will not; they specialize personnel to distinct points of view. The claim is valid that effective rational coordination of the federal administration, if possible to achieve at all, would require an agreed set of values[8]—if "rational" is defined as the practice of the root method of decision making. But a high degree of administrative coordination occurs as each agency adjusts its policies to the concerns of the other agencies in the process of fragmented decision making I have just described.

For all the apparent shortcomings of the incremental approach to policy alternatives with its arbitrary exclusion coupled with fragmentation, when compared to the root method, the branch method often looks far superior. In the root method, the inevitable exclusion of factors is accidental, unsystematic, and not defensible by any argument so far developed, while in the branch method the exclusions are deliberate, systematic, and defensible. Ideally, of course, the root method does not exclude; in practive it must.

Nor does the branch method necessarily neglect long-run considerations and objectives. It is clear that important values must be omitted in considering policy, and sometimes the only way long-run objectives can be given adequate attention is through the neglect of short-run considerations. But the values omitted can be either long-run or short-run.

SUCCESSION OF COMPARISONS (5b)

The final distinctive element in the branch method is that the comparisons, together with the policy choice, proceed in a chronological series. Policy is not made once and for all; it is made and remade end-

---

[7]The link between the practice of the method of successive limited comparisons and mutual adjustment of interests in a highly fragmented decision-making process adds a new facet to pluralist theories of government and administration.

[8]Herbert Simon, Donald W. Smithburg, and Victor A. Thompson, *Public Administration* (New York: Alfred A. Knopf, Inc., 1950), p. 434.

lessly. Policy making is a process of successive approximation to some desired objectives in which what is desired itself continues to change under reconsideration.

Making policy is at best a very rough process. Neither social scientists, nor politicians, nor public administrators yet know enough about the social world to avoid repeated error in predicting the consequences of policy moves. A wise policy-maker consequently expects that his policies will achieve only part of what he hopes and at the same time will produce unanticipated consequences he would have preferred to avoid. If he proceeds through a *succession* of incremental changes, he avoids serious lasting mistakes in several ways.

In the first place, past sequences of policy steps have given him knowledge about the probable consequences of further similar steps. Second, he need not attempt big jumps toward his goals that would require predictions beyond his or anyone else's knowledge, because he never expects his policy to be a final resolution of a problem. His decision is only one step, one that if successful can quickly be followed by another. Third, he is in effect able to test his previous predictions as he moves on to each further step. Lastly, he often can remedy a past error fairly quickly—more quickly than if policy proceeded through more distinct steps widely spaced in time.

Compare this comparative analysis of incremental changes with the aspiration to employ theory in the root method. Man cannot think without classifying, without subsuming one experience under a more general category of experiences. The attempt to push categorization as far as possible and to find general propositions which can be applied to specific situations is what I refer to with the word "theory." Where root analysis often leans heavily on theory in this sense, the branch method does not.

The assumption of root analysts is that theory is the most systematic and economical way to bring relevant knowledge to bear on a specific problem. Granting the assumption, an unhappy fact is that we do not have adequate theory to apply to problems in any policy area, although theory is more adequate in some areas—monetary policy, for example—than in others. Comparative analysis, as in the branch method, is sometimes a systematic alternative to theory.

Suppose an administrator must choose among a small group of policies that differ only incrementally from each other and from present policy. He might aspire to "understand" each of the alternatives—for example, to know all the consequences of each aspect of each policy. If so, he would indeed require theory. In fact, however, he would usually decide that, *for policy-making purposes*, he need know, as explained above, only the consequences of each of those aspects of the policies in which they differed from one another. For this much more modest aspiration, he requires no theory (although it might be helpful, if available), for he can proceed to isolate probable differences by examining the differences in consequences associated with past differences in policies, a feasible program because he can take his observations from a long sequence of incremental changes.

For example, without a more comprehensive social theory about juvenile delinquency than scholars have yet produced, one cannot possibly understand the ways in which a variety of public policies—say on education, housing, recreation, employment, race relations, and policing—might encourage or discourage delinquency. And one needs such an understanding if he undertakes the comprehensive overview of the problem prescribed in the models of the root method. If, however, one merely wants to mobilize knowledge sufficient to assist in a choice among a small group of similar policies—alternative policies on juvenile court procedures, for example—he can do so by comparative analysis of the results of similar past policy moves.

THEORISTS AND PRACTITIONERS

This difference explains—in some cases at least—why the administrator often feels that the outside expert or academic problem solver is sometimes not helpful and why they in turn often urge more theory on him. And it explains why an administrator often feels more confident when "flying by the seat of his pants" than when following the advice of theorists. Theorists often ask the administrator to go the long way round to the solution of his problems, in effect ask him to follow the best canons of the scientific method, when the administrator knows that the best available theory will work less well than more modest incremental comparisons. Theorists do not realize that the administrator is often in fact practicing a systematic method. It would be foolish to push this explanation too far, for sometimes practical decision-makers are pursuing neither a theoretical approach nor successive comparisons, nor any other systematic method.

It may be worth emphasizing that theory is sometimes of extremely limited helpfulness in policy making for at least two rather different reasons. It is greedy for facts; it can be constructed only through a great collection of observations. And it is typically insufficiently precise for application to a policy process that moves through small changes. In contrast, the comparative method both economizes on the need for facts and directs the analyst's attention to just those facts that are relevant to the fine choices faced by the decision-maker.

With respect to precision of theory, economic theory serves as an example. It predicts that any economy without money or prices would in certain specified ways misallocate resources, but this finding pertains to an alternative far removed from the kind of policies on which administrators need help. On the other hand, it is not precise enough to predict the consequences of policies restricting business mergers, and this is the kind of issue on which the administrators need help. Only in relatively restricted areas does economic theory achieve sufficient precision to go far in resolving policy questions; its helpfulness in policy making is always so limited that it requires supplementation through comparative analysis.

SUCCESSIVE COMPARISON AS A SYSTEM

Successive limited comparisons is, then, indeed a method or system; it is not a failure of method for which administrators ought to apologize. Nonetheless, its imperfections, which have not been explored in this paper, are many. For example, the method is without a built-in safeguard for all relevant values, and it also may lead the decision maker to overlook excellent policies for no other reason than that they are not suggested by the chain of successive policy steps leading up to the present. Hence, it ought to be said that under this method, as well as under some of the most sophisticated variants of the root method—operations research, for example—policies will continue to be as foolish as they are wise.

Why then bother to describe the method in all the above detail? Because it is in fact a common method of policy formulation, and is, for complex problems, the principal reliance of administrators as well as of other policy analysts.[9] And because it will be superior to any other decision-making method available for complex problems in many circumstances, certainly superior to a futile attempt at superhuman comprehensiveness. The reaction of the public administrator to the exposition of method doubtless will be less a discovery of a new method than a better acquaintance with an old. But by becoming more conscious of their practice of this method, administrators might practice it with more skill and know when to extend or constrict its use. (That they sometimes practice it effectively and sometimes not may explain the extremes of opin-

[9]Elsewhere I have explored this same method of policy formulation as practiced by academic analysts of policy ("Policy Analysis," *op. cit.*). Although it has been here presented as a method for public administrators, it is no less necessary to analysts more removed from immediate policy questions, despite their tendencies to describe their own analytical efforts as though they were the rational-comprehensive method with an especially heavy use of theory. Similarly, this same method is inevitably resorted to in personal problem solving, where means and ends are sometimes impossible to separate, where aspirations or objectives undergo constant development, and where drastic simplification of the complexity of the real world is urgent if problems are to be solved in the time that can be given to them. To an economist accustomed to dealing with the marginal or incremental concept in market processes, the central idea in the method is that both evaluaion and empirical analysis are incremental. Accordingly I have referred to the method elsewhere as "the incremental method."

ion on "muddling through," which is both praised as a highly sophisticated form of problem solving and denounced as no method at all. For I suspect that insofar as there is a system in what is known as "muddling through," this method is it.)

One of the noteworthy incidental consequences of clarification of the method is the light it throws on the suspicion an administrator sometimes entertains that a consultant or adviser is not speaking relevantly and responsibly when in fact by all ordinary objective evidence he is. The trouble lies in the fact that most of us approach policy problems within a framework given by our view of a chain of successive policy choices made up to the present. One's thinking about appropriate policies with respect, say, to urban traffic control is greatly influenced by one's knowledge of the incremental steps taken up to the present. An administrator enjoys an intimate knowledge of his past sequences that "outsiders" do not share, and his thinking and that of the "outsider" will consequently be different in ways that may puzzle both. Both may appear to be talking intelligently, yet each may find the other unsatisfactory. The relevance of the policy chain of succession is even more clear when an American tries to discuss, say, antitrust policy with a Swiss, for the chains of policy in the two countries are strikingly different and the two individuals consequently have organized their knowledge in quite different ways.

If this phenomenon is a barrier to communication, an understanding of it promises an enrichment of intellectual interaction in policy formulation. Once the source of difference is understood, it will sometimes be stimulating for an administrator to seek out a policy analyst whose recent experience is with a policy chain different from his own.

This raises a question only briefly discussed above on the merits of like-mindedness among government administrators. While much of organization theory argues the virtues of common values and agreed organizational objectives, for complex problems in which the root method is inapplicable, agencies will want among their own personnel two types of diversification: administrators whose thinking is organized by reference to policy chains other than those familiar to most members of the organization and, even more commonly, administrators whose professional or personal values or interests create diversity of view (perhaps coming from different specialties, social classes, geographical areas) so that, even within a single agency, decision making can be fragmented and parts of the agency can serve as watchdogs for other parts.

DISTRIBUTION, REGULATION, REDISTRIBUTION: THE FUNCTIONS OF GOVERNMENT

THEODORE J. LOWI

In the long run, all governmental policies may be considered redistributive, because in the long run some people pay in taxes more than they receive in services. Or, all may be thought regulatory because, in the long run, a governmental decision on the use of resources can only displace a private decision about the same resource or at least reduce private alternatives about the resource. But politics works in the short run, and in the short run certain kinds of government decisions can be made without regard to limited resources. Policies of this kind are called "distributive," a term first coined for nineteenth-century land policies, but easily extended to include most contemporary public land and resource policies; rivers and harbors ("pork barrel") programs; defense procurement and research and development programs; labor, business, and agricultural "clientele" services; and the traditional tariff. Distributive policies are characterized by the ease with which they can be disaggregated and dispensed unit by small unit, each unit more or less in isolation from other units and from any general rule. "Patronage" in the fullest meaning of the word can be taken as a synonym for "distributive." These are policies that are virtually not policies at all but are highly individualized decisions that only by accumulation can be called a policy. They are policies in which the indulged and the deprived, the loser and the recipient, need never come into direct confrontation. Indeed, in many instances of distributive policy, the deprived cannot as a class be identified, because the most influential among them can be accommodated by further disaggregation of the stakes.

Reprinted by permission from Randall B. Ripley, ed., PUBLIC POLICIES AND THEIR POLITICS *(New York: W. W. Norton & Company, 1966), pp. 27–40. Mr. Lowi is Professor of Political Science at the University of Chicago.*

Regulatory policies are also specific and individual in their impact, but they are not capable of the almost infinite amount of disaggregation typical of distributive policies. Although the laws are stated in general terms ("Arrange the transportation system artistically." "Thou shalt not show favoritism in pricing."), the impact of regulatory decisions is clearly one of directly raising costs and/or reducing or expanding the alternatives of private individuals ("Get off the grass!" "Produce kosher if you advertise kosher!"). Regulatory policies are distinguishable from distributive in that in the short run the regulatory decision involves a direct choice as to who will be indulged and who deprived. Not all applicants for a single television channel or an overseas air route can be propitiated. Enforcement of an unfair labor practice on the part of management weakens management in its dealings with labor. So, while implementation is firm-by-firm and case-by-case, policies cannot be disaggregated to the level of the individual or the single firm (as in distribution), because individual decisions must be made by application of a general rule and therefore become interrelated within the broader standards of law. Decisions cumulate among all individuals affected by the law in roughly the same way. Since the most stable lines of perceived common impact are the basic sectors of the economy, regulatory decisions are cumulative largely along sectoral lines; regulatory policies are usually disaggregable only down to the sector level.

Redistributive policies are like regulatory policies in the sense that relations among broad categories of private individuals are involved and, hence, individual decisions must be interrelated. But on all other counts there are great differences in the nature of impact. The categories of impact are much broader, approaching social classes. They are, crudely speaking, haves and havenots, bigness and smallness, bourgeoisie and proletariat. The aim involved is not use of property but property itself, not equal treatment but equal possession, not behavior but being. The fact that our income tax is in reality only mildly redistributive does not alter the fact of the aims and the stakes involved in income tax policies. The same goes for our various "welfare state" programs, which are redistributive only for those who entered retirement or unemployment rolls without having contributed at all. The nature of a redistributive issue is not determined by the outcome of a battle over how redistributive a policy is going to be. Expectations about what it *can* be, what it threatens to be, are determinative.

ARENAS OF POWER

Once one posits the general tendency of these areas of policy or governmental activity to develop characteristic political structures, a number of hypotheses become compelling. And when the various hypotheses are accumulated, the general contours of each of the three arenas begin quickly to resemble, respectively, the three "general" thories of political process. The arena that develops around distributive policies is best characterized in the terms of E. E. Schattschneider's findings on the politics of tariff legislation in the nineteen-twenties. The regulatory arena corresponds to the pluralist school,[1] and the school's general notions are found to be limited pretty much to this one arena. The redistributive arena most closely approximates, with some adaptation, an elitist view of the political process.

(1) The distributive arena can be identified in considerable detail from Schattschneider's case-study alone.[2] What he and his pluralist successors did not see was that the traditional structure of tariff politics is also in largest part the structure of politics of all those diverse policies identified earlier as distributive. The arena is "pluralistic" only in the sense that a large number of small, intensely organized interests are operating. In fact, there is even greater multiplicity of participants here than the pressure-group model can account for, because essentially it is a politics of every man for himself. The single person and the single firm are the major activists.

Although a generation removed, Schattschneider's conclusions about the politics of the Smoot-Hawley Tariff are almost one-for-one applicable to rivers and harbors and land development policies, tax exemptions, defense procurement, area redevelopment, and government "services." Since there is no real basis for discriminating between those who should and those who should not be protected [indulged], says Schattschneider, Congress seeks political support by "giving a limited protection [indulgence] to all interests strong enough to furnish formidable resistance." Decision-makers become "responsive to considerations of equality, consistency, impartiality, uniformity, precedent, and moderation, however formal and insubstantial these may be." Furthermore, a "policy that is so hospitable and catholic . . . disorganizes the opposition."

When a billion-dollar issue can be disaggregated into many millions of nickel-dime items and each item can be dealt with without regard to the others, multiplication of interests and of access is inevitable, and so is reduction of conflict. All of this has the greatest bearing on the relations among participants and, therefore, the "power structure." Indeed, coalitions must be built to pass legislation and "make policy," but what of the nature and basis of the coalitions? In the distributive arena,

[1][The "pluralist school" of American political science contends that public policy outcomes can be largely explained by looking at the pattern of group activity. Some treat government as merely the recorder of group triumphs. Others treat governmental units or groups themselves. *Editor*]

[2]E. E. Schattschneider, *Politics, Pressures, and the Tariff* (Hamden, Conn.: Shoe String, 1935).

political relationships approximate what Schattschneider called "mutual non-interference"—"a mutuality under which it is proper for each to seek duties [indulgences] for himself but improper and unfair to oppose duties [indulgences] sought by others." In the area of rivers and harbors, references are made to "pork barrel" and "log-rolling," but these colloquialisms have not been taken sufficiently seriously. A log-rolling coalition is not one forged of conflict, compromise, and tangential interest but, on the contrary, one composed of members who have absolutely nothing in common; and this is possible because the "pork barrel" is a container for unrelated items. This is the typical form of relationship in the distributive arena.

The structure of these log-rolling relationships leads typically, though not always, to Congress; and the structure is relatively stable because all who have access of any sort usually support whoever are the leaders. And there tend to be "elites" of a peculiar sort in the Congressional committees whose jurisdictions include the subject matter in question. Until recently, for instance, on tariff matters the House Ways and Means Committee was virtually the government. Much the same can be said for Public Works on rivers and harbors. It is a broker leadership, but "policy" is best understood as cooptation rather than conflict and compromise.

Distributive issues individualize conflict and provide the basis for highly stable coalitions that are virtually irrelevant to the larger policy outcomes; thousands of obscure decisions are merely accumulated into a "policy" of protection or of natural-resources development or of defense subcontracting. Congress did not "give up" the tariff; as the tariff became a matter of regulation (see below), committee elites lost their power to contain the particpants because obscure decisions became interrelated, therefore less obscure, and more controversy became built in and unvoidable.

(2) The regulatory arena could hardly be better identified than in the thousands of pages written for the whole polity by the pluralists. But, unfortunately, some translation is necessary to accommodate pluralism to its more limited universe. The regulatory arena appears to be composed of a multiplicity of groups organized around tangential relations or David Truman's "shared attitudes." Within this narrower context of regulatory decisions, one can even go so far as to accept the most extreme pluralist statement that policy tends to be a residue of the interplay of group conflict. This statement can be severely criticized only by use of examples drawn from non-regulatory decisions.

As I argued before, there is no way for regulatory policies to be disaggregated into very large numbers of unrelated items. Because individual regulatory decisions involve direct confrontations of indulged and deprived, the typical political coalition is born of conflict and compromise among tangential interests that usually involve a total sector of the economy. Thus, while the typical basis for coalition in distributive politics is uncommon interests (log-rolling), an entirely different basis is typical in regulatory politics.

Owing to the unrelatedness of issues in distributive politics, the activities of single participants need not be related but rather can be specialized as the situation warrants it. But the relatedness of regulatory issues, at least up to the sector level of the trade association, leads to the containment of all these within the association. When all the stakes are contained in one organization, constituents have no alternative but to fight against each other to shape the policies of that organization or actually to abandon it.

What this suggests is that the typical power structure in regulatory politics is far less stable than that in the distributive arena. Since coalitions form around shared interests, the coalitions will shift as the interests change or as conflicts of interest emerge. With such group-based and shifting patterns of conflict built into every regulatory issue, it is in most cases impossible for a Congressional committee, an administrative agency, a peak association governing board, or a social elite to contain all the participants long enough to establish a stable power elite. Policy outcomes seem inevitably to be the residue remaining after the reductions of demands by all participants have been made in order to extend support to majority size. But a majority-sized coalition of shared interests on one issue could not possibly be entirely appropriate for some other issue. In regulatory decision-making, relationships among group leadership elements and between them on any one or more points of governmental access are too unstable to form a single policy-making elite. As a consequence, decision-making tends to pass from administrative agencies and Congressional committees to Congress, the place where uncertainties in the policy process have always been settled. Congress as an institution is the last resort for breakdowns in bargaining over policy, just as in the case of parties the primary is a last resort for breakdowns in bargaining over nominations. No one leadership group can contain the conflict by an almost infinite subdivision and distribution of the stakes. In the regulatory political process, Congress and the "balance of power" seem to play the classic role attributed to them by the pluralists.

Beginning with reciprocity in the 1930's, the tariff began to lose its capacity for infinite disaggregation because it slowly underwent redefinition, moving away from its purely domestic significance towards that of an instrument of international politics. In brief, the tariff, especially following World War II and our assumption of peace time international leadership, became a means of regulating the domestic economy for international purposes. The significant feature here is not the international but the regulatory part of the redefinition. As the process of redefinition took place, a number of significant shifts in power relations took place as well, because it was no longer possible to deal with each dutiable item in isolation. Everything in Bauer, Pool, and Dexter points toward the expansion of relationships to the level of the sector.* The political problem of the South was the concentration of textile industry there. Coal, oil, and rails came closer and closer to coalition. The final shift came with the 1962 Trade Expansion Act, which enabled the President for the first time to deal with broad categories (to the sector) rather than individual commodities.

Certain elements of distributive politics remain, for two obvious reasons. First, there are always efforts on the part of political leaders to disaggregate policies because this is the best way to spread the patronage and to avoid conflict. (Political actors, like economic actors, probably view open competition as a necessary evil or a last resort to be avoided at almost any cost.) Second, until 1962, the basic tariff law and schedules were still contained in the Smoot-Hawley Act. This was amended by Reciprocal Trade, but only to the extent of allowing negotiated reductions rather than reductions based on comparative costs. Until 1962, tariff politics continued to be based on commodity-by-commodity transactions, and thus until then tariff coalitions could be based upon individual firms (or even branches of large and diversified firms) and log-rolling, unrelated interests. The escape clause and peril point were maintained in the 1950's so that transactions could be made on individual items even within reciprocity. And the coalitions of strange bedfellows continued: "Offered the proper coalition, they both [New England textiles and Eastern railroads] might well have been persuaded that their interest was in the opposite direction."

But despite the persistence of certain distributive features, the true nature of tariff in the 1960's emerges as regulatory policy with a developing regulatory arena. Already we can see some changes in Congress even more clearly than the few already observed in the group structure. Out of a committee (House Ways and Means) elite, we can see the emergence of Congress in a pluralist setting. Even as early as 1954–1955, the compromises eventually ratified by Congress were worked out, not in committee through direct cooptation of interests, but in the Randall Commission, a collection of the major interests in conflict. Those issues that could not be thrashed out through the "group process" also could not be thrashed out in committee but had to pass on to Congress and the floor. After 1954 the battle centered on major categories of goods (even to the extent of a textile management-union entente) and the battle took place more or less openly on the floor. The weakening of the Ways

*Raymond A. Bauer, Ithiel de Sola Pool, and Lewis Anthony Dexter, *American Business and Public Policy: The Politics of Foreign Trade* (New York: Atherton Press, 1963) [Editor's note].

and Means Committee as the tariff elite is seen in the fact that in 1955 Chairman Jere Cooper was unable to push a closed rule through. The Rules Committee, "in line with tradition," granted a closed rule but the House voted it down 207—178. Bauer, Pool, and Dexter saw this as a victory for protectionism, but it is also evidence of the emerging regulatory arena—arising from the difficulty of containing conflict and policy within the governing committee. The last effort to keep the tariff as a traditional instrument of distributive politics—a motion by Daniel Reed to recommit, with instructions to write in a provision that Tariff Commission rulings under the escape clause be final except where the President finds the national security to be involved—was voted down 206—199. After that, right up to 1962, it was clear that tariff decisions would not be made piecemeal. Tariff became a regulatory policy in 1962; all that remains of distributive politics now are quotas and subsidies for producers of specific commodities injured by general tariff reductions.

(3) Compared particularly with the regulatory area, very few case-studies of redistributive decisions have ever been published. This in itself is a significant datum—which C. Wright Mills attributes to the middle-level character of the issues that have gotten attention. But, whatever the reasons, it reduces the opportunities for elaborating upon and testing the scheme. Most of the propositions to follow are illustrated by a single case, the "welfare state" battle of the 1930's. But this case is a complex of many decisions that became one of the most important acts of policy ever achieved in the United States. A brief review of the facts of the case will be helpful. Other cases will be referred to in less detail from time to time.

As the 1934 mid-term elections approached, pressures for a federal social security system began to mount. The Townsend Plan and the Lundeen Bill had become nationally prominent and were gathering widespread support. Both schemes were severely redistributive, giving all citizens access to government-based insurance as a matter of right. In response, the President created in June of 1934 a Committee on Economic Security (CES) composed of top cabinet members with Secretary of Labor Perkins as chairman. In turn, they set up an Advisory Council and a Technical Board, which held hearings, conducted massive studies, and emerged on January 17, 1935, with a bill. The insiders around the CES were representatives of large industries, business associations, unions, and the most interested government bureaucracies. And the detailed legislative histories reveal that virtually all of the debate was contained within the CES and its committees until a mature bill emerged. Since not all of the major issues had been settled in the CES's bill, its members turned to Congress with far from a common front. But the role of Congress was still not what would have been expected. Except for a short fight over committee jurisdiction (won by the more conservative Finance and Ways and Means Committees) the legislative process was extraordinarily quiet, despite the import of the issues. Hearings in both Houses brought forth very few witnesses, and these were primarily CES members supporting the bill, and Treasury Department officials, led by Morgenthau, opposing it with "constructive criticism."

The Congressional battle was quiet because the real struggle was taking place elsewhere, essentially between the Hopkins-Perkins bureaucracies and the Treasury. The changes made in the CES bill had all been proposed by Morgenthau (the most important one being the principle of contribution, which took away the redistributive sting). And the final victory for Treasury and mild redistribution came with the removal of administrative responsibility from both Labor and Hopkins's Federal Emergency Relief Administration. Throughout all of this some public expressions of opinion were to be heard from the peak associations, but their efforts were mainly expended in the quieter proceedings in the bureaucracies. The Congress's role seems largely to have been one of ratifying agreements that arose out of the bureaucracies and the class agents represented there. Revisions attributable to Congress concerned such matters as exceptions in coverage, which are part of the distributive game that Congress plays at every opportunity. The *principle* of the Act was set in an interplay involving (quietly) top executives and business and labor leaders.

With only slight changes in the left-right positions of the participants, the same pattern has been observed in income tax decisions. Professor Stanley S. Surrey notes: "The question, 'Who speaks for tax equity and tax fairness?,' is answered today largely in terms of only the Treasury Department.'" "Thus, in tax bouts . . . it is the Treasury versus percentage legislation, the Treasury versus capital gains, the Treasury versus this constituent, the Treasury versus that private group. . . . As a consequence, the congressman . . . [sees] a dispute . . . only as a contest between a private group and a government department." Congress, says Surrey, "occupies the role of mediator between the tax views of the executive and the demands of the pressure groups." And when the tax issues "are at a major political level, as are tax rates or personal exemptions, then pressure groups, labor organizations, the Chamber of Commerce, the National Association of Manufacturers, and the others, become concerned." The "average congressman does not basically believe in the present income tax in the upper brackets," but rather than touch the principle he deals in "special hardship" and "penalizing" and waits for decisions on principle to come from abroad. Amidst the 1954–1955 tax controversies, for example, Ways and Means members decided to allow each member one bill to be favorably reported if the bill met with unanimous agreement.

Issues that involve redistribution cut closer than any others along

Table 1   Published expressions of Manufacturers' Association of Connecticut on selected issues

	Number of References in Ten-year Period (1934–40, 1946–48)		Per Cent of Favorable References
1. Unspecified regulation	378		7.7
2. Labor relations, general	297		0.0
3. Wages and hours	195		0.5
Total expressions, redistribution		870	
4. Trade practices	119		13.8
5. Robinson-Patman	103		18.4
6. Antitrust	72		26.4
7. Basing points	55		20.0
8. Fair-Trade (Miller-Tydings)	69		45.5
Total expressions, regulation		418	

Source: Robert E. Lane, *The Regulation of Businessmen* (New Haven, 1953), 38ff. The figures are his; their arrangement is mine.

class lines and activate interests in what are roughly class terms. If there is ever any cohesion within the peak associations, it occurs on redistributive issues, and their rhetoric suggests that they occupy themselves most of the time with these. In a ten-year period just before and after, but not including, the war years, the Manufacturers' Association of Connecticut, for example, expressed itself overwhelmingly more often on redistributive than on any other types of issues. Table 1 summarizes the pattern, showing that expressions on generalized issues involving basic relations between bourgeoisie and proletariat outnumbered expressions on regulation of business practices by 870 to 418, despite the larger number of issues in the latter category. This pattern goes contrary to the one observed by Bauer, Pool, and Dexter in tariff politics, where they discovered, much to their surprise, that self-interest did not activate both "sides" equally. Rather, they found, the concreteness and specificity of protectionist interests activated them much more often and intensely than did the general, ideological position of the liberal-traders. This was true in tariff, as they say, because there the "structure of the communications system favored the propagation of particular demands." But there is also a structure of communications favoring generalized and ideological demands; this structure consists of the peak associations, and it is highly effective when the issues are generalizable. This is the case consistently for redistributive issues, almost never for distributive issues, and only seldom for regulatory issues.

As the pluralists would argue, there will be a vast array of organized interests for any item on the policy agenda. But the relations among the interests and between them and government vary, and the nature of and conditions for this variation are what our political analyses should be concerned with. Let us say, in brief, that on Monday night the big associations meet in agreement and considerable cohesion on "the problem of government," the income tax, the Welfare State. On Tuesday, facing regulatory issues, the big associations break up into their constituent trade and other specialized groups, each prepared to deal with special problems in its own special ways, usually along subject-matter lines. On Wednesday night still another fission takes place as the pork barrel and the other forms of subsidy and policy patronage come under consideration. The parent groups and "catalytic groups" still exist, but by Wednesday night they have little identity. As Bauer, Pool, and Dexter would say, they have preserved their unanimity through overlapping memberships. They gain identity to the extent that they can define the issues in redistributive terms. And when interests in issues are more salient in sectoral or geographic or individual terms, the common or generalized factor will be lost in abstractness and diffuseness. This is what happened to the liberal trade groups in the tariff battles of the 1950's, when "the protectionist position was more firmly grounded in direct business considerations and . . . the liberal-trade position fitted better with the ideology of the times. . . ."

Where the peak associations, led by elements of Mr. Mills's power elite, have reality, their resources and access are bound to affect power relations. Owing to their stability and the impasse (or equilibrium) in relations among broad classes of the entire society, the political structure of the redistributive arena seems to be highly stabilized, virtually institutionalized. Its stability, unlike that of the distributive arena, derives from shared interests. But in contrast to the regulatory arena, these shared interests are sufficiently stable and clear and consistent to provide the foundation for ideologies. Table 2 summarizes the hypothesized differences in political relationships drawn above.

Many of the other distinctive characteristics of this arena are related to, perhaps follow from, the special role of the peak associations. The cohesion of peak associations means that the special differences among related but competing groups are likely to be settled long before the policies reach the governmental agenda. In many respects the upperclass directors perform the functions in the redistributive arena that are performed by Congressional committees in the distributive arena and by committees and Congress in the regulatory arena. But the differences are crucial. In distributive policies there are as many "sides" as there are tariff items, bridges and dams to be built, parcels of public land to be given away or leased, and so on. And there are probably as many elites as there are Congressional committees and subcommittees which have jurisdiction over distributive policies. In redistribution, there will never be more than two sides and the sides are clear, stable, and consis-

Table 2   Arenas and political relationships: a diagrammatic survey

Arena	Primary Political Unit	Relation Among Units	Power Structure	Stability of Structure	Primary Decisional Locus	Implementation
Distribution	Individual, firm, corporation	Log-rolling, mutual-non-interference, uncommon interests	Non-conflictual elite with support groups	Stable	Congressional committee and/ or agency**	Agency centralized to primary functional unit ("bureau")
Regulation*	Group	"The coalition," shared subject-matter interest, bargaining	Pluralistic, multi-centered, "theory of balance"	Unstable	Congress, in classic role	Agency decentralized from center by "delegation," mixed control
Redistribution	Association	The "peak association," class, ideology	Conflictual elite, i.e., elite and counterelite	Stable	Executive and peak associations	Agency centralized toward top (above "bureau"), elaborate standards

*Given the multiplicity of organized interests in the regulatory arena, there are obviously many cases of successful log-rolling coalitions that resemble the coalitions prevailing in distributive politics. In this respect, the difference between the regulatory and the distributive arenas is thus one of degree. The *predominant* form of coalition in regulatory politics is deemed to be that of common or tangential interest. Although the difference is only one of degree, it is significant because this prevailing type of coalition makes the regulatory arena so much more unstable, unpredictable, and non-elitist ("balance of power"). When we turn to the redistributive arena, however, we find differences of principle in every sense of the word.
**Distributive politics tends to stabilize around an institutional unit. In most cases, it is the Congressional committee (or subcommittee). But in others, particularly in the Department of Agriculture, the focus is the agency or the agency *and* the committee. In the cities, this is the arena where machine domination continues, if machines were in control in the first place.

tent. Negotiation is possible, but only for the purpose of strengthening or softening the impact of redistribution. And there is probably one elite for each side. The elites do not correspond directly to bourgeoisie and proletariat; they are better understood under Wallace Sayre's designation of "money-providing" and "service-demanding" groups. Nonetheless, the basis for coalition is broad, and it centers around those individuals most respected and best known for worth and wealth. If the top leaders did not know each other and develop common perspectives as a result of common schooling, as Mills would argue, these commonalities could easily develop later in life because the kinds of stakes involved in redistributive issues are always the same. So institutionalized does the conflict become that governmental bureaucracies themselves begin to reflect them, as do national party leaders and Administrations. Finally, just as the nature of redistributive policies influences politics towards the centralization and stabilization of conflict, so does it further influence the removal of decision-making from Congress. A decentralized and bargaining Congress can cumulate but it cannot balance, and redistributive policies require complex balancing on a very large scale. What William H. Riker has said of budget-making applies here: " . . . legislative governments cannot endure a budget. Its finances must be totted up by party leaders in the legislature itself. In a complex fiscal system, however, haphazard legislative judgments cannot bring revenue into even rough alignment with supply. So budgeting is introduced—which transfers financial control to the budget maker. . . ." Congress can provide exceptions to principles and it can implement those principles with elaborate standards of implementation as a condition for the concessions that money-providers will make. But the makers of principles of redistribution seem to be the holders of the "command posts."

None of this suggests a power elite such as Mills would have had us believe existed, but it does suggest a type of stable and continual conflict that can only be understood in class terms. The foundation upon which the social-stratification and power-elite school rested, especially when dealing with national power, was so conceptually weak and empirically unsupported that its critics were led to err in the opposite direction by denying the direct relevance of social and institutional positions and the probability of stable decision-making elites. But the relevance of that approach becomes stronger as the scope of its application is reduced and as the standards for identifying the scope are clarified. But this is equally true of the pluralist school and of those approaches based on a "politics of this-or-that policy."

CHAPTER SIXTEEN

HOW SPECIAL TAX PROVISIONS GET ENACTED

STANLEY S. SURREY

Recently there has been considerable criticism directed against the existence in our tax laws of provisions granting special treatment to certain groups or individuals. The purpose of this article is to consider the question of why the Congress enacts these special tax provisions.

SOME MAJOR FACTORS

High Rates of Tax
The high rates of the individual income tax, and of the estate and gift taxes, are probably the major factor in producing special tax legislation. This is, in a sense, a truism, for without something to be relieved of, there would be no need to press for relief. The point is that the average congressman does not basically believe in the present rates of income tax in the upper brackets. When he sees them applied to individual cases, he thinks them too high and therefore unfair. Any argument for relief which starts off by stating that these high rates are working a "special hardship" in a particular case or are "penalizing" a particular taxpayer—to use some words from the tax lobbyist's approved list of effective phrases—has the initial advantage of having a sympathetic listener.

Tax Polarity
The existence of two rate structures in the income tax and of two types of taxes on the transfer of wealth permits a congressman to favor a spe-

Reprinted by permission from Randall B. Ripley, ed., PUBLIC POLICIES AND THEIR POLITICS *(New York: W. W. Norton & Company, Inc., 1966), pp. 51–60. Copyright 1957 by the Harvard Law Review Association. Mr. Surrey was Assistant Secretary of the Treasury for Tax Policy during the Kennedy and Johnson Administrations and is now Jeremiah Smith, Jr., Professor of Law at the Harvard Law School.*

cial group by placing its situation under the lower rate structure or the less effective tax. Thus, the presence of the twenty-five-per-cent capital-gains rate enables Congress to shift an executive stock option from the high rates applying to executive compensation to the lower capital-gains rate. If there were no special capital-gains rate, or if we did not tax capital gains at all, this shift could not be made, since a congressman would not completely exempt the stock option. Similarly, the presence of a gift tax permits certain transfers of wealth, such as transferred life insurance, to be shifted from the higher estate tax to the lower gift tax.

As a consequence, given this congressional tendency, we reach the paradox that having a gift tax as well as an estate tax may, given the present lack of proper co-ordination of the two taxes, result in less effective taxation of certain transfers of wealth than if we relied only on an estate tax.

Technical Complexity

The high rates of tax, the complexities of modern business, the desires of the wealthy and middle-income groups for clear tax charts to guide their family planning, the Government's need for protection against tax avoidance, the claims of tax equity, and various other factors have combined to make the income, estate, and gift taxes exceedingly complex in technical detail. These technicalities involve the drawing of countless dividing lines. Consequently, a case on the high-tax side of a line may closely resemble the cases on the other side receiving more favorable tax treatment. The result is a fertile ground for assertions of inequity and hardship as particular taxpayers desire legislation to bend the dividing lines and thereby extend the favorable treatment to their situations. Also, faulty tax planning, ill-advised legal steps, or transactions concluded in ignorance of tax law can produce severe tax consequences. These "tax penalties" could have been averted under an informed tax guidance that would have taken the taxpayer safely through the technical tax maze. In these circumstances, the taxpayer facing severe monetary hurt because of a "mere technicality" (to use the phrase that will be pressed on the congressman) is quite likely to evoke considerable sympathy for his plight.

History and Politics

The accidents of tax history also play a major role in the existence of special provisions. Tax-exempt securities in large part achieved their favored status through the vagaries of constitutional interpretation and not through any special desire to relieve the wealthy. Percentage depletion for oil and gas and the deduction of intangible drilling expenses have their roots in legislative compromises and administrative interpretation which for the most part do not appear to have been planned as special-interest relief. It is only later that the extent of the tax generosity inherent in such provisions is comprehended. But by then they are in the law, the problem of the group benefited is one of defense rather than attack, and the strategic advantages are all with that group. This is especially so when the area involved touches on major political matters, as in the case of percentage depletion and tax-exempt securities.

Political considerations naturally overhang this whole area, for taxation is a sensitive and volatile matter. Any major congressional action represents the compromises of the legislator as he weighs and balances the strong forces constantly focused on him by the pressure groups of the country. Many special provisions—capital gains, for one—are caught in these swirling pressures.

Separation of Executive and Legislative Branches of Government

But many of the tax provisions we are considering do not lie at this political level. They are simply a part of the technical tax law. They are not of major importance in their revenue impact. But they are of major importance to the group or individual benefited and they are glaring in their departure from tax fairness. The inquiry, therefore, must here be directed toward some of the institutional features in the tax-legislation process which may be responsible for special provisions of this technical variety.

Congress occupies the role of mediator between the tax views of the executive and the demands of the pressure groups. This is so whether the tax issue involved is a major political matter or a minor technical point. The Congress is zealous in maintaining this position in the tax field.

The Congress regards the shaping of a revenue bill as very much its prerogative. It will seek the views of the executive, for there is a respect for the sustained labors of those in the executive departments and also a recognition, varying with the times, of the importance of presidential programs. But control over the legislation itself, both as to broad policies and as to details, rests with the Congress. Hence a congressman, and especially a member of the tax committees, is in a position to make the tax laws bend in favor of a particular individual or group despite strong objection from the executive branch. Under such a governmental system the importance to the tax structure of the institutional factors that influence a congressman's decision is obvious.

SOME INSTITUTIONAL FACTORS

The Congressman's Desire To Be Helpful

A congressman's instincts are to be helpful and friendly. If it were otherwise, he would not be in Congress. When a constituent, or some other person who is in a position to claim attention, seeks legislative action, the congressman likes to respond within reason. If the proposal presented to him is at all rational he will, in all probability, at least introduce it in bill form so as not to offend the constituent. If the congressman is not a member of one of the tax committees, that may end the matter—but it may not, for the proposal has been launched and lies ready to be pushed ahead by whatever pressures may be generated in its behalf.

Lack of Congressional Appreciation of Departure From Fairness

In many cases the congressman considering a special tax provision may not realize that tax fairness is at all involved. He sees only the problem of the particular constituent or group concerned. The case in this focus may be very appealing, for human beings are involved with human problems. The income tax, always an impersonal, severe, monetary burden, becomes an oppressive force bearing down on men in difficulty. The congressman may therefore not even appreciate that arguments of over-all fairness and equity have any relation to the question, or may very well think them too intangible and remote. Provisions for the relief of the blind and the aged are perhaps illustrations. Or the congressman, moved simply by a desire to help a constituent, may not understand the ramifications of the proposal. He is not a tax technician and he may view the proposal in isolation rather than perceive its relationship to the intricate technical structure of the revenue code. The proposal, so viewed, becomes merely a "little old amendment" which helps a constituent and does no harm. His brother congressmen are quite willing to be good fellows and go along, especially if the congressman urging the proposal is well-liked. After all, they too from time to time will have "little old amendments" to propose. Thus, in 1955 the Ways and Means Committee decided that in the initial consideration of members' bills dealing with technical matters it would allow each member one bill to be considered and then reported by the full committee if the bill met with unanimous agreement.

The Treasury Department's Presentation

The congressman's failure to recognize that tax fairness is at all involved may often be due to the inadequacy of the Treasury Department's presentation of the issues. This is not said critically, but by way of explanation. The problem facing the Treasury in these matters is formidable. The interested constituents or groups are generally skillful in presenting their cases in appealing form. Their energies are concentrated on one matter; they have time and money to devote to it; they may have the advantage of personal acquaintance, directly or through intermediaries, with the congressman; they can obtain skilled counsel informed on the ways of the Congress. The Treasury's tax staff must tackle all of these problems; its members are usually not chosen for skill in the presentation of issues or in handling congressmen; although on the whole remarkably good, considering the compensation, they are rarely among the ablest in the tax field, nor do they usually have the needed experience.

Lack of Omniscience on the Part of the Treasury

The treasury tax staff is not omniscient. Yet understanding approaching omniscience is needed to do its job. A lack of knowledge on any particular matter, a failure of skill at any moment, can be fatal. The approach of the average congressman is to hear the private group, find out in general what it wants, react sympathetically for a variety of reasons, and then ask the Treasury whether there is any objection to the proposal. If the Treasury is off its guard and acquiesces, the proposal becomes law. If the Treasury is unprepared and presents a weak case, the proposal becomes law. Equally serious is the in-between situation in which the Treasury acknowledges that some hardship is present in the particular situation, but points out that the difficulty is but a phase of a general problem and that it has not yet been able fully to analyze the general area. It therefore urges that the particular proposal be postponed until further study is given to the whole matter. But recognition of some hardship and of some merit in his particular proposal is all that the Congressman needs. His constituent wants relief from that admitted hardship now, and not years later when the whole matter has been thought through and his case fitted into a solution appropriate for many cases. Hence the congressman will seek approval of the proposal in the limited form necessary to solve the particular problem presented to him—and a special tax provision is thereby born.

Lack of Opposition Apart From the Treasury Department to Proponents of Special Tax Provisions

The critical importance that attaches to the level of treasury competence and the fatal consequences of any slip on its part derive from its unique position in tax legislation. The question, "Who speaks for tax equity and tax fairness?," is answered today largely in terms of only the Treasury Department. If that department fails to respond, then tax fairness has no champion before the Congress. Moreover, it must respond with vigor and determination, and after a full explanation of the matter it must take a forthright stand on the issues. A Treasury Department that contents itself with explaining the issues and then solemnly declaring the matter to be one for the policy determination of Congress abdicates its responsibility. The congressman understands aggressiveness and a firm position. He is often in the position of the small boy inwardly seeking parental bounds for his conduct while outwardly declaiming against them. He may not accept policy guidance from the treasury policy spokesman, but he wants it presented. He will invariably interpret a treasury statement that the matter is one for his own policy decision as a victory for the seeker of the special provision.

Thus, in the tax bouts that a congressman witnesses the Treasury is invariably in one corner of the ring. Assuming the Treasury decides to do battle, which is hardly a safe assumption at all times, it is the Treasury versus percentage depletion, the Treasury versus capital gains, the Treasury versus this constituent, the Treasury versus that private group. The effect on the congressman as referee is inevitable. He simply cannot let every battle be won by the Treasury, and hence every so often he gives the victory to the sponsors of a special provision. Moreover, the Treasury is not an impersonal antagonist—it is represented before the Congress by individuals. These individuals are constantly forced to say that enactment of this proposal will be unfair, and the same of the next, and the next. The congressman, being only human, is bound from time to time to look upon these individuals as the Cassandras of the tax world. To avoid this dilemma, the Treasury in a close case will sometimes concede the issue if the proposal can be narrowly confined. It feels compelled to say "yes" once in a while simply to demonstrate that it maintains a balanced judgment and possesses a sense of fairness. A special provision is thus enacted simply because it happens to have somewhat more merit than the numerous other special proposals before the committees and because an affirmative answer here by the Treasury will protect negative responses to the other proposals.

The Congressional Tax Staff

The description of the Treasury as the principal and often the sole defender of tax fairness calls for a consideration of the role of the congressional tax staff. Most of the congressional tax technicians are members of the staff of the Joint Committee on Internal Revenue Taxation and as such serve both the House Ways and Means Committee and the Senate Finance Committee. There are a few technicians attached to the separate committees, and the clerks of the committees can play a very important role if they are personally so inclined. But institutionally the chief guidance given to Congress by its own employees comes from this joint committee staff.

The members of this staff work closely with the treasury tax technicians. Their work on the details of proposals and drafts is highly important, but the task of policy formulation and policy guidance to the congressmen appears to be reserved exclusively to the chief of that staff. His role is a difficult and unenviable one. Many congressmen pass along to him the tax proposals that they are constantly receiving from their constituents. Undoubtedly, the Chief of Staff discreetly but effectively blocks many of these proposals from proceeding further. But he also, whatever his inclinations may be, cannot in his situation always say "no." Perhaps inevitably on the crucial issues his role tends to be that of the advocate of the congressman advancing a particular proposal on behalf of a special group. The special-interest groups cannot appear in the executive sessions of the committees, and the congressman sympathetic to their point of view is not technically equipped to present their case; he tends to look to the Chief of Staff to assume that task. Further, he looks to the Chief of Staff to formulate the technical compromises which will resolve the dispute between the special-interest group and the Treasury. The Chief of Staff must therefore work closely with the Congressmen and be "brilliantly sensitive to their views." He must necessarily be able to gauge the degree of interest that a congressman may have in a proposal and weigh that in the consideration of the guidance he will give.

Because of these institutional pressures the Chief of Staff is very often the opponent of the Treasury Department before the tax committees. As a result, the difficulties for the average congressman on the tax committees become even greater. The issues get more and more complex as the "experts" disagree, and the congressman can hardly follow the technical exchanges. He is quite often content to fall back on the comfortable thought that, since the congressional expert appears to disagree with the treasury experts, there is adequate technical justification for voting either way. Hence the congressman is free to be guided by his own sympathies and instincts. Since generally these sympathies are in favor of the private groups, their proposals obtain his vote.

Unfortunately agreement between the congressional Chief of Staff and the Treasury can sometimes present just as difficult a problem. When the two disagree, at least the congressman who is seeking to discover the real issues may find them exposed at some time through this disagreement of experts. But if the experts agree, the effect is often to foreclose any real committee consideration of the issues. The congressman may be lulled into thinking that no significant issues are involved, and the proposal therefore becomes law. But if the government experts have erred, or if they have incorrectly gauged the congressional sentiment, special benefits may well result which the congressman would not have sanctioned had he understood what was involved.

Lack of Effective Aid From the Tax Bar

The lack of any pressure-group allies for the Treasury in its representation of the tax-paying public could have been remedied in part by effective aid from the tax bar. Yet for a good many years the vocal tax bar not only withheld any aid but very often conducted itself as an ally of the special pressure groups. Many a lawyer representing a client seeking a special provision could without much difficulty obtain American Bar Association or local-bar-association endorsement for his proposal.

He could then appear before Congress and solemnly exhibit the blessing of the legal profession. In fact, the activity of the Bar Association in this respect became so obvious that it seemingly boomeranged—many a congressman began instinctively to smell mischief when presented with a Bar Association tax proposal or endorsement.

Lack of Public Knowledge of Special Tax Provisions

Perhaps the most significant aspect of the consideration of special tax provisions by the Congress is that it usually takes place without any awareness of these events by the general public. Almost entirely, these matters lie outside of the public's gaze, outside of the voter's knowledge. The special provisions which are enacted lie protected in the mysterious complex statutory jargon of the tax law. This technical curtain is impenetrable to the newspapers and other information media. The public hears of debate over tax reduction or tax increase and it may learn something about the general rate structure. But it seldom learns that the high rates have no applicability to much of the income of certain wealthy groups. Nor does it understand how this special taxpayer or that special group is relieved of a good part of its tax burden. All of these matters are largely fought out behind this technical curtain. Hence the congressman favoring these special provisions has for the most part no accounting to make to the voters for his action. He is thereby much freer to lend a helping hand here and there to a group which has won his sympathy or which is pressing him for results.

The Relationship of Special Tax Provisions to Private-Relief Bills

Some of these special provisions represent simply private-relief claims for the particular individual benefited. While phrased as amendments to the tax law, they are only money claims against the Government based on the equities asserted to exist. Thus, it is said of a senator skilled in congressional ways that he would ask the legislative draftsman preparing the draft of a particular tax provision to make the amendment as general in language and as specific in application as was possible. The tax committees and the Treasury have not solved the problem of how to handle these special bills. Curiously enough, some tax situations do come through the judiciary committees as private-relief bills along with other private-relief bills involving claims against the Government. These bills may involve, for example, a removal of the barrier of the statute of limitations in cases thought equitable, or the recovery of funds spent for revenue stamps lost in some fashion. Here they are subject to the criteria developed over the decades by those committees in the handling of private-claims bills. These criteria are reasonably strict, and few of the bills pass the Congress. Of those that do succeed, a number are vetoed, and a veto is customarily regarded as a final disposition of the bill.

Many situations come before the tax committees that are quite comparable, in that the tax proposal is equivalent to a money claim against the Government, equal to the tax to be saved, sought for a specific taxpayer on equitable grounds. This is especially true in the case of proposals of a retroactive character. In the tax committees these special proposals tend to take on the coloration of an amendment to the tax code of the same character as all the various substantive tax matters before these committees. In essence, all amendments to the tax laws that private groups push on their own behalf are designed to lower taxes for the proponents and thereby relieve them from a tax burden to which they are subject. The special proposals thus become simply one more amendment in the long list of changes to be considered. The proponents of these special proposals are thereby able to cloak the fact that they are presenting private-relief claims against the Government. This is especially so when the proposal is considered as merely one more item in a general revenue bill. Here it is also protected from the threat—and fate—of a presidential veto. Even when the proposal is considered as a separate bill, the fact that it is merely one of the bills before a tax committee that is considering a great many substantive bills involving amendments to the tax code generally produces the same result. The committee will tend to focus on the proposal as curing a substantive defect in the law and lose sight of the fact that the special proposal is essentially a private-relief bill.

CHAPTER SEVENTEEN

THE WALNUT GROWERS & THE CHICKEN FARMERS

CLEM MILLER

In today's world most people are ready to admit that, as much as they dislike the word "lobbying," the function carried on under this name is essential to government. (In fact, the right to lobby is protected by the First Amendment.) In recent months there has been a graphic contrast here in effectiveness of lobbying activity between two segments of agriculture important to the economic health of our district: walnut growers and poultrymen. Both groups are in economic trouble because of abundance.

The walnut growers have a large carry-over from last year which, if placed on top of this year's record production, would break the market. The growers wanted the government to buy walnuts for diversion into the school lunch program, to be financed from existing tariffs on foreign walnut imports.

In the poultry industry, overproduction led by huge combines of bankers and feed companies, with million-hen farms, has broken the egg and meat-bird markets wide open. Independent poultrymen are losing six to eight cents per dozen eggs and four to eight cents per pound of meat, and are going bankrupt in droves.

The walnut industry is well organized. They have been proud that they don't have supports and don't ask the government for "handouts." This is easy to understand. One marketing cooperative controls seventy per cent of the state's production. So, when the industry got in trouble

Reprinted by permission from MEMBER OF THE HOUSE: LETTERS OF A CONGRESS-MAN, *John W. Baker, ed. (New York: Charles Scribner's Sons, 1962), pp. 137–40. Clem Miller represented the First District of California in Congress from 1959 through 1962, when he was killed in an airplane crash while campaigning for re-election.*

and came to Washington, they came well prepared. Each California congressman received a personal, carefully reasoned, five-page letter. It was followed up by another shorter letter. Then, a telegram called attention to the letters. Finally, there was a telephone call, asking for comments on the letters. By this time, we were fairly wide awake. Quite properly, the group worked through the congressman in whose district the association offices and many growers are located. We received several calls from the congressman's staff, alerting us, keeping us posted, offering help in answering questions.

After this preliminary barrage, the walnut growers' representative was ready to come to town. He set up headquarters at a nearby hotel. He called on congressmen several times, accompanied by a gentleman from the packing and canning section of the industry. He talked to my legislative assistant. Then we were all invited to a luncheon at the hotel, where the plight of the industry was laid before us and it was announced that a meeting was set up with the Secretary of Agriculture. Meticulous care was taken to be sure that all congressmen and senators who represent walnut growers would be there. In a large Department of Agriculture conference room with numerous department officials present, a skillful "presentation" for the industry was made. Immediately afterward, the walnut congressmen jumped up to demand action. One was self-contained but bitter about department inaction. Another pointed out the illogical Administration position in caustic terms. In turn, each congressman added his bit to the complaint. The Administration was bland and quite self-righteous ("We have more confidence in the walnut grower than he has in himself."). The exasperation of the Republican congressmen toward the Republican Secretary of Agriculture mounted. "Would a 'shaded' market price have to become a rout before the government moved?" they wanted to know. Administration officials were apparently unshaken.

However, two weeks later, the Administration did act. The industry was delighted. The work of the lobby had been effective.

Let's contrast this with the way things are developing in the egg industry. Some time ago I received a long letter from a constituent asking what congressional action was expected in poultry. A check revealed that nothing was contemplated in Congress. Of the seven thousand bills in Congress, there was not one on poultry or eggs. No hearings were scheduled. My interest piqued, I discussed the situation with House Agriculture Committee staff members and with the acting chairman of the subcommittee. The prevailing view was that since there was no leadership in the industry, and no agreement on policy, hearings would serve no purpose. I urged that hearings be scheduled to see if policy might materialize. A day or so later, I heard that a group of distressed poultrymen from New Jersey were asking to meet with their government. The Georgia and Alabama broiler people also asked to be heard.

All of a sudden, we learned that there was to be a hearing. Citizens were petitioning their government for a redress of grievances. At the hearing a crowd of two hundred poultrymen swarmed into the Agriculture Committee room which had been designed for about seventy-five people. Poultrymen-witnesses testified that the lowest prices in eighteen years for eggs and chickens were bankrupting an industry. As one witness said, in 1957 we were separating the men from the boys; in 1959 it was the men from the giants. One poultryman gave a stark, moving account of his town's plight. He gestured to his friends, sitting somberly at his side. They had been against federal help until a month or so previously, he said. "We called the people who were down here in 1957 looking for handouts 'radicals.' Now, we are here ourselves."

Throughout two days the same depressing story was recounted as the farmer-witnesses, speaking for themselves and other small producers, took their turn. Technological advances, together with banker-feed company-grower integration, were destroying the independent poultryman. Then the Department of Agriculture spokesman told its story. He confirmed the growers' story but indicated that nothing could be done. It was the inexorable law of supply and demand. Significantly absent were representatives of the larger organized farm groups. At nightfall, the poultrymen had to return to their farms.

What was the next step? It is up to the interested congressmen, they told us. How come, we asked? What are we to do? The leader of the poultrymen said that we had been told the problem. Yes, was the response, but he and his friends should go to see the Secretary of Agriculture. Testimony had indicated that Congress had already given the Secretary all of the authority he needed to act. It would do no good to pass more laws, particularly since they would certainly end with Presidential vetoes.

All of the men were active poultrymen who had to get back to their flocks. They were leaving that night. Who was to carry the ball for them here in Washington during the next critical weeks? Who was going to do the telephoning? Who was going to coordinate policy between New Jersey, California, Alabama, Wisconsin, Georgia, and Kansas? The answer from them was, "No one." We had been given a problem. It was ours now. The result to date: a resolution of the Agriculture Committee urging the Secretary to "implement such programs of purchase, diversion, and export of poultry products as will lead toward improvement of the present critical situation." Results for the poultrymen: nothing.

CHAPTER EIGHTEEN

BUDGETARY STRATEGIES OF ADMINISTRATIVE AGENCIES

AARON B. WILDAVSKY

Budgetary strategies are actions by governmental agencies intended to maintain or increase the amount of money available to them. Not every move in the budgetary arena is necessarily aimed at getting funds in a conscious way. Yet administrators can hardly help being aware that nothing can be done without funds, and that they must normally do things to retain or increase rather than decrease their income.

Our major purpose in this chapter is to describe in an orderly manner the major budgetary strategies currently being employed and to relate them to the environment from which they spring. In this way we can, for the first time, describe the behavior of officials engaged in budgeting as they seek to relate their requirements and powers to the needs and powers of others. Strategies are the links between the intentions and perceptions of budget officials and the political system that imposes restraints and creates opportunities for them. When we know about strategies we are not only made aware of important kinds of behavior, we also learn about the political world in which they take place.

Strategic moves take place in a rapidly changing environment in which no one is quite certain how things will turn out and new goals constantly emerge in response to experience. In this context of uncertainty, choice among existing strategies must be based on intuition and hunch, on an "educated guess," as well as on firm knowledge. Assuming a normal capacity to learn, however, experience should eventually provide a more reliable guide than sheer guesswork. When we discover

Reprinted by permission from THE POLITICS OF THE BUDGETARY PROCESS *(Boston: Little, Brown and Company, 1964), pp. 63–84. Mr. Wildavsky is Professor of Political Science and Dean of the Graduate School of Public Affairs at the University of California at Berkeley.*

strategies that are practiced throughout the entire administrative apparatus, we suspect that officials have discovered paths to success which may not be wholly reliable but which have proved to be more advantageous than the available alternatives.

UBIQUITOUS AND CONTINGENT STRATEGIES

What really counts in helping an agency get the appropriations it desires? Long service in Washington has convinced high agency officials that some things count a great deal and others only a little. Although they are well aware of the desirability of having technical data to support their requests, budget officials commonly derogate the importance of the formal aspects of their work as a means of securing appropriations. Budget estimates that are well prepared may be useful for internal purposes—deciding among competing programs, maintaining control of the agency's operations, giving the participants the feeling they know what they are doing, finding the cost of complex items. The estimates also provide a respectable backstop for the agency's demands. But, as several informants put it in almost identical words, "It's not what's in your estimates but how good a politician you are that matters."

Being a good politician, these officials say, requires essentially three things: cultivation of an active clientele, the development of confidence among other governmental officials, and skill in following strategies that exploit one's opportunities to the maximum. Doing good work is viewed as part of being a good politician.

Strategies designed to gain confidence and clientele are ubiquitous; they are found everywhere and at all times in the budgetary system. The need for obtaining support is so firmly fixed a star in the budgetary firmament that it is perceived by everyone and uniformly taken into account in making the calculations upon which strategies depend.

"Contingent" strategies are particular; they depend upon conditions of time and place and circumstance; they are especially dependent upon an agency's attitude toward the opportunities the budgetary system provides for. Arising out of these attitudes, we may distinguish three basic orientations toward budgeting in increasing order of ambition. First, defending the agency's base by guarding against cuts in old programs. Second, increasing the size of the base by moving ahead with old programs. Third, expanding the base by adding new programs. These types of strategies differ considerably from one another. An agency might cut popular programs to promote a restoration of funds; it would be unlikely to follow this strategy in adding new programs. We shall take up ubiquitous and contingent strategies in turn.

CLIENTELE

Find a Clientele

For most agencies locating a clientele is no problem at all; the groups interested in their activities are all too present. But for some agencies the problem is a difficult one and they have to take extraordinary measures to solve it. Men and women incarcerated in federal prisons, for instance, are hardly an ideal clientele. And the rest of society cares only to the extent of keeping these people locked up. So the Bureau of Prisons tries to create special interest in its activities on the part of Congressmen who are invited to see what is going on. "I wish, Mr. Bow, you would come and visit us at one of these prison places when you have the time. . . . I am sure you would enjoy it." The United States Information Agency faces a similar problem—partly explaining its mendicant status—because it serves people abroad rather than directly benefiting them at home. Things got so bad that the USIA sought to organize the country's ambassadors to foreign nations to vouch for the good job it said it was doing.

Serve Your Clientele

For an agency that has a large and strategically placed clientele, the most effective strategy is service to those who are in a position to help them. "If we deliver this kind of service," an administrator declared, "other things are secondary and automatic." His agency made a point of organizing clientele groups in various localities, priming them to engage in approved projects, serving them well, and encouraging them to inform their congressmen of their reaction. Informing one's clientele of the full extent of the benefits they receive may increase the intensity with which they support the agency's request.

Expand Your Clientele

In order to secure substantial funds from Congress for domestic purposes, it is ordinarily necessary to develop fairly wide interest in the program. This is what Representative Whitten did when he became a member of the Appropriations Committee and discovered that soil conservation in various watersheds had been authorized but little money had been forthcoming: "Living in the watersheds . . . I began to check . . . and I found that all these watersheds were in a particular region, which meant there was no general interest in the Congress in this type of program. . . . It led me to go before the Democratic platform committee in 1952 and urge them to write into the platform a plank on watershed protection. And they did." As a result, Whitten was able to call on more general support from Democrats and increase appropriations for the Soil Conservation Service watersheds.

Concentrate on Individual Constituencies

After the Census Bureau had made an unsuccessful bid to establish a national housing survey. Representative Yates gave it a useful hint. The proposed survey "is so general," Yates said, "as to be almost useless to the people of a particular community. . . . This would help someone like Armstrong Cork, who can sell its product anywhere in the country . . . but will it help the construction industry in a particular area to know whether or not it faces a shortage of customers?" Later, the Bureau submitted a new program that called for a detailed enumeration of metropolitan districts with a sample survey of other areas to get a national total. Endorsed by mortgage holding associations, the construction material industry, and federal and state housing agencies, the new National Housing Inventory received enthusiastic support in Congress where Representative Preston exclaimed, "This certainly represents a lot of imaginative thinking on your part. . . ." In another case the National Science Foundation made headway with a program of summer mathematics institutes not only because the idea was excellent but also because the institutes were spread around the country, where they became part of a constituency interest congressmen are supposed to protect.

Secure Feedback

Almost everyone claims that his projects are immensely popular and benefit lots of people. But how do elected officials know? They can only be made aware by hearing from constituents. The agency can do a lot to ensure that its clientele responds by informing them that contacting congressmen is necessary and by telling them how to go about it if they do not already know. In fact, the agency may organize the clientele in the first place. The agency may then offer to fulfill the demand it has helped to create. Indeed, congressmen often urge administrators to make a show of their clientele.

> SENATOR WHERRY: Do you have letters or evidence from small operators . . . that need your service that you can introduce into the record? . . . Is that not the test on how much demand there is for your services?
>
> RALSTON [Bureau of Mines]: Yes. . . . If it is important, as a rule they come to talk.

When feedback is absent or limited, congressmen tend to assume no one cares and they need not bother with the appropriation. " . . . A dozen or more complaints do not impress me very much. . . . We cut

this out last spring and we did not hear any wild howls of distress. . . ."
When feedback is present it can work wonders, as happened with the
Soil Conservation Service's Small Watershed program. Representative
Andersen waxed enthusiastic:

> . . . Will you point again to Chippewa-Shakopee? I know that project
> well because it is in my district. I wish the members of this subcommittee
> could see that Shakopee Creek watershed as it is today. The farmers in
> that neighborhood were very doubtful when we started that project. Now
> many of them tell us, Mr. Williams, that the additional crops they have
> obtained . . . have more than repaid their entire assessment. . . .

Guarding the treasury may be all right but it becomes uncomfortable
when cuts return to haunt a congressman. This is made clear in Representative Clevenger's tale of woe.

> CLEVENGER: I do not want to economize on the Weather Bureau. I
> never did. I do want an economical administration. . . . I have been
> blamed for hurricane Hazel. My neighbor, who lived across the road
> from me for 30 years, printed in his paper that I was to blame for $500
> millions in damage and 200 lives. . . . His kids grew up on my porch and
> yet he prints that on the first page and it is not "maybe." I just "am." He
> goes back to stories that related to cuts that I made when I was chairman
> of the Committee.

Most agencies maintain publicity offices (under a variety of titles)
whose job is to inform interested parties and the general public of the
good things the agency is doing, creating a favorable climate of opinion.
There may be objections to this practice on the part of congressmen
who do not like an agency and/or its programs, but those who favor the
agency consider it desirable. House subcommittee Chairman Kirwan urged
this course on the Bureau of Indian Affairs in connection with its Alaskan
Native Service, a worthy but not overly popular program. "Why don't you
make some arrangement to tell the Americans every year," Kirwan suggested, "instead of telling this committee what is going on? If you write
a letter when you go back to Alaska . . . I will guarantee you the press
will get it." The Weather Bureau was urged to put out some publicity of
its own by Representative Flood, who observed that

> . . . forecasts . . . were obviously, literally, and figuratively all wet. Some-
> body pointed out in this [New York Times] editorial where this . . .
> forecast has been "a little cold, a little wet, a little snow, but not bad." . . .
> But something took place which . . . dumped the whole wagonload of
> snow on Broadway and made them very unhappy. This happened re-
> peatedly over a period of 30 days, which did not make you look very good,
> if I can understate it. . . . All right. Why do you not prepare a statement

for the many newspaper readers in the area and point out to them that you know the problem is there, and that this is what you want to do about it. . . .

A final example comes from a student who wrote away for a summer job and received in reply a letter from an administrator refusing him on account of budgetary limitations. "Because of our inadequate funds at this critical time," the official wrote, "many students, like yourself, who would otherwise receive the professional training that this work provides, will be deprived of that opportunity. . . . Only prompt action by Congress in increasing these funds can make the success of our mission possible."

Divided We Stand

The structure of administrative units may be so arranged as to obtain greater support from clientele. It may be advantageous for a department to create more bureaus or subunits so that there are more claimants for funds who can attract support. "We have had the rather disillusioning experience that too often when we create a new agency of Government or divide up an existing agency," a Representative concluded, "that we wind up with more people on the payroll than we ever had before. . . ." There can be little doubt the division of the NIH into separate institutes for heart research, cancer research, and so on has helped mobilize more support than lumping them together under a general title with which it would be more difficult for individuals to identify.

United We Fall

The Weather Bureau is an example of an agency that did rather poorly until it took the many suggestions offered by its supporters in Congress and established a separate appropriation for research and development. The new category was the glamorous one and it was easier to attract support alone; being lumped in with the others hurt its appeal. Indeed, putting projects under the same category may be a way of holding down the expenditures for some so that others will not suffer. One of the imposing difficulties faced in building up the Polaris missile program was the fear that it would deprive traditional Navy activities of resources.

Advisory Committees Always Ask for More

Get a group of people together who are professionally interested in a subject, no matter how conservative or frugal they might otherwise be, and they are certain to find additional ways in which money could be spent. This apparently invariable law was stated by Representative Thomas when he observed that "All architects [doctors, lawyers, scientists, Indian chiefs] are for more and bigger projects, regardless of type. I have not seen one yet that did not come into that classification."

Advisors may be used to gather support for a program or agency in various ways. They may directly lobby with Congress or the President. "I happened to have lunch with Dr. Farber [a member of the quasi-governmental advisory committee of the NIH] the other day," Congressman Fogarty reveals, "and I learned there is considerable sentiment for these [clinical research] centers." Congressman Cederberg did not know of "anyone who would in any way want to hamper these programs, because I had lunch with Dr. Farber. . . ." Advisors may provide a focus of respectability and apparent disinterest to take the onus of self-seeking from the proponents of greater spending. They may work with interest groups and, indeed, may actually represent them. They may direct their attempts to the public media of information as anyone can see by reading the many columns written by Howard Rusk, M.D., a writer on medical subjects for the *New York Times,* requesting greater funds for the NIH.

Do Not Admit Giving in to "Pressure"

CIVIL AERONAUTICS BOARD OFFICIAL: . . . One of the reasons there has been such substantial expansion in local airline service, believe it or not, is largely due to the members of Congress.

REPRESENTATIVE FLOOD: I hope you are talking about Hazelton, Pa.

CAB OFFICIAL: I am talking about Pennsylvania as well as every other state. I do not want to leave the impression here that there has been undue pressure or that we have been unduly influenced by members of Congress, but we have tried to cooperate with them.

REPRESENTATIVE FLOOD: I do not care what the distinction is.

But If They Press Make Them Pay

CAB OFFICIAL: . . . Senator . . . if there are any members of Congress apprehensive about the increasing level of subsidy, this has not been evident to the Board. . . . I cannot think of any local service case in which we have not had at least 15, 20, or 25 members of Congress each one urging an extension of the local service to the communities in his constituency as being needed in the public interest. . . . We felt that they, if anyone, knew what the public interest required . . . as to local service . . . with full knowledge that this would require additional subsidy.

Avoid Being Captured

The danger always exists that the tail will wag the dog and the agency must exercise care to avoid being captured. Rival interests and congressmen may be played against each other. New clientele may be recruited to replace the old. The President and influential congressmen may be persuaded to help out. Or the agency may just decide to say "no" and take the consequences. Dependence upon the support of clientele, however, implies some degree of obligation and the agency may have to make some compromises. The interests involved may also have to compromise because they are dependent upon the administrators for access to decisions, and they may have many irons in the fire with the agency so that it is not worth jeopardizing all of them by an uncompromising stand on one.

Spending and Cutting Moods

Unfortunately, no studies have been made about how cutting and spending moods are generated. Yet changes in the climate of opinion do have an impact on appropriations. Possibly a great many groups and individuals, working without much direct coordination but with common purpose, seize upon events like reaction to World War II controls and spending to create a climate adverse to additional appropriations, or upon a recession to create an environment favorable for greater expenditures.

Budget Balancing and End-Runs

It is clear that the slogan of the balanced budget has become a weapon in the political wars as well as an article of belief. This is not the place to inquire whether the idea has merit; this is the place to observe that as a belief or slogan budget balancing is one determinant of strategies.

When the idea of a balanced budget becomes imbued with political significance, the Administration may seek appropriations policies that minimize the short-run impact on the budget although total expense may be greater over a period of years. In the Dixon-Yates case a proposed TVA power plant was rejected partly because it involved large immediate capital outlays. The private power plant that was accepted involved much larger expenditures over a 25-year period, but they would have had comparatively little impact during the Eisenhower Administration's term of office.[1]

When clientele are absent or weak there are some techniques for making expenditures that either do not appear in the budget or appear much later on. The International Monetary Fund may be given a Treasury note that it can use at some future date when it needs money. Public buildings may be constructed by private organizations so that the rent paid is much lower in the short run than an initial capital expenditure. The Federal Government may guarantee local bond flotations. An agency and its supporters who fear hostile committee action may also seek out ways to avoid direct encounter with the normal budgetary process. This action is bitterly opposed, especially in the House Appropriations Committee, as back-door spending.

I do not mean to suggest that getting constituency support is all

[1]See the author's *Dixon-Yates: A Study in Power Politics* (New Haven, Conn.: Yale University Press, 1962).

that counts. On the contrary, many agencies lay down tough criteria that projects must meet before they are accepted. The point is that there are ordinarily so many programs that can be truly judged worthwhile by the agency's standards that its major task appears to be that of gaining political support. Priorities may then be assigned on the basis of the ability of the program and its sponsors to garner the necessary support.

CONFIDENCE

The sheer complexity of budgetary matters means that some people need to trust others because they can check up on them only a fraction of the time. "It is impossible for any person to understand in detail the purposes for which $70 billion are requested," Senator Thomas declared in regard to the defense budget. "The Committee must take some things on faith." If we add to this the idea of budgeting by increments, where large areas of the budget are not subject to serious questions each year, committee members will treat an agency much better if they feel that its officials will not deceive them. Thus the ways in which the participants in budgeting try to solve their staggering burden of calculation constrains and guides them in their choice of means to secure budgetary ends.

Administrative officials are unanimously agreed that they must, as a bare minimum, enjoy the confidence of the Appropriations Committee members and their staff. "If you have the confidence of your subcommittee your life is much easier and you can do your department good; if you don't have confidence you can't accomplish much and you are always in trouble over this or that." How do agency personnel seek to establish this confidence?

Be What They Think They Are

Confidence is achieved by gearing one's behavior to fit in with the expectations of committee people. Essentially, the desired qualities appear to be projections of the committee members' images of themselves. Bureaucrats are expected to be masters of detail, hard-working, concise, frank, self-effacing fellows who are devoted to their work, tight with the taxpayer's money, recognize a political necessity when they see one, and keep the congressmen informed. Where Representative Clevenger speaks dourly of how "fewer trips to the coffee shop . . . help make money in most of the departments . . .," Rooney demonstrates the other side of the coin by speaking favorably of calling the Census Bureau late at night and finding its employees "on the job far later than usual closing hours." An administrator is highly praised because "he always knows his detail and his work. He is short, concise, and to the point. He does not waste any words. I hope when it comes to the economy in your laundry soap it is as great as his economy in words."

To be considered aboveboard, a fair and square shooter, a frank man is highly desirable. After an official admitted that an item had been so far down on the priority list that it had not been discussed with him, Senator Cordon remarked, "All right, I can understand that. Your frankness is refreshing." An administrator like Val Peterson, head of the Federal Civil Defense Agency, will take pains to stress that, "There is nothing introduced here that is in the field of legerdemain at all. . . . I want . . . to throw the cards on the table. . . ."

The budget official needs to show that he is also a guardian of the treasury: sound, responsible, not a wastrel; he needs to be able to defend his presentations with convincing evidence and to at least appear to be concerned with protecting the taxpayer. Like the lady who gets a "bargain" and tells her husband how much she has saved, so the administrator is expected to speak of economies. Not only is there no fat in his budget, there is almost no lean. Witness Dewey Short, a former congressman, speaking on behalf of the Army: "We think we are almost down to the bone. It is a modest request . . . a meager request. . . ." Agency people soon catch on to the economy motif: "I have already been under attack . . for being too tight with this money . . ." Petersen said, "I went through it [a field hospital] very carefully myself to be sure there were no plush items in it, nothing goldplated or fancy."

If and when a subcommittee drops the most prevalent role and becomes converted into an outright advocate of a program, as with the Polaris missile system, the budget official is expected to shoot for the moon and he will be criticised if he emphasizes petty economies instead of pushing his projects. Democratic subcommittee Chairman Kirwan and ranking Republican Jensen complained that the Bureau of Land Management did not ask for enough money for soil conservation. "It is only a drop in the bucket," Kirwan said, "they are afraid to come in." "This committee has pounded for the seven years I know of," Jensen responded, "trying to get them to come in with greater amounts for soil conservation and they pay no attention to it." The norm against waste may even be invoked for spending, as when Kirwan proclaimed that, "It is a big waste and loss of money for the U.S. Government when only 6 million is requested for the management of fish and wild life." In 1948 the head of the Cancer Institute was told in no uncertain terms, "The sky is the limit . . . and you come in with a little amount of $5,500,000. . . ." It is not so much what administrators do but how they meet the particular subcommittee's or chairman's expectations that counts.

Play It Straight!

Everyone agrees that the most important requirement of confidence, at least in a negative sense, is to be aboveboard. As Rooney once said, "There's only two things that get me mad. One is hare-brained schemes; the other is when they don't play it straight." A lie, an attempt to blatantly cover up some misdeed, a tricky move of any kind, can lead to an irreparable loss of confidence. A typical comment by an administrator states, "It doesn't pay to try to put something over on them [committee members] because if you get caught, you might as well pack your bags and leave Washington." And the chances of getting caught (as the examples that follow illustrate) are considerable because interested committeemen and their staffs have much experience and many sources of information.

Administrators invariably mention first things that should not be done. They believe that there are more people who can harm them than can help and that punishments for failure to establish confidence are greater than the rewards for achieving it. But at times they slip up and then the roof falls in. When Congress limited the amount of funds that could be spent on personnel, a bureau apparently evaded this limitation in 1952 by subcontracting out a plan to private investors. The House subcommittee was furious:

> REPRESENTATIVE JENSEN: It certainly is going to take a housecleaning . . . of . . . all people who are responsible for this kind of business.
> OFFICIAL: We are going to do it, Mr. Chairman.
> REPRESENTATIVE JENSEN: I do not mean "maybe." That is the most disgraceful showing that I have seen of any department.
> OFFICIAL: I am awfully sorry.

If a committee feels that it has been misled, there is no end to the punitive actions it can take. Senator Hayden spoke of the time when a bureau was given a lump-sum appropriation as an experiment. "Next year . . . the Committee felt outraged that certain actions had been taken, not indicated in the hearings before them. Then we proceeded to earmark the bill from one end to the other. We just tied it up in knots to show that it was the Congress, after all, that dictated policy."

Four months after a House subcommittee had recommended funds for a new prison, a supplemental appropriation request appeared for the purchase of an institution on the West Coast that the Army was willing to sell. Rooney went up in smoke. "Never mentioned it at all, did you?" "Well," the Director replied, "negotiations were very nebulous at that time, Mr. Rooney." "Was that," Rooney asked, "because of the fact that this is a first-rate penal institution . . . and would accommodate almost 1,500 prisoners?" It developed that Rooney, catching sight of the proposed supplemental, had sent a man out to investigate the institution. The supplemental did not go through.

Integrity

The positive side of the confidence relationship is to develop the opinion that the agency official is a man of high integrity who can be trusted. He must not only give but must also appear to give reliable information.

He must keep confidences and not get a congressman into trouble by what he says or does. He must be willing to take blame but never credit. Like a brand name, a budget official's reputation comes to be worth a good deal in negotiation. (This is called "ivory soap value," that is, 99 and 44/100% pure.) The crucial test may come when an official chooses to act contrary to his presumed immediate interests by accepting a cutback or taking the blame in order to maintain his integrity with his appropriations subcommittee. It must not be forgotten that the budget official often has a long-term perspective and may be correct in trying to maximize his appropriations over the years rather than on every single item.

If you are believed to have integrity, then you can get by more easily.

> ROONEY: Mr. Andretta [Justice Department], this is strictly a crystal ball operation; is it?
> ANDRETTA: That is right.
> ROONEY: Matter of an expert guess?
> ANDRETTA: An expert guess. . . .
> ROONEY: We have come to depend upon your guesswork and it is better than some other guesswork I have seen.

A good index of confidence is ability to secure emergency funds on short notice with skimpy hearings. No doubt Andretta's achievement was related to his frequent informal contact with Rooney.

> ROONEY: I am one who believes we should keep in close contact with one another so we understand one another's problems.
> ANDRETTA: I agree.
> ROONEY: You very often get in touch with us during the course of the year when you do not have a budget pending, to keep us acquainted with what is going on.
> ANDRETTA: Exactly. . . .

Make Friends: The Visit

Parallel in importance to the need for maintaining integrity is developing close personal relationships with members of the agency's appropriations subcommittee, particularly the chairman. The most obvious way is to seek them out and get to know them. One official reports that he visited every member of his subcommittee asking merely that they call on him if they wanted assistance. Later, as relationships developed, he was able to bring up budgetary matters. Appropriations hearings reveal numerous instances of personal visitation. A few examples should suggest how these matters work. Representative Jensen: "Mr. Clawson [head of the Bureau of Land Management] came in my office the other day to visit with me. I don't know whether he came in purposely or whether he was just going by and dropped in, and he told me that he was asking for considerably more money for . . . administrative expenses and we had quite a visit. . . ." A subordinate employee of that bureau showed that he had caught the proper spirit when he told Representative Stockman, "If you would like some up-to-date information from the firing line, I shall be glad to call at your office and discuss the matter; will you like for me to do that?"

When columnist Peter Edson editorially asked why the Peace Corps did so well in appropriations compared to the difficult times had by the State Department and the Agency for International Development, he concluded that Sargent Shriver, head of the Corps, "has tried to establish congressional confidence in him and his agency. Of the 537 members of Congress, he has called on at least 450 in their offices."

The Pay-Off

Wherever possible, the administrators seek to accommodate the congressman and impress him with their interest and friendliness. This attitude comes through in an exchange between a man in the Fish and Wildlife Service and Senator Mundt.

> OFFICIAL: Last year at the hearings . . . you were quite interested in the aquarium there [the Senator's state], particularly in view of the centennial coming up in 1961.
> MUNDT: That is right.
> OFFICIAL: Rest assured we will try our best to have everything in order for the opening of that centennial.

The administrator recognizes and tries to avoid certain disagreeable consequences of establishing relationships with congressmen. The congressman who talks too much and quotes you is to be avoided. The administrator who receives a favor may get caught unable to return one the following year and may find that he is dealing with an enemy, not just a neutral.

I'd Love to Help You But . . .

Where the administrator's notion of what is proper conflicts with that of a congressman with whom it is desirable to maintain friendly relations, there is no perfect way out of the difficulty. Most officials try to turn the congressman down by suggesting that their hands are tied, that something may be done in the future, or by stressing some other project on which they are agreed. After Representative Natcher spoke for the second time of his desire for a project in his district, Don Williams of the Soil Conservation Service complimented him for his interest in watershed activity in Kentucky but was "sorry that some of the projects that were proposed would not qualify under the . . . law . . . but . . they are highly desirable."

The "it can't be done" line was also taken by the Weather Bureau in an altercation with Representative Yates.

> WEATHER BUREAU OFFICIAL: We cannot serve the public by telephone . . . because we cannot put enough telephone lines or the operators to do the job. . . . We expect them [the public] to get it through the medium of newspapers, radio, television. If you have six telephones you have to have six people to deal with them. You have no idea. . . .
>
> YATES: Yes; I do have an idea, because I have been getting calls from them. What I want to do is have such calls transferred to you. . . . But as long as you have only one phone, I shall get the calls and you will not. . . .
>
> WEATHER BUREAU OFFICIAL: We find we must do it on the basis of mass distribution.

Sometimes, action may be delayed to see if the committee member will protest. The Weather Bureau tried for a while to cut off weather reports from Savannah to the northern communities that constitute its major source of tourists despite the fact that the Bureau's House subcommittee chairman represented that city.

> REPRESENTATIVE PRESTON: I wrote you gentlemen . . . a polite letter about it thinking that maybe you would [restore it] . . . and no action was taken on it. Now, Savannah may be unimportant to the Weather Bureau but it is important to me. . . .
>
> WEATHER BUREAU OFFICIAL: I can almost commit ourselves to seeing to it that the Savannah weather report gets distribution in the northeastern United States.

Give and Take

At other times some compromise may be sought. Secretary of Commerce Averell Harriman was faced with the unpalatable task of deciding which field offices to eliminate. He first used internal Department criteria to find the lower one-third of offices in point of usefulness. Then he decided which to drop or curtail by checking with the affected congressmen, trying to determine the intensity of their reactions, making his own estimate of whom he could and could not afford to hurt. Harriman's solution was a nice mixture of internal and political criteria designed to meet as many goals as possible or at least to hold the Department's losses down.[2]

Truth and Consequences

In the end, the administrator may just have to face the consequences of opposing congressmen whose support he needs. Even if he were disposed to accommodate himself to their desires at times, he may find that other

[2]Kathryn Smul Arnow, *The Department of Commerce Field Offices*, The Inter-University Case Program, ICP Case Series, No. 21, February, 1954.

influential members are in disagreement. He may play them off against one another or he may find that nothing he can do will help. The best he may be able to do is to ride out the storm without compounding his difficulties by adding suspicions of his integrity to disagreements over his policies. He hopes, particularly if he is a career man, that the congressmen will rest content to damn the deed without damning the man.

Emphasis

The administrator's perception of congressional knowledge and motivation helps determine the kind of relationships he seeks to establish. The administrator who feels that the members of his appropriations subcommittees are not too well informed on specifics and that they evaluate the agency's program on the basis of feedback from constituents, stresses the role of supporting interests in maintaining good relations with congressmen. He may not feel the need to be too careful with his estimates. The administrator who believes that the congressmen are well informed and fairly autonomous is likely to stress personal relationships and demonstrations of good work as well as clientele support. Certain objective conditions may be important here. Some subcommittees deal with much smaller areas than others and their members are likely to be better informed than they otherwise would be. Practices of appointment to subcommittees differ between House and Senate and with passing time. Where congressmen are appointed who have direct and important constituency interests at stake, the information they get from back home becomes more important. If the composition of the committee changes and there are many members without substantial background in the agency's work, and if the staff does not take up the slack, the agency need not be so meticulous about the information it presents. This situation is reflected in the hearings in which much time is spent on presenting general background information and relatively little on specifics.

Subcommittee and Other Staff

Relationships of confidence between agency personnel and subcommittee staff are also vital and are eagerly sought after. Contacts between subcommittee staff and budget officers are often frequent, intensive, and close. Frequency of contacts runs to several times a day when hearings are in progress, once a day when the bill is before the committee, and several times a month during other seasons. This is the principal contact the committee staff has with the Executive Branch. Even when the staff seeks information directly from another official in the agency, the budget officer is generally apprised of the contact and it is channeled through him. Relationships between ordinary committee staff members and Budget Bureau personnel are infrequent, although the people involved know one another. The top-ranking staff members and the Budget

Bureau liaison man, however, do get together frequently to discuss problems of coordination (such as scheduling of deficiency appropriations) and format of budget presentation. At times, the BOB uses this opportunity to sound out the senior staff on how the committee might react to changes in presentation and policy. The staff members respond without speaking for the committee in any way. There also may be extensive contact between committee staff and the staff attached to individual congressmen, but there is not a stable pattern of consultations. House and Senate Appropriations Committee staff may check with one another; also, the staff attached to the substantive committees sometimes may go into the financial implications of new bills with appropriations staff.

When an agency has good relations with subcommittee staff it has an easier time in Congress than it might otherwise. The agency finds that more reliance is placed on its figures, more credence is given to its claims, and more opportunities are provided to secure its demands. Thus one budget officer received information that a million-dollar item had been casually dropped from a bill and was able to arrange with his source of information on the staff to have the item put back for reconsideration. On the other hand, a staff man can do great harm to an agency by expressing distrust of its competence or integrity. Asked if they would consider refusing to talk to committee staff, agency officials uniformly declared that this refusal would be tantamount to cutting their own throats.

PARTIES, ELECTIONS, AND VOTERS

Elections determine which political leaders will rule, whether a Nixon or a Humphrey or a Kennedy will wield the powers of the president, whether Democrats or Republicans will control Congress, whether judicial appointees will be predominantly liberal or conservative. Because voters are the ultimate arbiters in the United States, both their political opinions and their election day habits are of crucial interest to students of politics.

The most impressive contributions to knowledge made by modern political science have been in the study of the individual citizen. The development of sample survey techniques makes it possible to learn with precision and reliability the opinions and behavior of the electorate and its major components. This is neither the place to describe survey methods nor the place to defend them. Just as medicine has its quacks and amateur practitioners, so there are corrupt and inept pollsters. But in the hands of responsible specialists, the opinion survey has proved a reliable tool for examining areas of human behavior hitherto inaccessible to researchers.

Since 1948 the field of voting behavior research has blossomed. The recency of this development means that only a few elections have yet been studied; it is possible that some major findings will be modified as continuing research broadens the base of evidence. But it is already known that some considerations play a greater role in some elections than in others; for example, the 1948 election saw voters divided more along social class lines than in subsequent elections, while 1960 saw a peak of religious consciousness, and 1968 saw a high point of racial awareness. The following selections, however, are not explanations of the outcomes of particular elections. Instead, they illuminate various enduring characteristics of individual political behavior and, in so doing, contribute to a richer and more realistic understanding of the workings of democratic politics.

The first, third, and fourth selections are based on findings from nationwide sample surveys in which about 1700 adults were interviewed once before and once after a given election. The second selection is from a study in which about 750 adult residents of Elmira, New York were interviewed three times during the 1948 campaign and once just after the election.

The opening article emphasizes the importance of voter identification with either the Republican or Democratic party. This partisan loyalty is the most durable and important single feature of American voting behavior. Almost four out of five Americans have never changed party. This persistent affiliation influences not only the way they vote, but also how they perceive political events. Since party identification is a determinant of voting behavior somewhat independent of both interest group membership and attitudes on political issues, the durability of this loyalty contributes importantly to political stability and the persistence of the two-party system.

The second selection throws further light on how individual behavior contributes to the maintenance of two-party politics. Berelson and his associates show not only that most voters are ill-informed about the campaign positions taken by the two presidential candidates, but also that this ignorance falls into certain revealing patterns: Many voters misperceive their favored candidate's stands so as to make them compatible with the voters' own beliefs on various issues; similarly, when the opposing candidate takes stands that the voters agree with, they tend to reverse his position. This misperception helps accommodate a diversity of opinion within the framework of two major parties.

The first two selections are concerned with forces maintaining stability in voting; yet, obviously, some people change their votes since the same party does not always win the White House. In the third selection, Donald E. Stokes discusses the dynamic factors in presidential elections, particularly the changing images of the two parties and the personalities of the candidates. The past continues to affect many Americans' views of the parties; the Republicans carried the burden of the Depression a generation after Herbert Hoover left office, while for decades the Democrats' image has been haunted by the coincidence of wars and Democratic administrations. Contemporary reality has some influence on these heritages, however. The prosperity of the Eisenhower years eroded the Hoover heritage for the Republicans, while Senator Barry Goldwater's belligerent views removed for the 1964 election the long-term Democratic image as the "party of war." The Vietnam War in the Johnson Administration restored this stigma to the Democrats in 1968.

These shifts are not as dramatic in their impact as the personal appeals of the two presidential candidates, which are an almost wholly nonideological element in the determination of political victory in the United States.

While it may be useful to think of political policies or leaders as "liberal" or "conservative," these words clearly are not applicable to the primitive political thought of the bulk of the electorate. In the fourth selection V. O. Key shows that most Americans do not even hold consistent opinions on issues. He goes on to discuss the implications of this condition for the operation of democratic government. On the one hand, the fact that alignments on different issues do not coincide means that political conflict is likely to be less intense, since allies on one issue are enemies on the next. On the other hand, this criss-crossing means that political parties are likely to be composed of such a jumble of contradictory impulses that they will be unable to act. Key speculates that complete paralysis is avoided through the actions of political leaders.

Herbert McClosky and his associates support Key's speculations with findings from their study of both leaders and rank-and-file members of the two major parties. They show that, taken as groups, Republican and Democratic voters are not so very far apart in their attitudes on a number of issues. But leaders of the two parties fully live up to expectations of partisan division; the Republican leadership is largely conservative, the Democratic leadership, mostly liberal. This situation explains why the policies of the two parties are more divergent than the opinions of their followers and provides further proof of the crucial role played by political leaders in providing coherence for our two-party system.

CHAPTER NINETEEN

PARTY
IDENTIFICATION

BENJAMIN I. PAGE AND RAYMOND E. WOLFINGER

American political parties are notoriously weak as organizations, but as frames of reference for voters they are pervasive and powerful influences. Indeed, the most important fact about the average American's political perspectives is his sense of identification with one or the other of the two major parties. This psychic "membership" is remarkably resistant to change and affects a variety of political attitudes and behaviors. Above all it conditions how Americans vote.[1]

I

Like people everywhere, Americans are not very interested in government and are poorly informed about public affairs. For example, only half the people know the name of one of their United States Senators.[2] An even smaller fraction understand the meaning of "liberalism" and "conservatism,"[3] or report reading or hearing *anything* about even one candidate in a congressional campaign (see Chapter 4 for more on public familiarity with Congress). There is scarcely any political issue, no

---

[1]The concept of party identification is one of the many fundamental contributions from the national election studies conducted since 1952 by the Survey Research Center of the University of Michigan. The major reports of these studies are Angus Campbell, Philip E. Converse, Warren E. Miller, and Donald E. Stokes, *The American Voter* (New York: John Wiley & Sons, Inc., 1960); and, by the same authors, *Elections and the Political Order* (New York: Wiley, 1966).

[2]Hazel G. Erskine, "The Polls: Textbook Knowledge," *Public Opinion Quarterly*, Vol. 27 (Spring 1963), p. 138.

[3]Philip E. Converse, "The Nature of Belief Systems in Mass Publics," in *Ideology and Discontent*, ed. David E. Apter (New York: The Free Press, 1964), p. 223.

Written especially for this book; © *1970 by Benjamin I. Page and Raymond E. Wolfinger. Mr. Page is a Lecturer in Political Science at Stanford University.*

matter how important, conspicuous, emotional, or persistent, on which more than three out of five people have an opinion *and* know what the federal government's policy is.[4] Yet most people react to current events and vote periodically. How do they make political decisions without adequate information on which to base their responses to the political world?

The answer lies in the existence of two political parties whose nominees for a century have had a monopoly on control of government, thus permitting most citizens to make political responses on the basis of a simple cue: the party label. The party is what psychologists call a "reference group," that is, a collectivity with which many people identify and which helps its members define themselves. We all have a set of pictures of ourselves, as Americans, southerners, farmers, Catholics, workers, radicals, and so on. Any individual "belongs" to several reference groups, each of which is relevant in different contexts. In dealing with black strangers, for example, a white student would be much more likely to think of himself as white than when talking with a white professor, when he would be most conscious of his identity as a student. In the political context the most important reference group for most people most of the time is the party. People approach political news and decisions not as wholly objective and unbiased observers, but as Democrats or Republicans. Having considerable psychological involvement in these identities, voters do not lightly abandon them.

Almost three-quarters of adult Americans consider themselves Republicans or Democrats and an additional eleven to nineteen percent say that they lean toward one party or the other.[5] Identical questions on this point have been asked of representative samples almost every year since 1952, and similar questions were asked in the 1930s. The pattern of answers is very stable; not only do the mass of voters identify with one of the two parties, but each party's share of the electorate has remained almost constant for a generation. Since the early 1950s the proportion of adult Americans calling themselves Democrats has never fallen below 44 percent nor risen above 51 percent. For Republicans the upper and lower boundaries are 24 percent and 29 percent. In 1968, for example, 45 percent called themselves Democrats and 10 percent more leaned toward the Democratic party, while 24 percent identified with the Republican party and an additional 9 percent leaned in that direction.[6]

The most important consequence of this party affiliation is that peo-

[4]*The American Voter, op. cit.,* pp. 172–75.

[5]*Elections and the Political Order, op. cit.,* p. 13.

[6]*Ibid.* These and other findings for 1968 were computed by the authors from data gathered by the Michigan Survey Research Center, which is the source of the data on previous years. The 1968 data were obtained through the Inter-University

ple who identify with a party are very likely indeed to vote for its nominees for office. More than 70 percent of party identifiers report that they have always or usually voted for their party's presidential candidates.[7] In any single presidential election the overwhelming majority of voters remain loyal to their party, even when one candidate wins by a landslide. Table 1 shows how strong and weak Republicans and Democrats have voted in every election from 1952 through 1968. (Strength of party identification was measured by asking those who classified themselves in one party or the other whether they were "strong" or "not so strong" Democrats or Republicans) In 1968, for example, 96 percent of the strong Republican and 82 percent of the weak Republican voters cast their ballots for Nixon. Although 1968 was a Republican year and there was a third party candidate, 85 percent of the strong and 58 percent of the weak Democrats voted for Humphrey. In every election since 1952 over 80 percent of the strong party identifiers and a substantial majority of the weak identifiers voted with their party. An individual's vote can be predicted more accurately from his party affiliation than from any other personal characteristic such as race, religion, or social class. Moreover, it is a better predictor than attitudes on any of the political issues of the day.

Party identification does not merely guide voters to pull a particular lever on election day; it also colors their evaluations of the candi-

Table 1   Relation of Party Identification to Presidential Vote, 1952–1968

Percentage of Vote for Democratic Candidate

Year	Democrats[a] Strong %	Democrats[a] Weak %	Independents %	Republicans[a] Weak %	Republicans[a] Strong %
1952	84	62	33	6	1
1956	85	63	27	7	1
1960	91	72	46	13	2
1964	95	82	66	43	10
1968	85	57	26	10	3

[a]See text for definition of "strong" and "weak."
Source: Survey Research Center data obtained through the Inter-University Consortium for Political Research; the authors are solely responsible for computation and analysis.

Consortium for Political Research, which is not responsible for computation and interpretation.

Some observers contend that there has been a considerable increase in independents in the past few years and see in this supposed trend evidence that party identification is declining. In fact, the Survey Research Center's data show that 10.5 percent of American adults called themselves independents at the time of the 1968 election, a gain of only two to three percent over the late 1950's. This modest increase may reflect nothing more than the growing number of young people in the electorate, for youth tend to be less partisan than older voters—just as they are less likely to be interested in politics or to go to the polls on election day.

[7]*The American Voter, op. cit.,* p. 125.

dates throughout the campaign. People generally see favorable personal qualities in their party's candidate. Indeed, the simple fact of nomination seems to confer on candidates more positive images than they had prior to the national convention.[8] Similarly, when nonpolitical figures like General Eisenhower enter the political arena and become identified with one party, they are soon evaluated in partisan terms.[9]

When other kinds of information about an election are less available, party identification becomes more important as a guide to voters. In congressional campaigns the candidates are usually less visible than presidential aspirants and thus their party label is the only cue that most voters have. Consequently party-line voting is even more common than in presidential elections (see Chapter 4). Voting for more obscure officials like state legislators is also based heavily on party loyalty. One of the most striking demonstrations of the power of the party label occurred in California during the 1950s. For generations the state's laws had allowed candidates to run for nomination not only in their own party's primary but in the primary of the opposite party as well. If a candidate won in both primaries he was as good as elected and had no need to worry about the general election. This was no mere theoretical possibility, for under this system, called "cross-filing," winning election in the primary was commonplace. As many as 82 percent of the congressional candidates, 90 percent of those running for the state senate, and 78 percent of the lower house candidates were elected in the primary.[10] The lucky winners usually were incumbents and their easy success was due to the simple fact that, being already in office, they were far more likely to be known than their primary opponents *in either party*. Cross-filing was abolished in 1959, but an earlier change in the law effectively crippled the process and in so doing dramatically revealed the importance of party labels in situations where most voters are uninformed about the candidates for whom they vote. Beginning with the 1954 primaries candidates could still cross-file, but their affiliation had to be printed on the ballot. Thus voters in the Democratic primary knew which candidates were really Democrats and which were Republicans trying for a quick victory, and vice versa; and this all but killed cross-filing. The addition of just three letters—"Dem." or "Rep."—after each candidate's name on the ballot supplied all the information most Californians needed to keep them from voting for the opposition party's man in their own primary, and the number of candidates elected in the primary dwindled to a handful. Such is the influence of party identification when information is scarce.

[8]Bertram H. Raven and Philip S. Gallo, "The Effects of Nominating Conventions, Elections, and Reference Group Identifications Upon the Perception of Political Figures," *Human Relations*, Vol. 18 (August 1965), p. 219.

[9]*Elections and the Political Order, op. cit.*, p. 330–32.

[10]Robert J. Pitchell, "The Electoral System and Voting Behavior: The Case of California's Cross-Filing," *Western Political Quarterly*, Vol. 12 (June 1959), pp. 459–84.

Beyond elections, party identification has a powerful effect on people's evaluations of governmental performance. Members of the president's party always are more likely to approve the way he handles his job. Approval of specific governmental actions follows the same pattern. For example, while Lyndon Johnson was president, Democrats were less likely than Republicans to say that "the U.S. made a mistake sending troops to fight in Vietnam."[11] During the economic recession of 1957–58 Democrats were not only more critical of the Eisenhower Administration's conduct of economic affairs, but more frequently claimed that the recession affected their own personal financial condition.[12]

We have emphasized the importance of party identification as a source of cues to voters and a frame of reference for evaluating political reality. It is not the only such factor, however; if it were, the Democrats would always win national elections, since they are easily the majority party at present.[13] But obviously the fortunes of parties, politicians, and causes do ebb and flow. These trends in postwar presidential elections are described in Chapter 21. The author of that selection, Donald E. Stokes, summarizes the sources of flux:

> And yet the nation's response to a changing political world is not wholly governed by fixed party loyalties. Some elements of political reality not agreeing with these loyalties will get through the perceptual screen raised in the partisan voter. A war, a sharp recession, a rash of scandal will leave their mark on all shades of partisans, although the mark will not be deep enough to change the votes of more than some. . . . other identifications will at times lead the voter to perceive political objects in a way that contradicts his partisan bias. As they become relevant to politics, identifications of a racial or national or religious or class nature may counter the perceptual effects of long-term partisan loyalties in large segments of the electorate.[14]

As Table 1 shows, there are always some people who cross party lines in presidential voting. For the most part these people *continue to think of themselves as adherents of their party*; their defections are the product of short-term forces such as an extraordinarily appealing candidate of the opposite party and/or a war, scandal, or other embarrassment to their own party. These factors brought Eisenhower millions of votes in 1952 and 1956 from people who continued to identify with the Democratic

[11]*Gallup Opinion Index*, April 1968, p. 14.

[12]*The American Voter, op. cit.*, pp. 388–89. This partisan difference persisted when similar occupational groups were compared.

[13]For a discussion of "The Concept of a Normal Vote" see *Elections and the Political Order, op. cit.*, chap. 2. One persistent impediment to mobilization of the Democratic advantage is the generally lower level of political participation among most of the social groups that are predominantly Democratic. See Lester W. Milbrath, *Political Participation* (Chicago: Rand McNally & Co., 1965), chap. 5. In short, better-off people are more likely both to be Republicans and to vote.

[14]*Elections and the Political Order, op. cit.*, pp. 127–28.

party (and continued to vote for Democratic candidates for other offices). When these temporary forces are no longer present, the defectors are very likely to return to their customary partisan loyalties.[15] Votes from Democrats were responsible for Eisenhower's capture of 58 percent of the vote in 1956. Two years later, when his name was not on the ballot, Republican congressional candidates got only 43 percent of the votes cast. "Without strong national candidates, pressing issues, or circumstances to move the electorate, the voting decision was determined largely by the standing party loyalties of those voters sufficiently concerned with politics to go to the polls."[16] Short-term forces generally are most important in influencing the votes of people who are least interested in politics. The winning margin in such elections, then, tends to be composed disproportionately of people who may sit out elections where such forces are absent.[17]

As long as the connection between a present policy or situation and a political party is clear, Americans tend to evaluate the policy in partisan terms. Proposals about future policy, however, usually lack any such direct connection with a party. In the absence of party-related cues, party identification has less impact on attitudes and Republicans and Democrats thus do not differ so sharply on specific issues. One study found that on twenty-four major issues there were only seven in which the differences between Republicans and Democrats were as great as ten to fifteen percent (see Chapter 23). Three general conclusions about public opinion are highly relevant to the ideological meaning of party "membership" in the United States: (1) Those people who identify with one party or the other are far from unanimous on any particular issue. Those subjects where there is some partisan differentiation—government regulation of business, federal aid to education, minimum wage laws, and the like—are basic bread-and-butter issues related to the New Deal origins of current party alignments. But even here there is considerable diversity, and on such topics as foreign policy followers of the two parties rarely differ in their opinions. (2) Moreover, people are on different sides of different issues. There is little attitudinal consistency from one issue to the next, except perhaps among a relatively small group of very interested and active people; hence the basis for truly ideological parties is lacking (see Chapter 22). This is one of the reasons why our parties are so "undisciplined." (3) One of the mechanisms fostering the persistence

[15]Campbell and his associates call the Eisenhower landslides "deviating elections," since they were a temporary departure from the continuing balance of party loyalties. These contrast with "maintaining elections," where the result reflects the underlying partisan distribution, and "realigning elections," in which that distribution is more or less durably altered (*ibid.*, chap. 4). "Realigning elections" are discussed in the latter part of this selection.

[16]*Ibid.*, p. 53.

[17]*Ibid.*, pp. 52–57.

of party loyalty under these circumstances is systematic misperception of the candidates' positions so as to make them more consistent with the opinions of their supporters (see Chapter 20).

These findings show that party identification does not consistently determine specific policy preferences. By the same token, the findings make it hard to argue that a person's stands on the issues lead him to identify with a particular party; indeed, given that we have only two parties, and numerous combinations of opinions, this would be most improbable. This leads us to a key question: If citizens do not "rationally" choose a party that reflects their opinions, how do they come to identify with one party or the other?

II

It would not be too wide of the mark to say that party identification is something of a habit; and like many habits, it is learned early in life and may persist without any apparent reason for its retention. Children consider themselves "Republicans" and "Democrats" at an early age. The than a third of children in the second grade say that they are Republicans or Democrats, as do over half of fifth graders.[18] These children develop partisan loyalties long before they can describe any differences between the parties. They are like baseball fans, supporting a party because it is "theirs."

There is every reason to think that children acquire their party affiliations from their parents. Most report that their party is the same as their parents', and few say that they belong to the opposite party.[19] The same pattern is found among high school students.[20] Yet while parents seem to pass on their partisan loyalties, the same is not true of their opinions on political issues. Research on high school seniors reveals very weak relationships between the students' political opinions and those of their parents.[21] This fact, like other findings reported below, suggests the extent to which party identification reflects habit and is independent of attitudes on particular issues.

The majority of adults also belong to the same party as their parents and never change their affiliation; only one in ten identifies with the op-

---

[18]Robert D. Hess and Judith V. Torney, *The Development of Political Attitudes in Children*, Anchor edition (Garden City, N.Y.: Doubleday & Company, Inc., 1968), p. 103; see also Fred I. Greenstein, *Children and Politics* (New Haven, Conn.: Yale University Press, 1965), p. 71.

[19]Hess and Torney, *op. cit.*, p. 103.

[20]M. Kent Jennings and Richard G. Niemi, "The Transmission of Political Values from Parent to Child," *American Political Science Review*, Vol. 62 (March 1968), pp. 172–74.

[21]*Ibid.*, pp. 174–76. Jennings and Niemi conclude that parental transmission of party identification "is a prime exception" to their findings of discontinuities in political perspectives between parents and children (p. 183).

posite party.[22] Such impressive continuity is maintained partly by social reinforcement. Party loyalties have roots in many social groupings: occupational, religious, ethnic, and regional. Most Americans are brought up with, marry, work with, and associate with people who tend to share these characteristics and who—as a side effect—share and reinforce their party identification.

This is a highly mobile society and one might expect that party loyalties would change for those people who go to college, get better jobs, or move to different parts of the country. Some partisan shifts do occur among such people. But the surprising fact is that these new personal experiences have relatively mild partisan consequences. Inherited party loyalties are a powerful anchor dragging against individual social change.[23] "Upward social mobility"—increases in education, social status, and income—is not accompanied by commensurate political change. Members of the middle class from working-class backgrounds are far less likely to be Republicans than are people born into the middle class.[24] It appears that most people whose votes are "inconsistent" with their class position, i.e., working-class Republicans and middle-class Democrats, follow parental political preferences.[25]

The social bases of party identification reflect only probabilistic tendencies, not hard-and-fast differences. Richer people and those in white-collar jobs are likely to be Republicans; those with less money and in blue-collar jobs tend to be Democrats. Negroes, Catholics and Jews are mostly Democrats, a tendency which exists quite apart from differences in income or occupation. Southerners and city dwellers are mostly Democrats; Republicans predominate in small towns and in the Midwest.[26] The imperfect character of these relationships must be emphasized. All broad social groupings include sizable proportions of followers of both parties. This cross-cutting of social and political cleavages, more prevalent in America than in many other parts of the world, is thought to have a good deal to do with the relative stability and low temperature of American politics (see Chapter 25).

Both at the level of social groups and in many individual cases party loyalties persist long after the reasons for their formation have become irrelevant. The Civil War's impact on partisan alignments seems to have been particularly tenacious. Gratitude to the "party of Lincoln" kept

[22]*The American Voter, op. cit.*, pp. 147–48.

[23]See, e.g., *ibid.*, pp. 448–50.

[24]James A. Barber, Jr., *Social Mobility and Political Behavior* (Chicago: Rand McNally & Co., 1970).

[25]Bernard R. Berelson *et al., Voting* (Chicago: University of Chicago Press, 1954), p. 90. See also Arthur S. Goldberg, "Discerning a Causal Pattern Among Data on Voting Behavior," *American Political Science Review*, Vol. 60 (December 1966), pp. 913–22.

[26]*The American Voter, op. cit.*, pp. 158–60.

Negroes in the Republican party until the New Deal, and to this day the dogged Republicanism of the poor mountaineers in eastern Tennessee reflects their ancestors' dissent from the majority Confederate sentiment in that state. One of the most striking examples of this phenomenon is in the voting patterns of Indiana counties: For a century some have been Republican strongholds while others, apparently identical economically, are consistently Democratic. A well-known study uncovered the sources of these differences in the homes of Indiana's original settlers—New England or the South: "If one plots on the map of Indiana clusters of underground railroad stations and points at which Union authorities had difficulties in drafting troops, he separates, on the whole, Republican and Democratic counties."[27] The authors concluded that for many people voting choices are merely "a reaffirmation of past decisions"—in this case, decisions originally made by the voters' great-grandfathers.

The present proportions and social characteristics of Democrats and Republicans have been fairly stable for many years, but they have not been the same throughout our history, nor are they frozen for all time. At times in the past, usually marked by severe social or economic strains, party alignments have shifted, either through a fairly wholesale movement toward one party or realignment of a particular social group. Our two-party system in its present form emerged from the turmoil of the Civil War and its aftermath, which drove white southerners into the Democratic party and established the new Republican party as the only alternative. "The distribution of partisan attachments in the nation today, a century after the Civil War, follows the same regional lines laid down at that time."[28] The economic problems and controversies of the 1890s, focusing on the great debate about the free coinage of silver, strengthened the Republican hold on the Northeast and weakened the party in the West.[29] In 1928 the presidential candidacy of Al Smith (the first Catholic nominated for president) on the Democratic ticket brought anti-Catholic sentiment to a head. It had the far more durable consequence of bringing to the Democrats millions of immigrant votes, thus establishing the big cities as a Democratic stronghold, a role they continue to play today.[30] Shortly thereafter came the most widespread realignment of the twentieth century. The prolonged and shattering trauma of the Depression put an end to the Republicans' longstanding position as the country's majority party. Even this development was

[27]V.O. Key, Jr. and Frank Munger, "Social Determinism and Electoral Decision: The Case of Indiana," in *American Voting Behavior* eds. Eugene Burdick and Arthur J. Brodbeck (Glencoe, Ill.: The Free Press, 1959), p. 457n.

[28]*The American Voter, op. cit.*, p. 152.

[29]V. O. Key, Jr., "A Theory of Critical Elections," *Journal of Politics*, Vol. 17 (February 1955), pp. 3–18.

[30]*Ibid.*; and Samuel J. Eldersveld, "The Influence of Metropolitan Party Pluralities in Presidential Elections Since 1920: A Study of Twelve Cities," *American Political Science Review*, Vol. 43 (September 1949), p. 1196.

limited by the force of habit, however, for it seems that most of the millions who swelled the Democrats' ranks were not converted Republicans but either young people coming of age with the 1930s or previously apathetic citizens shocked into political consciousness by the Depression.[31] No matter how sweeping, electoral realignments in the United States are based on a heritage of past crises, loyalties, and resentments.

Along with these massive changes in party allegiances have come smaller-scale conversions. Jews, for example, voted Republican by a ratio of about four to one until the New Deal; since then they have been just as overwhelmingly Democratic.[32] Members of a nationality group in a particular locality sometimes transfer their partisan loyalties when one of their number is "recognized" by nomination for high office, thus making ethnicity both highly relevant and favorably related to one party.[33] Like so many other realignments, such changes may persist long after the candidate responsible has passed from the scene.

If most voters inherit party allegiance from their parents and cling to it despite changes in life-style and opinions, if the ultimate source of partisan loyalties often is some long-forgotten issue, party identification looks very much like a psychological crutch for the ignorant. It unquestionably *is* a support, but one would be wrong to consider party identifiers more ignorant and apathetic than independents. No myth has been more thoroughly demolished by voting behavior research than the civics-textbook-ideal independent voter, aloof from partisan attachments, who "votes for the man" only after careful attention to the campaign. The fact of the matter is that the average independent is *less* interested, involved, and knowledgeable about politics than the average party identifier.[34] Furthermore, most people whose votes switch from one election to the next are not among the more interested and informed segments of the electorate.[35] Party identification probably helps many people vote in accordance with their self interest. Political information is particularly costly to the uneducated, which means, of course, mainly the poor and members of minority groups. Party labels seem to be a shortcut that is especially helpful for those who are handicapped in mastering the intricacies of candidates and issues. In nonpartisan local elections—where candidates do not run with party designations—such people often stay away from the polls or vote for the best-known candidates, who may not share their goals. But cities with partisan elections have much higher

[31]*The American Voter, op. cit.*, pp. 153–56.

[32]*Ibid.*, p. 159.

[33]Raymond E. Wolfinger, "The Development and Persistence of Ethnic Voting," *American Political Science Review*, Vol. 59 (December 1965), pp. 896–908.

[34]*The American Voter, op. cit.*, pp. 143–45. There are some interested and well informed independents, but they are the exception.

[35]*Ibid.*, p. 264, ch. 20; *Elections and the Political Order, op. cit.*, ch. 8.

turnout.[36] The party label seems to give the working class in particular cues about which candidates are likely to represent its economic interests.[37]

As we said at the beginning of this article, party identification is something of an "economizing device," a cognitive shortcut to help people achieve a satisfactory orientation toward the political world. It provides a reference group in terms of which individuals can perceive and react to political phenomena. This frame of reference is so firmly established on the American political scene that it muffles existing social, economic, and ideological cleavages, since the principal means of political expression—voting—is so powerfully conditioned by ingrained party loyalties. Party identification also helps maintain the strength of the minority party in elections when an unpopular candidate might otherwise all but obliterate it. Thus, if the 1964 election had been only a referendum on Senator Goldwater's political views, the Republican party would virtually have ceased to exist in Congress and many state capitols.[38] In these ways, as in other respects, party identification has come to be a stabilizing force in American politics—for good and for bad.[39]

[36]Robert R. Alford and Eugene C. Lee, "Voting Turnout in American Cities," *American Political Science Review*, Vol. 62 (September 1968), pp. 796–813.

[37]Robert H. Salisbury and Gordon Black, "Class and Party in Partisan and Non-Partisan Elections: The Case of Des Moines," *American Political Science Review*, Vol. 57 (September 1963), pp. 584–92; and Eugene C. Lee, *The Politics of Nonpartisanship* (Berkeley and Los Angeles: University of California Press, 1960).

[38]Philip E. Converse *et al.*, "Electoral Myth and Reality: The 1964 Campaign," *American Political Science Review*, Vol. 59 (June 1965), 321–36.

[39]For a further discussion of the causes and consequences of stability in American politics see chaps. 24 and 25.

POLITICAL
PERCEPTION

BERNARD R. BERELSON, PAUL F. LAZARSFELD, AND WILLIAM N. McPHEE

. . . The modern political party in a town like Elmira has an effective existence more in the minds of the partisans than in the local community's formal political organizations. . . . This existence is primarily expressed through differences in attitudes toward political issues of the day.

But this is not the only way in which the partisans differentiate themselves. There is also the fact of political perception—how the voter *sees* events in the political world. Specifically, we are concerned here with how voters in 1948 saw the issues of the campaign and what difference that made in their political behavior.

Now this is not simply a nice psychological problem with little relevance for the political situation. The process of political perception can operate to increase cleavage or consensus within the community. It undoubtedly contributes directly to a "real" definition of the differences between the parties, in terms of what might be called their "political norms." . . .

Once again we encounter a brief glimpse of the spiral of cause and effect that constitutes political history—in this case the history of political issues: What the parties do affects what the voters think they are and what the voters think they are affects what they subsequently do. Out of this interaction between subjective perception and objective reality, mutually affecting one another over decades, emerges not only our definition but the reality of a political party's role. The popular

Reprinted by permission of the publisher from VOTING *(Chicago: University of Chicago Press, 1954), pp. 215–33. Copyright © 1954 by the University of Chicago Press. Mr. Berelson is vice president of The Population Council. Mr. Lazarsfeld is Quetelet Professor Emeritus of Social Science at Columbia University. Mr. McPhee is Professor of Sociology at the University of Colorado.*

image of "what Republicans (or Democrats) are like" helps to define and determine what they "really" are. Today's subjective unreality in the voters' minds affects tomorrow's objective reality in the political arena.

About thirty years ago an analyst of public opinion gained lasting distinction by elaborating the differences between "the world outside and the pictures in our heads." Walter Lippmann discussed what many theorists—philosophers, psychologists, sociologists, political scientists, an-thropologists—have noted and documented before and since: subjective perception does not always reflect objective reality accurately. Selective perception—sampling the real world—must be taken into account. The mirror that the mind holds up to nature is often distorted in accordance with the subject's predispositions. The "trickle of messages from the out-side is affected by the stored-up images, the preconceptions, and the prej-udices which interpret, fill them out, and in their turn powerfully direct the play of our attention, and our vision itself. . . . In the individual person, the limited messages from outside, formed into a pattern of stereotypes, are identified with his own interests as he feels and con-ceives them."[1] Another student of public opinion put it similarly: "Each looks at, and looks for, the facts and reasons to which his attention points, perceiving little, if at all, those to which his mind is not directed. As a rule, men see what they look for, and observe the things they expect to see."[2]

The world of political reality, even as it involves a presidential campaign and election, is by no means simple or narrow. Nor is it crystal-clear. Over a period of six months, and intensively for six weeks, the elec-torate is subjected to a wide variety of campaign events. Even if all the political events were unambiguous, there would still be a problem of po-litical perception; but, as it is, the campaign is composed (often de-liberately) of ambiguous as well as clear elements.

PERCEPTION AND VOTING

Just how clear was the objective field to be perceived in 1948? Some propagandists, and some students of propaganda, believe that ambiguity often promotes effectiveness, since each subject is then free to define the matter in terms satisfactory to himself. While a sharply clear statement may win some friends by its very decisiveness, it may also lose some peo-ple for the same reason. Now Truman and Dewey had both been public figures for some time and had taken public stands on many political

[1] Walter Lippmann, *Public Opinion* (New York: Harcourt, Brace, & World, 1922), p. 21.

[2] A. Lawrence Lowell, *Public Opinion in War and Peace* (Cambridge, Mass.: Harvard University Press, 1923), p. 22.

matters; yet their positions on the issues in the campaign were not equally clear.

In 1948 Truman took a more straightforward and more aggressive position on these issues than Dewey (Table 1). The latter spoke to a large extent on the need for unity, peace, and freedom, while Truman specified his position *for* price control and public housing and *against* the Taft-Hartley Law. And Truman used quite vigorous language in stating his position, whereas Dewey employed a more lofty rhetoric. Except perhaps for the Russian issue (which became involved with the spy and domestic Communist issue), there can be no question but that, objectively, Dewey's position was more amenable to misperception than Truman's.

Table 1   Positions Taken by Dewey and Truman on Four Issues During the Campaign

	Dewey	*Truman*
Price control	Causes of high prices were war, foreign aid, the administration's discouragement of production, governmental mismanagement Remedies: cut government spending, reduce national debt, increase production No reference to imposition of controls Only one major reference	Republicans would not act against inflation in Eightieth Congress or special session; they rejected the administration's program Called for price controls or anti-inflation measures on several occasions
Taft-Hartley Law	Referred to it as "Labor-Management Relations Act of 1947," never as "Taft-Hartley Law" Made abstract remarks about "labor's freedoms" which would be "zealously guarded and extended" Approved the law in general ("will not retreat from advances made") but left door open for improvements ("where laws affecting labor can be made a better instrument for labor relations . . . ")	Made the "shameful" and "vicious" law a major issue; recalled that Republicans passed it over his veto: "It ought to be repealed" Took this position in at least ten major campaign speeches during October
Policy toward U.S.S.R.	Took a strong anti-communism position; linked communism to administration Made this a major issue in about seven campaign speeches	Took an anti-communism position; major references twice
Public housing	Only minor references to need for more housing (Republican platform called for housing financed by private enterprise, with federal "encouragement" when private industry and local government were unable to fill need)	Republicans "killed" Taft-Ellender-Wagner Bill Called for public housing sponsored by government in at least ten major campaign speeches

Figure 1 The Voters' Own Stands on the Issues Affect Their Perception of the Candidates' Stands*

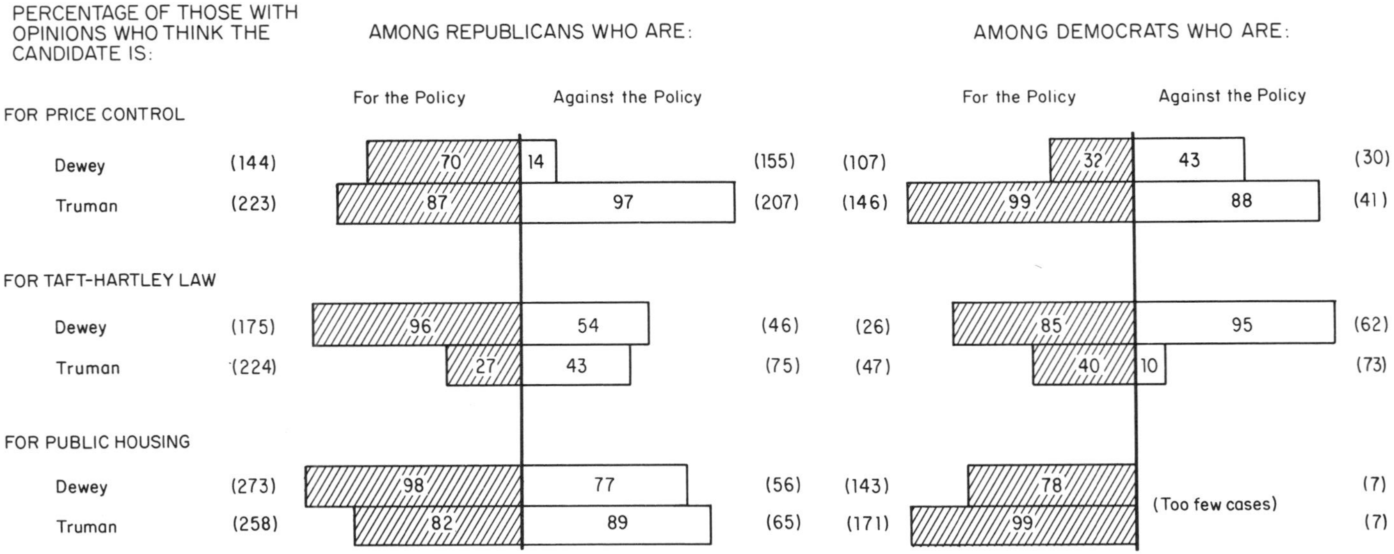
PERCENTAGE OF THOSE WITH OPINIONS WHO THINK THE CANDIDATE IS:
AMONG REPUBLICANS WHO ARE:
AMONG DEMOCRATS WHO ARE:
For the Policy
Against the Policy
For the Policy
Against the Policy
FOR PRICE CONTROL
Dewey (144) 70 14 (155) (107) 32 43 (30)
Truman (223) 87 97 (207) (146) 99 88 (41)
FOR TAFT-HARTLEY LAW
Dewey (175) 96 54 (46) (26) 85 95 (62)
Truman (224) 27 43 (75) (47) 40 10 (73)
FOR PUBLIC HOUSING
Dewey (273) 98 77 (56) (143) 78 (7)
Truman (258) 82 89 (65) (171) 99 (7)
(Too few cases)

*Note: For simplification and clarity, the "No stand" and the "Don't know" responses have been omitted from this chart. The omission does not affect the point of the data.

And this is reflected in the extent of nonperception of the candidates' stands.[3] On the four issues the proportion of respondents who do not know the candidates' stands averages about 10 per cent for Truman and about 25 per cent for Dewey. (This also reflects the fact that Truman's official position brought him before the public on such issues on numerous occasions; but a counterconsideration is that Dewey's position as governor of New York made him especially familiar to Elmirans.)

Perception and Own Stand

. . . Perception of the candidates' stands on issues may be affected by the respondents' own stands on them. The voters can thus manage to increase the consistency within their own political position, or at least the apparent consistency. And this is clearly the case. In almost every instance respondents perceive their candidate's stand on these issues as similar to their own and the opponent's stand as dissimilar—whatever their own position (Figure 1). For example, those Republicans who favor price control perceive Dewey as favoring price control (70 per cent), and few who oppose price control perceive Dewey as favoring controls (14 per cent). And the Republicans who are against controls perceive Truman as favoring them somewhat more than the Republicans who are for them. As with their perception of group support, so with their perception of the issues: the partisans manage to "pull" their own candidate and "push" the opposing candidate with considerable consistency. Overlaying the base of objective observation is the distortion effect—distortion in harmony with political predispositions. As Schumpeter says, "Information and arguments in political matters will 'register' only if they link up with the citizen's preconceived ideas."[4]

At the same time, some voters maintain or increase their perceptual defense on political issues by refusing to acknowledge differences with their own candidate or similarities to the opposition candidate. Such denial of reality, a defense utilized against uncongenial aspects of the environment, is well documented by case studies and laboratory experiments in the psychological literature of neurosis. Here we have evidence on its operation in the midst of a political campaign where motivation is less strong.

Take the two major issues of price control and the Taft-Hartley Law, on which the candidates took relatively clear positions. Objectively, an observer would say that Truman was for and Dewey against price con-

---

[3]The questions followed this form: "From what you know, is Truman (Dewey) for the Taft-Hartley Law or against it?" The respondent could say "Don't know" or state that the candidate had not taken any stand on the issue. The perception questions were asked in August, before the campaign proper; replies may have been different in October.

[4]Joseph Schumpeter, *Capitalism, Socialism, and Democracy*, 3rd ed. (New York: Harper & Row, 1950), p. 263.

trol and that Truman was against and Dewey for the Taft-Hartley Law. Yet, when our respondents are asked where the candidates stand, a certain proportion of them do not know or profess not to know. But—and this is the point—the "Don't knows" are more frequent among partisans who themselves take a different position from their own candidate or the same position as the opponent (Figure 2).

Perception and Strength of Feeling

This tendency to "misperceive" issues in a favorable direction does not operate in a uniform fashion within the electorate. The degree of affect attached to the election, in the form of intensity upon one's vote intention, also influences perception. Those voters who feel strongly about their vote intention perceive political issues differently from those who do not feel so strongly about the matter (Figure 3). With remarkable

Figure 2   Partisans Tend Not to Perceive Differences with Their Own Candidate or Similarities to the Opposition Candidate

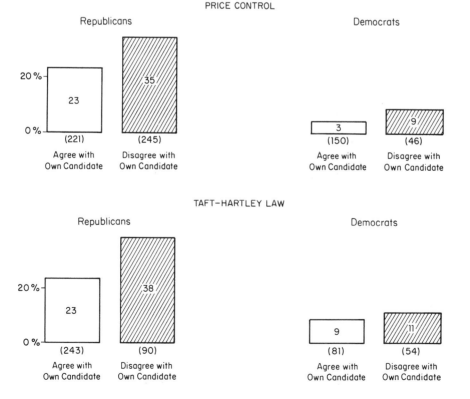

PERCENTAGE WHO "DON'T KNOW" THEIR OWN CANDIDATE'S STAND

PRICE CONTROL

Republicans — Democrats

20% 23 (221) Agree with Own Candidate | 35 (245) Disagree with Own Candidate | 3 (150) Agree with Own Candidate | 9 (46) Disagree with Own Candidate

TAFT-HARTLEY LAW

Republicans — Democrats

20% 23 (243) Agree with Own Candidate | 38 (90) Disagree with Own Candidate | 9 (81) Agree with Own Candidate | 11 (54) Disagree with Own Candidate

Figure 3   The Stronger the Political Affiliation, the Greater the Tendency to Perceive Political Issues Favorably to One's Self*

AMONG THOSE OBJECTIVELY IN DISAGREEMENT WITH THE GIVEN CANDIDATE

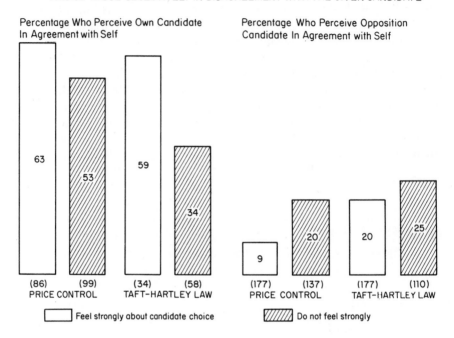

Percentage Who Perceive Own Candidate In Agreement with Self

Percentage Who Perceive Opposition Candidate In Agreement with Self

Note: Analogous results are obtained for the housing and "firmer with Russia" issues. This same tendency appears in the case of perception of the support given the candidates by various socioeconomic and ethnic groups. In almost every case strong partisans "pull" approved groups more than weak partisans.

consistency within each party, the intensely involved "pull" their own candidate and "push" the opponent more than the less involved. (Incidentally, it is probably not too much to suggest that this "pull" and "push" are equivalent to the psychological defense mechanisms of generalization and exclusion.)

For example, when objectively they are *not* in agreement with their own party, *strong* Republicans and Democrats perceive their candidate's stand on the issues as more in harmony with their own stand than do weak Republicans and Democrats in the same situation. But, by no means is this a general tendency to see everyone in agreement with themselves. When they objectively disagree with the *opposition* candidate, the strong partisans are quickest to perceive that disagreement. The stronger the partisanship, the *greater* the (mis)perception of agreement with one's own side and the *less* the (mis)perception of agreement with the opposition. Presumably, misperception makes for partisanship, and the reverse. Thus, the people strongest for a candidate —the ones most interested in and active for his election, the ones who make up the core of the party support—are the ones who take the least equivocal position on what their party stands for. And, at the same time, those who favor the party position as they see it are more likely to support the candidate strongly.

In the course of the campaign, then, strength of party support influences the perception of political issues. The more intensely one holds a vote position, the more likely he is to see the political environment as favorable to himself, as conforming to his own beliefs. He is less likely to perceive uncongenial and contradictory events or points of view and hence presumably less likely to revise his own original position. In this manner perception can play a major role in the spiraling effect of political reinforcement.

Necessarily, such partisanly motivated perception increases the recognized or believed differences between the parties. Strong Republicans and Democrats are farther apart in perception of political issues than weak Republicans and Democrats; they disagree more sharply in their perception of campaign events. Among the strongly partisan, then, the process of perception operates to make the opponent into more of an "enemy" and thus to magnify the potential for political cleavage. . . .

ACCURACY OF PERCEPTION

The question of "correct" and "incorrect" perception has been implicit in our discussion thus far, since differentiation in perception requires a degree of misperception on the part of some perceivers (assuming a definition of objective reality). But the question has not been given explicit consideration. Without retracing our steps, let us now summarize from this vantage point.

Analysis of the perception that occurs during a presidential campaign requires a definition of what is "correct" perception. In the case of political issues, perceiving the candidates' stands as they predominantly appear in the campaign speeches should serve. Since some stands are ambiguous, or at least contain an element of propagandistic vagueness, we use here two stands of Truman and Dewey that are reasonably straightforward and clear—those on the Taft-Hartley Law (with Truman against and Dewey for) and on price control (with Truman for and Dewey against). The index of correct perception on the issues is based upon the number of correct responses given out of the four possible.

In the first place, the amount of correct perception in the community is limited. Only 16 per cent of the respondents know the correct stands of both candidates on both issues, and another 21 per cent know them on three of the four. Over a third of the respondents know only one stand correctly or none at all. And these are crucial issues in the campaign, much discussed in the communication media. Thus, a good deal less than half the political perception in the community is reasonably accurate, by such definitions.[5]

But any such arbitrary measure is less useful for its absolute than for its relative value. Who are the people more and less likely to perceive political issues correctly? For example, what of attention to the campaign in the press and radio? Do the people who read and listen about politics more than others perceive more correctly, or does selective perception get in the way? It seems that communication exposure clarifies perception probably more than any other factor (Figure 4). This is an important consideration; the more reading and listening people do on campaign matters, the more likely they are to come to recognize the positions the candidates take on major issues. It is as though the weight of the media is sufficient to "impose" a certain amount of correct perception, regardless of the barrier presented by the voter's party preference (and despite the fact that those who do most of the reading and listening also feel most strongly for their candidate and are hence more amenable to selective perception). The more that people are *exposed* to political material, the more gets through.

Other characteristics also make for accurate perception. The intellectual training received in the classroom enables the voter to make clearer discriminations in the political arena. And, despite greater affect toward campaign affairs, the interested people manage to maintain a clearer view of the issues (see Figure 5). . . . But, of all these factors, the strongest is communication exposure. It is more effectively related to accurate perception of where the candidates stand than either education or interest. Reading and listening must make a difference.

INFERENCES: PSYCHOLOGICAL AND POLITICAL

What are the implications of this perceptual situation? Broadly speaking, there are two sets of conclusions which can be drawn.

The first deals with the psychology of political perception. For perceptual selection must serve a definite psychological function for the individual voter. As in other spheres of activity, so in the political: one function must be to avoid potential stress. The voter must do this, even though unconsciously, by using his perceptual opportunities as a defense or protection against the complexities, contradictions, and problems of the campaign. Indeed, the extent and nature of misperception suggest that the voter may even be aware of the attitudinal cross-pressures

[5]To repeat: these figures apply to the early campaign period of August. Similar data for October, at the end of the campaign, would almost certainly raise these estimates.

Figure 4   Several Characteristics Are Associated with Accurate Perception of the Candidates' Stands on Issues*

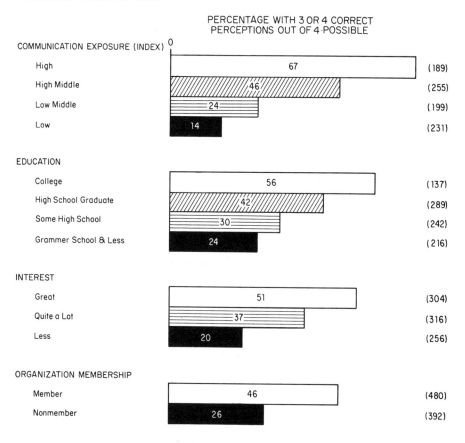

PERCENTAGE WITH 3 OR 4 CORRECT
PERCEPTIONS OUT OF 4 POSSIBLE

COMMUNICATION EXPOSURE (INDEX)

High	67	(189)
High Middle	46	(255)
Low Middle	24	(199)
Low	14	(231)

EDUCATION

College	56	(137)
High School Graduate	42	(289)
Some High School	30	(242)
Grammer School & Less	24	(216)

INTEREST

Great	51	(304)
Quite a Lot	37	(316)
Less	20	(256)

ORGANIZATION MEMBERSHIP

Member	46	(480)
Nonmember	26	(392)

*Note: Each of these characteristics works independently of the others.

to which the campaign subjects him from which he gains escape through perceptual processes. For the greater his affect toward the election (in terms of strength of feeling toward the candidates), the greater the degree of psychic protection. The voter tends to oversee or to invent what is favorable to himself and to distort or to deny much of what is unfavorable. This must leave him fewer internal conflicts to resolve —with, so to speak, a favorable balance of perception. In any event, the voters manage to use the materials of politics, even of a presidential campaign, for their own psychological protection—for the avoidance of some inconsistencies in their beliefs that otherwise would be manifest.

Then there are certain political implications of the patterning of perception. First, there are in a sense two political campaigns. One is the

Figure 5   Percentage with Three or Four Perceptions Correct

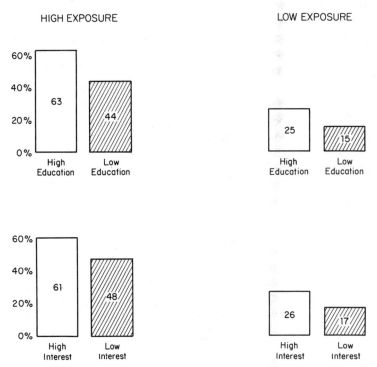

HIGH EXPOSURE

LOW EXPOSURE

objective campaign that is carried on in the "real" world, and the other is the campaign that exists in the voter's mind, that is, the "real" campaign as perceived. There is no one-to-one correspondence between them. Given the chance, some voters transform the objective campaign into a subjective one more satisfying to them. The campaign waged by the candidates—even when deliberately unambiguous—is not the one perceived by all the voters, but this does not make it any less "real" for the voters themselves. "If men define situations as real, they are real in their consequences."

Second, there is the meaning of perception for rational political judgment. Here its role must make the voter's political judgment *seem* more rational to him because it maximizes agreement with his own side and maximizes disagreement with the opposition. In other words, perception often operates to make the differences between the parties *appear* greater than they actually may be—and thus to make the voter's decision *appear* more rational (in one sense) than it actually is. In this way, paradoxical though it may seem, misperception contributes to a seeming "rationality" in politics.

Third, perception must reduce or even eliminate certain political cross-pressures before they come to the level of visibility—before they start pressing. If the voter finds himself holding opinions championed by opposing parties, it has been thought that he could do one of two things: remain in this "inconsistent" position (which is, of course, altogether legitimate) or remove the "inconsistency" by changing one opinion to fit the other. But he has another out: he can perceptually select, out of the somewhat ambiguous propaganda of the campaign, those political cues which remove the problem by defining it away. He can "see" that the candidates do not disagree on the issue at hand or that his candidate really agrees with him or that the opponent really disagrees or that he cannot tell where his candidate stands. Just as the process may reduce the voter's level of psychological tension, so may it reduce his political inconsistency.

Finally, this serves to introduce the major political implications of our perceptual material—its implications for the problem of cleavage and consensus in the democratic community. In an earlier section we dealt with this problem in the *evaluation* of political affairs; now we meet it in perception. The overall effect of political perception is to increase the amount of political consensus *within* the parties and to increase the amount of political cleavage *between* the parties—once again, homogeneity within and polarization between. Both are achieved by something like the mechanisms of generalization, exclusion, and denial—through the perceptual enlargement of the area of agreement with one's own candidate (generalization); through the misperceived rejection of the opponent's position (exclusion); and through the professed lack of knowledge of one's candidate's stand where disagreement is likely (denial).

Let us close this chapter by comparing it briefly with the chapter on the perception of groups. In each case the perceptions are likely to help voters to maintain their own position, without being too much concerned by contradiction. In the social case it is harmony with people; in the present case it is a harmony with ideas. With groups the matter was fairly simple: each respondent is surrounded by a primary group in which the large majority thinks like himself. No wonder, then, that he infers that "everyone" will vote as he does. (Of course, this tendency is tempered by a strong sense of reality; misperception is only superimposed upon it.) In the case of the candidates' stand, the voter gets his information from reading, listening, and discussion. This is subject to *selective* gathering of information, forgetting of disturbing elements, reinterpretation of what the candidate "really" means—all mechanisms familiar in social psychology. Probably, even, social selection reinforces the selected collection of information, as a result of discussion between like-minded people.

In a way, both phenomena can be subsumed under one heading. Voters cannot have contact with the whole world of people and ideas;

they must *sample* them. And the sampling is biased. People pick the people and the ideas to suit their personal equilibrium and then project that sample upon the universe. First, selective perception, then misperception, then the strengthening of opinion, and then, in turn, more selective perception. Fortunately, there are realities, competing concerns, and corrosion of existing beliefs that, under normal circumstances, do not permit this process to get far out of bounds.

In sum, then, the actual operation of political perception during a presidential campaign decreases tension in the individual and increases tension in the community—one might almost say, *by* increasing tension in the community. The voters, each in the solitude of his own mind, wish to see the campaign in a favorable way, and they use their perception of where the candidates stand to this end. "Democracy in its original form never seriously faced the problem which arises because the pictures inside people's heads do not automatically correspond with the world outside."[6]

[6]Lippmann, *op. cit.*, p. 21.

CHAPTER TWENTY-ONE

SOME DYNAMIC ELEMENTS OF CONTESTS FOR THE PRESIDENCY

DONALD E. STOKES

Despite the measured pace of American elections, there have now been a number of presidential campaigns since the advent of survey studies of voting. However sparingly, political history slowly has added to the set of distinct configurations of men and events which comprise a contest for the Presidency. The set is still small, whatever the impression created by massed thousands of interviews or by the accompanying files of election returns. Yet it is now large enough to be pressed hard for evidence about the sources of electoral change.

A primary virtue of measurements extended over a series of elections is that they can throw light on the problem of change. So long as the earliest voting studies were confined to cross-sectional relationships, they could deal only very inadequately with changes superimposed on these relationships or with changes in the relationships themselves. In the case of Lazarsfeld's enormously influential Erie County study in 1940, the natural limitations of a single-election study were compounded by the investigators' misfortune in choosing a campaign whose dominant personality and principal issues differed little from those of preceding elections. I have often wondered whether the static social determinism of *The People's Choice* would have emerged from a campaign in which the tides of short-term change were more nearly at flood.[1]

[1]Paul F. Lazarsfeld, Bernard Berelson, and Hazel Gaudet, *The People's Choice* (New York: Duell, Sloan and Pearce, 1944). It is paradoxical that Lazarsfeld and his associates should have come to so static a view of party preference, since the desire to observe changes of preference was so central to their original intentions. Had they worked within the context of an election such as that of 1952 it is entirely unlikely that they could have ignored the presence of massive inter-election change, overlaid on the social bases of preference summarized in the Index of Political Predisposition.

Reprinted by permission from the AMERICAN POLITICAL SCIENCE REVIEW, *60 (March 1966), 19–28. A statistical appendix and four methodological footnotes have been omitted.*

I shall examine here some sources of change which are richly evident in the presidential elections of the last two decades. In doing so I shall utilize several time series which can be extracted from the Survey Research Center's interview studies of the American electorate. The presidential contest of 1964 marked the fourth occasion on which the Center's national electoral studies have recorded the public's response to the issues and personalities of a presidential campaign.

This lengthening interval of electoral history contains material enough for the analyst of change. From the Eisenhower victories of the early 1950's, the high-point of presidential Republicanism since the Great Depression overwhelmed Hoover's party, the strength of Eisenhower's successors ebbed away in 1960 and sank in 1964 to a level which can only be regarded as one of the extreme lows of American national party competition. I shall examine some of the attitudinal factors in this extraordinary decline, focusing especially on the importance of changes in the issues and leaders which the electorate is asked to appraise. The relation of these "inputs" to the "output" of the presidential vote is exceedingly complex, but the moral of my piece is that this relationship introduces more dynamism into contests for the Presidency than the stability of party identification or of the social bases of party preference might lead us to expect.

In the course of discussion I shall utilize a statistical model which has proved useful for measuring various attitudinal forces on the nation's vote. Dealing with a type of behavior which is notoriously subject to multiple influences, this model seeks to discern the relative importance of several dimensions of attitude both for individual choice and for the nation's collective decision.[2] The model treats the behavior of the individual voter as governed in an immediate sense by the direction and strength of his attitudes toward the several political objects he is asked to appraise, attitudes which we have probed in these presidential elections by asking a series of free-answer questions about the parties and presidential candidates. Since a presidential campaign confronts the voter with four main objects—the two parties and the two candidates—it is natural to place each respondent along four dimensions of attitude, and many of the findings reported below will rely on such a four-dimensional model. For other purposes, however, it is more revealing of the content of political attitude to place each respondent along six attitudinal dimensions: (1) attitude toward the Democratic candidate as a person; (2) attitude toward the Republican candidate as a person; (3) attitude toward the parties and candidates which relates to the benefit of various groups; (4) attitude toward the parties and candi-

---

[2] For a report of the application of this model to the Eisenhower elections see Donald E. Stokes, Angus Campbell, and Warren E. Miller, "Components of Electoral Decision," *American Political Science Review*, Vol. 52 (June 1958), 367–87.

dates which relates to domestic policy; (5) attitude which relates to foreign policy; and (6) attitude which relates to the general performance of the parties in the nation's affairs. A detailed account of the procedure by which respondents are assimilated to these several dimensions appears in the appended note.

The appendix also describes the statistical operations by which we obtain definite estimates of each dimension's contribution to the winning majority—the means by which, in effect, the nation's collective decision is resolved into a set of attitudinal components. These methods must of course be regarded as approximate, for reasons of sampling if no other, and I advance no claim to exact measurement; none is really necessary to the central conclusion which I shall draw from the analysis. Nevertheless, the model's success in estimating the direction and size of the winning majority in each of a series of elections does increase our confidence that we have measured dimensions of popular feeling which are deeply involved in changes of party fortune.

The several dimensions of attitude, however, have by no means been equally involved in electoral change. Just as the various components of electoral decision can be very different in their direction and strength at a given point in time, they can exhibit a very different tendency to change over time. In the period of our research some have been relatively stable, others not. By examining the role of each attitude component over twelve years we form several time series which are extraordinarily suggestive of the sources of change during this interval of our national politics.

THE ATTITUDINAL COMPONENTS OVER TIME

The curves described by the components of the six-dimensional model arrange themselves into three interesting pairs. The first of these is a pair whose values have consistently favored the Democrats over the entire period. As shown by Figure 1, partisan evaluations relating to domestic issues and to group benefit have uniformly helped the Democrats more than the Republicans, although the extent of this aid has fluctuated from year to year. To an unusual degree these elements of the party images have roots in the past, extending back at least to the Roosevelt New Deal. Indeed, the benefit to the Democrats from their party's sponsorship of disadvantaged elements of American society is an antique theme of our party politics. Even in the mid-1950's and the early 1960's the volume of comment approving the Democrats and disapproving the Republicans in terms of the interests of the common man was impressive. In the two most recent elections, however, these class-related comments were diminished somewhat and were accompanied by references to religious and racial groups in which the arithmetic of group size was less

favorable to the Democrats. For these reasons the group curve in Figure
1 shows the party's advantage to be somewhat less in 1960 and 1964.

It will be apparent that the concept of "group" is defined here in
a very inclusive manner. Likewise, our net has been cast very widely in
coding references relating to domestic issues. In particular, many of the
comments giving substance to the domestic issue dimension are "valence"

Figure 1   Continuing Democratic Advantage: Groups and Domestic Policy

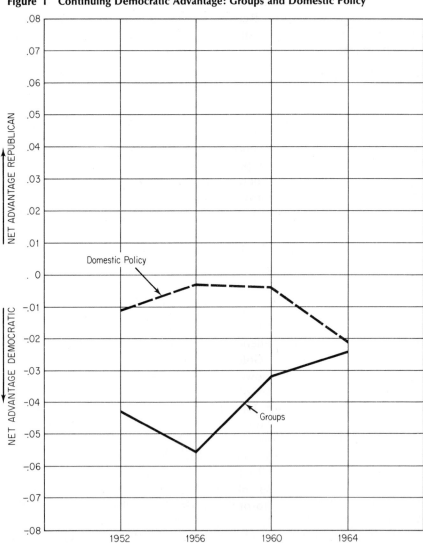

or "image" issues, in which the parties or candidates are linked with something which is uniformly approved or disapproved ("the Republicans are the party of depression") rather than "position" issues on which there are genuine differences of party policy. The leading image issue of domestic politics throughout this period was the association of the Democrats with good times, the Republicans with bad. This association, which probably had weakened steadily from the height of the Great Depression to the election of 1952, was further attenuated by the prosperity of Eisenhower's first term. But it revived again in the recession of 1958, before the Republican administration had left office, and it has been given fresh substance by the rising prosperity of the Kennedy and Johnson years.

The domestic issue dimension has not, however, been altogether lacking in genuine position issues. One of the peculiar qualities of the Goldwater candidacy is that it converted into position issues a number of image issues on which a broad consensus had hitherto coexisted between the parties. This fact was not lost upon the general public. Under the Goldwater challenge, the Democrats were rewarded more generously in 1964 than in any of the three prior elections for their sponsorship of social security and of the circle of other social and economic welfare policies which had wide popular approval. Primarily for this reason the domestic issue curve of Figure 1 shows a greater Democratic advantage in 1964 than in the years before.

A second pair of curves is traced by the movement of two components in which a strong initial Republican advantage is seen to have vanished over these four elections. As shown by Figure 2, the Republican party under Eisenhower enjoyed a substantial lead over the Democrats on foreign affairs—preeminently in terms of the great image issue of peace and war. This lead was not greatly lessened when Eisenhower's deputy sought the Presidency in 1960, but Nixon's legacy dissolved altogether in the contest of Goldwater and Johnson. It would be a misreading of the 1964 value, however, to suppose that widely-held foreign policy beliefs consistent with Goldwater's were nicely balanced by widely-held beliefs consistent with Johnson's. According to our evidence, foreign affairs did intrude on the public's consciousness in the 1964 campaign more than in any election since 1952, but popular references to foreign issues in 1964 still had only about a fourth the frequency of references to domestic issues. The loss of Republican advantage on this dimension was due to the final collapse of the belief that the party under Goldwater was more likely to bring peace than were the Democrats under Johnson.[3]

[3]For direct additional evidence on this point see Philip E. Converse, Aage R. Clausen, and Warren E. Miller, "Electoral Myth and Reality: The 1964 Election," *American Political Science Review*, Vol. 59 (June 1965), p. 332.

Figure 2   Decaying Republican Advantage: Foreign Policy and Party Performance

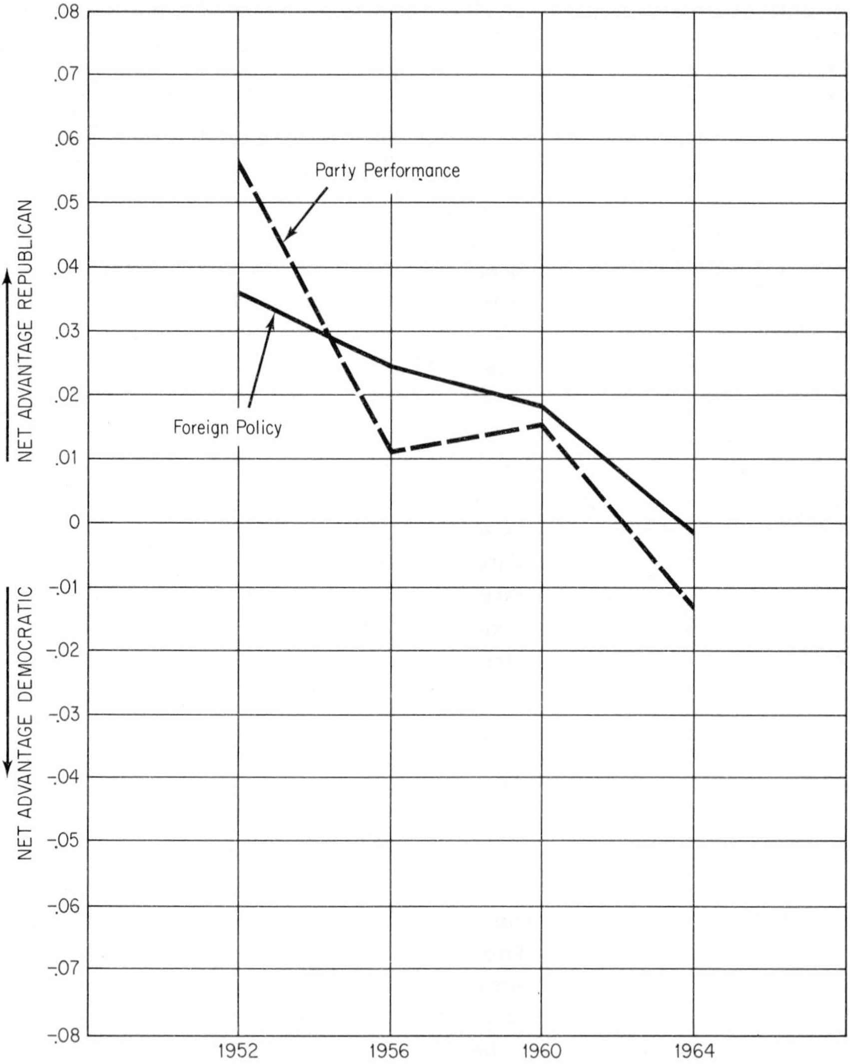

The loss of Republican advantage in foreign affairs is paralleled by the decay of the party's advantage in popular assessments of party performance. The Republicans began this series of elections immensely aided by the mood for a change in 1952. There is no more striking element in all of our attitudinal materials than the public's anger and frustration with the outgoing Democratic administration in that year. Whatever the validity of the public's grievance, it was real enough in motivational terms and contributed handsomely to Eisenhower's first victory. The force of this feeling was easily spent, however, once the

Democrats had been driven from office. Yet in 1956 and again in 1960 the Republicans still enjoyed an edge in terms of the electorate's general evaluations of current party performance, a fact which is the more remarkable in view of the stronger hold of the Democrats on the nation's underlying party identifications.[4] By 1964, however, this lingering advantage had been swept away and the Democrats by a modest margin were now seen as the party better qualified to conduct the country's affairs.

The third pair of curves is traced by the components having to do with popular reactions to the personal attributes of the candidates. As shown in Figure 3, there has been remarkable variety in the appeal of the Republican candidates. The values of this component in 1952 and 1956 attest to General Eisenhower's personal hold on the electorate, an attraction which, if anything, was even more wholly personal after Eisenhower had served four years as President. Mr. Nixon's appeal in 1960 was somewhat less, although his personal appeal to the electorate, especially the sense of his broad experience, was marked. If the eventual account given by the political histories is that Nixon was a weak candidate in 1960, it will be largely myth.

The response to Goldwater, however, was something else again. Whereas Nixon's personal stature helped bring his party to the verge of a third presidential victory against a party enjoying a clear advantage in the country's partisan identifications, popular reaction to Goldwater contributed to his party's electoral ruin. The detailed references to Goldwater are an impressive amalgam of doubts—a wild and erratic campaigner, muddled and unclear, unstable, poorly educated, and so on—with these themes very little offset by references to the advertised qualities of integrity, sincerity, and decisiveness. If our estimates are right, the transition from Nixon to Goldwater cost the Republicans something like 7 percent of the total vote.

Despite immense differences of personal style, the appeal of three successive Democratic candidates was much more nearly equal. And except for Stevenson's second campaign, the response to each of these candidates added to his strength at the polls. Certainly the movement of the Democratic curve in Figure 3 shows Johnson to have been an asset to his own candidacy in 1964: the response to Johnson's attributes apparently did the Democrats about as much good as the response to Goldwater's did. The combined effect of both appears to have moved the two-party vote roughly 5 percentage points toward Johnson.

To emphasize the dynamic implications for party competition of pairing successive candidates for President, Figure 4 combines the effect of the personal appeals of the two men seeking the office in each of these

---

[4]For evidence on the distribution of party identification in this period see "The Concept of the 'Normal Vote'," in A. Campbell, P. Converse, W. Miller, and D. Stokes, *Elections and the Political Order* (New York, 1966), Ch. 1.

Figure 3   Greatest Variation: Appeal of Candidates

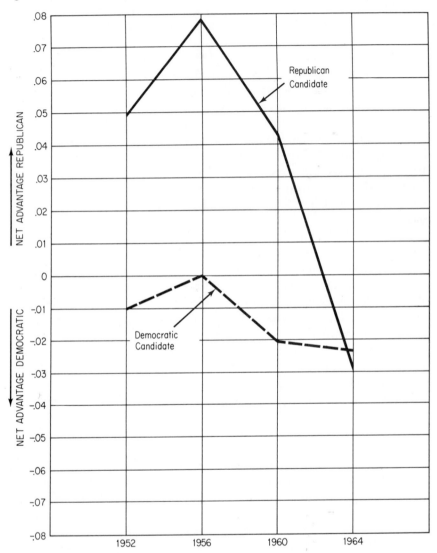

elections. The variation of this summary curve is impressive indeed. From a maximum Republican advantage of nearly 8 percent in the rematch of Eisenhower and Stevenson, the curve falls through more than 13 percentage points to a maximum Democratic advantage of more than 5 percent in the contest of Johnson and Goldwater. A more eloquent statistical comment on the personal contribution which candidates for President can make to electoral change could hardly be given.

It would be a mistake to read into these figures too simple an ex-

Figure 4   Net Impact of Candidates

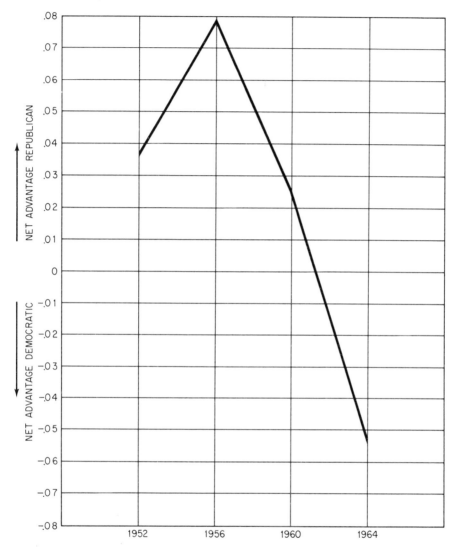

planation of the impact of candidate personality on the mass public. Certainly it would be grossly wrong to suppose that the properties of these "stimulus objects" are somehow immediately and directly impressed on the electorate's response. The relation of stimulus and response is remarkably complex, involving an interplay of several quite different factors. Before drawing some general conclusions about the problem of change it would be well to consider the interaction of the "actual" properties of the stimuli to which the electorate responds, certain response dispositions which the electorate has already learned, and some properties of the communication processes by which the electorate is informed of the objects of presidential politics.

STIMULUS PROPERTIES AND RESPONSE DISPOSITIONS IN THE ATTITUDE COMPONENTS

Although the comments below extend to the full range of stimuli to which the public is exposed, some of the subtleties of electoral response can most readily be observed in connection with candidate effects. The men seeking the Presidency bring to a campaign certain "real" properties as stimulus objects. Some of these belong to the past—the candidate's role as war hero, his success as governor or senator, his marital difficulties, and so on—although the communication of these things to much of the public may lie ahead. Other properties have to do with appearance, behavior, and personal style—the candidate's smile, the timbre of his voice, his smoothness in dealing with the teleprompter, his willingness to suffer fools gladly—knowledge of which can reach the electorate in numberless ways.

Impressions of these things, however, do not fall on wholly unprepared ground. Voters display a variety of response dispositions as they form their evaluation of the candidates. One type of response disposition is so evident as to require little comment. A wealth of research evidence, as well as familiar observation, attests the profound influence which partisan loyalties may have on the voter's perceptions of the men seeking office. The stronger the voter's party bias, the more likely he is to see the candidate of his own party as hero, the candidate of the other party as villain. No one who has talked with a sample of voters during a presidential campaign can have failed to note at every hand the processes by which cognitive balance is achieved.[5]

The voter's perceptual predispositions are not, however, limited to party bias. We are confronted at times by striking evidence of other identifications exerting a like influence on candidate images. A vivid example of these is the influence of religion on perceptions of John F. Kennedy during the 1960 election campaign. Because Kennedy was the Democratic candidate, voters identifying with the Democratic party

[5]Certainly evidence of it is plentiful enough in the Center's studies. See, for example, Angus Campbell, Philip E. Converse, Warren E. Miller and Donald E. Stokes, *The American Voter* (New York: John Wiley and Sons, 1960), pp. 120–45. An excellent general review of the achievement of cognitive congruence in political attitudes is given by Robert E. Lane and David O. Sears in their *Public Opinion* (Englewood Cliffs, N.J.: Prentice-Hall, 1964). An interesting application of these concepts to attitude change may be found in Denis G. Sullivan, "Psychological Balance and Reactions to the Presidential Nominations in 1960," in M. Kent Jennings and L. Harmon Zeigler (eds.), *The Electoral Process* (Englewood Cliffs, N.J.: Prentice-Hall, 1966), pp. 238–64.

tended to view him more favorably than did voters identifying with the Republican party. But Kennedy was seen by the electorate not only as a Democrat; he was seen as a Catholic as well. As a result, at every point along the party identification continuum, Catholics tended to perceive Kennedy in a more favorable light than did Protestants.

A demonstration of the joint biasing effects of religion and party in 1960 may be found in Figure 5. In that campaign we placed each of our sample respondents along a standard party identification scale, represented here by five ordered groups: Strong Republicans, Weak Republicans, Independents, Weak Democrats, and Strong Democrats. At the same time we placed each of our Protestant and Catholic respondents on a scale of religious identification defined here by four ordered groups: persons strongly identified with a Protestant Church, persons weakly identified with such a church, persons weakly identified with the Catholic Church, and persons strongly identified with the Catholic Church. These two forms of psychological identification are moderately correlated in American society (that is, Catholics are more likely than Protestants to be Democratic) but not more than moderately so. Crossing the two here yields twenty groups defined by religion and party at once in which we may examine the distribution of attitude toward Kennedy. Figure 5 displays the mean attitude toward Kennedy within each of these twenty groups.

The means exhibit a remarkable pattern. The fact that the curve for each religious group slopes upward to the right shows that, whatever the voter's religious identification, he is more likely to have perceived Kennedy favorably the closer he was to the Democratic end of the party identification dimension. And the march of the four religious curves up the figure shows that, whatever the voter's party identification, he is more likely to have perceived Kennedy positively the closer he was to the Catholic end of the religious dimension. There is even a pattern to the partial discontinuities: the regularity of the curves for weak Protestants and weak Catholics suggests that the biasing tendencies of party identification were generally effective among the mildly religious while the irregularity of the curves for strong Protestants and strong Catholics suggests that party loyalty could have a marked impact on the strongly religious only if a party faith were itself strongly held.

Figure 5 is so rich in evidence of selective perception that we may easily miss what it has to say about the element of Kennedy's image which was not the result of response dispositions based on religion and party. The fact that this element was a favorable one ought not to be obscured by the strong pattern of the figure. Any reasonable operation by which we might seek to reconstruct a mean attitude among persons who are religiously and politically neutral would show that Kennedy was likely to be positively seen when his image did not fall prey to strong negative

Figure 5   Influence of Party and Religious Identifications on Perceptions of Kennedy

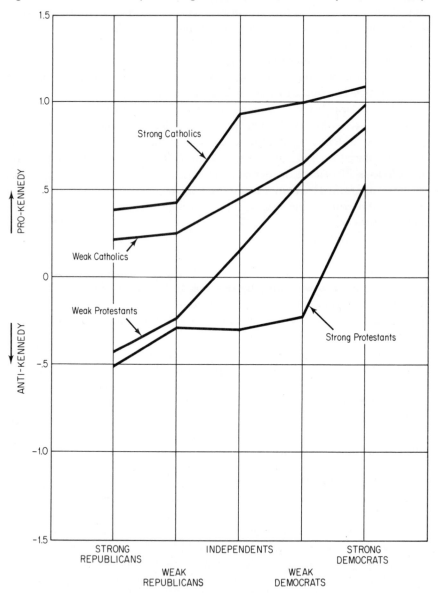

bias. For example, persons who were politically independent perceived Kennedy favorably even if they were weakly identified with a Protestant church.

We ought not to conclude from this that partisan and religious dispositions were the only response biases involved in the electorate's response to Kennedy or that, these dispositions aside, Kennedy was in some absolute sense an attractive candidate. In 1960, as any campaign year, many other kinds of response dispositions underlay the private impressions of the candidates formed by tens of millions of voters. We have identified two of the most important. It would not be difficult to suggest other factors which may have predisposed voters to react positively or negatively to something in the youthful, vigorous, Ivy-educated, Boston-accented stimulus which Kennedy presented.

Perhaps this point can be stated even more forcefully in terms of popular reaction to General Eisenhower, the most attractive presidential candidate since Franklin Roosevelt. The point is simply that "attractive" implies more than something about the candidate himself; it also implies something about the response dispositions of the electorate. Given the dominant values of contemporary American society, Eisenhower was enormously appealing. But we can at least imagine his having done very badly before an electorate less resonant to the military conqueror and less susceptible to the charm of a supremely other-directed personality who nevertheless evoked many of the traditional virtues. We might suppose, for example, that Eisenhower would have done very badly indeed before an electorate whose dominant values are those of American university faculties of social science.

Attitudes already formed toward some political objects are of course among the dispositions which can influence response to others. This seems especially true in the case of attitudes toward the candidates. When one rival for the Presidency already is well known, as an incumbent President will always be, the public's attitude toward his opponent will inevitably be colored by its response to the established figure. Thus, in 1940, Roosevelt-haters were quick to discover the virtues of Wendell Willkie when he was thrust onto the presidential stage, as Roosevelt's partisans were quick to discern Willkie's vices. And in the early 1950's, Adlai Stevenson had the misfortune to be paired with a much better-established rival who already enjoyed the highest public regard.[6]

Of course the complex relation of candidate stimulus to the public's response also involves important communication factors. In a sense, the only real candidate stimuli are those which reach the voter via the mass media and interpersonal conversation, stimuli which only rarely are complemented by direct voter contact with the candidate. Therefore, the benefit or harm done to a candidate's cause by his actual personal attributes is mediated not only by the response dispositions of the electorate; it is mediated as well by the manner in which these attributes are

---

[6]The voter's attitude toward a given political object may be influenced by the presence of other objects in his perceptual field even when no question of order is involved in the formation of attitude. In such a case, however, it is more reasonable to think of these effects as belonging to the configuration of stimulus objects, rather than to the voter's response dispositions.

communicated to the electorate. It is not hard to believe that some of the disarray of Goldwater's popular image was due to his extraordinarily bad press. The candidate properties communicated to the public are not a pure fiction of the media. But neither are they a pure reflection of the candidate himself, as he might have been seen at home in the desert.

What has been said of candidates can be said of any object which has electoral effects. Certainly the political role of domestic and foreign issues involves a similar interplay of stimulus properties, response tendencies, and communication processes. The Korean War's immense profit for the Republicans in 1952, for example, depended on much more than a set of objective events in the Far East and the parties' stand on those events. It depended too on a welter of response dispositions in the electorate—general isolationist or internationalist attitudes, hostility to communism, latent militarist tendencies, the anxieties of farmers over having sons away at harvest time, and the like—as well as the way in which the public was informed by the communications media of what was happening half a world away.

If the political effects of issues and personalities in the wider environment depend partly on what the electorate hears and how it is disposed to react to what it hears, it follows that changes in communication and response tendencies can at times alter the political effects of a stimulus which has not itself changed. A clear example of this is the rapid build-up of a candidate by the mass media when he steps into the charmed circle of leading contenders—or the opposite experience, which many potential candidates have had, of falling through the media's trap door to oblivion. Instances of marked change of response dispositions while political objects remain unchanged are more difficult to discern, but they undoubtedly occur. Herbert Hoover's high starched collars, a symbol of middle class prosperity in the booming twenties, probably looked quite different from the bread-lines of 1932.

Although changes of communication and of response dispositions can alter the electorate's response to a given political object, it is nevertheless true that a turnover of objects—of the personalities, issues, and events of national politics—is the more important source of short-term electoral change. This is the more true since a stimulus object can affect communication and response dispositions themselves. For example, quite apart from the sort of man he "really" is, a candidate can have wide influence on his treatment by the mass media. If the newspapers gave Mr. Goldwater extraordinarily rough treatment for a Republican candidate, Goldwater's own posture toward the press was part of the reason. Similarly, different candidates engage different response dispositions in the mass public. Unlike any Democratic candidate since Al Smith, Kennedy activated response dispositions based on Catholic and Protestant religious identifications, as we have seen. And candidates can lead the electorate to learn new dispositions, as Kennedy helped make the country receptive to a whole new generation of youthful, vigorous candidates for national and state office.

This type of change is vividly mirrored in the components of electoral decision given here for the past four presidential elections. The evidence of the changing personal impact of the candidates is especially impressive. Yet in a presidential system the turnover of candidates has implications reaching beyond sheer personal appeal. A candidate for the nation's great office is a focus for popular feeling about issues and questions of group benefit as well, and our measurements should be extended to take this fact into account.

RELATIVE CHANGE IN CANDIDATE AND PARTY ATTITUDE

It is hardly surprising that candidates for the Presidency should attract attitudes which are somewhat distinct from those attaching to the parties themselves. The platforms adopted by the nominating conventions are much less binding than the election manifestoes of a British party, for example, and a presidential candidate is notoriously at liberty to take his own stands on major issues and the problems of major social groupings. Equally, on matters requiring congressional action he is free to contradict positions taken by his party in the Senate and House. And on matters of foreign policy, the country is largely dependent on the candidate's record and views to know what his administration would be likely to do in the world. This is the stuff of which a presidential system is made.

Therefore, it is of interest to compare the variability of attitudes toward the parties and their presidential candidates. Neither has been constant over the period of our research, but the two have shown vastly different propensities to change. When we turn from a six- to a four-dimensional model, summarizing popular feeling according to the party or candidate toward which it is directed whether or not it concerns domestic or foreign issues, questions of group benefit, or other matters, the candidate components are found to have moved much more strongly from Republican to Democratic advantage.

This contrast is shown by Figure 6, in which each pair of party and candidate components of the four-dimensional model is added together at each election. The combined party curve has not by any means stood still. The public's full assessment of the parties showed a marked Republican advantage in the mood of 1952. But by 1956 the comparison of parties had moved to the Democrats' benefit, and this trend continued over the later two elections.

The combined candidate curve, however, describes a very much greater change. The public's full assessment of Eisenhower and Steven-

Figure 6   Variation of Party and Candidate Components

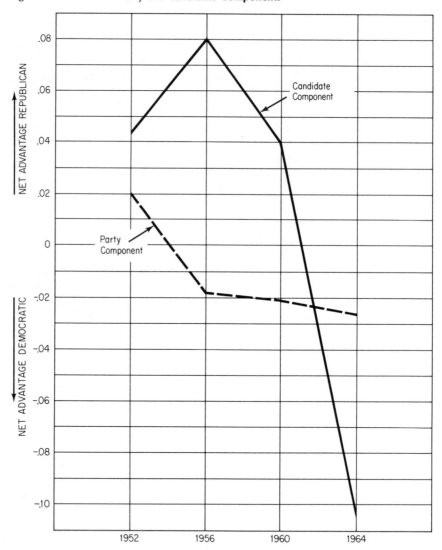

son, including issue and group perceptions as well as perceptions of personal qualities, was strongly Republican in 1952 and even more decisively
so four years later. In the 1960 election, the comparison of candidates
still favored the Republicans, although much more moderately. But between the Kennedy-Nixon campaign and the Johnson-Goldwater campaign the combined candidate component moved a most remarkable
distance to the Democrats' advantage. In each contest the candidate curve
was the farther removed from the zero-point: indeed, its average displacement from the neutral point has been more than 6 percent, whereas the

average displacement of the party curve has been about 2 percent. But the really arresting comparison has to do with relative change: over these elections the variance of the candidate curve has exceeded that of the party curve by more than 10 to 1.

It is therefore evident that the dynamism of popular attitude is peculiarly tied to the emergence of new candidates for the Presidency. The attitudes toward the parties are not inert. The shift in the relative assessment of the parties over the period of this research has been enough to alter the parties' strength by something like six million votes on a turnout equal to that of 1964. But this change, impressive as it is, nevertheless is moderate by comparison with the change induced by succeeding pairs of candidates. The fluctuations of electoral attitudes over these elections have to a remarkable degree focused on the candidates themselves.

All of this is quite out of keeping with the static perspective of the earliest studies of voting. Even if our findings are no more than approximately true, they argue strongly the dynamic implications of changes of the stimulus objects of national politics. This source of change has in fact brought spectacular shifts of presidential voting despite the fact that over the same period there has been almost no perceptible shift in the single most important type of response disposition, the electorate's enduring party loyalties. It may also be noted that the variations of attitude recorded here have been largely independent of secular changes in the structure of American society, although, as we have seen, a turnover of stimulus objects can alter dramatically the facts of social structure which are relevant to political choice. Taken together, changes in the several stimulus objects of presidential politics in this span of years have been quite enough to bring a change of party control, indeed to have induced a drastic transformation of party fortune in the contest for the Presidency.

INTERRELATIONS OF OPINION

V. O. KEY, JR.

When the distribution of opinion within the political system is viewed an issue at a time, an important aspect of public opinion is obscured. Opinions on different issues are distributed through the population in relation to each other; important dimensions of the opinion system may be identified by the simultaneous examination of opinion distributions on several issues. In speculation about political systems reflections recur about interrelations among political attitudes. Although political theoreticians seldom employ that phrase, they deal with the question in one guise or another. One line of thought centers on the interrelation of attitudes within an individual. Gilbert and Sullivan were talking about interrelations of attitude when they wrote of little Conservatives and little Liberals. Persons so named supposedly have within themselves an outlook or orientation that organizes their opinions in a characteristic manner toward specific issues as they arise. Though students of ideology become recondite as they conceive bodies of general doctrine to be mechanisms that control individual opinion and behavior, implicit in their analysis is the theme that opinions are organized in accord with some basic attitude pattern that characterizes the whole personality.

Other speculation concerns the consequences for a political order of opinion interrelationships within the society as a whole. Though the simple division of people into "conservatives" and "liberals" describes an aspect of the system as a whole as well as characteristics of individuals,

Reprinted by permission of the publisher from PUBLIC OPINION AND AMERICAN DEMOCRACY *(New York: Alfred A. Knopf, Inc., 1960), pp. 153–81. Copyright ©️ 1961 by V. O. Key, Jr. Mr. Key, who died in 1963, was Professor of Government at Harvard University.*

other and more complex problems are associated with the patterning of opinions within society. For example, when the lines of cleavage on many issues coincide, intensity of conflict within the social system will be relatively high. (The division of society into "liberals" and "conservatives," in effect, assumes this type of coincidence of conflict.) The contrary type of situation—one in which lines of cleavage do not coincide—may muffle political conflict. Enemies on the burning issue of today may be allies on the foremost questions of tomorrow. Antagonists will, in short, have common interests, and the mixture of antagonism and alliance may induce restraint in conflict.

Apart from such questions that may go to the roots of the nature of a political order, interrelations of opinions within the electorate may bear significantly on the party system. The workings of a dual party system may be profoundly affected by the degree to which cleavages on the many issues of politics do or do not coincide. And when cleavages coincide, the nature of the party battle may be influenced by the intensity with which opinions are held by opposing groups within the public. On the other hand, when popular cleavages do not coincide, party groups within the electorate may encounter the most serious difficulty in the maintenance of sufficient unity for effective action. Within the representative body party groups may be converted into a congeries of factions, no one of which possesses the power to govern. Under such circumstances, the skills of leadership will be taxed to construct new majorities as each new question arises. . . .

FOREIGN AND DOMESTIC POLICY: CONGRUENCE AND NONCONGRUENCE OF OPINION OF OPINION GROUPS

. . . Opinions on domestic welfare policy are commonly regarded as arrayed along a scale from extreme conservatism to extreme liberalism, whereas foreign-policy opinions are usually pictured as distributed along an isolationism-internationalism continuum. . . . The descriptive problem is to portray in some comprehensible way the manner in which the distributions of opinion on foreign and domestic policy are related within the population.

An attack on that problem may begin with an examination of the distribution of opinion on these two dimensions at the time of the 1952 presidential campaign. The distributions on the two dimensions took different forms. On external policy the modal opinion was isolationist, at least as measured by responses to the question on how people felt about whether "this country has gone too far in concerning itself with problems in other parts of the world." The largest bloc of persons thought that we had gone too far; a substantial number thought that we had not gone too far; and only a few answered in a pro-con manner—as may be seen from the left panel of Figure 1. It may be doubted the answers to the question meant that the country was isolationist in any absolute sense. Probably a majority responded favorably to the Republican exploitation in their campaign of the Korean issue; as they saw the situation of the moment, they thought the country had "gone too far." In contrast, on domestic policy a majority supported the prevailing degree of governmental activity in social welfare or favored even further action. The modal opinion was liberal as measured by responses to the question about whether the government had "done about right, too much, or not enough" in "trying to deal with such problems as unemployment, education, housing, and so on." About half the respondents thought the government had done "about right," as the right panel of Figure 1 indicates, while the remainder were about equally divided between those who thought it "should do more" or that it should "do less."

We need only to cross-tabulate the distributions of the responses on these two questions to identify the combinations of opinion within the electorate and to determine their size. The combinations of opinion supposed to make up the "four-party" system constituted the following percentages of the 1952 national sample:

Isolationist-liberal	14%
Internationalist-liberal	9
Isolationist-conservative	12
Internationalist-conservative	5

If those who regarded government policy in the social welfare field as being "about right" were to be classified as "liberal," a characterization not without basis, the sizes of the blocs of opinion would be:

Isolationist-liberal	41%
Internationalist-liberal	25
Isolationist-conservative	12
Internationalist-conservative	5

Although data for 1956 precisely comparable to those for 1952 are not available, by 1956 a change had occurred in the distribution of attitudes toward foreign involvement. The liquidation of the Korean incident altered the situation which people were appraising, and the Eisenhower Administration brought many Republicans to the support of a higher degree of participation in international affairs.[1] Nevertheless, other

---

[1]In 1954 the proportion of persons taking the position that the United States had gone "too far" in concerning itself with problems in other parts of the world was considerably smaller than in 1952, 41 per cent against 55 per cent. See Angus Campbell and Homer C. Cooper, *Group Differences in Attitudes and Votes* (Ann Arbor: University of Michigan Survey Research Center, 1956), p. 141.

Figure 1   Opinions on International Involvement and Social Welfare Activity, 1952

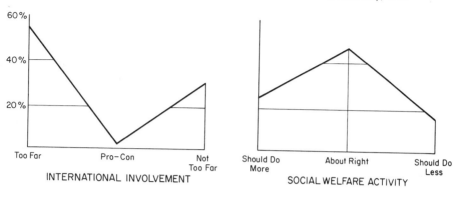

Data source: Survey Research Center, University of Michigan, 1952. For text of the questions, see Table 1. Percentage base includes those with no opinion.

measures made it clear that foreign-policy issues and domestic issues in 1956 still divided the people along different lines. In 1956 a national sample was rated along a scale of internationalism—or willingness to tolerate foreign involvement—and a scale of domestic liberalism. Those who ranked high on the liberalism scale were almost as likely to be high on the internationalism scale as were those who placed at the conservative end of the liberalism scale (see Table 2). The lines of cleavage in the two policy areas did not coincide.

Table 1   Relations Between Opinion on International Involvement and Opinion on Governmental Social Welfare Activity, 1952

Social Welfare Activity[a]	International Involvement[b]				
	Too Far	Pro-Con	Not Too Far	DK	Total
Should do more	14%[c]	*[d]	9%	2%	25%
About right	27	1	16	5	49
Should do less	12	*	5	1	18
DK†	3	*	2	3	8
TOTAL	56%	1%	32%	11%	100%

[a]"Some people think the national government should do more in trying to deal with such problems as unemployment, education, housing, and so on. Others think the government is already doing too much. On the whole, would you say that what the government has done has been about right, too much, or not enough?"
[b]"Some people think that since the end of the last world war this country has gone too far in concerning itself with problems in other parts of the world. How do you feel about this?"
[c]The entries are percentages of the total sample. $N = 1614$.
[d]Asterisk denotes less than 1/2 of 1 per cent.
Data source: Survey Research Center, University of Michigan, 1952.
†Don't know [Ed. note].

Table 2   Relation of Position on Domestic Liberalism Scale to Position on Internationalism Scale, 1956[a]

Internationalism	Liberalism		
	Low	Medium	High
High	50%	59%	58%
Medium	32	28	21
Low	18	13	21
TOTAL	100%	100%	100%
N	226	598	491

[a]For the construction and content of the scales, see Appendix II.
Data source: Survey Research Center, University of Michigan, 1956.

Foreign Policy and Fiscal Policy

Interrelations of opinions on foreign and domestic policies create problems in the contrivance of a program to command majority support. A domestic action may repel those whose support is needed in the foreign field, and action abroad may outrage those whose disposition might be to support policy at home. Another dimension of this conflict and congruence occurs in the relation between opinions on foreign issues and levels of taxation. Opinion in support of involvement abroad may be worthless unless it is accompanied by a willingness to pay the price.

Odd kinds of noncongruence exist between opinions on taxation and on foreign policy. Judgments of a national sample on taxation were obtained in 1956 by the ascertainment of agreement and disagreement with the proposition: "The government ought to cut taxes even if it means putting off some important things that need to be done." Reaction to the proposition was by no means a simple-minded reflex complaint against taxation: 45 per cent of the sample disagreed with the proposition; only 24 per cent agreed; the remainder either thought it would depend or expressed no opinion. No doubt the question had different meanings for different people, but it also probably isolated a bloc of people with a special kind of concern about taxation.

When responses to the tax question are tabulated against foreign-aid questions, some notion of the nature and size of blocs of opinion supportive of foreign involvement emerges. About one fifth of the total sample supported aid to "poorer countries" even though "they can't pay for it" and simultaneously vowed that taxes ought not to be cut at the expense of "important things that need to be done." Another technically consistent bloc, about one twelfth of the sample, opposed foreign aid and favored tax cuts. The odds are that the one tenth favoring both foreign aid and tax cuts were not steadfast supporters of foreign aid. The details of these relations appear in Table 3.

Table 3   Combinations of Opinion on Foreign Economic Aid and on Cutting Taxes

Cutting Taxes[a]	Foreign Aid[b]				
	Pro	Depends	Con	DK	Total
Pro	11%[c]	4%	8%	3%	26%
Depends	4	3	3	1	11
Con	22	8	11	4	45
DK	5	1	4	8	18
TOTAL	42%	16%	26%	16%	100%

[a]"The government ought to cut taxes even if it means putting off some important things that need to be done."
[b]"The United States should give economic help to the poorer countries of the world even if they can't pay for it."
[c]Entries are percentages of the total sample holding the indicated combinations of opinion. $N = 1764$.
Data source: Survey Research Center, University of Michigan, 1956.

The relationships may be put in another form. Consider the proportions of persons supporting certain types of foreign involvement who also support tax cuts "even if it means putting off some important things that need to be done." From one fourth to one third of the supporters of foreign involvement as measured by a series of questions also subscribed to the view that taxes ought to be cut "even if it means putting off some important things." For the details, see Table 4.

Consequences of Patterns In Interrelation of Foreign and Domestic Policy

These prosaic tables, indicative of the fact that foreign and domestic issues cut the population in different ways, point to characteristics of the structure of opinion important to the American political system. A basic

Table 4   Relation of Support for Foreign Involvement to Opinions on Cutting Taxes[a]

Cutting Taxes	Pro Foreign Aid	Pro Act Tough	Con Stay Home
Pro	26%	30%	21%
Depends	10	11	12
Con	52	46	59
No opinion; DK	12	13	8
TOTAL	100%	100%	100%
N	756	1,095	998

[a]For the wording of the issue propositions, see Appendix I.
Data source: Survey Research Center, University of Michigan, 1956.

consequence of the crisscrossing of the electorate by the two kinds of issues concerns the nature of the party system. Given the variety of noncongruent groups produced by these issue cleavages two parties each consisting of persons like-minded on all issues cannot be constructed. To the extent that these combinations of opinion are projected into the representative system, deference to public opinion can prevail only if legislative groups are fluid.[2] The ruling coalition in Congress must vary in its composition from issue to issue. The maneuvers persisting over two decades to maintain support of foreign policy by the construction of a wavering bipartisan coalition amply illustrate the proposition. . . .

INTERRELATIONS OF OPINIONS ON DOMESTIC POLICIES

Noncongruence between distributions of opinion on foreign and domestic policy creates vexing problems in the management of the political system. Within the domestic policy realm, too, people do not invariably divide along the same line on all issues. Hence a multiplicity of noncongruent cleavages in domestic affairs contributes toward results similar to those produced by the crisscrossing of lines of disagreement on foreign and domestic policy. The foundation of opinion patterns on domestic matters affects more significantly the character of the political system, for the basic structure of American politics rests on domestic issues. Foreign policy cleavages are only superimposed on that structure.

The Liberal-Conservative Continuum

Division of people into liberal and conservative categories is a great convenience in the description of political opinions. It is also misleading, for people do not divide into two camps, with members of one group in agreement on one side of all domestic economic issues and united to oppose the other group united within itself in opposition on the same issues. If such were the reality, our politics would probably be far different, as well as much more easily described. Instead, the liberal-conservative cleavage divides the population along different lines, depending on the matter at issue. The difference between liberal and conservative is one not of black and white but of degree. At the conservative end of the scale are those who may be agreed in support of all or most measures with a "conservative" tendency, while at the opposite end are those united in support of all or most liberal causes. Between the extremes are those with mixed opinions; they take, in varying combinations, the conservative view on some measures and the liberal on others. In a symmetrical distribution persons at the center of the scale would be half-liberal and

[2]Doubtless considerable variation prevails in the extent to which particular opinion patterns are projected into the representative apparatus. For example, the chances are that in the South political participation among those of isolationist sentiment is extremely low.

half-conservative in their outlooks on a set of issues. In short, the division of the population is peculiar for each liberal-conservative issue.

Domestic Welfare Policy and Fiscal Policy

. . . As in the realm of international policy, in domestic policy a balance has to be struck between the demand for public services and the propensity to resist payment of taxes. Those who advocate the enlargement of public services do not invariably support a correlative tax policy.

The odd combinations of opinion that develop about fiscal policy and welfare legislation find illustration in the relations between attitudes on the question of the government's role in assuring that those who want to work can find a job and on the proposition that taxes should be cut at the cost of "things that ought to be done." The various combinations of opinion on these two questions are shown as proportions of a 1956 sample in Table 5. Almost one fifth of the total sample (18 per cent) supported the idea that the government ought to see that those willing to work "can find a job" and adhered also to the notion that taxes ought to be cut. By contrast, another fifth of the sample (21 per cent) maintained a consistent position on both issues, a proportion of approximately the same size as that of the comparably consistent supporters of foreign aid. It may be that only about one fifth of the population can be relied upon to give a consistently sensible and firm support to interrelated policies of the kinds described.

Another tack on the interrelations of opinions on taxes and welfare policy may be taken by an examination of the views on the tax question of two groups: those who support and those who oppose welfare policy. The data appear for a series of policy propositions in Table 6. Obviously larger proportions of the pro-welfare than of the anti-welfare individuals concur in the proposition to cut taxes at the cost of important services. Doubtless at the two ends of the tax scale different views prevail on what public services are important. Nevertheless, when a

Table 5   Combinations of Opinion on Job Guarantee and on Cutting Taxes[a]

	Job Guarantee				
Cutting Taxes	Pro	Depends	Con	DK	Total
Pro	18%[b]	2%	5%	1%	26%
Depends	6	1	3	1	11
Con	21	4	17	3	45
DK	10	1	2	5	18
TOTAL	55%	8%	27%	10%	100%

[a]For wording of the issue questions, see Appendix I.
[b]Entries are percentages of the total sample. $N = 1764$.
Data source: Survey Research Center, University of Michigan, 1956.

Table 6   Relation of Opinion on Welfare Measures to Opinion
on Cutting Taxes[a]

Opinion on Welfare Measures

Tax Cutting	Job Guarantee		School Aid		Medical Care	
	Pro	*Con*	*Pro*	*Con*	*Pro*	*Con*
Pro	32%	20%	29%	21%	32%	20%
Depends	11	11	11	12	11	10
Con	38	62	43	59	38	65
No opinion; DK	19	7	17	8	19	5
TOTAL	100%	100%	100%	100%	100%	100%
N	996	471	1185	259	949	458

[a]For wording of the issue questions, see Appendix I.
Data source: Survey Research Center, University of Michigan, 1956.

third or so of those who support, for example, federal aid for school construction also feel that taxes ought to be cut at the cost of important services, doubt may be entertained about the solidity of the support for aid to education.

If the data are arranged in still another way, it appears that the tax cut question must isolate a necessitous group of people as well as an odd opinion combination. Let us focus attention on those persons who support the tax-cut proposition and ascertain their views on welfare issues. The persons supporting the tax-cut proposition consist in large measure, as may be seen from Table 7, of persons favorably disposed toward welfare measures. Almost one fifth of the electorate falls within this category of persons who commit themselves to self-defeat.[3] Yet from their standpoint their position is comprehensible. A simple calculus of self-interest makes simultaneous support of tax reduction and expansion of welfare activities entirely consistent for them. For the system as a whole, however, this type of opinion combination is irrational and creates problems in program-making. The freedom of action for government created by a permissive consensus on a welfare measure may be constricted by opinion on taxation. The existence of a cluster of persons holding this combination of opinions makes it possible for political leadership to befuddle a considerable bloc of people.

The substantial bloc of persons consisting of opponents of social welfare measures who also take the firm position that taxes should not

[3]In a study of Detroit, Janowitz finds that "the lower social strata and the lesser status groups demand an extension of the scope of government welfare services and yet simultaneously feel that the burdens imposed by government are not worth the services rendered." Further, "negative and hostile feelings" about the worth of government "were concentrated at the bottom of the social pyramid, where simultaneously the demands for more government administration predominate."—Morris Janowitz, *et al., Public Administration and the Public* (Ann Arbor, Mich.: University of Michigan Bureau of Government, 1958), pp. 40, 105.

Table 7   Opinions on Welfare Policies of Persons Who Support a Tax Cut Even If It Means Putting Off Some Important Things That Need To Be Done

Opinion on Welfare Proposition	School Aid	Job Guarantee	Medical Care
Pro	76%	70%	67%
Depends	7	5	6
Con	12	21	20
DK; no opinion	5	4	7
TOTAL	100%	100%	100%
N	453	453	453

Data source: Survey Research Center, University of Michigan, 1956.

be reduced at the cost of "important things that need to be done" attracts attention. Those persons may be attached to a restricted view of the proper scope of governmental functions, but they place a higher value on public services of which they approve than they do upon a tax cut. These views, of course, may be consistent for the individuals who hold them; they also make sense in terms of the requirements of the political system as a whole. If the weights of blocs of opinion could be nicely reckoned, it probably would turn out that those composed of opinions consistent with the needs of the political system as a whole carry a weight in the political process disproportionate to their numbers.

These interrelations of opinion suggest melancholy thoughts about the practical politics of the interaction of tax policy and substantive policy. Taxation to finance welfare programs meets opposition among those who favor welfare programs even more frequently than among those who oppose them. Progressive taxation is offered as the solution, but it meets opposition from persons who oppose both welfare programs and higher taxation of themselves, a combination of motives that increases intensity of feeling and probably exertions in the political process as well. The balance of forces drives policy makers back toward concealed and indirect taxation, which may be regressive in its incidence. Such an approach may have strategic advantage in that it may be safely assumed that most of these persons who both take the simple-minded position on taxes and support expansion of welfare activities have no impressive comprehension of the theory of the incidence of taxation.

Other Examples of Noncongruent Opinion Groupings

The crisscrossings of opinion cleavages that involve questions of taxation and of expenditure make a comparatively simple pattern; the same people simultaneously want increased expenditures and reduced taxes. If it were feasible to sample opinions on all issues and to construct some representation of their combinations within clusters of individuals in the society as a whole, we should have an incredibly complex picture of many kinds of opinion combinations that occur as different cleavages cut through the society in different planes. That task certainly cannot be essayed with the data at hand, but a few more examples may be set out to give some inkling of the nature of what is a complex reality.

In the field of general economic policy we have data on opinions on two related propositions: the proposition that government ought to see to it that big business corporations do not have much influence on the way government is run and the proposition that the government ought to see to it that everybody who wants to work can find a job. A priori, given the background of American political debate, we might expect that these questions would cut through the population in about the same way. One of the bugaboos of American politics has long been the big business corporation. It might be supposed that those who believe that the government ought to see to it that everybody who "wants to work can find a job" would join in the cry to restrain the influence of big business. In fact, those who opposed government action to assure jobs favored restraint on big business influence in about the same degree as did the pro-job-guarantee group (52 per cent against 56 per cent). Views on restraint of business were, as Table 8 shows, quite independent of views on the government job-guarantee question.

The medical-care and school-integration questions create another pair of noncongruent opinion cleavages within the population. Orthodox liberals advocate both medical care and school integration, but these combinations of opinion do not uniformly occur in the general population. The manner in which the cleavages fall on these issues illustrates the capacity of politics to make strange bedfellows. In the South well over half the supporters of government action in the field of medical care oppose federal intervention in school segregation. In the North the relationship was reversed; half of the supporters of medical care favored federal interposition in the problem of school segregation.

Table 8   Combinations of Opinion on Restraining Political Influence of Big Business and of Opinion on Job Guarantee

Job Guarantee[a]	Restrain Big Business Influence[b]				
	Pro	Depends	Con	DK	Total
Pro	31%	3%	8%	14%	56%
Depends	4	*	1	2	7
Con	14	2	7	4	27
DK	2	*	1	7	10
TOTAL	51%	5%	17%	27%	100%

[a]"The government in Washington ought to see to it that everybody who wants to work can find a job."
[b]"The government ought to see to it that big business corporations don't have much say about how the government is run."
Data source: Survey Research Center, University of Michigan, 1956.

Table 9   Combinations of Opinion on Medical Care and School Integration, North and South

School Integration	Medical Care[a]				
	Pro	Depends	Con	DK	Total
		North			
Pro[b]	25%[c]	4%	11%	4%	44%
Depends	3	1	1	1	6
Con	18	3	13	3	37
DK	5	1	2	5	13
TOTAL	51%	9%	27%	13%	100%
		South			
Pro	17	2	6	2	27
Depends	4	1	1	1	7
Con	35	5	14	4	58
DK	5	*	*	3	8
TOTAL	61%	8%	21%	10%	100%

[a]"The government ought to help people get doctors and hospital care at low cost."
[b]That is, those who disagreed with the proposition: "The government in Washington should stay out of the question of whether white and colored children go to the same school."
[c]Entries are percentages of the sample holding the specified combinations of opinion.
Data source: Survey Research Center, University of Michigan, 1956.

Many Southerners and Northerners who are allied on the medical-care question are at odds on the integration question. Similarly, many persons allied on the integration issue are at odds on the medical-care question. The relative sizes of the various opinion combinations on the two questions in the North and in the South are shown in Table 9.

Inferentially, these combinations of opinion and crisscrossing of cleavages throw some light on the old supposition that a man's political opinions are but an expression of some broad attitude or of some personality pattern. Studies of limited and highly indoctrinated populations, such as college undergraduates, once led to the conclusion that, since opinions on one specific issue permitted the prediction of opinions on other specific issues, a general or basic attitude governed these responses on individual issues. When the general population is sampled, that inference becomes less tenable. Or if the view is tenable, it is so only on the supposition that within the population there is an enormous variety of individual basic attitudes to produce the various combinations of opinions that exist on specific issues. Rather than to seek the explanation of issue opinions in some basic attitude pattern, it is as sensible to regard individual opinions on specific issues as the product of rationality, immediate self-interest, or other such factors.[4] Such generality or consistency

---

[4]See G. W. Allport, "The Composition of Political Attitudes," *American Journal of Sociology*, Vol. 35 (1929), 220–38; Ross Stagner, "Correlational Analysis of Nationalistic Opinions," *Journal of Social Psychology*, Vol. 12 (1940), 197–212. The skeptical

of attitude as prevails may come more from indoctrination by a political party or by other groups with programs than from any characteristic response by individuals to a range of questions.

ESCAPES FROM CONFLICT

Our data convey a dim and overly simple conception of the variety of clusters of opinion that exist within the population, but they suffice to identify several types of opinion combinations. An opinion combination may be technically consistent—that is, made up of opinions supportive of mutually dependent policy; for example, those persons who believe that the "government in Washington" should see to it that everybody has a job and who also take a negative position on tax cuts hold technically consistent opinions. On the other hand, opinion combinations may be technically inconsistent in that contradictory positions are held on operationally related questions. From another viewpoint, an opinion combination may be consistent in partisan terms in that on two or more issues a person holds positions that appear to parallel the leadership line of one party. Or an opinion combination may be inconsistent in partisan terms; for example, those persons who thought in 1952 that the government had "gone too far" in involvement in world affairs but not "far enough" in social-welfare legislation were certain, if they voted, to vote against some of their beliefs, but persons with opinions consistently organized in partisan terms would not have faced the same dilemma.

Escapes, both for the individual and for the system as a whole, mitigate the consequences of conflicts created by noncongruence of opinion groupings. For the individual in the voting situation the relative salience of issues may provide an escape from conflict or may, in fact, make what appears to be a conflict no conflict at all. To appreciate this possibility the nature of the data on which the preceding analyses rest must be kept in mind. Interviewers ask for judgments on questions about which the respondent may or may not have thought much one way or another. A person may have said that he strongly believed that the government ought to do more in the field of welfare, housing, etc., but foremost in his mind may have been an anxiety about when the Korean War would be brought to an end.[5] Issues of foreign policy may have been more salient to him than domestic issues, and for that individual the conflict would have been nonexistent. Perhaps he proceeded, insensible of internal

---

remarks about the controlling effects of basic attitudes should not be regarded as conflicting with the psychological finding that individuals tend to organize their opinions in a way to promote psychological comfort or to avoid internal conflict. The argument, rather, is that people often accommodate themselves handily to opinion combinations with which the politically sophisticated observer might find it difficult to live.

[5]A notion of the way issues change in salience comes from the question occasionally asked by the AIPO: "What do you think is the most important problem

conflict, to vote against himself on domestic matters, as doubtless several million persons did in 1952. Or salience may not be between issues but between issues and judgments of candidates or concern about the quality and tenor of government management.

An indication of how the relative salience of issues works in the determination of the vote is provided by analyses of responses in 1956 to open-ended questions on the parties and on the presidential candidates. In the course of their ruminations about the merits and demerits of the political parties and about the candidates, persons made references to foreign and domestic issues. From the number of references in these two policy areas, persons could be classified roughly according to whether foreign or domestic matters were salient for them. As the categorization proceeded, it became necessary to create pigeonholes for those with apparently equal attention on the two areas, as well as for those whose observations were devoid of policy content. The national sample divided in the following way.[6]

Foreign salience	16%
Domestic salience	47
Equal attention	8
No issue content	29

How persons in these several categories voted clearly indicates the bearing of salience on the individual voting decision. Over three fourths of those persons for whom foreign issues were salient voted Republican. Those for whom domestic concerns were more central gave Eisenhower a bare majority. Those who gave equal attention to the two fields also returned a heavy Republican majority. Given the fact that domestic issues were salient for most of the electorate, those who gave equal attention to domestic and foreign affairs had a relatively heavy focus of attention on external matters.[7]

---

facing this country today?" Responses just before and after the Little Rock episode were as follows:

	September, 1957	November, 1957
Keeping the peace	34%	26%
High cost of living	22	12
Racial problems	10	29

[6]The breakdown by type of issue salience in 1952 was almost precisely the same as in 1956: foreign, 17 per cent; domestic, 54 per cent; equal, 10 per cent; no issue content, 19 per cent.

[7]The Republican percentages of the 1956 presidential vote according to the types of issue salience listed in the text were: foreign, 78; domestic, 52; equal attention, 74; no issue content, 57. From these percentages, it is clear that factors other than issue salience accounted for most of the variance in the vote. It should also be said that the measure of salience, contrived *ad hoc* from data collected for other purposes, may have a character of circularity. Salience, as measured, may reflect in part a tendency of people to talk about those policy matters that best support their voting decisions.

Other investigators have identified the same phenomenon in other ways. Apart from relative salience, voters may have quite deliberate and conscious judgments about the relative importance of policy areas in which they are in attitudinal conflict in partisan terms. Berelson found, for example, that in Elmira those voters who were domestic liberals but inclined toward isolationism in foreign affairs tended to vote in the direction indicated by the relative importance they attached to domestic and foreign issues.[8] In other situations voters seem quite unaware that they are cross-pressured.[9] Some individuals work themselves out of the conflict situation by what the psychologists denominate a "distortion of perception"; that is, they see their candidate or their party as being in agreement with themselves even though informed observers may have contrary perceptions of the relationship.

To be differentiated from those actions that permit the individual to escape from conflict are those adjustments by which the political system as a whole adapts itself to the circumstances created by great groupings holding noncongruent attitudes. For example, governmental action may satisfy a majority on one issue and on a second issue go against the majority, which may be composed in part of some of those who make up the majority on the first issue. The broad record of the Eisenhower Administration provides a classic case of the simultaneous triumph and defeat of noncongruent majorities. Its foreign-policy performance brought majority approval in 1956, while its record on domestic policy as a whole evidently earned disapproval. Our governmental structure conveniently permitted the simultaneous expression of both phases of this electoral schizophrenia when in 1956 Eisenhower won reelection as the Democrats carried Congress. But public opinion is not self-executing, and in the determination of which of two noncongruent majorities is to prevail American constitutional arrangements permit the Executive to exercise wide discretion. Even the most friendly observer would not claim that the Eisenhower Administration was characterized by imaginative, venturesome, and energetic initiation of domestic policy. It made its bows to opinion majorities on domestic questions by mild proposals, most of which failed through the weakness of White House legislative leadership.[10] When Congress developed within itself sufficient cohesion to initiate controversial domestic measures, it met presidential veto.

In another fashion, the political system as a whole handles the di-

---

[8] Bernard Berelson, *et al., Voting* (Chicago: University of Chicago Press, 1954), p. 200. For a related finding, see Philip K. Hastings, "The Independent Voter in 1952: A Study of Pittsfield, Massachusetts," *American Political Science Review*, Vol. 47 (1953), 805–10.

[9] See Martin Kriesberg, "Cross-Pressures and Attitudes," *Public Opinion Quarterly*, Vol. 13 (1949), 5–16.

[10] The tricks of the art of governing include that of verbal deference to public opinion unaccompanied by correlative concrete action.

vergencies of objective manifest in inconsistent opinion groupings by taking some account of the relative weight of opinion clusters. It seems plain that some types of opinion are accorded less deference than others, even though the numbers of their holders in the population may be the same. That this is true there can be no doubt. Whether its truth can be satisfactorily established is another matter. Some of the combinations of opinion we have isolated invite speculation about their strength in the political process. One may suspect, for example, that in many jurisdictions, and perhaps in the nation as a whole, a relatively strong position may be occupied by those hardheaded individuals who oppose extension of the scope of welfare activities yet take a firm stand against tax cuts at the expense of important governmental functions. On the contrary, those clusters of persons who favor more extended welfare activity but can be seduced by promises of tax cuts probably do not weigh heavily in the balance of political forces. Technically inconsistent opinion clusters may not enjoy a strength proportionate to their numbers.

ELITES, PROGRAMS, EQUILIBRIUM

This excursion through the jungle of data on the interrelations of opinion doubtless has created some bewilderment, for the meaning of the facts is by no means self-evident. Nor can their meaning be stated with either simplicity or great assurance. Although the characteristics of opinion described probably have a profound bearing on the nature of the political order, the specification of that bearing requires leaps from the crude facts over dark and obscure terrain toward plausible conclusions whose connection with their point of origin is not readily demonstrable.

Noncongruent Cleavages and Cohesion in The Political Order

Some observers see in the circumstance of multifarious but noncongruent cleavage a source of cohesion within the political system. Obviously, the argument goes, if the state divides itself into two or more groups, each consisting of persons completely in agreement against outsiders on all issues, the potentialities for strident discord and disruptive friction may be great.[11] In the abstract, the hypothesis seems plausible if we assume that the issues involved are not all low-temperature questions. Less obvious, though, is the reasoning underlying the proposition that a multiplicity of cleavages may lend cohesion to the state.

In part, the cohesion hypothesis rests on the fact that crisscrossing cleavages make the same persons allies on some questions and opponents

---

[11]Bartlett observes that "where potentialities of division are very numerous, the possibility of serious splitting may be at a minimum, but where possible lines of division are few, the group may be in serious danger of radical deterioration."— *Political Propaganda* (Cambridge: Cambridge University Press, 1940), p. 8.

on others, a circumstance that supposedly serves either to mute the intensity of conflict or at least to require that it be conducted in accord with some limiting etiquette. . . . Throughout the social system enmities are paradoxically ameliorated by friendships and disruptive conflicts are offset by cohesive commonalities. An actual opinion situation, to be sure, would deviate from the model in many ways. Simultaneous consensus on a large proportion of issues, for example, would keep narrow the area of conflict.[12] Or the component of conflict might be enlarged by the bipolarization of attitudes on several issues. Yet, with noncongruent opinion groupings, connective links would in varying degrees span the gap between opponents.

These comments in terms of congruent- and noncongruent-opinion categories verge toward theories about the consequences for the nature of the political order of overlapping group membership. A Southern worker may be a member of a union (that advocates civil rights for Negroes) and of a white Citizens' Council (that urges the contrary viewpoint). Persons who maintain a position of conflicting loyalties may, in some instances, try to make the peace (or they may withdraw from one group or take other evasive action). Yet it may be seriously doubted whether the kinds of overlapping, or noncongruent, opinion groupings described in this chapter have a substantial effect on behavior through the population generally. The Southerner who allies himself with the Northerner on medical care and opposes him on integration is no less an ardent supporter of white supremacy for that fact. Or the internationalist who finds himself on the same side of foreign issues with a welfare stater whose views on domestic policy he detests is probably in the mass no less an opponent of the welfare state because of that alliance.

The effects upon the political order of multifarious opinion cleavages probably must be sought in their bearing on the behavior of leadership elements. Those who are most sensible of and most sensitive to the inconsistencies and conflicts of opinion groupings, the contradictory disciplines of cross pressures, are probably the influentials in both public and politically relevant private spheres of leadership. A Senator may have in his following both conservative-internationalists and liberal-internationalists, and other combinations as well. A Representative may have to worry about constituents who are enthusiastic advocates of public power and medical care and others who desire medical care legisla-

---

[12]For example, Sappenfield finds in a study of university students that those of different religions may be in disagreement on a narrow range of religious questions but united on a range of beliefs about democratic institutions.—"Ideological Agreement and Disagreement Among Religious Groups," *Journal of Abnormal and Social Psychology*, Vol. 38 (1943), 532–39. In the same vein, religious "differences may be minimized by the sharing of a large fund of non-religious values."—R. M. Williams, Jr., "Religion, Value-Orientation, and Intergroup Conflict," *Journal of Social Issues*, Vol. 12 (1956), 12–20.

tion but cannot stomach public power. Local union officials, urged to promote the international's policy on foreign affairs, may speak only softly to their unskilled brethren with a provincial outlook. A Democratic precinct captain in a suburban neighborhood may push aid to education and sound fiscal policy; another in a working-class precinct may soft-pedal foreign policy and talk up social welfare.

It is probably in the effects of these variegated opinion clusters on the levels of political leadership—using the term to cover a fairly large category of political activists—that one must seek the bearing of a multiplicity of political cleavages on the nature of the political order. Individuals can hold inconsistent opinions with no great personal discomfort. The political leader, though, must contrive some way to enact social welfare legislation to benefit his constituents without at the same time outraging them by the necessary levy of taxes. He must also, if he is a legislator, so conduct himself that he may tomorrow approach for support his enemy of today. If this stab in the dark is correct, to give credence to the hypothesis that multiplicity of cleavages conduces to cohesion, one must include in the explanatory model some account of the complex interactions between mass opinion and the political elite through whose actions the nature of the political order becomes manifest.

And, as we reflect in this vein, another consequence of a multiplicity of cleavage, not often noted, becomes apparent. The strange bedfellows attendant upon noncongruence of cleavage may over the long run muffle political conflict and induce cohesion within the political order. Yet in the short run, in which we spend most of our lives, multiplicity of cleavage may promote stasis if not paralysis within the state. By multiplication of the uncertainties and the risks for leadership, by subjection of elites to conflicting pressures and directives of dubious clarity, by creation of blocs of opinion susceptible to diversionary exploitation, a set of circumstances conducive to blockage of action comes into being. No majority nicely united on outstanding issues can be readily mobilized; a potential majority on one issue is often shattered by the inclination of some of its members to prefer to kill action on some other issue. Without determined and venturesome leadership, the great leviathan may stall on dead center. All this is not to deny that the Republic may, under some circumstances, flourish even though the government is stalled on dead center. The analysis points, rather, to the nature of checks and balances within the social structure that have to be neutralized when major action becomes necessary.

Elites and Coherent Political Action

The quilted pattern of opinion differentiation is projected upward to condition the behavior of political elites. By the same token these types of opinion patterns place obligations upon the political elite in a democracy. To govern, it must influence opinions as well as be influenced thereby. No aspect of public opinion demonstrates more persuasively the duty of leadership to educate, as well as to follow, than the characteristics of opinion examined in this chapter.

A modicum of consistency or coherence in the program of government as a whole must, of necessity, prevail. In one of its phases that consistency is a technical necessity, for one policy may depend upon another. That technical necessity permeates the detailed actions of government, most of which never come to wide public attention. But, even with the scant data examined, we have identified instances of policies of high visibility which technically demand coherent treatment. The most simple case is that of taxation and welfare policy. The pattern of opinion, whatever lack of faith we may have in the precision of our measurements, is not congruent on the two issues. Substantial numbers of proponents of welfare policies simultaneously rank tax reduction as an action to be taken at the expense of "important things that ought to be done." Obviously the advancement of the public weal requires sufficient skill and courage on the part of political elites to manage interrelated policies in a coherent manner and to win public consent for that action.

Another aspect of consistency in program is a matter not of administrative but of political necessity. A party requires for its existence an inner core of activists fairly well united on a wide range of issues. A degree of difference can be tolerated even within the party elite, but a party leadership cannot survive the centrifugal forces if the party activists are divided along as many lines as is the public generally. If the data were available on the top layers of political influentials—two or three million people—they would probably show, within each party, a much higher degree of consistency of opinion, along party lines, than either their supporters or the public generally. Such evidence as is available indicates that as political activity and political involvement increase, consistency of opinion—in partisan terms—tends to increase.[13] Moreover between the leadership echelons of the parties fairly consistent and sharp differences exist in broad outlook.[14]

[13]Angus Campbell, Gerald Gurin, and Warren E. Miller, *The Voter Decides* (New York: Harper & Row, Publishers, 1954), Ch. 8. The size of national samples does not permit the isolation from them of sufficient numbers of the thin layer of highly active partisans to demonstrate the degree of contrast in policy consistency between them and the rank and file of partisans. Yet perceptible differences in partisan consistency exist between even the broad strata of party identifiers that can be differentiated by crude measures of political involvement and of participation.

[14]See Herbert McClosky: "Conservatism and Personality," *American Political Science Review*, Vol. 52 (1958), 27–45; Angus Campbell, Philip E. Converse, Warren E. Miller, and Donald E. Stokes, *The American Voter* (New York: John Wiley & Sons, Inc., 1960), Ch. 9. The early work of S. P. Hayes, Jr., points in the same direction. His professional respondents showed a far higher degree of consistency of views among various policies—in partisan terms—than did factory workers. See "The Interrelation of Political Attitudes: II. Consistency in Voters' Attitudes," *Journal of Social Psychology*, Vol. 10 (1939), 359–78.

However consistently the party elite may subscribe to the party program, it must win the support of an electorate whose views are not so consistently organized in partisan terms. The task of winning popular consent is complicated by the existence of the kinds of noncongruent opinion clusters that we have identified; whatever combination of positions a party advocates, it will both repel and attract many of the same people. Hence we have considerable appeal to ambiguity, and, in truth, noncongruent opinion clusters create both the opportunity and the temptation to resort to humbuggery.

The technical tasks placed upon governing elites by the total pattern of noncongruent opinion distributions make patent the excessive simplicity of the customary conceptions of majority rule. Discussion of majority rule tends to assume the existence of a single great issue. Once opinion is ascertained, it remains only to take action in accord therewith. In fact, many questions exist simultaneously. If all issues fell into the same policy dimension, the problems of governments would be far simpler than they are. . . .

In reality, all issues do not fall in this manner. The cleavages crisscross, or, in other terms, opinions on some issues are not scalable. And, more important for the argument, it may be assumed that the distributions of opinion on different questions interact as action occurs. Those interactions condition the problem of organization of opinion to maintain support for a government. A policy on a domestic-welfare question may antagonize those sensitive to taxation. An action on segregation may drive away those who have been catered to by a welfare policy. A policy of foreign aid may gain the support of some persons antagonistic to the government's welfare actions and perhaps destroy the support of other persons favorable to the welfare actions. . . .

Knowledge about such interrelated movements in opinion distributions is practically nil. The odds are that the repercussions from government action in one opinion area on the shape of the distribution in another opinion area are not quickly felt. The process of interaction is doubtless slowed by the time required for perceptions of the new reality to percolate through the population, by the inattention of many persons, by nonpolicy attitudes such as party identification, and by other frictions. It may be, too, that the distributions of some types of opinions that are lightly held, as in some foreign-policy areas, may fairly quickly be altered by the effects of action or inaction in other realms. In any event, the entire discussion points to the complexity of the problem of maintaining the equilibrium of the political system—even if we interpret equilibrium to mean only the maintenance of 51 per cent of the vote on our side.

CHAPTER TWENTY-THREE

ISSUE CONFLICT AND CONSENSUS AMONG PARTY LEADERS AND FOLLOWERS

HERBERT McCLOSKY, PAUL J. HOFFMANN, AND ROSEMARY O'HARA

American political parties are often regarded as "brokerage" organizations, weak in principle, devoid of ideology, and inclined to differ chiefly over unimportant questions. In contrast to the "ideological" parties of Europe—which supposedly appeal to their followers through sharply defined, coherent, and logically related doctrines—the American parties are thought to fit their convictions to the changing demands of the political contest.[1] According to this view, each set of American party leaders is satisfied to play Tweedledee to the other's Tweedledum.

PRESSURES TOWARD UNIFORMITY AND CLEAVAGE

Although these "conclusions" are mainly derived from *a priori* analysis or from casual observations of "anecdotal" data (little systematic effort having been made so far to verify or refute them), they are often taken

This article is the first in a series reporting the findings of a national field study of political belief and affiliation among American party leaders and followers. The study was carried out through the Laboratory of Research in Social Relations at the University of Minnesota under grants made to the senior author by the Committee on Political Behavior of the School Science Research Council, and supplementary grants from the Graduate School Research Fund. The manuscript was prepared at the Survey Research Center, University of California, Berkeley, under a Fellowship in Legal and Political Philosophy awarded to the senior author by the Rockefeller Foundation.

[1]Maurice Duverger, *Political Parties, Their Organization and Activity in the Modern State* (New York: Wiley, 1954), p. 102.

Reprinted by permission from the AMERICAN POLITICAL SCIENCE REVIEW, *54 (June 1960), 406–27. Mr. McClosky is Professor of Political Science at the University of California at Berkeley. Mr. Hoffmann has left the academic world. Mrs. O'Hara is a social studies teacher at King High School in Tampa, Florida.*

as confirmed—largely, one imagines, because they are compatible with certain conspicuous features of American politics. Among these features is the entrenchment of a two-party system which, by affording both parties a genuine opportunity to win elections, tempts them to appeal to as many diverse elements in the electorate as are needed to put together a majority.[2] Since both parties want to attract support from the centrist and moderate segments of the electorate, their views on basic issues will, it is thought, tend to converge. Like giant business enterprises competing for the same market, they will be led to offer commodities that are in many respects identical.[3] It is one thing for a small party in a multi-party system to preserve its ideological purity, quite another for a mass party in a two-party system to do so. The one has little hope of becoming a majority, and can most easily survive by remaining identified with the narrow audience from which it draws its chief supporters; the other can succeed only by accommodating the conflicting claims of many diverse groups—only, in short, by blunting ideological distinctions.[4]

Constraints against enlarging intellectual differences also spring from the loosely confederated nature of the American party system, and from each national party's need to adjust its policies to the competing interests of the locality, the state, and the nation.[5] Many party units are more concerned with local than with national elections, and prefer not to be handicapped by clearcut national programs. Every ambitious politician, moreover, hopes to achieve a *modus vivendi* tailored to the particular and often idiosyncratic complex of forces prevailing in his constituency, an objective rarely compatible with doctrinal purity.[6] Often, too, local politics are largely nonpartisan or are partisan in ways that scarcely affect the great national issues around which ideologies might be expected to form.[7] The development and enforcement of a sharply delineated ideology is also hindered by the absence in either party of a firmly established, authoritative, and continuing organiza-

---

[2]The analysis of these and related tendencies associated with the American system is ably set forth in Pendleton Herring, *The Politics of Democracy* (New York: Norton, 1940), p. 102 and *passim*. Also, James M. Burns, *Congress on Trial: The Legislative Process and the Administrative State* (New York: Harper & Row, 1949), p. 34.

[3]See especially E. E. Schattschneider, *Party Government* (New York: Holt, Rinehart & Winston, 1942), p. 92 and *passim*; and V. O. Key, *Politics, Parties, and Pressure Groups* (4th ed.), (New York: Crowell-Collier, 1958), Ch. 8; Howard R. Penniman, *Sait's American Parties and Elections* (5th ed.), (New York: Appleton-Century-Crofts, 1952), p. 162.

[4]William Goodman, *The Two-Party System in the United States* (Princeton, N.J.: Van Nostrand, 1956), p. 43.

[5]Duverger, *op. cit.*, pp. 187, 418.

[6]Herring, *op. cit.*, p. 133.

[7]Belle Zeller (ed.), *American State Legislatures* (New York: Crowell-Collier, 1954); but see also Malcolm E. Jewell, "Party Voting in American State Legislatures," *American Political Science Review*, Vol. 49 (September, 1955), pp. 773–91.

tional center empowered to decide questions of doctrine and discipline.[8] Party affiliation is loosely defined, responsibility is weak or nonexistent, and organs for indoctrinating or communicating with party members are at best rudimentary.

Cultural and historical differences may also contribute to the weaker ideological emphasis among American, as compared with European, parties. Many of the great historical cleavages that have divided European nations for centuries—monarchism *vs.* republicanism; clericalism *vs.* anticlericalism; democracy *vs.* autocracy, etc.—have never taken root in this country. Apart from the slavery (and subsequently the race) issue, the United States has not experienced the intense class or caste conflict often found abroad, and contests of the capitalism *vs.* socialism variety have never achieved an important role in American politics. In addition, never having known a titled nobility, we have largely been freed from the conflicts found elsewhere between the classes of inherited and acquired privilege.

Consider, too, the progress made in the United States toward neutralizing the forces which ordinarily lead to sharp social, and hence intellectual and political, differentiation. The class and status structure of American society has attained a rate of mobility equalling or exceeding that of any other long-established society. Popular education, and other facilities for the creation of common attitudes, have been developed on a scale unequalled elsewhere. Improvements in transportation and communication, and rapid shifts in population and industry have weakened even sectionalism as a source of political cleavage. Rural-urban differences continue to exist, of course, but they too have been diminishing in force and have become less salient for American politics than the differences prevailing, for example, between a French peasant proprietor and a Parisian *boulevardier*.[9] In short, a great many Americans have been subjected in their public lives to identical stimuli—a condition unlikely to generate strong, competing ideologies.

The research reported here was designed not to refute these observations but to test the accuracy of the claim that they are sufficient to prevent differences in outlook from taking root in the American party system. We believed that the homogenizing tendencies referred to are strongly offset by contrary influences, and that voters are preponderantly led to support the party whose opinions they share. We further thought that the competition for office, though giving rise to similarities between

[8]Report of the Committee on Political Parties, American Political Science Association, *Toward A More Responsible Two-Party System* (New York: Holt, Rinehart & Winston, 1950), *passim.*

[9]Data bearing on these generalizations will be presented in companion articles which specifically deal with sectional and rural-urban influences on issue outlook.

the parties, also impels them to diverge from each other in order to sharpen their respective appeals. For this and other reasons, we expected to find that the leaders of the two parties, instead of ignoring differences alleged to exist within the electorate, would differ on issues more sharply than their followers would. We believed further that even in a brokerage system the parties would serve as independent reference groups, developing norms, values, and self-images to which their supporters could readily respond.[10] Their influence, we felt, would frequently exceed that of ethnic, occupational, residential, and other reference groups. In sum, we proceeded on the belief that the parties are not simply spokesmen for other interest groups, but are in their own right agencies for formulating, transmitting, and anchoring political opinions, that they attract adherents who in general share those opinions, and that through a feedback process of mutual reinforcement between the organization and its typical supporters, the parties develop integrated and stable political tendencies. Other hypotheses will be specified as we present and analyze our findings.

PROCEDURES

The questions considered in this paper were part of a large field study made in 1957–1958 on the nature, sources, and correlates of political affiliation, activity, and belief in the American party system (hereafter referred to as the PAB study). Pilot studies on Minnesota samples had led us to suspect that many "settled" notions about party affiliation and belief in America would not stand up under careful empirical scrutiny; further, we felt that little progress would be made in the exploration of this subject until a comprehensive portrait of party membership in America had been drawn. Accordingly, a nationwide study was launched to acquire a detailed description of party leaders and supporters, gathering data on their backgrounds, political experiences, personality characteristics, values, motivations, social and political attitudes, outlooks on key issues, and related matters.

For our samples of party "leaders" we turned to the Democratic and Republican national conventions, largely because they are the leading and most representative of the party organs, their delegates coming from every part of the United States and from every level of party and government activity. Our samples ranged from governors, Senators, and

---

[10]*Cf.* James W. Prothro, Ernest Q. Campbell, and Charles M. Grigg, "Two Party Voting in the South: Class vs. Party Identification," *American Political Science Review*, Vol. 52 (March, 1958), 131–39. Also, Peter H. Odegard and E. Allen Helms, *American Politics: A Study in Political Dynamics* (New York: Harper & Row, 1947), pp. 809–21.

national committeemen at the one end to precinct workers and local officials at the other. In the absence of comprehensive information about the characteristics of the party élites in America, no one can say how closely the convention delegates mirror the total party leadership. We felt it fair to assume, nevertheless, that the delegates represented as faithful a cross section of American party leadership as could be had without an extraordinary expenditure of money and labor. Using convention delegates as our universe of leaders also held some obvious advantages for research, since the composition of this universe (by name, address, party, state, sex, place of residence, and party or public office) can usually be ascertained from the convention calls. Of the 6,848 delegates and alternates available to be sampled, 3,193 actually participated; 3,020 (1,788 Democrats and 1,232 Republicans) completed and returned questionnaires that were usable in all respects.[11] The proportion of returns was roughly equivalent for both sets of party leaders.

The rank and file sample, which we wanted both for its intrinsic value and for its utility as a control group, was obtained by special arrangement with the American Institute of Public Opinion. In January 1958, Gallup interviewers personally distributed our questionnaire to 2,917 adult voters in two successive national cross-sectional surveys. Some 1,610 questionnaires were filled out and returned, of which 1,484 were completely usable. This sample closely matched the national population on such characteristics as sex, age, region, size of city, and party affiliation; and, though it somewhat oversampled the upper educational levels, we considered it sufficiently large and representative for most of our purposes. Of the 1,484 respondents, 821 were Democratic supporters (629 "pure" Democrats, plus 192 whom we classified as "independent" Democrats) and 623 were Republican supporters (479 "pure" Republicans, plus 144 "independent" Republicans). Forty respondents could not be identified as adherents of either party.

The lengthy questionnaire developed for the study was designed to be self-administered. It contained, in addition to questions on the respondents' personal backgrounds, a number of queries on their political history and experience, their attitudes toward the party system and toward such related matters as party organization, discipline and responsibility, their self-images with regard to social class and liberalism-conservatism, their reference group identifications, and their views on party

---

[11]This gratifyingly large number of returns of so lengthy and detailed a questionnaire was attained through a number of follow-up mailings and special letters. These and other procedures designed to check the adequacy of the sample will be fully described in the volume containing the report of the overall study. The difference in the number of returns from the two parties was largely a result of the greater number of Democratic delegates to begin with.

leadership and ideology. The largest part of the questionnaire consisted of 390 scale items, randomly arranged, which when sorted and scored fell into 47 scales for measuring the personality, attitude, and value characteristics of each of the respondents. We had validated and used all but three of these scales in earlier studies.

The questions most relevant for the present article were those which asked each respondent to express his attitudes toward twenty-four important national issues, and to state whether he believed support for each issue should be "increased," "decreased," or "remain as is." The list of issues and the responses of each sample will be found in Tables 1–5, where, for convenience of analysis, the issues have been grouped under five broad headings: public ownership, government regulation of the economy, equalitarianism and human welfare, tax policy, and foreign policy.

In tabulating the results, we first scored each individual on each issue and then computed aggregate scores for all the members of a given sample. To begin with, percentages were used to show the proportion who favored increasing, decreasing, or retaining the existing level of support on each issue. But as it was clumsy to handle three figures for each issue, we constructed a single index or "ratio of support" which would simultaneously take account of all three scores. The index was built by assigning a weight of 1.0 to each "increase" response in the sample, of 0 to each "decrease" response, and of .50 to each "remain as is" (or "same") response. Thus the ratio-of-support score shown for any given sample is in effect a mean score with a possible range of 0 to 1.0, in which support for an issue increases as the scores approach 1.0 and decreases as they approach 0. In general, the scores can be taken to approximate the following overall positions: .0 to .25—strongly wish to reduce support; .26 to .45—wish to reduce support; .46 to .55—satisfied with the *status quo*; .56 to .75—wish to increase support; and .76 to 1.00—strongly wish to increase support. Note that the differences in degree suggested by the categories refer not to the *strength of feeling* exhibited by individuals toward an issue but rather to the *numbers of people* in a sample who hold points of view favoring or opposing that issue.

Because they include "same" and "no code" as well as "increase" and "decrease" responses, our ratios of support sometimes flatten the differences between groups. Had we employed only the percentage scores for the "increase" or "decrease" responses, the differences between samples would in many instances have seemed larger. Nevertheless, the ratio of support offers so many advantages that we have employed it as our principal measure. For one thing, as the equivalent of a mean score, it takes into account all scores, omitting no respondent from the tabulation. For the same reason it enables us to assess the amount of dispersion or homogeneity exhibited by any sample and makes it easy to calculate significances of difference.[12] Reliance upon a single, uniform statistic also allows us to make ready comparisons not only *between* but *within* samples, and to determine quickly how large the differences actually are. By observing whether a ratio of support is above or below .50 we can see at once whether a particular group predominantly favors or opposes the issue in question, and how strongly it does so. The use of ratio scores also makes it possible to compare issues as well as groups, *e.g.*, to see whether one issue is more preferred than another.

For further information on the meaning of the issue responses, we also compared samples on a number of related scales and items. Tabulating and statistical operations were carried out to control for demographic influences like education, occupation, age, and sectionalism; to ascertain homogeneity of opinion within the several samples; to rank the issues according to the magnitude of the differences between samples; to compare members' positions on issues against official platform statements; and to determine whether leaders and followers are able to name the issues which actually divide the parties. Some of the findings yielded by these operations will be considered here, while others, for reasons of space, will have to be reserved for future publications.

A word of caution before we turn to the findings. The respondents were offered only the twenty-four issues that impressed us in February 1957, as most significant and enduring. However, they may not all be as salient today as they seemed at that time. Nor, within the limitations of a single questionnaire, could we explore every issue that informed observers might have considered important. Some presumably vital issues such as states rights, political centralization, and expansion of government functions could not be stated explicitly enough within our format to be tested properly. These are issues that are so generalized as to encompass many other specific issues, and so highly charged as to awaken a profusion of symbolic and emotive associations.

The *form* of our issue questions may also be open to criticism, for space limitations prevented our subjects from indicating how strongly they felt and how much they knew about each of the issues. This deficiency, however, may be less important than it appears, since for the groups we most wanted to compare (*e.g.*, Democratic *vs.* Republican

---

[12]The measure of dispersion used for this purpose was the standard deviation, which was computed by using the scores of 0, .50 and 1.00 as intervals in the calculations. To avoid having to calculate separate significances of difference for each of the comparisons we wanted to observe, we simply made the assumption—erring on the side of caution—that the maximum variance of .50 had occurred in each instance. The magnitude of the significance of difference is, in other words, often greater than we have reported. The significance test used in this procedure was the critical ratio. Unless otherwise indicated, all the differences reported are statistically significant at or beyond the .01 level.

leaders), the degree of political knowledge and intensity is likely to be rather similar. The difficulty is greater when comparing leaders with followers, but is somewhat offset by controlling for education and socio-economic status. Although some subtleties of interpretation are bound to be lost because these variables have been omitted, we are satisfied that our issue questions in their present form furnish a useful measure for assessing *group* (as distinguished from *individual*) opinion.

Finally, one may wonder about the value of opinions stated on a questionnaire compared with the worth of views formally expressed by an organization or implicit in the actions of its leaders. Advantages can be cited on both sides. The beliefs expressed in official party statements or in legislative roll calls, it might be claimed, represent the *operating* beliefs of the organization by virtue of having been tested in the market-place or in the competition of legislative struggle. Positions taken on issues on which a party stakes its future may be more valid evidence of what the party truly believes than are the opinions expressed by individual members under conditions of maximum safety. On the other hand, the responses to the issue and attitude questions in the PAB study represent the anonymous, private opinions of party leaders and followers uncomplicated by any need to make political capital, to proselytize, to conciliate critics, or to find grounds for embarrassing the opposition at the next election. Hence they may for some purposes represent the most accurate possible reflection of the "actual" state of party opinion. The controversy over the value of the two approaches is to some extent spurious, however, for they offer different perspectives on the same thing. In addition, considerable correspondence exists between the party positions evident in congressional roll calls and the privately expressed opinions of the party leaders in our study.[13]

FINDINGS: COMPARISONS BETWEEN LEADERS

No more conclusive findings emerge from our study of party issues than those growing out of the comparisons between the two sets of party leaders. Despite the brokerage tendency of the American parties, their active members are obviously separated by large and important differences. The differences, moreover, conform with the popular image in which the Democratic party is seen as the more "progressive" or "radical," the Republican as the more "moderate" or "conservative" of the

---

[13]See, for example, the congressional roll-call results reported by Julius Turner, *Party and Constituency: Pressures on Congress*, The Johns Hopkins University Studies in Historical and Political Science Series, Vol. 69 (1951). The complexities affecting the determination of party votes in Congress are thoroughly explored in David B. Truman, *The Congressional Party: A Case Study* (New York: John Wiley & Sons, Inc., 1959).

two.[14] In addition, the disagreements are remarkably consistent, a function not of chance but of systematic points of view, whereby the responses to any one of the issues could reasonably have been predicted from knowledge of the responses to the other issues.

Examination of Tables 1–5 shows that the leaders differ significantly on 23 of the 24 issues listed and that they are separated on 15 of these issues by .18 or more ratio points—in short, by differences that are in absolute magnitude very large. The two samples are furthest apart in their attitudes toward public ownership and are especially divided on the question of government ownership of natural resources, the Democrats strongly favoring it, the Republicans just as strongly wanting it cut back. The difference of .39 in the ratio scores is the largest for any of the issues tested. In percentages, the differences are 58 per cent (D) vs. 13 per cent (R) in favor of increasing support, and 19 per cent (D) vs. 52 per cent (R) in favor of decreasing support. Both parties preponderantly support public control and development of atomic energy, but the Democrats do so more uniformly.

V. O. Key, among others, has observed that the Republican party is especially responsive to the "financial and manufacturing commu-

Table 1   Comparison of Party Leaders and Followers on "Public Ownership" Issues, by Percentages and Ratios of Support

	Leaders		Followers	
Issues	Democrats N = 1,788	Republicans N = 1,232	Democrats N = 821	Republicans N = 623
Public ownership of natural resources				
Per cent favoring: increase	57.5	12.9	35.3	31.1
decrease	18.6	51.9	15.0	19.9
same, n.c.[a]	23.8	35.2	49.7	49.0
Support ratio	.69	.30	.60	.56
Public control of atomic energy				
Per cent favoring: increase	73.2	45.0	64.2	59.4
decrease	7.2	15.3	7.1	10.0
same, n.c.	19.6	39.7	28.7	30.6
Support ratio	.83	.65	.79	.75
Mean support ratios for the public ownership category	.76	.48	.70	.66

[a]n.c. = no code.

14Conservatism is here used not in the classical but in the more popular sense, in which it refers to negative attitudes toward government ownership, intervention, and regulation of the economy; resistance to measures for promoting equalitarianism and social welfare through government action; identification with property, wealth, and business enterprise, etc.

nity,"[15] reflecting the view that government should intervene as little as possible to burden or restrain prevailing business interests. The validity of this observation is evident throughout all our data, and is most clearly seen in the responses to the issues listed under government regulation of the economy, equalitarianism and human welfare, and tax policy. Democratic leaders are far more eager than Republican leaders to strengthen enforcement of anti-monopoly laws and to increase regulation of public utilities and business. Indeed, the solidarity of Republican opposition to the regulation of business is rather overwhelming: 84 per cent want to decrease such regulation and fewer than .01 per cent say they want to increase it. Although the Democrats, on balance, also feel that government controls on business should not be expanded further, the differences between the two samples on this issue are nevertheless substantial.

The two sets of leaders are also far apart on the farm issue, the Democrats preferring slightly to increase farm supports, the Republicans wanting strongly to reduce them. The Republican ratio score of .20 on this issue is among the lowest in the entire set of scores. The magnitude of these scores somewhat surprised us, for while opposition to agricultural subsidies is consistent with Republican dislike for state intervention, we had expected the leaders to conform more closely to the familiar image of the Republican as the more "rural" of the two parties.[16] It appears, however, that the party's connection with business is far more compelling than its association with agriculture. The Republican desire to reduce government expenditues and to promote independence from "government handouts" prevails on the farm question as it does on other issues, while the Democratic preference for a more regulated economy in which government intervenes to reduce economic risk and to stabilize prosperity is equally evident on the other side. Party attitudes on this issue appear to be determined as much by ideological tendencies as by deliberate calculation of the political advantages to be gained by favoring or opposing subsidies to farmers. Comparison of our findings with Turner's earlier data on farm votes in Congress[17] suggests, in addition, that the sharp party difference on the farm issue is neither a recent development nor a mere product of the personal philosophy of the present Secretary of Agriculture.

Having implied that agricultural policies partly result from principle, we must note that on three other issues in this category (trade

[15]Key, *op. cit.*, p. 239.

[16]The friendlier attitude toward farmers among Democratic leaders than Republican leaders is borne out in the responses to several other questions used in the study. For example, the Republican leaders list farmers as having "too much power" far more frequently than do the Democratic leaders. Equally, the Democrats are significantly more inclined to regard farmers as having "too little power."

[17]Turner, *op. cit.*, p. 64.

Table 2   Comparison of Party Leaders and Followers on "Government
Regulation of the Economy" Issues, by Percentages and Ratios of Support[a]

	Leaders		Followers	
	Democrats	Republicans	Democrats	Republicans
Issues	N = 1,788	N = 1,232	N = 821	N = 623
Level of farm price supports				
Per cent favoring: increase	43.4	6.7	39.0	23.0
decrease	28.1	67.4	27.6	40.3
same, n.c.	28.5	25.8	33.4	36.7
Support ratio	.58	.20	.56	.41
Government regulation of business				
Per cent favoring: increase	20.2	0.6	18.6	7.4
decrease	38.5	84.1	33.4	46.2
same, n.c.	41.3	15.3	48.0	46.4
Support ratio	.41	.08	.43	.31
Level of tariffs				
Per cent favoring: increase	13.0	19.2	16.6	15.2
decrease	43.0	26.3	25.3	21.3
same, n.c.	43.9	54.5	58.1	63.4
Support ratio	.35	.46	.46	.47
Restrictions on credit				
Per cent favoring: increase	24.8	20.6	26.1	25.7
decrease	39.3	20.6	22.2	23.8
same, n.c.	35.9	58.8	51.8	50.5
Support ratio	.43	.50	.52	.51
Mean support ratios for "government regulation of the economy" category	.59	.48	.58	.53

[a][Some items have been deleted from this table—Ed.]

unions, credit, and tariffs), principle seems to be overweighed by old-fashioned economic considerations. In spite of their distaste for government interference in economic affairs, the Republicans almost unanimously favor greater regulation of trade unions and they are more strongly disposed than the Democrats toward government intervention to restrict credit and to raise tariffs. Of course, party cleavages over the credit and tariff issues have a long history,[18] which may by now have endowed them with ideological force beyond immediate economic considerations.[19] The preponderant Democratic preference for greater regulation of trade unions is doubtless a response to recent "exposures" of corrupt

[18]See John B. Johnson, Jr., *The Extent and Consistency of Party Voting in the United States Senate*, Ph.D. thesis, University of Chicago, 1943. By applying the Rice Index-of-Likeness to Senate votes, Johnson finds the tariff to have been the most partisan issue before the Congress in the years 1880–1940.

[19]Corinne Silverman, "The Legislator's View of the Legislative Process," *Public Opinion Quarterly*, Vol. 18 (1954–1955), 180.

labor practices, though it may also signify that the party's perspective toward the trade unions is shifting somewhat.

The closer Republican identification with business, free enterprise, and economic conservatism in general, and the friendlier Democratic attitude toward labor and toward government regulation of the economy, are easily observed in the data from other parts of our questionnaire. Republican leaders score very much higher than Democratic leaders on, for example, such scales as economic conservatism, independence of government, and business attitudes. On a question asking respondents to indicate the groups from which they would be most and least likely to take advice, 41 per cent of the Democratic leaders but only 3.8 per cent of the Republican leaders list trade unions as groups from which they would seek advice. Trade unions are scored in the "least likely" category by 25 per cent of the Democrats and 63 per cent of the Republicans. Similarly, more than 94 per cent of the Republican leaders, but 56 per cent of the Democratic leaders, name trade unions as groups that have "too much power." These differences, it should be noted, cannot be accounted for by reference to the greater number of trade union members among the Democratic party leadership, for in the 1956 conventions only 14 per cent of the Democrats be-

Table 3   Comparison of Party Leaders and Followers on "Equalitarian and Human Welfare" Issues, by Percentages and Ratios of Support[a]

	Leaders		Followers	
Issues	Democrats N = 1,788	Republicans N = 1,232	Democrats N = 821	Republicans N = 623
Federal aid to education				
Per cent favoring: increase	66.2	22.3	74.9	64.8
decrease	13.4	43.2	5.6	8.3
same, n.c.	20.4	34.5	19.5	26.8
Support ratio	.76	.40	.85	.78
Minimum wages				
Per cent favoring: increase	50.0	15.5	59.0	43.5
decrease	4.7	12.5	2.9	5.0
same, n.c.	45.2	72.0	38.1	51.5
Support ratio	.73	.52	.78	.69
Enforcement of integration				
Per cent favoring: increase	43.8	25.5	41.9	40.8
decrease	26.6	31.7	27.4	23.6
same, n.c.	29.5	42.8	30.7	35.6
Support ratio	.59	.47	.57	.59
Mean support ratios for "equalitarian and human welfare" category	.71	.50	.70	.66

[a][Some items have been deleted from this table—Ed.]

longed to trade unions, and while an even smaller percentage (4 per cent) of the Republicans were trade unionists, this disparity is hardly great enough to explain the large differences in outlook. The key to the explanation has to be sought in the symbolic and reference group identifications of the two parties, and in their underlying values.

Nowhere do we see this more clearly than in the responses to the equalitarian and human welfare issues. The mean difference in the ratio scores for the category as a whole is .22, a very large difference and one that results from differences in the expected direction on all six issues that make up the category. On four of these issues—federal aid to education, slum clearance and public housing, social security, and minimum wages—the leaders of the two parties are widely separated, the differences in their ratio scores ranging from .36 to .21. The percentages showing the proportions who favor increased support for these issues are even more striking. In every instance the Democratic percentages are considerably higher: 66 *vs.* 22 per cent (education); 78 *vs.* 40 per cent (slum clearance and housing); 60 *vs.* 23 per cent (social security); and 50 *vs.* 16 per cent (minimum wages). The Democratic leaders also are better disposed than the Republican leaders toward immigration: twice as many of them (36 per cent *vs.* 18 per cent) favor a change in policy to permit more immigrants to enter. The overall inclination of both party élites, however, is to accept the present levels of immigration, the Democratic ratio score falling slightly above, and the Republican slightly below, the midpoint.

More surprising are the differences on the segregation issue, for, despite strong Southern influence, the Democratic leaders express significantly more support for enforcing integration than the Republicans do. Moreover, the difference between the two parties rises from .12 for the national samples as a whole to a difference of .18 when the Southern leaders are excluded. In his study of Congress, Turner found that the Republicans gave more support to Negro rights than the Democrats did.[20] The reversal of this finding in our data does not necessarily mean that a change has occurred since Turner made his study, but only that the votes of the congressional parties do not always reflect the private feelings of the national party leadership. Then, too, Southern influence is disproportionately stronger in the Democratic congressional party than in the national Democratic organization as a whole, and disproportionately weaker in the Republican congressional party than in the Republican organization as a whole.

Examination of the actual magnitude of the ratio scores in this category reveals that the Republicans want not so much to abrogate existing social welfare or equalitarian measures as to keep them from

[20]Turner, *op. cit.,* p. 54.

Table 4   Comparison of Party Leaders and Followers on "Tax Policy" Issues, by Percentages and Ratios of Support[a]

	Leaders		Followers	
Issues	*Democrats* N = 1,788	*Republicans* N = 1,232	*Democrats* N = 821	*Republicans* N = 623
Corporate income tax				
Per cent favoring: increase	32.3	4.0	32.0	23.3
decrease	23.3	61.5	20.5	25.7
same, n.c.	44.4	34.5	47.5	51.0
Support ratio	.54	.21	.56	.49
Mean support ratios for "tax policy" category	.36	.19	.42	.38

[a][Some items have been deleted from this table—Ed.]

being broadened. The Democrats, by comparison, are shown to be the party of social equality and reform, more willing than their opponents to employ legislation for the benefit of the underprivileged. Support for these inferences and for the greater liberalism of the Democrats can be found elsewhere in our data as well. Analysis of the scale results show Republican leaders scoring higher than Democratic leaders on such measures as chauvinism, elitism, conservatism, and right-wing values, and lower on tolerance, procedural rights, and faith in democracy. No differences worth noting, however, were found for ethnocentrism, faith in freedom, or the California F scale. The Democrats had a slightly higher average score on the left-wing scale, but the number of leaders in either party who scored high on this measure was fairly small.

The self-images and reference group identifications of the two parties also should be noted in this connection. For example, many more Democratic than Republican leaders call themselves liberal and state that they would be most likely to take advice from liberal reform organizations, the Farmers' Union, and (as we have seen) from the trade unions; only a small number consider themselves conservative or would seek advice from conservative reform organizations, the National Association of Manufacturers, or the Farm Bureau Federation. The Republicans have in almost all instances the reverse identifications: only a handful regard themselves as liberal or would seek counsel from liberal organizations, while more than 42 per cent call themselves conservative and would look to the NAM or to conservative reform organizations for advice. Almost two thirds of the Republicans (compared with 29 per cent of the Democrats) regard the Chamber of Commerce as an important source of advice. Businessmen are listed as having "too much power" by 42 per cent of the Democrats but by only 9 per cent of the Republicans. The Democrats are also significantly more inclined

Table 5   **Comparison of Party Leaders and Followers on "Foreign Policy" Issues, by Percentages and Ratios of Support**

Issues	Leaders		Followers	
	Democrats N = 1,788	Republicans N = 1,232	Democrats N = 821	Republicans N = 623
Reliance on the United Nations				
Per cent favoring: increase	48.9	24.4	34.7	33.4
decrease	17.6	34.8	17.3	19.3
same, n.c.	33.5	40.7	48.0	47.3
Support ratio	.66	.45	.59	.57
American participation in military alliances				
Per cent favoring: increase	41.5	22.7	39.1	32.3
decrease	17.6	25.7	14.0	15.4
same, n.c.	40.9	51.6	46.9	52.3
Support ratio	.62	.48	.62	.58
Foreign aid				
Per cent favoring: increase	17.8	7.6	10.1	10.1
decrease	51.0	61.7	58.6	57.3
same, n.c.	31.1	30.7	31.3	32.6
Support ratio	.33	.23	.26	.26
Defense spending[a]				
Per cent favoring: increase	20.7	13.6	50.5	45.7
decrease	34.4	33.6	16.4	15.4
same, n.c.	44.8	52.8	33.0	38.8
Support ratio	.43	.40	.67	.65
Mean support ratios for "foreign policy" category (excl. defense spending)	.54	.39	.49	.47

[a]See footnote 22.

than the Republicans to consider Catholics, Jews, and the foreign born as having "too little power." While self-descriptions and reference group identifications often correspond poorly with actual beliefs—among the general population they scarcely correspond at all, in fact—we are dealing, in the case of the leaders, with a politically informed and highly articulate set of people who have little difficulty connecting the beliefs they hold and the groups that promote or obstruct those beliefs.

Our fourth category, tax policy, divides the parties almost as severely as do the other categories. The mean difference for the category as a whole is .20, and it would doubtless have been larger but for the universal unpopularity of proposals to increase taxes on small and middle income groups. Table 4 shows that the differences between the parties on the tax issues follow the patterns previously observed and that tax policy is for the Democrats a device for redistributing income and promoting social equality. Neither party, however, is keen about raising taxes for *any* group: even the Democrats have little enthusiasm for new taxes on upper income groups or on business and corporate enterprises. The Republican leaders are overwhelmingly opposed to increased taxes for *any* group, rich *or* poor. This can be seen in their low ratio scores on the tax issues, which range from only .15 to .24. But while they are far more eager than the Democratic leaders to cut taxes on corporate and private wealth, they are less willing to reduce taxes on the lower income groups. These differences, it should be remarked, are not primarily a function of differences in the income of the two samples. Although there are more people with high incomes among the Republican leaders, the disproportion between the two samples is not nearly great enough to account for the dissimilarities in their tax views.

Of the five categories considered, foreign policy shows the smallest average difference, but even on these issues the divergence between Democratic and Republican leader attitudes is significant. Except for defense spending the Democrats turn out to be more internationalist than the Republicans, as evidenced in their greater commitment to the United Nations and to American participation in international military alliances like NATO. Twice as many Democrats as Republicans want the United States to rely more heavily upon such organizations, while many more Republicans want to reduce our international involvements. Both parties are predominantly in favor of cutting back foreign aid—a somewhat surprising finding in light of Democratic public pronouncements on this subject—but more Republicans feel strongly on the subject. Our data thus furnish little support for the claim that the parties hold the same views on foreign policy or that their seeming differences are merely a response to the demands of political competition.[21]

Nevertheless, it would be incorrect to conclude that one party believes in internationalism and the other in isolationism. The differences are far too small to warrant any such inference. Traces of isolationism, to be sure, remain stronger in the Republican party than in the Democratic party—an observation buttressed by the finding that twice as many Republicans as Democrats score high on the isolationism scale. The pattern of Republican responses on both the issue and scale items signifies, however, that the leaders of that party generally accept the degree of "internationalism" now in effect, but shrink from extending it further. Consider too, the similarities in the leaders' scores on defense spending,

---

[21]*Cf.* Turner, *op, cit.,* p. 56, in which he found differences on foreign policy difficult to assess in Congress, partly because of its tie with the executive branch; see also George Belknap and Angus Campbell, "Political Party Identification and Attitudes Toward Foreign Policy," *Public Opinion Quarterly,* Vol. 15 (Winter 1951–1952), 608–19.

for despite their greater leaning toward isolationism, the Republicans are no more inclined than the Democrats to leave the country defenseless.[22]

In treating issues in the Elmira election study of 1948, Berelson, Lazarsfeld, and McPhee[23] found it helpful to distinguish between "style" and "position" issues. "Style" issues principally yield symbolic, psychological, or subjective gratifications, and have relatively intangible consequences; "position" issues reflect direct, personal, and material interests, and have more objective consequences. According to the Elmira report, "position" issues (or what politicians might call "bread and butter" issues) divide voters more sharply than style issues. Most of the issues tested in the present study would have to be classified as "position" issues, but five of them—United Nations, international alliances, foreign aid, immigration, and segregation—could be classified as style issues. Four others—natural resources, atomic energy, education, and slum clearance—contain both symbolic and material elements and can best be described as "mixed."

Although the classification is crude, the findings it yields are generally consistent with the claims of the Elmira study. On the fourteen position issues—taxes, trade unions, tariffs, minimum wages, farm prices, social security, credit restrictions, and the regulation of business, public utilities, and monopolies—Democratic and Republican leaders show an average ratio score difference of .21. On the style issues the two parties differ by .13—a significantly smaller difference. Largest of all, however, are the differences for the "mixed" issues, which average more than .30. This result should occasion little surprise, for when ideology and interest are *both* at work, partisanship is likely to be intensified. Several considerations could account for the superiority of position over style issues as causes of political cleavage: they are "bread and butter" issues, and are thus more often subject to pressure by organized interest groups; they have immediate and tangible consequences, which

[22]The issue of defense spending has been kept separate from the other foreign policy issues because the magnitude of the scores for some of the leaders and all of the followers were obviously inflated by the launching of Sputnik I in November, 1957. The Sputnik incident occurred between the first and second wave of the leader survey and produced an increase in the number favoring defense spending of 40 per cent for the Democrats and 33 per cent for the Republicans. While this is a fascinating testimonial to the influence sometimes exercised by events on public opinion, its effect in this case was to distort scores in such a way as to make the leader and follower samples non-comparable. With proper caution, however, comparisons can be made between Democratic and Republican leaders, since both samples were affected in roughly the same way by Sputnik. For a similar reason we can also compare the Democratic followers with the Republican followers. Comparisons between leaders and followers on this issue cannot, however, be justified from our data.

[23]Bernard R. Berelson, Paul F. Lazarsfeld and William N. McPhee, *Voting* (Chicago: University of Chicago Press, 1954), Ch. 9.

may lead politicians to pay greater attention to them than they do to issues whose payoff is more uncertain; and, finally, they are not so likely to be part of the common core of values upon which the community structure rests.

COMPARISONS BETWEEN FOLLOWERS

So far we have addressed ourselves to the differences between Democratic and Republican *leaders*. In each of the tables presented, however, data are included from which the two sets of party *followers* may also be compared.

The observation most clearly warranted from these data is that the rank and file members of the two parties are far less divided than their leaders. Not only do they diverge significantly on fewer issues—seven as compared with 23 for the leader samples—but the magnitudes of the differences in their ratio scores are substantially smaller for every one of the 24 issues. No difference is larger than .14, and on the majority of the issues the disparity is smaller than .05. Insofar as they differ at all, however, the followers tend to divide in a pattern similar to that shown by the leaders, the correlation between their rank orders being .72. All the issues on which the followers significantly disagree are of the "bread and butter" variety, the more symbolic issues being so remotely experienced and so vaguely grasped that rank and file voters are often unable to identify them with either party. Policies affecting farm prices, business regulation, taxes, or minimum wages, by contrast, are quickly felt by the groups to whom they are addressed and are therefore more capable of arousing partisan identifications. It should also be noted that while the average differences are small for all five categories, they are smallest of all for foreign policy—the most removed and least well understood group of issues in the entire array.[24]

Democratic and Republican followers were also compared on a number of scales and reference group questions. The results, while generally consistent with the differences between the leaders, show the followers to be far more united than their leaders on these measures as well. Even on business attitudes, independence of government, and economic conservatism, the differences are small and barely significant. No differences were found on such scales as tolerance, faith in democ-

---

[24]For comparative data on party affiliation and issue outlooks among rank and file voters, see Angus Campbell, Phillip E. Converse, Warren E. Miller, and Donald E. Stokes, *The American Voter* (New York: John Wiley & Sons, Inc., 1960), especially Chs. 8 and 9 dealing with issues and ideology. The text of this important report on the 1956 election study carried out by the Michigan Survey Research Center unfortunately reached us too late to be used to full advantage in the present analysis. The findings of the Michigan and the PAB studies, relative to the role of issues and ideology among the general population, corroborate and supplement each other to a very great degree.

racy, procedural rights, conservatism-liberalism (classical), the California
F scale, and isolationism. The average Democrat is slightly more willing
than the average Republican to label himself a liberal or to seek advice
from liberal organizations; the contrary is true when it comes to adopting conservative identifications. Only in the differential trust they express toward business and labor are the two sets of followers widely
separated.

These findings give little support to the claim that the "natural
divisions" of the electorate are being smothered by party leaders.[25] Not
only do the leaders disagree more sharply than their respective followers, but the level of consensus among the electorate (with or without
regard to party) is fairly high. Inspection of the "increase" and "decrease" percentage scores (Tables 1-5) shows that substantial differences of opinion exist among the electorate on only five of the 24 issues
(credit restrictions, farm supports, segregation, and corporate and business taxes). Of course, voters may divide more sharply on issues at election
time, since campaigns intensify party feeling and may also intensify
opinions on issues. Available data from election studies allow no unequivocal conclusion on this point,[26] but even the party-linked differences
found among voters during elections may largely be echoes of the opinions announced by the candidates—transient sentiments developed for
the occasion and quickly forgotten.

LEADER CONFLICT AND FOLLOWER CONSENSUS: EXPLANATIONS

Considering the nature of the differences between the leader and follower samples, the interesting question is not why the parties fail to
represent the "natural division" in the electorate (for that question
rests on an unwarranted assumption) but why the party elites disagree
at all, and why they divide so much more sharply than their followers?

Despite the great pressures toward uniformity we have noted in
American society, many forces also divide the population culturally,
economically, and politically. The United States is, after all, a miscellany
of ethnic and religious strains set down in a geographically large and
diverse country. Many of these groups brought old conflicts and ideologies with them, and some have tried to act out in the new world the
hopes and frustrations nurtured in the old. Then, too, despite rapid

25*Cf.* Stephen K. Bailey, *The Condition of Our National Parties* (monograph),
Fund for the Republic, 1959.

26The data reported by the Elmira study of 1948 show the supporters of the
two parties to be largely in argeement on issues. See Berelson, *et al., op. cit.,* pp. 186,
190, 194, 211. The findings of the 1956 Michigan Survey suggest strongly that most
voters, even at election time, do not know much about issues and are unable to link
the parties with particular issues. Campbell and his associates conclude, for example,
that "many people fail to appreciate that an issue exists; others are insufficiently
involved to pay attention to recognized issues; and still others fail to make connections
between issue positions and party policy." Campbell, *et al., op. cit.,* Ch. 8.

social mobility, social classes have by no means been eliminated. No special political insight is needed to perceive that the two parties characteristically draw from different strata of the society, the Republicans from the managerial, proprietary, and to some extent professional classes, the Democrats from labor, minorities, low income groups, and a large proportion of the intellectuals.[27] Partly because the leaders of the two parties tend to over-respond to the modal values of the groups with which they are principally identified, they gradually grow further apart on the key questions which separate their respective supporters.[28] The Republican emphasis on business ideology is both a cause and a consequence of its managerial and proprietary support; the greater Democratic emphasis on social justice, and on economic and social levelling, is both the occasion and the product of the support the party enjoys among intellectuals and the lower strata. These interrelationships are strengthened, moreover, by the tendency for a party's dominant supporters to gain a disproportionate number of positions in its leadership ranks.[29]

The differences which typically separate Democratic from Republican leaders seem also to reflect a deep-seated ideological cleavage often found among Western parties. One side of this cleavage is marked by a strong belief in the power of collective action to promote social justice, equality, humanitarianism, and economic planning, while preserving freedom; the other is distinguished by faith in the wisdom of the natural competitive process and in the supreme virtue of individualism, "character," self-reliance, frugality, and independence from government. To this cleavage is added another frequent source of political division, namely, a difference in attitude toward change between "radicals" and "moderates," between those who prefer to move quickly or slowly, to reform or to conserve. These differences in social philosophy and posture do not always coincide with the divisions in the social structure, and their elements do not, in all contexts, combine in the same way. But, however crudely, the American parties do tend to embody these competing points of view and to serve as reference groups for those who hold them.

Party cleavage in America was no doubt intensified by the advent of the New Deal, and by its immense electoral and intellectual success. Not only did it weld into a firm alliance the diverse forces that were to be crucial to all subsequent Democratic majorities, but it also made explicit the doctrines of the "welfare state" with which the party was henceforth

[27]For an analysis of the connection between intellectuals and liberal politics, see Seymour M. Lipset, *Political Man* (Garden City, N.Y.: Doubleday & Company Inc., 1960), Ch. 10; also Paul F. Lazarsfeld and Wagner Thielens, Jr., *The Academic Mind* (New York: Free Press of Glencoe, 1958), Chs. 1 and 2.

[28]Samuel P. Huntington, "A Revised Theory of American Party Politics," *American Political Science Review*, Vol. 44 (1950), 676.

[29]PAB data supporting this generalization will be presented in a future publication.

to be inseparably identified. Because of the novelty of its program and its apparently radical threat to the familiar patterns of American political and economic life, it probably deepened the fervor of its Republican adversaries and drove into the opposition the staunchest defenders of business ideology. The conflict was further sharpened by the decline of left-wing politics after the war, and by the transfer of loyalties of former and potential radicals to the Democratic party. Once launched, the cleavage has been sustained by the tendency for each party to attract into its active ranks a disproportionate number of voters who recognize and share its point of view.

Why, however, are the leaders so much more sharply divided than their followers? The reasons are not hard to understand and are consistent with several of the hypotheses that underlay the present study.

(1) Consider, to begin with, that the leaders come from the more articulate segments of society and, on the average, are politically more aware than their followers and far better informed about issues.[30] For them, political issues and opinions are the everyday currency of party competition, not esoteric matters that surpass understanding. With their greater awareness and responsibility, and their greater need to defend their party's stands, they have more interest in developing a consistent set of attitudes—perhaps even an ideology. The followers of each party, often ignorant of the issues and their consequences, find it difficult to distinguish their beliefs from those of the opposition and have little reason to be concerned with the consistency of their attitudes. Furthermore, the American parties make only a feeble effort to educate the rank and file politically, and since no central source exists for the authoritative pronouncement of party policy,[31] the followers often do not know what their leaders believe or on what issues the parties chiefly divide. In short, if we mean by ideology a coherent body of informed social doctrine, it is possessed mainly by the articulate leadership, rarely by the masses.

(2) Differences in the degree of partisan involvement parallel the differences in knowledge and have similar consequences. The leaders, of course, have more party spirit than the followers and, as the election studies make plain, the stronger the partisanship, the larger the differences on issues. The leaders are more highly motivated not only to belong to a party appropriate to their beliefs, but to accept its doctrines and to learn how it differs from the opposition party. Since politics is more salient for leaders than for followers, they develop a greater stake in the outcome of the political contest and are more eager to discover the intellectual grounds by which they hope to make victory possible.

---

[30]For the effects of education on issue familiarity, see Campbell, *et al., op. cit.,* Ch. 8.

[31]Schattschneider, *op. cit., Toward A More Responsible Two-Party System, passim.*

Through a process of circular reinforcement, those for whom politics is most important are likely to become the most zealous participants, succeeding to the posts that deal in the formation of opinion. Ideology serves the instrumental purpose, in addition, of justifying the heavy investment that party leaders make in political activity. While politics offers rewards, it also makes great demands on the time, money, and energies of its practitioners—sacrifices which they can more easily justify if they believe they are serving worthwhile social goals. The followers, in contrast, are intellectually far less involved, have less personal stake in the outcome of the competition, have little need to be concerned with the "correctness" of their views on public questions, and have even less reason to learn in precisely what ways their opinions differ from their opponents'. Hence, the party elites recruit members from a population stratified in some measure by ideology, while the rank and file renews itself by more random recruitment and is thus more likely to mirror the opinions of a cross section of the population.

(3) Part of the explanation for the greater consensus among followers than leaders resides in the nature and size of the two types of groups. Whereas the leader groups are comparatively small and selective, each of the follower groups number in the millions and, by their very size and unwieldiness, are predisposed to duplicate the characteristics of the population as a whole. Even if the Republicans draw disproportionately from the business-managerial classes and the Democrats from the trade union movement, neither interest group has enough influence to shape distinctively the aggregate opinions of so large a mass of supporters. Size also affects the nature and frequency of interaction within the two types of groups. Because they comprise a smaller, more selectively chosen, organized, and articulate elite, the leaders are apt to associate with people of their own political persuasion more frequently and consistently than the followers do. They are not only less cross-pressured than the rank and file but they are also subjected to strong party group efforts to induce them to conform. Because their political values are continually renewed through frequent communication with people of like opinions, and because they acquire intense reference group identifications, they develop an extraordinary ability to resist the force of the opposition's arguments. While the followers, too, are thrown together and shielded to some extent, they are likely to mingle more freely with people of hostile political persuasions, to receive fewer partisan communications, and to hold views that are only intermittently and inconsistently reinforced. Since, by comparison with the leaders, they possess little interest in or information about politics, they can more easily embrace "deviant" attitudes without discomfort and without challenge from their associates. Nor are they likely to be strongly rewarded for troubling to have "correct" opinions. The followers, in short, are less often and less effectively indoctrinated than their leaders. The group processes

described here would function even more powerfully in small, sectarian, tightly organized parties of the European type, but they are also present in the American party system, where they yield similar though less potent consequences.

(4) Political competition itself operates to divide the leaders more than the followers. If the parties are impelled to present a common face to the electorate, they are also strongly influenced to distinguish themselves from each other.[32] For one thing, they have a more heightened sense of the "national interest" than the followers do, even if they do not all conceive it in the same way. For another, they hope to improve their chances at the polls by offering the electorate a recognizable and attractive commodity. In addition, they seek emotional gratification in the heightened sense of brotherhood brought on by the struggle against an "outgroup" whose claim to office seems always, somehow, to border upon usurpation. As with many ingroup-outgroup distinctions, the participants search for moral grounds to justify their antagonisms toward each other, and ideologies help to furnish such grounds. Among the followers, on the other hand, these needs exist, if at all, in much weaker form.

LEADERS VERSUS FOLLOWERS

In comparing each party elite with its own followers we were mainly interested in seeing how closely each body of supporters shared the point of view of its leaders, in order to test the hypothesis that party affiliation, even for the rank and file, is a function of ideological agreement. In predicting that the parties would tend to attract supporters who share their beliefs, we expected, of course, to find exceptions. We knew that many voters pay little attention to the ideological aspects of politics and that, in Gabriel Almond's phrase, a party's more "esoteric doctrines" are not always known to its followers.[33] Nevertheless we were not prepared for the findings turned up by this phase of the inquiry, for the differences between leaders and followers—among the Republicans at least—are beyond anything we had expected. Indeed, the conclusion is inescapable that the views of the Republican rank and file are, on the whole, much closer to those of the Democratic leaders than to those of the Republican leaders. Although conflicts in outlook also exist between Democratic leaders and followers, they are less frequent or severe.

If we turn once again to the table of rank order differences, we see that the Democratic followers differ significantly from their leaders on twelve of the 23 issues, and that the average difference in the ratio scores

---

[32]Schattschneider, *ibid.*, p. 192.
[33]Gabriel Almond, *The Appeals of Communism* (Princeton, N.J.: Princeton University Press, 1954), pp. 5–6, and Ch. 3.

of the two samples is .07. Democratic leaders and Republican followers differ significantly on only eleven of the 23 issues, with an average difference between them of only .08. Notice, by contrast, that Republican leaders and followers diverge significantly on 18 of 23 issues, and show an average difference of .16. To complete the comparison, the Republican leaders and Democratic followers were in disagreement on 19 of the 23 issues, their average difference being .20. As these comparisons make plain, there is substantial consensus on national issues between Democratic leaders and Democratic and Republican followers, while the Republican leaders are separated not only from the Democrats but from their own rank and file members as well.

Examination of the Democratic scores shows the leaders to be slightly more "progressive" than their followers on most of the issues on which differences appear. The leaders are, for example, more favorable to public ownership of natural resources, to regulation of monopolies and public utilities, to a reduction of tariffs, and to a liberalized credit policy. They are more internationalist on the foreign aid and United Nations issues and substantially more sympathetic to the maintenance and expansion of immigration. The results showing the relative radicalism of the two samples are not unequivocal, however, for on several issues—federal aid to education, minimum wages, and taxes on business enterprise and large incomes—the followers take the more radical view. Nor are the differences significant on such issues as atomic energy, slum clearance, segregation, farm price supports, government control of business and trade unions, and taxes on middle and small income groups. In general, the followers turn out more radical chiefly on a few of the bread and butter issues—a reflection, no doubt, of their lower socio-economic status. When we control for occupation, the differences between Democratic leaders and followers on these issues largely disappear.

Consideration of the scores of Republican leaders and followers shows not only that they are widely separated in their outlooks but also that the leaders are uniformly more conservative than their followers. Only on the immigration issue is this trend reversed. The followers hold the more "radical" ideas on the two public ownership issues, on five of the six equalitarian and human welfare issues, on four of the seven regulation-of-the-economy issues, and on four of the five tax policy issues. They are also more willing to place greater reliance upon the U.N. and upon international military alliances. Observe that the largest differences occur on those issues which have most sharply separated New Deal–Fair Deal spokesmen from the hard core of the Republican opposition—federal aid to education, redistribution of wealth through taxes on business, corporations, and the wealthy, public ownership of natural resources, public housing, regulation of business, social security, farm price supports, minimum wages, and trade union regulations.

In short, whereas Republican leaders hold to the tenets of business ideology and remain faithful to the spirit and intellectual mood of leaders like Robert A. Taft, the rank and file Republican supporters have embraced, along with their Democratic brethren, the regulatory and social reform measures of the Roosevelt and Truman administrations. This inference receives further support from the scores on our party ideology scale where, on a variety of attitudes and values which characteristically distinguish the leaders of the two parties, the Republican followers fall closer to the Democratic than to the Republican side of the continuum. Thus, in addition to being the preferred party of the more numerous classes, the Democrats also enjoy the advantage over their opponents of holding views that are more widely shared throughout the country.

Assuming the findings are valid, we were obviously wrong to expect that party differentiation among followers would depend heavily upon ideological considerations.[34] Evidently, party attachment is so much a function of other factors (*e.g.,* class and primary group memberships, religious affiliation, place of residence, mass media, etc.) that many voters can maintain their party loyalties comfortably even while holding views that contradict the beliefs of their own leaders.

Still, we are not entitled to conclude that issue outlook has no effect on the party affiliation of ordinary members. It is conceivable, for example, that the Republican party has come to be the minority party partly because the opinions of its spokesmen are uncongenial to a majority of the voters. We have no way of knowing from our data—collected at only a single point in time—how many "normally" Republican voters, if any, have defected to the Democrats or fled into independency because they disapprove of Republican beliefs. At the present stage of the analysis, we have no grounds for going beyond the proposition that political affiliation without conformity on issues is possible on a wide scale. In future analyses we shall attempt to learn more about the nature of the relationship between belief and party affiliation by stratifying voters according to the frequency with which they conform to the beliefs of their party leaders. We hope, in this way, to discover whether those who conform least are also less firm in their party loyalties.

THE HOMOGENEITY OF SUPPORT
FOR LEADERS AND FOLLOWERS

So far we have only considered conflict and agreement *between* groups. We should now turn to the question of consensus *within* groups. To what extent is each of our samples united on fundamental issues?

34See the discussion bearing on this conclusion in Campbell *et al., op. cit.,* Chs. 8 and 9. Also, Avery Leiserson, *Parties and Politics, An Institutional and Behavioral Approach* (New York: Alfred A. Knopf, Inc., 1958), pp. 162–66.

In order to assess homogeneity of opinion within party groups, standard deviation scores were computed on each issue for each of the four samples. The higher the standard deviation, of course, the greater the disagreement. The range of possible sigma scores is from 0 (signifying that every member of the sample has selected the same response) to .500 (signifying that all responses are equally divided between the "increase" and "decrease" alternatives). If we assume that the three alternative responses had been randomly (and therefore equally) selected, the standard deviations for the four samples would fall by chance alone around .410. Scores at or above this level may be taken to denote extreme dispersion among the members of a sample while in the neighborhood of .300 or below suggest that unanimity within the sample is fairly high. By these somewhat arbitrary criteria we can observe immediately . . . that consensus within groups is greater on most issues than we would expect by chance alone, but that it is extremely high in only a few instances. Although the Republican leaders appear on the average to be the most united and the Democratic leaders the least united of the four groups, the difference between their homogeneity scores (.340 vs. .310) is too small to be taken as conclusive. The grounds are somewhat better for rejecting the belief that leaders are more homogeneous in their outlooks than their followers, since the hypothesis holds only for one party and not for the other.

While generalizations about the relative unity of the four samples seem risky, we can speak more confidently about the rank order of agreement *within* samples. . . . We have ranked the issues according to the degree of consensus exhibited toward them by the members of each of the four party groups. There we see that the leaders of the Republican party are most united on the issues that stem from its connections with business—government regulation of business, taxes (especially on business), regulation of trade unions, and minimum wages. The Democratic leaders are most united on those issues which bear upon the support the party receives from the lower and middle income groups—taxes on small and middle incomes, anti-monopoly, slum clearance, social security, and minimum wages. The Republican leaders divide most severely on federal aid to education, slum clearance, U.N. support, segregation, and public control of atomic energy and natural resources; the Democratic leaders are most divided on farm prices, segregation, credit restrictions, immigration, and the natural resources issue. Among the followers the patterns of unity and division are very similar, as attested by the high correlation of .83 between the rank orders of homogeneity scores. Both Republican and Democratic followers exhibit great cohesion, for example, on taxes on small and middle incomes, social security, slum clearance, and minimum wages. Both divide rather sharply on segregation, farm price supports, defense spending, U.N. support, and taxes on large incomes.

The two sets of followers, in short, are alike not only in their opinions on issues but in the degree of unanimity they exhibit toward them.

Inspection of the homogeneity data furnishes additional evidence on the between-group comparisons made earlier. Whereas Democratic and Republican followers divide on issues in approximately the same way, the two sets of leaders differ from each other in this respect also (the correlation between their rank orders on homogeneity is only .28). Democratic leaders and followers tend to unite or divide on the same issues for the most part (r equals .77), but Republican leaders and followers are not parallel in this respect either (r equals .30). The pattern of homogeneity and dispersion among Republican followers is, in fact, much closer to that of the Democratic leaders (r equals .75).

In computing scores for homogeneity we were in part concerned to test the belief that political parties develop greatest internal solidarity on those questions which most separate them from their opponents. According to this hypothesis, external controversy has the effect of uniting the members further by confronting them with a common danger. Whether or not this hypothesis would be borne out in a study of small, sectarian parties we cannot say, but it receives no support from the present study of the American mass parties. Comparisons of the rank order data . . . show that there is no consistent connection between inter-party conflict and intra-party cohesion. The correlations between the rank orders of difference and the rank orders of homogeneity are in every case insignificant.[35]

SUMMARY AND CONCLUSIONS

The research described in this paper—an outgrowth of a nationwide inquiry into the nature and sources of political affiliation, activity, and belief—was principally designed to test a number of hypotheses about the relation of ideology to party membership. Responses from large samples of Democratic and Republican leaders and followers were compared on twenty-four key issues and on a number of attitude questions and scales. Statistical operations were carried out to assess conflict and consensus among party groups and to estimate the size and significance of differences. From the data yielded by this inquiry, the following inferences seem most warranted:

1. Although it has received wide currency, especially among Europeans, the belief that the two American parties are identical in principle and doctrine has little foundation in fact. Examination of the opinions

35For an interesting set of comparative data on the relation of internal party cohesion to issue outlook, see Morris Davis and Sidney Verba, "Party Affiliation and International Opinions in Britain and France, 1947–1956," *Public Opinion Quarterly*, Vol. 24 (Winter 1960–1961), 590–604.

of Democratic and Republican leaders shows them to be distinct communities of co-believers who diverge sharply on many important issues. Their disagreements, furthermore, conform to an image familiar to many observers and are generally consistent with differences turned up by studies of congressional roll calls. The unpopularity of many of the positions held by Republican leaders suggests also that the parties submit to the demands of their constituents less slavishly than is commonly supposed.

2. Republican and Democratic leaders stand furthest apart on the issues that grow out of their group identification and support—out of the managerial, proprietary, and high-status connections of the one, and the labor, minority, low-status, and intellectual connections of the other. The opinions of each party elite are linked less by chance than by membership in a common ideological domain. Democratic leaders typically display the stronger urge to elevate the lowborn, the uneducated, the deprived minorities, and the poor in general; they are also more disposed to employ the nation's collective power to advance humanitarian and social welfare goals (*e.g.*, social security, immigration, racial integration, a higher minimum wage, and public education). They are more critical of wealth and big business and more eager to bring them under regulation. Theirs is the greater faith in the wisdom of using legislation for redistributing the national product and for furnishing social services on a wide scale. Of the two groups of leaders, the Democrats are the more "progressively" oriented toward social reform and experimentation. The Republican leaders, while not uniformly differentiated from their opponents, subscribe in greater measure to the symbols and practices of individualism, *laissez-faire*, and national independence. They prefer to overcome humanity's misfortunes by relying upon personal effort, private incentives, frugality, hard work, responsibility, self-denial (for both men and government), and the strengthening rather than the diminution of the economic and status distinctions that are the "natural" rewards of the differences in human character and fortunes. Were it not for the hackneyed nature of the designation and the danger of forcing traits into a mold they fit only imperfectly, we might be tempted to describe the Republicans as the chief upholders of what Max Weber has called the "Protestant ethic."[36] Not that the Democrats are insensible to the "virtues" of the Protestant-capitalistic ethos, but they embrace them less firmly or uniformly. The differences between the two élites have probably been intensified by the rise of the New Deal and by the shift of former radicals into the Democratic party following the decline of socialist and other left-wing movements during and after the war.

---

[36]Max Weber, *Protestant Ethic and the Spirit of Capitalism* (London: Routledge & Kegan Paul, 1948), Ch. 5.

3. Whereas the leaders of the two parties diverge strongly, their followers differ only moderately in their attitudes toward issues. The hypothesis that party beliefs unite adherents and bring them into the party ranks may hold for the more active members of a mass party but not for its rank and file supporters. Republican followers, in fact, disagree far more with their own leaders than with the leaders of the Democratic party. Little support was found for the belief that deep cleavages exist among the electorate but are ignored by the leaders. One might, indeed, more accurately assert the contrary, to wit: that the natural cleavages between the leaders are largely ignored by the voters. However, we cannot presently conclude that ideology exerts no influence over the habits of party support, for the followers do differ significantly and in the predicted directions on some issues. Furthermore, we do not know how many followers may previously have been led by doctrinal considerations to shift their party allegiances.

4. Except for their desire to ingratiate themselves with as many voters as possible, the leaders of the two parties have more reason than their followers to hold sharply opposing views on the important political questions of the day. Compared with the great mass of supporters, they are articulate, informed, highly partisan, and involved; they comprise a smaller and more tightly knit group which is closer to the wellsprings of party opinion, more accessible for indoctrination, more easily rewarded or punished for conformity or deviation, and far more affected, politically and psychologically, by engagement in the party struggle for office. If the leaders of the two parties are not always candid about their disagreements, the reason may well be that they sense the great measure of consensus to be found among the electorate.

5. Finding that party leaders hold contrary beliefs does not prove that they *act* upon those beliefs or that the two parties are, in practice, governed by different outlooks. In a subsequent paper we shall consider these questions more directly by comparing platform and other official party pronouncements with the private opinions revealed in this study. Until further inquiries are conducted, however, it seems reasonable to assume that the views held privately by party leaders can never be entirely suppressed but are bound to crop out in hundreds of large and small ways—in campaign speeches, discussions at party meetings, private communications to friends and sympathizers, statements to the press by party officials and candidates, legislative debates, and public discussions on innumerable national, state, and local questions. If, in other words, the opinions of party leaders are as we have described them, there is every chance that they are expressed and acted upon to some extent. Whether this makes our parties "ideological" depends, of course, on how narrowly we define that term. Some may prefer to reserve that designation for parties that are more obviously preoccupied

with doctrine, more intent upon the achievement of a systematic political program, and more willing to enforce a common set of beliefs upon their members and spokesmen.

6. The parties are internally united on some issues, divided on others. In general, Republican leaders achieve greatest homogeneity on issues that grow out of their party's identification with business, Democratic leaders on issues that reflect their connection with liberal and lower-income groups. We find no support for the hypothesis that the parties achieve greatest internal consensus on the issues which principally divide them from their opponents.

In a sequel to this paper we shall offer data on the demographic correlates of issue support, which show that most of the differences presented here exist independently of factors like education, occupation, age, religion, and sectionalism. Controlling for these influences furnishes much additional information and many new insights but does not upset our present conclusions in any important respect. Thus, the parties must be considered not merely as spokesmen for other interest groups but as reference groups in their own right, helping to formulate, to sustain, and to speak for a recognizable point of view.

PART SIX

CONSENSUS, STABILITY, AND PROTEST

This section pursues one of the themes implicit in much of Part Five: How can a political system accommodate a diversity of beliefs without repression or chaos? In the past few years political dissatisfaction has been amplified to the point of widespread alienation and disorder. Growing out of disgust with the war in Vietnam and impatience with the continued privations of Negroes, the wave of protest has directed attention to the character, sources, and consequences of political stability and change in America. This interest also has led to research that attempts to place the new techniques of protest within the more general framework of American politics.

In the first selection Herbert McClosky explores the level of consensus in the United States, the extent to which voters and political leaders understand and accept such fundamental values as equality, majority rule, free speech, and due process. He finds that agreement with these and other lofty values shrinks drastically when voters are asked concrete questions about specific situations involving these principles. Leaders, on the other hand, are more devoted to democratic values and "rules of the game." In short, consensus on the democratic creed is lacking among the electorate as a whole; its presence among the "articulate classes" is far more pronounced. In a long and thoughtful analysis of these findings McClosky discusses their implications for the maintenance of democracy.

Acceptance of democratic values is only part of the explanation for the maintenance of political equilibrium in the United States, as Robert Dahl argues in the second selection. He attributes the level of stability to "three sets of factors: (1) The characteristic pattern of consensus. (2) The characteristic pattern of cleavage. (3) The structure of government and politics." (Much of the evidence on these points can be found in Chapters 19, 20, 22, 23, and 24 of this reader.) While there have been periods of intense conflict in our past, for the most part all three of the above factors tended to muffle political passions and facilitate compromise. Yet, as Dahl points out, there is a fine line between moderating conflict and frustrating the impassioned demands of minorities. The forces maintaining stability may also prevent timely governmental action to deal with the grievances of individuals who feel oppressed. Thus while we have largely solved the problem of national unity, this achievement has not been without its price. The most important cost is the scanty attention paid the needs of minority groups which lack adequate political resources and whose needs are outside the principal concerns of most voters. The most obvious group of this kind is, of course, Negroes.

There was a time just a few years ago when it was widely believed that the full enfranchisement of black voters would give them political power commensurate with their numbers and thus provide the means of ending their second-class status. The flaws in this assumption are explored by Donald R. Matthews and James W. Prothro, authors of a massive study of the development of Negro political participation in the contemporary South. Their analysis of the relationships between voting power and public policy is not limited to any region of the country, but applies with equal relevance to the political aspirations of minorities anywhere.

If the ability to vote does not provide any group with adequate means of pressing its claims on the government, then we are likely to see a threat to political stability, if not to due process and civil liberties. There is, however, one political resource other than the vote that is available to deprived groups: protest. Michael Lipsky defines protest as an objection to policies or conditions "characterized by showmanship or display of an unconventional nature," and designed to attract the sympathetic intervention of "third parties." In the final selection Lipsky discusses the leadership styles, organizational problems, tactics, targets, and constituents of protest as a political technique by groups too poor and unaccomplished to use any other means to get their way.

CHAPTER TWENTY-FOUR

CONSENSUS AND IDEOLOGY IN AMERICAN POLITICS

HERBERT McCLOSKY

The belief that consensus is a prerequisite of democracy has, since de Tocqueville, so often been taken for granted that it is refreshing to find the notion now being challenged. Prothro and Grigg,[1] for example, have questioned whether agreement on "fundamentals" actually exists among the electorate, and have furnished data which indicate that it may not. Dahl,[2] reviewing his study of community decision-makers, has inferred that political stability does not depend upon widespread belief in the superiority of democratic norms and procedures, but only upon their *acceptance*. From the findings turned up by Stouffer,[3] and by Prothro and Grigg, he further conjectures that agreement on democratic norms is greater among the politically active and aware—the "political stratum" as he calls them—than among the voters in general. V. O.

This is a revised version of a paper initially prepared for delivery at the Annual Meeting of the American Political Science Association, Washington D.C., September 1962. The research on which it is based has been processed and analyzed through the Survey Research Center, University of California, Berkeley. Major support for the research was made available by the Social Science Research Council; supplementary support was given by the Rockefeller Foundation and the Institute of Social Sciences, University of California. I am indebted to my research assistant, Beryl L. Crowe, for assistance in the preparation of the research materials. This article may be referred to as number A22 in the Survey Research Center's publication series.

[1]James W. Prothro and C. W. Grigg, "Fundamental Principles of Democracy: Bases of Agreement and Disagreement," *Journal of Politics*, Vol. 22 (Spring, 1960), pp. 276–94.

[2]Robert A. Dahl, *Who Governs?* (New Haven, 1961), ch. 28.

[3]Samuel A. Stouffer, *Communism, Conformity, and Civil Liberties* (New York, 1955).

Reprinted by permission from the AMERICAN POLITICAL SCIENCE REVIEW, *58 (June 1964), 361–79. Two methodological appendices have been omitted.*

Key,[4] going a step further, suggests that the viability of a democracy may depend less upon popular opinion than upon the activities and values of an "aristocratic" strain whose members are set off from the mass by their political influence, their attention to public affairs, and their active role as society's policy makers. "If so, any assessment of the vitality of a democratic system should rest on an examination of the outlook, the sense of purpose, and the beliefs of this sector of society."

Writers who hold consensus to be necessary to a free society have commonly failed to define it precisely or to specify what it must include. Even Tocqueville[5] does not go deeply enough into the matter to satisfy these needs. He tells us that a society can exist and, *a fortiori*, prosper only when "the minds of all the citizens [are] rallied and held together by certain predominant ideas; . . . when a great number of men consider a great number of things from the same aspect, when they hold the same opinions upon many subjects, and when the same occurrences suggest the same thoughts and impressions to their minds"—and he follows this pronouncement with a list of general principles he believes Americans hold in common. Elsewhere, he speaks of the "customs" of the American nation (its "habits, opinions, usages, and beliefs") as "the peculiar cause which renders that people able to support a democratic government." But nowhere does he set forth explicitly the nature of the agreement upon which a democratic society presumably depends.

Later commentators have not clarified matters much. Some, like A. Lawrence Lowell,[6] have avoided Tocqueville's emphasis upon shared ideas, customs, and opinions in favor of the less demanding view that popular government requires agreement mainly "in regard to the legitimate character of the ruling authority and its right to decide the questions that arise." Consensus, in this view, becomes merely a synonym for legitimacy. Others speak of consensus as a sense of solidarity or social cohesion arising from a common ethos or heritage, which unites men into a community.[7] Political scientists have most frequently employed the term

[4]V. O. Key, "Public Opinion and the Decay of Democracy," *Virginia Q. Rev.*, Vol. 37 (Autumn, 1961), pp. 481–94. See also David B. Truman, "The American System in Crisis," *Political Science Quarterly*, Vol. 74 (Dec., 1959), pp. 481–97. John Plamenatz, "Cultural Prerequisites to a Successfully Functioning Democracy: a Symposium," *American Political Science Review*, 50 (March, 1956), 123.

[5]Alexis deTocqueville, *Democracy in America* (ed. Phillips Bradley, New York, 1945), II, p. 8; I, pp. 392, 322. The difficulty of specifying the values which underly democracy, and on which consensus is presumed to be required, is illustrated in the exchange between Ernest S. Griffith, John Plamenatz, and J. Roland Pennock, cited above, pp. 101–37. The problem of certifying the "fundamentals" of democratic consensus is directly discussed by Pennock, pp. 132–3. See also Peter Bachrach, "Elite Consensus and Democracy," *Journal of Politics*, Vol. 24 (August, 1962), pp. 449–52.

[6]A. L. Lowell, *Public Opinion and Popular Government* (New York, 1926), p. 9.

[7]Cf., for example, Louis Wirth, *Community Life and Social Policy* (Chicago, 1956), pp. 201–3, 381–2. For a critique of "consensus theory" and the several definitions of consensus see Irving L. Horowitz, "Consensus, Conflict, and Cooperation: a Sociological Inventory," *Social Forces*, Vol. 41 (Dec., 1962), pp. 177–88.

to designate a state of agreement about the "fundamental values" or "rules of the game" considered essential for constitutional government. Rarely, however, have writers on consensus attempted to state what the fundamentals must include, how extensive the agreement must be, and *who* must agree. Is agreement required among all men or only among certain of them? Among the entire electorate or only those who actively participate in public affairs? Is the same type of consensus essential for all democracies at all times, or is a firmer and more sweeping consensus needed for periods of crisis than for periods of calm, for newer, developing democracies than for older stable ones?

While certain of these questions are beyond the scope of this paper (no one, in any event, has done the systematic historical and comparative research needed to answer them satisfactorily), something might be learned about the relation of ideological consensus to democracy by investigating the subject in at least one major democracy, the United States. In the present paper I wish to explore further some of the questions raised by the writers I have cited and to present research findings on several hypotheses relating to those questions.

I. HYPOTHESES AND DEFINITIONS

We expected the data to furnish support for the following hypotheses, among others:

> That the American electorate is often divided on "fundamental" democratic values and procedural "rules of the game" and that its understanding of politics and of political ideas is in any event too rudimentary at present to speak of ideological "consensus" among its members.

> That, as Prothro and Grigg report for their samples, the electorate exhibits greater support for general, abstract statements of democratic belief than for their specific applications.

> That the constituent ideas of American democratic ideology are principally held by the more "articulate" segments of the population, including the political influentials; and that people in these ranks will exhibit a more meaningful and far reaching consensus on democratic and constitutional values than will the general population.

> That consensus is far from perfect even among the articulate classes, and will be evidenced on political questions more than on economic ones, on procedural rights more than on public policies, and on freedom more than equality.

> That whatever increases the level of political articulateness—education, S.E.S., [socioeconomic status—Ed.] urban residence, intellectuality, political activity, etc.—strengthens consensus and support for American political ideology and institutions.

Whether a word like ideology can properly be employed in the American context depends, in part, on which of its many connotations one chooses to emphasize. Agreement on the meaning of the term is far from universal, but a tendency can be discerned among contemporary writers to regard ideologies as *systems* of belief that are elaborate, integrated, and coherent, that justify the exercise of power, explain and judge historical events, identify political right and wrong, set forth the interconnections (causal and moral) between politics and other spheres of activity, and furnish guides for action.[8] While liberal democracy does not fulfill perfectly the terms of this definition, it comes close enough, in my opinion, to be considered an ideology.[9] The elements of liberal democratic thought are not nearly so vague as they are sometimes made out to be, and their coalescence into a single body of belief is by no means fortuitous. American democratic "ideology" possesses an elaborately defined theory, a body of interrelated assumptions, axioms, and principles, and a set of ideals that serve as guides for action. Its tenets, postulates, sentiments, and values inspired the great revolutions of the seventeenth and eighteenth centuries, and have been repeatedly and explicitly set forth in fundamental documents, such as the Constitution, the Declaration of Independence, and the Federalist Papers. They have been restated with remarkable unanimity in the messages of Presidents, in political speeches, in the pronouncements of judges and constitutional commentators, and in the writings of political theorists, historians, and publicists. They are so familiar that we are likely to see them not as a coherent union of ideas and principles embodying a well-defined political tendency, but as a miscellany of slogans and noble sentiments to be trotted out on ceremonial occasions.

Although scholars or Supreme Court justices might argue over fine points of interpretation, they would uniformly recognize as elements of American democratic ideology such concepts as consent, accountability, limited or constitutional government, representation, majority rule, minority rights, the principle of political opposition, freedom of thought, speech, press, and assembly, equality of opportunity, religious toleration, equality before the law, the rights of juridical defense, and individual self-determination over a broad range of personal affairs. How widely such elements of American liberal democracy are approved, by whom

---

[8] *Cf.* Daniel Bell, *The End of Ideology* (Glencoe, 1960), pp. 369–75; Edward Shils, "Ideology and Civility: on the Politics of the Intellectual," *Sewanee Review*, Vol. 66 (Summer, 1958), pp. 450–1; Louis Wirth, *op. cit.*, pp. 202–3.

[9] A persuasive case for considering liberal democracy as an ideology is made by Bernard Williams, "Democracy and Ideology," *Political Science Quarterly*, Vol. 32 (October–December, 1961), pp. 374–84. The nature of ideology in America and some of the other questions addressed in the present paper are discussed by Robert G. McCloskey, "The American Ideology," in Marian D. Irish (ed.), *Continuing Crisis in American Politics* (Englewood Cliffs, N.J., 1963), pp. 10–25.

and with what measure of understanding, is another question—indeed, it is the central question to be addressed in this paper. But that they form an integrated body of ideas which has become part of the American inheritance seems scarcely open to debate.[10]

The term consensus will be employed in this paper to designate a state of agreement concerning the aforementioned values. It has principally to do with shared beliefs and not with feelings of solidarity, the willingness to live together, to obey the laws, or to accept the existing government as legitimate. Nor does it refer to an abstract or universal state of mind, but to a measurable state of concurrence around values that can be specified. Consensus exists in degree and can be expressed in quantitative form. No one, of course, can say how close one must come to unanimity before consensus is achieved, for the cutting point, as with any continuous variable, is arbitrary. Still, the term in ordinary usage has been reserved for fairly substantial measures of correspondence, and we shall take as a minimal requirement for consensus a level of agreement reaching 75 per cent. This figure, while also arbitrary, recommends itself by being realistically modest (falling as it does midway between a bare majority and unanimity), and by having been designated in this country and elsewhere as the extraordinary majority required for certain constitutional purposes.

Since I shall in subsequent pages frequently (and interchangeably) employ such terms as the "articulate minority," the "political class," the "political elite," the "political influentials," and the "political stratum," I should also clarify what they are intended to signify. I mean them to refer to those people who occupy themselves with public affairs to an unusual degree, such as government officials, elected office holders, active party members, publicists, officers of voluntary associations, and opinion leaders. The terms do not apply to any definable social class in the usual sense, nor to a particular status group or profession. Although the people they designate can be distinguished from other citizens by their activity and concerns, they are in no sense a community, they do not act as a body, and they do not necessarily possess identical or even harmonious interests. "Articulates" or "influentials" can be found scattered throughout the society, at all income levels, in all classes, occupations, ethnic groups, and communities, although some segments of the population will doubtless yield a higher proportion of them than others.

---

[10]See Gunnar Myrdal, *An American Dilemma: The Negro Problem and American Democracy* (New York, 1944), ch. 1. For a comprehensive review of the American value system and evidence concerning its stability over time, see Clyde Kluckhohn, "Have There Been Discernible Shifts in American Values during the Past Generation?" in E. E. Morison (ed.), *The American Style: Essays in Value and Performance* (New York, 1958), pp. 145–217. Kluckhohn concludes (p. 152) that despite some changes, the American value system has been "remarkably stable" since the 18th century and remains "highly influential in the life of the United States."

I scarcely need to add that the line between the "articulates" and the rest of the population cannot always be sharply drawn, for the qualities that distinguish them vary in form and degree and no single criterion of classification will satisfy every contingency.

The data for the present inquiry have been taken from a national study of political actives and supporters carried out in 1957–58. I have in a previous paper described the procedures of that study in some detail,[11] and will not trouble to repeat that description here. Perhaps it will suffice for present purposes merely to note the following: national surveys were carried out on two separate samples, the first a sample of over 3,000 political "actives" or "leaders" drawn from the delegates and alternates who had attended the Democratic and Republican conventions of 1956; the second a representative national sample of approximately 1,500 adults in the general population drawn by the American Institute of Public Opinion (Gallup Poll). Gallup interviewers also delivered and introduced the questionnaire to all respondents, discussed its contents with them, and furnished both oral and written instructions for its self-administration and completion. (For sample characteristics, see Appendix B [deleted here—Ed.].)

The party actives may be considered an especially pure sample of the "political stratum," for every person in the sample has marked himself off from the average citizen by his greater political involvement. Although the general population sample may be regarded as a sample of "inarticulates," to be compared with the sample of leaders, there are within it, of course, many persons who by virtue of education, profession, organizational activities, etc. can be classified as "articulates." We shall for certain purposes consider them in this light in order to provide further tests for our hypotheses.

Both samples received the same questionnaire—a lengthy instrument containing questions on personal background, political experience, values, attitudes, opinions, political and economic orientation, party outlooks, and personality characteristics. Many of the questions were direct inquiries in the standard form, but most were single sentence "items" with which the respondent was compelled to express his agreement or disagreement. While each of these items can stand alone and be regarded in its own right as an indicator of a person's opinions or attitudes, each of them is simultaneously an integral element of one of the 47 "scales" that was expressly fashioned to afford a more refined and reliable assessment of the attitude and personality predispositions of every respondent. Each of the scales (averaging approximately nine items) has been independently validated either by empirical validation procedures employing appropriate criterion groups, or by a modified Gutt-

---

[11] Herbert McClosky, Paul J. Hoffmann, and Rosemary O'Hara, "Issue Conflict and Consensus Among Party Leaders and Followers," *American Political Science Review*, Vol. 54 (June, 1960), pp. 406–27 [chap. 23 in this book—Ed].

man reproducibility procedure (supplemented, in some instances, by a "face validity" procedure utilizing item ratings by experts).

Data on the *scale* scores are presented in Table IV and are to be distinguished from the *"percentage agree"* scores for *individual items* presented in the remaining tables.

II. FINDINGS

"Rules of the Game" and Democratic Values

Although the so-called "rules of the game" are often separated from other democratic values, the distinction is to some extent arbitrary. One might, for example, reasonably regard as "rules of the game" many of the norms governing free speech, press, social and political equality, political toleration, and the enforcement of justice. For convenience, nevertheless, we shall treat separately those responses that stand out from the general body of democratic attitudes by their particular emphasis upon fair play, respect for legal procedures, and consideration for the rights of others. A sample of items expressing these values is presented in Table I.

Table I   Political Influentials vs. The Electorate: Response to Items Expressing "Rules of the Game"*

Items	Political Influentials (N = 3020)	General Electorate (N = 1484)
	% Agree	
There are times when it almost seems better for the people to take the law into their own hands rather than wait for the machinery of government to act.	13.3	26.9
The majority has the right to abolish minorities if it wants to.	6.8	28.4
We might as well make up our minds that in order to make the world better a lot of innocent people will have to suffer.	27.2	41.6
If congressional committees stuck strictly to the rules and gave every witness his rights, they would never succeed in exposing the many dangerous subversives they have turned up.	24.7	47.4
I don't mind a politician's methods if he manages to get the right things done.	25.6	42.4
People ought to be allowed to vote even if they can't do so intelligently.	65.6	47.6

*Since respondents were forced to make a choice on each item, the number of omitted or "don't know" responses was, on the average, fewer than one percent, and thus has little influence on the direction or magnitude of the results reported in this and subsequent tables. [Some items have been deleted from this table—Ed.]

The responses to these items show plainly that while a majority of the electorate support the "rules of the game," approval of such values is significantly greater and more uniform among the influentials. The latter have achieved consensus (as we have defined it) on eight of the twelve items and near consensus on three of the remaining four items. The electorate, by contrast, does not meet the criterion for consensus on a single item.

Although the *scales* (as distinguished from individual *items*) cannot appropriately be used to measure *consensus*, comparison of the scores on those scales which most nearly embody the "rules of the game" furnishes additional evidence that the political class responds to such norms more favorably than does the electorate. The proportion scoring high[12] on a scale of "faith in direct action" (a scale measuring the inclination to take the law into one's own hands) is 26.1 per cent for the active political minority and 42.5 per cent for the general population. On a scale assessing the willingness to flout the rules of political integrity, the proportions scoring high are 12.2 per cent and 30.6 per cent respectively. On "totalitarianism," a scale measuring the readiness to subordinate the rights of others to the pursuit of some collective political purpose, only 9.7 per cent of the political actives score high compared with 33.8 per cent of the general population.

These and other results which could be cited support the claim advanced by earlier investigators like Prothro and Grigg, and Hyman and Sheatsley,[13] that a large proportion of the electorate has failed to grasp certain of the underlying ideas and principles on which the American political system rests. Endorsement of these ideas is not unanimous among the political elite either, but is in every instance greater than that exhibited by the masses.

The picture changes somewhat when we turn from "rules of the game" to items which in a broad, general way express belief in freedom of speech and opinion. As can be seen from Table II, support for these values is remarkably high for both samples. Both groups, in fact, respond so overwhelmingly to abstract statements about freedom that one is tempted to conclude that for these values, at least, a far-reaching consensus has been achieved.[14] These results become even more striking when

[12]"High" refers to a score made by the upper third of the popular distribution on the scale in question. For example, in the case of the "political indulgence" scale approximately one-third (actually 30.6%) received scores of five or above. Hence, anyone making a score of five or above on this scale is considered to have scored high on "political indulgence." "Low" refers to scores made by the lower third of the distribution.

[13]Prothro and Grigg, *loc. cit.*; Herbert Hyman and Paul B. Sheatsley, "The Current Status of American Public Opinion," in Daniel Katz *et al.* (eds.), *Public Opinion and Propaganda* (New York, 1954) pp. 33–48.

[14]*Cf.* Robert Lane's report on his "Eastport" sample, in *Political Ideology* (New York, 1962), pp. 461–2.

Table II   Political Influentials vs. The Electorate: Responses to Items Expressing Support for General Statements of Free Speech and Opinion[a]

Items	Political Influentials (N = 3020)	Electorate (N = 1484) General
	% Agree	
People who hate our way of life should still have a chance to talk and be heard.	86.9	81.8
No matter what a person's political beliefs are, he is entitled to the same legal rights and protections as anyone else.	96.4	94.3
I would not trust any person or group to decide what opinions can be freely expressed and what must be silenced.	79.1	64.6
Freedom of conscience should mean freedom to be an atheist as well as freedom to worship in the church of one's choice.	87.8	77.0

[a][Some items have been deleted from this table—Ed.]

we consider that the items in the table are not mere clichés but statements which in some instances closely paraphrase the arguments developed in Mill's essay, *On Liberty*. We cannot, therefore, dismiss them as mere responses to familiar, abstract sentiments which commit the respondent to nothing in particular.

Still, as can readily be discerned from the items in Table III, previous investigators have been partially correct, at least, in observing that the principles of freedom and democracy are less widely and enthusiastically favored when they are confronted in their specific, or applied, forms.[15] As Dahl remarks, it is a "common tendency of mankind . . . to qualify universals in application while leaving them intact in rhetoric."[16] This observation, of course, also holds for the political articulates, but to a lesser degree. Not only do they exhibit stronger support for democratic values than does the electorate, but they are also more consistent in applying the general principle to the specific instance.[17] The average citizen has greater difficulty appreciating the importance of certain procedural or juridical rights, especially when he believes the country's internal security is at stake.

Findings which underscore and amplify these conclusions are yielded by a comparison of the scale scores. The data presented in Table IV

[15]See Hyman and Sheatsley, *op. cit.*, pp. 40–2; Prothro and Grigg, *op. cit.*

[16]Robert A. Dahl. *loc. cit.* For data on the failure of some people to perceive the relevance of democratic principles for concrete situations see G. D. Wiebe, "The Army-McCarthy Hearings and the Public Conscience," *Public Opinion Quarterly*, Vol. 22 (Winter, 1958–59), pp. 490–502.

[17]See also Stouffer, *op. cit.*, ch. 2.

Table III   Political Influentials vs. The Electorate: Response to Items Expressing Support for Specific Applications of Free Speech and Procedural Rights[a]

Items	Political Influentials (N = 3020)	General Electorate (N = 1484)
	% Agree	
Freedom does not give anyone the right to teach foreign ideas in our schools.	45.5	56.7
A man oughtn't to be allowed to speak if he doesn't know what he's talking about.	17.3	36.7
A book that contains wrong political views cannot be a good book and does not deserve to be published.	17.9	50.3
If a person is convicted of a crime by illegal evidence, he should be set free and the evidence thrown out of court.	79.6	66.1
In dealing with dangerous enemies like the Communists, we can't affort to depend on the courts, the laws and their slow and unreliable methods.	7.4	25.5

[a][Some items have been deleted from this table—Ed.]

confirm that the influentials not only register higher scores on all the pro-democratic scales (faith in freedom, faith in democracy, procedural rights, tolerance), but are more likely to reject antidemocratic sentiments as well. Although they are themselves an elite of a sort, they display greater faith in the capacity of the mass of men to govern themselves, they believe more firmly in political equality, and they more often disdain the "extreme" beliefs embodied in the Right Wing, Left Wing, totalitarian, elitist, and authoritarian scales. Their repudiation of antidemocratic attitudes is by no means unanimous either, but their responses are more uniformly democratic than are those expressed by the electorate.

Equalitarian Values

If Americans concur most strongly about liberty in the abstract, they disagree most strongly about equality. Examples of equalitarian values are presented in Table V. Both the political stratum and the public divide sharply on these values, a finding which holds for political, as well as for social and economic equality. Both are torn not only on the empirical question of whether men are *in fact* equal but also on the normative issue of whether they should be *regarded* as equal. Neither comes close to achieving consensus on such questions as the ability of the people to rule themselves, to know their best interests in the long run, to understand the issues, or to pick their own leaders wisely. Support for these equalitarian features of "popular" democracy, however, is greater among the elite than among the masses.

Table IV   Political Influentials vs. The Electorate: Percentages Scoring High and Low on Democratic and Anti-Democratic Attitude Scales*

Scale	Political Influentials (N = 3020)	General Electorate (N = 1484)	Scale	Political Influentials (N = 3020)	General Electorate (N = 1484)
	(%s down)			(%s down)	
Faith in Democracy			Elitism		
% High*	40.1	18.5	% High	22.8	38.7
% Low	14.4	29.7	% Low	41.0	22.4
Procedural Rights			Totalitarianism		
% High	58.1	24.1	% High	9.7	33.8
% Low	12.3	31.3	% Low	60.1	28.4
Tolerance			Right Wing		
% High	61.3	43.1	% High	17.5	33.1
% Low	16.4	33.2	% Low	45.3	28.9
Faith in Freedom			Left Wing		
% High	63.0	48.4	% High	6.7	27.8
% Low	17.1	28.4	% Low	68.7	39.3
Ethnocentrism			California F-Scale		
% High	27.5	36.5	% High	14.7	33.5
% Low	46.9	36.3	% Low	48.0	23.5

*For explanation of % High and Low see footnote 12. The middle group has been omitted from this table. Differences between the influentials and the electorate on all the scales in this table are, by Kolmogorov-Smirnov and chi-square tests, statistically significant at or beyond the .01 percent level of significance.

The reverse is true for the values of economic equality. Among the political stratum, indeed, the weight of opinion is against equality—a result strongly though not exclusively influenced by the pronounced economic conservatism of the Republican leaders in the sample. Support for economic equality is only slightly greater among the electorate. The pattern, furthermore, is extremely spotty, with some policies strongly favored and others as strongly rejected. Thus approval is widespread for public policies (such as social security) that are designed to overcome gross inequalities, but is equally strong for certain features of economic life that promote inequality, such as private enterprise, economic competition, and unlimited pursuit of profit.[18] On social and ethnic equality, both samples are deeply split.

In short, both the public and its leaders are uncertain and ambiva-

---

[18]These inferences are drawn not only from the few items presented in Table V, but from data previously reported by H. McClosky, P. J. Hoffmann, and R. O'Hara, op. cit., p. 413; and from the responses to dozens of items in the present study that express attitudes and opinions toward the private enterprise system, taxes, private property, profits, socialism, etc. On the whole, little enthusiasm is registered among either the elite or the masses for a drastic revision of the economy or a major redistribution of the wealth.

Table V   Political Influentials vs. The Electorate: Responses to Items Expressing Belief in Equality

Items	Political Influentials (N = 3020)	General Electorate (N = 1484)
	% Agree	
Political Equality		
The main trouble with democracy is that most people don't really know what's best for them.	40.8	58.0
Few people really know what is in their own best interest in the long run.	42.6	61.1
"Issues" and "arguments" are beyond the understanding of most voters.	37.5	62.3
Most people don't have enough sense to pick their own leaders wisely.	28.0	47.8
It will always be necessary to have a few strong, able people actually running everything.	42.5	56.2
Social and Ethnic Equality		
We have to teach children that all men are created equal but almost everyone knows that some are better than others.	54.7	58.3
Just as is true of fine race horses, some breeds of people are just naturally better than others.	46.0	46.3
Regardless of what some people say, there are certain races in the world that just won't mix with Americans.	37.2	50.4
When it comes to the things that count most, all races are certainly not equal.	45.3	49.0
The trouble with letting certain minority groups into a nice neighborhood is that they gradually give it their own atmosphere.	49.8	57.7
Economic Equality		
Labor does not get its fair share of what it produces.	20.8	44.8
Every person should have a good house, even if the government has to build it for him.	14.9	28.2
I think the government should give a person work if he can't find another job.	23.5	47.3
The government ought to make sure that everyone has a good standard of living.	34.4	55.9
There will always be poverty, so people might as well get used to the idea.	40.4	59.4

lent about equality. The reason, I suspect, lies partly in the fact that the egalitarian aspects of democratic theory have been less adequately thought through than other aspects, and partly in the complications connected with the concept itself. One such complication arises from the historical association of democracy with capitalism, a commingling of egalitarian and inegalitarian elements that has never been (and perhaps never can be) perfectly reconciled. Another complication lies in the diffuse and variegated nature of the concept, a result of its application to at least four separate domains: political (*e.g.*, universal suffrage), legal (*e.g.*, equality before the law), economic (*e.g.*, equal distribution of property or opportunity), and moral (*e.g.*, every man's right to be treated as an end and not as a means). Accompanying these are the confusions which result from the common failure to distinguish equality as a *fact* from equality as a *norm.* ("All men are created equal," for example, is taken by some as an empirical statement, by others as a normative one.) Still other complications arise from the differential rewards and opportunities inevitable in any complex society, from the differences in the initial endowment individuals bring into the world, and from the symbolism and fears that so often attend the division of men into ethnic compartments. All these confound the effort to develop a satisfactory theory of democratic equality, and further serve to frustrate the realization of consensus around egalitarian values.

Faith in the Political System

Another perspective on the state of ideology and consensus in America may be obtained by observing how people respond to the political system. How do Americans feel about the political and social institutions by which they are ruled? Do they perceive the system as one they can reach and influence? Are they satisfied that it will govern justly and for the common good?

Sample items relating to these questions are contained in Tables VI and VII. An assessment of the responses, however, is confounded by an ambivalence in our tradition. Few will question that Americans are patriotic and loyal, that they accept the political system as legitimate, and that they are inclined to shy away from radical or extreme movements which aim to alter or to overthrow the constitutional foundations of the system. Yet Americans are also presumed to have a longstanding suspicion of government—a state of mind which some historians trace back

Table VI   Political Influentials vs. The Electorate: Responses to Items Expressing Cynicism Toward Government and Politics[a]

Items	Political Influentials (N = 3020)	General Electorate (N = 1484)
	% Agree	
Most politicians are looking out for themselves above all else.	36.3	54.3
Both major parties in this country are controlled by the wealthy and are run for their benefit.	7.9	32.1
Many politicians are bought off by some private interest.	43.0	65.3
Most politicians can be trusted to do what they think is best for the country.	77.1	58.9
Most politicians don't seem to me to really mean what they say.	24.7	55.1
Most political parties care only about winning elections and nothing more.	28.3	46.2
All politics is controlled by political bosses.	15.6	45.9

[a][Some items have been deleted from this table—Ed.]

**Table VII   Political Influentials vs. The Electorate: Responses to Items
Expressing a Sense of Political Futility[a]**

Items	Political Influentials (N = 3020)	General Electorate (N = 1484)
	% Agree	
It's no use worrying my head about public affairs; I can't do anything about them anyhow.	2.3	20.5
I feel that my political leaders hardly care what people like myself think or want.	10.9	39.0
Nothing I ever do seems to have any effect upon what happens in politics.	8.4	61.5
It seems to me that whoever you vote for, things go on pretty much the same.	21.1	51.3

[a][Some items have been deleted from this table—Ed.]

to the depredations of George III and to the habits of self-reliance forced upon our ancestors by frontier life.[19]

It is impossible in the present context to determine the extent to which the scores contained in these tables signify genuine frustration and political disillusionment and the extent to which they represent familiar and largely ritualistic responses. It is plain, however, that Americans are, verbally at least, both confused and divided in their reactions to the political system. Many feel themselves hopelessly ineffectual politically. Approximately half perceive government and politicians as remote, inaccessible, and largely unresponsive to the electorate's needs or opinions.[20] About the same proportion regard politics as squalid and seamy, as an activity in which the participants habitually practice deception, expediency, and self-aggrandizement. Yet by a curious inconsistency which so frequently frustrates the investigator searching the data for regularities, 89.6 per cent express confidence that the government will do what is right. However strongly they mistrust the men and the procedures through which public policies are fashioned, most voters seem not to be greatly dissatisfied with the outcome. They may be cynical about the operation of the political system, but they do not question its legitimacy.[21]

[19]Evidence is accumulating that the distrust of politics, often thought to be peculiar to the United States, is also found in many other countries. In fact, Gabriel Almond and Sidney Verba report in their cross-cultural study of citizenship that political interest is higher in the United States than it is in the four other countries they studied (United Kingdom, West Germany, Italy, and Mexico); and that Americans, if anything, are less negative toward politics than are the citizens of the other countries. See *The Civic Culture* (1963), chs. III–IV.

[20]See also the Michigan data on voters' sense of "political efficacy" in Angus Campbell, Gerald Gurin, and Warren E. Miller, *The Voter Decides* (Evanston, 1954), pp. 187–94.

[21]For other data on ambivalent attitudes toward government, see Hyman and Sheatsley, *op. cit.*

Although the influentials do not unanimously endorse American political practices either, they are substantially less suspicious and cynical than is the electorate. Indeed, they have achieved consensus or come close to achieving it on most of the items in the two tables. These results are further borne out by the *scale* scores: only 10.1 per cent of the articulates score "high" on the political cynicism scale, as contrasted with 31.3 per cent of the general population; on political suspiciousness the scores are 9.0 per cent high versus 26.7 per cent; on pessimism they are 12.6 per cent versus 26.7 per cent; and on sense of political futility the influentials score (understandably enough) only 3.1 per cent high compared with 30.2 per cent high for the electorate. The active minority also exhibits a stronger sense of social responsibility than the people do (their respective percentage high scores are 40.7 per cent versus 25.8 per cent) and, as previously noted, they are less tolerant of infractions against ethical political procedures.

Should we not, however, have expected these results as a matter of course, considering that the influentials were selected for study precisely because of their political experience and involvement? Possibly, except that similar (though less pronounced) differences emerge when we distinguish articulates from inarticulates by criteria other than actual political activity. Voters, for example, who have been to college, attained high status occupations or professions, or developed strong inintellectual interests are, by a significant margin, also likely to possess more affirmative attitudes toward government, politics, and politicians.[22] They display a greater sense of social and political responsibility, are more optimistic, and are less indulgent of shoddy political methods. The political actives who are highly educated exhibit these attitudes even more strongly. Familiarity, it seems, far from breeding contempt, greatly increases respect, hope and support for the nation's political institutions and practices. Inferential support for this generalization is available from the findings turned up by Almond and Verba in all five countries they investigated in their comparative study of citizenship.[23]

Coherence and Consistency of Attitudes
So far we have explored the question of ideology and consensus mainly from the point of view of agreement on particular values. This, however, is a minimum criterion. Before one can say that a class or group or nation has achieved consensus around an ideology, one should be satisfied

[22]Similar findings are reported by Robert E. Agger, Marshall N. Goldstein and Stanley A. Pearl, "Political Cynicism: Measurement and Meaning," *Journal of Politics*, Vol. 23 (1961), 477–506.

[23]Almond and Verba, *op. cit.*, ch. IV. One can, of course, imagine circumstances, such as political disorganization or revolutionary crises, in which the generalization would not hold—in which, indeed, the political elite might lead the struggle *against* the existing governing institutions. I am speaking, in the present context, of politics under "normal" conditions in established democracies.

that they understand its values in a coherent and correct way. It is a poor consensus in which generalities and slogans are merely echoed with little appreciation of their significance. It seemed appropriate, therefore, to compare the influentials and voters concerning their information and understanding, the relation of their opinions to their party preferences, and the consistency of their views on public affairs.

To begin with, the influentials are more likely than the electorate to have opinions on public questions. For example, 28 per cent of the public are unable (though a few may only be *unwilling*) to classify themselves as liberal, middle of the road, or conservative; while only 1.1 per cent of the articulates fail to make this classification. Forty-eight percent of the voters, compared to 15 per cent of the actives, do not know in which direction they would turn if the parties were reorganized to reflect ideological differences more clearly. Forty-five per cent of the electorate but only 10.2 per cent of the influentials cannot name any issue that divides the parties. By ratios of approximately three or four to one the electorate is less likely to know which level of government they are mainly interested in, whether they prefer their party to control Congress or the presidency, whether they believe in party discipline and of what type, whether control of the parties should rest at the national or local levels, and so on.

As these and other of our findings suggest, active political involvement heightens one's sense of intellectual order and commitment. This inference is further supported by the data on partisanship. One example may suffice to illustrate the point: when the articulates and the electorate are ranged on a scale assessing their orientation toward 14 current liberal-conservative issues, the political actives tend to bunch up at the extreme ends of the distribution (the Democratic actives at the "liberal" end, the Republican actives at the "conservative" end), while the rank and file supporters of both parties fall more frequently into the middle or conflicted category. The political influentials, in short, display issue orientations that are more partisan and more consistent with their party preferences.

Essentially the same effect is achieved among the general population by increases in education, economic status, or other factors that raise the level of articulateness. College-educated Democrats and Republicans, for example, disagree more sharply on issues than grade school Democrats and Republicans do. Partisan differences are greater between the informed than between the uninformed, between the upper-class supporters of the two parties than between the lower-class supporters, between the "intellectuals" in both parties than between those who rank low on "intellectuality."

Increases in political knowledge or involvement, hence, cause men not so much to waver as to choose sides and to identify more unswervingly with one political tendency or its opposite. Inarticulateness and distance from the sources of political decision increase intellectual uncertainty and evoke political responses that are random rather than systematic. We are thus led by the findings to a pair of conclusions that may at first appear contradictory but that in reality are not: the political class is more united than the electorate on fundamental political values but divides more sharply by party affiliation on the issues which separate the two parties.[24] Both facts—the greater consensus in the one instance and the sharper cleavage in the other—testify to its superior ideological sophistication.

Not only are the articulates more partisan, but they are also more consistent in their views. Their responses to a wide range of political stimuli are to a greater extent intellectually patterned and informed. They are, for example, better able to name reference groups that correspond with their party affiliation and doctrinal orientation: approximately twice as many active Democrats as ordinary Democratic voters name liberal, Democratically oriented organizations as groups they would seek advice from (*e.g.*, trade unions, Farmers Union, etc.); and by equally large or larger ratios they *reject* as sources of advice such conservative or Republican oriented organizations as the NAM, the Farm Bureau, and the Chamber of Commerce. With some variations, similar findings emerge when Republican leaders are compared with Republican voters. If we also take into account the liberal or conservative issue-orientation of the respondents, the differential ability of party leaders and followers to recognize reference groups becomes even more pronounced. Clearly, the political stratum has a better idea than the public has of who its ideological friends and enemies are. The capacity to recognize sympathetic or hostile reference groups is not highly developed among the public at large.

Compared with the influentials, ordinary voters also show up poorly in their ability to classify themselves politically. For example, among Democratic actives who score as "liberals" in their views on issues, 82.2 per cent correctly describe themselves as "liberals," while 16.7 per cent call themselves "middle of the roaders" and only 1.1 per cent misclassify themselves as "conservatives." Among Democratic *voters* who actually hold liberal views, only 37.0 per cent are able to label themselves correctly. The disparity is less striking between Republican leaders and followers but bears out no less conclusively that most voters lack the sophistication to recognize and label accurately the tendency of their own political views. Even their choice of party is frequently discrepant with their actual ideological views: as we reported in a previous paper,[25] not

---

[24]See also V. O. Key, *Public Opinion and American Democracy* (New York, 1961), pp. 51–52.

[25]McClosky, Hoffmann, and O'Hara, *op. cit.* [chap. 23 in this book—Ed.].

only do Democratic and Republican voters hold fairly similar opinions on issues, but the latter's opinions are closer to the opinions of Democratic leaders than to those of their own leaders.

Data we have gathered on patterns of support for individual political leaders yield similar conclusions: the articulates are far better able than the electorate to select leaders whose political philosophy they share. Often, in fact, voters simultaneously approve of two or more leaders who represent widely different outlooks—for example, Joseph McCarthy and Dwight D. Eisenhower. In a similar vein, a surprisingly large number of voters simultaneously score high on a Right Wing scale and a liberal issues scale, or hold other "discrepant" outlooks. Such inconsistencies are not unknown among the political actives either, but they are much less frequent. Not only does the public have less information than the political class but it does not succeed as well in sorting out and relating the information it does possess.[26]

Most of the relationships reported in the foregoing have been tested with education, occupation, and sometimes with other demographic variables controlled, but the introduction of these factors does not change the direction of the findings, although it sometimes affects the magnitude of the scores.

Comparisons of scores for the two samples have also been made with "acquiescent" response-set controlled. Acquiescence affects the results, but does not eliminate the differences reported or alter the direction or significance of the findings. (See Appendix A [deleted here—Ed.].)

III. SUMMARY AND DISCUSSION

Several observations can be offered by way of summarizing and commenting upon the data just reported:

1. American politics is widely thought to be innocent of ideology, but this opinion more appropriately describes the electorate than the active political minority. If American ideology is defined as that cluster of axioms, values and beliefs which have given form and substance to American democracy and the Constitution, the political influentials manifest by comparison with ordinary voters a more developed sense of ideology and a firmer grasp of its essentials. This is evidenced in their stronger approval of democratic ideas, their greater tolerance and regard for proper procedures and citizen rights, their superior understanding and acceptance of the "rules of the game," and their more affirmative attitudes toward the political system in general. The electorate displays a substantial measure of unity chiefly in its support of freedom in the

---

[26]For other findings on the state of ideological development among the electorate, see Angus Campbell, Philip E. Converse, Warren E. Miller and Donald E. Stokes, *The American Voter* (New York, 1960), chs. 8–10.

abstract; on most other features of democratic belief and practice it is sharply divided.

The political views of the influentials are relatively ordered and coherent. As liberals and conservatives, Democrats and Republicans, they take stands on issues, choose reference groups, and express preferences for leaders that are far more consistent than the attitudes and preferences exhibited by the electorate. The latter's opinions do not entirely lack order but are insufficiently integrated to meet the requirements of an ideology.[27] In contrast to the political elite, which tends to be united on basic values but divided on issues by party affiliation (both of which testify to a measure of ideological sophistication), the voters divide on many basic political values and adopt stands on issues with little reference to their party affiliation.

The evidence suggests that it is the articulate classes rather than the public who serve as the major repositories of the public conscience and as the carriers of the Creed. Responsibility for keeping the system going, hence, falls most heavily upon them.[28]

2. Why should consensus and support for democratic ideology be stronger among the political stratum than among the electorate? The answer plainly has to do with the differences in their political activity, involvement and articulateness.

Some observers complain that Americans have little interest in political ideas because they are exclusively concerned with their own personal affairs. Evidence is becoming available, however, that political apathy and ignorance are also widespread among the populations of other countries and may well be endemic in all societies larger than a city-state. It is difficult to imagine any circumstance, short of war or revolutionary crisis, in which the mass of men will evince more interest in the community's affairs than in their own concerns. This is not because they are selfish, thoughtless, or morally deficient, but because the stimuli they receive from public affairs are relatively remote and intangible. One can scarcely expect ordinary men to respond to them as intensively as they respond to the more palpable stimuli in their own everyday lives, which impinge upon them directly and in ways they can understand and do something about. The aphorism which holds man to be a political animal may be supportable on normative grounds but is scarcely defensible as a description of reality. Political apathy seems

---

[27]For a similar conclusion on this point, see V. O. Key, *Public Opinion and American Democracy* (New York, 1961), pp. 41, 49. The second chapter of this volume contains an excellent discussion of opinion consensus among the electorate, and touches on a number of the points dealt with in this paper. Evidence on the infrequency of "ideological" thinking among the voters is presented in Campbell, Converse, Miller, and Stokes, *op. cit.*, p. 249. By the criteria used the authors were able to classify only 3.5% of the voters as "ideologues" and 12% as "near-ideologues."

[28]V. O. Key, "Public Opinion and the Decay of Democracy," *loc cit.*

for most men the more "natural" state. Although political matters are in a sense "everyone's concern," it is just as unreasonable to hope that all men will sustain a lively interest in politics as it would be to expect everyone to become addicted to chamber music, electronics, poetry, or baseball. Since many voters lack education, opportunity, or even tangible and compelling reasons for busying themselves with political ideas, they respond to political stimuli (if they respond at all) without much reflection or consistency. Their life-styles, furthermore, tend to perpetuate this state of affairs, for they are likely to associate with people like themselves whose political opinions are no more informed or consistent than their own. As inarticulates, they are also inclined to avoid the very activities by which they might overcome their indifference and develop a more coherent point of view.

Many voters, in addition, feel remote from the centers of political decision and experience an acute sense of political futility. They know the political world only as a bewildering labyrinth of procedures and unceasing turmoil in which it is difficult to distinguish the just from the wicked, the deserving from the undeserving. The political questions about which they are asked to have opinions are complex and thorny; every solution is imperfect and exacts its price; measures that benefit some groups invariably aggrieve others. The principles which govern the political process seem vague, recondite and impossible to relate to actual events. All this obviously deters voters from developing ideologically, from acquiring insights into the subtleties of the democratic process, and from achieving consensus even on fundamental values.

Although the influentials face some of the same obstacles, they are better able to overcome them. As a group they are distinguished from the mass of the electorate by their above-average education and economic status, their greater political interest and awareness, and their more immediate access to the command posts of community decision. Many of them participate not only in politics but in other public activites as well. This affords them, among other benefits, a more sophisticated understanding of how the society is run and a more intimate association with other men and women who are alert to political ideas and values. Political concepts and abstractions, alien to the vocabulary of many voters, are for the elite familiar items of everyday discourse.

Consider also that the political stratum is, by almost every social criterion we have examined, more homogeneous than the electorate. This promotes communication among them and increases a common body of attitudes.[29] As Newcomb[30] has remarked, "the actual conse-

[29]For additional data on the homogeneity of social characteristics and values among American elite groups, see James N. Rosenau, "Consensus-Building in the American National Community: Hypotheses and Supporting Data," *Journal of Politics,* Vol. 24 (November, 1962), 639–61.

[30]Theodore M. Newcomb, "The Study of Consensus," in R. K. Merton *et al.* (eds.), *Sociology Today* (New York, 1959), pp. 277–92.

quences of communication, as well as the intended ones, are consensus-increasing." Among many segments of the general population, however, communication on matters of political belief either occurs not at all or is so random and cacophonus as to have little utility for the reinforcement of political values. If Louis Wirth is correct in observing that "the limits of consensus are marked by the range of effective communication,"[31] it becomes easier to understand why the active minority achieves consensus more often than the voters do.

Compared with the electorate, whose ordinary members are submerged in an ideological babble of poorly informed and discordant opinions, the members of the political minority inhabit a world in which political ideas are vastly more salient, intellectual consistency is more frequently demanded, attitudes are related to principles, actions are connected to beliefs, "correct" opinions are rewarded and "incorrect" opinions are punished. In addition, as participants in political roles, the actives are compelled (contrary to stereotype) to adopt opinions, to take stands on issues, and to evaluate ideas and events. As *articulates* they are unavoidably exposed to the liberal democratic values which form the main current of our political heritage. The net effect of these influences is to heighten their sensitivity to political ideas and to unite them more firmly behind the values of the American tradition. They may, as a result, be better equipped for the role they are called upon to play in a democracy than the citizens are for *their* role.

The findings furnish little comfort for those who wish to believe that a passion for freedom, tolerance, justice and other democratic values springs spontaneously from the lower depths of the society, and that the plain, homespun, uninitiated yeoman, worker and farmer are the natural hosts of democratic ideology. The mystique of the simple, unworldly, "natural" democrat has been with us since at least the rise of Christianity, and has been assiduously cultivated by Rousseau, Tolstoy, Marx, and numerous lesser writers and social reformers. Usually, the simpler the man, the lower his station in life, and the greater his objective need for equality, the more we have endowed him with a capacity for understanding democracy. We are thus inclined to give the nod to the farmer over the city man, the unlearned over the educated, the poor man over the man of wealth, the "people" over their leaders, the unsophisticated over the sophisticated. Yet every one of these intuitive expectations turns out, upon investigation, to be questionable or false. Democratic beliefs and habits are obviously not "natural" but must be learned; and they are learned more slowly by men and women whose lives are circumscribed by apathy, ignorance, provincialism and social or physical distance from the centers of intellectual activity. In the absence of knowledge and experience—as we can readily observe

[31] *Op. cit.*, p. 201.

from the fidgety course of growth in the newly emerging nations—the presuppositions and complex obligations of democracy, the rights it grants and the self-restraints it imposes, cannot be quickly comprehended. Even in a highly developed democratic nation like the United States millions of people continue to possess only the most rudimentary understanding of democratic ideology.

3. While the active political minority affirms the underlying values of democracy more enthusiastically than the people do, consensus among them is far from perfect, and we might well inquire why this is so.

Despite the many forces impelling influentials toward agreement on basic ideological values, counteracting forces are also at work to divide them. Not all influentials are able to comprehend democratic ideas, to apply them to concrete contexts, or to thread their way through the complexities of modern political life. Nor is communication perfect among them either, despite their greater homogeneity. Many things divide them, not least of which are differences in education, conflicting economic and group interests, party competition, factional cleavages and personal political ambitions.

In demonstrating that the influentials are better prepared than the masses to receive and reflect upon political ideas, we run the risk of overstating the case and of exaggerating their capacity for ideological reasoning. Some members of the political class obviously have no more intellectual concern with politics than the masses do; they are in it for "the game," for personal reasons, or for almost any reason except ideology.

Then, too, while most democratic ideas are in their most general form simple enough for almost all members of the elite to understand, they become considerably more puzzling when one sets out to explicate them, to relate them to each other or to apply them to concrete cases. Only a few of the complications need to be cited to illustrate the point: several of the ideas, such as equality, are either inherently vague or mean different things in different contexts. Some democratic (or constitutional) values turn out in certain situations to be incompatible with other democratic values (*e.g.*, the majority's right to make and enforce the laws at times clashes with individual rights, such as the right to stand on one's religious conscience). As this suggests, democratic ideas and rules of the game are ordinarily encountered not in pure form or in isolation but in substantive contexts that are bound to influence the ways in which we react to them.[32] Many businessmen who consider the regulation of business as an unconstitutional invasion of freedom look upon the regulation of trade unions as a justifiable curb upon lawlessness; trade unionists, needless to say, lean to the opposite view.

---

[32]For a discussion of this point, see Peter Bachrach, "Elite Consensus and Democracy," *Journal of Politics*, Vol. 24 (August, 1962), 439–52.

Consider, too, what a heavy burden we place upon a man's normal impulses by asking him to submit unconditionally to democratic values and procedures. Compliance with democratic rules of the game often demands an extraordinary measure of forbearance and self-discipline, a willingness to place constraints upon the use of our collective power and to suffer opinions, actions, and groups we regard as repugnant. The need for such self-restraint is for many people intrinsically difficult to comprehend and still more difficult to honor. Small wonder, then, that consensus around democratic values is imperfect, even among the political influentials who are well situated to appreciate their importance.

4. We turn now to the most crucial question suggested by the research findings, namely, what significance must be assigned to the fact that democratic ideology and consensus are poorly developed among the electorate and only imperfectly realized among the political influentials?

Our first and most obvious conclusion is that, contrary to the familiar claim, a democratic society can survive despite widespread popular misunderstanding and disagreement about basic democratic and constitutional values. The American political system survives and even flourishes under precisely these conditions, and so, we have reason to think, do other viable democracies. What makes this possible is a more conjectural question, though several observations can be offered by way of answering it.

Democratic viability is, to begin with, saved by the fact that those who are most confused about democratic ideas are also likely to be politically apathetic and without significant influence. Their role in the nation's decision process is so small that their "misguided" opinions or non-opinions have little practical consequence for stability. If they contribute little to the vitality of the system, neither are they likely to do much harm. Lipset[33] has pointed out that "apathy undermines consensus," but to this one may add the corollary observation that apathy also furnishes its own partial corrective by keeping the doubters from acting upon their differences. In the United States, at least, their disagreements are *passive* rather than *active,* more the result of political ignorance and indifference than of intellectual conviction or conscious identification with an "alien" political tendency. Most seem not even to be aware of their deviations from the established values. This suggests that there may, after all, be some utility in achieving agreement on large, abstract political sentiments, for it may satisfy men that they share common values when in fact they do not. Not only can this keep conflicts from erupting, but it also permits men who disagree to continue to communicate and thus

[33]Seymour Martin Lipset, *Political Man*, (New York, 1960), p. 27. Chapter I of this volume provides a stimulating and valuable discussion of the relation of conflict and consensus to the operation of democracy.

perhaps to convert their pseudo-consensus on democratic values into a genuine consensus.

I do not mean to suggest, of course, that a nation runs no risks when a large number of its citizens fail to grasp the essential principles on which its constitution is founded. Among Americans, however, the principal danger is not that they will reject democratic ideals in favor of some hostile ideology, but that they will fail to understand the very institutions they believe themselves to be defending and may end up undermining rather than safeguarding them. Our research on "McCarthyism," for example, strongly suggests that popular support for the Senator represented less a conscious rejection of American democratic ideals than a misguided effort to defend them. We found few McCarthy supporters who genuinely shared the attitudes and values associated with his name.[34]

Whether consensus among the influentials is either a necessary or sufficient condition for democratic stability is not really known. Since the influentials act, make public decisions, are more organized, and take political ideas more seriously, agreement among them on constitutional values is widely thought to be essential for viability. At present, however, we do not have enough information (or at least we do not have it in appropriately organized form) to state with satisfactory precision what the actual relation is between elite consensus and democratic stability. Some democratic governments, *e.g.*, Weimar Germany, crumbled when faced with ideological conflicts among their political classes; others, *e.g.*, post-war Italy and France, have until now managed to weather pronounced ideological cleavages. The opinion has long prevailed that consensus is needed to achieve stability, but the converse may be the more correct formulation, *i.e.*, that so long as conditions remain stable, consensus is not required; it becomes essential only when social conditions are disorganized. Consensus may strengthen democratic viability, but its absence in an otherwise stable society need not be fatal or even particularly damaging.

It should also be kept in mind that the existence of intellectual disagreements—even among the influentials—does not necessarily mean that they will be expressed or acted upon. In the United States (and doubtless elsewhere as well), numerous influences are at work to prevent ideological cleavages from assuming an important role in the nation's political life. This is certainly the tendency of such political institutions as federalism, checks and balances, separation of powers, bicameralism, the congressional committee system, the judiciary's practice of accomodating one discrepant law to another, and a system of elec-

[34] Herbert McClosky, "McCarthyism: The Myth and the Reality," unpublished paper delivered at the American Psychological Association, New York, September, 1957. See also Wiebe, *loc. cit.*

tions more often fought around local issues and personalities than around urgent national questions. Our two-party system also functions to disguise or soften the genuine disagreements that distinguish active Democrats from active Republicans. The American social system contributes to the same end, for it is a model of the pluralistic society, a profuse collection of diverse groups, interests and organizations spread over a vast and variegated territory. Consensus in such a society becomes difficult to achieve, but by the same token its absence can also more easily be survived. The complexities of a highly pluralistic social and political order tend to diminish the impact of intellectual differences, to compel compromise, and to discourage the holders of divergent views from crystalizing into intransigent doctrinal camps. Thus it seems, paradoxically enough, that the need for consensus on democratic rules of the game increases as the conflict among competing political tendencies becomes sharper, and declines as their differences become more diffused. Italy, by this reasoning, has greater need of consensus than the United States, but has less chance of achieving it. A democratic nation may wisely prefer the American model to the Italian, though what is ideally desired, as Lipset observes[35] is a balance between cleavage and consensus—the one to give reality and force to the principle of opposition, the other to furnish the secure framework within which that principle might be made continuously effective. Countervailing power within a structure of shared political values would, by this logic, be the optimal condition for the maintenance of a democratic society.

5. But even giving this much weight to consensus may exaggerate the role which intellectual factors play in the attainment of democratic stability. The temptation to assign a controlling influence to the place of ideas in the operation of democracy is very great. Partly this results from our tendency to confuse the textbook model of democracy with the reality and to assume the high order of rationality in the system that the model presupposes (*e.g.*, an alert citizenry aware of its rights and duties, cognizant of the basic rules, exercising consent, enjoying perfect information and choosing governers after carefully weighing their qualifications, deliberating over the issues, etc.). It is not my purpose to ridicule this model but to underscore the observation that it can easily mislead us into placing more weight than the facts warrant upon cognitive elements—upon ideas, values, rational choice, consensus, etc.— as the cementing forces of a democratic society. An *ad hominem* consideration may also be relevant here: as intellectuals and students of politics, we are disposed both by training and sensibility to take political ideas seriously and to assign central importance to them in the operation of the state. We are therefore prone to forget that most people take

---

[35]Lipset, *op. cit.*, pp. 21–2.

them less seriously than we do, that they pay little attention to issues, rarely worry about the consistency of their opinions and spend little or no time thinking about the values, pre-suppositions, and implications which distinguish one political orientation from another. If the viability of a democracy were to depend upon the satisfaction of these intellectual activities, the prognosis would be very grim indeed.

Research from many different lines of inquiry confirms unequivocally that the role heretofore assigned to ideas and to intellectual processes in general has been greatly exaggerated and cannot adequately explain many political phenomena which, on *a priori* grounds, we have expected them to explain. Witness, for example, the research on the non-rational factors which govern the voting decision, on the effects—or rather the non-effects—of ideology on the loyalty and fighting effectiveness of German and American soldiers, on the differences between the views of party leaders and followers, on the influence of personality on political belief, and on group determinants of perception.[36] We now have evidence that patriotism and the strength of one's attachment to a political community need not depend upon one's approval of its intellectual, cultural, or political values. Indeed, our present research clearly confirms that the men and women who express "patriotism" in extreme or chauvinistic form usually have the least knowledge and understanding of American democratic ideals, institutions, and practices.

Abundant anecdotal data from the observation of dictatorial and other nations further corroborates the conclusion that men may become attached to a party, a community, or a nation by forces that have nothing to do with ideology or consensus. Many of these forces are so commonplace that we often neglect them, for they include family, friends, home, employment, property, religion, ethnic attachments, a common language, and familiar surroundings and customs. These may lack the uplifting power of some political doctrines, but their ability to bind men to a society and its government may nevertheless be great. This observation, of course, is less likely to hold for the intelligentsia than for the inarticulates, but even the political behavior of intellectuals is never governed excusively by appeals to the mind.

The effect of ideas on democratic viability may also be diminished by the obvious reluctance of most men to press their intellectual differences to the margin and to debate questions that may tear the community

---

36*Cf.*, for example, Campbell *et al.*, *op. cit.*; Bernard R. Berelson, Paul F. Lazarsfeld, and William N. McPhee, *Voting* (Chicago, 1954), especially ch. 14; Edward A. Shils and Morris Janowitz, "Cohesion and Distintegration in the German Wehrmacht in World War II," *Public Opinion Quarterly*, Vol. 12 (1948), 280–315; Herbert McClosky, "Conservatism and Personality," *American Political Science Review*, Vol. 52 (March, 1958), 27–45; T. W. Adorno *et al.*, *The Authoritarian Personality*, (New York, 1950), ch. XVII; Richard Crutchfield, "Conformity and Character," *American Psychologist*, Vol. 10 (1955), 191–98.

apart. So long as no urgent reason arises for bringing such differences to the surface, most men will be satisfied to have them remain dormant. Although there are men and women who are exceptions to this generalization, and who cannot bear to leave basic questions unresolved, they are likely to be few, for both the principles and practices of an "open society" strongly reinforce tolerance for variety, contingency and ambiguity in matters of belief and conscience. As our data on freedom of opinion suggest, few Americans expect everyone to value the same things or to hold identical views on public questions. The tendency to ignore, tolerate, or play down differences helps to create an illusion of consensus which for many purposes can be as serviceable as the reality.[37]

6. To conclude, as we have in effect, that ideological awareness and consensus are overvalued as determinants of democratic viability is not to imply that they are of no importance. While disagreements among Americans on fundamental values have tended to be passive and, owing to apathy and the relative placidity of our politics, easily tolerated; while they do not follow party lines and are rarely insinuated into the party struggle; and while no extremist movement has yet grown large enough to challenge effectively the governing principles of the American Constitution, this happy state of affairs is not permanently guaranteed. Fundamental differences could *become* activated by political and economic crises; party differences could *develop* around fundamental constitutional questions, as they have in France and other democracies; and powerful extremist movements are too familiar a phenomenon of modern political life to take for granted their eternal absence from the American scene.

Obviously a democratic nation also pays a price for an electorate that is weakly developed ideologically. Lacking the intellectual equipment to assess complex political events accurately, the unsophisticated may give support to causes that are contrary to their own or to the national interest. In the name of freedom, democracy, and the Constitution, they may favor a McCarthy, join the John Birch Society, or agitate for the impeachment of a Supreme Court Justice who has worked unstintingly to uphold their constitutional liberties. They may also have difficulty discriminating political integrity from demagoguery, maturity and balanced judgment from fanaticism, honest causes from counter-

---

[37]Robert G. McCloskey, *loc. cit.*, suggests that the American political tradition is marked by "ambivalence" toward certain of our fundamental values and that this may discourage the achievement of "consensus" in the usual sense. He believes, however, that Americans have learned to live with, and even to ignore, inconsistencies in the value system, in keeping with our "pragmatic spirit." Whether this ability is uniquely American or whether it is characteristic of all "open," democratic societies is a question well worth investigating. It could, conceivably, be a natural outgrowth of democratic ideology itself, no element of which can be conceived and enforced absolutely without infringing other elements. On this last point, see Sidney Hook, *The Paradoxes of Freedom* (Berkeley, 1962), pp. 14–62.

feits. Our findings on the attitudes shown by ordinary Americans toward "extreme" political beliefs (Left Wing beliefs, Right Wing beliefs, totalitarianism, isolationism, etc.) verify that the possibilities just cited are not merely hypothetical. Those who have the least understanding of American politics subscribe least enthusiastically to its principles, and are most frequently "misled" into attacking constitutional values while acting (as they see it) to defend them.

There is, however, reason to believe that ideological sophistication and the general acceptance of liberal democratic values are increasing rather than declining in the United States. Extreme ideological politics of the type associated with Marxism, fascism and other doctrinaire networks of opinion may be waning, as many sociologists believe,[38] but the same observation does not hold for the influence of democratic ideas. On the contrary, democratic ideology in the United States, linked as it is with the articulate classes, gives promise of growing as the articulate class grows. Many developments in recent American life point to an increase in "articulateness": the extraordinary spread of education, rapid social mobility, urbanization, the proliferation of mass media that disseminate public information, the expansion of the middle class, the decline in the size and number of isolated rural groups, the reduction in the proportion of people with submarginal living standards, the incorporation of foreign and minority groups into the culture and their increasing entrance into the professions, and so on. While these developments may on the one side have the effect of reducing the tensions and conflicts on which extreme ideologies feed, they are likely on the other side to beget a more articulate population and a more numerous class of political influentials, committed to liberal democracy and aware of the rights and obligations which attend that commitment.

[38]*Cf.* Daniel Bell, *The End of Ideology* (Glencoe, 1960), pp. 369–75; S. M. Lipset, *op. cit.*, pp. 403–17; Edward Shils, *loc. cit.*

CHAPTER TWENTY-FIVE

THE AMERICAN OPPOSITIONS: AFFIRMATION AND DENIAL

ROBERT A. DAHL

The normal pattern of oppositions in the United States is roughly this:

> Oppositions seek limited *goals* that do not directly challenge the major institutions or the prevailing American system of beliefs.

> Oppositions employ a wide variety of *strategies*: they combine a heavy emphasis on winning presidential and congressional elections with an equally heavy emphasis on bargaining, logrolling, and pressure-group activities in policy-making.

> Oppositions are not usually very *distinctive*; they are not even clearly identifiable as oppositions; they melt into the system.

> Oppositions are not combined into a single organization of high *cohesion*; they usually work through one or both major parties, each of which has rather low internal unity.

> These two parties are highly *competitive* in national elections but in Congress members of different parties are both *competitive* and *co-operative*.

> Oppositions try to gain their objectives by seeking out encounters with policy-makers at a great variety of official *sites*—bureaucratic, congressional, presidential, judicial, local, etc.

A distinctive, persistent, unified structural opposition scarcely exists in the United States. Overt and organized oppositions ordinarily affirm their support for the prevailing ideology and the basic social, economic, and

Reprinted by permission from Robert A. Dahl, ed., POLITICAL OPPOSITIONS IN WESTERN DEMOCRACIES *(New Haven, Conn.: Yale University Press, 1966), pp. 34–35, 48–50, 53–69.*

political institutions; these oppositions concentrate on limited changes within the established framework of ideas and institutions. Oppositions, then, are typically opposed only to specific policies or the personnel of government. Thus it is nearly always impossible to refer precisely to "the" opposition, for the coalition that opposes the government on one matter may fall apart, or even govern, on another. To say where "the government" leaves off and "the opposition" begins is an exercise in metaphysics.

So far I have been speaking of "normal" oppositions. There are, however, other chapters in the story of oppositions in the United States. For example, groups opposed to existing polities and frustrated by their inability to achieve changes sometimes go beyond the conventional strategies of American politics: they defy national law, call the legitimacy of one or more major institutions into question, and even resort to individual or collective violence.

These oppositional groups shade off into an indeterminate collection of alienated Americans whose opposition is even more out of line with the pattern of normal opposition described a moment ago. Even if we put to one side the small radical or revolutionary parties and political movements that have existed from time to time on the fringes of American political life, commitment to the prevailing ideology and institutions among the general population is highly uneven. There are, and probably always have been, Americans who reject some or most of the key elements in the dominant ideology and some or most of the major institutions. The size and social content of this group probably varies from one generation to another. Since it is extremely difficult for these individuals and groups to express their opposition through the usual processes of American politics, they may either resort to other means or lapse into apathy and withdraw from politics. These Americans are the neglected side of the American political system.

To explain the normal pattern of opposition, and its dark underside, I propose to rely mainly on three sets of factors:

1. The characteristic pattern of consensus.
2. The characteristic pattern of cleavage.
3. The structure of government and politics.

CONSENSUS

That American opinions tend to converge has been emphatically stressed by foreign observers ever since Tocqueville and Harriet Martineau visited the United States in the 1830s. If caution and even skepticism are justified in evaluating their assertions as to what Americans believe or once believed, it is nonetheless difficult to explain American politics without invoking the familiar proposition that a predominant number of Americans arrived fairly early in their national history at a rough concordance on attitudes on some important political questions—questions of a kind that have led to profound and enduring cleavages in other countries.

What usually strikes foreign observers is the extent to which Americans profess the virtues of a government ruled by the elected representatives of the people, that is, popular government or "democracy." Americans publicly disagree about liberty; they do not, in this strict sense, publicly disagree over "democracy." . . .

CLEAVAGE

The ambience of unity that has just been described is impressive. It is, nonetheless, something of an illusion. The traditional ideology, which appears so monolithic, is a patchwork of ambiguities and potential contradictions that not only permit but even encourage a wide variety of conflicts.

European (and American) observers have often underestimated the pervasiveness of conflict in American politics because political conflict in the United States does not follow the expected patterns of class and ideological politics. The American "working class" is obviously not arrayed against "the bourgeoisie." The sound of conflict is muffled by the outward consensus on ideology: everyone seems to be employing the same ideology, the same phrases, even the same words.

Nevertheless, an examination of cleavage patterns in American politics suggests three conclusions:

1. Certain types of questions or issues have been the subject of political conflict for relatively long periods of time.
2. These questions have led to extremely severe conflict about once every generation.
3. Ordinarily, however, the severity of political conflicts is greatly reduced by, among other things, the pattern of cleavage, which encourages conciliation rather than conflict.

The Persistent Subjects of Conflict

Dispute over specific concrete policy questions tends to be of a rather short-run nature. The particular issues that provoke controversy in one decade are likely to be superseded in the next by other specific questions. Nevertheless, certain types of issues have been recurrent subjects of conflict in American politics.

One of these is the nature and extent of democratic processes. This question has persistently reappeared in American politics in a multitude of forms. It was one of the basic cleavages of the Constitutional Convention itself, where a question at issue was whether the republic to be established under the new constitution was to be democratic or aristocratic in character. The Convention and the Constitution left the issue unsettled. A major difference between the Federalists and the Republicans during the first several decades under the new Constitution was the way they answered this question.[1] After the demise of the Federalists, aristocratic themes were muted—at least in public. But even if the outward form of the dispute changed, differences have persisted to the present day over the extent, distribution, and kinds of civil and political rights and liberties that should be guaranteed. On matters of this kind, the seemingly massive consensus about "democracy" quickly breaks down; as we saw above, although certain general propositions in the American ideology are given well-nigh universal lip service, any attempt to apply these general principles to concrete cases reveals sharp differences. Thus a problem on which there has never been much deep agreement is the proper balance between the rights and duties of majorities and minorities. Spokesmen for regional minorities (the South, for example) frequently challenge the constitutional or moral authority of the Congress, the President, or the Supreme Court (or all three) to impose a national policy on the whole country. The rights of dissident, radical, or revolutionary opposition groups are invariably in dispute. Although conflicts over liberties and rights almost always wind up in the courts, and often produce epochal Supreme Court decisions, these conflicts are inescapably political as well. A recent example was supplied by Senator Joseph McCarthy, who formed the nucleus of an opposition movement on the Right that challenged existing government policies and procedures for dealing with Communists, alleged Communists, and other individuals and groups who, it was charged, endangered the national security.

Another highly visible kind of issue that generates conflict is the specific or general role of the government in the regulation and control of the economy. The absence of a sizable socialist movement in the United States and any large-scale challenge to the basic economic institutions can easily be misleading, for consensus breaks down here too. Ever since Alexander Hamilton, the first Secretary of the Treasury, presented his economic programs to the First Congress, government economic policies have stimulated sharp controversy. Indeed, probably conflict in national politics has occurred more frequently in this domain than in any other.

[1]Some historians would probably disagree with the preceding three sentences, which telescope a complex development into a few words. The relevant literature is too vast to cite here. I am developing each of these points at length in a forthcoming book on American politics.

The single most concrete, persistent, and explosive issue in American politics from the Constitutional Convention to the present has, however, been the place of the Negro in American life, whether as slave or as freeman. Although the question has sometimes been removed from national debate by tacit understandings among white leaders, it seems safe to say that no other issue has exerted such a steady force on the patterns of coalition and opposition in American politics. To protect its peculiar institution, whether slavery before the Civil War or white supremacy afterward, the South has always had to maneuver so as to prevent the triumph of a majority hostile to the racial practices of the White South. The South has steadily and skillfully used its political strength in Congress and in the presidential elections to bargain with the North and West for protection of—or at least acquiescence in—its treatment of the Negro. On only two occasions has this strategy failed. It failed (at least in the eyes of some Southern leaders) just before and after the election of 1860; as a result these leaders induced the South to choose the path of secession and finally war. The second failure occurred during the period beginning with the Supreme Court decision outlawing segregation in the schools in 1954 and culminating in the passage of the Civil Rights Act in 1964. The eventual results of this second failure may prove to have important consequences for American politics.[2]

Finally, foreign policy, though a dormant question for long periods, sometimes generates fairly sharp conflicts. During the early years from 1789 to 1815 foreign policy was an important source of conflict between Federalists and Republicans. During the century that followed, widespread acceptance of neutrality, isolationism, and the Monroe Doctrine tended to inhibit sharp and persistent controversy over foreign affairs. But from the First World War onward, American foreign policies have frequently been the subject of political conflict: neutrality, the arming of merchant ships, and entry into the First World War; the Treaty of Versailles and the League of Nations; neutrality and aid to the Allies prior to our entry in World War II; since then the dimensions of foreign aid, how to deal with Communist nations, the wars in Korea and Viet Nam —all have provoked controversy.

The Recurrence of Intense Conflict

One of the commonest beliefs about American politics (rather widely shared by Americans themselves) is that although conflict does occur over these issues, it is rarely if ever very intense. Because there are no precise ways of measuring the severity or intensity of a conflict, and it is therefore difficult to compare the severity or intensity of one conflict with that of another, the validity of this belief is not easy to challenge.

[2]See pp. 431–432.

Yet if one is prepared to accept as indices threats or moves to disrupt the constitutional system, threatened or actual violence against or on behalf of national policies, or expressions by sober and informed observers or participants that a given conflict will lead to disruption, revolution, or civil war, then the weight of historical evidence seems to offer solid support to a contrary proposition:

> From the very first years under the new Constitution American political life has undergone, about once every generation, a conflict over national politics of extreme severity. . . .

Whoever supposes, then, that American politics has been nothing more than a moving consensus, a sort of national Rotary Club luncheon, has not sufficiently reflected on the recurrence of intense conflict, crisis, and violence in American history.

The Pattern of Cleavage

If cleavages have been persistent, and if at times they have led to intense conflicts, why, one might inquire, has the system not been disrupted more often? Why have American oppositions been, on the whole, so moderate? Why don't oppositions "debate the great issues" and "present clear-cut alternatives," as critics so often demand? Why is it that "opposition" and "government" are often so hard to distinguish from one another?

One reason was discussed in the preceding section: the ambience of consensus in which government and oppositions operate. As long as oppositions employ substantially the same ideology and accept much the same set of values as the administration, it is difficult for them to force debate on the great issues (for alternatives clearly outside the common ideology are excluded).

A second reason, which will be discussed briefly in the next section, is the structure of government and politics in the United States.

But a third reason is to be found in the very patterns of cleavage that lead to conflict. Even though, as we have seen, Americans divide quite often on questions of democratic rights and privileges, on the place of Negroes in American life, and on the economic role of the government, and divide somewhat less often on foreign policy, these and other issues do not ordinarily divide them into exclusive camps. For two reasons, it seems, American politics is almost never highly polarized.

1. Differences in political attitudes and actions are not highly related to differences in socioeconomic characteristics—region, status, occupation, etc. Even though there is some relationship, it is usually weak: people in the same regions, or the same status groups, or the same broad occupational categories do not form distinct, homogeneous clusters of attitudes. Consequently, polarization of politics along socioeconomic lines is inhibited.

2. Differences in political attitudes and loyalties are not highly inter-related among themselves. That is, persons who hold the same attitudes on one question frequently hold different attitudes on other questions. To overstate the point, every ally is sometimes an enemy and every enemy is sometimes an ally. Thus polarization of politics along ideological lines is inhibited.

As to the first explanation, it is difficult to find any distinctive and persistent clusters of attitudes in different regions of the United States, except on the question of the Negro. Regional differences in political attitudes do, of course, exist; but the differences are, on the whole, weak. Southerners are not, for example, more conservative about the economic role of the government than people in other regions. In fact, on the basis of 1956 survey evidence, V. O. Key suggested that "on some questions the South turns out to be a shade more 'liberal' than other regions." Key also pointed out, incidentally, that "even with respect to the Negro the unity of the South varies from aspect to aspect of race policy. Southerners take a far stronger position on school segregation than on such questions as the protection of the economic rights of Negroes."[3] Nor, despite its reputation, has the Midwest remained (assuming that it once was) notably more isolationist or less internationalist than the rest of the country.[4] The reputation of the Midwest was created in part by its representatives in Congress, of whom a larger percentage opposed foreign aid in the period before and after World War II than among the representatives from other regions. Yet much of this congressional isolationism was more closely related to party than to region: Democratic congressmen from the Midwest have been, unlike their Republican colleagues, predominantly internationalist.[5]

Relationships are often found between political attitudes and various indices of occupation, socioeconomic status, and class. But strong relationships are rare, and often they are surprisingly weak. Thus in 1956 percentages of persons who ranked high on a scale of internationalism did not seem to vary a great deal according to whether the occupations were white-collar, blue-collar, or farming.[6] As in other countries, how-

[3]V. O. Key, *Public Opinion and American Democracy* (New York: Alfred A. Knopf, Inc., 1960), pp. 102–3.

[4]On a scale of "internationalism," the percentages in each region which ranked high in 1956 were 53 per cent in the Midwest, compared with 59 per cent in the Northeast, 58 per cent in the Far West, and 56 per cent in the South. Key, *Public Opinion and American Democracy*, p. 107.

[5]Leroy N. Rieselbach, "The Demography of the Congressional Vote on Foreign Aid, 1939–1958," *American Political Science Review*, 58 (September 1964) 577–88, esp. 582–83.

[6]White-collar workers who identified themselves as middle class ranked a little higher in internationalism; otherwise, differences were negligible. See Key, *Public Opinion and American Democracy*, Table 6.11, p. 144.

Table 1   Socioeconomic Status and Support for Stronger Economic Role of Government*

Occupation of head of family	Class with which respondent identified himself	
	Working	*Middle*
White-collar	40%	22%
Blue-collar	50%	35%
Farm operator	41%	32%

*Entries are percentages ranking high in support for government aid to cities and towns for building more schools; to Negroes for fair treatment in jobs and housing; in guaranteeing everyone a job; for medical care; and in providing electric power and housing.
Source: Key, *Public Opinion and American Democracy*, p. 143.

ever, manual workers tend to diverge from nonmanual workers in their views on the proper economic policies of the government. The effects of class identification seem to be even greater than the effects of occupation; in 1956 a white-collar worker who identified himself as a member of the working classes was somewhat more likely to be in favor of government intervention in the economy on a variety of fronts than a blue-collar worker who identified himself as middle class. (See Table 1.) Yet because class identity is weak, manual workers do not differ as sharply from nonmanual workers in their voting for candidates and parties as they do in a number of countries. Among the major English-speaking democracies, class voting seems to be lower in the United States than in Britain and Australia (though higher than in Canada).[7]

Ethnic and religious loyalties and identifications introduce heterogeneity into regions and status groups. The common belief that distinctive ethnic and religious identifications are weakening in the United States as the descendants of the various immigrants become assimilated into American life has been recently challenged in a study of ethnic groups in New York; the authors conclude:

> Religion and race seem to define the major groups into which American society is evolving as the specifically national aspect of ethnicity [*i.e.*, the specific nation from which one's ancestors came] declines. In our large American cities, four major groups emerge: Catholics, Jews, white Protestants, and Negroes.[8]

Yet, like region, status, occupation, and economic position, ethnic and religious loyalties do not as such produce sharp political cleavages.

[7]"A number of public opinion surveys taken between 1952 and 1962 indicate that class voting is consistently higher in Australia and Great Britain than in Canada and the United States. The countries may be ranked in the following order: Great Britain, Australia, the United States, and Canada." Robert R. Alford, *Party and Society*, pp. 101–2.

[8]Nathan Glazer and Daniel Patrick Moynihan, *Beyond the Melting Pot* (Cambridge, Mass., the MIT Press and Harvard University Press, 1963), p. 314.

Voting patterns are very much more distinctive than political attitudes. Jews and Catholics vote more heavily Democratic than Protestants; Negroes vote more heavily Democratic than whites; and voters of Irish, Italian, Polish, German, and Scandinavian descent often seem to have somewhat distinctive voting patterns. The differences may be more apparent in local elections than in national elections, and most distinctive when a representative of their own ethnic group—or an enemy of their ethnic group—has a leading place on one ticket.[9]

The extent to which religious differences cut across class differences is revealed in a very general way by the data in Tables 2 and 3. In national elections over the past generation, among both manual workers and nonmanual workers, Catholics have voted Democratic in considerably higher proportions than Protestants (Table 2). The discrepancy was greatest between middle-class (nonmanual) Catholics and Protestants; many Catholics who had moved into nonmanual occupations maintained their traditional loyalties as Democratic voters. The differences between Catholics and Protestants were smallest in the elections of 1952 and 1956, when General Eisenhower was the Republican candidate, and as might be expected, greatest in 1960 when John F. Kennedy, a Catholic, was the Democratic candidate.

To look at the same data in another way (Table 3), Protestants split most sharply along class lines in 1936 in the midst of the Great Depression, when Franklin Roosevelt was running for a second term. Catholics split most sharply in 1952 when many middle-class Catholics succumbed to the appeal of Eisenhower; in 1960, on the other hand, Kennedy all but

Table 2   Religious Voting by Occupational Categories, 1936–1960
(Non-Southern Whites Only): 7 Presidential, 2 Congressional Elections

*Religious voting: % Catholics voting Democratic
minus % Protestants voting Democratic*

	Manual workers	*Nonmanual*	*Farmers*
High	41% (1960)	59% (1960)	39% (1956)
Median	20% ('52, '54)	28% (1956)	14% (1958)
Low	16% (1956)	17% (1952)	— 5% (1954)

Source: Data taken from Table II, pp. 92–94, in Seymour M. Lipset, "Religion and Politics in the American Past and Present," in Robert Lee and Martin Marty, eds., *Religion and Social Conflict* (New York, Oxford University Press, 1964).

[9]See the evidence in Louis Harris, *Is There a Republican Majority, Political Trends, 1952–1956* (New York, Harper, 1954), Ch. 6; Angus Campbell and Homer C. Cooper, *Group Differences in Attitudes and Votes, A Study of the 1954 Congressional Election* (Ann Arbor, Survey Research Center, 1956), Ch. 3; Alford, *Party and Society*, pp. 241 ff.; Campbell *et al.*, *The American Voter*, pp. 319 ff. In the 1964 presidential election the fears aroused among Negroes by the candidacy of Senator Goldwater amplified to near unanimity their predisposition to vote Democratic.

Table 3   Class Voting by Catholics and Protestants, 1936–1960 (Non-Southern Whites Only): 7 Presidential, 2 Congressional Elections

*Class voting: % manual workers voting Democratic
minus % nonmanual voting Democratic*

	Catholics	Protestants
High	28% (1952)	29% (1936)
Median	16% (1948)	23% (1956)
Low	6% (1960)	18% (1954)

Source: See Table 2.

obliterated the appeal of class among Catholics by his appeal as a fellow Catholic.

Thus religion or ethnic identity may either amplify the effects of class and status on voting, as in the case of Negroes or working-class Catholics; or, conversely, religion or ethnic identity may depress the significance of class and status by providing a crosscutting cleavage, as in the case of middle-class Catholics and Jews or white working-class Protestants. Moreover, just as the impact of occupation and economic position on voting may vary depending on the state of the economy, so the impact of religion and ethnic identity is not a constant but a varying factor depending on current issues and on the candidates themselves.

More important, differences in voting and partisan loyalties among ethnic and religious groups do not seem to reflect significant differences in ideology or attitudes about policy. This is not to say that there are *no* discernible differences in political predispositions and beliefs among the different groups. It has been conjectured that "the sympathy which Catholic doctrine has had for trade union objectives, as contrasted with the greater emphasis on individualism inherent in Protestantism may in some part explain why even non-union middle-class Catholics are more supportive of union rights in this country."[10] In New York City, it has been said, "what attracts Jews is liberalism, using the term to refer to the entire range of leftist positions, from the mildest to the most extreme."[11] The kind of Christian pacifism exemplified by Martin Luther King's strategy of nonviolence quite possibly could not have succeeded with any other group of Americans as well as it did with Negroes.

Nonetheless, differences in attitudes and beliefs often reflect other factors like education and economic position; or else the differences are highly specific and depend on some particular issue that impinges di-

[10]Lipset, "Religion and Politics," *The First New Nation*, p. 113. Lipset cites the following finding: "Ohio's counties were segregated (for analytic purposes) into twenty different levels of urbanism, income ,and rural farm, and in all twenty of these groups the more Catholic counties exceeded the least Catholic in their opposition to right-to-work" (i.e. anti-union) legislation in a 1958 referendum. See also John H. Fenton, *The Catholic Vote* (New Orleans, Hauser Press, 1960), pp. 37–38.

[11]Glazer and Moynihan, *Beyond the Melting Pot*, p. 167.

rectly on the group, as in the case of Catholic views on governmental aid to parochial schools or the views of Negroes on civil rights. On the whole, when these factors are removed it is difficult to find much distinctiveness in the political attitudes of the various ethnic and religious groups.[12]

In short, then, differences in political attitudes and actions are related to a number of different social and economic characteristics, but they are not highly related to any, and the variety of social and economic characteristics of any broad category of the population makes for a high degree of political heterogeneity. Hence polarization along social and economic lines is inhibited.

The second factor mentioned a moment ago—that differences in political attitudes and loyalties are not highly interrelated—contributes further to this process. Despite the relatively low level of differences in political attitudes and actions among people in different regions, occupations, classes, religions, and ethnic groups, it is conceivable that Americans might divide into two distinctive ideological blocs, each of which was internally a rather heterogeneous (though not random) mixture of socio-economic groups. In a very rough way this might serve as a description of the Democratic and Republican parties. The difficulty is, however, that until the present the ideological distinctiveness of these blocs has been blurred because even on major issues persons who hold the same attitudes on one question diverge on others. Two issues of great recent salience—integration and medical care—furnish illustrations. One might speculate that at least in the North economic liberals who would favor medical care would also be civil libertarians who would favor racial integration in the public schools; conversely, the prosegregationists might also be economic conservatives. Doubtless there is some tendency of this kind. The relations are, however, very shaky. In a 1956 sample, among Northerners who favored medical care about half also favored racial integration in the schools; but more than a third opposed it. Hence a Northern medical care coalition would, in the extreme case, lose a third of its support when it endorsed racial integration. Conversely, Northerners who opposed a federal medical care program were almost evenly divided on the question of racial integration; hence their coalition would (in principle) split wide open if it took any definite stand on the issue of segregation.[13]

Unless attitudes are highly polarized, it is impossible to divide a

[12]See, for example, the generalizations based on data from a survey made during the 1954 congressional elections in Campbell and Cooper, *Group Differences*, pp. 79–80.

[13]V. O. Key, *Public Opinion and American Democracy*, p. 170. In the 1964 election the voters in California supported President Johnson against Senator Goldwater by six to four and at the same time supported by two to one an amendment to the state constitution permanently nullifying all state legislation to eliminate racial discrimination in the sale of housing. ·

population into two like-minded collections of people. No matter what criterion is used for dividing people, as long as there are only two categories or collections, then within each category there will be many conflicting views. Given the existence of a two-party system, it follows inevitably that, unless attitudes are highly polarized, each of the two parties can hope to win only by constructing an electoral coalition made up of people whose views coincide on some questions but diverge on others. This is exactly what happens most of the time in the United States. And as long as (1) political attitudes are not polarized and (2) only two major parties exist, there can be no escape from two parties each with heterogeneous followings.

Is the pattern I have been describing a recent one? It is difficult to say, for we have surveys and election studies only for the past quarter-century. Yet there is substantial reason for thinking that low polarization has been the usual condition of American politics, and that the reasons for low polarization have been about the same in the past as they are now: large socioeconomic groups have generally been heterogeneous in political attitudes, and persons who agree on one question disagree on others.[14]

Presumably there have been historical fluctuations; the tide of polarization ebbs and flows. Polarization has probably risen to high points during each of the major crises described earlier, and then receded. But polarization is rarely high in American politics and, it would appear, never persistent.

STRUCTURE OF GOVERNMENT AND POLITICS

After the patterns of consensus and cleavage, the third major factor that helps to account for the characteristics of oppositions in the United States is the structure of government and politics: structure in large part prescribed by the Constitution but in some measure amplified by practice and tradition.

One critical element in this structure is of course the two major parties. Parties other than the two largest have less impact on politics in the United States than in any other country examined in this volume. The two parties are, however, decentralized; they do not command as high a degree of voting support from their members in Congress as most European parties seem to do; they tend to be pragmatic, even opportunistic, in approach; they seek and retain highly heterogeneous followings. Some of these characteristics, as we shall see, result from—or at

[14]Although it covers only a limited period, a recent study of Jacksonian Democracy lends support to this interpretation. See Lee Benson, *The Concept of Jacksonian Democracy: New York as a Test Case* (Princeton: Princeton University Press, 1961), particularly Ch. 13, "Outline for a Theory of American Voting Behavior."

any rate are strengthened by—the kinds of factors discussed up to this point. But the reasons an almost exclusive two-party system exists and persists in the United States are too complex and debatable to enter into here. I propose therefore to consider the two-party system as a given, and not try to account for it. Its existence helps us explain the characteristics of oppositions.

The other aspect of the structure of government and politics that bears most heavily on the characteristics of oppositions is the fragmentation of power that it facilitates. As everyone knows, the structure provides a great many checkpoints at which one set of officials can block, slow up, or significantly modify the actions of other officials—the White House, the executive agencies, the independent commissions, the House, the Senate, the rules of procedure in each house, the standing committees, conference committees of the two houses, the federal courts—and not least the federal system itself, in which all these features are in greater or lesser degree duplicated in 50 different states with a rather extensive amount of authority and power.

These features reinforce the heterogeneous character of the parties, primarily by providing to leaders who hold these offices, or can influence officeholders, an extensive opportunity to bargain for advantages by threatening to block, slow up, or modify the policies of other leaders who need their support, constitutionally or from long-standing tradition, practice, or law.

Illustrations abound. Ever since 1938 Democratic Presidents have suffered defeats at the hands of conservatives in Congress. In President Kennedy's first two years in office, a conservative coalition of Northern Republicans and Southern Democrats voted together on about one-fourth of the roll-call votes in the Senate and about one-sixth of the roll-call votes in the House. Considering only these votes, the coalition defeated the President by winning in the Senate more than half the time and in the House nearly two times out of three. The victories of the conservative coalition included measures dealing with foreign aid, farm laborers from Mexico, mass transportation, and aid to depressed areas.[15] Or to take the example of civil rights: until 1964 opponents of laws designed to strengthen Negro rights regularly defeated these measures even when they had majority backing; the instruments were usually the House Rules Committee (controlled by a coalition of Southern Democrats and conservative Republicans) and the filibuster in the Senate. It was the Supreme Court, not the Congress, that ordered the principal changes in Southern patterns of segregation. Yet the Southern states, aided by the

---

[15]*Congressional Quarterly Weekly Report, 21* (Week Ending April 17, 1964), "On Conservative Coalition," pp. 737–40. It should be pointed out that the victories of the conservative coalition were sometimes only marginal changes in the President's proposals, not outright defeats of the whole measure.

institutions of federalism, generally refused to comply; with relatively weak presidential leadership and enforcement under President Eisenhower, their opposition was on the whole successful. Southerners who defied the Court argued, moreover, that they were only obeying the law: the law of their own state.

CONSEQUENCES FOR THE STRATEGY AND TACTICS OF OPPOSITION

The strategy and tactics of opposition in the United States have been largely determined, I have suggested, by

1. The characteristic pattern of consensus
2. The characteristic pattern of cleavage
3. The structure of government and politics

Let me now describe some of the consequences in more detail.

First, a group opposed to existing American institutions is unlikely to gain much support if it mounts a comprehensive attack on the prevailing American ideology, or if it is widely perceived as doing so. To the extent that such a group is pragmatic and realistic in orientation, it will try to reduce its apparent divergence from the prevailing ideology by stressing aspects more consistent with its own ideology and objectives. Since the prevailing ideology is not all of one piece, it lends itself fairly readily to such treatment. However, the result within a radical opposition group is to create an esoteric ideology and an exoteric one; and this produces difficulties when naive followers attracted by the exoteric ideology are repelled by the esoteric one. To some extent this has been a problem with the Communist Party.[16] Alternatively, an opposition that does not accommodate itself to the prevailing ideology is likely to be so unrealistic in its general behavior that its following is minuscule and made up of a disproportionate number of individuals low in political skills, realism, and effectiveness. The result is that few Americans are ever exposed to a presentation of an alternative ideology that involves extensive criticism of the prevailing institutions or the belief-system that legitimizes these institutions.

Second, opposition is likely to be successful in bringing about the changes it seeks only if it affirms its support for the prevailing ideology and the basic institutions of American life, and concentrates its fire on some specific aspect of existing institutions, practices, or beliefs, e.g., free land for homesteaders, slavery, national regulation of banks, child labor, the sale of alcoholic beverages, and so on.

---

[16]Irving Howe and Lewis Coser, *The American Communist Party, A Critical History* (New York, Praeger, 1962), pp. 538 ff.

Third, given the dominance of two parties, low polarization, and the particular structure of government and politics, opposition is likely to be successful only if it enters directly into one of the two parties or bargains with both parties.

Although the option of forming a new party is theoretically open, there is not a single case in American history where an opposition has formed a third party, pushed one of the major parties aside, and subsequently won a national election. The electoral record of third parties in the United States is one of nearly total failure.[17] Of all the party systems in the world, the American two-party system has the longest continuous history of rivalry between the same two major parties. To anyone contemplating the formation of a third party, this historical fact should be (though evidently it not always is) a melancholy prospect to contemplate.

The upshot is, then, that to be effective in a concrete way an opposition will usually have to operate in league with, and make concessions to, leaders of groups whose attitudes on some questions will be in conflict with attitudes among its own followings.

Fourth, it is difficult or impossible to make a sharp distinction between "loyal opposition" and "government." Both merge imperceptibly into a system of coalitions, bargaining, and compromise in which no one coalition can be said to "govern" and none is definitely and persistently in opposition. Significantly, in Congress, in the state legislatures, and with rare exceptions in the press, Americans do not speak of "the loyal opposition" or even "the opposition." The closest terms are "the majority party" and "the minority party"; and even these terms cannot refer to both President and Congress during those periods when President, Senate, and House are not of the same party, which has been the case one-fourth of the time since 1789.

SOME CONSEQUENCES FOR THE SYSTEM

Thus, just as the pervasive ideology provides support for the political system, so too the operation of the political system, in the ways I have just examined, provides support for the prevailing ideology.

To overstate the point somewhat: opposition cannot change the institutions because of the ideology; yet opposition cannot change the ideology because of the political institutions. Since most of the electorate

---

[17]One might object that the Republicans began in 1854–56 as a third party, but the point is only technically true and of little relevance, for the Republican Party did not destroy the Whigs and take their place. The Whigs were destroyed by the slavery controversy, and the Republicans built their party, like Phoenix, on the ruins of the Whigs. This could perhaps happen again. The leaders of some third parties have impatiently awaited their Phoenix for a very long time. But after a full century the phenomenon has not yet been repeated.

accepts roughly the same ideology, it is possible (with the assistance of institutional factors such as presidential elections and single-member districts) for a two-party system—of a kind—to exist. Yet given the existence of only two major parties competing for votes, and given the initial acceptance of a single ideology among the electorate, competition between the two parties in turn undoubtedly reinforces the ideology.

This familiar process of reinforcement might be illustrated in the following way. Suppose we were to classify American adults according to the number of major propositions in the prevailing ideology with which each person disagrees: for example, support for popular government, for the constitutional system, for change by constitutional means, for private property, and for the desirability and possibility of personal success. Although we do not have the exact data we need, the evidence presented earlier suggests that most voters would not disagree with any of the major propositions; some, however, would disagree with one; a few with two or three; almost none with all five. A distribution would look something like Figure 1.

In conditions like these both parties direct their appeals to the great body of voters piled up on the left of the distribution. For either party to make any other appeal is to run the risk of losing a vast number of votes in order to gain a much smaller number among the political deviants.[18] When a party or a presidential candidate misreads the distribution, as Senator Goldwater did in 1964, the election confirms the risk of "extremism" by producing a resounding defeat. Further, the very fact that both parties are driven by the logic of numbers to adhere to

Figure 1

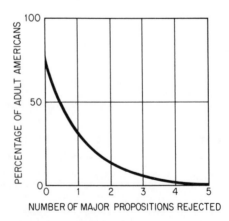

NUMBER OF MAJOR PROPOSITIONS REJECTED

[18]This point was strongly stressed by E. E. Schattschneider in *Party Government* (New York, Rinehart, 1942).

roughly the same ideology means that the ideology is constantly reinforced, or, at the very least, that alternative ideologies are severely handicapped. Thus a typical election, far from generating long-lasting ideological tensions and conflicts as in many other countries, instead tends in the long run to strengthen the traditional ideology. For both major parties emphasize the virtues of that ideology and their faithful adherence to it.

The result is, then, that Americans have solved over long periods the problem of national unity that has weakened and even destroyed many other attempts to operate representative government. If the price for this success is high, the costs of failure could be even higher. Americans have their Civil War to remind them what failure can cost: one out of every dozen males of military age dead, an entire section of the country devastated, and the major question at issue, the place of Negroes in American life, given no more than a superficial, unstable, and morally intolerable solution. The twentieth century has revealed once more what enormous costs may be imposed on the people of a country, and on the world, when representative institutions fail from internal conflicts: Italy, Spain, and Germany, to mention only the three major European examples. The American achievement is all the more significant because of the differences in race, ethnic group, religion, and national origin of the American people, their sheer numbers, the vast size of the country, and the degree of economic specialization that has much of the time existed in the different regions.

Yet the costs of success (in this sense) are high—higher than most Americans are aware of, I think, and quite possibly higher than they need to be. For there are several additional consequences that must, I think, be weighed in the balance.

First, the system makes it easy for political leaders to ignore groups of people whose problems lie outside the attention, loyalties, values, and identifications of the great mass of voters, particularly if these groups lack bargaining power because of poor organization, low status, isolation, ignorance, lack of political incentives, and so on. In practical political terms, the political leader who seeks to find solutions for the problems of marginal groups runs the risk of gaining less support than he loses. It seems highly unlikely, for example, that the deprivation of Negro rights could have gone on so long, with so little national attention, if the United States had had cabinet government, proportional representation, three or four major political parties, and more sources of ideological dissent. To say that this alternative would also have generated costs (costs that many of us would regard as excessive) does not gainsay the costs of the present system.

Second, criticism of the major structures and institutions of the United States tends to be rather limited and examination of structural alternatives is ordinarily rather slight. The point is, no doubt, a familiar one; yet to weigh the balance of advantage and disadvantage flowing out of this consequence is not as easy as it is sometimes made to appear. Extensive, severe, and persistent criticism of the major social, economic, and political structures would put a serious strain on any democratic polity. Moreover, comprehensive and persistent criticism is almost inevitably grounded in ideologies; yet ideological controversy, like religious controversy, is rarely conducive to rational presentation, consideration, and appraisal of alternatives. Although nationwide shouting matches put a heavy burden on a democracy, they do not even compensate for that disadvantage by improving the grasp of the alternatives among citizens and leaders. Is it, as a practical matter, possible to have a rational, orderly examination in national politics of great structural alternatives? The question poses, I think, an unsolved problem. But to say that it is unsolved does not mean that the American solution is desirable. At one extreme, Italy, France, and Germany have in the past all incurred very high costs from implacable ideological controversy. At the opposite extreme, the immunity from comprehensive criticism that the major structures of American social, economic, and political life seem to possess may also impose heavy costs.

Third, if severe ideological cleavages often stimulate irrational controversy, it seems more than likely that the overwhelming ideological consensus of the kind I have described in this essay also encourages irrationalities. It may do so by compelling political dissenters to choose between futility and the two-party politics of compromise, thereby increasing their sense of frustration and political alienation. One enters here a doubtful terrain, and what follows is speculative. It is usually assumed that pragmatic, two-party politics American-style encourages reasonable compromises that mitigate frustration by yielding something to all the parties to a conflict. Yet this is surely not the whole story. Consider the lot of the political dissenter in the light of all that has been said up to this point. If he enters into a third party he is condemned to political impotence. If he enters into one of the two major parties, he constantly sees his principles compromised or even forfeited. He has no satisfactory choice among candidates in elections. From his point of view, the relevant policy alternatives are rarely posed; national leaders, it seems, are unwilling to take his alternatives seriously. Differences among national leaders that are important to voters closer to the center of the political spectrum are, to our political dissenter, too small to be noticeable. It is natural for him to interpret political conflict among national leaders as sham battles within a unified power elite—or, as the American Right often calls it, taking a leaf from the British Left, the Establishment (Eastern, Liberal).

For the political dissenter, continued political impotence and rejection breed frustration. Frustration may produce apathy and withdrawal from politics, but frustration may also turn to hostility, resentment, vengefulness, and even hatred for national leaders in both parties. The political dissenter, then, is likely to become alienated from the political system—from its prevailing practices, its institutions, its personnel, and their assumptions. "Betrayed" by the leaders who dominate the system of politics, the politically alienated dissenters look to some new leader for deliverance—a leader who, like them, will shake off the shackles of two-party, pragmatic, compromising politics and offer a radical and uncompromising alternative. In 1948 Henry Wallace may have briefly tapped a reservoir of politically alienated voters on the Left; an alienated Right evidently responded to a Joe McCarthy in 1952, to a Barry Goldwater in 1964.

It is reasonable to surmise (if one continues this line of speculation) that from the defeat of Populism in 1896 until the New Deal, the largest alienated group in the United States was on the Left. Populism was in many ways the American equivalent of European social democracy.[19] And when it went down to defeat in 1896, the Left was confronted with the familiar alternatives of supporting a separate socialist party that could not win elections or entering one of the two major parties and compromising with all the heterogeneous elements that made up these parties.

Since the advent of the New Deal, however, it is evidently the Right that has been alienated, perhaps increasingly. Except for the fact that this new Right is almost exclusively white, its composition seems to be socially and economically heterogeneous. Attempts to locate the new Right in particular social, economic, or educational strata have on the whole proved unsuccessful. What distinguishes the new Right most sharply is not its social-economic position but simply its dissenting ideology; and its alienation stems from a total inability to win national elections or, until 1964, even to secure presidential candidates who would espouse its obviously deviant minority views.[20]

[19]Norman Pollack argues: "Had Populism succeeded, it could have fundamentally altered American society in a socialist direction." *The Populist Response to Industrial America* (Cambridge, Harvard University Press, 1962), p. 12.

[20]This interpretation deliberately stresses the political sources of the radical Right. Attempts to locate the socioeconomic sources of the new Right have been unsuccessful. In the first edition of *The Radical Right*, ed. by Daniel Bell (New York, Criterion Books, 1955), the authors suggested such sources as anxieties over status and the new rich. But the evidence for these hypotheses was slight; in the second edition (New York, Anchor Books, 1964) the authors themselves are inclined to doubt them. As Lipset remarks, efforts to test their hypotheses about the effects of status incongruities "with the data now available proved unfruitful" (*The Radical Right*, p. 402). Oddly, in the first edition the authors all but ignored the most obvious possibility: the frustration of conservative Republicans unable to win elections. In 1960 Nelson Polsby

In national elections, the Right has had to look, in the North, to the Republican Party; in the South, to the Republicans or to a Southern third-party "Dixiecrat" movement. The Dixiecrats, like other third parties, have proved to be a political failure. As for the Republican Party, until 1964 it refused to nominate a presidential candidate wholly satisfactory to its right wing. The defeat of Senator Taft at the Republican convention in 1952, and the nomination and election of General Eisenhower, were dramatic and unmistakable victories for the moderates —the "Eastern, Liberal Establishment." Because Eisenhower was a Republican President, his attitudes and policies were perhaps all the more displeasing to the Right, since they demonstrated the ineffectiveness of the Right within its own party. In 1964, the Right at last had its way in the nomination of Barry Goldwater. The consequence was—as most responsible observers outside the Right predicted from the outset—overwhelming defeat.

In the conventional liberal-democratic theory of politics, political dissenters are a valuable source of enlightenment; by posing currently unpopular alternatives they force citizens and leaders to examine possibilities they could otherwise ignore. In the United States, however, it is doubtful whether the process has worked quite this way. Frustration and alienation seem to encourage paranoid interpretations of political life,[21] emotionalism and styles of thought that do not produce debate and discussion but hostility and rejection. The moderates close ranks against the threat. In the end, the attack of the political dissenters, far from clarifying alternatives by debate and discussion, may actually reinforce the prevailing ideology.

---

called attention to the fact that the most significant distinction beween those who supported and opposed McCarthy in various surveys was party identification: his supporters were mainly regular Republicans, while most Democrats opposed him. ("Towards an Explanation of McCarthyism," *Political Studies*, 8 [1960].) Lipset, after acknowledging Polsby's finding, says that two surveys "suggest that the most important single attribute associated with opinion of McCarthy was education, while a 1954 national study . . . indicated that religious affiliation was of greater significance than party." (*The Radical Right*, p. 398. The findings were: the more educated the respondents, the more anti-McCarthy they were, and Protestants were more anti-McCarthy than Catholics.) In a more recent study of persons who attended a "San Francisco Bay Region School of Anti-Communism" (an extreme right-wing group) in 1962, the authors found that this particular group of right-wingers were Republicans of relatively high socioeconomic status and education. Their most salient characteristic was their support for Republican candidates. Ninety-two per cent of those who voted in the 1960 presidential election supported the Republican candidate, Richard Nixon, and two-thirds identified themselves as Republicans, 19 per cent as independents, and only 8 per cent as Democrats. Raymond E. Wolfinger, Barbara Kaye Wolfinger, Kenneth Prewitt, and Sheilah Rosenhack, "America's Radical Right: Politics and Ideology" in David E. Apter, ed., *Ideology and Discontent* (New York, The Free Press, 1964), pp. 262–93.

[21]Richard Hofstadter, "The Paranoid Style in American Politics," *Harper's Magazine* (November 1964), pp. 77–86.

CHANGES

In emphasizing the recurring patterns of the American system, I have inevitably portrayed that system as more static over the long run than in fact it is. The system does change. Opinions change as to what the government should be doing in the issue-areas mentioned earlier—democratic rights and privileges, the Negro, the role of the government in the economy, foreign policy. And the policies enforced by the government also change.

An attempt to explain changes in political opinions and policies would take us into a vast area, important but not well charted. However, it might be useful to conjecture whether there are likely to be any important changes in the three main sets of explanatory factors discussed earlier. Of these three kinds of factors, the pattern of cleavages seems to offer the greatest likelihood of significant changes.

The pattern described earlier seems likely to change in two ways. First, it is reasonable to project a trend of gradually declining salience of objective differences within the American population as a result of affluence, widespread education, mass communications, the expansion of white-collar employment and declining proportions of farmers and manual workers. If this trend continues, then objective differences will become even less related than they are at present to differences in voting patterns and, more important, to political attitudes. Subjective factors only related in a loose way to these objective characteristics—values, ideology, psychological predispositions—may then become relatively more important. To the extent that this occurs, the appropriate strategy for the political parties will be to pay less attention to the presumed desires of particular socioeconomic categories in the population and more and more to general attitudes, aspirations, and policy-oriented views that cut across socioeconomic categories to like-minded voters in each of these categories. In this sense, American politics may become more, not less, "ideological." As a result of this change the parties may be even more heterogeneous than at present in the socioeconomic characteristics of their support, and at the same time less heterogeneous and more unified in the policies for which they can secure the support of their voters. To put it another way, one's political allies and opponents today would remain one's allies and opponents tomorrow.

This change might well be the result of two other changes that are very likely to occur in American politics: the removal of the ancient issue of Negro rights from its central (if not always public) place in politics by defeating the South on this question and providing such powerful juridical guarantees for the Negro that the process cannot be reversed, as it was after 1876; and the development of a two-party system in the South.

For one condition above all created the pattern of cleavage that has dominated American politics in which today's allies are tomorrow's opponents. This was the power of the one-party South in elections and in Congress and its virtually unbreakable unity on the institutions of white supremacy in the South. A party that would not do business with the South on its own terms, i.e., yield to white supremacy in the South, has for nearly a hundred years stood in perpetual danger of being defeated in elections or in Congress, or both, by a party that would. Both parties yielded to this imperative. As a result, the South was at once a permanent opposition (on all questions involving racial segregation) and a permanent partner in government.

If, however, the issue that has made this inevitable is removed from politics, and if the Republican Party gains an increasingly strong foothold in the South (not merely in presidental elections but also in elections to Congress and the state legislatures), there will be little left to distinguish Northern liberals and progressives from Southern liberals and progressives, Northern moderates from Southern moderates, or Northern conservatives from Southern conservatives. The parties may then regroup along lines of greater ideological and programmatic consistency.

Should this take place, however, it is not likely to produce two sharp differentiated parties with distinct ideologies. The kind of consensus, even pseudo-consensus, discussed earlier, makes this unlikely. The content of the beliefs at the center may—indeed, undoubtedly will—change. But the tendency for opinions and beliefs to converge will probably continue. The center will then continue to dominate political life, and dissenters will continue to be frustrated and alienated.

TRANSLATING VOTES INTO PUBLIC POLICY

DONALD R. MATTHEWS and JAMES W. PROTHRO

Political pundits have assumed that the vote will automatically give southern Negroes influence over public policy commensurate with their numbers. Once Negroes are voting in substantial numbers, the argument goes, southern state and local officials will either respond to Negro demands or suffer at the polls. Negroes will then be able to use their political leverage to force governments to eliminate segregation in other realms of life. Hence the special significance of the vote to southern Negroes.

Attractive as this argument is, it is much too simple. The linkages between mass attitudes, as expressed in elections, and public policy are exceedingly complex and little understood. The best research we have suggests that the translation of votes into power, and power into policy, is by no means automatic, and that public officials and political leaders have far more freedom of maneuver in dealing with their constituents than had been initially realized.[1] The governmental response to Negro votes, then, may not be at all automatic in the South or anywhere else. The experience of northern Negroes—who have been voting in large numbers for many decades and yet are still distinctly "second-class citizens"—is not very comforting to those who would place primary reliance on the vote as the "solution" to the Negro problem in the South.

[1]See, for example, L. A. Dexter, "The Representative and His District," *Human Organization*, Vol. 16 (1947), pp. 2–13; V. O. Key, Jr., *Public Opinion and American Democracy* (New York: Alfred A. Knopf, 1961), Chap. 21; W. E. Miller and D. Stokes, "Constituency Influence in Congress," *American Political Science Review*, Vol. 57 (1963), pp. 45–56.

Reprinted by permission from NEGROES AND THE NEW SOUTHERN POLITICS *(New York: Harcourt, Brace & World, Inc., 1966), pp. 477–81. Messrs. Matthews and Prothro are Professors of Political Science at the University of North Carolina.*

THE VOTE AS A POLITICAL RESOURCE

A number of resources can be translated into political power—votes, money, prestige, information, skill, organization, and so on.[2] Individuals and groups possess varying amounts of these resources. The amount of *potential* political power they have is *not* directly determined by the amount of *any one resource* they have. Rather, it depends on how much of *all* these resources they control. (In the typical case there is likely to be a good deal of dispersion, with those having a great deal of one resource not having much of the others.) People's actual power depends, further, not just on the level of their total resources but also on whether they choose to expend these resources to further their political goals. The local millionaire, for example, may have a tremendous power *potential* because he is wealthy, but little actual power because he is more interested in chasing nubile blondes and buying yachts than in seeking political influence. It is therefore possible for individuals and groups with limited political resources who invest them heavily in politics to be more influential than those with vast power potential but no inclination to use their resources for political purposes. In the usual case, the proportion of all political resources actually used for political purposes tends to be small. The result is a great deal of "slack" (or unexpended resources) in the political system.

Southern Negroes have but one political resource in abundance—votes. Southern whites, most of whom still oppose the Negro's political objectives, tend to have the lion's share of *all* political resources, including votes. The competition between the two groups for control over public policy will tend to be very uneven unless southern whites fail to use their overwhelmingly superior resources for political ends. No doubt there has been a great deal of "slack" in the utilization of political resources by southern whites in the past. But the more threatened they feel by evidence of rising Negro political power in the future, the more their disproportionate resources will be invested in politics and the less "slack" there will be. Racial inequalities in political resources other than the vote, then, probably will result in southern Negroes' receiving less influence over policy than their proportionate share of the electorate would seem to dictate.

Even the vote itself has limitations as a political resource for southern Negroes. They are in a minority almost everywhere in the South. (In the relatively few communities where Negroes are potentially a clear majority of the electorate, white resistance to Negro voting tends to be most vehement, and the barriers to the effective use of the ballot, once

---

[2]This discussion of political resources and their relationship to power follows R. A. Dahl, *Who Governs?* (New Haven: Yale University Press, 1961), chs. 19–28.

achieved, are likely to be greatest.) In order to win, southern Negroes generally have to enter into coalitions with at least some white politicians and voters. In situations characterized by an overwhelming white consensus in favor of segregation, biracial coalition-building is almost impossible. A good many Negroes in the South may finally win the right to vote only to find themselves in a more or less permanent political minority.

Where a significant minority of moderate and integrationist whites is in being—as in Peripheral South cities like Urbania [Urbania is a fictitious name.]—Negro-white political coalitions are easier to arrange. But opponents of biracial coalitions need merely take steps to increase the salience of the racial issue to the electorate at large, and the Negro-white coalition usually dissolves. In view of the corrosive effects of the racial issue and the lack of other stable political structures in one-party systems, Negroes in the South may have to rely primarily on joining *ad hoc* coalitions on an issue-by-issue basis. On many state, local, and "style" issues,[3] for example, the Negroes' most likely allies are the economically conservative but racially moderate middle classes; in presidential politics and on class issues, however, they may receive greater benefits from highly volatile, "populistic" coalitions with heavily segregationist white workers.

Such a complex and fluid political situation, characterized by high tension levels and limited "slack," places heavy demands on political leaders. For one thing, bargaining and negotiations between white and Negro leaders must be almost continuous and call for highly developed political skills. In the second place, followers may become confused by rapidly shifting strategies and alliances. They must be given clear cues and constant guidance lest they inadvertently throw their votes away. All these things southern Negro leaders must be able to do, and do well, before the Negro vote can have a major impact on public policy, *even in areas where biracial coalitions are formed.* The desperate shortage of capable Negro leaders . . . and the possibility that this shortage will become even more severe in the future . . . not only affect how often Negroes go to the polls, but how effectively they use their votes once they get there.

TYPES OF NEGRO GOALS

Southern Negroes seem to have a better chance of achieving some types of racial objectives than others by way of the ballot box. Other modes of

[3]The distinction between "style" and "class" (or "position") issues is from B. Berelson, P. F. Lazarsfeld, and W. N. McPhee, *Voting* (Chicago: University of Chicago Press, 1954), pp. 194ff.

attack—litigation, demonstrations, and federal intervention—are likely
to be more fruitful than the vote in grappling with many kinds of civil
rights problems.

First, Negro votes are an effective resource in altering segregationist
practices when *the costs of abandoning segregation are relatively low for
the white community*. For example, police brutality tends to decline and,
to a lesser extent, the entire administration of justice tends to improve
after southern Negroes become active members of the electorate.[4] The
psychic and monetary costs of such reforms for whites are modest. Where,
on the other hand, the white community perceives the costs of abandoning segregation as high—such as in the areas of housing or school desegregation—the Negro vote seems to have little impact. The coefficient of
correlation between the proportion of the Negro adult population
registered to vote and the existence of desegregated schools, by county, in
1958 was $+.03$! Change in this area tends to be brought about through
litigation and federal action. Negro political muscle demonstrated at
the local polls seems entirely irrelevant.

A second factor that affects the ability of the Negro vote to bring
about desegregation is the *visibility of the issue to the white community*.
If the benefits of the reform are confined to the Negro ghetto, and if the
change can be brought about without a great deal of publicity, then the
Negro vote seems to carry more punch. Negro policemen for example,
have been hired in many southern communities and assigned to responsibilities in Negro residential areas with scarcely any publicity or controversy. Hiring Negro firemen, however, tends to be much more difficult.
Either Negro and white firemen must share the same living quarters or
else the community must build a new firehouse. And a new firehouse
takes money, often a bond issue. So hiring Negro firemen is both more
costly and more visible, and hence harder to achieve.

Third, the power of the Negro vote increases to *the extent that
whites perceive the issue as involving matters of fairness and impartiality*. One of the greatest resources of Negroes in their struggle for equality
is the obvious congruence of many of their demands with the "democratic" and "good government" ethos. Reforms that can be justified by
simple and clear appeals to the whites' sense of fair play and impartiality
have a relatively good chance of being adopted. Thus nondiscrimination
in public hiring practices is far easier to achieve than a policy of com-
pensatory opportunities that seems, on its face, to discriminate in favor

[4]In this section we rely heavily on W. R. Keech, "The Negro Vote as a Political
Resource: The Case of Durham" (Unpublished Dissertation, University of Wiscon-
sin, 1966). See also U. S. Commission on Civil Rights, *1961 Report*, Vol. I, "Voting,"
(Washington, D.C.: U.S. Government Printing Office, 1961), part III, pp. 143–99;
H. S. Whitaker, "A New Day: The Effects of Negro Enfranchisement in Selected
Mississippi Counties" (Unpublished Dissertation, Florida State University, 1965); A.
Sindler, "Protest Against the Political Status of the Negro," *Annals*, Vol. 357 (1965),
pp. 48–54.

of Negroes. Police brutality and discrimination in electoral administration are obviously unfair, and very few white southerners are prepared to defend either practice as inherently desirable.

Finally, the vote can help southern Negroes to achieve racial equality only in the *public sector of community life*. Even a responsive government is of little help in altering injustice in areas where the government has no legal authority or informal influence. As the more blatant, legal, "southern" forms of segregation are replaced by more subtle, *de facto*, "northern" forms, the vote as a weapon in the civil rights struggle will become less and less potent.

THE VALUE OF THE VOTE

This is not to argue that the vote is of little or no value to southern Negroes. It is to argue, however, that the concrete benefits to be derived from the franchise—under the conditions that prevail in the South—have often been exaggerated.

To be sure, much of the extravagant talk about the vote being *the* key that will unlock the door to racial equality for southern Negroes should be discounted as political hyperbole. It is dangerous talk nonetheless. Statements to this effect by responsible public officials, from the President of the United States on down, and by scores of prominent Negro leaders, just might be taken at face value. The result might be to lull nonsoutherners into thinking that the southern Negroes' struggle for equality has been won when the tide of battle has merely begun to shift, to lead southern Negroes to expect miracles from the vote and to become deeply embittered when the miracles fail to materialize, and to lead southern whites to panic at the prospect of a "black domination" of the region that will never come. The vote for southern Negroes is a necessary but not a sufficient condition for racial progress in the South. So are continued pressures from the non-South and realism and understanding from Negro and white southerners.

The concrete, measurable payoffs from Negro voting in the South will *not* be revolutionary. But these are not the only reasons for valuing the franchise. The effects of taking part in the process of self-government *on the participant*—on his self-esteem and his sense of civic responsibility—must not be ignored. One middle-aged Negro interviewed in the course of this study was asked why he so deeply wanted to vote. He replied simply: "To be a man." This is reason enough to justify all the efforts and sacrifices that have been made to reenfranchise the Negroes of the South. Race will remain a serious problem in the South until southerners—Negro as well as white—accept the moral worth of Negroes as a matter of course. The vote and its exercise by southern Negroes will help both groups move toward this new day.

CHAPTER TWENTY-SEVEN

PROTEST AS A POLITICAL RESOURCE

MICHAEL LIPSKY

The frequent resort to protest activity by relatively powerless groups in recent American politics suggests that protest represents an important aspect of minority group and low income group politics.[1] At the same

This article is an attempt to develop and explore the implications of a conceptual scheme for analyzing protest activity. It is based upon my studies of protest organizations in New York City, Washington, D.C., Chicago, San Francisco, and Mississippi, as well as extensive examination of written accounts of protest among low-income and Negro civil rights groups. I am grateful to Kenneth Dolbeare, Murray Edelman, and Rodney Stiefbold for their insightful comments on an earlier draft. This paper was developed while the author was a Staff Associate of the Institute for Research on Poverty at the University of Wisconsin. I appreciate the assistance obtained during various phases of my research from the Rabinowitz Foundation, the New York State Legislative Internship Program, and the Brookings Institution.

[1]"Relatively powerless groups" may be defined as those groups which, relatively speaking, are lacking in conventional political resources. For the purposes of community studies, Robert Dahl has compiled a useful comprehensive list. See Dahl, "The Analysis of Influence in Local Communities," *Social Science and Community Action*, Charles R. Adrian, ed. (East Lansing, Michigan, 1960), p. 32. The difficulty in studying such groups is that relative powerlessness only becomes apparent under certain conditions. Extremely powerless groups not only lack political resources, but are also characterized by a minimal sense of political efficacy, upon which in part successful political organization depends. For reviews of the literature linking orientations of political efficacy to socioeconomic status, see Robert Lane, *Political Life* (New York, 1959), ch. 16; and Lester Milbrath, *Political Participation* (Chicago, 1965), ch. 5. Further, to the extent that group cohesion is recognized as a necessary requisite for organized political action, then extremely powerless groups, lacking cohesion, will not even appear for observation. Hence the necessity of selecting for intensive study a protest movement where there can be some confidence that observable processes and results can be analyzed. Thus, if one conceives of a continuum on which political groups are placed according to their relative command of resources, the focus of this essay is on those groups which are near, but not at, the pole of powerlessness.

Reprinted by permission from the AMERICAN POLITICAL SCIENCE REVIEW, *Vol. 62 (December 1968), pp. 1144–58. Mr. Lipsky is Assistant Professor of Political Science at the University of Wisconsin.*

time that Negro civil rights strategists have recognized the problem of using protest as a meaningful political instrument,[2] groups associated with the "war on poverty" have increasingly received publicity for protest activity. Saul Alinsky's Industrial Areas Foundation, for example, continues to receive invitations to help organize low income communities because of its ability to mobilize poor people around the tactic of protest.[3] The riots which dominated urban affairs in the summer of 1967 appear not to have diminished the dependence of some groups on protest as a mode of political activity.

This article provides a theoretical perspective on protest activity as a political resource. The discussion is concentrated on the limitations inherent in protest which occur because of the need of protest leaders to appeal to four constituencies at the same time. As the concept of protest is developed here, it will be argued that protest leaders must nurture and sustain an organization comprised of people with whom they may or may not share common values. They must articulate goals and choose strategies so as to maximize their public exposure through communications media. They must maximize the impact of third parties in the political conflict. Finally, they must try to maximize chances of success among those capable of granting goals. The tensions inherent in manipulating these four constituencies at the same time form the basis of this discussion of protest as a political process. It is intended to place aspects of the civil rights movement in a framework which suggests the general political processes in which such organizations operate.

I. "PROTEST" CONCEPTUALIZED

Protest activity as it has been adopted by elements of the civil rights movement and others has not been studied extensively by social scientists. Some of the most suggestive writings have been done as case studies of protest movements in single southern cities.[4] These works generally lack

---

[2]See, e.g., Bayard Rustin, "From Protest to Politics: The Future of the Civil Rights Movement," *Commentary* (February, 1965), 25–31; and Stokely Carmichael, "Toward Black Liberation," *The Massachusetts Review* (Autumn, 1966).

[3]On Alinsky's philosophy of community organization, see his *Reveille for Radicals* (Chicago, 1945); and Charles Silberman, *Crisis in Black and White* (New York, 1964), ch. 10.

[4]See, e.g., Jack L. Walker, "Protest and Negotiation: A Case Study of Negro Leadership in Atlanta, Georgia," *Midwest Journal of Political Science*, 7 (May, 1963), 99–124; Jack L. Walker, *Sit-Ins in Atlanta: A Study in the Negro Protest*, Eagleton Institute Case Studies, No. 34 (New York, 1964); John Ehle, *The Free Men* (New York, 1965) [Chapel Hill]; Daniel C. Thompson, *The Negro Leadership Class* (Englewood Cliffs, N.J., 1963) [New Orleans]; M. Elaine Burgess, *Negro Leadership in a Southern City* (Chapel Hill, N.C., 1962) [Durham].

a framework or theoretical focus which would encourage generalization from the cases. More systematic efforts have been attempted in approaching the dynamics of biracial committees in the South,[5] and comprehensively assessing the efficacy of Negro political involvement in Durham, N.C. and Philadelphia, Pa.[6] In their excellent assessment of Negro politics in the South, Matthews and Prothro have presented a thorough profile of Southern Negro students and their participation in civil rights activities.[7] Protest is also discussed in passing in recent explorations of the social-psychological dimensions of Negro ghetto politics[8] and the still highly suggestive, although pre-1960's, work on Negro political leadership by James Q. Wilson.[9] These and other less systematic works on contemporary Negro politics,[10] for all of their intuitive insights and valuable documentation, offer no theoretical formulations which encourage conceptualization about the interaction between recent Negro political activity and the political process.

Heretofore the best attempt to place Negro protest activity in a framework which would generate additional insights has been that of James Q. Wilson.[11] Wilson has suggested that protest activity be conceived as a problem of bargaining in which the basic problem is that Negro groups lack political resources to exchange. Wilson called this "the problem of the powerless."[12]

While many of Wilson's insights remain valid, his approach is limited in applicability because it defines protest in terms of mass action or response and as utilizing exclusively negative inducements in the bargaining process. Negative inducements are defined as inducements which are not absolutely preferred but are preferred over alternative possibilities.[13] Yet it might be argued that protest designed to appeal to

[5]Lewis Killian and Charles Grigg, *Racial Crisis in America: Leadership in Conflict* (Englewood Cliffs, N.J., 1964).

[6]William Keech, "The Negro Vote as a Political Resource: The Case of Durham" (unpublished Ph.D. Dissertation, University of Wisconsin, 1966); John H. Strange, "The Negro in Philadelphia Politics 1963–65" (unpublished Ph.D. Dissertation, Princeton University, 1966).

[7]Donald Matthews and James Prothro, *Negroes and the New Southern Politics* (New York, 1966). Considerable insight on these data is provided in John Orbell, "Protest Participation among Southern Negro College Students," *American Political Science Review*, 61 (June, 1967), 446–56.

[8]Kenneth Clark, *Dark Ghetto* (New York, 1965).

[9]*Negro Politics* (New York, 1960).

[10]A complete list would be voluminous. See, e.g., Nat Hentoff, *The New Equality* (New York, 1964); Arthur Waskow, *From Race Riot to Sit-in* (New York, 1966).

[11]The Strategy of Protest: Problems of Negro Civic Action," *Journal of Conflict Resolution*, 3 (September, 1961), 291–303. The reader will recognize the author's debt to this highly suggestive article, not least Wilson's recognition of the utility of the bargaining framework for examining protest activity.

[12]*Ibid.*, p. 291.

[13]*Ibid.*, pp. 291–92.

groups which oppose suffering and exploitation, for example, might be offering positive inducements in bargaining. A few Negro students sitting at a lunch counter might be engaged in what would be called protest, and by their actions might be trying to appeal to other groups in the system with positive inducements. Additionally, Wilson's concentration on Negro civic action, and his exclusive interest in exploring the protest process to explain Negro civic action, tend to obscure comparison with protest activity which does not necessarily arise within the Negro community.

Assuming a somewhat different focus, protest activity is defined as a mode of political action oriented toward objection to one or more policies or conditions, characterized by showmanship or display of an unconventional nature, and undertaken to obtain rewards from political or economic systems while working within the systems. The "problem of the powerless" in protest activity is to activate "third parties" to enter the implicit or explicit bargaining arena in ways favorable to the protesters. This is one of the few ways in which they can "create" bargaining resources. It is intuitively unconvincing to suggest that fifteen people sitting uninvited in the Mayor's office have the power to move City Hall. A better formulation would suggest that the people sitting in may be able to appeal to a wider public to which the city administration is sensitive. Thus in successful protest activity the *reference publics* of protest *targets* may be conceived as explicitly or implicitly reacting to protest in such a way that target groups or individuals respond in ways favorable to the protesters.[14]

It should be emphasized that the focus here is on protest by relatively powerless groups. Illustration can be summoned, for example, of activity designated as "protest" involving high status pressure groups or hundreds of thousands of people. While such instances may share some of the characteristics of protest activity, they may not represent examples of developing political resources by relatively powerless groups because the protesting groups may already command political resources by virtue of status, numbers or cohesion.

It is appropriate also to distinguish between the relatively restricted use of the concept of protest adopted here and closely related political strategies which are often designated as "protest" in popular usage. Where groups already possess sufficient resources with which to

---

[14]See E. E. Schattschneider's discussion of expanding the scope of the conflict, *The Semisovereign People* (New York, 1960). Another way in which bargaining resources may be "created" is to increase the relative cohesion of groups, or to increase the perception of group solidarity as a precondition to greater cohesion. This appears to be the primary goal of political activity which is generally designated "community organization." Negro activists appear to recognize the utility of this strategy in their advocacy of "black power." In some instances protest activity may be designed in part to accomplish this goal in addition to activating reference publics.

bargain, as in the case of some economic boycotts and labor strikes, they may be said to engage in "direct confrontation."[15] Similarly, protest which represents efforts to "activate reference publics" should be distinguished from "alliance formation," where third parties are induced to join the conflict, but where the value orientations of third parties are sufficiently similar to those of the protesting group that concerted or coordinated action is possible. Alliance formation is particularly desirable for relatively powerless groups if they seek to join the decision-making process as participants.

The distinction between activating reference publics and alliance formation is made on the assumption that where goal orientations among protest groups and the reference publics of target groups are similar, the political dynamics of petitioning target groups are different than when such goal orientations are relatively divergent. Clearly the more similar the goal orientations, the greater the likelihood of protest success, other things being equal. This discussion is intended to highlight, however, those instances where goal orientations of reference publics depart significantly, in direction or intensity, from the goals of protest groups.

Say that to protest some situation, A would like to enter a bargaining situation with B. But A has nothing B wants, and thus cannot bargain. A then attempts to create political resources by activating other groups to enter the conflict. A then organizes to take action against B with respect to certain goals. *Information concerning these goals must be conveyed through communications media* (C, D, and E) *to F, G, and H, which are B's reference publics.* In response to the reactions of F, G, and H, or in anticipation of their reactions, B responds *in some way*, to the protesters' demands. This formulation requires the conceptualization of protest activity when undertaken to create bargaining resources as a political process which requires communication and is characterized by a multiplicity of constituencies for protest leadership.

A schematic representation of the process of protest as utilized by relatively powerless groups is presented in Figure 1. In contrast to a simplistic pressure group model which would posit a direct relationship between pressure group and pressured, the following discussion is guided by the assumption (derived from observation) that protest is a highly indirect process in which communications media and the reference publics of protest targets play critical roles. It is also a process characterized by reciprocal relations, in which protest leaders frame strat-

---

[15]For an example of "direct confrontation," one might study the three-month Negro boycott of white merchants in Natchez, Miss., which resulted in capitulation to boycott demands by city government leaders. See *The New York Times*, December 4, 1965, p. 1.

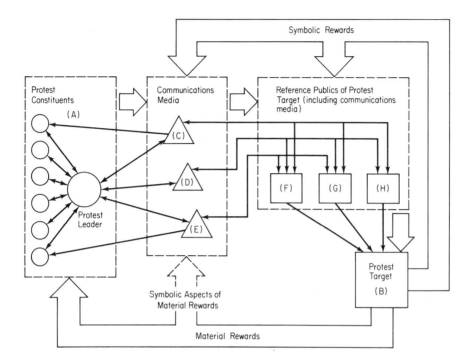

Figure 1   Schematic Representation of the Process of Protest by Relatively Powerless Groups

egies according to their perception of the needs of (many) other actors.

In this view protest constituents limit the options of protest leaders at the same time that the protest leader influences their perception of the strategies and rhetoric which they will support. Protest activity is filtered through the communications media in influencing the perceptions of the reference publics of protest targets. To the extent that the influence of reference publics is supportive of protest goals, target groups will dispense symbolic or material rewards. Material rewards are communicated directly to protest constituents. Symbolic rewards are communicated in part to protest constituents, but primarily are communicated to the reference publics of target groups, who provide the major stimuli for public policy pronouncements.

The study of protest as adopted by relatively powerless groups should provide insights into the structure and behavior of groups involved in civil rights politics and associated with the "war on poverty." It should direct attention toward the ways in which administrative agencies respond to "crises." Additionally, the study of protest as a political resource should influence some general conceptualizations of American political pluralism. Robert Dahl, for example, describes the "normal American political process" as

> one in which there is a high probability that an active and legitimate group in the population can make itself heard effectively at some crucial stage in the process of decision.[16]

Although he agrees that control over decisions is unevenly divided in the population, Dahl writes:

> When I say that a group is heard "effectively" I mean more than the simple fact that it makes a noise; I mean that one or more officials are not only ready to listen to the noise, but expect to suffer in some significant way if they do not placate the group, its leaders, or its most vociferous members. To satisfy the group may require one or more of a great variety of actions by the responsive leader: pressure for substantive policies, appointments, graft, respect, expression of the appropriate emotions, or the right combination of reciprocal noises.[17]

These statements, which in some ways resemble David Truman's discussion of the power of "potential groups,"[18] can be illuminated by the study of protest activity in three ways. First, what are the probabilities that relatively powerless groups can make themselves heard effectively? In what ways will such groups be heard or "steadily appeased"?[19] Concentration on the process of protest activity may reveal the extent to which, and the conditions under which, relatively powerless groups are likely to prove effective. Protest undertaken to obstruct policy decisions, for example, may enjoy greater success probabilities than protest undertaken in an effort to evoke constructive policy innovations.[20]

Second, does it make sense to suggest that all groups which make noises will receive responses from public officials? Perhaps the groups which make noises do not have to be satisfied at all, but it is other groups which receive assurances or recognition. Third, what are the probabilities that groups which make noises will receive tangible rewards, rather than symbolic assurances?[21] Dahl lumps these rewards to-

---

[16]*A Preface to Democratic Theory* (Chicago, 1956), pp. 145–46.
[17]*Ibid.*
[18]*The Governmental Process* (New York, 1951), p. 104.
[19]See Dahl, *A Preface to Democratic Theory*, p. 146.
[20]Observations that all groups can influence public policy at some stage of the political process are frequently made about the role of "veto groups" in American politics. *See Ibid.*, pp. 104 ff. See also David Riesman, *The Lonely Crowd* (New Haven, 1950), pp. 211 ff., for an earlier discussion of veto-group politics. Yet protest should be evaluated when it is adopted to obtain assertive as well as defensive goals.
[21]See Murray Edelman, *The Symbolic Uses of Politics* (Urbana, Ill., 1964), ch. 2.

gether in the same paragraph, but dispensation of tangible rewards clearly has a different impact upon groups than the dispensation of symbolic rewards. Dahl is undoubtedly correct when he suggests that the relative fluidity of American politics is a critical characteristic of the American political system.[22] But he is less precise and less convincing when it comes to analyzing the extent to which the system is indeed responsive to the relatively powerless groups of the "average citizen."[23]

The following sections are an attempt to demonstrate the utility of the conceptualization of the protest process presented above. This will be done by exploring the problems encountered and the strains generated by protest leaders in interacting with four constituencies. It will be useful to concentrate attention on the maintenance and enhancement needs not only of the large formal organizations which dominate city politics,[24] but also of the ad hoc protest groups which engage them in civic controversy. It will also prove rewarding to examine the role requirements of individuals in leadership positions as they perceive the problems of constituency manipulation. In concluding remarks some implications of the study of protest for the pluralist description of American politics will be suggested.[25]

II. PROTEST LEADERSHIP AND ORGANIZATIONAL BASE

The organizational maintenance needs of relatively powerless, low income, ad hoc protest groups center around the tension generated by the need for leadership to offer symbolic and intangible inducements to protest participation when immediate, material rewards cannot be anticipated, and the need to provide at least the promise of material rewards. Protest leaders must try to evoke responses from other actors in the political process, at the same time that they pay attention to participant organizational needs. Thus relatively deprived groups in the

[22]See Dahl, *Who Governs?* (New Haven, 1961), pp. 305 ff.

[23]In a recent formulation, Dahl reiterates the theme of wide dispersion of influence. "More than other systems, [democracies] . . . try to disperse influence widely to their citizens by means of the suffrage, elections, freedom of speech, press, and assembly, the right of opponents to criticize the conduct of government, the right to organize political parties, and in other ways." *Pluralist Democracy in the United States* (Chicago, 1967), p. 373. Here, however, he concentrates more on the availability of options to all groups in the system, rather than on the relative probabilities that all groups in fact have access to the political process. See pp. 372 ff.

[24]See Edward Banfield, *Political Influence* (New York, 1961), p. 263. The analysis of organizational incentive structure which heavily influences Banfield's formulation is Chester Barnard, *The Functions of the Executive* (Cambridge, Mass., 1938).

[25]In the following attempt to develop the implications of this conceptualization of protest activity, I have drawn upon extensive field observations and bibliographical research. Undoubtedly, however, individual assertions, while representing my best judgment concerning the available evidence, in the future may require modification as the result of further empirical research.

political system not only receive symbolic reassurance while material rewards from the system are withheld,[26] but protest leaders have a stake in perpetuating the notion that relatively powerless groups retain political efficacy despite what in many cases is obvious evidence to the contrary.

The tension embraced by protest leaders over the nature of inducements toward protest participation accounts in part for the style adopted and goals selected by protest leaders. Groups which seek psychological gratification from politics, but cannot or do not anticipate material political rewards, may be attracted to militant protest leaders. To these groups, angry rhetoric may prove a desirable quality in the short run. Where groups depend upon the political system for tangible benefits, or where participation in the system provides intangible benefits, moderate leadership is likely to prevail. Wilson has observed similar tendencies among Negro leaders of large, formal organizations.[27] It is no less true for leadership of protest groups. Groups whose members derive tangible satisfactions from political participation will not condone leaders who are stubborn in compromise or appear to question the foundations of the system. This coincides with Truman's observation:

> Violation of the "rules of the game" normally will weaken a group's cohesion, reduce its status in the community, and expose it to the claims of other groups.[28]

On the other hand, the cohesion of relatively powerless groups may be strengthened by militant, ideological leadership which questions the rules of the game and challenges their legitimacy.

Cohesion is particularly important when protest leaders bargain directly with target groups. In that situation, leaders' ability to control protest constituents and guarantee their behavior represents a bargaining strength.[29] For this reason Wilson stressed the bargaining difficulties of Negro leaders who cannot guarantee constituent behavior, and pointed out the significance of the strategy of projecting the image of group solidarity when the reality of cohesion is a fiction.[30] Cohesion is less significant at other times. Divided leadership may prove productive by bargaining in tandem[31] or by minimizing strain among groups in

---

[26]As Edelman suggests, cited previously.

[27]*Negro Politics*, p. 290.

[28]*The Governmental Process*, p. 513.

[29]But cf. Thomas Schelling's discussion of "binding oneself," *The Strategy of Conflict* (Cambridge, Mass., 1960), pp. 22 ff.

[30]"The Strategy of Protest," p. 297.

[31]This is suggested by Wilson, "The Strategy of Protest," p. 298; St. Clair Drake and Horace Cayton, *Black Metropolis* (New York, 1962, rev. ed.), p. 731; Walker, "Protest and Negotiation," p. 122. Authors who argue that divided leadership is dysfunctional have been Clark, p. 156; and Tilman Cothran "The Negro Protest Against Segregation in the South," *The Annals*, 357 (January, 1965), p. 72.

the protest process. Further community divisions may prove less detrimental to protest aims when strong third parties have entered the dispute originally generated by protest organizations.

The intangible rewards of assuming certain postures toward the political system may not be sufficient to sustain an organizational base. It may be necessary to renew constantly the intangible rewards of participation. And to the extent that people participate in order to achieve tangible benefits, their interest in a protest organization may depend upon the organization's relative material success. Protest leaders may have to tailor their style to present participants with tangible successes or with the appearance of success. Leaders may have to define the issues with concern for increasing their ability to sustain organizations. The potential for protest among protest group members may have to be manipulated by leadership if the group is to be sustained.[32]

The participants in protest organizations limit the flexibility of protest leadership. This obtains for two reasons. They restrict public actions by leaders who must continue to solicit active participant support and they place restraints on the kinds of activities which can be considered appropriate for protest purposes. Poor participants cannot commonly be asked to engage in protest requiring air transportation. Participants may have anxieties related to their environment or historical situation which discourages engagement in some activities. They may be afraid of job losses, beatings by the police, or summary evictions. Negro protest in the Deep South has been inhibited by realistic expectations of retribution.[33] Protests over slum housing conditions are undermined by tenants who expect landlord retaliation for engaging in tenant organizing activity.[34] Political or ethical mores may conflict with a proposed course of action, diminishing participation.[35]

[32]This observation is confirmed by a student of the Southern civil rights movement: "Negroes demand of protest leaders constant progress. The combination of long-standing discontent and a new-found belief in the possibility of change produces a constant state of tension and aggressiveness in the Negro community. But this discontent is vague and diffuse, not specific; the masses do not define the issues around which action shall revolve. This the leader must do." Lewis Killian, "Leadership in the Desegregation Crises: An Institutional Analysis," in Muzafer Sherif (ed.), *Intergroup Relations and Leadership* (New York, 1962), p. 159.

[33]Significantly, southern Negro students who actively participated in the early phases of the sit-in movement "tended to be unusually optimistic about race relations and tolerant of whites [when compared with inactive Negro students]. They not only *were* better off, objectively speaking, than other Negroes but *felt* better off." Matthews and Prothro, *op. cit.*, p. 424.

[34]This is particularly the case in cities such as Washington, D.C., where landlord-tenant laws offer little protection against retaliatory eviction. See, e.g., Robert Schoshinski, "Remedies of the Indigent Tenant: Proposal for Change," *Georgetown Law Journal*, 54 (Winter, 1966), 541 ff.

[35]Wilson regarded this as a chief reason for lack of protest activity in 1961. He wrote: ". . . some of the goals now being sought by Negroes are least applicable to those groups of Negroes most suited to protest action. Protest action involving such

On the other hand, to the extent that fears are real, or that the larger community perceives protest participants as subject to these fears, protest may actually be strengthened. Communications media and potential allies will consider more soberly the complaints of people who are understood to be placing themselves in jeopardy. When young children and their parents made the arduous bus trip from Mississippi to Washington, D.C. to protest the jeopardizing of Head Start funds, the courage and expense represented by their effort created a respect and visibility for their position which might not have been achieved by local protest efforts.[36]

Protest activity may be undertaken by organizations with established relationship patterns, behavior norms, and role expectations. These organizations are likely to have greater access to other groups in the political system, and a demonstrated capacity to maintain themselves. Other protest groups, however, may be ad hoc arrangements without demonstrated internal or external relationship patterns. These groups will have different organizational problems, in response to which it is necessary to engage in different kinds of protest activity.

The scarcity of organizational resources also places limits upon the ability of relatively powerless groups to maintain the foundations upon which protest organizations develop. Relatively powerless groups, to engage in political activity of any kind, must command at least some resources. This is not tautological. Referring again to a continuum on which political groups are placed according to their relative command of resources, one may draw a line somewhere along the continuum representing a "threshold of civic group political participation." Clearly some groups along the continuum will possess some political resources (enough, say, to emerge for inspection) but not enough to exercise influence in civic affairs. Relatively powerless groups, to be influential, must cross the "threshold" to engage in politics. Although the availability of group resources is a critical consideration at all stages of the protest process, it is particularly important in explaining why some groups seem to "surface" with sufficient strength to command attention. The following discussion of some critical organizational resources should illuminate this point.

Skilled professionals frequently must be available to protest organizations. Lawyers, for example, play extremely important roles in enabling protest groups to utilize the judicial process and avail themselves of adequate preparation of court cases. Organizational reputation may de-

---

tactics as mass meetings, picketing, boycotts, and strikes rarely find enthusiastic participants among upper-income and higher status individuals": "The Strategy of Protest," p. 296.

[36]See *The New York Times*, February 12, 1966, p. 56.

pend upon a combination of ability to threaten the conventional political system and of exercising statutory rights in court. Availability of lawyers depends upon ability to pay fees and/or the attractiveness to lawyers of participation in protest group activity. Volunteer professional assistance may not prove adequate. One night a week volunteered by an aspiring politician in a housing clinic cannot satisfy the needs of a chaotic political movement.[37] The need for skilled professionals is not restricted to lawyers. For example, a group seeking to protest an urban renewal policy might require the services of architects and city planners in order to present a viable alternative to a city proposal.

Financial resources not only purchase legal assistance, but enable relatively powerless groups to conduct minimum programs of political activities. To the extent that constituents are unable or unwilling to pay even small membership dues, then financing the cost of mimeographing flyers, purchasing supplies, maintaining telephone services, paying rent, and meeting a modest payroll become major organizational problems. And to the extent that group finances are supplied by outside individual contributions or government or foundation grants, the long-term options of the group are sharply constrained by the necessity of orienting group goals and tactics to anticipate the potential objections of financial supporters.

Some dependence upon even minimal financial resources can be waived if organizations evoke passionate support from constituents. Secretarial help and block organizers will come forward to work without compensation if they support the cause of neighborhood organizations or gain intangible benefits based upon association with the group. Protest organizations may also depend upon skilled non-professionals, such as college students, whose access to people and political and economic institutions often assists protest groups in cutting across income lines to seek support. Experience with ad hoc political groups, however, suggests that this assistance is sporadic and undependable. Transient assistance is particularly typical of skilled, educated, and employable volunteers whose abilities can be applied widely. The die-hards of ad hoc political groups are often those people who have no place else to go, nothing else to do.

Constituent support will be affected by the nature of the protest target and whether protest activity is directed toward defensive or assertive goals. Obstructing specific public policies may be easier than successfully recommending constructive policy changes. Orientations

[37] On housing clinic services provided by political clubs, see James Q. Wilson, *The Amateur Democrat: Club Politics in Three Cities* (Chicago, 1962), pp. 63–64, 176. On the need for lawyers among low income people, see e.g., *The Extension of Legal Services to the Poor*, Conference Proceedings (Washington, D.C., n.d.), esp. pp. 51–60; and "Neighborhood Law Offices: The New Wave in Legal Services for the Poor," *Harvard Law Review*, 80 (February, 1967), 805–50.

toward defensive goals may require less constituent energy, and less command over resources of money, expertise and status.[38]

III. PROTEST LEADERSHIP AND COMMUNICATIONS MEDIA

The communications media are extremely powerful in city politics. In granting or withholding publicity, in determining what information most people will have on most issues, and what alternatives they will consider in response to issues, the media truly, as Norton Long has put it, "set . . . the civic agenda."[39] To the extent that successful protest activity depends upon appealing to, and/or threatening, other groups in the community, the communications media set the limits of protest action. If protest tactics are not considered significant by the media, or if newspapers and television reporters or editors decide to overlook protest tactics, protest organizations will not succeed. Like the tree falling unheard in the forest, there is no protest unless protest is perceived and projected.

A number of writers have noticed that the success of protest activity seems directly related to the amount of publicity it receives outside the immediate arena in which protest takes place. This view has not been stated systematically, but hints can be found in many sources. In the literature on civil rights politics, the relevance of publicity represents one of the few hypotheses available concerning the dynamics of successful protest activity.[40]

When protest tactics do receive coverage in the communications media, the way in which they are presented will influence all other actors in the system, including the protesters themselves. Conformity to standards of newsworthiness in political style, and knowledge of the prejudices and desires of the individuals who determine media coverage in political skills, represent crucial determinants of leadership effectiveness.

The organizational behavior of newspapers can partly be understood by examining the maintenance and enhancement needs which direct them toward projects of civic betterment and impressions of ac-

[38]An illustration of a low income group protest organization mobilized for veto purposes is provided by Dahl in "The Case of the Metal Houses." See *Who Governs?*, pp. 192 ff.

[39]Norton Long, "The Local Community as an Ecology of Games," in Long, *The Polity*, Charles Press, ed. (Chicago, 1962), p. 153. See pp. 152–54. See also Roscoe C. Martin, Frank J. Munger, *et al.*, *Decisions in Syracuse: A Metropolitan Action Study* (Garden City, N.Y., 1965) (originally published: 1961), pp. 326–27.

[40]See, e.g., Thompson, *op. cit.*, p. 134, and *passim*; Martin Oppenheimer, "The Southern Student Movement: Year I," *Journal of Negro Education*, 33 (Fall, 1964), p. 397; Cothran, *op. cit.*, p. 72; Pauli Murray, "Protest Against the Legal Status of the Negro," *The Annals*, 357 (January, 1965), p. 63; Allan P. Sindler, "Protest Against the Political Status of the Negro," *The Annals*, 357 (January, 1965), p. 50.

complishment.[41] But insight may also be gained by analyzing the role requirements of reporters, editors, and others who determine newspaper policy. Reporters, for example, are frequently motivated by the desire to contribute to civic affairs by their "objective" reporting of significant events; by the premium they place on accuracy; and by the credit which they receive for sensationalism and "scoops."

These requirements may be difficult to accommodate at the same time. Reporters demand newsworthiness of their subjects in the short run, but also require reliability and verifiability in the longer run. Factual accuracy may dampen newsworthiness. Sensationalism, attractive to some newspaper editors, may be inconsistent with reliable, verifiable narration of events. Newspapers at first may be attracted to sensationalism, and later demand verifiability in the interests of community harmony (and adherence to professional journalistic standards).

Most big city newspapers have reporters whose assignments permit them to cover aspects of city politics with some regularity. These reporters, whose "beats" may consist of "civil rights" or "poverty," sometimes develop close relationships with their news subjects. These relationships may develop symbiotic overtones because of the mutuality of interest between the reporter and the news subject. Reporters require fresh information on protest developments, while protest leaders have a vital interest in obtaining as much press coverage as possible.

Inflated reports of protest success may be understood in part by examining this relationship between reporter and protest leader. Both have role-oriented interests in projecting images of protest strength and threat. In circumstances of great excitement, when competition from other news media representatives is high, a reporter may find that he is less governed by the role requirement of verification and reliability than he is by his editor's demand for "scoops" and news with high audience appeal.[42]

On the other hand, the demands of the media may conflict with the needs of protest group maintenance. Consider the leader whose constituents are attracted solely by pragmatic statements not exceeding what they consider political "good taste." He is constrained from making militant demands which would isolate him from constituents. This constraint may cost him appeal in the press.[43] However, the leader whose or-

---

41See Banfield, *op. cit.*, p. 275.

42For a case study of the interaction between protest leaders and newspaper reporters, see Michael Lipsky, "Rent Strikes in New York City: Protest Politics and the Power of the Poor" (unpublished Ph.D. dissertation, Princeton University, 1967), pp. 139–49. Bernard Cohen has analyzed the impact of the press on foreign policy from the perspective of reporters' role requirements; see his *The Press and Foreign Policy* (Princeton, N.J., 1963), esp. chs. 2–3.

43An example of a protest conducted by middle-class women engaged in pragmatic protest over salvaging park space is provided in John B. Keeley, *Moses on the Green*, Inter-University Case Program, No. 45 (University, Ala., 1959).

ganizing appeal requires militant rhetoric may obtain eager press coverage only to find that his inflammatory statements lead to alienation of potential allies and exclusion from the explicit bargaining process.[44]

News media do not report events in the same way. Television may select for broadcast only thirty seconds of a half-hour news conference. This coverage will probably focus on immediate events, without background or explanatory material. Newspapers may give more complete accounts of the same event. The most complete account may appear in the weekly edition of a neighborhood or ethnic newspaper. Differential coverage by news media, and differential news media habits in the general population,[45] are significant factors in permitting protest leaders to juggle conflicting demands of groups in the protest process.

Similar tensions exist in the leader's relationships with protest targets. Ideological postures may gain press coverage and constituency approval, but may alienate target groups with whom it would be desirable to bargain explicitly. Exclusion from the councils of decision-making may have important consequences, since the results of target group deliberations may satisfy activated reference publics without responding to protest goals. If activated reference publics are required to increase the bargaining position of the protest group, protest efforts thereafter will have diminished chances of success.

IV. PROTEST LEADERSHIP AND "THIRD PARTIES"

I have argued that the essence of political protest consists of activating third parties to participate in controversy in ways favorable to protest goals. In previous sections I have attempted to analyze some of the tensions which result from protest leaders' attempts to activate reference publics of protest targets at the same time that they must retain the interest and support of protest organization participants. This phenomenon is in evidence when Negro leaders, recognized as such by public officials, find their support eroded in the Negro community because they have engaged in explicit bargaining situations with politicians.

[44]This was the complaint of Floyd McKissick, National Director of the Congress of Racial Equality, when he charged that ". . . there are only two kinds of statements a black man can make and expect that the white press will report. . . . First . . . is an attack on another black man. . . . The second is a statement that sounds radical, violent, extreme—the verbal equivalent of a riot. . . . [T]he Negro is being rewarded by the public media only if he turns on another Negro and uses his tongue as a switchblade, or only if he sounds outlandish, extremist or psychotic." Statement at the Convention of the American Society of Newspaper Editors, April 20, 1967, Washington, D.C., as reported in *The New York Times*, April 21, 1967, p. 22. See also the remarks of journalist Ted Poston, *ibid.*, April 26, 1965, p. 26.

[45]Matthews and Prothro found, for example, that in their south-wide Negro population sample, 38 percent read Negro-oriented magazines and 17 percent read newspapers written for Negroes. These media treat news of interest to Negroes more completely and sympathetically than do the general media. See pp. 248 ff.

Negro leaders are thus faced with the dilemma that when they be-have like other ethnic group representatives they are faced with loss of support from those whose intense activism has been aroused in the Negro community, yet whose support is vital if they are to remain credible as leaders to public officials.

The tensions resulting from conflicting maintenance needs of pro-test organizations and activated third parties present difficulties for pro-test leaders. One way in which these tensions can be minimized is by dividing leadership responsibilities. If more than one group is engaged in protest activity, protest leaders can, in effect, divide up public roles so as to reduce as much as possible the gap between the implicit de-mands of different groups for appropriate rhetoric, and what in fact is said. Thus divided leadership may perform the latent function of minimizing tensions among elements in the protest process by permit-ting different groups to listen selectively to protest spokesmen.[46]

Another way in which strain among different groups can be mini-mized is through successful public relations. Minimization of strain may depend upon ambiguity of action or statement, deception, or upon ef-fective inter-group communication. Failure to clarify meaning, or fal-sification, may increase protest effectiveness. Effective intragroup com-munication may increase the likelihood that protest constituents will "understand" that ambiguous or false public statements have "special meaning" and need not be taken seriously. The Machiavellian circle is complete when we observe that although lying may be prudent, the ap-pearance of integrity and forthrightness is desirable for public relations, since these values are widely shared.

It has been observed that "[t]he militant displays an unwillingness to perform those administrative tasks which are necessary to operate an organization. Probably the skills of the agitator and the skills of the administrator . . . are not incompatible, but few men can do both well."[47] These skills may or may not be incompatible as personality traits, but they indeed represent conflicting role demands on protest leader-ship. When a protest leader exhausts time and energy conducting fre-quent press conferences, arranging for politicians and celebrities to ap-pear at rallies, delivering speeches to sympathetic local groups, college symposia and other forums, constantly picketing for publicity and gen-erally making "contacts," he is unable to pursue the direction of office routine, clerical tasks, research and analysis, and other chores.

The difficulties of delegating routine tasks are probably directly re-lated to the skill levels and previous administrative experiences of group members. In addition, to the extent that involvement in protest or-

---

[46]See footnote 31 above.
[47]Wilson, *Negro Politics,* p. 225.

ganizations is a function of rewards received or expected by individuals because of the excitement or entertainment value of participation, then the difficulties of delegating routine, relatively uninteresting chores to group members will be increased. Yet attention to such details affects the perception of protest groups by organizations whose support or assistance may be desired in the future. These considerations add to the protest leader's problem of risking alienation of protest participants because of potentially unpopular cooperation with the "power structure."

In the protest paradigm developed here, "third parties" refers both to the reference publics of target groups and, more narrowly, to the interest groups whose regular interaction with protest targets tends to develop into patterns of influence.[48] We have already discussed some of the problems associated with activating the reference publics of target groups. In discussing the constraints placed upon protest, attention may be focused upon the likelihood that groups seeking to create political resources through protest will be included in the explicit bargaining process with other pressure groups. For protest groups, these constraints are those which occur because of class and political style, status, and organizational resources.

The established civic groups most likely to be concerned with the problems raised by relatively powerless groups are those devoted to service in the public welfare and those "liberally" oriented groups whose potential constituents are either drawn from the same class as the protest groups (such as some trade unions), or whose potential constituents are attracted to policies which appear to serve the interest of the lower class or minority groups (such as some reform political clubs).[49] These civic groups have frequently cultivated clientele relationships with city agencies over long periods. Their efforts have been reciprocated by agency officials anxious to develop constituencies to support and defend agency administrative and budgetary policies. In addition, clientele groups are expected to endorse and legitimize agency aggrandizement. These relationships have been developed by agency officials and civic groups for mutual benefit, and cannot be destroyed, abridged or avoided without cost.

Protest groups may well be able to raise the saliency of issues on the civic agenda through utilization of communications media and successful appeals or threats to wider publics, but admission to policy-making councils is frequently barred because of the angry, militant rhetorical style adopted by protest leaders. People in power do not like to sit down with rogues. Protest leaders are likely to have phrased de-

[48]See Wallace Sayre and Herbert Kaufman, *Governing New York City* (New York, 1960), pp. 257 ff. Also see Banfield, *op. cit.*, p. 267.

[49]See Wilson, *The Amateur Democrat*, previously cited. These groups are most likely to be characterized by broad scope of political interest and frequent intervention in politics. See Sayre and Kaufman, *op. cit.*, p. 79.

mands in ways unacceptable to lawyers and other civic activists whose cautious attitude toward public policy may reflect not only their good intentions but their concern for property rights, due process, pragmatic legislating or judicial precedent.

Relatively powerless groups lack participation of individuals with high status whose endorsement of specific proposals lends them increased legitimacy. Good causes may always attract the support of high status individuals. But such individuals' willingness to devote time to the promotion of specific proposals is less likely than the one-shot endorsements which these people distribute more readily.

Similarly, protest organizations often lack the resources on which entry into the policy-making process depends. These resources include maintenance of a staff with expertise and experience in the policy area. This expertise may be in the areas of the law, planning and architecture, proposal writing, accounting, educational policy, federal grantsmanship or publicity. Combining experience with expertise is one way to create status in issue areas. The dispensing of information by interest groups has been widely noted as a major source of influence. Over time the experts develop status in their areas of competence somewhat independent of the influence which adheres to them as information-providers. Groups which cannot or do not engage lawyers to assist in proposing legislation, and do not engage in collecting reliable data, cannot participate in policy deliberations or consult in these matters. Protest oriented groups, whose primary talents are in dramatizing issues, cannot credibly attempt to present data considered "objective" or suggestions considered "responsible" by public officials. Few can be convincing as both advocate and arbiter at the same time.

V. PROTEST LEADERSHIP AND TARGET GROUPS

The probability of protest success may be approached by examining the maintenance needs of organizations likely to be designated as target groups.[50] For the sake of clarity, and because protest activity increasingly is directed toward government, I shall refer in the following paragraphs exclusively to government agencies at the municipal level. The

---

[50]Another approach, persuasively presented by Wilson, concentrates on protest success as a function of the relative unity and vulnerability of targets. See "The Strategy of Protest," pp. 293 ff. This insight helps explain, for example, why protest against housing segregation commonly takes the form of action directed against government (a unified target) rather than against individual homeowners (who present a dispersed target). One problem with this approach is that it tends to obscure the possibility that targets, as collections of individuals, may be divided in evaluaion of and sympathy for protest demands. Indeed, city agency administrators under some circumstances act as partisans in protest conflicts. As such, they frequently appear ambivalent toward protest goals: sympathetic to the ends while concerned that the means employed in protest reflect negatively on their agencies.

assumption is retained, however, that the following generalizations are applicable to other potential target groups.

Some of the constraints placed on protest leadership in influencing target groups have already been mentioned in preceding sections. The lack of status and resources that inhibit protest groups from participating in policy-making conferences, for example, also helps prevent explicit bargaining between protest leaders and city officials. The strain between rhetoric which appeals to protest participants and public statements to which communications media and "third parties" respond favorably also exists with reference to target groups.

Yet there is a distinguishing feature of the maintenance needs and strategies of city agencies which specifically constrains protest organizations. This is the agency director's need to protect "the jurisdiction and income of his organization [by] . . . [m]anipulation of the external environment."[51] In so doing he may satisfy his reference groups without responding to protest group demands. At least six tactics are available to protest targets who are motivated to respond in some way to protest activity but seek primarily to satisfy their reference publics. These tactics may be employed whether or not target groups are "sincere" in responding to protest demands.

1. Target groups may dispense symbolic satisfactions. Appearances of activity and commitment to problems substitute for, or supplement, resource allocation and policy innovations which would constitute tangible responses to protest activity. If symbolic responses supplement tangible pay-offs, they are frequently coincidental, rather than intimately linked, to projection of response by protest targets. Typical in city politics of the symbolic response is the ribbon cutting, street corner ceremony or the walking tour press conference. These occasions are utilized not only to build agency constituencies,[52] but to satisfy agency reference publics that attention is being directed to problems of civic concern. In this sense publicist tactics may be seen as defensive maneuvers. Symbolic aspects of the actions of public officials can also be recognized in the commissioning of expensive studies and the rhetorical flourishes with which "massive attacks," "comprehensive programs," and "coordinated planning" are frequently promoted.

City agencies establish distinct apparatus and procedures for dealing with crises which may be provoked by protest groups. Housing-related departments in New York City may be cited for illustration. It is usually the case in these agencies that the Commissioner or a chief deputy, a press secretary and one or two other officials devote whatever time is necessary to collect information, determine policy and respond quickly to reports of "crises." This is functional for tenants, who, if they

[51]Sayre and Kaufman, *op. cit.*, p. 253.
[52]See *ibid.*, pp. 253 ff.

can generate enough concern, may be able to obtain shortcuts through lengthy agency procedures. It is also functional for officials who want to project images of action rather than merely receiving complaints. Concentrating attention on the maintenance needs of city politicians during protest crises suggests that pronouncements of public officials serve purposes independent of their dedication to alleviation of slum conditions.[53]

Independent of dispensation of tangible benefits to protest groups, public officials continue to respond primarily to their own reference publics. Murray Edelman has suggested that:

> Tangible resources and benefits are frequently not distributed to unorganized political group interests as promised in regulatory statutes and the propaganda attending their enactment.[54]

His analysis may be supplemented by suggesting that symbolic dispensations may not only serve to reassure unorganized political group interests, but may also contribute to reducing the anxiety level of organized interests and wider publics which are only tangentially involved in the issues.

2. Target groups may dispense token material satisfactions. When city agencies respond, with much publicity, to cases brought to their attention representing examples of the needs dramatized by protest organizations, they may appear to respond to protest demands while in fact only responding on a case basis, instead of a general basis. For the protesters served by agencies in this fashion it is of considerable advantage that agencies can be influenced by protest action. Yet it should not be ignored that in handling the "crisis" cases, public officials give the appearance of response to their reference publics, while mitigating demands for an expensive, complex *general* assault on problems represented by the cases to which responses are given. Token responses, whether or not accompanied by more general responses, are particularly attractive to reporters and television news directors, who are able to dramatize individual cases convincingly, but who may be unable to "capture" the essence of general deprivation or of general efforts to aleviate conditions of deprivation.

3. Target groups may organize and innovate internally in order to blunt the impetus of protest efforts. This tactic is closely related to No. 2 (above). If target groups can act constructively in the worst cases, they will then be able to pre-empt protest efforts by responding to the

---

[53]See Lipsky, *op. cit.*, chs. 5–6. The appearance of responsiveness may be given by city officials *in anticipation* of protest activity. This seems to have been the strategy of Mayor Richard Daley in his reaction to the announcement of Martin Luther King's plans to focus civil rights efforts on Chicago. See *The New York Times*, February 1, 1966, p. 11.

[54]See Edelman, *op. cit.*, p. 23.

cases which best dramatize protest demands. Alternatively, they may designate all efforts which jeopardize agency reputations as "worst" cases, and devote extensive resources to these cases. In some ways extraordinary city efforts are precisely consistent with protest goals. At the same time extraordinary efforts in the most heavily dramatized cases or the most extreme cases effectively wear down the "cutting-edges" of protest efforts.

Many New York City agencies develop informal "crisis" arrangements not only to project publicity, as previously indicated, but to mobilize energies toward solving "crisis" cases. They may also develop policy innovations which allow them to respond more quickly to "crisis" situations. These innovations may be important to some city residents, for whom the problems of dealing with city bureaucracies can prove insurmountable. It might be said, indeed, that the goals of protest are to influence city agencies to handle every case with the same resources that characterize their dispatch of "crisis" cases.[55]

But such policies would demand major revenue inputs. This kind of qualitative policy change is difficult to achieve. Meanwhile, internal reallocation of resources only means that routine services must be neglected so that the "crisis" programs can be enhanced. If all cases are expedited, as in a typical "crisis" response, then none can be. Thus for purposes of general solutions, "crisis" resolving can be self-defeating unless accompanied by significantly greater resource allocation. It is not self-defeating, however, to the extent that the organizational goals of city agencies are to serve a clientele while minimizing negative publicity concerning agency vigilance and responsiveness.

4. Target groups may appear to be constrained in their ability to grant protest goals.[56] This may be directed toward making the protesters appear to be unreasonable in their demands, or to be well-meaning individuals who "just don't understand how complex running a city really is." Target groups may extend sympathy but claim that they lack resources, a mandate from constituents, and/or authority to respond to protest demands. Target groups may also evade protest demands by arguing that "If-I-give-it-to-you-I-have-to-give-it-to-everyone."

The tactic of appearing constrained is particularly effective with established civic groups because there is an undeniable element of truth to it. Everyone knows that cities are financially undernourished. Established civic groups expend great energies lobbying for higher levels of funding for their pet city agencies. Thus they recognize the validity of this constraint when posed by city officials. But it is not inconsistent to point out that funds for specific, relatively inexpensive programs, or for the expansion of existing programs, can often be found if pressure is in-

[55]See Lipsky, *op. cit.*, pp. 156, 249 ff.
[56]On the strategy of appearing constrained, see Schelling, *op. cit.*, pp. 22 ff.

creased. While constraints on city government flexibility may be extensive, they are not absolute. Protest targets nonetheless attempt to diminish the impact of protest demands by claiming relative impotence.

5. Target groups may use their extensive resources to discredit protest leaders and organizations. Utilizing their excellent access to the press, public officials may state or imply that leaders are unreliable, ineffective as leaders ("they don't really have the people behind them"), guilty of criminal behavior, potentially guilty of such behavior, or are some shade of "left-wing." Any of these allegations may serve to diminish the appeal of protest groups to potentially sympathetic third parties. City officials, in their frequent social and informal business interaction with leaders of established civic groups, may also communicate derogatory information concerning protest groups. Discrediting of protest groups may be undertaken by some city officials while others appear (perhaps authentically) to remain sympathetic to protest demands. These tactics may be engaged in by public officials whether or not there is any validity to the allegations.

6. Target groups may postpone action. The effect of postponement, if accompanied by symbolic assurances, is to remove immediate pressure and delay specific commitments to a future date. This familiar tactic is particularly effective in dealing with protest groups because of their inherent instability. Protest groups are usually comprised of individuals whose intense political activity cannot be sustained except in rare circumstances. Further, to the extent that protest depends upon activating reference publics through strategies which have some "shock" value, it becomes increasingly difficult to activate these groups. Additionally, protest activity is inherently unstable because of the strains placed upon protest leaders who must attempt to manage four constituencies (as described herein).

The most frequent method of postponing action is to commit a subject to "study." For the many reasons elaborated in these paragraphs, it is not likely that ad hoc protest groups will be around to review the recommendations which emerge from study. The greater the expertise and the greater the status of the group making the study, the less will protest groups be able to influence whatever policy emerges. Protest groups lack the skills and resource personnel to challenge expert recommendations effectively.

Sometimes surveys and special research are undertaken in part to evade immediate pressures. Sometimes not. Research efforts are particularly necessary to secure the support of established civic groups, which place high priority on orderly procedure and policy emerging from independent analysis. Yet it must be recognized that postponing policy commitments has a distinct impact on the nature of the pressures focused on policy-makers.

IV. CONCLUSION

In this analysis I have agreed with James Q. Wilson that protest is correctly conceived as a strategy utilized by relatively powerless groups in order to increase their bargaining ability. As such, I have argued, it is successful to the extent that the reference publics of protest targets can be activated to enter the conflict in ways favorable to protest goals. I have suggested a model of the protest process which may assist in ordering data and indicating the salience for research of a number of aspects of protest. These include the critical role of communications media, the differential impact of material and symbolic rewards on "feedback" in protest activity, and the reciprocal relationships of actors in the protest process.

An estimation of the limits to protest efficacy, I have argued further, can be gained by recognizing the problems encountered by protest leaders who somehow must balance the conflicting maintenance needs of four groups in the protest process. This approach transcends a focus devoted primarily to characterization of group goals and targets, by suggesting that even in an environment which is relatively favorable to specific protest goals, the tensions which must be embraced by protest leadership may ultimately overwhelm protest activity.

At the outset of this essay, it was held that conceptualizing the American political system as "slack" or "fluid," in the manner of Robert Dahl, appears inadequate because of (1) a vagueness centering on the likelihood that any group can make itself heard; (2) a possible confusion as to which groups tend to receive satisfaction from the rewards dispensed by public officials; and (3) a lumping together as equally relevant rewards which are tangible and those which are symbolic. To the extent that protest is engaged in by relatively powerless groups which must create resources with which to bargain, the analysis here suggests a number of reservations concerning the pluralist conceptualization of the "fluidity" of the American political system.

Relatively powerless groups cannot use protest with a high probability of success. They lack organizational resources, by definition. But even to create bargaining resources through activating third parties, some resources are necessary to sustain organization. More importantly, relatively powerless protest groups are constrained by the unresolvable conflicts which are forced upon protest leaders who must appeal simultaneously to four constituencies which place upon them antithetical demands.

When public officials recognize the legitimacy of protest activity, they may not direct public policy toward protest groups at all. Rather, public officials are likely to aim responses at the reference publics from which they originally take their cues. Edelman has suggested that regulatory policy in practice often consists of reassuring mass publics while at the same time dispensing specific, tangible values to narrow interest groups. It is suggested here that symbolic reassurances are dispensed as much to wide, potentially concerned publics which are not directly affected by regulatory policy, as they are to wide publics comprised of the downtrodden and the deprived, in whose name policy is often written.

Complementing Edelman, it is proposed here that in the process of protest symbolic reassurances are dispensed in large measure because these are the public policy outcomes and actions desired by the constituencies to which public officials are most responsive. Satisfying these wider publics, city officials can avoid pressures toward other policies placed upon them by protest organizations.

Not only should there be some doubt as to which groups receive the symbolic recognitions which Dahl describes, but in failing to distinguish between the kinds of rewards dispensed to groups in the political system, Dahl avoids a fundamental question. It is literally fundamental because the kinds of rewards which can be obtained from politics, one might hypothesize, will have an impact upon the realistic appraisal of the efficacy of political activity. If among the groups least capable of organizing for political activity there is a history of organizing for protest, and if that activity, once engaged in, is rewarded primarily by the dispensation of symbolic gestures without perceptible changes in material conditions, then rational behavior might lead to expressions of apathy and lack of interest in politics or a rejection of conventional political channels as a meaningful arena of activity. In this sense this discussion of protest politics is consistent with Kenneth Clark's observations that the image of power, unaccompanied by material and observable rewards, leads to impressions of helplessness and reinforces political apathy in the ghetto.[57]

Recent commentary by political scientists and others regarding riots in American cities seems to focus in part on the extent to which relatively deprived groups may seek redress of legitimate grievances. Future research should continue assessment of the relationship between riots and the conditions under which access to the political system has been limited. In such research assessment of the ways in which access to public officials is obtained by relatively powerless groups through the protest process might be one important research focus.

The instability of protest activity outlined in this article also should inform contemporary political strategies. If the arguments presented here are persuasive, civil rights leaders who insist that protest activity is a shallow foundation on which to seek long-term, concrete

[57]Clark, *op. cit.*, pp. 154 ff.

gains may be judged essentially correct. But the arguments concerning the fickleness of the white liberal, or the ease of changing discriminatory laws relative to changing discriminatory institutions, only in part explain the instability of protest movements. An explanation which derives its strength from analysis of the political process suggests concentration on the problems of managing protest constituencies. Accordingly, Alinsky is probably on the soundest ground when he prescribes protest for the purpose of building organization. Ultimately, relatively powerless groups in most instances cannot depend upon activating other actors in the political process. Long-run success will depend upon the acquisition of stable political resources which do not rely for their use on third parties.